PRIVATE ENFORCEMENT OF ANTITRUST LAW IN THE UNITED STATES

Private Enforcement of Antitrust Law in the United States

A Handbook

Edited by

Albert A. Foer

President, The American Antitrust Institute, Washington DC, USA

Randy M. Stutz

Director of Special Projects, The American Antitrust Institute, Washington DC, USA

Edward Elgar

Cheltenham, UK • Northampton, MA, USA

Published by
Edward Elgar Publishing Limited
The Lypiatts
15 Lansdown Road
Cheltenham
Glos GL50 2JA
UK

Edward Elgar Publishing, Inc.
William Pratt House
9 Dewey Court
Northampton
Massachusetts 01060
USA

A catalogue record for this book
is available from the British Library

Library of Congress Control Number: 2012930609

MIX
Paper from
responsible sources
FSC
www.fsc.org
FSC® C018575

ISBN 978 0 85793 959 3 (cased)

Typeset by Servis Filmsetting Ltd, Stockport, Cheshire
Printed and bound by MPG Books Group, UK

Contents

Detailed Contents

Contributors

Wendy K. Arends is an Associate at Godfrey & Kahn SC in Madison, Wisconsin.

Adam C. Briggs is an attorney in Singapore and formerly an Associate at Godfrey & Kahn SC in Madison, Wisconsin.

W. Joseph Bruckner is a Partner at Lockridge Grindal Nauen PLLP in Minneapolis, Minnesota.

Patrick B. Clayton is an Associate at Zelle Hofmann Voelbel & Mason LLP in San Francisco, California.

Craig C. Corbitt is a Partner at Zelle Hofmann Voelbel & Mason LLP in San Francisco, California.

Eric L. Cramer is a Managing Shareholder at Berger & Montague PC in Philadelphia, Pennsylvania.

Michael B. Eisenkraft is an Associate at Cohen Milstein Sellers & Toll PLLC in New York City.

Albert A. Foer is the President of the American Antitrust Institute in Washington D.C.

Anthony J. Gaughan is a law professor at Drake University and formerly an Associate at Godfrey & Kahn SC in Madison, Wisconsin.

Pamela Gilbert is a Director of the American Antitrust Institute and a Partner at Cuneo Gilbert & LaDuca LLP in Washington D.C.

Joseph Goldberg is a Partner at Freedman Boyd Daniels Hollander Goldberg Ives & Duncan, PA in Albuquerque, New Mexico.

Dan E. Gustafson is a Member of Gustafson Gluek PLLC in Minneapolis, Minnesota.

Michael D. Hausfeld is Chairman of Hausfeld LLP in Washington D.C.

Katherine Kinsella is the President of Kinsella Media LLC in Washington D.C.

Robert H. Lande is a Director of the American Antitrust Institute and the Venable Professor of Law at the University of Baltimore School of Law in Baltimore, Maryland.

James Langenfeld is a Managing Director at Navigant Economics and Adjunct Professor at Loyola University Chicago School of Law in Chicago, Illinois.

Scott Martin is a Shareholder at Greenberg Traurig LLP in New York City.

Kevin J.L. O'Connor is the Chair of the Antitrust and Trade Regulation Practice Group at Godfrey & Kahn SC in Madison, Wisconsin.

Hannah L. Renfro is an attorney with the Wisconsin Department of Commerce and formerly an Associate at Godfrey & Kahn SC in Madison, Wisconsin.

J. Douglas Richards is the Managing Partner of the New York office of Cohen Milstein Sellers & Toll PLLC in New York City.

Victoria Romanenko is an Associate at Cuneo Gilbert & LaDuca, LLP in Washington D.C.

Jonathan L. Rubin is the Managing Member at Rubin PLLC in Washington D.C.

Matthew R. Salzwedel is Corporate Counsel at HomeServices of America, Inc., in Minneapolis, Minnesota.

Abigail E. Shafroth is an Associate at Cohen Milstein Sellers & Toll PLLC in Washington D.C.

Daniel C. Simons is an Associate at Berger & Montague, PC in Philadelphia, Pennsylvania.

Stacey P. Slaughter is a Partner at Robins, Kaplan, Miller & Ciresi LLP in Minneapolis, Minnesota.

Randy M. Stutz is the Director of Special Projects at the American Antitrust Institute in Washington D.C.

Bonny E. Sweeney is a Partner at Robbins Geller Rudman & Dowd LLP in San Diego, California.

Joseph Tabacco is the Managing Partner at Berman DeValerio in San Francisco, California.

Michael J. Waters is a Shareholder at Vedder Price PC in Chicago, Illinois.

Shannon Wheatman is a Vice President of Kinsella Media, LLC in Washington D.C.

K. Craig Wildfang is a Partner at Robins, Kaplan, Miller & Ciresi LLP in Minneapolis, Minnesota.

Gregory G. Wrobel is a Shareholder and the Antitrust Practice Group Leader at Vedder Price PC in Chicago, Illinois.

Judith A. Zahid is a Partner at Zelle Hofmann Voelbel & Mason LLP in San Francisco, California.

Preface

This Handbook has a history. In 2010, the American Antitrust Institute (AAI) published *The International Handbook on Private Enforcement of Competition Law*.[1] This comparative law volume contained 11 original essays on private enforcement in the United States, where the bulk of the world's experience with private enforcement is located, and 19 essays on private enforcement in countries scattered around the rest of the world. As we edited the American essays, we realized that we had something surprisingly new and valuable on our hands.

Our treatment of the U.S. experience seemed to be the first resource in which practitioners explain in a systematic and highly detailed way how a private antitrust case is put together and pursued, canvassing practical, procedural, and substantive considerations from inception to final resolution. Step-by-step, in more or less chronological order, the collection of essays explains how a case moves from suspicion to proof and from complaint to trial, or more likely to dismissal or settlement, and nearly everything in between. It even deals with how claims are administered and how lawyers are compensated. It is simultaneously about law, economics, procedure, and practical life within the antitrust community, covering almost everything a serious antitrust student or an inexperienced antitrust practitioner would want to know. In short, it was a resource that the various editors wished we had encountered much earlier in our careers.

Naturally, then, we advised Edward Elgar that we would like to present an expanded and updated version of the collected American essays, to be tailored specifically to the American market. This Handbook is the result. The expansion and updating occurs in all the earlier chapters, which were revised by their original authors. Some important new cases intervened between books, especially relating to class actions, and these were incorporated, bringing the book current as of September 2011. But we also added new chapters by new authors, including on the role of economists and expert witnesses, settlement practice, cy pres remedies, and proposals for reform. The chapter on settlement practice, co-authored by an experienced plaintiff-side class action lawyer and an experienced defense-side class action lawyer, represents an entirely new contribution to the field; despite the fact that antitrust cases rarely go to trial, very little has previously been written about the strategic aspects of reaching settlement in an antitrust case.

While it is true that the resolution of private antitrust cases (prior to trial) is consistent and fairly predictable, the substantive and procedural law in the field is quite dynamic, and the student or practitioner who engages with this Handbook engages with private enforcement at a time when the field is arguably in a heightened state of flux. In the wake of the Supreme Court's October 2010 term, for example, some contend that two opinions

[1] The American Antitrust Institute, The International Handbook on Private Enforcement of Competition Law (Albert A. Foer & Jonathan W. Cuneo eds., 2010).

– *Wal-Mart Stores, Inc. v. Dukes*[2] and *AT&T Mobility LLC v. Concepcion*[3] – threaten to fundamentally alter the use of what has been the primary procedural mechanism for the private redress of widespread harm caused by antitrust violations: the Rule 23 class action. While the field thus will not hold still for a portrait painting, we use the remainder of this preface to sketch the broad contours of the private enforcement landscape.

* * *

It has been a mantra over the years that at least nine out of 10 antitrust cases in the United States are brought privately, rather than by a government agency. Indeed, in the AAI's 2008 *Transition Report on Competition Policy to the 44th President*, we stated that the number of private antitrust cases actually exceeds the number of U.S. government actions (civil and criminal) by more than 25 to 1.[4] However, we also wrote in 2008 that the number of private actions filed had "declined significantly since 1978," and the number of government actions had fallen "even more sharply (in percentage terms)."[5] Since 2008, the number of private actions, including class actions, has continued to decline dramatically, while the number of Justice Department antitrust investigations has declined to a lesser degree. And yet the number of cases filed by the Justice Department has actually increased. This requires some explication.

According to data provided by the Administrative Office of the U.S. Courts, the total number of private antitrust cases filed in federal district courts between 2008 and 2010 has declined annually in recent years, from 1,287 in 2008, to 792 in 2009, to 523 in 2010.[6] The 523 private antitrust cases filed in 2010 constitutes a 10-year low.[7] Antitrust class actions filed in federal court have also declined dramatically during the same period.[8] There were 767 antitrust class actions filed in 2008, 376 in 2009, and 202 in 2010.[9] The 202 antitrust class actions in 2010 likewise constitutes a 10-year low.[10]

---

2 Wal-Mart Stores, Inc. v. Dukes, 131 S. Ct. 2541, 2551 (2011).

3 AT&T Mobility LLC v. Concepcion, 131 S. Ct. 1740 (2011).

4 The American Antitrust Institute, The Next Antitrust Agenda: The American Antitrust Institute's Transition Report on Competition Policy to the 44th President 222 (Albert A. Foer ed., 2008), *available at* http://www.antitrustinstitute.org/content/next-antitrust-agenda.

5 *Id.* (citing Sourcebook of Criminal Justice Statistics Online, Table 5.41.2007, http://www.albany.edu/sourcebook/pdf/t5412007.pdf).

6 Sourcebook of Criminal Justice Statistics Online, Table 5.41.2010; Antitrust Cases Filed in U.S. District Courts, http://www.albany.edu/sourcebook/pdf/t5412010.pdf (citing the Administrative Office of the United States Courts, Judicial Business Annual Reports, for each applicable year).

7 *See id.; but see infra* note 10. The average number of private antitrust cases filed in federal district court annually from 2001–2010 was 836. *See id.* The range of annual filings during that time was from 523 to 1,287. *See id.*

8 LexisNexis, CourtLink, Nature of Suit Strategic Profile, Other Statutes – Antitrust (All Courts), http://lexisnexis.com/courtlink (available with subscription).

9 *Id.*

10 *Id.* The combined average number of antitrust class actions filed in federal court annually from 2001–2010 was 407. *See id.* The range of annual filings during that time was from 202 to 767. *See id.* It bears noting, however, that data concerning class action filings is often flawed in

Assuming that the number of private cases is somehow related to the number of government cases, it is probably more useful to focus on the Antitrust Division of the Department of Justice (DOJ or the Antitrust Division) rather than the Federal Trade Commission (FTC) or the states as the best indicator of government activity that private cases are likely to track. That is because litigated judgments in cases brought by the DOJ constitute prima facie evidence of violations in private follow-on actions, while FTC actions have no collateral estoppel effect in subsequent antitrust actions.[11] Moreover, even without the benefit of this rule, private actions are more likely to follow Antitrust Division cases because the Division brings more cases involving claims of price-fixing and other per se violations of Section 1 of the Sherman Act, claims in which follow-on private plaintiffs can more easily establish a prima facie case as compared to a rule of reason case. There is no reason to believe that cases initiated by the states lead to many follow-on private cases; on the contrary, state cases are frequently follow-on actions themselves.

According to its workload statistics, the Antitrust Division initiated a total of 208 investigations in 2008, 214 in 2009, and 158 in 2010.[12] The 158 investigations in 2010 constitutes a 10-year low.[13] In 2008 and 2009, respectively, 76 of the 208 investigations, or 37 percent, and 92 of the 214 investigations, or 43 percent, concerned Sherman Act Section 1 conduct.[14] In 2010, 53 of the 158 investigations, or 34 percent, concerned Section 1 conduct.[15] It bears noting, however, that fluctuations in the number of investigations initiated do not necessarily correspond to fluctuations in the number of cases filed by the Antitrust Division. For example, the Division filed 19 civil cases – a 10-year high – in 2008, and it filed 14 civil cases – a runner-up to the 10-year high – in 2010.[16] Likewise,

---

one important respect. Because a great many class actions will be consolidated before the Judicial Panel on Multidistrict Litigation (JPML) and resolved prior to trial, a count of class action *filings* will necessarily include overlapping and duplicate class actions that should properly be conceived as a single class action that is pursued in a single MDL proceeding. *See* The American Antitrust Institute, *supra* note 5, at 229 n.35 (citing Emery G. Lee II & Thomas E. Willging, *The Impact of the Class Action Fairness Act of 2005 on the Federal Courts: Fourth Interim Report to the Advisory Comm. on Civil Rules* (April 2008), http://www.fjc.gove/public/pdf.nsf/lookup/cafa0408.pdf/$file/cafa0408.pdf (electing to eliminate overlapping and duplicate proceedings that were consolidated in MDL proceedings for purposes of calculating class action statistics in a report to the Federal Judicial Center)). This point is elucidated in § 1.01 of Chapter 1 of this Handbook, which notes that, in 2010, 137 class actions concerning a range of specified products were ultimately consolidated into just five class action proceedings before the JPML. To the degree that the data discussed *supra* in notes 7–8 and accompanying text includes overlapping and duplicate class action filings, it too may be flawed.

11 *See* 15 U.S.C. § 16.

12 U.S. Dep't of Justice, Antitrust Div. Workload Statistics FY 2001–2010 1, http://www.justice.gov/atr/public/workload-statistics.pdf.

13 *See id.* Figures do not include business reviews or premerger notifications, but do include investigations initiated as a result of premerger notifications. The average number of total investigations initiated annually from 2001–2010 was 234. *See id.* The range of total investigations initiated annually during that time was from 158 to 283. *See id.*

14 *Id.*

15 *Id.* A substantial majority of the remaining investigations concerned Clayton Act Section 7 conduct. *See id.*

16 *Id.* at 5.

the Division filed a 10-year high of 72 criminal cases in 2009, and a runner-up to the 10-year high – 60 criminal cases – in 2010.[17] Thus, while the number of investigations initiated by DOJ seems to be declining as of 2010, the Division's "percentage-of-cases-filed-per-investigation" was higher in 2010 than in any of the previous 10 years, and it filed as many or more combined civil and criminal cases than in any of the previous 10 years other than 2009.

Why is the number of private antitrust cases in decline over the last few years while the combined number of civil and criminal cases filed by the Antitrust Division, to which private plaintiffs may "follow on," is on the rise?

One answer is that private enforcers, contrary to the perceptions of some, do not always follow an easy trail blazed by government enforcers. As Professor Robert Lande ably illustrates in the Introduction to this Handbook, oftentimes private plaintiffs "stand alone" rather than "follow on," or the government may follow a trail blazed by private plaintiffs. This helps to explain why trends in private enforcement do not always lag trends in public enforcement.

Some other possible answers double as the recurring themes that are found throughout the remainder of this Handbook. Such themes may help to further explain the dramatic decline in private actions and private class actions after 2008, and to fill in the contours of our existing private enforcement landscape. These include:

(1) Judicial opinions that raise threshold hurdles for plaintiffs in pursuing their claims in court.[18]
(2) A whipsaw effect, from the costs of litigation continually going up while the odds of winning are continually going down, and an altered cost/benefit analysis necessary to justify a contingent fee case, leading to fewer cases being filed.
(3) Changed dynamics of class action filings after the Class Action Fairness Act of 2005.
(4) More stringent litigation hurdles for plaintiffs, including a rigorous class certification hearing where merits issues may be resolved, and heightened expert admissibility standards under *Daubert*[19] and Rule 702 of the Federal Rules of Evidence.[20]
(5) The judiciary's decreasing reliance on per se rules of illegality (reflected in Supreme Court opinions like *Leegin*[21]).[22]

---

17 *Id.* at 7.

18 This is particularly evident with respect to pleading requirements after the Supreme Court's opinion in *Bell Atlantic Corp. v. Twombly*, 550 U.S. 544 (2007), but other judicial opinions have hindered private plaintiffs in the areas of standing, antitrust injury, burden of production, and burden of proof. *See* Andrew I. Gavil, Professor of Law, Howard University School of Law, *Then and Now: Have We Lost Faith in the Antitrust Private Right of Action?*, Presentation at the American Antitrust Institute 4th Annual Future of Private Antitrust Enforcement Conference, slide 7 (Dec. 7, 2010) (citing *Brunswick, Illinois Brick, Matsushita, Sylvania, BMI, Brooke Group, Trinko*, and *Leegin*), *available at* http://www.antitrustinstitute.org/~antitrust/sites/default/files/GAVIL%20slides.pdf.

19 Daubert v. Merrell Dow Pharmaceuticals, Inc., 509 U.S. 579 (1993).

20 Gavil, *supra* note 18, at slide 7.

21 Leegin Creative Leather Products, Inc. v. PSKS, Inc., 551 U.S. 877 (2007).

22 Gavil, *supra* note 18, at slide 7.

(6) The judiciary's increasing deference to regulation (reflected in Supreme Court opinions like *Trinko*[23]).[24]

Still other possible answers are doubtless available to the willing researcher. As Professor Gavil has noted in discussing the above, there are trends reflected in the Supreme Court's rhetoric that go well beyond the last three years or even the last 10 years.[25] We encourage readers to seek clearer answers to these kinds of questions, and to appreciate the macro complexities attending this dynamic area of the law.

* * *

Apart from helping readers to appreciate the macro complexities of private antitrust enforcement, it is our hope that this Handbook will go a very long way toward unraveling all the important micro complexities in the field. After Professor Lande's Introduction, which examines the benefits of private antitrust enforcement by reference to an empirical study of 40 large, private cases,[26] the ensuing 15 chapters attempt to follow a more or less chronological order, each answering a question:

What acts constitute violations of U.S. antitrust law?
What investigative and other activities typically occur before a complaint is filed?
What parties are entitled to pursue an antitrust claim?
What decisions are involved in the initiation of a private action?
How are claims aggregated, and what is the current state of class action law?
What types of motions typically arise during the pre-trial phase?
How is evidence obtained?
What role do economists and expert witnesses play?
How are damages proved and other remedies obtained?
How is antitrust litigation funded?
How do private and public enforcement efforts interact?
What are the strategic and practical considerations associated with settlement?

---

23 Verizon Commc'ns, Inc. v. Law Offices of Curtis. V. Trinko, LLP, 540 U.S. 398 (2004).

24 Gavil, *supra* note 18, at slide 7.

25 Gavil, *supra* note 18, at slides 3–4 (comparing the Court's language in 1979 in *Reiter v. Sonotone* Corp., 442 U.S. 330, 344–45 (1979) ("Congress created the treble damages remedy of § 4 precisely for the purpose of encouraging private challenges to antitrust violations. These private suits provide a significant supplement to the limited resources available to the Department of Justice for enforcing the antitrust laws and deterring violations.") with the Court's language in 2004 in *Trinko*, 540 U.S. at 414 ("Against the slight benefits of antirust intervention here, we must weigh a realistic assessment of its costs. . . . The cost of false positives counsels against an undue expansion of § 2 liability.")).

26 An updated study reviewing an additional 20 such cases will be available on AAI's website, www.antitrustinstitute.org, prior to the publication of this Handbook. Apart from this work by Professor Lande and Professor Joshua P. Davis of the University of San Francisco School of Law, the amount of empirical information about private enforcement is surprisingly slight. We call your attention to a new book, highly critical of private enforcement, Daniel A. Crane, The Institutional Structure of Antitrust Enforcement (2011), which provides both empirical and anecdotal information.

What happens after there is a fund to distribute?
What happens when there are still funds left over?
What types of proposals have been made to reform the current system?

The Handbook is a product of the American Antitrust Institute, a 501(c)(3) research, education, and advocacy organization founded in 1998.[27] The co-editors are Albert A. Foer, President of the AAI, a former senior FTC official, lawyer, and business leader; and Randy M. Stutz, Director of Special Projects for the AAI, an antitrust lawyer formerly with a national law firm. We have been blessed with the strong administrative assistance of Sarah Frey, the AAI's Manager of Communications. We are most indebted, of course, to the various authors whose names appear in the list of contributors. We also want to thank a variety of volunteers who helped us with the editing of specific chapters: Kevin Kim, Evan Schultz, Edmond Wybaillie, Ke Li, Flavia Fortes, Nigel Barella, Niranjan Adhikari, and Benjamin Van Rompuy.

Albert A. Foer and Randy M. Stutz
Washington D.C., October 21, 2011

[27] For more, see the AAI website, www.antitrustinstitute.org.

Introduction: Benefits of private enforcement[1]

Robert H. Lande[2]

Many commentators, especially members of the defense bar, have criticized the existing United States system of private antitrust litigation. Some assert that private actions all too often result in remedies that provide lucrative fees for plaintiffs' lawyers but secure no significant benefits for overcharged victims.[3] Others suggest that private litigation merely follows an easy trail blazed by government enforcers and adds little of public benefit to government sanctions.[4] Yet others contend that, in light of government enforcement,

---

[1] This chapter is a condensation and revision of two articles by Robert H. Lande & Joshua P. Davis: *Benefits From Private Antitrust Enforcement: An Analysis of Forty Cases*, 42 USF. L. Rev. 879 (2008), *available at* http://papers.ssrn.com/sol3/papers.cfm?abstract_id=1090661 [hereinafter *Benefits: An Analysis*], and *Comparative Deterrence from Private Enforcement and Criminal Enforcement of the U.S. Antitrust laws*, 2010 BYU L. Rev. 315 (2011), *available at* http://papers.ssrn.com/sol3/papers.cfm?abstract_id=1565693 [hereinafter *Comparative Deterrence*]. For summaries of the individual case studies analyzed in this article, see *Benefits from Antitrust Private Antitrust Enforcement: Forty Individual Case Studies*, http://papers.ssrn.com/sol3/papers.cfm?abstract_id=1105523 [hereinafter *Benefits: Individual Case Studies*].

[2] Venable Professor of Law, University of Baltimore Law School; Board of Directors, American Antitrust Institute. The author is grateful to Gary Stapleton and Thomas Weaver for excellent research assistance.

[3] Professor Cavanagh ably summarized this belief: "Many class action suits generate substantial fees for counsel but produce little, if any, benefit to the alleged victims of the wrongdoing. Coupon settlements, wherein plaintiffs settle for 'cents off' coupons while their attorneys are paid their full fees in cash . . . are of dubious value to the victims of antitrust violations . . . [and] defendants are not forced to disgorge their ill gotten gains when coupons are not redeemed." Edward Cavanagh, *Antitrust Remedies Revisited*, 84 Or. L. Rev. 147, 214 (2005) (footnote omitted). However, Professor Cavanagh provides only an anecdote to support these conclusions. He offers no data to show the type of antitrust settlements he describes as typical or to demonstrate how often they result in useless coupons.

[4] John C. Coffee, Jr. at one point subscribed to this view, but later concluded the evidence was to the contrary. John C. Coffee, Jr., *Understanding the Plaintiff's Attorney: The Implications of Economic Theory for Private Enforcement of Law Through Class and Derivative Actions*, 86 Colum. L. Rev. 669, 681 n.36 (1986) ("Although the conventional wisdom has long been that class actions tend to 'tag along' on the heels of governmentally initiated suits, a recent study of antitrust litigation by Professors Kauper and Snyder has placed this figure at '[l]ess than 20 percent of private antitrust actions filed between 1976 and 1983.'") (citation omitted).

private cases lead to excessive deterrence.[5]

One common criticism of private actions in general – and of class actions in particular – is that they are a form of legalized blackmail or extortion, one in which plaintiffs' attorneys coerce defendants into settlements based not on meritorious claims, but rather on the cost of litigation or fear of an erroneous and catastrophic judgment.[6] These actions also are said to discourage legitimate competitive behavior.[7] For these and related reasons, many members of the antitrust community call for the curtailment of private enforcement;[8] some even call for its abolition.[9]

Although these criticisms are widespread, they have been made without any systematic empirical evidence.[10] Those who point to the alleged flaws of our system of private antitrust enforcement support their arguments only with anecdotes, many of which are self-serving or questionable. These arguments have never been supported with reliable data.

---

[5] As the Antitrust Modernization Commission noted: "[S]ome have argued that treble damages, along with other remedies, can overdeter some conduct that may not be anticompetitive and result in duplicative recovery. No actual cases or evidence of systematic overdeterrence were presented to the Commission, however." ANTITRUST MODERNIZATION COMM'N, REPORT AND RECOMMENDATIONS 247 (2007), *available at* http://govinfo.library.unt.edu/amc/report_recommendation/amc_final_report.pdf (footnotes omitted). For reasons why "treble damages" do not lead to excessive deterrence but on the contrary should be increased, see Robert H. Lande, *Five Myths about Antitrust Damages*, 40 USF. L. REV. 651 (2006), *available at* http://papers.ssrn.com/sol3/papers.cfm?abstract_id=1263478.

[6] *See* John H. Beisner & Charles E. Borden, *Expanding Private Causes of Action: Lessons from the U.S. Litigation Experience*, U.S. Chamber Institute for Legal Reform, www.instituteforlegalreform.com/get_ilr_doc.php?id=1034. However, Beisner and Borden and others who embrace this view provide no systematic empirical basis for its factual predicates.

[7] AMC Commissioner Cannon once wrote:

> Private plaintiffs are very often competitors of the firms they accuse of antitrust violations, and have every incentive to challenge and thus deter hard competition that they cannot or will not meet. . . . [L]itigation is expensive and courts and juries may erroneously conclude that procompetitive or competitively neutral conduct violates the antitrust laws. . . . [P]otential defendants . . . will refrain from engaging in some forms of potentially procompetitive conduct in order to avoid the cost and risk of litigation.

W. Stephen Cannon, *A Reassessment of Antitrust Remedies: The Administration's Antitrust Remedies Reform Proposal: Its Derivation and Implications*, 55 ANTITRUST L.J. 103, 106 (1986).

[8] HERBERT HOVENKAMP, THE ANTITRUST ENTERPRISE: PRINCIPLE AND EXECUTION 59 (Cambridge: Harvard Univ. Press 2005).

[9] *See* William Breit & Kenneth G. Elzinga, *Private Antitrust Enforcement: The New Learning*, 28 J.L. & ECON. 405, 440 (1985).

[10] One prominent critic, former ABA Antitrust Section Chair Janet McDavid, candidly admitted this: "[The] issue [of class action abuse] was never directly presented in these cases, but many of these issues arise in the context of class actions in which the potential for abusive litigation is really pretty extraordinary." C. Scott Hemphill, Janet L. McDavid, Andrew J. Pincus & Ronald A. Stern, panelists, *Roundtable Discussion – Mark D. Whitener and Andrew I. Gavil, Moderators*, 22 ANTITRUST 8, 12–13 (Fall 2007). When asked by Professor Andrew Gavil about empirical evidence, McDavid said: "I'm not aware of empirical data on any of those issues. My empirical data are derived from cases in which I am involved." *Id.*

Some critics' anecdotes surely are true. Private antitrust enforcement, which constitutes in most years more than 90 percent of antitrust cases in the United States,[11] certainly is imperfect.[12] However, objective observers should not confuse anecdotes with data. A balanced view would also consider the systematic benefits of private actions in terms of both compensating victimized consumers and businesses, and deterring future anticompetitive conduct.

The purpose and design of the AAI private enforcement study

This chapter discusses a study that serves as a first step towards providing the empirical data necessary to assess the benefits of private antitrust enforcement. With the support of the American Antitrust Institute and a variety of research assistants, the authors of the study analyzed the compensation and deterrence effects from a group of 40 recent, successful, large-scale private antitrust cases. Among other things, the authors examined the amount of money recovered for victims, what proportion of the money was recovered from foreign entities, whether the private litigation was preceded by government action, and on whose behalf money was recovered (direct purchasers, indirect purchasers, or a competitor). To our knowledge, no similar study has ever been undertaken.

It is important to note that this study does not purport to be comprehensive or in any way definitive. It does not analyze every recent significant private antitrust case, assess a random sample of cases, or even include all of the largest or "most important" ones.[13] The authors simply tried to assemble and evaluate 40 of the largest and most successful cases that concluded between 1990 and 2007.[14]

The study was not intended to demonstrate that private litigation often has established important legal precedents: other studies have done this convincingly.[15] The "first cut," instead, was to look for recent private cases that were final, including appeals, and that recovered at least $50 million in cash for victims of anticompetitive behavior. The

---

[11] *See* SOURCEBOOK OF CRIMINAL JUSTICE STATISTICS ONLINE, Table 5.41, http://www.albany.edu/sourcebook/pdf/t5412004.pdf (Antitrust Cases filed in U.S. District Courts, by type of case, 1975–2004).

[12] Government enforcement also is imperfect.

[13] For example, we were not able to include an analysis of the consumer class action suits against Microsoft, even though a highly respected journalist reported that together these cases recovered more than $1.5 billion for victims. *See* Todd Bishop, *Microsoft antitrust payouts, the grand total*, THE MICROSOFT BLOG (July 7, 2006, 6:50 AM), http://blog.seattlepi.com/microsoft/2006/07/07/microsoft-antitrust-payouts-the-grand-total/.

[14] In one case, the final settlement was approved within this time frame, but the final award of fees and costs to the attorneys did not occur until January 2008. *See In re* Auto. Refinishing Paint Antitrust Litig., 2008 U.S. Dist. LEXIS 569 (E.D. Pa. Jan. 3, 2008).

[15] For an excellent analysis, see Stephen Calkins, *Coming to Praise Criminal Antitrust Enforcement*, European University Institute 11th EU Competition Law and Policy Workshop (Florence, Italy, June 2–3, 2006), *available at* http://www.eui.eu/RSCAS/Research/Competition/2006%28pdf%29/200610-COMPed-Calkins.pdf. Professor Calkins found that, of leading antitrust cases decided before 1977, 12 were private and 27 were government. Of the leading cases decided in 1977 or later, however, he found that 30 were private cases and only 15 were government cases. *Id.* at 17.

authors included only the recovery of money in their results; awards of products, services, discounts, coupons, and injunctive relief were not treated as "benefits."[16]

Results of the study: Compensation

The 40 cases (or groups of cases)[17] analyzed in the study provided U.S. consumers and businesses a cumulative recovery in the range of at least $18.006 to $19.639 billion in allegedly[18] illegally acquired wealth.[19] (Expressed in 2010 dollars, the corresponding range would be $21.887 to $23.862 billion.[20]) Of this, more than $5.706 to $7.056 billion came from 18 cases involving foreign companies that allegedly violated U.S. antitrust laws. In other words, without private enforcement of the antitrust laws, this money would have remained with foreign alleged lawbreakers instead of being returned to U.S. consumers and businesses.[21]

Interestingly, a large proportion of the total amount recovered – at least 42 to 46 percent or $7.631 to $8.981 billion – came from the 15 cases that did not follow publicly disclosed U.S. or EU government enforcement actions.[22] In all such cases, private plaintiffs apparently uncovered the alleged violations and initiated and pursued the litigation, with the government following the private plaintiffs' lead or playing no role at all. Another $4.212 billion came from cases with a mixed private/public origin.[23] Only about a third of the total private recovery – $6.163 to $6.446 billion – came from cases that were purely public in origin.

Still other private cases followed a government investigation but provided significantly greater relief than the government action (if, indeed, the government brought an action). Some cases also expanded the scope of inquiry into the challenged conduct and the claims against the defendant, or they helped plaintiffs to obtain relief from parties not included

---

16 Securities were counted in one case because they had a readily ascertainable market value.

17 To arrive at this number we counted related cases as being a single "case." For example, there have been many separate legal actions involving vitamins cartels. However, this report analyzes and counts them all together as one "case."

18 For simplicity we are calling all of the charges "allegations," even the ones proven in court.

19 All figures include the awarded attorneys' fees. Although a federal court verdict would produce treble damages for victims, almost all of our cases involved settlements, and in no case did a court determine the percentage overcharge. We know of no way to determine whether any of the settlements exceeded single damages.

20 *See Comparative Deterrence*, *supra* note 1, at Table 14.

21 Cases were not selected for this project on the basis of whether a foreign defendant was likely to be involved.

22 When conduct gave rise to both government and private litigation, we tried to ascertain who first uncovered the antitrust violation. However, because government records are confidential and the enforcers usually do not reveal or discuss their investigations, we could not always make definitive classifications. Because we had access only to publicly available information, some of our classifications could be mistaken. For further discussion of the interplay between public and private enforcement, see Chapter 11 of this Handbook.

23 For example, *In re Polypropylene Carpet Antitrust Litig.*, 93 F. Supp. 2d 1348 (N.D. Ga. 2000), started as a result of a different private antitrust suit, which led to a government investigation in the polypropylene carpet market, that in turn led to the private litigation analyzed in this report. *See Benefits: An Analysis*, *supra* note 1, Table 5, for other examples.

in the government actions. The high proportion of private actions that supplanted, co-originated with, or enhanced government enforcement is perhaps surprising. There were still other instances where the authors of the study were not able to ascertain the origin of a case.[24]

The authors documented a total of $18.006 to $19.639 billion (using nominal dollars) in recoveries by direct purchasers, indirect purchasers, or competitors.[25] Direct purchasers, in 32 cases, recovered $12.088 to $13.438 billion (67 to 68 percent of the total). Indirect purchasers, in six cases, recovered $1.815 billion. Competitors, in six cases, recovered $4.028 to $4.311 billion. All but six of the cases were class actions.

Some of the cases analyzed also involved substantial non-monetary relief. For example, one case generated coupons, fully redeemable in cash if not used for five years. Another case resulted in a $125 million energy rate reduction for consumers. To be very conservative, the authors did not count any part of the coupons[26] or the rate reduction[27] in the study's "cash" recovery totals. Some cases also yielded extremely useful cy pres grants,[28] which likewise were left out of results.

Many other cases led to the restructuring of industries in ways that, according to the judge presiding over the litigation, provided improvements for competition even more beneficial than the monetary relief conferred on the victims. For example, the *Visa/MasterCard* case was settled in April 2003 for "$3,383,400,000 in compensatory relief, plus additional injunctive relief valued at $25 to $87 billion or more."[29] Similarly, the *NASDAQ* case decreased the spreads received by market makers, the *Insurance* litigation

---

24 *See, e.g., Benefits: Individual Case Studies, supra* note 1, at 77–87 (*El Paso* case summary).

25 Direct purchasers are customers who bought a good or service directly from a defendant, and indirect purchasers are customers who purchased a good or service further down the chain of distribution. In the U.S., in general only direct purchasers and competitors can bring claims for damages under federal law, and indirect purchasers can bring claims for damages only under state law (most, but not all, U.S. states allow indirect purchaser actions). For further discussion of direct and indirect purchaser claims, see Chapter 3 of this Handbook.

26 *See Benefits: Individual Case Studies, supra* note 1, at 13–18 (*Auction House* case summaries). These coupons traded for a value that reflected their discounted present value. They also comprised 20 percent of the legal fees paid to prevailing attorneys, who said they will redeem them for cash after the expiration of the mandatory five-year waiting period.

27 *See id.* at 77–87 (*El Paso* case summary).

28 *See, e.g., id.* at 110–113 (*Insurance* case summary). This case resulted in a cash settlement with a creative remedy that: (1) funded the development of a public entity that provides risk management education and technical services to small businesses, public entities, and non-profits; and (2) provided funding to states to develop a risk database for municipalities and local governments. *Id.*

Cy pres is a type of remedy that is available in some class actions where there are funds left over after the class members have been compensated, or the funds are insufficient to distribute to the class members in an economically efficient manner. The court has discretion to award these funds to the "next best" usage consistent with the purposes of the case. *See* Albert A. Foer, *Enhancing Competition Through the Cy Pres Remedy: Suggested Best Practices* (American Antitrust Institute, Working Paper No. 07-11, 2007), *available at* http://www.antitrustinstitute.org (search "Working Paper No. 07-11"). For further discussion of cy pres remedies, see Chapter 14 of this Handbook.

29 Wal-Mart Stores, Inc. v. Visa USA & MasterCard Int'l, 396 F.3d 96, 111 (2d Cir. 2005). The case is described in detail by the lead attorney for the plaintiffs, Lloyd Constantine, in PRICELESS (Kaplan Publishing 2009).

eliminated restrictions on insurance policies, and the *NCAA* case eliminated caps on pay to college coaches.[30] The generic drug cases – *Buspirone, Cardizem, Oncology (Taxol), Relafen, Remeron,* and *Terazosin* – collectively discouraged collusion between brand name and generic drug manufacturers, saving consumers many hundreds of millions of dollars in drug costs.[31]

Results of the study: Deterrence

In addition to its important role in compensating victims of past antitrust violations, private enforcement also helps deter future antitrust violations. The study therefore assesses the deterrence effects of private antitrust enforcement. Although to some degree the deterrence value of private recoveries can be measured by reference to the very same compensation figures discussed earlier in this chapter, the authors sought to contextualize these figures by comparing the deterrence value of private recoveries to the deterrence value of what is widely viewed as the gold standard for antitrust or competition law enforcement worldwide: the DOJ anti-cartel enforcement program. This includes individual fines, corporate fines, and even hard-to-value prison time and house arrest secured by DOJ enforcers.

Although EU cartel enforcement has become increasingly successful in recent years,[32] DOJ enforcement against horizontal collusion is roundly lauded as perhaps the premier enforcement program of its kind in the world. In the United States, even among critics who believe that monopolization and vertical restraints never should be challenged, unkind words for the DOJ's anti-cartel program are rare and relatively minor. This lavish praise, which, it should be noted, is exceptionally well deserved, stands in sharp contrast to the harsh criticism of private enforcement presented at the beginning of this chapter.[33] An objective observer might therefore be surprised to discover that private enforcement probably deters more anticompetitive conduct than the widely praised DOJ anti-cartel program. Indeed, the study suggests that this may well be true despite the DOJ's ability to bring cases that result in prison sentences, house arrest, and individual as well as corporate fines![34]

Before concluding that private enforcement almost deserves the same, nearly ubiquitous praise typically reserved for the DOJ anti-cartel program, one might well ask an additional important question. We are confident that federal anti-cartel prosecutions indeed

---

30 *See Benefits: Individual Case Studies*, *supra* note 1, at 135–39; Arthur R. Kaplan, *Antitrust as a Public-Private Partnership: A Case Study of the NASDAQ Litigation*, 52 Case W. Res. L. Rev. 111 (2001) (describing the *NASDAQ* case).

31 *See Benefits: Individual Case Studies*, *supra* note 1, at 135–39.

32 For an analysis of EU anti-cartel enforcement generally, see John M. Connor & Robert H. Lande, *The Size of Cartel Overcharges: Implications for U.S. and EU Fining Policies*, 51 Antitrust Bull. (in S.C.) 983, 993–1003 (2006), *available at* http://papers.ssrn.com/sol3/papers.cfm?a bstract_id=988722.

33 *See supra* notes 3–10 and accompanying text.

34 U.S. Dep't of Justice Antitrust Div., Antitrust Division Mission, *available at* http://www.justice.gov/atr/about/mission.html (last visited Sept. 29, 2011). The Antitrust Division also can secure disgorgement of cartel overcharges, but this remedy is rare. *See e.g.*, U.S. v. Keyspan, 763 F. Supp. 2d 633 (S.D.N.Y. 2011).

target anticompetitive conduct, but can we be confident that private cases do the same? Defendants often characterize these cases as non-meritorious and against the public interest, and such cases almost always end in settlement rather than a decision by a judge, jury, or the Federal Trade Commission.[35] The question of whether private cases actually target anticompetitive conduct will be addressed near the end of this chapter.

1. Deterrence from the DOJ criminal anti-cartel enforcement program

The total amount of criminal corporate fines imposed in DOJ anti-cartel cases from 1990 to 2007 was approximately $4.2 billion.[36] There is no way to measure how many cartels were never formed due to the deterrence effects of these fines. Surely, however, $4.2 billion in fines was enough to deter a large amount of anticompetitive conduct. During this same period, these same cases also resulted in individual fines that totalled $67 million,[37] and defendants were required to return another $118 million to overcharged government entities in the form of restitution payments.[38]

DOJ prosecutions resulting in prison sentences and house arrests also significantly deter illegal activity. Criminal antitrust prosecutions from 1990–2007 resulted in 520 prison sentences totalling roughly 330 years,[39] and another 97 years of "house arrest or confinement to a halfway house."[40]

In attempting to compare the deterrence value of private enforcement to the deterrence value of DOJ criminal enforcement, the authors of the study faced the vexing task of setting a value – or a disvalue, cost, or disincentive effect – on prison time and house arrest. To the extent that prison time is incomparable to anything that can be valued monetarily, the task may be impossible. But the authors of the study at least attempted to make a rough approximation.

As a starting point, it is clear that prison time should not be valued – or disvalued – infinitely. Cartelists do not act as if they infinitely fear prison time because they often decide to form cartels and risk that outcome. Rather, potential offenders appear to calculate, at least to some very uncertain degree, their chances of getting caught and the prison sentences and fines they are likely to face.[41] They balance this, in some extremely rough way that only they know, against cartel rewards. Because it is common knowledge that people often go to prison for fixing prices, and yet corporate officials continue attempting to form new cartels, the deterrence effects of prison time must be less than infinite.

---

35 *Comparative Deterrence*, *supra* note 1, at 3.

36 U.S. Dep't of Justice, Antitrust Div. Workload Statistics FY 1990–1999 12, *available at* http://www.justice.gov/atr/public/246419.pdf; U.S. Dep't of Justice, Antitrust Div. Workload Statistics FY 2000–2009 14, *available at* http://www.justice.gov/atr/public/256139.pdf.

37 Workload Statistics FY 1990–1999, *supra* note 36, at 12; Workload Statistics FY 2000–2009, *supra* note 36, at 14.

38 Workload Statistics FY 1990–1999, *supra* note 36, at 12; Workload Statistics FY 2000–2009, *supra* note 36, at 14.

39 Workload Statistics FY 1990–1999, *supra* note 36, at 13; Workload Statistics FY 2000–2009, *supra* note 36, at 15.

40 Workload Statistics FY 1990–1999, *supra* note 36, at 13; Workload Statistics FY 2000–2009, *supra* note 36, at 15; *Comparative Deterrence*, *supra* note 1, at app. 1, table 5.

41 *See supra* notes 38–40.

The authors of the study identified five possible approaches to valuing prison time. All five approaches were incorporated into the study in the hope that doing so would increase the reliability of results. The approaches include: (1) the valuations for lives and years of life that are used for various regulatory and public policy purposes; (2) tort awards for loss of a life in wrongful death cases; (3) awards made by the September 11th Victim Compensation Fund to victims' families; (4) the compensation provided to people who have been wrongly imprisoned; and (5) similar estimates by scholars in the field.[42]

The five approaches yielded estimates that are broadly consistent with one another.[43] To be conservative, the authors of the study took the highest of these estimates for the disvalue or deterrence equivalent of a year in prison, $1,500,000 per year, and increased it to $2 million.[44] They used $1 million for the disvalue or deterrence equivalent of a year of house arrest.

Although it is frequently assumed that corporations always engage in profit maximizing behavior, the authors of the study also allowed that executives might care much more about personal consequences than consequences to their corporations. This is in keeping with other common exceptions to profit maximization assumptions, such as the effects of agent/principal relationships. Although it is not possible to correct for these problems precisely, the authors took the arbitrary step of tripling the deterrence effects of all individual sanctions relative to corporate sanctions. As a result, a year of prison time was valued – or disvalued – at $6 million[45] rather than $2 million, and a year of house arrest at $3 million rather than $1 million. The authors also tripled the individual fine figures.[46]

Using these estimates and simple arithmetic, the deterrence value of the 330 years of prison time, $4.2 billion in corporate fines, $67 million in individual fines (artificially trebled), and $118 million in restitution imposed for cartel offences, for the entirety of the DOJ anti-cartel program from 1990–2007, is approximately $6.8 billion. Although it is impossible to know how many cartels were deterred by the equivalent of $6.8 billion in sanctions, surely the number must be substantial.

---

42 *See* Lande & Davis, *Comparative Deterrence, supra* note 1.

43 *Id.*

44 Two million dollars is probably significantly more than the true cost or deterrence value of a year in prison, but this figure was used in order to take a conservative and relatively non-controversial approach.

45 Valuing a year's worth of life at $6 million would mean that a 20-year prison sentence would be valued at $120 million, a figure far in excess of the amount that society places on an individual's life.

46 This assumes that the individuals actually pay their own fines. It is, however, difficult to determine whether the antitrust fines imposed on corporate employees are ultimately paid by the employees, or are often or usually directly or indirectly paid by their employers. This area of law is exceedingly complex, and, of course, even if indemnification is illegal, this does not mean that it does not occur regularly. *See* 1 Roger Magnuson, Shareholder Litigation § 9:37 (West 2009); Pamela H. Bucey, *Corporate Executives Who Have Been Convicted of Crimes: An Assessment and Proposal*, 24 Ind. L. Rev. 279 (1991); Note, *Indemnification of Directors: The Problems Posed By Federal Securities and Antitrust Legislation*, 76 Harv. L. Rev. 1403 (1963).

2. *Deterrence from private antitrust litigation*

As discussed earlier in this chapter, empirical research into the deterrence value of private antitrust litigation, during any period, is virtually nonexistent. However, the 40 cases that concluded between 1990 and 2007, which formed the basis for the study, can provide an extremely low floor on this amount. The study documented between $18.006 billion and $19.639 billion in cash paid by defendants in these 40 private U.S. antitrust cases alone (in nominal dollars).[47]

In other words, the deterrence effects from just the cash awards from these 40 private cases nearly tripled the estimated total deterrence value of the DOJ anti-cartel program, a figure that includes the deterrence effects of corporate fines, individual fines (artificially trebled), restitution, prison time valued at $6 million per year, and house arrest valued at $3 million per year. Note that this is not a comparison of the full deterrence effects from these 40 private cases to the full deterrence effects secured by the DOJ in the same 40 cases. This is a comparison of only the cash-based deterrence effects from just 40 private cases to the full estimated deterrence effects from every DOJ cartel case filed during the same 17-year period.

It is true that not all of these 40 cases were against cartels; some were against monopolies and other arrangements. The 25 collusion cases in the study secured a total of $9.200 to $10.600 billion.[48] Comparing this amount to the DOJ total of $6.800 billion shows that even these 25 private collusion cases alone probably deterred more anticompetitive behavior than the entire DOJ anti-cartel enforcement program. Moreover, because this study surveyed only 40 private cases, it significantly underestimates the deterrence effects of all private enforcement during the same period. Also recall that the study conservatively valued coupons, discounts, products and injunctive relief as being worth nothing.

One important complication with these results is worth noting, however: Many of these private cases were follow-ups to government prosecutions.[49] As a result, some of the credit for the deterrence caused by these private recoveries should go to the government enforcers for uncovering and prosecuting the violations. But even where the government discovered the cartels, private cases ultimately secured the damages. Private plaintiffs therefore should get much of the credit for the resulting deterrence in these cases, though the credit should be shared with the government enforcers.

Were the private actions good cases?

It is very difficult for critics of private enforcement to make a credible case that the combination of public and private enforcement in the United States has caused over-deterrence. The area of antitrust most affected by private enforcement is horizontal collusion, and responsible analysts believe that only approximately 25 percent of cartels are even detected.[50] Critics argue that despite this general under-deterrence of cartels,

---

[47] *See supra* notes 19–21 and accompanying text.

[48] *See* Lande & Davis, *Comparative Deterrence*, *supra* note 1, at 23.

[49] *Id.* at 29.

[50] Judge Ginsburg & Professor Wright recently analyzed the empirical literature on cartel detection and concluded that only 25 percent of cartels currently are detected, in both the EU and the

most private actions are not good cases because, for example, private plaintiffs miss cartels and instead sue firms that have done nothing wrong. If this were true, not only would private enforcement fail to discourage illegal behavior, it would even discourage beneficial conduct. However, there are many reasons to believe that most, if not all, of the 40 private cases in the study were meritorious cases. And there are no valid reasons to conclude the reverse.

First, every one of the settlements among the 40 cases was approved as being in the public interest by a federal judge.[51] Of the 45 judges who presided over part or all these settlements, 27 were appointed by Republican presidents.[52] Second, most were at least partially validated through various means other than settlement. For example, in 13 of the 40 cases, defendants also received a criminal penalty for the same conduct.[53] Where a criminal penalty was imposed, it is hard to believe that defendants did nothing wrong. In 12 cases, government enforcers obtained a civil victory.[54] In nine cases, defendants lost at trial in the private litigation or in a very closely related private case.[55] In nine cases, plaintiffs survived or prevailed on a motion for summary judgment, most of which were argued almost as rigorously as a trial on the merits.[56] In at least three cases, plaintiffs survived a motion to dismiss.[57]

In sum, 34 of the 40 cases – 31 if you do not include the motions to dismiss – had at least one indicator that plaintiffs' case was probably meritorious. (The number of cases with indicators does not add up to 34 (or 31) because eight cases had more than one indicator.) All told, it is much more likely that most if not all of the recoveries reflect defendants' perceptions that they could well lose on the merits, not only at trial but also on appeal. How likely is a firm that did nothing wrong to nevertheless pay $50 million or even $500 million in settlement? While this could happen on occasion, the argument loses credibility as settlements get higher.

At the same time, objective observers should ask to see evidence that most private cases lack merit, as critics suggest. Scant such evidence exists. Defendants' self-serving anecdotes, assertions, and protestations should carry no more weight than those of their plaintiff counterparts.

Conclusions

This chapter has not attempted to perform an overall cost/benefit analysis of U.S. private antitrust enforcement. To be sure, private enforcement has many flaws and problems, and many private actions have not been in the public interest. However, the debate over private enforcement should have balance, and it should be grounded in empiricism. The study discussed in this chapter suggests that the flaws of U.S. private antitrust enforcement have

---

United States. See Douglas H. Ginsburg & Joshua D. Wright, *Antitrust Sanctions*, 6 Competition Pol'y Int'l 3, 8 (2010).

[51] *See* Lande & Davis, *Comparative Deterrence*, *supra* note 1, at 25.

[52] *Id.*

[53] *Id.* at 23.

[54] *Id.* at 27.

[55] *Id.*

[56] *Id.*

[57] *Id.*

been greatly exaggerated, on the basis of no evidence except the self-serving anecdotes of parties who frequently have an interest in restricting it.

Private enforcement is virtually the only way to compensate the victims of conduct that violates the antitrust laws. It is responsible for the recovery of billions of dollars that otherwise would have remained with companies that violated the antitrust laws. Many of these lawbreakers were foreign companies. Government enforcement is wonderful, but it rarely helps victims recover the amount taken from them by practices that violate the antitrust laws. The billions of dollars defendants pay in private cases also help to deter future anticompetitive conduct. In fact, in the United States, private enforcement might well deter even more anticompetitive conduct than the DOJ criminal antitrust enforcement program.

As to the possibility that U.S. private enforcement could lead to over-deterrence, it is important to remember that, for practical purposes, victims have only a nominal right to recover "treble damages." In reality, various constraints on recovery mean that, even after trebling of a judgment at trial, plaintiffs likely recover less than single actual damages.[58] To get closer to a full recovery, for example, these settlements would have to compensate victims for unawarded prejudgment interest.[59] They also should compensate victims for difficult-to-quantify and unawarded damages items such as the allocative inefficiency effects of market power,[60] and the value of victims' time expended pursuing litigation.[61]

---

[58] To the extent the purpose of the remedy is compensation, the "damages" caused by an antitrust violation should consist of the sum of all relatively predictable harms caused by that violation affecting anyone other than the defendants. Damages should include the wealth transferred from consumers to the violator(s), as well as the allocative inefficiency effects felt by society, whether caused directly, or indirectly via "umbrella" effects. Plaintiffs' attorneys' fees, the value of plaintiffs' time spent pursuing the case, and the cost to the American taxpayer of administering the judicial system should also be included. When all these adjustments are made it is likely that the United States "treble" damages remedy actually is less than single damages. *See* Robert H. Lande, *Are Antitrust "Treble" Damages Really Single Damages?*, 54 OHIO ST. L.J. 115, 122–24, 158–68 (1993), *available at* http://papers.ssrn.com/sol3/papers.cfm?abstract_id=1134822.

[59] In the United States, interest is only awarded from the time of a judicial decision and the rate is usually quite low. *Id.* at 130.

[60] For an explanation of the allocative inefficiency effects of market power, see *id.* at 119–21, 152–54. Allocative inefficiency is another name for the suboptimal use of societal resources that results from anticompetitive pricing:

> To raise prices a monopoly reduces output from the competitive level. The goods no longer sold are worth more to would-be purchasers than they would cost society to produce. This foregone production of goods worth more than their cost is pure social loss and constitutes the "allocative inefficiency" of monopoly. For example, suppose that widgets cost $1.00 in a competitive market (their cost of production plus a competitive profit). Suppose a monopolist would sell them for $2.00. A potential purchaser who would have been willing to pay up to $1.50 will not purchase at the $2.00 level. Since a competitive market would have sold those widgets for less than they were worth to him, the monopolist's reduced production has decreased the consumer's satisfaction without producing any countervailing benefits for anyone. This pure loss is termed "allocative inefficiency."

Robert H. Lande, *The Rise and (Coming) Fall of Efficiency as the Ruler of Antitrust*, 33 ANTITRUST BULL. 429, 433–34 n.17 (1988); *see also* EDWIN MANSFIELD, MICROECONOMICS: THEORY AND APPLICATIONS 277–92 (W.W. Norton & Co., Inc., 4th ed. 1982) (1970).

[61] *See* Lande, *supra* note 58, at 130–36. As the Antitrust Modernization Commission noted: "Indeed, in light of the fact that some damages may not be recoverable (e.g., compensation for

Over-deterrence seems implausible when you consider that victims are unlikely even to be made fully whole. So called treble damages awards not only fail to cross any theoretical over-deterrence threshold that exists beyond victim compensation, they almost never even reach the starting point.

Further, antitrust verdicts producing even nominal treble damages are rare,[62] and it is likely that few of the overwhelming majority of antitrust cases that settle do so for more than single actual damages.[63] Especially in light of estimates that only 25 percent of cartels are even detected,[64] over-deterrence remains, as the Antitrust Modernization Commission noted, only an unproven assertion.[65] On the contrary, in the United States, anticompetitive conduct occurs far too frequently, despite the deterrence effects of our present system of private litigation.

Another benefit from private cases is that they have saved taxpayers a significant amount of money in foregone enforcement costs. Although government enforcers often will be best suited to uncover and win particular cases, sometimes government enforcers will lack the necessary resources. Sometimes, due to their relatively low salaries, high turnover involving the very best government lawyers may harm the government's chances of victory. Sometimes government enforcers lack the industry expertise of private attorneys and their clients. Sometimes government enforcers may have a political agenda that leads them not to bring or settle a case on easy terms. Sometimes government enforcement efforts will be unduly affected by budgetary constraints[66] and undue fear of losing cases.[67]

---

interest prior to judgment, or because of the statute of limitations and the inability to recover 'speculative' damages) treble damages help ensure that victims will recover at least their actual damages." ANTITRUST MODERNIZATION COMM'N, REPORT AND RECOMMENDATIONS, *supra* note 5, at 246 (footnote omitted).

62 For a list of antitrust verdicts that calculated damages amounts, see John M. Connor & Robert H. Lande, *How High Do Cartels Raise Prices? Implications for Optimal Cartel Fines*, 80 TUL. L. REV. 513, app. at 565 (2005), *available at* http://papers.ssrn.com/sol3/papers.cfm?abstract_id=787907.

63 This is especially true when inflation is considered. For an analysis of this issue, see Robert H. Lande, *Why Antitrust Damage Levels Should Be Raised*, 16 LOY. CONSUMER L. REV. 329 (2004), *available at* http://papers.ssrn.com/sol3/papers.cfm?abstract_id=1118902.

64 *See* Ginsburg & Wright, *supra* note 50.

65 Recall the Conclusion of the U.S. Antitrust Modernization Commission: "No actual cases or evidence of systematic over deterrence were presented to the Commission . . . ." ANTITRUST MODERNIZATION COMM'N, REPORT AND RECOMMENDATIONS, *supra* note 5, at 247 (2007) (citation omitted).

66 This is especially true in the current climate of tight federal budgets.

67 Professor Calkins notes:

> Governmental agencies also hesitate to litigate because of fear of defeat. Courtroom setbacks can demoralize agency staff, raise questions in the eyes of observers, and impose political costs. Few agency annual reports boast about the well-fought loss, and, in an era in which governmental accountability is fashionable, it is challenging to characterize losses as accomplishments. All too often, agencies worry about their win rates. . . . [A]nd general counsels who are nominated for higher office like to claim that their agency won a high percentage of its cases. Everyone wants a good batting average. Unfortunately, a single loss can ruin a good batting average compiled with few at-bats.

Stephen Calkins, *In Praise of Antitrust Litigation: The Second Annual Bernstein Lecture*, 72 ST. JOHN'S L. REV. 1 (1998) (citations omitted).

Not surprisingly, a vigorous private antitrust regime is likely to confer significant benefits over and above those conferred by a system reliant solely upon government enforcement. The United States' distinctive system of private antitrust enforcement is substantially underappreciated. It has produced tremendous benefits for the U.S. economy – for consumers and for businesses of all sizes. It has enabled U.S. businesses and consumers to protect themselves from economic exploitation, both by those who subvert the free market in general and by foreign cartels in particular.[68] Although negative assertions about the efficacy of private U.S. antitrust litigation have been very well publicized, this might well be due less to the merits of these allegations than to the power of the economic interests that stand to benefit from a curtailment of private enforcement.

[68] *See* John M. Connor & Robert H. Lande, *The Size of Cartel Overcharges: Implications for U.S. and EU Fining Policies*, 51 ANTITRUST BULL. 983 (2007), *available at* http://papers.ssrn.com/sol3/papers.cfm?abstract_id=988722. Historically, depending upon the data set used and the methodology employed, cartels in the United States have overcharged an average of 18 percent to 37 percent. By contrast, the overcharges of European cartels averaged in the 28 percent to 54 percent range, and cartel overcharges within a single European country averaged 16 percent to 48 percent. *Id.*

1 Defining antitrust violations in the United States

Bonny E. Sweeney[1]

§ 1.01 Introduction

Private lawsuits have played a critical role in the enforcement of U.S. antitrust laws ever since the Sherman Act was enacted in 1890. The Supreme Court and federal and state enforcement authorities have repeatedly recognized the role Congress envisioned for the private plaintiff when it provided private parties a treble-damage remedy. As the Supreme Court put it, "the purpose of giving private parties treble-damage and injunctive remedies

[1] Bonny E. Sweeney is a partner at Robbins Geller Rudman & Dowd LLP in San Diego, California, where she specializes in antitrust class action litigation.

was not merely to provide private relief, but was to serve as well the high purpose of enforcing the antitrust laws."[2]

This central role is reflected in the number of private cases and their success. Between 1975 and 2010, private antitrust litigants filed more than 30,000 cases in federal courts, accounting for more than 75 percent of all federal antitrust cases filed during that period.[3] Between 1990 and 2007, private plaintiffs recovered more than $18 billion in damages.[4] As a result of its domination of federal antitrust dockets, private litigation has profoundly affected the substantive law of antitrust. Over the last four decades, the Supreme Court has decided 90 antitrust cases. Of these, more than two-thirds were initiated by private plaintiffs.

This chapter outlines the elements the private antitrust plaintiff must prove in litigating antitrust claims. While the focus is on federal law, state law will be discussed briefly, primarily where it diverges from federal law. The chapter is organized along two main themes: (1) joint conduct among two or more actors and (2) unilateral or single-firm conduct. This structure mimics the federal Sherman Act, which separately regulates concerted conduct (under § 1) and single-firm conduct (under § 2).[5]

§ 1.02 Restraints of trade: Agreements that restrict competition

Under federal law, agreements that restrict competition are typically evaluated under § 1 of the Sherman Antitrust Act, which declares illegal "[e]very contract, combination in the

---

[2] Zenith Radio Corp. v. Hazeltine Research, Inc., 395 U.S. 100, 130–31 (1969); *see also* Perma Life Mufflers Inc. v. Int'l Parts Corp., 392 U.S. 134, 139 (1968) ("[T]he purposes of the antitrust laws are best served by insuring that the private action will be an ever-present threat to deter anyone contemplating business behavior in violation of the antitrust laws."). In criminal prosecutions brought by the Department of Justice's Antitrust Division, the Division typically waives the Sentencing Guidelines requirement that the defendant pay restitution to victims because compensation is available through private litigation. *See, e.g.*, Plea Agreement in United States v. Hsu, No. CR 11-0061 RS (N.D. Cal. Mar. 30, 2011) ("The United States and the defendant agree that, pursuant to U.S.S.G. Section 5E1.1(b), the defendant should not be ordered to pay restitution in light of the civil cases filed . . . which potentially provide for a recovery of a multiple of actual damages."), *available at* http://www.justice.gov/atr/cases/f269400/269486.htm.

[3] SOURCEBOOK OF CRIMINAL JUSTICE STATISTICS (2010), *available at* http://www.albany.edu/sourcebook/pdf/t5412010.pdf. According to the raw statistics, private cases account for more than 90 percent of all federal antitrust case filings during this period. These statistics, however, overstate the number of private actions because they individually count pre consolidation class action filings that all challenge the same conduct. In 2010, for example, private plaintiffs filed 137 separate class actions in antitrust cases involving photochromic lens, potatoes, polyurethane foam, silver futures, and American Express. These 137 cases were ultimately consolidated into just five class actions. UNITED STATES JUDICIAL PANEL ON MULTIDISTRICT LITIGATION, *available at* (with log-in) https://ecf.jpml.uscourts.gov/cgi-bin/JPML_MDLCaseRpt.pl?48165531251463-L_570_0-1 (accessed June 10, 2011). Thus, the number of private antitrust cases filed in 2010 was 391, rather than the reported 523. These 391 cases accounted for just over 78 percent of all antitrust cases filed in federal courts.

[4] Robert H. Lande & Joshua P. Davis, *Benefits from Private Enforcement: An Analysis of Forty Cases*, 42 U.S.F. L. REV. 879, 879–891 (2008).

[5] This chapter will also briefly touch upon private challenges to mergers and acquisitions. These lawsuits comprise a very small proportion of private antitrust litigation in the United States and are rarely successful. See the discussion *infra* at § 1.02.5(d).

form of trust or otherwise, or conspiracy, in restraint of trade or commerce among the several States, or with foreign nations."[6] To prevail on a § 1 claim, the government must prove three elements: (1) the existence of an agreement between two or more separate parties that (2) unreasonably restricts competition and (3) affects interstate or foreign commerce. A private plaintiff must additionally prove either that he has been "injured in his business or property" as a result of the unlawful agreement, or that such harm is imminent.[7]

1.02.1 "Contract, combination, or conspiracy"

Section 1 is potentially applicable to all types of joint action between two or more persons or entities, including open agreements such as agreements among members of a joint venture, and secret agreements, such as price-fixing cartels. It applies to horizontal agreements (agreements among competitors) and to vertical agreements (agreements between participants in a supply chain, such as a manufacturer and its distributor). It also applies to coerced "agreements," such as tying arrangements. Section 1 typically does not apply to agreements among members of a single corporate entity, such as an agreement between a parent corporation and its wholly-owned subsidiary, because the parent and subsidiary "have a complete unity of interest," and so are incapable of conspiring under Section 1.[8] However, the mere fact that legally distinct entities have organized themselves under a "single umbrella" or into a "structured joint venture" does not immunize them from scrutiny under § 1. Rather, the court must determine whether the agreement joins together "independent sources of decisionmaking."[9] If so, the entities are capable of conspiring together under § 1, and the finder of fact must determine whether the agreement unreasonably restrains trade.[10]

A plaintiff may prove the existence of a contract, combination, or conspiracy through direct or circumstantial evidence. A secret agreement will nearly always need to be proven through circumstantial evidence.[11] The agreement need not be in writing, and it need not even be express.[12] But there must be sufficient evidence to prove that the parties acted

---

[6] 15 U.S.C. § 1.

[7] Section 4 of the Clayton Act permits "any person . . . injured in his business or property by reason of anything forbidden in the antitrust laws" to recover treble damages. 15 U.S.C. § 15(a). Section 16 of the Clayton Act entitles "[a]ny person . . . upon . . . a showing that the danger of irreparable loss or damage is immediate . . . by a violation of the antitrust laws" to obtain an injunction. 15 U.S.C. § 26.

[8] Am. Needle, Inc. v. NFL, 560 U.S. __, 130 S. Ct. 2201, 2211–12 (2010). In "rare cases," however, even agreements within a single firm "can constitute concerted action covered by § 1 when the parties to the agreement act on interests separate from those of the firm itself." *Id.* at 2215.

[9] *Am. Needle*, 130 S. Ct. at 2212 (quoting Copperweld Corp. v. Independence Tube Corp., 467 U.S. 752, 769 (1984)).

[10] *Id.*

[11] *See, e.g.,* United States v. Wash., 586 F.2d 1147, 1153 (7th Cir. 1978) ("By its nature conspiracy is conceived and carried out clandestinely, and direct evidence of the crime is rarely available. Thus, circumstantial evidence from which the jury could reasonably infer the existence of an agreement is permissible.").

[12] United States v. General Motors Corp., 384 U.S. 127, 142–43 (1966) ("explicit agreement is not a necessary part of a Sherman Act conspiracy").

in concert. Specifically, the plaintiff "must present evidence that 'tends to exclude the possibility' that the alleged conspirators acted independently."[13]

It is not unlawful under the Sherman Act for businesses in a highly concentrated industry to engage in similar or even identical behavior, including pricing their products identically, so long as they have not agreed to do so. This conduct – "conscious parallelism" – can be found unlawful, however, if the plaintiff proves enough additional indicia of agreement – called "plus factors" – to enable the fact finder to infer an agreement. The following "plus factors" are often alleged, in addition to consciously parallel behavior, in support of a conspiracy allegation: (1) evidence that the defendants engaged in behavior that would have been against each defendant's self-interest if it had acted alone, but in all defendants' self-interest if they act together; (2) opportunities to conspire; (3) a motive to conspire, including poor economic performance prior to the conspiracy; (4) the exchange of price information; and (5) structural features that make collusion (that is, an agreement to fix prices, allocate markets, or otherwise restrain competition) more likely, such as a limited number of suppliers and a homogeneous product.[14]

In its 2007 decision in *Bell Atlantic Corp. v. Twombly*,[15] the Supreme Court clarified the standards for pleading a § 1 antitrust conspiracy claim in the context of conscious parallelism. The Court held that allegations of parallel conduct combined with a "bare assertion of conspiracy" were insufficient, even at the pleading stage, to sustain a complaint:

> [A]n allegation of parallel conduct and a bare assertion of conspiracy will not suffice. Without more, parallel conduct does not suggest conspiracy, and a conclusory allegation of agreement at some unidentified point does not supply facts adequate to show illegality. Hence, when allegations of parallel conduct are set out in order to make a § 1 claim, they must be placed in a context that raises a suggestion of a preceding agreement, not merely parallel conduct that could just as well be independent action.[16]

In addition to allegations of parallel conduct, the complaint must include "plausible grounds to infer an agreement" or "enough factual matter (taken as true) to suggest that an agreement was made."[17] The Court concluded that the conspiracy alleged by the plaintiff was not plausible because each of the defendants had a rational economic incentive to engage unilaterally in each of the parallel acts alleged by plaintiff to be suggestive of conspiracy.

---

[13] Matsushita Elec. Indus. Co. v. Zenith Radio Corp., 475 U.S. 574, 588 (1986) (quoting Monsanto Co. v. Spray-Rite Serv. Corp., 465 U.S. 752, 768 (1984)).

[14] *In re* Coordinated Pretrial Proceedings in Petroleum Prods. Antitrust Litig., 906 F.2d 432, 445–50 (9th Cir. 1990); *see* Richard A. Posner, Antitrust Law 69–79 (2001); *In re* High Fructose Corn Syrup Antitrust Litig., 295 F.3d 651, 657 (7th Cir. 2002).

[15] Bell Atl. Corp. v. Twombly, 550 U.S. 544 (2007).

[16] *Twombly*, 550 U.S. at 556–57. In *Ashcroft v. Iqbal*, 552 U.S. 662 (2009), the Court made clear that the *Twombly* standard applies to all civil actions, and not just antitrust cases.

[17] *Twombly*, 550 U.S. at 556. The Court "retired" the pleading standard of *Conley v. Gibson*, 355 U.S. 41 (1957), which had long held that in a notice pleading case, "a complaint should not be dismissed for failure to state a claim unless it appears beyond doubt that the plaintiff can prove no set of facts in support of his claim which would entitle him to relief." *Twombly*, 550 U.S. at 561. For a discussion of Rule 12(b)(6) motions to dismiss pursuant to *Twombly*, see Chapter 6 of this Handbook.

In its subsequent decision in *Ashcroft v. Iqbal*, the Court explained that the plausibility standard it articulated in *Twombly* is "not akin to a probability requirement."[18] Lower court decisions interpreting *Twombly* and *Iqbal* have similarly made clear that motions to dismiss antitrust claims are still governed by the notice pleading standard of Rule 8 of the Federal Rules of Civil Procedure.[19]

1.02.2 Affecting interstate or foreign commerce

The requirement that the challenged agreement affect interstate or foreign commerce is easily satisfied. Even if an agreement is limited by its terms to conduct within a state, it will be found to affect interstate or foreign commerce if the parties or the commerce affected by the restraint have some relation to interstate or foreign commerce.[20]

1.02.3 Unreasonably restrains competition

As the Supreme Court has repeatedly recognized, § 1, if read literally, could apply to "every instance of cooperation between two people."[21] But that is not how the Court has interpreted the statute. Rather, the Sherman Act only prohibits those agreements that are "unreasonably restrictive of competitive conditions."[22] An agreement can unreasonably restrict competitive conditions if it has the effect of raising prices, restricting output, diminishing quality, limiting choice, or creating, maintaining, enhancing, or preserving an entity's market power.

1.02.4 Rule of reason vs. per se analysis

In determining whether an agreement unreasonably restrains competition under § 1 of the Sherman Act, courts employ one of two standards of analysis. The "rule of reason" standard, which is used in most cases, analyzes the market and then weighs all of the harmful effects of the restraint against its benefits to determine whether the restraint "is one that promotes competition or one that suppresses competition."[23]

---

18 129 S. Ct. at 1949.

19 *See, e.g.*, Aktieselskabet AF 21 Nov. 2001 v. Fame Jeans Inc., 525 F.3d 8, 15 (D.C. Cir. 2008) ("*Twombly* leaves the long-standing fundamentals of notice pleading intact"); Airborne Beepers & Video, Inc. v. AT&T Mobility LLC, 499 F.3d 663, 667 (7th Cir. 2007) ("*Twombly* did not signal a switch to fact-pleading"); Starr v. Sony BMG Music Entm't, 592 F.3d 314, 323 (2d Cir. 2010) ("[P]laintiffs were not required to mention a specific time, place or person involved in each conspiracy allegation.").

20 *See, e.g.*, McLain v. Real Estate Bd., Inc., 444 U.S. 232 (1980) (local real estate brokers' agreement to fix the price of sales commissions affected interstate commerce because the commission rates affected local residential real estate sales, which in turn affected interstate demand for financing and title insurance).

21 Am. Needle, Inc. v. NFL, 560 U.S. __, 130 S. Ct. 2201 (2010).

22 Standard Oil Co. v. United States, 221 U.S. 1, 58 (1911).

23 Nat'l Soc'y of Prof'l Eng'rs v. United States, 435 U.S. 679, 691 (1978). The Supreme Court first articulated the standard in *Board of Trade of Chicago v. United States*, 246 U.S. 231, 238 (1918):

To prove a § 1 case under the rule of reason standard, the plaintiff must first define the relevant product and geographic markets[24] affected by the challenged restraint, and demonstrate that the defendant or defendants have market power in those markets.[25] Next, the plaintiff must prove that the challenged restraint has a substantial anticompetitive

---

The true test of legality is whether the restraint imposed is such as merely regulates, and perhaps thereby promotes competition, or whether it is such as may suppress or even destroy competition. To determine that question the court must ordinarily consider the facts peculiar to the business to which the restraint is applied, its condition before and after the restraint is imposed, the nature of the restraint, and its effect, actual or probable.

[24] Definition of the relevant market has long been considered necessary to provide the context in which to assess the competitive effect of the restraint. Cont'l T.V., Inc. v. GTE Sylvania, 433 U.S. 36, 53 n.21 (1977). Relevant market analysis is also employed under § 2 of the Sherman Act (monopolization), § 3 of the Clayton Act (certain tying and exclusive dealing agreements), § 7 of the Clayton Act (mergers and acquisitions), the Robinson-Patman Act (price discrimination), and § 5 of the FTC Act (unfair methods of competition). The standards for determining the relevant product and geographic markets are nearly identical under these statutes, and courts conducting a relevant market analysis rely on cases decided under each. While a thorough description of relevant market analysis is beyond the scope of this chapter, "[t]he outer boundaries of a product market are determined by the reasonable interchangeability of use or the cross-elasticity of demand between the product itself and substitutes for it." Brown Shoe Co. v. United States, 370 U.S. 294, 325 (1962). A similar test is used to determine the relevant geographic market, which the Supreme Court has described as "the 'area of effective competition . . . in which the seller operates, and to which the purchaser can practicably turn for supplies.'" United States v. Philadelphia Nat'l Bank & Trust, 374 U.S. 321, 359 (1963); *Brown Shoe Co.*, 370 U.S. at 336–37 ("The criteria to be used in determining the appropriate geographic market are essentially similar to those used to determine the relevant product market . . . .").

In recent years, the federal antitrust enforcement agencies have moved away from strict reliance on careful market definition and market share analysis in assessing competitive effects. The recently-issued Horizontal Merger Guidelines (August 19, 2010), for example, state that "[s]ome of analytical tools used by the Agencies to assess competitive effects do not rely on market definition. . . ." U.S. Dep't of Justice & Fed. Trade Comm'n, Horizontal Merger Guidelines at 7, *available at* http://www.ftc/gov/os/2010/08/100819hmg.pdf. Commentators have long criticized the market definition/market share framework of analysis, and one recent article concludes that the market definition process is "incoherent as a matter of basic economic principles and hence should be abandoned entirely." Louis Kaplow, *Why (Ever) Define Markets?*, 124 Harv. L. Rev. 437 (2010); *see also id.* at notes 78–80 (describing prior critiques).

[25] Market power is "the ability to raise prices above those that would be charged in a competitive market." Nat'l Collegiate Athletic Ass'n v. Board of Regents, 468 U.S. 85, 109 n.38 (1984) (*NCAA*). Market power can be proven by evidence of a high market share and barriers to new entry. What constitutes a sufficiently high market share to raise competitive concerns has never been definitively answered by the Supreme Court, and varies according to the type of restraint under review. For horizontal restraints, the courts and the enforcement agencies (the Federal Trade Commission (FTC) and the Antitrust Division of the Department of Justice (DOJ)) typically require that the competitors whose conduct is being challenged have a combined market share of at least 20 percent. For vertical restraints like tying arrangements and exclusive dealing, the threshold is at least 30 percent. For monopolization claims the threshold is generally considered to be 70 percent. ABA Section of Antitrust Law, Antitrust Law Developments 230–32 (5th ed. 2002).

Where the plaintiff can prove that the restraint caused "actual detrimental effects, such as a reduction of output," no inquiry into market power is required, because the market power inquiry is merely "a surrogate for detrimental effect." FTC v. Ind. Fed'n of Dentists, 476 U.S. 447, 460–61 (1986) (citation omitted).

effect.[26] If the plaintiff demonstrates that the agreement has a substantially harmful effect on competition (and not just individual competitors), and in addition demonstrates injury or imminent threat of injury to its business or property, it has established a prima facie case under § 1. The burden then shifts to the defendant to proffer a "procompetitive justification." In other words, the defendant must show that the restraint benefits competition by, for example, promoting interbrand competition, enhancing efficiency, increasing output, or making available a product or products that would not otherwise be available. If the defendant successfully proffers a non-pretextual procompetitive justification for the restraint, the burden shifts back to the plaintiff to show either that the defendant can advance the proffered procompetitive justification through less restrictive means, or that the anticompetitive harm of the conduct outweighs the procompetitive benefits.[27]

A few categories of agreements are deemed so harmful to competition that they are per se unlawful without analysis either of market conditions or their actual competitive effects.[28] Price-fixing, bid-rigging, and market and customer allocation agreements among horizontal competitors are per se unlawful.[29] In addition, some restraints can be analyzed either under a rule of reason or a modified per se standard of illegality.

The modified per se standard, also referred to as the "quick look" rule of reason standard, is more rigorous than the per se standard but less rigorous than a full blown rule of reason analysis. Under a "quick look," an analysis of market power is not required because the restraint at issue – typically one that increases price or reduces output – is

---

26 United States v. Topco Assocs., Inc., 405 U.S. 596, 606 (1972) (practices that "in some insignificant degree" restrain competition are not unlawful). The plaintiff must also show that the restraint has a substantially adverse impact on the competitive process, as opposed to a competitor or a group of competitors. Brunswick Corp. v. Pueblo Bowl-O-Mat, Inc., 429 U.S. 477 (1977).

27 Cal. Dental Ass'n v. FTC, 526 U.S. 756 (1999). In *California Dental*, the Court instructed courts applying a rule of reason analysis to use a "sliding scale" at each step of the burden-shifting test, so that the degree of proof required depends on the nature of the conduct considered and the degree of proof offered at the previous step. The Court stated that sometimes the analysis can be conducted in "the twinkling of an eye" and that the analysis can be truncated if at any point the outcome is clear. *Cal. Dental Ass'n*, 526 U.S. at 780, 781 n.15. In *United States v. Microsoft Corp.*, 253 F.3d 34 (D.C. Cir. 2001), a § 2 monopolization case, the Court of Appeals for the D.C. Circuit described a rule of reason analysis that is more structured and sequential than the analysis often employed by courts under § 1. Under this approach, after the plaintiff has established that the defendant's conduct has caused anticompetitive effects, the burden shifts to the defendant to proffer a procompetitive justification for its conduct. If it succeeds in showing a procompetitive justification, the burden shifts back to the plaintiff to show that the defendant can advance its procompetitive justification through less restrictive means. If plaintiff can meet this burden, it will prevail. If not, plaintiff must then demonstrate that the anticompetitive harm of the conduct outweighs the procompetitive benefits. *Microsoft*, 253 F.3d at 58–59.

28 A practice that "appears to be one that would always or almost always tend to restrict competition and decrease output" rather than "increase economic efficiency and render markets more, rather than less, competitive," is subject to the per se rule and is deemed illegal without any inquiry into the purported business justifications or the competitive injury. Broadcast Music, Inc. v. Columbia Broad. Sys., Inc., 441 U.S. 1, 19–20 (1979) (citation omitted).

29 FTC v. Superior Ct. Trial Lawyers Ass'n, 493 U.S. 411, 421–23 (1990) (agreement to restrict output); Arizona v. Maricopa Cty Med. Soc'y, 457 U.S. 332, 357 (1982) (price fixing); United States v. Koppers Co., 652 F.2d 290, 294 (2d Cir. 1981) (bid rigging); Palmer v. BRG of Ga., Inc., 498 U.S. 46, 49–50 (1990) (agreement to allocate markets).

obviously harmful to competition. On the other hand, the agreement may have some procompetitive benefits, making application of the per se standard inappropriate. For example, the Supreme Court held that a National Collegiate Athletic Association (NCAA) rule limiting the number of football games its member schools could televise was a naked restriction on output that had "significant potential for anticompetitive effect . . . ."[30] But because the rule was imposed in an industry "in which horizontal restraints on competition are essential if the product is to be available at all," application of the per se rule was inappropriate.[31]

Determining which standard of analysis applies has profound implications for private litigation. A full-blown rule of reason analysis requires extensive economic analysis of the relevant product and geographic markets, market power, and the competitive impact of the challenged agreement. This analysis is costly and increases significantly the length and uncertainty of litigation. Thus, a private plaintiff will always attempt to fit its claims within one of the categories of claims that are subject to per se analysis. And the defendant, in turn, will virtually always contend that the case must be analyzed under the rule of reason.

1.02.5 Horizontal restraints

Horizontal restraints are agreements among actual or potential competitors. Vertical restraints, in contrast, are agreements between parties who stand at different levels in a chain of distribution, such as an agreement between a manufacturer and its distributor. Because vertical restraints are almost never analyzed under a per se standard of illegality, the distinction is critical.[32] Several types of horizontal agreements that may be illegal are discussed below.

1.02.5(A) Cartels

Organizations of horizontal competitors that conspire to fix prices, restrict output, rig bids, or allocate customers or territorial or product markets have long been considered the "supreme evil of antitrust."[33] In the United States, the only criminal enforcement of antitrust laws is targeted against cartels. Cartel members who fix prices, agree on output restrictions, allocate customers or markets, or rig bids are all subject to felony prosecution and criminal fines.[34] The DOJ's Antitrust Division makes cartel prosecution a top priority, and its criminal prosecution of cartel members has resulted in sharply increased fines

---

30 Nat'l Collegiate Athletic Ass'n v. Board of Regents, 468 U.S. 85, 104 (1984). *See also* FTC v. Ind. Fed'n of Dentists, 476 U.S. 447 (1986) (quick look rule of reason applied to agreement among members of a dentists' association to withhold x-rays requested by insurers evaluating claims).

31 *NCAA*, 468 U.S. at 100–06.

32 As discussed below, some tying arrangements, which consist of a vertical agreement between a supplier and a customer, and hub-and-spoke conspiracies, which consist of both vertical and horizontal agreements, are analyzed under a per se or modified per se standard.

33 Verizon Commc'n Inc. v. Law Offices of Curtis V. Trinko, LLP, 540 U.S. 398, 408 (2004).

34 Division Update: Spring 2011, *available at* http://www.justice.gov/atr/public/division-update/2011/index.html (accessed Oct. 13, 2011). During fiscal year 2010, the Division filed 60 criminal cases and charged 63 individuals and 21 corporations. Though fewer than in 2009, the number of criminal cases brought by the Division in 2010 was the second-highest in the period

and jail time in recent years. In the period 2000–2010, the Antitrust Division obtained over $4.5 billion in criminal fines, with more than a dozen individual corporate fines of more than $100 million.[35] Over that same period, the percentage of defendants serving jail time has steadily trended upward, from 38 percent in 2000 to 78 percent in 2010. In 2010, the average jail sentence for an antitrust violator was 30 months.[36] Each of the offenses targeted for criminal prosecution is analyzed under a per se standard of illegality.

Cartels also give rise to a significant percentage of private antitrust litigation in the United States. When a criminal investigation becomes public, private individuals and businesses that have been harmed by the cartel's conduct will often file private actions – including class actions – to recover their damages.[37] In some instances, private litigation precedes the government investigation.[38]

2001–2010. ANTITRUST DIVISION WORKLOAD STATISTICS FY 2001–2010, *available at* http://www.justice.gov/atr/public/workload-statistics.pdf.

[35] Division Update, *supra* note 34; Antitrust Division: Sherman Act Violations Yielding a Corporate Fine of $10 Million or More, *available at* http://www.justice.gov/atr/public/criminal/sherman10.pdf.

[36] Scott D. Hammond, Deputy Asst. Att'y Gen., Antitrust Div., U.S. Dep't of Justice, Remarks at the 24th Annual National Institute on White Collar Crime: The Evolution of Criminal Antitrust Enforcement Over the Last Two Decades (Feb. 25, 2010), *available at* http:/www.usdoj.gov/atr/public/speeches/255515.htm; U.S. DEP'T OF JUSTICE, ANTITRUST DIV., CRIMINAL ENFORCEMENT: FINE AND JAIL CHARTS 2000–2010, *available at* www.justice.gov/atr/public/criminal/264101.html. The Antitrust Division's leniency program, begun in 1978 and modified in 1993 and 1994, enables corporations and individuals to avoid criminal convictions, fines and jail time by being the first to confess participation in a criminal antitrust violation. The leniency applicant must admit participation in a criminal violation of the antitrust laws before receiving a conditional leniency letter, and must demonstrate that it has satisfied its obligation to pay restitution before it will be granted final leniency. The program has been highly successful in encouraging companies and individuals to come forward and report cartel behavior. The Antitrust Division describes the Corporate Leniency Program as the Division's "*most* effective investigative tool" and states that cooperation from leniency applicants "has cracked more cartels than all other tools at our disposal combined." Scott D. Hammond, Presentation to the OECD Competition Committee: Cracking Cartels With Leniency Programs at 2 (Oct. 18, 2005), *available at* http://www.usdoj.gov/atr/public/speeches/212269.pdf (emphasis in original).

The leniency program impacts private litigation not only by exposing more cartels; it also sometimes facilitates cooperation with private plaintiffs. A leniency applicant may qualify for detrebling of damages if the applicant cooperates with plaintiffs in their civil action, while the applicant's former co-conspirators will remain liable for treble damages on a joint and several basis. SCOTT D. HAMMOND & BELINDA A. BARRETT, FREQUENTLY ASKED QUESTIONS REGARDING THE ANTITRUST DIVISION'S LENIENCY PROGRAM AND MODEL LENIENCY LETTERS (NOV. 19, 2008), *available at* http://www.justice.gov/atr/public/criminal/239583.htm.

[37] The victim of a price-fixing cartel is the customer that paid an inflated price. Because there are many victims, and because individual damages may be relatively modest, many victims pursue recovery through the class action device. Private litigation often begins within weeks or even days of a public announcement of a federal investigation into suspected cartel activity. While the Antitrust Division does not usually announce the inception of a criminal antitrust investigation, pre-dawn raids of targeted companies, often coordinated with antitrust authorities in other countries, are often reported in the press. Such investigations also become public because federal securities laws require publicly held companies to disclose such investigations in their quarterly filings. For further discussion of pre-complaint investigation, see Chapter 2 of this Handbook.

[38] *See In re* Nasdaq Market-Makers Antitrust Litig., 187 F.R.D. 465 (S.D.N.Y. 1998) (private

The claim most commonly alleged in private cartel litigation is price-fixing. Because price-fixing agreements are often accompanied by or implemented through agreements to restrict output as well as agreements to allocate customers or territorial markets, these claims are also common in private litigation. Least common among per se offenses is private litigation challenging bid-rigging. While the DOJ frequently prosecutes businesses and individuals for bid-rigging, the effects are often localized, making nationwide class actions less likely. The episodic nature of bid-rigging may render class certification difficult as well.

1.02.5(B) JOINT VENTURES

Joint ventures are collaborative undertakings among competitors in which otherwise independent firms seek to achieve a specific business objective (or objectives) through partial integration of their resources or risks. Joint ventures are "more integrated than cartels but less integrated than mergers."[39] Private parties injured by the formation of a joint venture or by subsequent agreements among venture participants can sue the participants or the joint venture itself under § 1 or § 2 of the Sherman Act, or under § 7 of the Clayton Act.[40] They can also assert state law claims under parallel statutory and common law rules. Most cases are brought under § 1.

The first step in evaluating the legality of a joint venture agreement under § 1 is to determine whether the venture participants engage in the requisite concerted conduct or instead operate as a single entity immune from scrutiny under § 1. In *American Needle, Inc. v. NFL*,[41] the Supreme Court, in a unanimous opinion, reversed a ruling by the Seventh Circuit that had held that § 1 did not apply to the NFL teams' joint agreements to develop and market their intellectual property. The teams formed National Football League Properties (NFLP) to develop and market their intellectual property, and agreed to share revenues equally or give the proceeds to charity. In 2000, the teams voted to allow NFLP to grant exclusive licenses, and NFLP granted Reebok an exclusive 10-year license to produce and sell trademarked hats and other headwear for all 32 teams. American Needle, a former licensee, sued the NFL, the 32 member teams, NFLP, and Reebok, alleging a violation of § 1. The district court granted summary judgment for the defendants, holding that the teams had sufficiently integrated their licensing operations so as to constitute a single entity immune from § 1 scrutiny.[42] The Seventh Circuit affirmed, finding that because the NFL teams shared an economic interest in promoting NFL football over other forms of entertainment, "only one source of economic power controls the

---

class action litigation preceded any publicly-known government investigation); *In re* Aftermarket Automotive Lighting Products Antitrust Litig., No. 2:09-ml-02007-GW (PGG) (C.D. Cal.) (private action preceded federal enforcement action). As another example, the FTC's 2009 lawsuit against Intel was preceded by private litigation by Intel's main rival, AMD, and by class action litigation (in addition to enforcement actions in the European Union, Korea, and Japan).

[39] *See* Thomas A. Piraino, Jr., *A Proposed Antitrust Approach to Collaborations Among Competitors*, 86 IOWA L. REV. 1137 (2001).

[40] The formation of the joint venture is subject to challenge under § 7 if the parties acquire voting securities in the newly formed entity. United States v. Penn-Olin Chem. Co., 378 U.S. 158 (1964).

[41] 130 S.Ct. 2201 (2010).

[42] Am. Needle, Inc. v. New Orleans La. Saints, 496 F. Supp. 2d 941, 943 (2007).

promotion of NFL football." Thus, according to the Seventh Circuit, the NFL acted as a single entity in the context of licensing its member teams' intellectual property.[43]

Rejecting the Seventh Circuit's conclusion, the Supreme Court emphasized that the determination whether an entity is capable of conspiring under § 1 requires a substantive inquiry into whether the challenged agreement "joins together 'independent centers of decisionmaking.' If it does, the entities are capable of conspiring under Section 1, and the court must decide whether the restraint of trade is an unreasonable and therefore illegal one."[44] The Court found that the NFL teams did "not possess either the unitary decision-making quality or the single aggregation of economic power characteristic of independent action."[45] Rather, each of the teams was "a substantial, independently owned, and independently managed business."[46] With respect to the licensing of their intellectual property, the Court also found that the teams compete in that market.[47] Nor did the fact that the NFL and its member teams formed a legally separate entity that centralized the management of their intellectual property immunize their conduct from § 1: "An ongoing § 1 violation cannot evade § 1 scrutiny simply by giving the ongoing violation a name and label."[48] Though it was a closer question, the Court held that decisions by NFLP could also constitute concerted activity covered by § 1, because such decisions were made by the 32 teams – potential competitors of one another in the intellectual property market – each of which owned its share of the jointly managed assets.[49]

If the joint venture is subject to § 1, it can be analyzed under a per se standard, a "quick look" rule of reason standard, or a full-blown rule of reason standard.[50] Merely labeling

---

[43] Am. Needle, Inc. v. NFL, 538 F.3d 736, 744 (7th Cir. 2008).

[44] Am. Needle, Inc. v. NFL, 560 U.S. __, 130 S. Ct. 2201, 2212 (2010) (quoting Copperweld Corp. v. Independence Tube Corp., 467 U.S. 752, 769 (1984)).

[45] *Id.* at 2212.

[46] *Id.*

[47] *Id.*

[48] *Id.* at 2213.

[49] *Id.* at 2215.

[50] *See, e.g.,* Broadcast Music Inc. v. CBS, Inc., 441 U.S. 1 (1979) (agreement by thousands of authors and composers to grant a joint venture a blanket license to all their musical compositions analyzed under a rule of reason standard because the agreement reflected integration of sales, addressed a free-rider problem, and created a product that would otherwise not have been available); Nat'l Collegiate Athletic Ass'n v. Board of Regents, 468 U.S. 85, 100–01 (1984) (NCAA rule limiting member universities' football game telecasts analyzed under quick look rule of reason rather than a per se standard because the "case involve[d] an industry in which horizontal restraints on competition are essential if the product is to be available at all"). Most recently, in *Texaco, Inc. v. Dagher*, 547 U.S. 1, 8 (2006), the Court held that a pricing arrangement that Shell and Texaco entered into after they consolidated their operations in the Western United States did not "fall within the narrow category of activity that is per se unlawful" because the joint venture (already reviewed by the antitrust authorities) had already eliminated all relevant competition between the parties. They had "agreed to pool their resources and share the risks of and profits from . . . [the joint venture's] activities," and shared those profits in their role as investors, not competitors. *Dagher*, 547 U.S. at 4, 8.

The FTC and DOJ's jointly issued Antitrust Guidelines for Collaboration Among Competitors similarly treat joint ventures differently depending on whether the parties integrate their economic resources and the nature and extent of any efficiencies created by the joint venture. FED. TRADE COMM'N & U.S. DEP'T OF JUSTICE, ANTITRUST GUIDELINES FOR COLLABORATIONS AMONG

a collaboration among competitors a joint venture, however, will not protect it from per se illegality under the Sherman Act if it involves joint price-setting or restrictions on output.[51]

As with any other conduct analyzed under the rule of reason, an evaluation of the legality of a joint venture agreement requires a fact-specific analysis. If the agreement has obvious anticompetitive effects or the plaintiff can show that it has already caused anticompetitive harm, the court may apply a "quick look" rule of reason standard, dispensing with any detailed market analysis.[52] Otherwise, the plaintiff must first define the relevant market (along both product and geographic dimensions) and then demonstrate that the joint venture has (or will have) market power in that market.[53] If the joint venture meets the threshold market power requirement, the court will then examine the nature of the agreement to determine whether it is likely to cause substantial anticompetitive harm. If yes, then the court will consider any procompetitive benefits proffered by the defendant, and determine whether those benefits can be achieved by a less restrictive alternative.[54]

The Competitor Collaboration Guidelines, issued jointly by the FTC and DOJ in 2000, set out the standards of review the enforcement agencies rely upon in evaluating the legality of concerted conduct. While the Guidelines are not binding on the courts, they have been cited in some published decisions (though not yet by the United States Supreme Court) and provide a useful framework for analysis because they are based on existing law. The Guidelines explain that the Agencies will challenge agreements "of a type that always or almost always tends to raise price or reduce output," such as price-fixing, bid-rigging, and market-allocation agreements, under a per se standard of illegality, "without inquiring into their claimed business purposes, anticompetitive harms, procompetitive benefits, or overall competitive effects."[55] On the other hand, the Agencies will not challenge an

---

COMPETITORS 4 (2000), *available at* http://www.ftc.gov/os/2000/04/ftcdojguidelines.pdf [hereinafter COMPETITOR COLLABORATION GUIDELINES or "Guidelines"] (agreements that "are reasonably related to, and reasonably necessary to achieve procompetitive benefits from, an efficiency-enhancing integration of economic activity" are analyzed under the rule of reason).

[51] Timken Roller Bearing Co. v. United States, 341 U.S. 593 (1951). *See also* Arizona v. Maricopa County Med. Soc'y, 457 U.S. 332 (1982) (agreement among medical doctors to set a maximum fee schedule constituted per se illegal price fixing); *but see Dagher*, 571 U.S. 1 (legality of joint venture between two previously competing companies that set a single price for jointly-produced product subject to rule of reason, not per se analysis, because the companies participated in the relevant market jointly through investment in joint venture and shared in profits as investors).

[52] *See Am. Needle,* 130 S. Ct. at 2216–17 (remanding determination of legality of league's joint licensing of intellectual property under § 1, the Supreme Court suggested applicability of "quick look" standard but also noted that the NFL's interest in maintaining a competitive balance among member teams might save the restraint); *Ind. Fed'n of Dentists*, 476 U.S. at 460–61 (analysis of market power not necessary where there is proof of actual anticompetitive effect); *Cal. Dental Ass'n*, 526 U.S. at 770 (court of appeals erred in applying quick look analysis where joint venture's advertising restrictions did not have obvious anticompetitive effects).

[53] If the combined market share of the joint venture and its members exceeds 20 percent, that is sufficient to continue the analysis. ABA SECTION OF ANTITRUST LAW, JOINT VENTURES: ANTITRUST ANALYSIS OF COLLABORATIONS AMONG COMPETITORS 47 (2006).

[54] *See, e.g.*, Sullivan v. Nat'l Football League, 34 F.3d 1091, 1103 (1st Cir. 1994) ("[A] given restriction is not reasonable, that is, its benefits cannot outweigh its harm to competition, if a reasonable, less restrictive alternative . . . exists."); *see also* Law v. NCAA, 134 F.3d 1010, 1019 (10th Cir. 1998).

[55] COMPETITOR COLLABORATION GUIDELINES at 8.

agreement "that is reasonably related" to an "efficiency-enhancing integration of economic activity" and "reasonably necessary" to achieve its procompetitive benefits under a flexible rule of reason standard.[56]

Under the Guidelines' flexible rule of reason standard, the Agencies begin their analysis by examining the business purpose of the challenged agreement and inquiring whether the agreement has caused anticompetitive harm. If the nature of the agreement and the absence of market power[57] demonstrate the absence of anticompetitive harm, the Agencies will not challenge the agreement. If the agreement has already caused anticompetitive harm, or if the "likelihood of anticompetitive harm is evident from the nature of the agreement," the Agencies will challenge the agreement without a detailed market analysis.[58] If the agreement raises competitive concerns but cannot be analyzed without a detailed market analysis, the Agencies will define relevant markets, calculate market shares and concentration levels, inquire whether the venture and its participants have the "ability and incentive to compete independently," evaluate the likelihood and impact of competitive entry, and "assess any other market circumstances that may foster or impede anticompetitive harms."[59] If this analysis indicates no potential for anticompetitive harm, the Agencies will discontinue the investigation. Otherwise, the Agencies will "examine whether the relevant agreement is reasonably necessary to achieve procompetitive benefits that likely would offset anticompetitive harms."[60]

Two federal statutes – the National Cooperative Research and Production Act (NCRPA)[61] and the Standards Development Organization Advancement Act (SDOA)[62] – provide limited antitrust safe harbors for certain kinds of joint ventures. The NCRPA provides limited antitrust immunity to research and development and production joint ventures that meet its criteria and that register with the DOJ and FTC. A joint venture that meets the NCRPA criteria and files the requisite notice is not subject to the per se standard. If it is adjudged to be in violation of the antitrust laws under a rule of reason standard, it is liable for only actual damages, rather than treble damages. Further, if a private plaintiff unsuccessfully challenges the legality of a qualified NCRPA joint venture, the defendant may recover its attorneys' fees and costs.[63] The SDOA extends the protections of the NCRPA to qualifying standard setting organizations.[64]

---

56 *Id.*

57 In this initial inquiry, the Agencies may be able to determine that there is no market power without defining a relevant market. For example, if there are no barriers to entry, or there is no plausible market power no matter how the market is defined, the Agencies may discontinue the inquiry without further analysis. *Id.* at 10 n.26.

58 This analysis is similar to the Supreme Court's "quick look" rule of reason analysis. *Id.* at 10.

59 *Id.* at 11.

60 *Id.* at 11–12.

61 15 U.S.C. §§ 4301–4305.

62 15 U.S.C. § 4301(a)(7).

63 15 U.S.C. §§ 4301–4305. Normally, the antitrust defendant must pay its own attorneys' fees and costs, even if it prevails. (The Clayton Act's exception to the "American Rule" entitles prevailing plaintiffs, not defendants, to attorneys' fees and costs. 15 U.S.C. § 15.)

64 15 U.S.C. § 4302.

1.02.5(C) Concerted refusals to deal

Concerted refusals to deal, also known as group boycotts, are agreements among horizontal competitors not to do business with certain other firms or individuals, or to do so only under specified terms. For many years group boycotts were considered illegal per se.[65] Under current law, however, they may be evaluated under either the per se or rule of reason standard, depending on the market power of the defendants, and the purpose and effect of the boycott: "the per se approach has generally been limited to cases in which firms with market power boycott suppliers or customers in order to discourage them from doing business with a competitor . . . ."[66] A per se approach will also be applied to group boycotts that constitute or enforce a price-fixing agreement or other agreement that is illegal per se.[67]

1.02.5(D) Mergers and acquisitions

While regulation of mergers and acquisitions is mostly left to federal and state antitrust authorities,[68] private litigants may also challenge them under federal and state law. Private plaintiffs may seek injunctive relief preventing or undoing the merger, and may seek damages.[69] The principal statute governing mergers and acquisitions is § 7 of the Clayton Act, which prohibits any merger or acquisition where "the effect of such acquisition may be substantially to lessen competition, or to tend to create a monopoly."[70] Private plaintiffs can also challenge a merger or acquisition as an unreasonable restraint of trade, monopolization, or attempted monopolization under §§ 1 or 2 of the Sherman Act,[71] and seek damages and injunctive relief under the Clayton Act.[72]

A plaintiff challenging a merger or acquisition must define a relevant market along product and geographic dimensions,[73] identify the market participants, and show that the merger is likely to substantially lessen competition in the relevant markets.[74] If the

---

[65] *See, e.g.*, Klor's, Inc. v. Broadway-Hale Stores, Inc., 359 U.S. 207, 212 (1959) (group boycotts "have long been held to be in the forbidden category" of restraints as to which courts need not inquire into anticompetitive effects).

[66] *Ind. Fed'n of Dentists*, 476 U.S. at 458 ("quick look" rule of reason analysis applied to agreement among a group of dentists not to forward x-rays to insurers).

[67] FTC v. Superior Ct. Trial Lawyers Ass'n, 493 U.S. 411, 436 n.19 (1990) (agreement among lawyers to stop representing indigent clients unless government increased fees illegal per se).

[68] The FTC, DOJ, and state attorneys general may seek injunctive relief preventing or undoing a merger or acquisition under § 16 of the Clayton Act, and may seek damages under § 4 of the Clayton Act. 15 U.S.C. §§ 26, 15.

[69] 15 U.S.C. §§ 26, 15. *See, e.g.*, Taleff v. Southwest Airlines Co., No. 3:11-cv-02179-JW (N.D. Cal. Nov. 30, 2011) (airline ticket purchasers unsuccessfully sued Southwest Airlines and AirTran Airways under § 7 of the Clayton Act to undo their merger, alleging that ticket purchasers suffered imminent threat of loss or damage "in the form of higher ticket prices and diminished service").

[70] 15 U.S.C. § 18. Section 7 applies broadly to transactions involving acquisitions of stock, assets or partnership interests, including those transactions which resemble mergers, and those in which only some assets or interests are acquired. *Id.*

[71] The government can challenge a merger under Section 5 of the Federal Trade Commission Act, 15 U.S.C. § 45.

[72] 15 U.S.C. §§ 1, 2, 15, 26.

[73] United States v. E.I. Du Pont de Nemours & Co., 353 U.S. 586, 593 (1957); Brown Shoe Co., Inc. v. United States, 370 U.S. 294, 324 (1962).

[74] United States v. Oracle Corp., 331 F. Supp. 2d 1098, 1164 (N.D. Cal. 2004) (citing United States v. Penn-Olin Chem. Co., 378 U.S. 158, 171 (1964)). While early Supreme Court cases held

defendant proffers evidence that the merger will create efficiencies and other procompetitive benefits, the plaintiff must show that the anticompetitive effects of the merger would outweigh any procompetitive benefits.[75]

The DOJ and FTC's recently-issued Horizontal Merger Guidelines (August 19, 2010) set forth the agencies' enforcement policy with respect to mergers and acquisitions involving actual or potential competitors.[76] The Horizontal Merger Guidelines, together with the agencies' 2006 Commentary on the earlier Guidelines, provide a useful framework for analysis.[77] The Guidelines describe the kinds and sources of evidence the agencies review in analyzing a merger,[78] the consideration to be given to the existence of price discrimination,[79] the methods the agencies use to define the relevant markets and assess market concentration,[80] how they assess unilateral and coordinated effects,[81] and the tools they use to analyze ease of entry.[82]

In addition to proving all of the elements that a government plaintiff must prove, the private plaintiff challenging a merger or acquisition faces the additional challenge of showing that it has standing. Just as in any other private antitrust action, the plaintiff must show that it has suffered or is likely to suffer antitrust injury as a result of the challenged merger or acquisition.[83] Because of this additional hurdle, competitor challenges to mergers and acquisitions have rarely succeeded since the mid-1980s.[84]

---

that mergers resulting in an entity with a market share comprising more than 30 percent of the relevant market and increasing concentration by more than 33 percent were presumptively illegal (*see, e.g.,* United States v. Philadelphia Nat'l Bank, 374 U.S. 321 (1963)), the Court retreated from that position in 1974 (*see* United States v. Gen. Dynamics Corp., 415 U.S. 486 (1974)), and in recent decades courts have permitted mergers in markets far more concentrated initially, and in which the merger resulted in far greater concentration. *See, e.g.,* United States v. Baker Hughes, Inc., 908 F.2d 981 (D.C. Cir. 1990) (no § 7 violation where post-acquisition market share exceeded 75 percent). The new Horizontal Merger Guidelines reflect the courts' and enforcement agencies' shift away from a focus on market shares and market concentrations to a broader, more fact-specific analysis of the competitive circumstances surrounding the proposed merger. *See* Carl Shapiro, *The 2010 Horizontal Merger Guidelines: From Hedgehog to Fox in Forty Years*, 49 Antitrust L.J. 77 (2010).

[75] The Horizontal Merger Guidelines and Merger Commentary make clear that the agencies will consider the nature and extent of any efficiencies created by a merger in analyzing its competitive effects, and will avoid "unnecessary interference with mergers that are either competitively beneficial or neutral." U.S. Dep't of Justice & Fed. Trade Comm'n, Horizontal Merger Guidelines, *supra* note 24, at 1; Commentary on Horizontal Merger Guidelines 49–59 (2006), *available at* http://www.ftc.gov/os/2006/03/CommentaryontheHorizontalMergerGuidelinesMarch2006.pdf.

[76] Horizontal Merger Guidelines, *supra* note 24.

[77] *Id.* at 1 n.1 (the Commentary remains a "valuable supplement").

[78] *Id.* §§ 1, 2.

[79] *Id.* § 3.

[80] *Id.* §§ 4, 5.

[81] *Id.* §§ 6, 7.

[82] *Id.* § 9.

[83] Brunswick Corp. v. Pueblo Bowl-O-Mat, Inc., 429 U.S. 477 (1977) (where acquisition of a competing but failing bowling alley harmed plaintiff by eliminating its opportunity for additional profits, but benefited competition, plaintiff has not shown antitrust injury and has no standing under the antitrust laws); Cargill, Inc. v. Monfort of Colo., Inc., 479 U.S. 104 (1986) (where post-merger conduct did not threaten antitrust injury, rival that challenged merger not entitled to injunctive relief under Clayton Act).

[84] In its 1986 decision in *Cargill, Inc.*, 479 U.S. 104, the Supreme Court denied injunctive relief

1.02.6 Vertical agreements

Vertical restraints are agreements among firms standing at different levels in the chain of distribution. They may be challenged under § 1 (unreasonable restraint of trade) or § 2 (monopolization or attempted monopolization) of the Sherman Act. As discussed below, § 2 challenges are always assessed under the fact-intensive rule of reason standard of illegality. Until recently, vertical restraints involving concerted conduct and restraints on output or price could be assessed under a per se standard of illegality. Since the Supreme Court's decision in *Leegin*,[85] however, most vertical restraints are now challenged under a rule of reason standard. Several types of vertical agreements that may be illegal are discussed below.

1.02.6(A) Hub-and-spoke price-fixing agreements

The only vertical price restraint that continues to be evaluated under a pure per se standard of illegality is the so-called "hub-and-spoke" conspiracy. A hub-and-spoke conspiracy is a price-fixing or market allocation cartel involving both vertical and horizontal agreements. At the center, or "hub", of the conspiracy is a dominant supplier or distributor, which enters into a series of vertical agreements with its distributors or suppliers (the "spokes"). Without more, these vertical restraints – even if they dictate prices – are not actionable under § 1.[86] If, however, the "spokes" enter into horizontal agreements with one another to adhere to the vertical restraint (the "rim" of the conspiracy), the series of agreements are per se unlawful.[87]

1.02.6(B) Resale price maintenance

One of the most commonly challenged vertical price restraints is resale price maintenance, in which a manufacturer and its distributor agree on minimum or maximum prices to be charged for the manufacturer's products.[88] Maximum resale price maintenance

---

to a plaintiff rival challenging a proposed merger, holding that the plaintiff had not shown that the merged entity's conduct was likely to cause it antitrust injury, even though both lower courts had found that the merger was illegal under § 7 of the Clayton Act. (Section 7 prohibits a merger where the effect "may be substantially to lessen competition, or to tend to create a monopoly." 15 U.S.C. § 18.) The competitor-plaintiff's threatened injury of reduced profits (caused by the merged entity's ability to lower prices) did not constitute antitrust injury. *Cargill, Inc.*, 479 U.S. at 114–15.

[85] Leegin Creative Prods. v. PSKS, Inc., 551 U.S. 877 (2007).

[86] United States v. Colgate & Co., 250 U.S. 300 (1919) (manufacturers may announce pricing policies to their distributors and terminate any distributor that fails to follow the policy without liability under § 1, unless the distributor manifests agreement)

[87] Interstate Circuit, Inc. v. United States, 306 U.S. 208 (1939); Toys "R" Us, Inc v. FTC, 221 F.3d 928 (7th Cir. 2000) (where major toy retailer negotiated series of agreements with leading toy manufacturers that they would not sell to discount warehouse club stores, and there was evidence that seven of those manufacturers accepted the restriction on the condition that their competitors would do the same, agreements were illegal per se).

[88] An agreement is an essential element of a claim under § 1. Thus, if a manufacturer unilaterally announces a minimum or maximum price for its products, and then terminates distributors that do not comply with the pricing policy, there is no agreement, and hence no liability under § 1. *Colgate & Co.*, 250 U.S. 300. (There may, however, be liability under § 2 of the Sherman Act.). If, however, the manufacturer demands assent, and receives it, there is an agreement that can be

agreements are analyzed under a rule of reason analysis.[89] Until recently, minimum resale price maintenance agreements were considered so harmful to consumers that they were analyzed under a per se standard of illegality. In *Leegin*,[90] however, the Supreme Court reversed 96 years of precedent, holding that minimum resale price maintenance agreements are now subject to the rule of reason.[91] In addition to noting that it has in recent decades reduced the number of practices that are subject to a per se standard of antitrust illegality, the Court reasoned that resale price maintenance policies often have procompetitive benefits, such as promoting interbrand competition by eliminating intrabrand competition.[92]

The *Leegin* decision was controversial when written and continues to be met with opposition at both the federal and state levels. As the dissent noted, requiring courts to apply a rule of reason analysis forces the parties to engage in "one of the most costly procedures in antitrust practice,"[93] and has the effect of making a plaintiff victory unlikely.[94] *Leegin* was followed by three failed attempts to pass federal legislation repealing the decision and reinstating the per se rule for minimum resale price maintenance.[95] A fourth attempt is currently before the Senate Committee on the Judiciary.[96] Some state courts have held that their own state laws governing resale price maintenance are not subject to a rule of reason analysis, and the appropriate standard of review remains an open question in many other jurisdictions.[97] Despite this uncertainty, and the fact that *Leegin* does not immunize minimum resale price maintenance agreements from liability, the number of manufacturers setting minimum retail prices has reportedly increased since 2007.[98]

1.02.6(c) Non-price vertical agreements

Vertical agreements that do not constrain price are typically assessed under a rule of reason standard of illegality, because of their "real potential to stimulate interbrand

---

challenged under § 1 of the Sherman Act. *See, e.g.*, *Leegin*, 551 U.S. 877 (manufacturer adopted a "Colgate policy," that is, a policy stating it would sell its products only to retailers that followed its suggested retail prices, but then took the additional step of demanding a "pledge" of compliance, which Leegin gave, then broke).

[89] State Oil Co. v. Khan & Assoc., Inc., 522 U.S. 3 (1997) (overturning nearly 30 years of precedent, Court held that maximum resale price maintenance agreements were subject to rule of reason, rather than per se, analysis).

[90] *Leegin*, 551 U.S. 877.

[91] *Id.*

[92] *Id.* at 889–91.

[93] *Id.* at 915–17 (Breyer J., dissenting).

[94] Albert A. Foer, President, American Antitrust Institute, Testimony Before the Maryland Senate Judiciary Committee on Senate Bill 239 (Feb. 25, 2009), *available at* http://www.antitrustinstitute.org/node/11041 (follow "Read the testimony" hyperlink).

[95] S. 2261, 110th Cong. § 1 (2007); S. 148, 111th Cong. § 1 (2009); H.R. 3190, 111th Cong. § 2 (2009).

[96] S. 75, 112th Cong. § 3 (2011). For further discussion of *Leegin*-related legislation and other reform proposals, see Chapter 15 of this Handbook.

[97] For a survey of current resale price maintenance statutes and case law in each of the 50 states and the District of Columbia, see Michael A. Lindsay, *Overview of State RPM*, Antitrust Source (Apr. 2011), *available at* http://www.americanbar.org/content/dam/aba/publishing/antitrust_source/apr11-lindsaychart_4-20f.authcheckdam.pdf.

[98] H.R. Rep. No. 111-676, at 3 (2010).

competition."[99] The most commonly challenged non-price vertical restraints are agreements among manufacturers and their distributors not to permit other entities to distribute the manufacturer's goods (exclusive distributorships) and agreements among manufacturers and their distributors limiting each distributor's customers or geographic sales territory (territorial and customer restrictions).

In determining whether an exclusive distributorship constitutes an unreasonable restraint of trade under the rule of reason, courts will consider the nature and extent of interbrand competition, the duration of the agreement, and the geographic scope covered by the exclusive distributorship.[100] In assessing the legality of territorial and customer restraints, courts have examined the purpose of the restrictions (for example, a restriction that promotes a legitimate business reason such as improving efficiency, reducing free riding, or promoting consumer safety is more likely to be upheld), the effect of the restriction in limiting competition in the relevant market, the market power of the supplier, and the impact on competition.[101]

1.02.6(D) Tying arrangements

A tying arrangement is a vertical "agreement" between seller and buyer in which the seller agrees to sell a product to the buyer "only on the condition that the buyer also purchases a different (or tied) product, or at least agrees that he will not purchase that product from any other supplier."[102] The buyer's agreement, though coerced, is sufficient to satisfy § 1's requirement of joint action. In order to prove a tying claim, a plaintiff must show (1) a tie between two separate products or services; (2) that the defendant has appreciable market power in the tying product market; and (3) that the tie has a "not insubstantial" effect on commerce in the tied product market.[103] Implicit in the first element is the requirement that the buyer was coerced into buying a product he or she did not want, or would have preferred to buy on other terms.

Tying arrangements are usually evaluated under a modified per se standard of illegality. Unlike the standard applied to a horizontal price-fixing agreement, a plaintiff in a tying case must show that the defendant has sufficient market power in the tying product market "to force a purchaser to do something he would not do in a competitive market."[104] While

---

[99] Bus. Elecs. Corp. v. Sharp Elec. Corp., 485 U.S. 717, 724 (1988).

[100] United States v. Chicago Tribune-N.Y. News Syndicate, Inc., 309 F. Supp. 1301, 1307–08 (S.D.N.Y. 1970) (whether territorial scope of agreement was "arbitrary and unreasonably broad" was fact question); Paddock Publ'ns v. Chicago Tribune Co., 103 F.3d 42, 47 (7th Cir. 1996) (enduring exclusive distribution contracts characterize markets that are recognized as competitive); Murphy v. Bus. Cards Tomorrow Inc., 854 F.2d 1202, 1205 (9th Cir. 1988) (restraint not unreasonable where substantial interbrand competition existed and there were low entry barriers).

[101] *Murphy*, 854 F.2d at 1205 (so long as there is sufficient interbrand competition, negative impact on intrabrand competition irrelevant); Clairol, Inc. v. Boston Disc. Ctr. of Berkley, 608 F.2d 1114, 1125 (6th Cir. 1979) (customer restrictions that promoted consumer safety and customer goodwill not unreasonably restrictive); Bi-Rite Oil Co. v. Ind. Farm Bureau Coop. Ass'n, 908 F.2d 200, 204 (7th Cir. 1990) (no violation where supplier lacked market power).

[102] N. Pac. Ry. Co. v. United States, 356 U.S. 1, 5–6 (1958).

[103] Eastman Kodak Co. v. Image Tech. Servs., Inc., 504 U.S. 451, 461–62 (1992); Jefferson Parish Hosp. Dist. No. 2 v. Hyde, 466 U.S. 2 (1984).

[104] *Hyde*, 466 U.S. at 13–14 (internal citation omitted). Market power can be demonstrated by a large market share or proof that the defendant offers a unique product that competitors cannot

the plaintiff must show appreciable market power in the tying product market, however, there is no requirement (in contrast to a rule of reason case) to demonstrate the anticompetitive effects of the tie. Moreover if the defendant does not have market power in the tying product, the plaintiff can still assert a rule of reason claim.[105]

Tying law has evolved from a state in which courts assumed that "[t]ying arrangements serve hardly any purpose beyond the suppression of competition,"[106] to one in which the potential procompetitive benefits of tying arrangements are widely recognized.[107] However, courts have not adopted the recommendation of some commentators to abandon entirely the modified per se standard in favor of a pure rule of reason analysis.[108]

§ 1.03 Single firm conduct

1.03.1 Elements of a § 2 monopolization claim

Section 2 of the Sherman Act[109] makes it illegal to "monopolize, or attempt to monopolize, or combine or conspire . . . to monopolize." A monopoly is illegal only if it was "willfully" acquired or maintained. "Willfully" refers to improper conduct that excludes or drives rivals from the market on some basis other than competition on the merits.[110]

In order to make out a monopolization claim, the government or a private plaintiff must prove that the defendant (1) possesses monopoly power in a relevant market; and (2) willfully acquired or maintained that power, instead of acquiring monopoly power through "growth or development as a consequence of a superior product, business acumen, or historic accident."[111] The private plaintiff must also prove that it was injured by reason of defendant's monopolization conduct, or that such harm is imminent.[112]

---

provide. Market power in a tying case will not be inferred from a market share of less than 30 percent. *Id.* at 26–29.

105 *Id.* at 21.

106 Fortner Enterprises, Inc. v. United States Steel Corp., 394 U.S. 495, 498–99 (1969).

107 Ill. Tool Works v. Indep. Ink, Inc., 547 U.S. 28, 37 (2006) (tracing the history of the Court's treatment of tying arrangements and noting that "[t]he assumption that '[t]ying arrangements serve hardly any purpose beyond the suppression of competition'" has not been endorsed by the Supreme Court since 1969 (internal citation omitted)).

108 The Antitrust Modernization Commission, established by Congress in 2002 to review federal antitrust law, recommended in 2007 that all tying cases be analyzed under a rule of reason standard. Antitrust Modernization Comm'n, Report and Recommendations 105 (2007). The AAI, in contrast, urges retention of the current modified per se rule for tying, with certain caveats. The Next Antitrust Agenda 81 (Albert A. Foer ed., 2008), *available at* http://www.antitrustinstitute.org/node/11001.

109 15 U.S.C. § 2.

110 Aspen Skiing Co. v. Aspen Highlands Skiing Corp., 472 U.S. 585, 605 n.32 (1985).

111 United States v. Grinnell Corp., 384 U.S. 563, 570–71 (1966).

112 As in any antitrust case, the plaintiff must also prove that the challenged conduct has an "anticompetitive effect" or causes "antitrust injury," that is, it harms not merely other competitors, but the competitive process itself. Spectrum Sports, Inc. v. McQuillan, 506 U.S. 447, 458 (1993) (the Sherman Act is not directed at "conduct which is competitive, even severely so, but against conduct which unfairly tends to destroy competition itself."); Brunswick Corp. v. Pueblo Bowl-O-Mat, Inc., 429 U.S. 477, 487–88 (1977) (plaintiff must show that the injury caused by defendant's challenged conduct is of "the type that the statute was intended to forestall").

1.03.1(A) MONOPOLY POWER IN A RELEVANT MARKET

The first step in determining whether a firm possesses monopoly power requires defining the "relevant market" along both product and geographic dimensions.[113] The relevant market must include all products "reasonably interchangeable by consumers for the same purposes."[114] Products in another market may also be included in the relevant market definition if the producer of those products can quickly and cheaply shift to production of the defendant's product (or a reasonably interchangeable substitute).[115]

After it has defined a proper relevant market along both product and geographic dimensions, the plaintiff must prove that the defendant possesses "monopoly power"[116] in that market. The Supreme Court has defined monopoly power as "the power to control prices or exclude competition."[117] In some cases the plaintiff will be able to rely on direct evidence to prove that the defendant has the power to control prices or exclude competition.[118] Usually, however, monopoly power is inferred from a firm's possession of a dominant share of a market characterized by barriers to entry.[119] A firm that controls 70 percent or more of a relevant market protected by entry barriers likely has monopoly

---

[113] Definition of the relevant market is often a critical dispute in monopoly cases. *See* Jonathan B. Baker, *Market Definition: An Analytical Overview*, 74 ANTITRUST L.J. 129 (2007) (the outcome of more cases has surely turned on market definition than on any other substantial issues); Pamela J. Harbour & Tara I. Koslov, *Section 2 in a Web 2.0 World: An Expanded Vision of Relevant Product Markets*, 76 ANTITRUST L.J. 769, 772 ("In any industry, product market definition is capable of determining the outcome of an antitrust inquiry or enforcement action."). In *United States v. Microsoft Corp.*, 253 F.3d 34 (D.C. Cir. 2001), the court defined the relevant market as the licensing of all Intel-compatible PC operating systems worldwide, a market in which Microsoft possessed a 95 percent market share. The court rejected Microsoft's argument that other products, specifically non-Intel compatible operating systems such as Apple's Macintosh operating system, operating systems for non-PC devices, and middleware, should be included in the market. *Microsoft*, 253 F.3d at 53–54. If the Court had accepted Microsoft's proposed market definition, Microsoft would have prevailed. *Cf.* United States v. Oracle Corp., 331 F. Supp. 2d 1098, 1158–61 (N.D. Cal. 2004) (holding that plaintiff did not meet its burden of proof in establishing relevant market).

[114] United States v. E.I. Du Pont de Nemours & Co., 351 U.S. 377, 395 (1956).

[115] *See* Rebel Oil Co. v. Atl. Richfield Co., 51 F.3d 1421, 1436 (9th Cir. 1995) (explaining "supply-side substitutability").

[116] Courts have used the terms "monopoly power" and "market power" interchangeably, although they arguably carry different burdens of proof. *See, e.g.*, *Grinnell Corp.*, 384 U.S. at 570 (Section 2 violation requires proof of "monopoly power"); *Hyde*, 466 U.S. at 16–17 (tying arrangement is illegal only if seller has "market power" in the tying product); *NCAA*, 468 U.S. at 109 n.38 (in § 1 case, Court defined market power as "the ability to raise prices above those that would be charged in a competitive market"); *E.I. Du Pont de Nemours & Co.*, 351 U.S. at 391 (in § 2 case, Court defined monopoly power as "the power to control prices or exclude competition").

[117] *E.I. Du Pont de Nemours & Co.*, 351 U.S. at 391.

[118] *See, e.g.*, FTC v. Mylan Labs., 62 F. Supp. 2d 25, 55 (D.D.C. 1999) (allegations that defendant successfully raised prices above competitive level and constricted supply of two drugs by denying competitor access to essential ingredient sufficient to allege monopoly power), *modified on other grounds*, 99 F. Supp. 2d 1 (D.D.C. 1999); *Rebel Oil Co.*, 51 F.3d at 1434; *Ind. Fed'n of Dentists*, 476 U.S. at 460–61 (in a § 1 rule of reason case, Court held that "the finding of actual, sustained adverse effects on competition . . . is largely sufficient to support a finding that the challenged restraint was unreasonable even in the absence of elaborate market analysis.").

[119] *Grinnell*, 384 U.S. at 571 ("existence of [monopoly] power ordinarily may be inferred from the predominant share of the market").

power.[120] Entry barriers include large initial capital outlays, regulatory barriers, control by the incumbent of a necessary input or intellectual property rights necessary to produce the product, or network effects that discourage new entry.[121]

1.03.1(B) Acquired, enhanced, or maintained through exclusionary conduct

A determination that the defendant possesses monopoly power in a relevant market does not, however, end the inquiry. As the Supreme Court has emphasized, the mere possession of monopoly power is not unlawful:

> Simply possessing monopoly power and charging monopoly prices does not violate § 2; rather the statute targets "the willful acquisition or maintenance of that power . . .".[122]

Rather, the plaintiff must prove that the defendant acquired, enhanced, or maintained its monopoly power through exclusionary conduct. There is no "general rule for distinguishing between exclusionary acts, which reduce social welfare, and competitive acts, which increase it."[123] Because "the means of illicit exclusion . . . are myriad," a plaintiff is not limited in identifying the types of anticompetitive conduct that can satisfy the "willfulness" element of § 2.

1.03.2 Examples of potentially exclusionary conduct

Case law has, however, identified certain practices that can constitute exclusionary conduct. Predatory pricing,[124] refusals to deal,[125] product disparagement or displacement,[126] anti-

---

[120] *E.I. Du Pont*, 351 U.S. at 404; *Grinnell Corp.*, 384 U.S. 563 (87 percent); *Eastman Kodak Co.*, 504 U.S. 451 (80 percent); Int'l Audiotext Network v. AT&T, 893 F. Supp. 1207 (S.D.N.Y. 1994), *aff'd*, 62 F.3d 69 (2d Cir. 1995) ("As a general proposition, a market share of 70 percent should be an adequate (if barely adequate) basis, at the pleading stage for an inference of power in a relevant market."). The concept of domination in the European context may be established at considerably lower market shares. *See* Einer Elhauge & Damien Geradin, Global Antitrust Law and Economics 270 (2007).

[121] *See, e.g., Microsoft*, 253 F.3d at 55 ("applications barrier to entry" protected Microsoft's monopoly position in the operating system market).

[122] Pac. Bell Tel. Co. v. Linkline Commc'ns, Inc., 555 U.S. 438, 129 S. Ct. 1109, 1118 (2009) (quoting *Grinnell Corp.*, 384 U.S. at 570–71.

[123] *Microsoft*, 253 F.3d at 58.

[124] Brooke Group Ltd. v. Brown & Williamson Tobacco Corp., 509 U.S. 209, 222–23 (1993) (predatory pricing may violate § 2).

[125] *See, e.g., Aspen Skiing Co.*, 472 U.S. 585 (Aspen ski resort that operated three of the four area ski resorts violated § 2 when it terminated a long-standing joint marketing arrangement with its smaller competitor, and the jury found no business justification for its conduct); *Eastman Kodak Co.*, 504 U.S. 451 (a monopolist's refusal to sell parts to independent service organizations that competed against it in servicing copiers could be a violation of § 2); *but see Trinko*, 540 U.S. 398 (Verizon's failure to comply with the mandate of the Telecommunications Act of 1996 to share its network with competitors on a non-discriminatory basis did not violate § 2).

[126] *See, e.g.*, Conwood Co. v. U.S. Tobacco Co., 290 F.3d 768, 783–88 (6th Cir. 2002) (distribution of misleading information about competing products, displacement of competitors' advertising, and other conduct violated § 2); Am. Prof'l Testing Serv., Inc. v. Harcourt Brace Jovanovich Legal & Prof'l Publ'ns, 108 F.3d 1147, 1151–53 (9th Cir. 1997) (distribution of disparaging leaflets about competitor). The Sixth Circuit noted in *Conwood* that these kinds of tortious acts will

competitive litigation,[127] denial of access to an essential facility,[128] enforcement of a fraudulently obtained patent,[129] vertical agreements that foreclose competition,[130] tying,[131] bundling,[132] and monopoly leveraging[133] have all been held to constitute exclusionary conduct that can support a monopoly claim under § 2.

In some cases, there are relatively precise rules for determining whether a defendant has acquired or maintained a monopoly through anticompetitive conduct. For example, a plaintiff alleging predatory pricing under § 2 must meet the exacting standard set by the Supreme Court in *Brooke Group* in 1993. In addition to establishing all of the other elements of a monopoly claim, the plaintiff must prove both that the defendant has set its prices so low that they are below "an appropriate measure of its . . . costs,"[134] and that there is a "dangerous probability" that the defendant will recoup the losses it incurs through low pricing by driving out rivals, thereby enabling it to charge monopoly prices.[135]

Though courts, commentators and federal enforcement officials have at times advocated the adoption of a single, all-purpose test to determine whether conduct is exclusionary under § 2, no single standard has been adopted. Courts and the antitrust enforcement agencies have sometimes used a balancing test derived from the § 1 "rule of reason" standard.[136] In one case, the Supreme Court used, with the support of several commentators, a

---

violate § 2 "only in 'rare gross cases.'" *Conwood*, 290 F.3d 783–84 (quoting 3A Areeda & Turner, Antitrust Law 782(a), at 272 (2002)). *See* Maurice E. Stucke, *When a Monopolist Deceives*, 76 Antitrust L.J. 823, 823–46 (2010) (criticizing the presumption in some circuits and the Areeda Treatise that the competitive harm from deception is generally de minimus).

127 *Cal. Motor Transp. Co. v. Trucking Unlimited*, 404 U.S. 508 (1972) (claim for conspiracy to monopolize could be based on concerted action by defendants to file federal and state actions seeking to preclude plaintiff from market).

128 MCI Commc'ns Corp. v. AT&T, 708 F.2d 1081 (7th Cir. 1983) (Section 2 violation where a monopolist controlled an essential facility but refused to permit access to competitor).

129 Walker Process Equip., Inc. v. Food Mach. & Chem. Corp., 382 U.S. 172, 176 (1965) (monopolist that knowingly brought infringement action on basis of invalid patent violated § 2).

130 *Microsoft*, 253 F.3d 34 (licensing agreements between Microsoft and original equipment manufacturers that contained terms making use of rival browser software difficult or impossible were anticompetitive and violated § 2).

131 *Hyde*, 466 U.S. at 9 (tying may violate § 2).

132 LePage's, Inc. v. 3M, 324 F.3d 141 (3d Cir. 2003) (bundled discounts violated § 2).

133 Image Tech. Servs., Inc. v. Eastman Kodak Co., 125 F.3d 1195, 1208–13 (9th Cir. 1997); *but see In re* Independent Serv. Orgs. Antitrust Litig., 203 F.3d 1322, 1327 (Fed. Cir. 2000) (rejecting monopoly leveraging theory in the absence of below-cost pricing); Schor v. Abbott Labs., 457 F.3d 608, 613–14 (7th Cir. 2006) (same); *Trinko*, 540 U.S. at 415 n. 4 (monopoly leveraging theory inapplicable where no proof of "dangerous probability of success" in monopolizing second market).

134 *Brooke Group*, 509 U.S. at 222–23 (an "appropriate measure" of cost has been held to be either the defendant's average variable cost, or its marginal cost).

135 *Id.*

136 *Microsoft*, 253 F.3d at 58–59. As in a § 1 rule of reason case, this balancing approach employs shifting burdens. After the plaintiff has demonstrated that the monopolist's conduct has caused anticompetitive effects in the relevant market, the burden shifts to the monopolist to proffer a "procompetitive justification" for its conduct, for example, "a non-pretextual claim that its conduct is indeed a form of competition on the merits," because, for example, it enhances efficiency or consumer appeal. If the defendant successfully proffers a non-pretextual procompetitive justification, the burden shifts back to the plaintiff to show that the monopolist can advance the proffered procompetitive justification through less restrictive means. If the plaintiff successfully rebuts

"profit sacrifice" test, which asks whether the defendant is willing to "sacrifice short-run benefits and consumer goodwill in exchange for a perceived long-run impact on its smaller rival."[137] The DOJ under a previous administration advocated a "disproportionality" test, which treats single-firm conduct as exclusionary only if its anticompetitive effects "substantially outweigh" any procompetitive benefits.[138] This standard was repudiated by the succeeding Assistant Attorney General for the DOJ's Antitrust Division, who did not propose a single test for evaluating all conduct under § 2, but advocated "balanced analyses" like the one applied in the *Microsoft* case.[139]

1.03.3 Elements of a § 2 attempted monopolization claim

A plaintiff in an attempted monopolization case (just like in a monopolization case) must prove that the defendant "has engaged in predatory or anticompetitive conduct."[140] The plaintiff must also prove that the defendant acted with "a specific intent to monopolize," and that there was a "dangerous probability" that the defendant would achieve monopoly power.[141]

In evaluating whether the defendant possessed the requisite intent, evidence that the defendant displayed an intent "to compete vigorously" is insufficient.[142] Instead, the plaintiff must show a "specific intent to destroy competition or build monopoly."[143] Intent may be proven by direct or circumstantial evidence, and must be supported by evidence of conduct corroborating the alleged intent.[144]

The principal factor in assessing whether a defendant had a "dangerous probability of success" is market share. A market share of 50 percent or more, together with barriers to entry, is often a starting point for this finding. A market share of between 30 and 50

---

the monopolist's procompetitive justifications, the plaintiff will prevail. If the plaintiff cannot rebut the defendant's procompetitive justification, it must then demonstrate that the anticompetitive harm of the conduct outweighs the procompetitive benefits. *Id.*

This balancing approach has been adopted by other courts and advocated by some antitrust enforcers and scholars. *See, e.g.,* United States v. Dentsply Int'l, Inc., 399 F.3d 181, 189, 191–96 (3d Cir. 2005) (using balancing approach); Jonathan M. Jacobson & Scott A. Sher, *"No Economic Sense" Makes No Sense for Exclusive Dealing*, 73 ANTITRUST L.J. 799 (2006); *In re* Rambus Inc., Docket No. 9302, Opinion of the Commission, at 30–31 (FTC Aug. 2, 2006) (using balancing approach); Christine A. Varney, [former] Asst. Att'y Gen. Antitrust Div., U.S. Dep't of Justice, Vigorous Antitrust Enforcement in this Challenging Era, Remarks as Prepared for the U.S. Chamber of Commerce (May 12, 2009), *available at* http://www.justice.gov/atr/public/speeches/245777.pdf [hereinafter *Varney Speech*].

137 *Aspen Skiing*, 472 U.S. at 610–11; A. Douglas Melamed, *Exclusionary Conduct Under the Antitrust Laws: Balancing, Sacrifice, and Refusals to Deal*, 20 BERKELEY TECH. L.J. 1247 (2005).

138 *See* the now withdrawn U.S. DEP'T OF JUSTICE, COMPETITION AND MONOPOLY: SINGLE-FIRM CONDUCT UNDER SECTION 2 OF THE SHERMAN ACT 45–46 (2008), *available at* http://www.usdoj.gov/atr/public/reports/236681.pdf.

139 *Varney Speech, supra* note 136.

140 *Spectrum Sports*, 506 U.S. at 456.

141 *Id.*

142 *Id.* at 459.

143 Times-Picayune Publ'g Co. v. United States, 345 U.S. 594, 626 (1953).

144 William Inglis & Sons Baking Co. v. ITT Cont'l Baking Co., 668 F.2d 1014, 1027, 1028 (9th Cir. 1981).

percent will rarely suffice, and a market share of less than 30 percent is always insufficient to support a finding of "dangerous probability of success."[145]

1.03.4 Price discrimination

The Robinson-Patman Act[146] is the principal federal statute regulating price discrimination. Criticized by many as inimical to the goals of modern competition policy because it protects competitors and can lead to increased prices to consumers, antitrust law's "illegitimate child"[147] is still on the books, despite numerous calls for its repeal.[148] Although the FTC and the DOJ both have enforcement authority, the FTC (which is the only federal agency that has enforced the Act since the 1960s) has sharply reduced its enforcement activity under the Act in recent years, bringing only one case since 1992.[149] Hence, it is enforced primarily through private litigation.

The Robinson-Patman Act prohibits a seller from offering different prices to different buyers for commodities of "like grade and quality," where the effect of such price discrimination may be to injure competition.[150] Different prices are allowed only if (1) the lower price is available to all buyers;[151] (2) a lower price is justified by lower costs of selling to a particular buyer;[152] (3) a lower price is offered in a good faith attempt to meet competition;[153] or (4) a lower price is justified by a change in market conditions, such as impending bankruptcy or perishability of goods.[154]

There are two kinds of price discrimination claims: primary-line discrimination (involving competition at the seller's level) and secondary-line discrimination (involving competition at the buyer's level). In a primary-line price discrimination claim, a competing seller challenges its rival's pricing policies; in a secondary-line claim, a disfavored buyer (or its customer) challenges the seller's discriminatory pricing.

In sharp contrast to other federal antitrust claims, a secondary-line buyer challenging price discrimination may prove the requisite injury to competition simply by showing its own injury: the statute prohibits price discrimination if its effect "may be substantially to lessen competition or tend to create a monopoly in any line of commerce, *or to injure,*

---

145 ANTITRUST LAW DEVELOPMENTS, *supra* note 25, at 312–315.

146 15 U.S.C. § 13 *et seq.*

147 XIV HERBERT HOVENKAMP, ANTITRUST LAW, ¶2300 (2006).

148 Following earlier calls for substantial overhaul of the Act, in 1977, a Department of Justice report stated that "serious consideration" should be given to its repeal. In 2007, the Antitrust Modernization Commission recommended that it be repealed in its entirety. ANTITRUST MODERNIZATION COMM'N, REPORT AND RECOMMENDATIONS 20, 312 (Apr. 2007). The position of the AAI is that the Robinson-Patman Act should be revised but not repealed. THE NEXT ANTITRUST AGENDA 130 (Albert A. Foer ed., 2008), *available at* http://www.antitrustinstitute.org/node/11001. For further discussion of legislative proposals affecting the Robinson-Patman Act, see Chapter 15 of this Handbook.

149 ANTITRUST MODERNIZATION COMM'N, REPORT AND RECOMMENDATIONS 316.

150 15 U.S.C. § 13(a).

151 *See, e.g.,* FTC v. Morton Salt Co., 334 U.S. 37, 42 (1948).

152 15 U.S.C. § 13(a).

153 *Id.* § 13(b).

154 *Id.* § 13(a).

destroy, or prevent competition with any person . . . ."[155] Thus, a plaintiff can prevail if it can show that a single competitor lost sales as a result of the discriminatory pricing, and need not show injury to competition.[156]

In order to recover damages, a secondary-line plaintiff must show that it lost sales or profits as a result of the price discrimination. Merely showing that it paid a higher price than its competitor is insufficient.[157]

The plaintiff alleging primary-line price discrimination must prove, in addition to the four elements required of secondary-line claims (price differential applied to commodities of like grade and quality that are sold in interstate commerce and which differential causes injury), that the differential pricing is *predatory*. That is, the plaintiff must prove "that the prices complained of are below an appropriate measure of its rival's costs" and that the competitor has a "reasonable prospect . . . of recouping its investment in below-cost prices . . . ."[158] This standard, nearly identical to the requirements imposed on a plaintiff alleging predatory pricing under § 2 of the Sherman Act,[159] has sharply curtailed these cases and "has largely eliminated calls for further reform regarding primary-line claims."[160]

§ 1.04 State law

All states have their own antitrust laws. Many state antitrust statutes are similar or identical to federal antitrust statutes, and are interpreted by their courts to be consistent with federal law. There are, however, notable distinctions. Many states do not, for example, have monopolization statutes analogous to § 2 of the Sherman Act.[161] In at least some of those states, however, monopolies may be challenged under state common law, or under

---

155 *Id.* (emphasis added).

156 *Morton Salt Co.*, 334 U.S. at 49; Volvo Trucks N. Am., Inc. v. Reeder-Simco GMC, Inc., 546 U.S. 164 (2006); *see also, e.g.*, J.F. Feeser, Inc. v. Serv-A-Portion, Inc., 909 F.2d 1524, 1535 (3d Cir. 1990) ("evidence of injury to a competitor may satisfy the component of competitive injury necessary to show a violation of the Robinson-Patman Act"). *Cf. Brunswick Corp.*, 429 U.S. at 488 (the purpose of the antitrust laws is to protect overall competition, not individual competitors). Even if the defendant can show that competition was not harmed, a plaintiff can prevail so long as there was injury to individual buyers. Chroma Lighting v. GTE Prods., 111 F.3d 653, 658 (9th Cir. 1977). In addition, injury can be inferred from proof that a "favored competitor received a significant price reduction over a substantial period of time." *Volvo Trucks*, 546 U.S. at 177.

157 XIV Herbert Hovenkamp, Antitrust Law ¶2331 79–93 (2006) ("The statute does not prohibit a price discrimination that merely 'injures or destroys' the disfavored *purchaser*. Rather, the discrimination must injure or destroy the disfavored purchaser's *ability to compete* with the favored purchaser.") (emphasis in original). *See* J. Truett Payne Co. v. Chrysler Motors Corp., 451 U.S. 557, 562 (1981) (to recover damages under § 4 of the Clayton Act, plaintiff "must make some showing of actual injury attributable to something the antitrust laws were designed to prevent").

158 *Brooke Group*, 509 U.S. at 222, 224.

159 A plaintiff in a § 2 predatory pricing case must also prove below-cost pricing and probable recoupment via supracompetitive pricing. Unlike the Robinson-Patman Act plaintiff, however, the § 2 plaintiff must show a "dangerous probability" of recoupment, instead of a merely "reasonable prospect." *Id.*

160 Antitrust Modernization Comm'n, Report and Recommendations 315.

161 California, for example, has no § 2 analog. *See* XIV Herbert Hovenkamp, Antitrust Law, ¶2414a 351–52 (2006); Bondi v. Jewels by Edwar, Ltd., 267 Cal. App. 2d 672 (1968) (Cartwright Act requires "combination").

state antitrust statutes that regulate concerted conduct.[162] Another significant difference is in state-law treatment of resale price maintenance. In some states minimum resale price maintenance remains per se illegal even after the Supreme Court's *Leegin* decision; in others, state legislatures are considering or have already enacted statutes directly rejecting *Leegin's* rule-of-reason standard.[163] Another significant difference is state law treatment of price discrimination. Some states' laws are more aggressively protective of individual competitors. In some states, for example, a primary-line price discrimination plaintiff (claim by a rival seller) need only prove that the defendant sold its goods at a discounted price that was below its fully-allocated cost, as opposed to its marginal or average variable cost (as required under the Robinson-Patman Act).[164] This is a far easier burden for plaintiffs to satisfy. Another significant difference is the treatment of parties who are indirectly injured by antitrust violations. Under federal law, indirect purchasers are barred from recovering their damages under the Clayton Act (though they may still seek injunctive relief).[165] A number of states have explicitly rejected the federal bar to indirect purchaser recovery, adopting "Illinois Brick repealers" or interpreting their statutes in a manner contrary to federal law.[166]

§ 1.05 Exempt industries

Despite broad agreement that the goal of antitrust law is to protect competition rather than competitors, there are currently more than 30 statutory and judge-made exemptions to the federal antitrust laws.[167] Insurance, agriculture, charitable giving, exports, fishing,

---

[162] As a practical matter, the absence of a state monopoly statute matters only when a party seeks to take advantage of other features of state law that are different from federal law. For example, a plaintiff may prefer to sue under a state rather than federal antitrust statute because of the availability, in many states, of a damages remedy for indirect purchasers.

[163] *See supra* note 97 and accompanying text.

[164] XIV Herbert Hovenkamp, Antitrust Law ¶2414b 352–55 (2006).

[165] Illinois Brick Co. v. Illinois, 431 U.S. 720 (1977) (only persons directly injured by conduct illegal under the Sherman Act may recover damages).

[166] *See* compilation of state laws in Gerald E. Hawxhurst, *A State-By-State Look At The Law on Indirect Purchaser Damage Actions*, 15 J. of the Antitrust & Unfair Competition L. Section of the State Bar of Cal. 41, 41–58 (2006); *see also* Michael A. Lindsay, *Overview of State RPM*, *supra* note 97. In some states that allow damages recovery for indirect purchases, defendants may be barred from defending against direct purchaser claims on the ground that the direct purchaser passed on the overcharge to its customers. Clayworth v. Pfizer, Inc., 233 P.3d 1066 (Cal. 2010).

[167] The Antitrust Modernization Commission Report, Annex A, identifies the following exemptions:

Statutory Exemptions from the Antitrust Laws: Agricultural Marketing Agreement Act, 7 U.S.C. §§ 608b–608c; Anti-Hog-Cholera Serum and Hog-Cholera Virus Act, 7 U.S.C. § 852; Capper-Volstead Act, 7 U.S.C. §§ 291–92; Charitable Donation Antitrust Immunity Act, 15 U.S.C. §§ 37–37a; Defense Production Act exemption, 50 U.S.C. app § 2158; Export Trading Company Act, 15 U.S.C. §§ 4001–21; Fishermen's Collective Marketing Act, 15 U.S.C. §§ 521–22; Health Care Quality Improvement Act, 42 U.S.C. §§ 11101–52; Labor exemptions (statutory and non-statutory), 15 U.S.C. § 17; 29 U.S.C. §§ 52, 101–15, 151–69; (and common law); Local Government Antitrust Act, 15 U.S.C. §§ 34–36; Medical resident matching program exemption, 15 U.S.C. § 37b; National Cooperative Research and Production Act, 15 U.S.C. §§ 4301–06; Need-Based Educational Aid Act, 15 U.S.C. § 1 note; Newspaper Preservation Act, 15 U.S.C. §§ 1801–04; Non-profit agricultural

health care, labor, local governments, college financial aid, medical resident matching programs, small businesses, soft drink distributors, railroads, shippers, professional baseball teams, and local governments all enjoy some measure of protection from federal antitrust liability.

One important statutory exemption is the Capper-Volstead Act of 1922, which immunizes an agricultural co-operative or association from antitrust liability unless it "monopolizes or restrains trade to such an extent that the price of any agricultural product is unduly enhanced." The coverage of the Act is broad. It applies to "[p]ersons engaged in the production of agricultural products as farmers, planters, ranchmen, dairymen, nut, or fruit growers," and it allows them collectively to process, prepare for market, handle, and market agricultural products in interstate and foreign commerce.[168] Enacted in 1922 – when demand for agricultural products was down from its war-time peak – the purpose of the Act was to permit agricultural co-operatives to join together to increase their bargaining strength against large corporate buyers. While antitrust advocates generally view exemptions as contrary to the goals of United States competition policy, there has been little movement to repeal or substantially modify the Act.[169]

More controversially, the McCarran-Ferguson Act exempts a wide swath of insurer conduct from antitrust scrutiny. The Act provides that the Sherman, Clayton, and FTC Acts "shall be applicable to the business of insurance,[170] [only] to the extent that such business is not regulated by State law."[171] With extensive state regulation of insurance,

---

cooperatives exemption, 15 U.S.C. § 17; Small Business Act exemption, 15 U.S.C. §§ 638(d), 640; Soft Drink Interbrand Competition Act, 15 U.S.C. §§ 3501–03; Sports Broadcasting Act, 15 U.S.C. §§ 1291–95; Standard Setting Development Organization Advancement Act, 15 U.S.C. §§ 4301–05, 4301 note; Webb-Pomerene Export Act, 15 U.S.C. §§ 61–66.

Statutory Exemptions Created as Part of a Regulatory Regime: Air Transportation Exemption, 49 U.S.C. §§ 41308–09, 42111; McCarran-Ferguson Act, 15 U.S.C. §§ 1011–15; Motor transportation exemption, 49 U.S.C. §§ 13703, 14302–03; Natural Gas Policy Act exemption, 15 U.S.C. § 3364(e); Railroad transportation exemption, 49 U.S.C. §§ 10706, 11321(a); Shipping Act, 46 U.S.C. app. §§ 1701–1719.

Judicially Created Exemptions: Baseball exemption; Filed-rate/*Keogh* doctrine; *Noerr-Pennington* Immunity; State Action Doctrine; Various implied immunities created in specific regulatory settings.

[168] 7 U.S.C. § 291. The exemption does not apply to agreements that include non-covered participants. *See, e.g.*, *In re* Mushroom Direct Purchaser Antitrust Litig., 621 F. Supp. 2d 274 (E.D. Pa. 2009) (non-farmer presence in mushroom cooperative made exemption inapplicable).

[169] In 2010, the DOJ and United States Department of Agriculture held a series of joint public workshops to address competition issues in agriculture. *See* Department of Justice, Agriculture and Antitrust Enforcement Issues in Our 21st Century Economy, *available at* http://www.usdoj.gov/atr/public/workshops/ag2010/index.html (accessed Oct. 13, 2011). While several state attorneys general urged the DOJ and the Department of Agriculture to review the Capper-Volstead Act to ensure that it continues to protect and benefit farmers, there has been no call for its repeal. Department of Justice, Final Comments of the Several States, http://www.justice.gov/atr/public/workshops/ag2010/016//AGW-15683.html.

[170] *See In re* Ins. Brokerage Antitrust Litig., 618 F.3d 300 (3d Cir. 2010) (alleged bid-rigging and steering practices did not constitute the "business of insurance" because they did not pertain to the spreading of risk).

[171] 15 U.S.C. § 1012(b).

the exception is broad. The Act does have a limiting provision, however: the Sherman Act still applies "to any agreement to boycott, coerce, or intimidate."[172] Furthermore, because the Act only exempts "the business of insurance," conduct by insurers that does not have the effect of spreading risk, is not integral to the policy relationship between the insurer and the insured, or includes entities outside the insurance industry, may not be exempt.[173] Numerous attempts to repeal or reduce the scope of the insurance exemption have not succeeded.

Another important exemption is organized labor. Federal statutes provide that labor unions are not combinations or conspiracies in restraint of trade and exempt specific union acts, including picketing and boycotts, from the antitrust laws.[174] The exemption does not extend to combinations among unions and non-labor groups. In addition to the statutory exemptions, courts have held that labor unions and employer groups have limited immunity from federal antitrust laws for conduct that is necessary to make the collective bargaining process work.[175]

Export activities also enjoy limited immunity from antitrust scrutiny under two related statutes, the Foreign Trade Antitrust Improvement Act (FTAIA)[176] and the Export Trading Company Act (ETCA).[177] Under the ETCA, a company engaged in export activities can obtain immunity from federal and state enforcement actions by obtaining a Certificate of Review from the Department of Commerce (which the Department of Commerce issues only with the concurrence of the DOJ). If subsequently sued by a private entity, a company that has obtained a Certificate of Review is entitled to a rebuttable presumption that it has complied with the statute, a shorter statute of limitations for antitrust claims, and a prohibition against treble damages.[178]

The FTAIA makes the Sherman and FTC Acts inapplicable to exporting activities unless those activities have a "direct, substantial, and reasonably foreseeable effect" on domestic commerce or a domestic firm competing for foreign trade.[179]

---

172 15 U.S.C. § 1013(b).

173 Randy Stutz, *Market Allocation in the Health Insurance Industry and the McCarran-Ferguson Act*, 89 Or. L. Rev. 885, 894 (2011).

174 *See* 15 U.S.C. § 17 (the labor of a human being is not a commodity or article of commerce and cannot be construed as an illegal combination or conspiracy in restraint of trade); 29 U.S.C. § 104 (no court shall have jurisdiction to issue a restraining order or permanent injunction in any case arising out of or involving a labor dispute), 29 U.S.C. § 105 (court does not have jurisdiction to issue restraining order or permanent injunction upon the grounds of a labor dispute that constitutes an unlawful combination or conspiracy).

175 Brown v. ProFootball, Inc., 50 F.3d 1041 (D.C. Cir. 1995), *aff'd*, 518 U.S. 231 (1996). *Cf.* California *ex rel.* Brown v. Safeway, Inc., 615 F.3d 1171 (9th Cir. 2010) (exemption did not apply to agreement among grocery stores to contribute to a fund for labor strikes because profit sharing is not necessary to make the collective bargaining process work).

176 15 U.S.C. §§ 6(a), 45(a).

177 15 U.S.C. §§ 4001–53.

178 *Id.*

179 15 U.S.C. § 6(a).

§ 1.06 Conclusion

Private enforcement of antitrust laws remains robust and effective in the United States. While judicial decisions have in recent years imposed stricter pleading standards, eliminated categories of conduct from the less stringent per se standard of review, and imposed heavier evidentiary burdens on plaintiffs seeking to certify a class, private plaintiffs continue to play an important role in enforcing the antitrust laws and deterring anticompetitive conduct.

2 Pre-complaint activities

Craig C. Corbitt, Judith A. Zahid, and Patrick B. Clayton[1]

§ 2.01 Introduction

The lofty goals of antitrust are not self-executing. They require careful planning and preparation by plaintiffs' counsel and the client. Most antitrust litigation is highly complex, takes years to resolve, and is very expensive. Success in an antitrust case starts with the right plaintiff, with the right claim. This chapter describes how private antitrust litigation typically begins, including client contact and retention, pre-filing investigation, and strategic considerations that typically are considered in determining the specific claims to file, and equally importantly, where to file them.[2]

§ 2.02 Meeting clients: Class and non-class actions

There are two common ways for the potential antitrust plaintiff and the antitrust lawyer to get together. First, a potential plaintiff who perceives an unfair competition issue may contact an antitrust lawyer, either directly or through a referral from a non-antitrust lawyer, to find out whether there is a basis for a claim. Second, especially in class actions, an antitrust lawyer who is aware of a potential claim may search for a potential plaintiff, subject to certain ethical restrictions discussed below. The former is the more traditional way, while the latter is a more recent trend that sometimes has

[1] Mr. Corbitt and Ms. Zahid are partners, and Mr. Clayton is an associate, in the San Francisco office of Zelle Hofmann Voelbel & Mason LLP. Zelle Hofmann has served as plaintiffs' counsel in some of the cases cited in this chapter.

[2] In starting out to build a case, plaintiffs' counsel must consider a broad range of legal and practical issues, many of which arise in earnest at different stages of the litigation process. This chapter touches on many of these concerns, despite their being addressed in detail in other chapters of this Handbook. As the reader will come to understand, it is vital that plaintiffs' counsel address these concerns at the outset, no matter how remote they may seem.

been met with criticism. Both are central to private antitrust enforcement in the United States.

A variety of individuals and companies may seek out an antitrust lawyer. For example, a project manager who senses that a competitive bidding process is not yielding competitive bids, a company that has been cut off from a supplier or a distribution outlet, a company that believes its larger competitor is engaging in unfair business tactics, or a customer who observes uncannily close price increases by suppliers. All of the preceding may have reason to contact an antitrust lawyer. A market participant's mere perceptions of anticompetitive practices often turn out to be just that – perceptions – which are not a good basis for an antitrust suit. An experienced antitrust lawyer usually can determine from an initial interview or after minimal fact investigation that there is no case. However, these competitor perceptions can sometimes lead to a very big case, e.g., *Advanced Micro Devices, Inc. v. Intel Corp.*,[3] and *Conwood v. United States Smokeless Tobacco Corp.*[4]

Sometimes the potential client is a "whistleblower," that is, an insider who observes abusive practices first-hand and is determined to bring such practices to light, often in hope of a reward.[5]

A potential client may approach an antitrust lawyer, or vice versa, when antitrust litigation (brought either by the government or private plaintiffs) has already commenced, and the client has potential claims similar to those already being litigated. When the existing litigation is a class action, a large company with substantial purchases from one or more defendants (usually direct purchases) may be advised by an antitrust lawyer to "opt out," i.e., remove itself from the class and either negotiate its own settlement without initiating litigation or file its own individual action against the same defendants, which usually proceeds alongside the class action in the same court. Opt-out plaintiffs, especially those with whom the defendants want to maintain an ongoing business relationship, can often recover more money on their own than if they had remained in the class. Fee agreements between law firms and opt-out plaintiffs are typically wholly or partially contingent on a successful outcome. Because of the size of potential recoveries by opt-out plaintiffs and the corresponding potential for large fees, law firms, even quite large ones, often seek out and contact potential opt-out plaintiffs in the hopes of representing them.[6]

The potential plaintiff often initially contacts a lawyer or a law firm that he or she has previously used in connection with other legal matters. If that lawyer is not experienced in antitrust litigation, the matter is likely to be referred to an antitrust specialist, sometimes in return for a referral fee.[7] An antitrust practitioner's demonstrated track record of success can lead to new clients and cases.

---

3 No. 05-441 (D. Del. filed June 27, 2005) (unlawful monopolization case, settled before trial by Intel in November 2009 for $1.25 billion plus business considerations).

4 290 F.3d 768 (6th Cir. 2002), *cert. denied*, 537 U.S. 1148 (2003) (judgment entered after jury trial of $1.1 billion in treble damages in unlawful monopolization case).

5 *See, e.g.*, Sabry Lee, Inc. v. Genera Corp., et al., No. 2:08-CV-05758 (C.D. Cal. filed Sept. 3, 2008) (price-fixing claim against group of after-market auto parts makers where plaintiff was a former distributor allegedly terminated for refusing to go along with the conspiracy).

6 For a discussion of common funding arrangements for opt-out plaintiffs and other types of private antitrust litigants, see Chapter 10 of this Handbook.

7 ABA Model Rules of Prof'l Conduct R. 1.5(e) (2002) (applies to referral fees).

Class action lawyers sometimes are approached by a potential client in the first instance, but more often lawyers who specialize in class actions actively seek out potential clients to act as class representatives, either by contacting other lawyers who may provide a referral or by initiating direct contact with the potential client. Class action lawyers often race to sign up class representatives as quickly as possible in order to increase their chances of being appointed by the court as class counsel, also known as the lead or co-lead counsel in the litigation. This position is highly sought-after by class action lawyers because of the potential for significantly higher fees. Class counsel "must fairly and adequately represent the interests of the class,"[8] which means running all aspects of the case from the pleading stage through discovery and trial or settlement, and supervising the other law firms representing the class. Especially in a large case, there may be a number of other law firms simultaneously representing the class under lead counsel's direction. In addition to the increased workload, being appointed lead counsel carries with it increased responsibility for funding the litigation, which can cost millions of dollars and greatly increase the potential risk. The involvement of multiple law firms spreads the risk among plaintiffs' counsel.

The relevant criteria for appointment of lead counsel are set forth in Rule 23(g) of the Federal Rules of Civil Procedure. They place a premium on "the work counsel has done in identifying or investigating potential claims in the action," along with counsel's knowledge, experience, resources, and other factors.

Many firms specialize in representing class action plaintiffs, and are commonly called "class action firms." Such firms are usually small, with a handful or at most a few dozen lawyers, compared with the large multinational law firms with hundreds of lawyers that typically represent corporate defendants. Some firms regularly represent both class plaintiffs and opt-out plaintiffs (although not in the same case), and a few firms also represent defendants as well as plaintiffs in class actions and other matters.

Rival class action firms often compete for appointment as class counsel. A group of firms may form an alliance in order to present an agreed upon choice to the court in return for promises by the selected firm or firms to favor its allies with work assignments, thereby increasing their potential fees. A class action firm that has done more of the initial investigation, signed up more class representatives, has a track record of success, is able to fund the litigation, or is located in the venue where the litigation is or is likely to be pending, is often rewarded by its peers with support for the lead counsel application. The court usually, but not always, will accept this "private ordering."[9] Sometimes rival groups will submit applications to be appointed, accompanied by attacks on the qualifications of their rivals.

Courts may also appoint interim class counsel. This role grants leadership status when multiple actions are pending and classes have not yet been certified. Interim class counsel is generally appointed in instances where a large number of actions have been

---

8 FED. R. CIV. P. 23(g)(4).

9 Alternatively, a few courts have made lead counsel appointment decisions following submissions by counsel that propose competing fee schedules, with the final selection from among otherwise-qualified counsel based on the proposal that offers the greatest percentage recovery to the class. *See, e.g., In re* Auction Houses Antitrust Litig., 197 F.R.D. 71 (S.D.N.Y. 2000).

consolidated or are otherwise pending before a single court.[10] In practice, the appointment of interim class counsel is decided in the earliest stages of the case, often before the filing of a consolidated class action complaint and the ensuing defense challenges to the pleadings.[11]

Class action plaintiffs can be either "direct purchasers" or "indirect purchasers." As the name implies, direct purchasers are those that bought directly from the alleged cartel members or abusive monopolist. Conversely, indirect purchasers have typically bought from resellers and tend to be consumers and businesses which do not resell the product at issue.[12] Indirect purchaser plaintiffs may not have bought the allegedly price-fixed product separately, but instead bought a product into which the product at issue was a component, e.g., a personal computer sold with Microsoft Windows.[13]

The Supreme Court's decision in *Illinois Brick v. Illinois*[14] barred indirect purchasers from recovering under federal antitrust law. However, a number of state legislatures and appellate courts reacted to that decision by permitting indirect purchasers to sue under their respective state laws, and the right of states to enforce their laws was upheld by the Supreme Court in *California v. ARC America Corp.*[15] For many years, it was common for direct purchaser cases to be heard in federal court and indirect purchaser cases to be heard in state court. That changed with the enactment by Congress of the Class Action Fairness Act, which expanded the jurisdiction of federal courts to cover most large indirect purchaser class actions.[16] As a result, direct purchaser class actions under the Sherman Act and indirect purchaser class actions under state antitrust laws now commonly end up before the same federal court, and separate lead counsel are usually appointed for each group.[17]

Indirect purchaser litigation is usually more complex than direct purchaser litigation,

---

10 *In re* TFT-LCD (Flat Panel) Antitrust Litig., No. M:07-CV-01827 (N.D. Cal. filed April 20, 2007); *In re* Flash Memory Antitrust Litig., No. 4:07CV000086 (N.D. Cal. filed January 5, 2007).

11 *See* MANUAL FOR COMPLEX LITIGATION, FOURTH § 21.11 (Initial Case Management Orders).

12 Indirect purchasers at an intermediate level also have standing under "Illinois-Brick repealer" state laws, but such claims are more difficult to pursue because of the complexity of proving that the overcharges they paid were not passed on to downstream purchasers. *See, e.g.*, Clayworth v. Pfizer Inc., 49 Cal.4th 758, 787 (2010) ("In instances where multiple levels of purchasers have sued . . . trial courts and parties have at their disposal and may employ joinder, interpleader, consolidation, and like procedural devices to bring all claimants before the court. In such cases, if damages must be allocated among various levels of injured purchasers, the bar on consideration of pass-on evidence must necessarily be lifted; the defendants may assert a pass-on defense as needed to avoid duplication in the recovery of damages.").

13 For a detailed discussion of issues affecting direct and indirect purchasers, see Chapter 3 of this Handbook.

14 431 U.S. 720 (1977).

15 490 U.S. 93 (1989).

16 28 U.S.C. §§ 1332(d), 1453, and 1711–15.

17 This trend has led some commentators, including the Antitrust Modernization Commission, to advocate the repeal of *Illinois Brick* and the symmetrical decision in *Hanover Shoe, Inc. v. United Shoe Machinery Corp.*, 392 U.S. 481 (1968), which prohibits antitrust defendants from asserting that the direct purchaser "passed on" overcharges to indirect purchasers, so that damages can be allocated between the various vertical plaintiff groups. *Findings and Recommendations of the Antitrust Modernization Commission: Hearing Before the Antitrust Task Force of the H. Comm. on the Judiciary*, 110th Cong. (2007). For further discussion of the Class Action Fairness Act, see Chapter 4 and Chapter 5 of this Handbook.

both because the laws of a number of different states may be at issue, and because it may be challenging to prove how much of the overcharge was "passed through" from the direct purchasers to end-user consumers and businesses. An additional complexity can arise when the defendant is a vertically-integrated manufacturer (e.g., a maker of component parts as well as finished products) and there is ambiguity as to which purchasers can be considered direct and indirect.[18] Federal judges who are familiar with *Illinois Brick*'s admonition about the complexity of indirect purchaser cases, and who have little or no experience with such cases, may be more hostile to class certification. Defendants in a few cases also have successfully challenged the standing of consumers who purchased the product at issue as a component of another product.[19] On the other hand, it is usually easier for antitrust class action lawyers to find appropriate indirect purchasers to represent, since they are more abundant. The potential class-wide damages may be much greater in an indirect than in a direct purchaser class action, because large direct purchasers frequently opt out of the class, and because the direct purchasers are often foreign companies that resold to consumers in the United States.

For the typical cartel-based class litigation, the total number of indirect purchaser class action cases filed is usually much higher than the total number of direct purchaser cases. This is true not only because it is easier to sign up an indirect purchaser plaintiff, but also because cases are usually filed initially in many district courts around the country because of the various state laws at issue. Direct purchaser cases tend to be fewer in number, but unless the industry is such that there are only a small handful of direct purchaser plaintiffs (e.g., the *Intel* and *Microsoft* cases), there are almost always multiple direct and indirect cases filed. When more than one federal district court is involved, the cases will be consolidated for pretrial proceedings in one court before one federal judge by the United States Judicial Panel on Multidistrict Litigation.[20]

---

[18] *See, e.g., In re* Optical Disk Drive Antitrust Litig., No. 3:10-md-02143 (N.D. Cal. Aug. 3, 2011); *In re* Refrigerant Compressors Antitrust Litig., No. 2:09-md-02042 (E.D. Mich. June 13, 2011).

[19] *See In re* Dynamic Random Access Memory (DRAM) Antitrust Litig., 516 F.Supp.2d 1072 (N.D. Cal. 2007) ("*DRAM I*") and 536 F.Supp.2d 1129 (N.D. Cal. 2008) ("*DRAM II*"). In the *DRAM I* and *DRAM II* decisions, the district court held that the indirect-purchaser plaintiffs who bought technology products containing DRAM did not have standing to maintain a class action against the defendant manufacturers of DRAM. The court applied the United States Supreme Court's *Associated General Contractors* ("AGC") factors, *see infra* notes 84–88 and accompanying text, to the state-law claims of the indirect-purchaser plaintiffs and concluded that the indirect-purchaser plaintiffs who purchased computers or other products in which DRAM was a component lacked standing as a matter of law, because they did not "participate" in the same market as the defendants who manufactured and sold DRAM chips. *DRAM II*, 536 F.Supp.2d at 1141. Other courts have reached a contrary result. *See e.g., In re* Graphics Processing Units Antitrust Litig., 527 F.Supp.2d 1011, 1097–98 (N.D. Cal. 2007); *In re* TFT-LCD Antitrust Litig., 586 F.Supp.2d 1109, 1123 (N.D. Cal. 2008).

[20] *See* 28 U.S.C. § 1407 ("When civil actions involving one or more common questions of fact are pending in different districts, such actions may be transferred to any district for coordinated or consolidated pretrial proceedings."). Accordingly, in an indirect-purchaser class action seeking damages under state law, a federal judge will face the added complexity of applying various state laws that, while generally consistent, may have variations that require in-depth state-by-state analyses in deciding dispositive and class certification motions.

§ 2.03 Ethical restrictions and fee arrangements

When the client contacts the lawyer or law firm in the first instance, the principal ethical issue that needs to be addressed is the potential for conflicts of interest. The American Bar Association's Model Rules of Professional Conduct should be consulted, along with the ethical rules of the particular states where the lawyer practices or where the case may be filed, which usually are similar to the Model Rules but may have slight variations.[21] Generally, conflicts rules prohibit lawyers from representing clients which have adverse or potentially adverse relationships with each other, unless each gives informed consent in writing. Larger law firms typically have a computerized system in place to identify potential adverse client relationships in order to ensure that they do not run afoul of this rule. With the increased mobility of lawyers from firm to firm, unforeseen conflicts may arise due to a lawyer's prior representation of an adverse client at another firm. Often this issue can be addressed through the creation of an ethical "wall" between the affected lawyer and the rest of his or her new firm. Under certain circumstances, however, this conflict will be imputed to his new firm and lead to the entire firm's disqualification.[22]

When the lawyer contacts a potential class representative or other potential client, the same conflicts rules apply, plus an additional ethical consideration, the rules against client solicitation.

Generally, a lawyer may solicit an existing client but is severely restricted from directly contacting potential clients with whom there is no prior relationship.[23] However, a lawyer may ask existing clients or colleagues in other firms to refer potential plaintiffs, and may even advertise in order to attract potential plaintiffs (attorney advertising is more common in product defect or other mass tort litigation than in antitrust litigation).[24]

Shortly after discussing any possible claim with a potential client, counsel should address options for fee arrangements. At one end of the spectrum are pure by-the-hour agreements, and at the other are "fee upon success," or straight contingent fee agreements, where the lawyer advances all costs and does not recover anything unless the client or class recovers something. Between these two extremes are so-called "blended" fee agreements,

---

[21] Model Rule 1.7(a) applies to conflicts of interest involving current clients. ABA MODEL RULES OF PROF'L CONDUCT R. 1.7(a) (2002)*; see also id.* at R. 1.8 (providing more specific conflicts rules for current clients).

[22] Schiessle v. Stephens, 717 F.2d 417 (7th Cir. 1983); *In re* Compact Disc Minimum Price Antitrust Litig., 2001 WL 243494 (D. Me. 2001); Central Milk Producer Co-op. v. Sentry Food Stones, Inc., 573 F.2d 988 (8th Cir. 1978); Pfarr v. Island Services Co., Inc., 124 F.R.D. 24 (D.R.I. 1989); Fred Webner, Inc. v. Shell Oil Co., 432 F. Supp. 694 (E.D. Mo. 1977).

[23] ABA MODEL Rule 7.3 (applies to direct contact with prospective clients).

[24] In 2007, at least four partners in the prominent national plaintiffs' securities litigation firm formerly known as Milberg Weiss were indicted on federal charges of participating in a scheme to pay millions of dollars in secret kick-backs to several individuals in exchange for them serving as named plaintiffs in more than 225 class-action and shareholder derivative-action lawsuits that were filed across the United States. The case shined a spotlight on the potential for abuse in recruiting class representatives. *See, e.g.,* PRESS RELEASE, U.S. ATTORNEY'S OFFICE, CENT. DIST. OF CAL., MELVYN WEISS, CO-FOUNDER OF MILBERG WEISS LAW FIRM, INDICTED IN SECRET KICKBACK SCHEME INVOLVING NAMED PLAINTIFFS IN CLASS ACTION LAWSUITS (Sept. 20, 2007), *available at* http://www.justice.gov/usao/cac/pressroom/pr2007/116a.html.

which can contain a mix of reduced-rate hourly billing and sliding-scale "percentage-of-recovery" arrangements that are tied to case milestones (pre-filing, post-complaint, pre-summary judgment, pre- and post-trial, etc.).

Antitrust cases today often cost millions of dollars to litigate and may not reach a resolution for five to 10 years. To spread the risk in class actions, groups of plaintiffs' law firms often form joint ventures or de facto working groups, sometimes but not always by written agreement, in order to litigate a case together and share the risks and costs. A plaintiffs' law firm or group of firms must be confident that it has sufficient resources, in both lawyers and money, to staff and fund lengthy and costly litigation that may drag on for many years. There is certainly a greater risk assumed by the plaintiff's attorney who sues a corporate giant for unlawful monopolization or takes on a large industry for price fixing, compared with the attorney who files a duplicative, tag-along action along with dozens of others, without giving any serious thought to running the case. Such "tag-along" firms may be assigned work and assessed money toward costs, but at a greatly reduced level. Lead counsel are subject to court orders and must see the case through to the end even if it turns out to be a poor investment, but tag-along firms usually can decide well before then to cut their losses and stop working on the case.

For plaintiff cases brought by individual firms on a non-class basis, sometimes the client agrees to pay a straight hourly fee plus expenses. However, because antitrust cases are very expensive but also potentially very lucrative, the client and the lawyer often negotiate a "blended" fee that may call for client payment of costs plus a reduced hourly rate, with a contingent fee depending on results. Some large opt-out cases, however, have been undertaken by law firms on a straight contingent fee basis, which can result in very large fees when tens of millions of dollars are recovered.[25]

§ 2.04 Investigative tools

A plaintiff's antitrust attorney should investigate and consider multiple factors before agreeing to represent either an individual client or a proposed class representative. First and foremost, the plaintiff's attorney must determine if it is a good case. Experience with similar cases helps greatly in this judgment, but even for an experienced antitrust lawyer it is not always obvious that the case is worth undertaking. In part this is because the antitrust laws have been established largely through decisions of the Supreme Court and lower federal appellate courts, and decisions may change over time or be applied inconsistently. The circuit where the case is filed, and even the identity of the district judge, can make a huge difference in the outcome. Even a seemingly strong case on the merits may be uneconomical to pursue, at least on a contingent fee basis, because the damages are not high enough, the anticipated expenses for discovery and experts are too high, or the case is otherwise too risky to pursue. Despite the pressure in class actions in particular to get a case on file as soon as possible, the prudent antitrust lawyer will carefully consider the relevant facts and law before filing it, and thoroughly research unsettled legal issues.

---

[25] For further discussion of fee arrangements and the funding of cases, see Chapter 10 of this Handbook.

A successful antitrust attorney must become as knowledgeable as possible about the particular market and industry involved in the case. It is critical that the attorney gathers and analyzes information on the market, the industry players and channels of distribution, pricing and market trends, and volume of commerce, both foreign and domestic. Discovery of unusual market conditions or pricing trends, for example, can validate a client's or an attorney's suspicions that anticompetitive behavior is taking place. Unnatural price increases or supply restrictions, the consolidation of participants or the dominance of one participant, and high barriers to enter a market are all factors that lend themselves to imperfect competition. Some of this information can be collected online, or purchased from third-party vendors that specialize in tracking and analyzing prices in a particular market. Developing this pre-filing body of information can take many months in some cases, and cost tens of thousands of dollars.

Information should be obtained from a variety of sources. The starting place, particularly in a non-class case, is the client. The plaintiff's attorney should gather all documents and information in the client's custody and thoroughly explore any potential weaknesses. A potential plaintiff that is a competitor or terminated distributor of the proposed defendant will certainly be attacked by the defendants as having brought on its own problems through mismanagement or worse, and the evidence pertaining to this defense must be thoroughly and candidly reviewed with the client. Class representatives on the other hand, particularly consumers, are unlikely to have much relevant information beyond being able to substantiate their purchases of the product or service at issue.[26] This information should also be gathered before the case is filed. Occasionally, class representatives also have dubious backgrounds and can be disqualified.[27] Consequently, any prior litigation history, arrest records, etc. should be explored.

The Internet is another primary investigatory tool. With just an online connection, attorneys and their staffs can investigate industries and markets around the world, and can quickly and inexpensively gather information about market participants, pricing history, supply shortages, capacity constraints, product demand, and a host of other relevant issues. The plaintiff's law firm should diligently scour the websites of U.S. and international competition regulators as well as news websites and financial websites such as Bloomberg or Market Watch. In addition, for a relatively small investment, lawyers can subscribe to international news services which also provide inside reports on industries in which the antitrust violation is believed to have occurred. The exponential growth of online information has substantially increased the ability of antitrust lawyers to gather relevant information before filing a case and to make more informed decisions about strategy.

---

[26] Of course, this purchase documentation should be reviewed with particular attention to the presence of any dispute resolution restrictions that may preclude participation in class action litigation or class arbitration. *See* AT&T Mobility LLC v. Concepcion, 563 U.S. ___ (2011).

[27] In the context of class certification, courts will examine the adequacy of the proposed class representatives, and are particularly sensitive to the existence of a financial relationship between the representative and class counsel that could compromise the representation of the absent class members. FED. R. CIV. P. 23(a)(4).

Expert economists are another critical resource in antitrust litigation.[28] It is very important for the plaintiff's lawyer to retain a good economist as quickly as possible when it appears litigation will be commenced. Preferably this will be done before filing the lawsuit. A number of economists specialize in competition economics, or more generally in industrial organization, and are experienced expert witnesses. Some are generally known to be more sympathetic to plaintiffs' cases than others. In addition to providing the theoretical and factual support to the underlying allegations of the case and the potential damages, economists typically provide opinions on whether common issues predominate over individual issues for purposes of class certification, and on the appropriate measure and amount of damages. In big cases, several testifying economists and other experts may be retained for different issues. Testifying expert economists are usually supported by large staffs at economic consulting firms, which "crunch the numbers" to support the testimony. The total expenses for economic advice and testimony over the course of the litigation can easily be millions of dollars. Unlike the lawyers, these economists cannot work on a contingent basis, lest they be accused of being biased for having a financial incentive in the outcome of the case (under ethical rules, lawyers cannot split fees with non-attorneys).[29]

It is a good (but expensive) idea to seek advice from an economist before filing a case. For example, economists can assist in determining whether a suspected market is conducive to collusion, whether pricing history is suspect, whether a suspected monopolist has sufficient market power in a definable relevant market, or whether there is a pro-competitive rationale for the defendants' conduct, and can otherwise assist in formulating the liability case. Industry experts, along with economists, can help analyze the various products in a market, the distribution channels, manufacturing processes and costs, and can identify potential roadblocks, such as atypical product specifications or potential problems in proving pass-through to indirect purchasers.

Plaintiffs' attorneys also sometimes hire private investigators prior to filing a suit. These investigators can conduct informal interviews of ex-employees or industry participants, or uncover evidence of concealed activities. Care must be taken to stay within ethical rules in these situations.

Private investigators are particularly susceptible to violations arising from conversations with parties represented by opposing counsel or using improper surveillance methods. Counselors who hire private investigators must remain cognizant of the laws and principles that guide the conduct of undercover investigations.[30] The attorney remains responsible for controlling investigations, and repercussions of an investigator's unethical behavior may be imputed to the attorney.[31]

---

[28] For a full discussion of the role of the expert in antitrust litigation, see Chapter 8 of this Handbook.

[29] *See* ABA Model Rule 5.4.

[30] *See* ABA Model Rule 4.2 ("In representing a client, a lawyer shall not communicate about the subject of the representation with a person the lawyer knows to be represented by another lawyer in the matter, unless the lawyer has the consent of the other lawyer or is authorized to do so by law or a court order."); *see also, e.g.*, N.J.S.A. § 2A:156A-1 *et seq.* and 18 Pa. Cons. Stat. Ann. § 5702 *et seq.* (wiretapping and electronic surveillance control acts).

[31] *In re* Complaint of PMD Enterprises, Inc., 215 F.Supp.2d 519, 527 (D. N.J. 2002) (revocation of attorney's pro hac vice admission was appropriate sanction after attorney's private investigator engaged in improper ex parte conversation with members of opponents' litigation control group).

News travels fast in the antitrust plaintiffs' community when a government agency announces that it is investigating suspected anticompetitive activity, when a news outlet reports a rumor of anticompetitive activity, or when a company announces in a regulatory filing that it has been subpoenaed in connection with an antitrust investigation. This information is readily available online. The activities of the Department of Justice (DOJ), the Federal Trade Commission (FTC), and state attorneys general can be monitored through news sites and the receipt of electronic alerts through various e-mail-based services. News of a "dawn raid" or other coordinated activity by the DOJ, the European Commission (EC) and/or other competition regulators around the world including the Canadian Bureau of Competition, Japanese Fair Trade Commission (JFTC), and the Korean Fair Trade Commission (KFTC) often leads to attempts by plaintiffs' lawyers to quickly get cases on file. These agencies also report the status of their investigations online. The public companies being investigated by a governmental entity typically disclose this news in corporate press releases and in Securities and Exchange Commission (SEC) and other regulatory filings.[32]

The announcement that a company is cooperating with the DOJ under the Antitrust Criminal Penalty Enhancement and Reform Act of 2004 (ACPERA) also draws the particular attention of plaintiffs' attorneys. ACPERA was designed to give leniency to a company that has engaged in criminal anticompetitive behavior but has voluntarily come forward and reported the activity.[33] The news of such cooperation can validate a plaintiff's attorney's belief that there is an underlying conspiracy, and can also suggest that the defendant may cooperate in a subsequent lawsuit. Under ACPERA, an amnesty applicant that cooperates with private litigants can avoid treble damages and joint-and-several liability in private litigation. Even though the appropriate level and the timing of such cooperation have not been clearly defined by the statute or case law, there is a reasonable expectation that when a named defendant is identified as being the ACPERA applicant, cooperation will be forthcoming.[34]

News of such government raids or investigations usually prompts plaintiffs' lawyers to do some independent analysis to see whether there is a basis for a lawsuit. However,

---

[32] Government agencies have the primary advantage over private litigants in that once they have the appropriate level of suspicion – for the DOJ it is the belief "that a criminal violation of the antitrust laws has occurred," 1 ANTITRUST DIVISION GRAND JURY PRACTICE MANUAL I.(B.)(1.) (2011 ed.) – they may launch an investigation, which immediately allows them access to the internal workings of a company. The European Commission's unannounced inspections (intriguingly referred to as "dawn raids") have been instrumental in breaking open many of the international cartels that plaintiffs' attorneys learn about and ultimately litigate here in the U.S.

Because the illegal operations of cartelists and monopolists are inherently kept secret, learning the details of a violation of the antitrust laws can be one of the biggest challenges for antitrust practitioners. Making this challenge more difficult is the fact that the anticompetitive activities at the heart of today's cases now span continents and reside in multiple levels of huge, international corporations. For cartels in particular, the details of "who met with who?" and "what was agreed to?" are jewels of knowledge that are sometimes never fully uncovered by regulatory bodies or teams of plaintiffs' attorneys.

[33] ACPERA is currently due to expire in June 2020.

[34] For a discussion of the utility of the leniency program and ACPERA as evidence gathering tools, see Chapter 7 of this Handbook; for a discussion of how the leniency program and ACPERA impact the interplay of public and private enforcement generally, see Chapter 11 of this Handbook.

more than a raid or an announced grand jury investigation is required before a case can be filed. Courts have held such news to be an insufficient basis standing alone to sustain a complaint against a motion to dismiss.[35]

In earlier years, class actions filed in response to announcements of government investigations or even findings of liability were not filed as quickly and frequently as they are today. Counsel would usually wait to see what developed from a government investigation before filing. For example, everyone in the plaintiffs' bar knew in 1999 that the government was investigating Microsoft and that a lengthy monopolization trial was underway in federal district court. Notwithstanding this knowledge, only one class action, in California state court, was on file. After Judge Jackson announced his findings against Microsoft in the government's case, however, dozens of cases were filed around the country within weeks.[36] Ten years later, with a faster flow of information (facilitated by the Internet, e-mail notices of case filings and government action, actions of foreign regulatory investigations, and access to foreign periodicals) and more competition among plaintiffs' lawyers, there is a tendency to pull the trigger much faster, sometimes, regrettably, with insufficient grounds to do so.

Nevertheless, the criticism from some quarters that class action lawyers merely piggyback on the efforts of government agencies is misguided. Many successful cases have not depended on prior government action at all, while in others the recoveries by private plaintiffs were well above the fines obtained by the government.[37]

After the case is filed, the plaintiff's lawyer must continue to regularly monitor reports of government actions against the suspected cartelist or monopolist. News of indictments or fines can bolster a case already on file. However, certainly not all regulatory investigations lead to guilty pleas, corporate fines, or criminal indictments. When some do, often the result will not obtain until a substantial amount of time has passed from the date that the investigation was opened or the complaint was filed. Therefore, counsel often must engage in years of aggressive and expensive litigation before a government action is concluded.[38]

---

35 *See, e.g.*, *In re* Graphics Processing Units Antitrust Litig., 253 F.R.D. 478, 482 (N.D. Cal. 2008); *In re* Static Random Access Memory (SRAM) Antitrust Litig., 580 F.Supp.2d 896, 902 (N.D. Cal. 2008).

36 Microsoft Corp. Antitrust Litg., No. 00-5594 (Hennepin Co. Dist. Ct., Minn.); Microsoft Corp. Antitrust Litig., No. CL 82311 (Polk Co. Dist. Ct., Iowa); Microsoft Corp. Antitrust., No. 05-CV-010927 (Wis. Cir. Ct.); Microsoft Cases, J.C.C.P. No. 4106 (Ca. Sup. Ct.).

37 *See, e.g.*, Robert H. Lande & Joshua P. Davis, *Benefits From Private Enforcement: An Analysis Of Forty Cases*, 42 U.S.F. L. Rev. 879 (2008).

38 Parallel government activities do not always benefit plaintiffs in an antitrust case. They can disrupt private actions, including through government interventions and discovery stays, and they can potentially weaken a private action if the investigation ends without any indictments or guilty pleas. The government can also negotiate terms of pleas that limit the scope of the conspiracy and create somewhat artificial boundaries within a private litigation. Private party discovery can also be severely limited by prior government investigations. For example, companies that have been subpoenaed by a grand jury must produce documents to the DOJ. These productions are negotiated and limited according to discussions had with the government representatives. When that finite universe is produced to the DOJ, it often serves as the benchmark for what private plaintiffs will first receive pursuant to a request for production of documents in their litigation. Since the documents are already collected by these companies, they can usually be produced quite quickly, but plaintiffs

The presence or absence of prior government action can influence the courts in their decisions. One federal court noted in its decision denying class certification that, unlike the Microsoft cases in which very similar classes had been certified, in the case at hand the government had dropped its investigation without bringing any charges.[39]

§ 2.05 Financial considerations

In addition to the extraordinary but necessary cost of expert economists discussed above, discovery costs for document review and depositions in antitrust cases are enormous. Antitrust cases have always been notorious for massive and expensive discovery.[40] The shift to discovery of electronic information has made the once dirty and time consuming work by junior associates of digging through hundreds of boxes in dusty warehouses seem quaint, but ironically has largely increased the cost of document review. Now, document productions consist of massive amounts of electronic information, comprised of e-mails and similar electronic data. This requires plaintiffs to invest in sophisticated and expensive electronic databases for document review. Some larger plaintiffs' firms have internal systems for such review, but in most cases the law firms hire third-party vendors to provide this service at a cost that can range into millions of dollars. Due to the international scope of some of today's cartel cases, these documents are often in multiple foreign languages, so they require costly translation software, paid interpreters, or teams of bilingual attorneys and paralegals. The sheer volume of these document productions, which may involve millions of pages and are measured in gigabytes or even terabytes, requires many months for review.

Dozens or even hundreds of contract attorneys are sometimes hired by plaintiffs' firms. This is a risk-reducing strategy because the firm has no obligation to retain the contract lawyer beyond the duration of the review. For solo-practitioners, in particular, employing this model is usually the only option for staying active in today's large antitrust cases. Hiring qualified contract attorneys ensures that a firm will continue to be given work by the lead counsel.

The global scope of contemporary cartels also increases the cost of litigation. Antitrust actions now typically involve multiple global companies, making the task of obtaining discovery that much more difficult and expensive. Hundreds of depositions are often taken in major antitrust cases, sometimes requiring travel throughout the world. Costs for court reporters and videographers can be thousands of dollars for each deposition taken. In addition, dozens of companies are often subpoenaed as third parties, either to obtain facts that bear on the liability allegations or, particularly in indirect purchaser cases, to obtain purchase and sale information relevant to establishing pass through and damages.

---

will fight an uphill battle to supplement such productions for any reason down the line – whether to increase the time period, learn of how the original production was queried, expand on a particular request, or the like.

[39] *GPU*, *supra* note 19, at 482. For further discussion of how plaintiffs' attorneys may obtain evidence, see Chapter 7 of this Handbook.

[40] *See, e.g.*, Bell Atl. Corp. v. Twombly, 550 U.S. 554, 558 (2007) ("proceeding to antitrust discovery can be expensive."). For further discussion of funding considerations associated with discovery, see Chapter 10 of this Handbook.

The out-of-pocket costs associated with conducting discovery and working with experts in major antitrust cases can easily amount to several million dollars.[41] In class actions and other contingency cases, these and all litigation costs are borne entirely by the plaintiffs' attorneys.

Each firm that participates in a large contingency antitrust case is expected to contribute regularly to a common litigation fund, from which expert and discovery costs are paid. These assessments have become increasingly larger, making it more difficult for smaller firms to keep up. Plaintiffs' attorneys that win court-appointed leadership roles can be expected to pay hundreds of thousands more dollars to the common fund than their co-counsel. Although they are rewarded with significantly higher fees if the case is successful, they are also the ones left holding the bag if the case does not reach a favorable resolution. Experts, court reporters, and document vendors expect to get paid, win or lose.

In addition to providing financial support, a plaintiff's law firm in a class action is often expected to provide attorney power to help fuel large discovery efforts. Attorney reviewers are regularly needed to donate substantial hours to the electronic discovery review, which also can be particularly taxing on smaller firms.

§ 2.06 Defining the claims to be asserted

After the client has been retained, the fee agreement has been signed, the legal and factual investigation has commenced, and the financial risks have been assessed, the final step before actually starting the litigation is to decide how to define the claims to be asserted.

Most private antitrust cases fall into one of two categories: (1) claims against a group of firms, operating as a *cartel* in restraint of trade; or (2) claims against a single firm, operating as a *monopoly* in restraint of trade.[42] The Sherman Act makes both illegal, and the Clayton Act confers upon certain victims the right of private enforcement to collect damages and enjoin future harm.[43] Other kinds of anticompetitive activity such as tying arrangements, vertical dealer terminations, and price discrimination are also outlawed by antitrust law, but private challenges to these activities are relatively rare.[44] The statutes, however, tell the antitrust plaintiff only part of the story.[45]

The sweeping language in § 1 of the Sherman Act – "[e]very contract, combination . . . or conspiracy, in restraint of trade . . . is declared to be illegal" – has been narrowed by a century of precedent that limits the category of forbidden contracts, combinations,

---

41 *See, e.g.*, Microsoft I-V, J.C.C.P. No. 4106 (document production costs and the costs for experts and consultants were $853,110.39 and $6,088,480.74, respectively).

42 *See* 15 U.S.C. §§ 1, 2.

43 *See* 15 U.S.C. §§ 15, 26.

44 Private plaintiffs can sue to block mergers under § 7 of the Clayton Act, but damages are not recoverable in such cases. Normally merger cases are brought by the DOJ or the FTC. However, companies that can afford to pay for them sometimes bring them in a private capacity and it is not unheard of for law firms to file on behalf of smaller plaintiffs on a contingent basis. Attorneys' fees are awarded by statute to a successful plaintiff, and the cases sometimes are settled through payment by the merging defendants to the plaintiff to drop the case.

45 For simplicity, this discussion focuses on federal antitrust law. The antitrust laws of the various states, and in particular those states whose antitrust laws afford standing to indirect purchasers, require careful consideration as well when defining the claims to be asserted.

and conspiracies to only those that *unreasonably* restrain trade.[46] In a similar fashion, the courts read § 15 of the Clayton Act, which declares that "any person who shall be injured in his business or property by reason of anything forbidden in the antitrust laws may sue therefore in any district court," with the gloss that "any person" means "any person *with antitrust standing*."[47] Thus, a lavish body of antitrust jurisprudence fleshes out these statutes' bare language.[48]

Just as the antitrust law has refined the definitions of who may sue for what, it has also drawn distinctions regarding the antitrust plaintiff's burden of proof. The elements of a typical cartel claim are: (1) existence of a contract, combination, or conspiracy; (2) that unreasonably restrained trade; (3) affecting interstate commerce; and (4) causing antitrust injury to the plaintiff.[49]

Yet not all claims are created equal. Some cartel claims – those alleging agreements among horizontal competitors to fix prices or to divide markets – fall into the category of automatic, or "per se," illegal conduct. These practices, the courts have concluded, "lack any redeeming virtue," and "always or almost always tend to restrict competition and decrease output."[50] Accordingly, the antitrust plaintiff alleging, for example, that a group of competitors entered into a horizontal price-fixing conspiracy need only prove the existence of the conspiracy in order to establish that the conspiracy was an unreasonable restraint of trade. The plaintiffs must still prove injury and damages in order to prevail.

By contrast, the balance of cartel claims (vertical price-fixing agreements, exclusivity arrangements, group boycotts, tying, etc.) and all monopoly claims proceed under a "rule of reason" or other non-per se test of illegality.[51] This means that the antitrust plaintiff alleging, for example, that firms in a vertical distribution chain agreed to set minimum prices, must not only prove the existence of the agreement, but must then prove that, under the circumstances, the conspiracy worked an unreasonable restraint of trade. That

[46] *See* Standard Oil Co. v. United States, 221 U.S. 1 (1911); State Oil Co. v. Khan, 522 U.S. 3 (1997).

[47] *See* Associated General Contractors of California, Inc. v. California State Council of Carpenters, 459 U.S. 519 (1983) (describing five-factor test to satisfy antitrust standing); Illinois Brick Co. v. Illinois, 431 U.S. 720 (1977) (limiting right to seek federal antitrust damages to plaintiffs who purchased directly from defendants).

[48] For further discussion of unreasonable restraints of trade, see Chapter 1 of this Handbook; for further discussion of antitrust standing, see Chapter 3 and Chapter 6 of this Handbook.

[49] *See, e.g.,* William O. Gilley Enterprises, Inc. v. Atlantic Richfield Co., 561 F.3d 1004, 1009 (9th Cir. 2009); *cf.* Cost Management Services, Inc. v. Washington Natural Gas Co., 99 F.3d 937, 949–950 (9th Cir. 1996) (identifying the elements of typical monopoly claim as: (1) possession of monopoly power in the relevant market; (2) wilful acquisition or maintenance of such power; and (3) causing antitrust injury to the plaintiff).

[50] Leegin Creative Leather Products, Inc. v. PSKS, Inc., 551 U.S. 877 (2007).

[51] Certain cases are judged under various other tests that have been articulated by the Supreme Court and appellate courts. *See, e.g.,* California Dental Ass'n v. F.T.C., 526 U.S. 756, 770 (1999) (explaining the abbreviated or "quick-look" analysis under the rule of reason); Brooke Group Ltd. v. Brown & Williamson Tobacco Corp., 509 U.S. 209, 222–23 (1993) (describing analysis for predatory pricing claims as requiring (1) below-cost pricing by a competitor and (2) a dangerous probability that the competitor will recoup its investment in below-cost prices); Continental T.V. Inc. v. GTE Sylvania Inc., 433 U.S. 36, 49 (1977) (under the rule of reason, "the factfinder weighs all of the circumstances in deciding whether a restrictive practice should be prohibited as imposing an unreasonable restraint on competition.").

is, the plaintiff must foreclose the possibility that the pro-competitive effects of the agreement outweigh the anticompetitive effects.

While the bumper-sticker phrase "rule of reason = plaintiff loses" has been disproved in several high-profile antitrust cases proceeding under the rule,[52] the underlying sentiment highlights the special care with which a rule of reason claim must be litigated. Although the rule of reason is described as the "standard" antitrust approach, with the per se rule as the exception, in practice, per se horizontal price-fixing cartel conspiracy claims, whether filed by private or government enforcers, dominate the antitrust docket.[53] The reason for this is clear: with fewer elements to prove, the risk analysis favors the plaintiff and increases the defendant's potential exposure to an adverse outcome. Therefore, the first task of the antitrust plaintiff's lawyer is to determine whether the per se rule will apply and, if not, evaluate the added complexity that will attend a claim proceeding under the rule of reason or another, more stringent standard of proof.[54]

§ 2.07 Anticipating defenses

With the claim in mind, the antitrust plaintiff must anticipate the roadblocks the defendants are likely to mount at the pleading stage and how to overcome them. The responsive Rule 12(b) motion seeking dismissal of the complaint is a standard feature of antitrust litigation. The grounds for a motion to dismiss the complaint are varied but familiar, including: (1) not plausible (*Twombly v. Bell Atlantic*);[55] (2) not connected to this country (FTAIA); (3) not justiciable (preemption); and (4) not the right plaintiff (*AGC*). The well-pleaded antitrust complaint anticipates and neutralizes each of these grounds as much as possible.

In *Twombly*, the Supreme Court used the context of a Sherman Act cartel claim to refine the "notice pleading" standard under Rule 8:

> While a complaint attacked by a Rule 12(b)(6) motion to dismiss does not need detailed factual allegations, a plaintiff's obligation to provide the "grounds" of his "entitlement to relief" requires more than labels and conclusions, and a formulaic recitation of the elements of a cause of action will not do. Factual allegations must be enough to raise a right to relief above the speculative level.[56]

Twombly directs the courts to review the allegations of a complaint and determine whether the plaintiff has "nudged" its claims "across the line from conceivable to plausible."[57] The courts have been grappling with this new standard ever since.[58]

---

[52] *See, e.g.*, the *Microsoft* private antitrust cases.

[53] *See, e.g.*, Antitrust Resource Manual § 8, *in* 7 U.S. Attorneys' Manual (1997) ("The most common violations of the Sherman Act – and the violations most likely to be prosecuted criminally – are price fixing, bid riggings, and territorial or customer allocation among competitors (commonly described as 'horizontal agreements').").

[54] For further discussion of the elements of antitrust claims and rule of reason versus per se analysis, see Chapter 1 of this Handbook.

[55] 550 U.S. 544, 555 (2007).

[56] *Id.* at 555 (internal citation omitted).

[57] *Id.* at 570.

[58] *See also* Ashcroft v. Iqbal, 129 S.Ct. 1937 (2009) (holding the *Twombly* pleading standard applies to all civil complaints under Fed. R. Civ. P. 8).

"Plausibility" under *Twombly* is often in the eye of the (district judge) beholder. Clearly, the more factual detail included in a complaint the better – yet even this aphorism does not explain fully the outcome of recent *Twombly* motions in antitrust cases.[59] Consider the orders on motions to dismiss in the remarkably similar cases of *In re LTL Shipping Services AntitrustLitigation*[60] and *In re Rail Freight Fuel Surcharge Antitrust Litigation.*[61] Both complaints alleged that a group of shippers (truckers and railroads, respectively) with dominant market shares conspired to coordinate near-lock-step fuel surcharges levied on the plaintiff customers. To support these allegations, the plaintiffs in both complaints noted the defendants' membership in industry trade groups and routine posting of surcharge announcements on the Web.

The district courts split in their rulings on the defendants' respective *Twombly* motions to dismiss. The *LTL* court concluded that, "[i]n sum, Plaintiffs' allegations do not show enough facts for the Court to find that agreement was plausible,"[62] whereas the *Railroad* court held that, "[t]he direct purchaser plaintiffs have provided robust factual details in their complaint supporting their 'independent allegation of actual agreement' from which the Court can infer that it is plausible that an actual agreement existed."[63] In light of the striking similarity of the complaints, these outcomes are difficult to reconcile.

The presence of government investigative activity has similarly proven to be an unreliable indicator of how a court will rule on a *Twombly* motion. In *In re Municipal Derivatives Antitrust Litigation*, for example, the court dismissed the complaint despite multiple pending enforcement proceedings against several defendants by the DOJ, the SEC, and the Internal Revenue Service.[64] Yet where plaintiffs alleged a price-fixing conspiracy by makers of "flash" memory chips and noted that many of the defendants were already under government investigation for price-fixing other kinds of memory chips, the court denied the *Twombly* motion: "At bottom, while these facts may not prove the existence of a conspiracy with respect to NAND flash memory, they are properly pleaded for the purpose of establishing the plausibility that such a conspiracy

---

59 *See also In re* Text Messaging Antitrust Litig., 630 F.3d 622, 629 (7th Cir. 2010) (noting the tension between "plausibility" as required under *Twombly*, and "probability" which is not required: "[t]his is a little unclear because plausibility, probability, and possibility overlap. Probability runs the gamut from a zero likelihood to a certainty. What is impossible has a zero likelihood of occurring and what is plausible has a moderately high likelihood of occurring. The fact that the allegations undergirding a claim could be true is no longer enough to save a complaint from being dismissed; the complaint must establish a nonnegligible probability that the claim is valid; but the probability need not be as great as such terms as 'preponderance of the evidence' connote.").

60 No. 1:08-MD-01895 (N.D. Ga. filed Jan. 28, 2009).

61 587 F.Supp.2d 27 (D.D.C. 2008).

62 *LTL*, No. 1:08-MD-01895.s

63 *Rail Freight*, 587 F.Supp.2d at 34 (internal citation omitted); *see also In re* Hawaiian & Guamanian Cabotage Antitrust Litig., 647 F.Supp.2d 1250 (W.D. Wash. 2009) (dismissing complaint under *Twombly* standard where allegations centered on parallel movements in fuel surcharges).

64 620 F.Supp.2d 499, 514 (S.D.N.Y. 2009) ("Named Plaintiffs' citations to these investigations do not constitute factual averments of a § 1 claim that would allow such a claim to survive a motion to dismiss.").

existed."[65] Only the most basic insights for the antitrust plaintiff can be salvaged from the *Twombly* landscape, but they bear great importance: investigate and plead every fact available and be satisfied that the complaint is "plausible" as the courts of the relevant venue understand and apply the standard.

While *Twombly* is probably the most often cited grounds for a motion to dismiss, the rise of a global economic system has resulted in an increase in the filing of motions to dismiss based on the once obscure Foreign Trade Antitrust Improvements Act (FTAIA).[66] The statute should be consulted whenever any potential antitrust claim will name a foreign defendant. "The FTAIA seeks to make clear to American exporters (and to firms doing business abroad) that the Sherman Act does not prevent them from entering into business arrangements (say, joint-selling arrangements), however anticompetitive, as long as those arrangements adversely affect only foreign markets."[67]

The statute itself is a muddle of double negatives and exceptions that has been politely described as "inelegantly phrased."[68] The Supreme Court has summarized the FTAIA as "removing from the Sherman Act's reach, (1) export activities and (2) other commercial activities taking place abroad, unless those activities adversely affect domestic commerce, imports to the United States, or exporting activities of one engaged in such activities within the United States."[69]

In considering a potential antitrust claim that involves a foreign party, there are, in general, two alternative paths for avoiding the application of an FTAIA dismissal. The first, and simplest, path to avoidance is to bring the claim within the "import trade or import commerce" exception, whereby the antitrust defendants, although located and acting abroad, are alleged to have imported goods or services into the U.S.[70]

The second, and more complicated, path to avoidance is to plead that the foreign conduct of the defendants, although not directly involving defendants' importation of goods or services into the U.S., nonetheless "(1) has a 'direct, substantial, and reasonably foreseeable effect' on domestic commerce, and (2) 'such effect gives rise to a [Sherman Act] claim.'"[71] This "domestic effects" exception analysis is elaborate and is discussed in greater detail later in this Handbook. The preliminary consideration to keep in mind, however, is that the link between defendants' foreign conduct and the domestic effects must be clear and strong.[72]

---

65 *In re* Flash Memory Antitrust Litig., 643 F.Supp.2d 1133, 1149 (N.D. Cal. 2009); *see also In re* Chocolate Confectionary Antitrust Litig., 602 F.Supp.2d 538, 576 (M.D. Pa. 2009) (denying motion to dismiss where complaint detailed the Canadian government's investigation of defendants, because "[d]efendants' alleged conduct in Canada enhances the plausibility of the alleged U.S. price-fixing conspiracy").

66 15 U.S.C. § 6a.

67 F. Hoffmann-La Roche Ltd. v. Empagran S.A., 542 U.S. 155, 161 (2004).

68 Carpet Group Intern. v. Oriental Rug Importers Ass'n, Inc., 227 F.3d 62, 69 (D.N.J. 2000).

69 *Empagran*, 542 U.S. at 161.

70 *See Carpet Group*, 227 F.3d at 71 (holding that claims against foreign association of importers and wholesalers of oriental rugs invoked the import trade or commerce exception).

71 *Empagran*, 542 U.S. at 158–159 (quoting 15 U.S.C. § 6a(1)(A), (2)).

72 *See* U.S. v. LSL Biotechnologies, 379 F.3d 672, 680 (9th Cir. 2004) (discussing meaning of "direct" effect).

Moreover, where the U.S. market for a good or service is just one of many affected by a foreign, global conspiracy, many courts have been hostile to allowing the antitrust claim to go forward.[73] These cases should cause the antitrust plaintiff contemplating a claim involving a foreign defendant to evaluate whether the claim will reasonably fall within an exception to the FTAIA.[74] Certain other statutes and legal doctrines can likewise frustrate attempts to sue foreign defendants that are directly or indirectly controlled by a foreign state.[75]

While the presence of a foreign defendant in a potential antitrust claim should trigger research as to the effect of the FTAIA and other legal defenses to the claim, the presence of a defendant subject to some type of federal regulation or oversight should alert the antitrust plaintiff to the possibility of antitrust preemption. Several industries enjoy some form of immunity from private antitrust claims under a grant of express antitrust preemption. For example, agricultural producers are free to form cooperative organizations for purposes of marketing such goods because of the Capper-Volstead Act, which places such conduct beyond the reach of the antitrust laws.[76] The airline industry, as a result of deregulation in the late 1970s, also enjoys limited immunity from state law claims relating to the rates, routes, or service of an airline under the Airline Deregulation Act;[77] however, this immunity does not extend to *federal* antitrust claims.[78]

In other circumstances, the courts have held that a regulatory system works an implied preemption of antitrust laws in favor of the regulated entity. In *Credit Suisse Securities (USA) LLC v. Billing*,[79] the Supreme Court held that an antitrust claim against securities brokers was preempted due to a "plain repugnancy" between the antitrust laws and the specific regulations of brokers under the securities laws. The Court applied a four-factor analysis for determining if the goals of the securities laws and the antitrust claim could be reconciled. Concluding that reconciliation was not possible, the Court held that the more general antitrust laws had to yield to the specific securities regulation.[80]

---

73 *See, e.g.,* Dee-K Enters., Inc. v. Heveafil Snd. Bhd., 299 F.3d 281, 295 (4th Cir. 2002) (affirming judgment for foreign defendants because under the domestic effects test, "these links to the United States are mere drops in the sea of conduct that occurred in Southeast Asia (and around the world)"), *cert denied*, 539 U.S. 969 (2003).

74 Another point of caution associated with the FTAIA comes with trying to predict whether the court will view the statute as a jurisdictional prerequisite, or instead as an additional element of the substantive claim and thus subject to a more lenient review. *See* Animal Science Prods., Inc. v. China Minmetals Corp., 654 F.3d 462 (3d Cir. 2011), *cert. denied*, 132 S.Ct. 1744 (2012) (splitting with other circuits and holding the FTAIA to be non-jurisdictional in nature). For further discussion of *Twombly*, the FTAIA, and procedural defenses generally, see Chapter 6 of this Handbook.

75 *See, e.g.,* Foreign Sovereign Immunities Act, 28 U.S.C. § 1602 *et seq.;* Mannington Mills v. Congoleum Corp., 595 F.2d 1287, 1293 (3rd Cir. 1979) (explaining concept of "foreign sovereign compulsion doctrine" as concerning immunities arising when a foreign government compels a business to violate U.S. antitrust laws).

76 *See* 7 U.S.C. § 291.

77 49 U.S.C. § 41713(b)(1).

78 *See, e.g., In re* Korean Air Lines Co. Antitrust Litig., No. 08-56385, 2011 U.S. App. LEXIS 7887 (9th Cir. Apr. 18, 2011) (affirming dismissal of state-law antitrust claims against airlines due to the Airline Deregulation Act).

79 551 U.S. 264, 127 S.Ct. 2383 (2007).

80 *Id.* at 2392.

Closely related to the concept of implied preemption is the filed rate doctrine. This judicially created rule provides that a carrier whose rates are subject to certain federal regulation cannot be sued for antitrust damages arising from those rates.[81] The doctrine applies to some federally regulated railroads and motor carriers, electricity wholesalers and pipeline operators, and telecommunications providers.

The rationale for applying the filed rate doctrine to dismiss rate challenging lawsuits is twofold: (1) it prevents the carriers from collecting different rates among like customers; and (2) it preserves the exclusivity of the regulatory agency's power to determine rate reasonableness by placing the rate-making process beyond the reach of the courts. Courts hearing antitrust and other substantive law claims against regulated carriers look at whether granting relief will require the court to determine the reasonableness of a rate subject to federal regulation. If so, the filed rate doctrine bars the claim.[82]

The common theme across the various antitrust pre-emption doctrines is that courts will engage in a close analysis before concluding an antitrust claim is pre-empted. Moreover, often there are significant exceptions and limitations on such pre-emption. If relevant, the antitrust plaintiff should dig deep into the pre-emption issue to locate these exceptions and limitations in order to keep the claim viable.

Another type of challenge interposed by defendants at the pleading stage with some frequency relates to the antitrust standing of the plaintiff to bring the claim. This type of challenge is typically shorthanded as an "*AGC*" motion, stemming from the Supreme Court's decision in *Associated General Contractors of California, Inc. v. California State Council of Carpenters*.[83] There, the Court held that a trade union did not have standing to pursue an antitrust claim alleging that a contractors' association conspired to restrain the union's activities. The Court balanced five factors, summarized as: "(1) the nature of the plaintiff's alleged injury; that is, whether it was the type the antitrust laws were intended to forestall; (2) the directness of the injury; (3) the speculative measure of the harm; (4) the risk of duplicative recovery; and (5) the complexity in apportioning damages."[84]

The typical *AGC* motion now arises most often in state law claims brought in federal court on behalf of *indirect* purchasers (who cannot sue under the Sherman Act).[85] *AGC*, a case interpreting federal antitrust law, has been held to apply to the standing requirements of some states' antitrust laws.[86] The application of federal standing law to state substantive claims is unsettled and the subject of controversy.[87] The antitrust plaintiff considering a claim under state substantive law (usually an indirect purchaser claim) therefore must

---

81 *See* Keogh v. Chicago and Northwestern Ry., 260 U.S. 156, 163–164 (1922) (announcing the doctrine); Square D Co. v. Niagara Frontier Tariff Bureau, Inc., 476 U.S. 409 (1986) (upholding the doctrine).

82 *See* E. & J. Gallo Winery v. EnCana Corp., 503 F.3d 1027 (9th Cir. 2007) (holding that filed rate doctrine is limited to claims involving rates subject to federal agency's jurisdiction, but does not apply to rates beyond the jurisdiction of the federal agency).

83 459 U.S. 519 (1983).

84 American Ad. Mgmt., Inc. v. General Tel. Co. of Cal., 190 F.3d 1051, 1054 (9th Cir. 1999) (citing *AGC*, 459 U.S. at 535).

85 Recall that state-law indirect purchaser claims are frequently heard in federal court pursuant to the Class Action Fairness Act. *See supra* note 16 and accompanying text.

86 *See In re* Flash Memory Antitrust Litig., No. 4:07CV000086 (N.D. Cal. filed January 5, 2007).

87 *See supra* note 18 and accompanying text.

investigate whether *AGC* may apply to the particular state statute, and whether, if so, the five-factor *AGC* analysis weighs in favor of standing.

Antitrust cases seeking to be certified as class actions are faced with much more difficult standards under recent case law.[88] A plaintiffs' lawyer overseeing a class action case must be prepared to meet the higher hurdles and tremendous costs associated with demonstrating Rule 23 class certification requirements, such as common impact. It is not uncommon for practitioners to submit hundreds of pages of economic expert reports in addition to undergoing days of evidentiary hearings.

§ 2.08 Deciding where to file the case

Antitrust cases can be filed in any federal district court.[89] As a practical matter, though, cases are usually filed where the plaintiff is located if it is a non-class case, unless the law is more favorable in another location.[90] Sometimes a defendant is strongly identified with its principal place of business, e.g., Microsoft and the State of Washington, and the plaintiff's lawyer probably will want to avoid bringing the case in that jurisdiction.

Although the law is theoretically the same in all federal district courts, certain districts and circuits have a reputation for being more plaintiff-friendly than others. Often this is based on a track record of success by plaintiffs' lawyers in a particular court, or on more favorable appellate decisions by the circuit court of appeals with jurisdiction over those districts. Plaintiffs' lawyers in both class and non-class cases should give careful thought to selecting the most favorable venue.

Would-be class actions are often filed in multiple district courts around the country, often depending on the locations of the law firms filing them. When this happens, the United States Judicial Panel on Multidistrict Litigation, colloquially called the MDL Panel, which consists of district judges from various parts of the country, will choose one district court in which to centralize them. Just as plaintiffs will advocate assignment to a district perceived as more plaintiff-friendly, defense counsel will advocate assignment to a more conservative venue. Groups of plaintiffs' lawyers often will form alliances to back a particular destination over another, in return for promises of support for a significant role in the leadership of the case. The MDL Panel considers a number of factors in making its decision, including convenience of the parties and potential witnesses, how many cases have been filed in each of the various districts, whether significant activity already has occurred in one of the candidate transferee courts, the experience of the district judge

---

[88] *See, e.g.*, *In re* Hydrogen Peroxide Antitrust Litig., 552 F.3d 305 (3rd Cir. 2008); *but see also* Behrend v. Comcast Corp., No. 10-2865, 2011 U.S. App. LEXIS 17524 (3rd Cir. Aug. 23, 2011).

[89] 15 U.S.C. § 7; Blumstock Bros. Advertising Agency v. Curtis Pub, 252 U.S. 436, 440 ("The Sherman Anti-Trust Act [*sic*] created a cause of action in favor of any person to recover by suit in any District Court"); *see also* The Clayton Act, 15 U.S.C. § 15 ("[A]ny person who shall be injured in his business or property by reason of anything forbidden in the antitrust laws may sue therefore in any district court.").

[90] *AMD v. Intel* was filed in the district court in Delaware even though both companies are located in the Bay Area, presumably because AMD thought that the applicable law was more favorable in light of *United States v. Dentsply Int'l, Inc.*, 399 F.3d 181 (3d Cir. 2005) and *LePages, Inc., v. 3M Company, Inc.*, 324 F.3d 141 (3d Cir. 2003).

who potentially may supervise the case, and the relative volume of complex cases already on file in the various districts.[91]

§ 2.09 Conclusion

Pre-complaint analysis is more important than ever. Antitrust litigation has always posed high risks for defendants, because of joint and several liability, the general rule against contribution, and the potential for treble damages. Those risks have not diminished. The expense of litigation has always been a significant factor for the plaintiff in deciding whether to file a case at all, and for both sides in deciding whether to settle before trial. In the past decade, however, legal risks and expenses have increased greatly, especially for plaintiffs. It is more important than ever that before filing a complaint, the prospective plaintiff or class counsel thoroughly assess the merits, the potential damages, and the different pleading, class certification, and summary judgment standards that may be applied in particular jurisdictions or by particular judges who may decide the case. A realistic assessment should also be made of the potential lawyer time, and of the out of pocket expenses likely to be necessary for the litigation, especially for discovery, document review, and experts. Sometimes the best cases are those that are not filed.

---

91 *See* John G. Heyburn II, *A View from the Panel: Part of the Solution*, 82 TUL. L. REV. 2225 (2008) (reviewing recent trends and explaining the process by which the Panel makes its decisions). For further discussion of the Judicial Panel on Multidistrict Litigation, see Chapter 4 and Chapter 5 of this Handbook.

3 Parties entitled to pursue a claim

Eric L. Cramer and Daniel C. Simons[1]

§ 3.01 Introduction

Antitrust violations often reverberate widely throughout a market and the economy more generally, impacting a multitude of market participants in a broad variety of ways. Hence, for a single violation, there may be multiple victims, each with potentially cognizable antitrust claims.

Under the literal and broad terms of the federal antitrust laws, all persons or entities suffering harm as a result of anticompetitive conduct theoretically have a claim, either to

[1] Eric L. Cramer and Daniel C. Simons are, respectively, a managing shareholder and an associate at Berger & Montague, P.C. Both focus their practices on antitrust and complex litigation.

seek an injunction under Section 16 of the Clayton Act (15 U.S.C. § 26), or to recover three times their damages resulting from the illegal conduct under Section 4 of the Clayton Act (15 U.S.C. § 15).

However, the courts have placed prudential limits on both the types of entities that can bring suit for violations of the Sherman Act and the circumstances under which such suits can be brought. These limitations come in the form of a multi-pronged test that examines the claimant, the linkage between the alleged harm and the challenged conduct, the type of claim asserted, and, in certain circumstances, the complexity of the proof needed to prove the claim. Because of this test, determining whether a plaintiff has standing to bring an antitrust claim can sometimes present complex and difficult issues,[2] and thus has generated a myriad of decisions over the years.

Chief among the restrictions on who can bring a claim is the need for the private antitrust plaintiff to demonstrate "antitrust injury." For that, the law first looks to see if a private plaintiff has sustained the type of injury the antitrust laws are meant to prevent.[3] Second, the plaintiff's injury must flow from that which makes the defendant's acts unlawful.[4] This portion of the test asks whether the alleged injury is connected to the purposes of the antitrust laws: the protection of competition.[5] A showing of antitrust injury – or the threat of such injury – flowing from the antitrust violation is a prerequisite for obtaining damages or injunctive relief under the federal antitrust laws.

Antitrust injury alone, however, is not sufficient to entitle a plaintiff to treble damages under § 4 of the Clayton Act.[6] An antitrust violation can send "ripples" of harm throughout various levels and segments of the economy. Courts have observed that permitting multiple damage claims for similar injuries arising from an antitrust violation could lead to duplicative recoveries or complex proceedings to apportion damages among claimants. Therefore, the Supreme Court has required a claimant to meet several "prudential" factors before it is allowed to bring a claim for treble damages under the Clayton Act.[7] Those plaintiffs who meet these factors are said to possess "antitrust standing."

One group of claimants has almost universally been recognized to have antitrust standing for both injunctive relief and money damages: those who purchased a product that's price was artificially inflated by alleged anticompetitive conduct *directly* from the accused monopolist or cartel member, i.e., "direct purchasers." Direct purchasers typically claim harm and seek damages measured by overcharges, which are measured as the difference between the price actually paid to the defendant for the affected product and the price that would have prevailed *but for* the illegal conduct.[8] Thus, the recovery sought by direct purchasers is directly related to the harm to competition due to anticompetitive practices,

---

[2] Arroyo-Melecio v. Puerto Rican Am. Ins. Co., 398 F.3d 56, 72 (1st Cir. 2005) ("[I]n many ways the standing question is the most difficult issue in [a] case.").

[3] Brunswick Corp. v. Pueblo Bowl-O-Mat, Inc., 429 U.S. 477, 489 (1977).

[4] *Id.*

[5] II Phillip E. Areeda & Herbert Hovenkamp, Antitrust Law 362 (1995).

[6] 15 U.S.C. § 15.

[7] Associated Gen. Contractors of Cal. v. Cal. State Council of Carpenters, 459 U.S. 519 (1983).

[8] *See, e.g.*, American Bar Ass'n, Proving Antitrust Damages 171 (1996) ("[T]he plaintiff's damages depend on the difference between the actual price paid and the competitive price, or the price that would have been charged absent the illegal agreement.").

i.e., the higher prices that flow from competitive restrictions. In addition, because the harm is direct, it is nearly always found to "flow" from the antitrust violation. For reasons discussed below, direct purchasers are the only purchasers in the chain of distribution entitled to recover overcharges resulting from antitrust violations under federal law. As a result, they are permitted to recover the entire overcharge, without a set-off reflecting the extent to which the direct purchaser may have "passed on" the overcharge down the chain of distribution or benefitted economically from the challenged conduct.

In contrast with direct purchasers, under federal law, *indirect* purchasers must show a sufficient causal nexus between the anticompetitive conduct and their injuries before they are granted antitrust standing. Even then, standing is almost always restricted to equitable relief. The corollary to the Supreme Court's ruling allowing direct purchasers to recover the entire overcharge is that indirect purchasers are not entitled to monetary relief under the Sherman Act.[9] However, indirect purchasers are permitted to recover damages under the laws of many states.[10]

Those in competition with a monopolist or cartel are also commonly permitted to pursue claims to recover for injuries they may have suffered due to the anticompetitive conduct. However, a competitor cannot merely show that its business or market share was adversely impacted by an anticompetitive practice. Even if the defendant otherwise violated the antitrust laws, if the competitor's claimed harm constituted losses incurred as a result of competition on the merits, there can be no antitrust injury.[11]

Finally, several other types of claimants have appeared as plaintiffs in antitrust suits alleging harm flowing from antitrust violations, including shareholders of corporations, suppliers, employees, terminated distributors, unions, trade groups, and others. Antitrust standing for such claimants is sometimes granted and sometimes not, depending on the nature of the claim and the relationship of the alleged harm to the violation.

This chapter first discusses the *sine qua non* of any private antitrust claim: antitrust injury. Second, the chapter looks at the standing requirements for those seeking injunctive relief under the federal antitrust laws. Third, we explore the necessary showing for standing to bring damage claims.[12] Fourth, we observe that direct purchasers are frequently granted antitrust standing, and catalog the few scenarios where direct purchaser antitrust recoveries have been questioned. Fifth, standing of indirect purchasers to pursue claims is examined, as well as possible exceptions to the federal bar on indirect purchaser damages actions and other means of potential recovery (including recovery under state law). Sixth, we discuss antitrust standing issues concerning competitors bringing claims, and the types of recoveries they have standing to seek. And, finally, we canvass the various other types of plaintiffs that have brought antitrust suits, and discuss how courts have dealt with each group's standing to bring antitrust claims.

---

[9] Ill. Brick Co. v. Illinois, 431 U.S. 720 (1977) (disallowing damage claims by indirect purchasers); Hanover Shoe, Inc. v. United Shoe. Mach. Corp., 392 U.S. 481 (1968) (reaffirming that direct purchasers are entitled to recover and banning defense that they passed on any overcharge downstream).

[10] *See* discussion *infra* § 3.06.

[11] *See* discussion *infra* § 3.07.

[12] *See supra* note 7.

§ 3.02 Antitrust injury: Harm to competition, not competitors

As the oft-quoted adage goes: the antitrust laws were designed for the protection of competition, not competitors.[13] The idea behind this proposition is that antitrust laws are not intended to protect competitors for their own sake. Rather, antitrust is concerned about the loss of competitors in a market only where that loss harms consumer welfare through higher prices, restricted output, or reduced choice.[14]

The Supreme Court elaborated on this principle in *Brunswick Corp. v. Pueblo Bowl-O-Mat, Inc.*[15] In that case, the owner of a handful of bowling alleys alleged that a rival's purchase of a large number of bowling centers violated the antitrust laws because it substantially lessened competition in certain regions. The plaintiff sought as damages the income it had lost to the alleged monopolist due to the violation. The Supreme Court found that the plaintiff could not recover because there was no demonstration that the defendant's conduct had created any anticompetitive effects and thus its "injury was not of the type that the statute was intended to forestall."[16] Moreover, the plaintiff was seeking damages *because* the challenged acquisitions actually preserved otherwise failing bowling alleys and thus preserved competition and decreased market concentration. Because the plaintiff's claimed harm flowed from the promotion of competition and not its elimination, allowing the plaintiff to recover would have been contrary to the very purpose of the antitrust laws – the protection of competition, not competitors.[17] As a result, to bring an antitrust claim, a plaintiff has to demonstrate, as a threshold matter, that it sustained "antitrust injury," defined as injury of the type the antitrust laws were intended to prevent, and which flows from that which makes defendants' acts unlawful.[18]

Accordingly, a plaintiff must demonstrate not only harm to itself, but that the harm suffered resulted from conduct that diminished competition and harmed consumer welfare generally.[19] Indeed, "[w]henever the plaintiff and consumers have divergent rather than congruent interests, there is a potential problem in finding 'antitrust injury'. . . . When the plaintiff is a poor champion of consumers, a court must be especially careful not to grant relief that may undercut the proper functions of antitrust."[20] Harm to competition is typically in the form of higher prices, reduced output, or reduced choice.[21]

---

[13] Brown Shoe v. United States, 370 U.S. 294, 320 (1962).

[14] "Congress designed the Sherman Act as a 'consumer welfare prescription.'" Reiter v. Sonotone Corp., 442 U.S. 330, 343 (1979) (quoting Robert H. Bork, The Antitrust Paradox 66 (1978)). *See also* Broadcom Corp. v. Qualcomm Inc., 501 F.3d 297, 308 (2007) ("The primary goal of antitrust law is to maximize consumer welfare by promoting competition among firms."). Other scholars have countered that the primary goal should not be end-user welfare, but rather, "protect[ing] the people by protecting the competitive process." Gregory J. Werden, *Monopsony and the Sherman Act: Consumer Welfare in a New Light*, 74 Antitrust L.J. 707, 735 (2007); *see also* Albert A. Foer, *The Goals Of Antitrust: Thoughts On Consumer Welfare In The U.S.*, *in* Handbook of Research in Trans-Atlantic Antitrust 566, 566–593 (Philip Marsden ed., 2006).

[15] 429 U.S. 477 (1977).

[16] *Id.* at 487–88 (internal quotes and citation omitted).

[17] *Id.* at 488.

[18] *Id.* at 489.

[19] *See supra* note 14 and accompanying text.

[20] Ball Mem'l Hosp. v. Mut. Hosp. Ins., 784 F.2d 1325, 1334 (7th Cir. 1986).

[21] NicSand, Inc. v. 3M Co., 507 F.3d 442, 451–52 (6th Cir. 2007) (harm to competition deemed

To show antitrust injury, some courts have imposed an additional requirement that the plaintiff must be a participant in the market in which the alleged restraint was carried out.[22] However, if "two markets are so closely related," anticompetitive behavior in the first market may give rise to antitrust injury for participants in another market.[23]

Establishing antitrust injury is only a first step in determining whether the plaintiff is an appropriate party. A plaintiff must also meet additional requirements to establish that it has standing to seek injunctive relief or money damages for violations of the Sherman Act. These requirements are discussed below.

§ 3.03 Standing for injunctive relief

The right to injunctive relief is established by § 16 of the Clayton Act:

> Any person, firm, corporation, or association shall be entitled to sue for and have injunctive relief . . . against threatened loss or damage by a violation of the antitrust laws, . . . when and under the same conditions and principles as injunctive relief against threatened conduct that will cause loss or damage is granted by courts of equity, under the rules governing such proceedings[.][24]

A plaintiff seeking an injunction must show antitrust injury, as well as (1) a threatened loss or injury cognizable in equity (2) proximately resulting from the alleged antitrust injury.[25]

Thus, whereas a plaintiff seeking damages under § 4 of the Clayton Act must demonstrate damage to "business or property," injunctive relief is available merely upon a showing of "*threatened* loss or damage."[26] And because the harm need not specifically be to "business or property," the threatened harm may not even be economic at all; it simply must result from an antitrust violation.

The distinction between damage to "business or property" and the lesser showing of "threatened loss or damage" is rooted in more than simply linguistic differences between §§ 4 and 16 of the Clayton Act. The right to obtain treble damages is restricted due to the prospect of overlapping or duplicative recoveries and the potential need for complex proofs to sort them out. These concerns are absent in the injunction context, however.

---

absent because plaintiff alleged harm flowing from lower prices); Yellow Page Solutions, Inc. v. Bell Atl. Yellow Pages Co., No. 00-Civ.-5663(MBM), 2001 U.S. Dist. LEXIS 18831, at *34 (S.D.N.Y. Nov. 19, 2001) (antitrust plaintiff's claim for lost profits fails unless plaintiff also shows harm to competition); Cancall PCS, LLC v. Omnipoint Corp., No. 99-Civ.-3395(AGS), 2000 WL 272309, at *6 (S.D.N.Y. Mar. 10, 2000) (dismissing antitrust claims for want of allegation that "consumers in general were charged higher prices").

22 *See, e.g.*, Legal Econ. Evaluations, Inc. v. Metro. Life Ins. Co., 39 F.3d 951, 956 (9th Cir. 1994) (no antitrust injury because "the asserted harm to competition takes place in different markets" than alleged injury).

23 Sanner v. Board of Trade of Chicago, 62 F.3d 918, 929 (7th Cir. 1995). *See also* Doe v. Abbott Labs., 2004 U.S. Dist. LEXIS 29129, *11 (N.D. Cal. Oct. 21, 2004) (plaintiffs permitted to sue for injuries on one product where harm was "inextricably intertwined" with anticompetitive activity concerning related product).

24 15 U.S.C. § 26.

25 McCarthy v. Recordex Serv., Inc., 80 F.3d 842, 856 (3d Cir. 1996).

26 Cargill, Inc. v. Monfort of Colo., Inc., 479 U.S. 104, 112 (1986) (emphasis added).

As to the possible multiplicity of claims, "one injunction is as effective as 100, and, concomitantly, . . . 100 injunctions are no more effective than one."[27]

Of course, a plaintiff seeking an injunction must still demonstrate antitrust injury.[28] Thus, in *Cargill*, the plaintiff, a would-be competitor, was denied an injunction because the harm it alleged – the defendants' decision to lower prices resulting in the plaintiffs' loss of profits – was not a cause of concern under the antitrust laws.[29] By contrast, direct purchasers are permitted to seek injunctive relief flowing from the charging of allegedly "supra-competitive prices."[30]

Moreover, the threatened harm must be proximately caused by the antitrust violation. Like § 4 of the Clayton Act, § 16 requires that the threatened harm come about "*by* a violation of the antitrust laws,"[31] which has been read to require a showing of proximate causation.[32] Thus, despite the "relaxed" requirements for injunctive relief (as compared to damages claims), inability to show proximate causation can still doom a potential antitrust action.[33]

Section 16 also requires that the plaintiff show that it would be entitled to an injunction under traditional principles of equity.

§ 3.04 Standing for damages claims

Demonstrating standing to obtain antitrust damages, in contrast, requires a somewhat greater showing than is required for an injunction. As the Supreme Court has explained, "[a] showing of antitrust injury is necessary, but not always sufficient, to establish standing under § 4 [of the Clayton Act], because a party may have suffered antitrust injury but may not be a proper plaintiff under § 4 for other reasons."[34]

The nature of some of those limitations appeared in the Supreme Court's decision in *Hawaii v. Standard Oil Co.*,[35] where the court denied the State of Hawaii standing to seek damages for harm to its "general economy" as the result of an antitrust violation. The Court found the alleged harm was "no more than a reflection of injuries to the 'business

---

27 *Id.* at 111 n.6. As discussed elsewhere in this chapter, it is for this reason that an indirect purchaser plaintiff has traditionally been allowed to pursue claims for injunctive relief for violations of the antitrust laws even though it is barred from seeking money damages. *See* discussion *infra* § 3.06.1.

28 *Cargill*, 479 U.S. at 111–112.

29 *Id.* at 115.

30 *See, e.g.*, *In re* Rail Freight Fuel Surcharge Antitrust Litig., 593 F. Supp. 2d 29, 41 (D.D.C. 2008).

31 15 U.S.C. § 26 (emphasis added).

32 *In re* Warfarin Sodium Antitrust Litig., 214 F.3d 395, 399–401 (3d Cir. 2000); Catlin v. Wash. Energy Co., 791 F.2d 1343, 1350 (9th Cir. 1986); Mid-West Paper Prods. Co. v. Cont'l Group, Inc., 596 F.2d 573, 591–92 (3d Cir. 1979); Reibert v. Atl. Richfield Co., 471 F.2d 727, 731 (10th Cir. 1973).

33 *See, e.g.*, Pocahontas Supreme Coal Co., Inc. v. Bethlehem Steel Corp., 828 F.2d 211, 220 (4th Cir. 1987) (affirming denial of injunction because claimed harm "too attenuated to be considered proximate"); *Catlin*, 791 F.2d 1350–51 (Reinhardt, J. concurring) (injunction appropriately denied where plaintiff did not establish causation).

34 *Cargill*, 479 U.S. at 110.

35 405 U.S. 251 (1972).

or property' of consumers, for which they may recover themselves under § 4."[36] Even a "lengthy and expensive trial" could not address the potential problems of "double recovery" inherent in permitting such a claim.[37]

The potential for double recovery and complex proofs again proved to be determinative in *Illinois Brick Co. v. Illinois*.[38] There, the Court disallowed treble damage claims by indirect purchasers because of the risk of duplicative recovery by both direct and indirect purchasers flowing from a single overcharge by the alleged violator.[39] That, and the unwieldy and expensive proofs that would be involved in attempting to allocate damages among direct and indirect purchaser plaintiffs, led the Court to adopt a rule barring indirect purchasers from recovering damages under the antitrust laws. Instead, the Court hewed to the rule it had announced in *Hanover Shoe, Inc. v. United Shoe Machinery Corp.*,[40] that direct purchasers – those most likely to "effectively enforce" the antitrust laws – were the appropriate plaintiffs to bring damages claims.[41]

The "direct purchaser rule" of *Illinois Brick* applies only to claims by downstream purchasers in the chain of distribution and has not been held to restrict all damages claims by consumers. For instance, in *Blue Shield of Virginia v. McCready*, the Court allowed a claim for treble damages by a patient seeking reimbursement from her health plan for her psychologist's services. McCready claimed that her health plan was restraining trade in the psychotherapy services market, by providing reimbursement only for psychiatric therapy (or psychological therapy administered through a physician's office). None of the factors of *Hawaii* or *Illinois Brick* prohibited McCready's claim even though McCready was not a "direct purchaser" from her health plan. Moreover, although the excluded psychologists and McCready's employer (who paid for the health plan) might also have standing, the plan was purchased for McCready's benefit, and thus she had standing as a consumer.[42] She faced a "Hobson's choice" between foregoing treatment by a psychologist or foregoing reimbursement. This rendered her injury "inextricably intertwined" with the injury the alleged conspirators sought to inflict on the market.[43]

After *McCready*, the Supreme Court further explicated the requirements for standing to bring a treble damages claim in *Associated General Contractors of California v. California State Council of Carpenters.*[44] First, the Court emphasized the need for a "causal

---

36 *Id.* at 264.

37 *Id.* Of course, this is not to say a state could *never* be a proper plaintiff to recover antitrust damages. For instance, if a state or its agent had directly purchased goods or services from a cartel, it would have standing as much as any other direct purchaser. These were exactly the facts in Chattanooga Foundry & Pipe Works v. Atlanta, 203 U.S. 390 (1906). Moreover, in the wake of *Hawaii v. Standard Oil*, Congress amended the Clayton Act to permit state attorneys general to bring damage actions, as *parens patriae*, on behalf state residents who would otherwise have claims under Section 4 of the Clayton Act. *See* 15 U.S.C. § 15c; *see also* Illinois Brick Co. v. Illinois, 431 U.S. 720, 734 n.14 (1977) (explaining Section 15c). For further discussion of attorney general actions, see Chapter 4 and Chapter 11 of this Handbook.

38 431 U.S. 720 (1977).

39 *Id.* at 730–31.

40 392 U.S. 481 (1968).

41 *Ill. Brick*, 431 U.S. at 735.

42 *McCready*, 457 U.S. at 480.

43 *Id.* at 483–84.

44 459 U.S. 519 (1983).

connection" between the asserted violation and the alleged harm.[45] Second, the Court repeated its focus on the "nature of the plaintiff's alleged injury," and that it must comport with the antitrust laws' purpose of "assur[ing] customers the benefits of price competition" and "protecting the economic freedom of participants in the relevant market."[46] Third, it examined the "directness or indirectness of the asserted injury," and whether the injury and alleged restraint were directly connected or attenuated by "several somewhat vaguely defined links."[47] Fourth, the Court looked for more "immediate victims of coercion by defendants," whose injuries would be "direct" and who would hold a right to obtain damages of their own. Fifth, the Court referred to the potentially speculative nature of the harm alleged.[48] Finally, the Court expressed concern about keeping the "scope of complex antitrust trials within judicially manageable limits," avoiding "duplicate recoveries on the one hand," and "the danger of complex apportionment of damages on the other."[49]

The courts of appeal have each construed the *Associated General* factors as guidelines, but not a comprehensive "checklist." For instance, in *In re Lower Lake Erie Iron Ore Antitrust Litigation*,[50] the Third Circuit noted that the various factors should be "weighed and balanced," with no "specific weight" assigned to any particular factor.[51] The court then took each of the factors in turn and assessed how well the plaintiffs and their asserted injuries fit with each factor.[52]

Over time, courts of appeal began to view these factors not only as a gauge of standing, but as part of an effort to find "efficient enforcers" of the antitrust laws.[53] That is, courts now use these factors to test the strength of the plaintiffs' motivation and ability to enforce the antitrust laws. With that in mind, we turn to the various types of plaintiffs that have appeared in private antitrust litigation over the years, and discuss how their ability to establish injury and standing has fared.

---

45 *Id.* at 537. The Court offered no precise test for causation, instead referring to the general law of proximate cause in torts. This generally means that the violation was a material factor in causing the plaintiff's injury, and that the plaintiff's injury was foreseeable by the alleged violator. *See* Nelson v. Monroe Reg'l Med. Ctr., 925 F.2d 1555, 1563–64 (7th Cir. 1991).

46 *Associated Gen.* 459 U.S. at 538 (citations omitted).

47 *Id.* at 540.

48 *Id.* at 542.

49 *Id.* at 543–44. Different circuits enumerate the factors in different ways. *See, e.g., In re* Lower Lake Erie Iron Ore Antitrust Litig., 998 F.2d 1144, 1165–66 (3d Cir. 1993) (five factors). The Serpa Corp. v. McWane, Inc., 199 F.3d 6, 10 (1st Cir. 1999) (grouping factors under six headings); Andrx Pharms., Inc. v. Biovail Corp., 256 F.3d 799, 806–817 (D.C. Cir. 2001) (five factors); Am. Ad Mgmt., Inc. v. Gen'l Tel. Co., 190 F.3d 1051, 1054 (9th Cir. 1999) (same), Paycom Billing Servs., Inc. v. MasterCard Int'l, Inc., 467 F.3d 283, 290–291 (2d Cir. 2006) (four factors).

50 998 F.2d at 1166.

51 *Id.*; *see also Paycom*, 467 F.3d at 291 ("the weight to be given the various factors will necessarily vary with the circumstances of particular cases") (alteration in original) (citation omitted); *Am. Ad Mgmt.*, 190 F.3d at 1055 ("To conclude that there is antitrust standing, a court need not find in favor of the plaintiff on each factor . . . . Generally no single factor is decisive[,]" but noting "great weight" is given to the nature of plaintiff's injury) (internal quotes and citations omitted).

52 *Lower Lake Erie*, 998 F.2d at 1167–1171. Notably, even if one factor weighed against standing, the court balanced it against the other factors as a whole, rather than treating each factor as a necessity. *See id.* at 1170 ("[C]omplex apportionment is not a sufficient reason to deny standing.").

53 *Paycom*, 467 F.3d at 290; Abraham v. Intermountain Health Care, Inc., 461 F.3d 1249, 1268 (10th Cir. 2006); Todorov v. DCH Healthcare Auth., 921 F.2d 1438, 1449 (11th Cir. 1991).

§ 3.05 Direct purchasers

It is by now well-settled that the prototypical "efficient enforcers" of the antitrust laws are the entities or persons that purchase directly from the alleged violator of the antitrust laws, i.e., the "direct purchasers."[54] It is so well established, in fact, that direct purchasers need not show they are "efficient enforcers" under the facts of any particular case; it is simply presumed.[55]

The foundations for the status of direct purchasers to bring antitrust damages claims were set over one hundred years ago in *Chattanooga Foundry & Pipe Works v. City of Atlanta*,[56] where the plaintiff city claimed injury to its "business or property" because an illegal conspiracy among the defendants "led [the city] to pay more than the worth of the pipe."[57] The Supreme Court agreed, concluding, "A person whose property is diminished by a payment of money wrongfully induced is injured in his property."[58]

Direct purchasers' standing to bring damage claims was reaffirmed and bolstered by the Court's decision in *Hanover Shoe, Inc. v. United Shoe Machinery Corp.*[59] There, the defendant had argued that the plaintiff, who purchased directly from the defendant, should not be entitled to recover because it had "passed on" any overcharge to the plaintiff's own customers in the distribution chain.[60] The Court began with the notion that "[t]he general tendency of the law, in regard to damages at least, is not to go beyond the first step."[61] Rejecting the notion that the possibility the purchaser passed on an overcharge requires recognition of the "pass on" defense, the Court noted that "[a] wide range of factors influence a company's pricing policies."[62] If the "passing-on" defense were recognized, an antitrust plaintiff seeking to recover damages would need to retain an economist to compute what the plaintiff's sales prices and volumes would have been absent the challenged conduct – a task which "would normally prove insurmountable," requiring "additional long and complicated proceedings involving massive evidence and complicated theories."[63] Also, if a direct purchaser would be subject to a defense that it passed on the overcharge to its own customers, the damage claim would keep running down the distribution chain to the "ultimate consumers" who only buy a tiny amount of the affected product and "would have only a tiny stake in a lawsuit and little interest in

---

[54] Blue Shield of Va. v. McCready, 457 U.S. 465, 474 (1982) (direct purchasers are plaintiffs most likely to "press their claims with . . . vigor"). For the sake of simplicity, we speak of the direct purchaser as the potential plaintiff and the seller as the violator. However, if the violation alleged involves monopsonistic conduct, potential plaintiffs include the seller who was forced to part with his goods at too low a price. *E.g.*, Mandeville Island Farms Inc. v. Am. Crystal Sugar Co., 334 U.S. 219 (1948).

[55] *See, e.g.*, Del. Valley Surgical Supply, Inc. v. Johnson & Johnson, 523 F.3d 1116, 1121–23 (9th Cir. 2008). One of the authors of this chapter (Mr. Cramer) was counsel for the direct purchaser class plaintiffs in this case.

[56] 203 U.S. 390 (1906).

[57] *Id.* at 396.

[58] *Id.*

[59] 392 U.S. 481 (1968).

[60] *Id.* at 488.

[61] *Id.* at 490 n.8 (internal quotes omitted).

[62] *Id.* at 492.

[63] *Id.* at 492–93.

attempting a class action."[64] As a result, the Court held that the direct purchaser had a claim for the entire amount its price was inflated due to the anticompetitive conduct, i.e., the entire overcharge.[65]

Having allowed damage claims by direct purchasers even if the plaintiffs had passed on all or part of their overcharge, the Court in *Illinois Brick* barred *indirect* purchasers from seeking some or all of those same damages under Clayton Act § 4.[66] The Court understood that an overcharge could cause "ripples of harm," affecting parties throughout the distribution chain, but nonetheless limited the reach of § 4 of the Clayton Act to the first level, i.e., direct, purchaser. The direct purchaser could thus recover the entire amount of the overcharge despite the "pass on" or other effects of the challenged conduct on the business of the direct purchaser,[67] but, as noted above, more attenuated purchasers down the chain of distribution could not recover for any harms flowing from the anticompetitive conduct, in light of the potential for double recovery and the complex proof needed to allocate injuries to purchasers along the distribution chain.[68] In sum, only direct purchaser damages claims were allowed.[69]

Direct purchaser claims were not at issue in *Associated General*, but the Court seems to have taken pains to reinforce the primacy of direct purchasers to private antitrust enforcement. First, in describing the nature of harms most closely associated with the purposes of the Sherman Act, the Court stated that "the Sherman Act was enacted to assure customers the benefits of price competition, and our prior cases have emphasized the central interest in protecting the economic freedom of participants in the relevant market."[70] Second, in describing the types of claims associated with complex apportionment and duplicative recovery, the Court pointed to the *indirect purchaser* damages claims it had banned in *Illinois Brick*, reaffirming impliedly that direct purchaser claims would yield no such complexities.

The Supreme Court further expanded on purchaser standing in *Reiter v. Sonotone Corp.*,[71] where an attempt was made to cabin purchaser standing to businesses and

---

64 *Id.* at 494.

65 *Id.*

66 *Ill. Brick*, 431 U.S. at 729–30.

67 Courts interpreting *Hanover Shoe* and *Illinois Brick* have made clear that those decisions prohibit not only use of the "passing on" defense, but also the subtle variation thereon that the direct purchasers somehow benefitted from the anticompetitive conduct (like increased revenues from reselling goods at the artificially inflated price). *See* Sports Racing Servs., Inc. v. Sports Car Club of Am., Inc., 131 F.3d 874, 884–885 (10th Cir. 1997) (rejecting argument that plaintiff benefitted from alleged violation and therefore lacked injury because "[t]hat reasoning is directly contrary to the Supreme Court's holding in *Hanover Shoe*. *Hanover Shoe* precludes the argument that [plaintiff] did not suffer cognizable antitrust injury merely because it passed overcharges on to its customers or otherwise was shielded from competition by the defendants' anticompetitive behavior"); Meijer, Inc. v. Abbott Labs., 251 F.R.D. 431, 435 (N.D. Cal. 2008); *In re* Relafen Antitrust Litig., 346 F. Supp. 2d 349, 369 (D. Mass. 2004). The authors of this chapter were counsel to the plaintiffs in the latter two cases.

68 *Ill. Brick*, 431 U.S. 720.

69 *Id.* at 724 ("[A] direct purchaser suing for treble damages under § 4 of the Clayton Act is injured within the meaning of § 4 by the full amount of the overcharge paid by it.").

70 *Associated Gen.*, 459 U.S. at 538.

71 442 U.S. 330.

foreclose claims by purchasing consumers. The defendants had argued that a consumer could not be injured in her "business or property" because a consumer had no "business" to injure. The Court disagreed, finding it was precisely for consumers that the Sherman Act was enacted:

> We described the Sherman Act as "conceived of primarily as a remedy for '[t]he people of the United States as individuals,' especially consumers," and the treble-damages provision of the Clayton Act as "conceived primarily as 'open[ing] the door of justice to every man . . . and giv[ing] the injured party ample damages for the wrong suffered.'"[72]

Thus, even if the purchaser is a consumer "injured only in terms of . . . a wrongful deprivation of money because the price . . . was artificially inflated by reason of [the] anticompetitive conduct," that is sufficient injury under the Clayton Act.[73]

3.05.1 Determining direct purchaser status

Direct purchasers are "the immediate buyers from the alleged antitrust violators."[74] Generally, a direct purchaser will take possession of that inventory for resale at prices that the manufacturer and direct purchaser negotiate. Sometimes, however, a manufacturer may negotiate price directly with one customer, but sell to that customer through an intermediary distributor. Courts have held that an entity which negotiates purchase price terms with a manufacturer and enters into a contract with that manufacturer that calls for the products to be distributed through an intermediary is not a "direct purchaser" from that manufacturer – the intermediary is the direct purchaser. Indeed, such a "contract customer" will not be considered a direct purchaser even if the intermediary doesn't actually physically take possession of products for re-delivery, but where the customer places purchase orders through the intermediary and that intermediary takes title to the product and retains the right to set a portion of its own prices.[75] Even if the contract customer has the product "drop-shipped" directly from the monopolist, that does not render the sale a direct sale.[76]

---

72 *Id.* at 343 (quoting *Brunswick Corp.*, 429 U.S. at 486 n.10).

73 *Id.* at 342. The Supreme Court did not address whether the direct purchaser rule applied to Reiter, nor what effect that rule might have on Reiter's ability to bring a claim (noting only that whether a person or entity was a "direct purchaser" and whether that same person or entity suffered "antitrust injury" were distinct questions). *See id.* at 337 n.3. Later decisions have made clear that a consumer must still satisfy *Illinois Brick*. *See, e.g.*, Campos v. Ticketmaster Corp., 140 F.3d 1166, 1169, 1171–72 (8th Cir. 1998) (recognizing that consumers could sue under *Reiter*, but barring consumers who were indirect purchasers from recovering damages).

74 *UtiliCorp*, 497 U.S. at 207; *Del. Valley*, 523 F.3d at 1121.

75 Warren Gen. Hosp. v. Amgen, Inc.., 643 F.3d 77, 88–89 (3d Cir. 2011); *see also* Del. Valley Surgical Supply, Inc. v. Johnson & Johnson, 523 F.3d at 1122 (denying direct purchaser status where plaintiff hospitals had a contract with the manufacturer that contained price terms but bought through an intermediary which intermediary both paid the manufacturer directly for its inventory and took title to the products before reselling them to the plaintiff hospitals, and where plaintiff hospitals paid the intermediary); St. Francis Med. Ctr. v. C.R. Bard, Inc., 657 F. Supp. 2d 1069, 1105–06 (E.D. Mo. 2009) (plaintiffs who had contracts with manufacturer that contained price terms but who had purchased through a distributor denied direct purchaser standing).

76 *Warren Gen. Hosp.*, 643 F.3d at 88–89; Howard Hess Dental Laboratories Inc. v. Dentsply

Another question that has recently arisen is whether a purchaser of a product incorporating a price-fixed component has direct purchaser standing to bring an antitrust claim against the manufacturer. The Third Circuit answered in the affirmative, upholding the standing of those that had purchased food products containing sugar from alleged members of a price-fixing cartel for sugar.[77] Were the rule otherwise, "producers would be free to fix the price of component prices, provided those components were later incorporated into another finished product."[78] Nevertheless, one court has required that an entity purchasing only a derivative product (i.e., a product that contains as an input the price-fixed product) is a direct purchaser only where it sues a defendant that produces the finished product as well as the price-fixed input.[79]

3.05.2 Overcharge damages

The form of damages most frequently sought by direct purchasers is an "overcharge," that is, the difference between the price actually paid to the antitrust defendant for the affected product and the price which would have prevailed but for the illegal conduct.[80]

Overcharges are intended to reflect the very essence of the societal harm done to the general economy: injuries flowing from the higher prices the cartel or monopolist was able to impose due to its anticompetitive activity. "Since the very purpose of antitrust law is to ensure that the benefits of competition flow to purchasers of goods affected by the violation, buyers have usually been preferred plaintiffs in private antitrust litigation, and a purchaser's standing to recover for an overcharge paid directly to an illegal cartel or monopoly is seldom doubted."[81] Thus, injuries in the form of overcharges are "of the type the antitrust laws were intended to prevent and that flows from that which makes defendants' acts unlawful."[82]

Int'l, Inc., 424 F.3d 363, 372 (3d Cir. 2005) (purchasers could not "avoid *Illinois Brick* by claiming they were direct purchasers of drop shipments when their complaint specifically alleges that they did not directly purchase from [the monopolist").

[77] *In re* Sugar Industry Antitrust Litig., 579 F.2d 13, 17–18 (3d Cir. 1978); *see also* Loeb Indus. v. Sumitomo Corp., 306 F.3d 469, 495 (7th Cir. 2002) (that plaintiff had purchased reshaped form of product did not render its injuries indirect); *In re* TFT-LCD Antitrust Litig., 267 F.R.D. 291, 306 (N.D. Cal. 2010); General Refractories Co. v. Stone Container Corp., No. 98 C 3543, 1999 U.S. Dist. LEXIS 238, at *10 (N.D. Ill. Jan. 8, 1999) (permitting suit alleging price-fixing of linerboard, a determinant of the prices for the corrugated sheets plaintiffs purchased).

[78] *TFT-LCD Antitrust Litig.*, 267 F.R.D. at 306.

[79] *In re* Refrigerant Compressors Antitrust Litig., No. 2:09 md 02042, 2011 U.S. Dist. LEXIS 63297, *38–39 (E.D. Mich. Jun. 13, 2011).

[80] *See supra* note 8 and accompanying text. *See also* PROVING ANTITRUST DAMAGES 202 ("Overcharge damages can be calculated . . . by determining a hypothetical competitive price, subtracting it from the actual price, and multiplying the resulting number by the quantity actually purchased.").

[81] *In re* Cardizem CD Antitrust Litig., 105 F. Supp. 2d 618, 650–651 (E.D. Mich. 2000) (internal quotes and citations omitted).

[82] Cordes & Co. Fin. Servs. v. A.G. Edwards & Sons, Inc., 502 F.3d 91, 107 (2d Cir. 2007) (quoting *Brunswick Corp.*, 429 U.S. at 489). *See also In re* Warfarin Sodium Antitrust Litig., 214 F.3d 395, 401 (3d Cir. 2000) ("The excess amount paid by" purchasers (there, indirect purchasers) was "not only . . . 'inextricably intertwined' with the injury [the monopolist] aimed to inflict [on its competitor], the overcharge was the aim of [the] preclusive conduct. It is difficult to imagine a more

3.05.3 Damages for supra-competitive prices from non-conspirators

While direct purchaser standing is generally recognized, one form of damage claim has generated some controversy among courts: damages sustained due to high prices charged by sellers who did not join a conspiracy.

Suppose, for instance, Firms A, B, and C – the only sellers in the market – entered into a conspiracy to fix prices above competitive levels. A purchase from any one of the conspirators is made at supra-competitive prices and thus gives rise to antitrust damages.

However, if Firms A and B conspire, but not Firm C, prices set by all three may still be at supra-competitive levels. This is because Firm C prices its product in relation to the prevailing market price. As Firms A and B are conspiring, this leaves Firm C free to raise its prices as well under the "umbrella" of the artificially inflated prices caused by the conspiracy between A and B. Given that Firm C can be expected to set its price as high as the market will profitably allow, it will do so. Purchasers from Firm C may have overpaid, and ostensibly should be able to sue the conspirators for such overcharges if they flow from the illegal conduct.

Many courts have recognized that such claims for "umbrella damages" are merely another form of the anticompetitive harm that can result from a conspiracy in restraint of trade, and have held such overcharges are recoverable.[83] Other courts have barred such recoveries, determining that, under the facts of those cases, the harm is too far removed from the alleged violation, that there is a risk of duplicative recoveries, or that there would be a need for complex reapportionment of damages.[84]

Some courts have expressed concerns about the difficulty of proving the price the non-conspirator would have charged absent the alleged conspiracy.[85] But, this raises an issue about the ability to calculate damages and should provide no basis for disallowing recovery entirely. Moreover, computing the price the non-conspirator actually charged

---

formidable demonstration of antitrust injury."). For further discussion of forms of damages and calculation of damages, see Chapter 9 of this Handbook.

[83] *See, e.g.*, Loeb Indus., Inc. v. Sumitomo Corp., 306 F.3d 469 (7th Cir. 2002); Lower Lake Erie, 998 F.2d 1144; *In re* Beef Indus. Antitrust Litig., 600 F.2d 1148, 1166 n.24 (5th Cir. 1979); *In re* Online DVD Rental Antitrust Litig., No. M 09-2029 PJH, 2009 U.S. Dist. LEXIS 111602 (N.D. Cal. Dec. 1, 2009) ("the court is not persuaded that there is a categorical bar precluding the umbrella liability theory" in direct purchaser case); *In re* Relafen Antitrust Litig., Master File No. 01-12238-WGY, Order at 2 (D. Mass. Dec. 19, 2003) (Young, C.J.); *In re* Ariz. Dairy Prods. Antitrust Litig., 627 F. Supp. 233, 236 (D. Ariz. 1985); *In re* Uranium Antitrust Litig., 552 F. Supp. 518, 525 (N.D. Ill. 1982); Oberweis Dairy v. Assoc. Milk Producers, 553 F. Supp. 962, 973–74 (N.D. Ill. 1982); Pollock v. Citrus Assoc. of New York, 512 F. Supp. 711, 719 (S.D.N.Y. 1981); Strax v. Commodity Exch., 524 F. Supp. 936, 939–40 (S.D.N.Y. 1981); *In re* Bristol Bay, Alaska Salmon Fishery Antitrust Litig., 530 F. Supp. 36, 38–39 (W.D. Wash. 1981); Wash. v. Am. Pipe & Constr. Co., 280 F. Supp. 802, 806–07 (W.D. Wash. 1968). *See also* II PHILLIP AREEDA, ANTITRUST LAW § 347 (2007) (LEXIS Ed.); AMERICAN BAR ASS'N, PROVING ANTITRUST DAMAGES 192 (1996) ("[T]he weight of authority seems now to be on the side of recognizing the claim for damages.").

[84] *See, e.g.*, Mid-West Paper Prods., 596 F.2d at 583; FTC v. Mylan Labs., 62 F. Supp. 2d 25, 39–42 (D.D.C. 1999); Antoine L. Garabet, M.D., Inc., v. Autonomous Tech. Corp., 116 F. Supp. 2d 1159, 1168–70 (C.D. Cal. 2000); *In re* Vitamins Antitrust Litig., 2001 WL 855463, at *3–4 (D.D.C. Jul. 2, 2001); *In re* Folding Carton Antitrust Litig., 88 F.R.D. 211, 218–220 (N.D. Ill. 1980).

[85] *E.g.*, *Mid-West Paper Prods.*, 596 F.2d at 584.

and what it would have charged absent the conspiracy is not materially different from evaluating the price a conspirator would have charged in the but-for world.[86] Finally, other courts have expressed concerns about imposing liability on defendants for harm from which they received no direct benefit.[87] But courts have long held that antitrust violators must bear the full extent of the injuries they caused, regardless of whether the violators directly profited.[88]

Rather than creating a default rule, in our view, recovery of "umbrella damages" from non-conspirators should be assessed on a case-specific basis, as required by *Associated General*.

3.05.4 Direct purchaser standing in cases alleging fraud on the patent office

Despite the long tradition of recognizing direct purchaser standing, a small number of courts have questioned such standing when a direct purchaser pursues antitrust claims predicated on the fraudulent procurement of a patent.[89] Such claims are grounded in antitrust law, rather than patent law.[90] Hence, conventional antitrust standing doctrines adhere.

The Second Circuit in *DDAVP* correctly recognized that direct purchasers are entitled to sue for the injuries they sustained due to anticompetitive conduct. The court applied the factors from *Associated General*, finding that the direct purchasers were "efficient enforcers under any formulation,"[91] and that there is no reason antitrust law would deny them standing. Stating that increasing the number of possible challengers to a patent's validity might disturb incentives for innovation, the court nonetheless held that that consideration was outweighed by the "potential 'to leave a significant antitrust violation undetected or unremedied.'"[92] Noting that the patent at issue in *DDAVP* had been found in a previous case to have been obtained through inequitable conduct and was therefore unenforceable, the court upheld the direct purchaser plaintiffs' antitrust standing.[93]

The holding in *DDAVP* comports with basic antitrust principles. Direct purchasers seek

---

86 *See Loeb*, 306 F.3d at 491 ("One need only know two pieces of information: the amount of cathode purchased by [the plaintiff] and the amount of cathode purchased and sold by those who sold cathode to [the plaintiff]. From there, reasonable estimates of damages are the order of the day."); *Uranium*, 552 F. Supp. at 525 (calculating but for prices of nonconspirators "is no more problematic than determining damages in any price-fixing case" and "[i]n the most pedestrian price fixing case, the trier of fact must calculate the price the defendants would have charged but for the conspiracy"); Areeda, Antitrust Law § 347.

87 *See, e.g.*, *Folding Carton Antitrust Litig.*, 88 F.R.D. at 220.

88 Areeda, Antitrust Law § 347.

89 Fraudulent procurement of the patent was recognized as one form of anticompetitive conduct in *Walker Process Equip., Inc. v. Food Mach. & Chem. Corp.*, 382 U.S. 172 (1965).

90 *Id.* at 176 ("The gist of [the antitrust plaintiff's] claim is that since [the defendant] obtained its patent by fraud it cannot enjoy the limited exception to the prohibitions of § 2 of the Sherman Act, but must answer under that section and § 4 of the Clayton Act in treble damages to those injured by any monopolistic action taken[.]").

91 *In re* DDAVP Direct Purchaser Antitrust Litig., 585 F.3d 677, 689 (2d Cir. 2009).

92 *Id.* at 691 (quoting *Associated Gen'l*, 459 U.S. at 542).

93 *DDAVP*, 585 F.3d at 691.

to vindicate directly the competitive harm caused by a defendant's monopolistic conduct, whereas a competitor plaintiff's interests sometimes diverge from those of consumers.[94] Indeed, direct purchasers' interests are typically directly aligned with those of stringent antitrust enforcement, whereas competitors may benefit from anticompetitive conduct (or, as discussed below, suffer "harm" from increased competition).

Moreover, a competitor could not, even in theory, bring a claim for overcharges that result from the enforcement of the fraudulently obtained patent at issue. A competitor would instead seek to recover its own lost profits flowing from the challenged anticompetitive conduct.[95] Thus, to have standing, the competitor must show that its attempts to compete were somehow inhibited by the presence of the fraudulent patent, i.e., that the fraudulent patent was somehow enforced in a way detrimental to the rival, causing it to lose sales.[96] But even if a rival were successful in suit, its recovery would be limited to profits lost from sales foregone; i.e., the difference between profits it actually made and profits it would have earned in a market free from anticompetitive restraint. The rival could not claim the difference between the but-for competitive price and the monopoly price actually charged to purchasers.

However, courts in two recent decisions, *In re Remeron Antitrust Litigation*[97] and *In re Plavix Antitrust Litigation*,[98] denied direct purchasers standing to pursue monopolization claims based on *Walker Process* theories, restricting standing to competitors. But the reasoning of these district courts is suspect given that they offered no explanation as to why the overcharges alleged by these direct purchasers did not constitute traditional antitrust injury, nor did these courts find that such purchasers could not meet the *Associated General* test.

These cases denying standing to direct purchasers to pursue monopolization claims under *Walker Process* theories commit a variety of mistakes. First, they "mistakenly appl[y] the antitrust rules for competitor standing to cases involving consumer standing."[99] *Remeron*, for instance, relied solely on cases where prospective competitors alleged patent fraud.[100] Unlike a purchaser, however, a competitor seeks to recover lost

---

94 Glaberson v. Comcast Corp., Civ. A. No. 03-6604, 2006 WL 2559479, at *7 (E.D. Pa. Aug. 31, 2006) ("Plaintiffs' injuries, which consist of overcharges, are distinct from [the excluded competitor's] injuries, which likely consist of lost profits."); *In re* Cardizem CD Antitrust Litig., 200 F.R.D. 297, 309–310 (E.D. Mich. 2001) (explaining that direct purchasers claim overcharges, while excluded competitors would seek "lost sales and lost profits").

95 *See DDAVP*, 585 F.3d at 689.

96 *See, e.g.*, Indium Corp. of Am. v. Semi-Alloys, Inc., 566 F. Supp. 1344, 1350 (N.D.N.Y. 1983), *modified in part*, 591 F. Supp. 608 (N.D.N.Y. 1984), *aff'd*, 781 F.2d 879 (Fed. Cir. 1985). *See also Indium*, 591 F. Supp. at 614 ("[I]t would be a mistake to interpret 'enforcement' too narrowly, and thereby limit the remedy of a *Walker Process* type antitrust action.").

97 335 F. Supp. 2d 522 (D.N.J. 2004). However, the court did permit the plaintiffs to pursue a claim for a "scheme to monopolize" that included the alleged "*Walker Process* violation" as part of the scheme. *Id.* at 528.

98 701 F. Supp. 938 (S.D. Ohio Mar. 26, 2010) (denying standing where patent had been affirmatively upheld as valid in prior litigation). The authors were counsel for the direct purchaser class plaintiffs in *Remeron*, *Plavix*, and *DDAVP*.

99 *See* I HERBERT HOVENKAMP, MARK D. JANIS, & MARK A. LEMLEY, IP AND ANTITRUST § 11.4b (Supp. 2008).

100 *Remeron*, 335 F. Supp. 2d at 529 (collecting cases involving competitor standing).

profits and therefore must show that the use of the patent caused it to lose business. Hence, there must be enforcement of the patent that affects the competitor plaintiff's sales and profits. This concern, however, does not apply to purchasers, who are harmed whenever the patent is unlawfully used to impede competition and artificially inflates the prices they pay.

Second, as discussed above, a competitor could not seek to vindicate the harm done to competition in the form of supra-competitive prices borne by the public. "Denying [direct purchasers] a remedy in favor of a suit by competitors would thus be 'likely to leave a significant antitrust violation undetected or unremedied.'"[101]

Third, some of these cases take rules for standing to initiate a declaratory judgment action under *patent law*[102] and improperly import those standards into *antitrust* standing analysis. But this conceives of antitrust claims that include *Walker Process* allegations as a kind of patent claim: the very error which the Seventh Circuit made – and the Supreme Court reversed, in *Walker Process*.[103]

Fourth, it is claimed that patentees need to be protected from unwanted litigation. But *Walker Process* itself dispelled this argument: an "interest in protecting patentees from 'innumerable vexatious suits' [may not] be used to frustrate the assertion of rights conferred by the antitrust laws."[104] In sum, as one court cogently explained: "Viewed properly as an antitrust claim, there is little reason to think that standing requirements for *Walker Process* claims differ from standing requirements in more conventional antitrust actions."[105]

3.05.5 Reduction in output and quality

Rather than proving it paid too high a price, a purchaser may also suffer cognizable antitrust injury by showing that it was directly affected by a reduction in output or product quality. The reduction in output is itself harmful to competition, as reduced volume can also lead to increased prices and reduced consumer choice. Reduced quality that results from collusion or monopolization can likewise constitute a cognizable anticompetitive effect, as a reduction in quality means that the purchaser is getting less value for the same

---

101 *DDAVP*, 585 F.3d at 689 (quoting *Associated Gen'l*, 459 U.S. at 542).

102 *E.g.*, Amana Refrigeration, Inc. v. Quadlux, Inc., 172 F.3d 852, 855 (Fed. Cir. 1999) (standard for standing to sue to invalidate patent when bringing action grounded in patent laws); Lang v. Pac. Marine & Supply Co., Ltd., 895 F.2d 761, 763–64 (Fed. Cir. 1990).

103 *See* Food Mach. & Chem. Corp. v. Walker Process Equip., Inc., 335 F.2d 315, 316 (7th Cir. 1964), *rev'd*, 382 U.S. 172 (1965). The Court of Appeals had affirmed dismissal of the antitrust claims, reasoning that the suit sought the cancellation of a patent, and standing to seek such relief was then restricted to the U.S. government. The Supreme Court reversed. *See supra* note 89.

104 *Cf. Walker Process*, 382 U.S. at 176. *See also* Ritz Camera & Image, LLC v. Sandisk Corp., No. 5:10-cv-02787-JF/HRL, 2011 U.S. Dist. LEXIS 18399, at *13 (N.D. Cal. Feb. 24, 2011) (applying the same principle to direct purchaser suits).

105 Molecular Diagnostics Labs. v. Hoffmann-LaRoche, Inc., 402 F. Supp. 2d 276, 280–81 (D.D.C. 2005); *see also* Ritz Camera & Image, 2011 U.S. Dist. LEXIS 18399, (N.D. Cal. Feb. 24, 2011) (permitting purchaser standing for *Walker Process* allegations); *In re* Netflix Antitrust Litig., Nos. C 07-00643 WHA, C 07-01266 WHA, C 07-01978 WHA, 2007 WL 1725422 (N.D. Cal. Jun. 14, 2007) (same).

money – with effects similar to a price increase.[106] Thus, purchaser claims can be based on losses of consumer choice or reduction in quality, as well as price increases.[107]

§ 3.06 Indirect purchasers

An indirect purchaser is one who is not the "immediate buyer[] from the alleged antitrust violator[],"[108] or who "[does] not purchase [the affected product] directly from the [antitrust] defendant[.]"[109]

In contrast with direct purchasers, indirect purchasers are barred from pursuing treble damage claims under Clayton Act § 4 due to the *Illinois Brick* doctrine.[110] Thus, if a direct purchaser suffered an overcharge and passed that overcharge on to its own customers, the latter would lack standing to sue for damages under the Clayton Act. Unlike *Associated General*, which requires a factual, case-by-case analysis for standing, the rule in *Illinois Brick* establishes a legal bar. The Supreme Court found that the presence of more direct victims, and the complications of apportioning overcharges between direct and indirect purchasers, mandates the bar.

Nevertheless, the Court in *Illinois Brick* stated that there are potential exceptions providing for indirect purchaser standing to pursue damage claims under the federal antitrust laws.

First, an indirect purchaser plaintiff may have standing if it was committed to what the Supreme Court referred to as a "preexisting cost-plus contract" with the direct

---

[106] Int'l Bhd. of Teamsters Local 734 Health & Welfare Trust Fund v. Philip Morris Inc., 196 F.3d 818, 823 (7th Cir. 1999) (Easterbrook, J.) ("Paying too much, or getting an inferior product for the same money, or getting a product that causes deferred injury . . ., causes a loss of one's money, which is 'property.'"); AD/SAT v. Associated Press, 181 F.3d 216, 230 (2d Cir. 1999) (equating injury to competition with "higher prices or reduced output or quality" (quoting III Areeda, Antitrust Law ¶652; Mathias v. Daily News, L.P., 152 F. Supp. 2d 465, 478 (S.D.N.Y. 2001) ("[T]he prototypical example of antitrust injury is an allegation by consumers that they have had to pay higher prices (or experienced a reduction in the quality of service) as a result of a defendant's anticompetitive conduct.").

[107] *See, e.g.*, *Nelson*, 925 F.2d at 1563–64 (patients alleged standing because illegal conduct led them to be deprived of treatment by physicians of their choice); *cf.* Ross v. Bank of Am., 524 F.3d 217, 223–25 (2d Cir. 2008) (where conspiracy imposed certain terms into credit card agreements, injury could be based on fact cardholders would be deprived of the choice of a card without such a term). Although Ross dealt with Article III standing, the concept applies to antitrust standing as well.

[108] Kansas v. Utilicorp United, Inc., 497 U.S. 199, 207 (1990).

[109] California v. ARC Am. Corp., 490 U.S. 93, 97 (1989). *See also Del. Valley Surgical Supply, Inc.*, 523 F.3d at 1124–25 (noting that indirect purchasers purchased through, and were invoiced by, wholesalers). In contrast, a direct purchaser buys from the antitrust violator without any intermediary. *See, e.g.*, *In re* Lorazepam & Clorazepate Antitrust Litig., 202 F.R.D. 12, 23 (D.D.C. 2001) (class members afforded standing as direct purchasers "to the extent that they purchased directly from [the defendant] for their own account[,]" i.e., they were billed by and paid the defendant directly); McCarthy v. Recordex Serv., 80 F.3d 842, 852 (3d Cir. 1996) (purchaser using a buying agent which "received a flat monthly fee, unrelated to the quantity of toilets ordered, and kept no inventory" meant that the purchaser, rather than the buying agent, would have standing).

[110] *Ill. Brick*, 431 U.S. 720.

purchaser, in which the indirect buyer "commit[s] to buying a fixed quantity."[111] Critical to this potential exception is the requirement of a "cost plus" arrangement, under which "a product is sold at a specified mark up above the seller's own cost."[112] Importantly, the indirect purchaser must also have bound itself to purchase a "fixed quantity" of the affected good. The buyer is thus pre-committed to pay a set mark up on a set number of goods. A "requirements contract," however – under which the buyer commits to buy all (or a set share) of its needs for a product from a particular seller – does not satisfy the "cost plus" exception.[113]

The viability of this exception was thrown into serious doubt by the Supreme Court's decision in *Kansas v. Utilicorp United, Inc.*,[114] where the Court denied an indirect purchaser standing even though it had allegedly absorbed 100 percent of the price increase. In the wake of *Utilicorp*, some courts have expressly questioned whether the "cost plus" exception still exists at all.[115]

Second, the indirect purchaser may be permitted to sue in lieu of the direct if the antitrust defendant owns or controls the direct purchaser.[116] The "owned and controlled" exception is limited, however, to "relationships involving such functional economic or other unity between the direct purchaser and either the defendant or the indirect purchaser that there effectively has been only one sale."[117]

There are other instances where *Illinois Brick* does not apply. When an ostensible direct purchaser is also a member of the antitrust conspiracy, many courts have recognized that it is the first innocent purchaser that has antitrust standing.[118] This is less an exception to

---

[111] *Id.* at 736; *In re* Wyoming Tight Sands Antitrust Cases, 866 F.2d 1286, 1290 (10th Cir. 1989) (cost plus exception requires fixed quantity).

[112] *Mid-West Paper Prods.*, 596 F.2d at 577.

[113] *UtiliCorp.*, 497 U.S. at 217 (contract for requirements of natural gas failed to meet exception); Lefrak v. Arabian Am. Oil Co., 487 F. Supp. 808, 823 n. 21 (E.D.N.Y. 1980). Requirements contracts "often create uncertainty as to meaning and effect" and "are designed to avoid the exactness imposed by the Supreme Court for determining the existence of a cost plus contract." *Id.* By the same token, a purchase order placed under a requirements contract dated after the anticompetitive conduct at issue will not likely fall within the "cost plus" exception. This is not the sort of pre-existing, fixed quantity contract the court spoke of in *Illinois Brick*.

[114] 497 U.S. 199 (1990).

[115] McCarthy v. Recordex Serv., 80 F.3d 842, 855 (3d Cir. 1996) ("The vitality of the 'pre existing cost plus contract' exception is doubtful, however, in light of *Utilicorp*.").

[116] *Id.* at 736 n.16. *See also* Freeman v. San Diego Ass'n of Realtors, 322 F.3d 1133, 1145–46 (9th Cir. 2003) (describing exception where "there is no realistic possibility that the direct purchaser will sue its supplier over the antitrust violation").

[117] Jewish Hosp. Assn. v. Stewart Mech. Enterps., 628 F.2d 971, 975 (6th Cir. 1980). Similarly, in *Royal Printing Co. v. Kimberly-Clark Corp.*, those indirect purchaser plaintiffs who could demonstrate that the wholesaler was a subsidiary of the defendant could proceed; plaintiffs who had purchased through an independent wholesaler, however, were denied suit. 621 F.2d 323, 326–28 (9th Cir. 1980).

[118] Paper Systems, Inc. v. Nippon Paper Indus. Co., Ltd., 281 F.3d 629, 631–32 (7th Cir. 2002); Lowell v. Am. Cyanamid Co., 177 F.3d 1228, 1233 (11th Cir. 1999) ("*Illinois Brick* is inapplicable to the present case where the complaint alleges a vertical conspiracy with no pass-on."); *In re* Brand Name Prescription Drugs Antitrust Litig., 123 F.3d 599, 604 (7th Cir. 1997) (Posner, C.J.) ("[A]ny indirect-purchaser defense would go by the board, since the [plaintiffs] would then be direct purchasers from the conspirators."); Ariz. v. Shamrock Foods Co., 729 F.2d 1208, 1212–14 (9th Cir.

Illinois Brick than a proper understanding and application of the rule. In such instances, the first-level party purchasing from a member of a conspiracy is the true direct purchaser. Indeed, the fundamental goal underlying *Illinois Brick* – the effective enforcement of federal antitrust laws – would be stood on its head were this not the rule. Otherwise, no innocent purchaser could maintain a claim.

Finally, an indirect purchaser may acquire standing to sue for damages by receiving an assignment from a direct purchaser.[119] An assignment of an antitrust claim must be "express" and specifically refer to the antitrust claims.[120] Once an assignment is in place, the indirect purchaser "stands in the shoes" of the direct purchaser, and has standing to the same extent as the assignor.[121]

It is unlikely any further exceptions to *Illinois Brick* will be recognized by the courts. The Supreme Court has cautioned lower federal courts against creating new exceptions to the *Illinois Brick* rule: "The rationales underlying *Hanover Shoe* and *Illinois Brick* will not apply with equal force in all cases. We nonetheless believe that ample justification exists for our stated decision not to carve out exceptions to the [direct purchaser] rule."[122]

3.06.1 Indirect purchaser injunctive relief

Illinois Brick was fundamentally a decision addressing § 4 of the Clayton Act, which governs damages. In *Cargill,* the Supreme Court distinguished between a competitor's

---

1984); Fontana Aviation, Inc. v. Cessna Aircraft Co., 617 F.2d 478, 481 (7th Cir. 1980); *see also* II Phillip E. Areeda, Antitrust Law ¶346h, at 369 (2d ed. 2000) ("Whether one adopts a coconspirator exception or regards this situation as outside *Illinois Brick's* domain, there is no tracing or apportionment to be done."); *In re* Wyoming Tight Sands Antitrust Cases, 695 F. Supp. 1109, 1117 (D. Kan. 1988) (noting that it is not an "'exception' at all" to grant standing; if "the direct purchaser participated in the allegedly illegal activities, the indirect purchaser would be the proper plaintiff"). *See also* Howard Hess Dental Labs. Inc. v. Dentsply Int'l, Inc., 424 F.3d 363, 379–81 (3d Cir. 2005) (recognizing limited co-conspirator exception). *Cf.* Dickson v. Microsoft Corp., 309 F.3d 193 (4th Cir. 2002) (dicta that exception would apply in price fixing cases).

A number of courts require that the middleman co-conspirator must be named as a defendant before standing may be conferred upon the middleman's customers. *McCarthy*, 80 F.3d at 854–55; *Campos*, 140 F.3d at 1171 n.4; *In re* Midwest Milk Monopolization Litig., 730 F.2d 528, 529–30 (6th Cir. 1984); *Beef Indus. Antitrust Litig.*, 600 F.2d at 1163.

119 Gulfstream III Assocs., Inc. v. Gulfstream Aerospace Corp., 995 F.2d 425, 437 (3d Cir. 1993) (Greenberg, J.) ("There is no serious doubt that an antitrust claim can be expressly assigned."); *In re* Fine Paper Litig., 632 F.2d 1081, 1090 (3rd Cir. 1980); La. Farmers' Protective Union, Inc., v. Great Atl. & Pac. Tea Co. of Am., Inc., 131 F.2d 419, 423 (8th Cir. 1942).

120 *Gulfstream III*, 995 F.2d at 440.

121 *Cordes*, 502 F.3d at 101 ("[Assignees] Cordes and Creditors Trust stood before the district court in the shoes of [assignors] Western Pacific and EqualNet."); Meijer, Inc. v. Warner Chilcott Holdings Co. III, 246 F.R.D. 293, 296 (D.D.C. 2007); *In re* Urethane Antitrust Litig., 237 F.R.D. 440, 448 (D. Kan. 2006).

122 *Utilicorp*, 497 U.S. at 216 (internal quotation marks omitted). For instance, one court declined to create an exception for the medical device industry, where certain indirect purchasers purportedly purchased the product in question under contracts with the manufacturers setting forth some terms of the sale, but nevertheless bought through middlemen. *Del. Valley*, 523 F.3d at 1122.

ability to seek treble damages and a plaintiff's right to seek an injunction. This distinction applies with equal force to indirect purchasers. None of the underlying rationales of *Illinois Brick* – such as, for example, the complications in allocating damages to different levels of the distribution chain, or the problems inherent in allowing duplicative recovery – prohibits an indirect purchaser from seeking *injunctive* relief. As the Third Circuit explained:

> [I]n contrast to the treble damage action, a claim for injunctive relief does not present the countervailing considerations such as the risk of duplicative or ruinous recoveries and the spectre of a trial burdened with complex and conjectural economic analyses that the Supreme Court emphasized when limiting the availability of treble damages.[123]

Hence, indirect purchasers are generally permitted to seek injunctive relief,[124] provided they meet the other requirements to establish standing to seek such relief outlined above.[125]

3.06.2 Restitution and disgorgement

Barred from seeking damages, some indirect purchasers have attempted instead to seek monetary relief in equitable forms, such as in the form of restitution or disgorgement, under § 16 of the Clayton Act. These remedies, in essence, seek to force the defendant to give up allegedly ill-gotten gains.

However, plaintiffs' pursuit of these remedies has not fared well. In *In re Multidistrict Vehicle Air Pollution Litigation*,[126] the Ninth Circuit, while recognizing that "restitution is indeed an equitable remedy," barred it as a vehicle for monetary relief under § 16:

> [Section] 16 limits the equitable remedies available under its terms to those against "threatened loss or damage." Here, the "reimbursement" would be awarded for the loss which has already occurred, at the time the car owner paid to have his vehicle retrofitted; it would not be relief "against threatened loss or damage." Recovery for past losses is properly covered under § 4; it comes under the head of "damages."[127]

In other words, the court viewed a claim for "reimbursement" as little more than a prohibited damages claim in equitable clothing. Moreover, courts have been skeptical of using equitable theories as a basis for damage claims because the practice would run afoul of the duplicative recovery concerns of *Illinois Brick*.[128]

---

[123] *Mid-West Paper Prods.*, 596 F.2d at 590.

[124] *Id.* at 592; *see also Dickson*, 309 F.3d at 214 n.24; *Campos*, 140 F.3d at 1172 ("Indirect purchaser status does not bar the plaintiffs from seeking injunctive relief under § 16 of the Clayton Act.").

[125] *See* discussion *supra* § 3.03.

[126] 538 F.2d 231 (9th Cir. 1976).

[127] *Id.* at 234.

[128] *Mylan Labs.*, 62 F. Supp. 2d at 41–42. For further discussion of equitable remedies for antitrust violations, see Chapter 9 of this Handbook.

3.06.3 Damages recovery under state law

While the federal antitrust laws bar damages recovery for indirect purchasers, indirect purchasers may be able to recover damages resulting from anticompetitive conduct under the laws of various states.

The ruling in *Illinois Brick* prohibiting indirect purchaser damage claims was criticized for limiting the "broad objective[]" of the antitrust laws: "to compensate victims of antitrust violations" – including consumers – "and to deter future violations."[129] As Justice Brennan noted in his dissent, "the brunt of antitrust injuries is borne by indirect purchasers, often ultimate consumers of a product, as increased costs are passed along the chain of distribution."[130] In contrast, the "middlemen" may "have little incentive to sue suppliers so long as they pass on the bulk of the illegal overcharges."[131] Calculating and then allocating damages between direct and indirect purchasers was said to be no more difficult or complex than other antitrust issues.[132] Some of these criticisms have either not been borne out by the facts (e.g., there is little evidence that direct purchasing middlemen are failing to bring cases that indirect purchasers would have brought), or fail to grapple with some of the procedural and other hurdles that sometimes impede indirect purchaser cases. For instance, in antitrust cases involving "inputs," such as, for example, hydrogen peroxide, sorbates, high fructose corn syrup, or lysine, several players are involved along the chain of processing the input and transforming it to an end product. Each might bear *some* of the overcharge as the product is resold, but the overcharge would then be spread thinly amongst all of the parties in the chain with the result being that the overcharge becomes a miniscule part of the finished product. Were indirect purchasers allowed to sue to recover their portion of the overcharge, entities at each link in the chain of processing and distribution might each have small fractions of the overcharge claim but no one entity or level of the distribution chain would have a claim large enough – or clear enough – to be worthy of suit. Hence, eliminating the rule that allows for concentrating the overcharge claim into a single level of the chain could, for all practical purposes, prevent any recovery at all for the vast bulk of the harm caused.

Nevertheless, in light of criticisms of *Illinois Brick*, a number of states passed "*Illinois Brick* repealer" acts, designed to give consumers standing even if they did not purchase directly. It is estimated that approximately 70 percent of the American population lives in states where a right of action is permitted by some or all indirect purchasers.[133]

The Supreme Court grappled with the repealer statutes in *California v. ARC America Corp.*[134] Notwithstanding its decision in *Illinois Brick*, and despite the possibility of duplicative recoveries, the Court found that states were not barred from enacting laws to afford standing to indirect purchasing consumers.

The *Illinois Brick* repealer statutes take several different forms. Many states simply permit indirect purchaser plaintiffs to pursue damage claims. For instance, California's

---

129 *Ill. Brick Co.*, 431 U.S. at 748 (Brennan, J. dissenting).
130 *Id.* at 749 (Brennan, J. dissenting).
131 *Id.* (Brennan, J. dissenting).
132 *Id.* at 758–60 (Brennan, J., dissenting).
133 Antitrust Modernization Comm'n, Report and Recommendations 279 n.22 (Apr. 2007).
134 490 U.S. 93 (1989).

Cartwright Act explicitly permits suits by "[a]ny person who is injured in his or her business or property by reason of anything forbidden or declared unlawful by this chapter, regardless of whether such injured person dealt directly or indirectly with the defendant."[135] Likewise, in the wake of *Illinois Brick*, the Minnesota legislature amended its antitrust act to specify that a plaintiff can sue for a violation of the antitrust law whether "injured directly or indirectly."[136] Other states authorize such damage claims if brought or joined by the Attorney General or another government authority,[137] or if the government is the indirect purchaser.[138]

In states where no specific statute is in force, courts have sometimes permitted indirect purchaser damage claims nevertheless.[139] The Tennessee Supreme Court, for instance, interpreted its state statute, which gave a right of action to "[a]ny person who is injured or damaged" by an antitrust violation, as "affording a remedy to the ultimate victims of the

---

135 Cal. Bus. & Prof. Code § 16750(a). *See also, e.g.*, Ala. Code § 6-5-60; D.C. Code Ann. § 28-4509; Haw. Rev. Stat. § 480-13 (permitting indirect purchaser recovery but limiting class actions to purview of attorney general); 740 Ill. Comp. Stat. 10/7(2) (authorizing private suits but providing "no person other than the Attorney General of this State shall be authorized to maintain a class action in any court of this State for indirect purchasers asserting claims under this Act"; *see infra* note 148 and accompanying text regarding class claims); Me. Rev. Stat. Ann., tit. 10, § 1104(1); Mich. Comp. Laws. Ann. § 445.778; Minn. Stat. § 325D.57; Miss. Code Ann. § 75-21-9; Nev. Rev. Stat. § 598A.210; N.M. Stat. Ann. § 57-1-3A; N.Y. Gen. Bus. Law § 340(6) (authorizing individual claims; *see infra* note 148 and accompanying text regarding class claims); N.C. Gen. Stat. § 75-16 (as construed in *Hyde v. Abbott Labs., Inc.*, 473 S.E.2d 680 (N.C. Ct. App. 1996)); N.D. Cent. Code § 51-08.1-08(3); S.D. Codified Laws § 37-1-33; Utah Code Ann. § 76-10-919(1)(a); Vt. Stat. tit. 9, § 2465; Wis. Stat. Ann. § 133.18(1). The West Virginia statute is silent on the matter, but its attorney general has promulgated a legislative rule extending standing to "any person who is injured directly or indirectly by reason of a violation of the West Virginia Antitrust Act." W. Va. Code R. § 142-9-2. *Cf. In re* New Motor Vehicles Canadian Exp. Antitrust Litig., 350 F. Supp. 2d 160, 173–74 (D. Me. 2004); *In re* Chocolate Confectionary Antitrust Litig., 602 F. Supp. 2d 538, 582 n.55 (M.D. Pa. 2009). Other states simply subsume indirect purchaser recovery under their general consumer protection or unfair trade laws, which is generally outside the scope of this chapter.

136 Minn. Stat. § 325D.57. *See also* State by Humphrey v. Philip Morris, Inc., 551 N.W.2d 490, 497 (Minn. 1996) ("After *Illinois Brick* was decided . . . Minnesota acted to change its law to allow anyone to sue in antitrust.").

137 *E.g.*, Alaska Stat. § 45.50.577(b); Ark. Code Ann. § 4-75-315(b); Colo. Rev. Stat. § 6-4-111; Idaho Code § 48-108(2), Siena v. Microsoft Corp., 796 A.2d 461, 463–65 (R.I. 2002) (Rhode Island Attorney General may bring suit on behalf of indirect purchasers); Va. Code Ann. § 59.1-9.15(d). *See also* 740 Ill. Comp. Stat. 10/7(2) (indirect purchasers can sue, and attorney general can bring class action); Gaebler v. N.M. Potash Corp., 676 N.E.2d 228, 230 (Ill. Ct. App. 1996) (construing this provision to preclude private class actions for indirect purchasers).

138 *E.g.*, Md. Code Ann. Com. Law § 11-209(b)(2); Davidson v. Microsoft Corp., 792 A.2d 336, 341 (Md. Ct. App. 2002) (governments permitted to sue whether they dealt "directly or indirectly" with defendant, but noting legislature had rejected a bill that would have repealed *Illinois Brick* generally).

139 *E.g.*, Freeman Indus., LLC v. Eastman Chem. Co., 172 S.W.3d 512, 517–20 (Tenn. 2005); Bunker's Glass Co. v. Pilkington, 47 P.3d 1119, 1124 (Ariz. App. 2002). *See also* Elkins v. Microsoft Corp., 817 A.2d 9, 16–20 (Vt. 2002) (indirect purchaser standing existed under Vermont law even prior to passage of repealer statute).

antitrust conduct."[140] It deemed them to be "the real victims of the antitrust violations," with "the true incentive to bring suit."[141]

On the other hand, courts in several states have adopted *Illinois Brick* and barred indirect purchaser claims. For instance, Florida courts have adopted the policy of *Illinois Brick* in construing their own state antitrust law.[142] In *Free v. Abbott Laboratories*,[143] the Fifth Circuit predicted Louisiana would follow a similar path.[144] Some courts have pointed to the legislature's failure to enact *Illinois Brick* repealer legislation as an indication that indirect plaintiffs ought not to have standing.[145] Other state legislatures have commanded their courts generally to follow federal antitrust law, which the courts have read to adopt *Illinois Brick*.[146] And in some states, the law remains murky.[147]

Until recently, certain other states statutorily barred indirect purchasers from bringing private *class* actions to recover treble damages.[148] However, the Supreme Court recently ruled that to the extent that such statutes attempt to regulate procedural aspects of litigation brought in federal court, they may be pre-empted by Federal Rule of Civil Procedure 23.[149] Which statutes restricting private indirect purchaser class actions are preempted remains an area of dispute. The New York statute, which was squarely at issue in *Shady Grove*, has been deemed preempted where claims are filed in federal courts. Yet, according to one court, an Illinois statute barring indirect purchaser class actions is not preempted.[150]

---

140 *Freeman*, 172 S.W.3d at 517, 520.

141 *Id.* at 520.

142 *E.g.*, Mack v. Bristol-Myers Squibb Co., 673 So. 2d 100, 110 (Fla. Dist. Ct. App. 1996). Nevertheless, indirect purchasers may still seek to recover under Florida's Deceptive and Unfair Trade Practices Act, Fla. Stat. §§ 501.201, et seq. *See In re* Wellbutrin XL Antitrust Litig., Civ. A. No. 08-2433, 2009 U.S. Dist. LEXIS 66676, at *49–54 (E.D. Pa. Jul. 31, 2009).

143 176 F.3d 298 (5th Cir. 1999).

144 *Id.* at 299. *Accord New Motor Vehicles*, 350 F. Supp. 2d at 170; FTC v. Mylan Labs., Inc., 99 F. Supp. 2d 1, 6–8 (D.D.C. 1999).

145 Vacco v. Microsoft Corp., 793 A.2d 1048, 1059–60 (Conn. 2002).

146 *See, e.g.*, Major v. Microsoft Corp., 60 P.3d 511, 513 (Okla. Ct. Civ. App. 2002).

147 *Compare In re* K-Dur Antitrust Litig., 2008 U.S. Dist. LEXIS 71767, at *22–23 (D.N.J. Feb. 25, 2008) (Orlofsky, J. Special Master) ("Pennsylvania has no general antitrust statute, nor any statute creating a private right of action against restraints of trade. Plaintiffs have not cited, nor have I located, any case awarding damages under Pennsylvania law for antitrust violations.") *with* Collins v. Main Line Bd. of Realtors, 304 A.2d 493, 498 (Pa. 1973) (suggesting record in that case did "not provide any legal basis for an award of damages," but not stating rule that such damages are never available).

148 *See, e.g.*, N.Y. Civ. P. Law § 901(b); 740 Ill. Comp. Stat. 10/7 (2) (proscribing indirect purchaser class actions brought "in any court of this State" unless brought by the state attorney general).

149 *Shady Grove Orthopedic Assocs., P.A. v. Allstate Ins. Co., 130 S. Ct. 1431 (2010). See also* Holster v. Gatco, Inc., 618 F.3d 214, 216–17 (2d Cir. 2010) (Calabresi, J.); *In re* Wellbutrin XL Antitrust Litig., 2010 U.S. Dist. LEXIS 135566, at *25 (E.D. Pa.; Dec. 22, 2010); *In re* Static Random Access Memory Antitrust Litig., 2010 U.S. Dist. LEXIS 97398, at *30–33 (N.D. Cal. Aug. 4, 2010).

150 *Wellbutrin XL*, 2010 U.S. Dist. LEXIS 135566, at *19–20. The court found "the Illinois restrictions on indirect purchaser actions are intertwined with Illinois substantive rights and remedies" and therefore not preempted. *Id.* at *19.

3.06.4 Do the **Associated General** *factors apply to a damages claim brought under a state* **Illinois Brick** *repealer statute?*

Although *Illinois Brick* repealers may avoid the total bar to recovery that exists under federal law, some courts have found that indirect purchasers may nonetheless be too remote from the anticompetitive conduct to recover, even under a repealer statute. Thus, in *In re Dynamic Random Access Memory Antitrust Litigation* (DRAM),[151] the court recognized that California's Cartwright Act contained an *Illinois Brick* repealer. It stated:

> However, while the Cartwright Act directly contradicts federal law insofar as indirect purchaser standing is generally concerned, it does not follow from this either that indirect purchaser status is itself sufficient under California law to establish antitrust standing, or that California law necessarily eschews the general test for antitrust standing as set forth in [*Associated General*]. For as defendants point out, the question whether indirect purchasers have standing under state law, and the question whether antitrust plaintiffs – which may include indirect purchasers – have antitrust standing for a particular claim, are two "analytically distinct" issues.[152]

The court pointed to a California decision which suggested that, the repealer notwithstanding, California's antitrust standing rules were in flux.[153] Thus, according to the *DRAM* court, an indirect purchaser must still meet "efficient enforcer" factors like those announced in *Associated General*, even when pursuing an antitrust claim for damages under California state law.[154]

Judge Hamilton's opinion quickly drew fire from a fellow jurist. Judge Alsup, writing in *In re Graphics Processing Units Antitrust Litigation* (GPU),[155] refused to follow *DRAM*, observing that "*Associated General Contractors* arose under the federal Clayton Act. It is far from clear that *Associated General Contractors* should be automatically read into the substantive antitrust law of each and every state."[156] Judge Alsup continued:

> Standing under each state's antitrust statute is a matter of that state's law. It would be wrong for a district judge, in *ipse dixit* style, to bypass all state legislatures and all state appellate courts and to pronounce a blanket and nationwide revision of all state antitrust laws. The rule urged by the defense may (or may not) be sound policy but that is a matter for the state policy makers to decide, not for a federal judge to impose by fiat.[157]

---

[151] 516 F. Supp. 2d 1072 (N.D. Cal. 2007).

[152] *Id.* at 1087.

[153] *Id.* at 1087–88 ("[T]he exact parameters of 'antitrust injury' under [the Cartwright Act] have not yet been established through either court decisions or legislation." (quoting Cellular Plus, Inc. v. Superior Court of San Diego County, 18 Cal. Rptr. 2d 308, 313 (Cal. Ct. App. 1993))).

[154] *See also In re* Intel Corp. Microprocessor Antitrust Litig., 496 F. Supp. 2d 404, 409 (D. Del. 2007) ("[I]t is appropriate to apply the AGC factors if not directly, at least as a guide, in evaluating Class Plaintiffs' state law antitrust claims."). *But see infra* notes 160–67 and accompanying text.

[155] 527 F. Supp. 2d 1011 (N.D. Cal. 2007).

[156] *Id.* at 1025.

[157] *Id.* at 1026. *See also In re* TFT-LCD Antitrust Litig., 586 F. Supp. 2d 1109, 1123 (N.D. Cal. 2008) ("The Court agrees with Judge Alsup that it is inappropriate to broadly apply the AGC test to plaintiffs' claims under the repealer states' laws in the absence of a clear directive from those states' legislatures or highest courts."); Moniz v. Bayer Corp., 484 F. Supp. 2d 228, 231 (D. Mass. 2007); D.R. Ward Const. Co. v. Rohm & Haas, Co., 470 F. Supp. 2d 485, 500–02 (E.D. Pa. 2006) (doubting *Associated General* applies to Vermont's antitrust statute).

Judge Alsup acknowledged that two states – Iowa and Nebraska – had adopted the *Associated General* test as their own for purposes of antitrust standing,[158] but declined to adopt the *Associated General* test on behalf of any other state.[159]

Some state courts have expressly considered – and rejected – application of the *Associated General* standing factors in the context of state antitrust claims.[160]

Other courts, however, have referenced those factors when evaluating whether a plaintiff has antitrust standing. As one court reasoned, the *Illinois Brick* repealer simply removed the absolute bar, but "d[id] not address the standing issue," which must be resolved through the application of a test like *Associated General*.[161] Notably, the court viewed itself as bound by statute to give "due deference to interpretations given by the federal courts to comparable antitrust statutes."[162]

This issue is currently before the Ninth Circuit in the *DRAM* case, which accepted the indirect purchaser plaintiffs' interlocutory appeal. The American Antitrust Institute (AAI) has filed an *amicus curiae* brief supporting reversal.[163] AAI argued that under *Erie Railroad Co. v. Tompkins*,[164] the role of federal courts is to apply existing state law policies articulated by the respective state legislatures, and not to create new rules of law in derogation of such policies.[165] This issue is noteworthy, in part, because the *Illinois Brick*

---

158 *GPU*, 540 F. Supp. 2d at 1097 (citing Southard v. Visa U.S.A., Inc., 734 N.W.2d 192, 199 (Iowa 2007) and Kanne v. Visa U.S.A., Inc., 723 N.W.2d 293, 302–03 (Neb. 2006)). *See also In re* Potash Antitrust Litig., 667 F. Supp. 2d 907, 945–46 (N.D. Ill. 2009) (agreeing that Iowa has adopted *Associated General* factors).

159 *Id. See also In re* Flash Memory Antitrust Litig., 43 F. Supp. 2d 1133, 1152 (N.D. Cal. 2009) (declining to adopt AGC factors for any states other than Iowa, Nebraska, and California). The court observed that one intermediate court appeared to use the *Associated General* factors, suggesting California would adopt them as well.

160 Teague v. Bayer AG, 671 S.E.2d 550, 557 (N.C. Ct. App. 2009) ("We hold the [*Associated General*] factors do not apply in determining which indirect purchasers have standing to sue under the North Carolina antitrust statutes."); Lorix v. Crompton, 736 N.W. 2d 619, 627–28 (Minn. Aug. 2, 2007).

161 Stark v. Visa U.S.A. Inc., No. 03-055030-CZ, 2004 WL 1879003, at *4 (Mich. Cir. Ct. July 23, 2004). *See also* Duvall v. Silvers, Asher, Sher & McLaren, M.D., 998 S.W.2d 821, 824–25 (Mo. Ct. App. 1999) (referencing *Associated General's* requirement for directness of injury, but not adopting multi-factor test); County of Cook v. Philip Morris, Inc., 817 N.E.2d 1039, 1043–46 (Ill. App. Ct. 2004) (incorporating remoteness analysis and dismissing Illinois antitrust claim); Ho v. Visa U.S.A., Inc., No. 112316/00, 2004 N.Y. Misc. LEXIS 577, at *2–3 (N.Y. Sup. Ct. Apr. 21, 2004) (applying *Associated General* factors to indirect purchasers). One trial court referenced the *Associated General* factors, but indirect purchaser standing was not before the court; as the opinion notes, the plaintiff had "not actually acquired the product or service that is alleged to be tainted by unlawful trade." Fucile v. Visa U.S.A. Inc., No. S1560-03 CNC, 2004 WL 3030037, at *1–2 (Vt. Sup. Ct. Dec. 27, 2004).

162 *Stark*, 2004 WL 1879003, at *4. At least one federal court has declined to follow *Stark*, citing the absence of an appellate law adopting the AGC factors. *See Potash*, 667 F. Supp. 2d at 943–44 ("Absent any ruling or indication by the state supreme court or state appellate courts, this Court is reluctant to apply the federal AGC test to Indirect Purchaser Plaintiffs' Michigan antitrust claim.").

163 Brief for the American Antitrust Institute as Amicus Curiae in Support of Appellants and Reversal, *In re* Dynamic Random Access Memory (DRAM) Antitrust Litig., Appeal No. 08-16478 (9th Cir. filed Mar. 5, 2009) [hereinafter *AAI DRAM Br.*].

164 304 U.S. 64 (1938).

165 *AAI DRAM Br.* at 5–9.

repealer acts, including California's, were specifically passed to abrogate the federal indirect purchaser bar with its attendant concerns of complexities of proof, and to permit indirect purchasers to recover.[166] The *Associated General* standard, on the other hand, "essentially applies the same considerations that underlay the *Illinois Brick* rule, which were obviously rejected by the repealer states."[167] How federal courts interpret and apply state antitrust laws is of increasing concern now that many state law antitrust class actions are removed to federal court under the Class Action Fairness Act (CAFA).[168] Thus, there is the increased danger of impediments being erected in federal court that hinder the enforcement of state antitrust laws and policies.

§ 3.07 Competitors

Competitors have been recognized as among the classic groups of plaintiffs authorized to bring antitrust suits.[169]

Like any other antitrust plaintiff, competitors must establish antitrust injury, i.e., they must show "injury of the type the antitrust laws were intended to prevent and that flows from that which makes defendants' acts unlawful."[170] In other words, the competitor plaintiff must show harm from conduct that impedes competition and should "reflect the anticompetitive effect either of the violation or of the anticompetitive acts made possible by the violation."[171] Competitor plaintiffs must also demonstrate that their asserted claims satisfy the factors enumerated in *Associated General*.

Thus, a competitor plaintiff cannot survive merely by showing that it lost profits or business as a result of ostensibly anticompetitive activity.[172] After all, the antitrust laws are designed to preserve and foster competition, not inhibit it. "The antitrust laws . . . were enacted for the 'protection of competition, not competitors.'"[173] Antitrust law "ensure[s] competition in general" and is "not narrowly focused to protect individual competitors . . . ."[174]

Following these general rules, courts have been hostile to claims for lost business brought by competitors if the defendant's actions were actually favorable to consumers or consumer welfare generally – a point which was dispositive in *Brunswick*.[175]

For instance, in *Cargill, Inc. v. Monfort of Colorado, Inc.*, a plaintiff competitor could not show antitrust injury where a merged company (presumed to be illegal) threatened

---

166 *Id.* at 9–16.

167 *Id.* at 17.

168 Pub. L. 109-2, 119 Stat. 4 (2005). For further discussion of CAFA, see Chapter 4 and Chapter 5 of this Handbook.

169 "[G]enerally only competitors and consumers will suffer antitrust injury . . . ." Carpet Group Int'l v. Oriental Rug Imps. Ass'n, Inc., 227 F.3d 62, 77 (3d Cir. 2000).

170 *Brunswick Corp.*, 429 U.S. at 489 (1977); *see also* Atl. Richfield Co. v. U.S. Petroleum Co., 495 U.S. 328 (1990).

171 *Brunswick Corp.*, 429 U.S. at 489.

172 *Atl. Richfield*, 495 U.S. at 338; *Cargill*, 479 U.S. at 115.

173 *Brunswick Corp*, 429 U.S. at 488 (internal citation omitted).

174 Capital Imaging Assocs., P.C. v. Mohawk Valley Med. Assoc., Inc., 996 F.2d 537, 543 (2d Cir. 1993).

175 *See Brunswick Corp.*, 429 U.S. at 488–89; *see also supra* notes 15–20 and accompanying text.

to engage in vigorous price competition, which would have allegedly caused the plaintiff to lose substantial profits. The plaintiff's threatened injuries flowed from the defendant's offer of its products at low prices, but as long as those prices were not predatory, the defendant's conduct was not "activity forbidden by the antitrust laws."[176] As a result, the competitor plaintiff had not alleged cognizable antitrust injury.

Likewise, lower courts have disallowed competitor claims arising out of the operation of competition rather than its suppression. In *NicSand, Inc. v. 3M Co.*,[177] the plaintiff alleged that a monopolist gave customers up-front cash payments and signed them to multi-year contracts.[178] As to the cash payments (which were discounts) and multi-year provisions (which allowed the purchasers to "buy in bulk" and thus earn a lower price), the court reasoned that "cutting prices in order to increase business often is the very essence of competition" and penalizing such activity would "chill the very conduct the antitrust laws are designed to protect."[179] According to the court, the exclusive supplier arrangements were not part of the defendant's anticompetitive design, but in fact had arisen due to customer demand (and the plaintiff had previously enjoyed their operation). Accordingly, the competitor plaintiff had not alleged cognizable antitrust injury.

In sum, a competitor plaintiff must allege an injury that parallels the harm done to consumers, rather than simply bemoan lost profits or income to itself.

3.07.1 New entrants to the market

A frequent question that emerges is when a plaintiff, rather than claiming that it was forced out of the market, asserts that it is being kept from entering the market in the first place. To be sure, "the law does not condone the purchase of protection from uncertain competition any more than it condones the elimination of actual competition."[180] However, the prospective competitor must do more than simply claim it wishes to compete. "A 'nascent' business – one that is merely a gleam in the eye and a hope in the heart of its promoters – does not possess the property to which antitrust injury can be done."[181] Hence, "most courts . . . have required a company that has not actually entered the market to show that it intended to enter and was prepared to do so within a reasonable time."[182]

---

176 479 U.S. at 115–16.

177 507 F.3d 442 (6th Cir. 2007).

178 *Id.* at 451–54.

179 *Id.* at 452 (quoting Matsushita Elec. Indus. Co. v. Zenith Radio Corp., 475 U.S. 574, 594 (1986)).

180 XII Herbert Hovenkamp, Antitrust Law ¶2030b at 213 (2d ed. 2005). *Accord* United States v. Microsoft Corp., 253 F.3d 34, 79 (D.C. Cir. 2001) (en banc); Sullivan v. Nat'l Football League, 34 F.3d 1091, 1100 (1st Cir. 1994); Engine Specialties Inc. v. Bombardier, Ltd., 605 F.2d 1, 9 (1st Cir. 1979). Further illustrating this point is *Andrx Pharmaceuticals, Inc. v. Biovail Corp. Int'l*, 256 F.3d 799 (D.C. Cir. 2001). There, the plaintiff was a prospective rival ready to compete that was foreclosed from the market due the challenged conduct. The plaintiff claimed injury in the form of profits it had lost on sales it was prevented from making by the conduct. Such lost profits were deemed antitrust injury even though the rival had not yet entered the market. The court recognized that the foreclosure of even potential rivals constituted harm to the competitive process. *See id.* at 813; *see also In re* Cardizem CD Antitrust Litig., 332 F.3d 896, 910 (6th Cir. 2002).

181 Bourns, Inc. v. Raychem Corp., 331 F.3d 704, 712 (9th Cir. 2003).

182 Grip-Pak, Inc. v. Ill. Tool Works, Inc., 694 F.2d 466, 475 (7th Cir. 1982). *See also Bourns*,

§ 3.08 Other types of antitrust claimants

Although competitors and purchasers are among the most common antitrust plaintiffs, the courts have never foreclosed other members of the public from bringing suit. As the Supreme Court long ago observed: "The [Clayton Act] does not confine its protection to consumers, or to purchasers, or to competitors, or to sellers. . . . The Act is comprehensive in its terms and coverage, protecting all who are made victims of the forbidden practices by whomever they may be perpetrated."[183]

3.08.1 Shareholders

One of the earliest cases relating to antitrust injury denied standing to shareholders seeking relief due to harms done to the corporation. The court in *Loeb v. Eastman Kodak Co.*[184] reasoned that any injuries sustained were borne by the corporation itself, which was capable of vindicating its own interests if it so chose. By contrast (foretelling the remoteness factors which later came into play in *Associated General*), the shareholder's interest was only "indirect, remote, and consequential."[185]

3.08.2 Suppliers

Courts have been divided on whether suppliers to market participants have standing to pursue antitrust claims. Of course "a seller may well have a claim if victimized by a price-fixing ring composed of buyers that lowered the market price: in such a case the seller is a participant in the very market where competition is impaired."[186] However, a different result pertains if the anticompetitive conduct targets the downstream market rather than upstream. Thus, if the supplier's customer fails (or loses business, curtailing purchases from the supplier) because of an antitrust violation, "usually the conduct was deemed an antitrust violation because of the threat to the customer, not the supplier."[187] Hence, the customer – i.e., the excluded rival – would have antitrust standing, but not the supplier.[188]

---

331 F.3d at 711 (noting plaintiff's intent but that it was "unprepared to enter the business"); *Andrx Pharms.*, 256 F.3d at 808 (plaintiff "*can* allege facts sufficient to indicate its intent and preparedness") (emphasis in original); Jayco Sys., Inc. v. Savin Bus. Mach. Corp., 777 F.2d 306, 313 (5th Cir. 1985) ("Where a business expansion . . . is contemplated, there must be a showing of intent to expand and of preparedness for the expansion.") (internal quotations and citation omitted); Huron Valley Hosp., Inc. v. City of Pontiac, 666 F.2d 1029, 1033 (6th Cir. 1981) (citations omitted).

[183] Mandeville Island Farms, Inc. v. Am. Crystal Sugar Co., 334 U.S. 219, 236 (1948)

[184] 183 F. 704, 709 (3d Cir. 1910).

[185] *Id.* at 709. Loeb was specifically cited in *Associated General* as an example of an injury deemed too "remote." 459 U.S. at 533–34. Courts applying the *Associated General* factors have accordingly denied standing to shareholders as well. *E.g.*, Meyer Goldberg, Inc. of Lorain v. Goldberg, 717 F.2d 290, 294 (6th Cir. 1983) (sole shareholder of bankrupt corporation lacked antitrust standing).

[186] SAS of P.R. v. P.R. Tel. Co., 48 F.3d 39, 44 (1st Cir. 1995). *See also Mandeville Island*, 334 U.S. at 236; *Beef Indus.*, 600 F.2d 1148; II Areeda & Hovenkamp, Antitrust Law ¶375b.

[187] *SAS of P.R.*, 48 F.3d at 44.

[188] *See id.*

To like effect, no standing was found for a landlord who wanted to supply real estate to a retailer's rivals, but could not because that retailer had previously leased the property, left it vacant and refused to surrender the lease, diminishing the rental value of all of the rental spaces on the property.[189] Applying *Associated General*, the court found such an injury too remote to confer standing on the landlord wishing to supply space to the potential rival. Consumers and market participants were more immediately affected and could bring suit if they chose.[190] Also, the asserted injury – the diminution in rental values at the shopping center – was considered too speculative.

Thus, some courts have stated that "[s]uppliers to direct market participants typically cannot seek recovery under the antitrust laws because their injuries are too secondary and indirect to be considered 'antitrust injuries.'"[191]

However, the view is not unanimous. In *Chemi SpA v. GlaxoSmithKline*,[192] the court permitted the supplier of an excluded rival to sue. The court viewed the injury as one the Sherman Act was designed to forestall and inextricably intertwined with the harm to the market: "In our view the antitrust laws are intended to provide a remedy to the manufacturers and sellers of a product where the monopoly was specifically designed to prevent the sale of that very product in the marketplace."[193]

3.08.3 Terminated dealers and distributors

Another recurring fact pattern is where a manufacturing company has been acquired by (or otherwise fallen prey to) a monopolist. The manufacturer may have contracted with dealers and distributors to disseminate the former company's product to the public. However, once acquired by a monopolist, the distributors are cut off, as the monopolist begins to use its own distribution channels. The dealer or distributor then attempts to sue the monopolist.

Such attempts often fail because this is not deemed to be "antitrust injury" associated with the anticompetitive harm – higher prices or reduced output. "Dealers in this situation lack standing because their particular injury was not caused by an exercise of the defendant's newly acquired power to raise prices . . . Instead, the dealer's injury was caused by the manufacturer's decision to terminate their relationship, something the manufacturer could have just as well done without having monopoly power."[194] In contrast, distributors

---

189 Southaven Land Co. v. Malone & Hyde, Inc., 715 F.2d 1079, 1085–88 (6th Cir. 1983).

190 *See id.* at 1087.

191 Serfecz v. Jewel Food Stores, 67 F.3d 591, 597 (7th Cir. 1995); *see also* R.C. Dick Geothermal Corp. v. Thermogenics, Inc., 890 F.2d 139, 148 (9th Cir. 1989); SignaPharm, Inc. v. Mutual Pharm. Co., Civ. No. 10-430, U.S. Dist. LEXIS 21267 (E.D. Pa. Mar. 2, 2011); Asahi Glass Co., Ltd. v. Pentech Pharms., Inc., 289 F. Supp. 2d 986, 990–91 (N.D. Ill. 2003) (Posner, J., sitting by designation) (denying standing to supplier of prospective generic product); Delco LLC v. Giant of Md., LLC, Civ. No. 07-3522 (JBS), 2007 WL 3307018, at *10 (D.N.J. Nov. 8, 2007).

192 356 F. Supp. 2d 495 (E.D. Pa. 2005).

193 *Id.* at 501. *See also* Ethypharm S.A. France v. Abbott Labs., 598 F. Supp. 2d 611, 617 (D. Del. 2009) (recognizing standing for excluded foreign supplier selling through U.S. distributor).

194 Port Dock & Stone Corp. v. Oldcastle Northeast, Inc., 507 F.3d 117, 123 (2d Cir. 2007); *see also* Atl. Richfield Co. v. USA Petroleum Co., 495 U.S. 328, 345–46 (1990); Norris v. Hearst Trust, 500 F.3d 454, 465–66 (5th Cir. 2007); The Serpa Corp., 199 F.3d at 11–12; Florida Seed Co.

and consumers buying from the monopolists *would* have antitrust injury, because they are paying higher prices due to the reduction in competition.

3.08.4 Employees

As with suppliers (employees are suppliers of labor), employee standing depends on the type of claim being pressed. An employee would be entitled to sue were there a conspiracy between the employer and others to suppress wages or fix other conditions of employment.[195] Thus, in *Eichorn v. AT&T Corp.*,[196] employees were granted standing to challenge a "no hire" agreement – an agreement among competitors not to hire a particular set of prospective employees – which suspended competition for their technical services. Quoting Areeda and Hovenkamp, the Court concluded:

> Antitrust law addresses employer conspiracies controlling employment terms precisely because they tamper with the employment market and thereby impair the opportunities of those who sell their services there. Just as antitrust law seeks to preserve the free market opportunities of buyers and sellers of goods, so also it seeks to do the same for buyers and sellers of employment services. It would be perverse indeed to hold that the very object of the law's solicitude and the persons most directly concerned – perhaps the only persons concerned – could not challenge the restraint.[197]

In contrast, employees may not sue for injuries sustained in the market into which their employers sold product. Thus, former employees of a car dealership driven out of business by an antitrust conspiracy were denied standing in *Peck v. General Motors Corp.*[198]

3.08.5 Unions and trade associations

Likewise, unions generally do not have standing for injuries sustained by their members. Indeed, enhanced competition – and the consequent drive by manufacturers to lower prices by reducing production costs – may be in tension with a union's *raison d'être* of increased wages and benefits for its members.[199] Thus, if the claim is for lost work or reduced wages, the injury may not be one that the antitrust laws were meant to prevent. This is particularly true if the employees themselves lack standing.[200] However, when the

---

v. Monsanto Co., 105 F.3d 1372, 1375 n.3 (11th Cir. 1997); John Lenore & Co. v. Olympia Brewing Co., 550 F.2d 495, 500 (9th Cir. 1977).

195 *See* Areeda and Hovenkamp, Antitrust Law ¶377a.

196 248 F.3d 131 (3d Cir. 2001).

197 *Id.* at 141 (quoting Areeda & Hovenkamp, Antitrust Law ¶377c); *see also* Doe v. Ariz. Hosp. & Healthcare Ass'n, No. CV 07-1292-PHX-SRB, 2009 U.S. Dist. LEXIS 42871, *19–23 (D. Ariz. Mar. 19, 2009) (allowing claims by proposed class of nurses alleging that defendants fixed the price of their wages below competitive levels).

198 894 F.2d 844 (6th Cir. 1990). *See also* G.K.A. Beverage Corp. v. Honickman, 55 F.3d 762, 766 (2d Cir. 1995) ("[M]erely derivative injuries sustained by employees, officers, stockholders, and creditors of an injured company do not constitute 'antitrust injury' sufficient to confer antitrust standing.").

199 *Associated Gen.*, 459 U.S. at 539.

200 *See* discussion *supra* § 3.08.4.

claimed injury is that the union purchased products that were the subject of anticompetitive conduct, standing has been upheld.[201]

Trade associations have had mixed success as antitrust plaintiffs. While some courts have permitted them to seek an injunction for harm sustained by their members,[202] U.S. law does not generally allow such entities to recover damages sustained by their members.[203] The claim is deemed to belong to the affected members, who would be able to sue in their own right either individually or as part of a class. This stands in contrast to proposals within the European Union that would permit certain damage claims for anticompetitive conduct by consumer groups, but not by their constituent members.[204]

§ 3.09 Conclusion

The list of potential claimants under the antitrust laws is as long and varied as the means by which the antitrust laws can be violated. But there are limits. To have a cognizable claim, a plaintiff would need to first and foremost establish that it has suffered the requisite type of injury, namely an antitrust injury.

---

201 *See, e.g.*, *In re* Warfarin Sodium Antitrust Litig., 391 F.3d 516, 531 (3d Cir. 2004).

202 *See, e.g.*, Associated Gen. Contractors v. Otter Tail Power Co., 611 F.2d 684, 690 (8th Cir. 1979) (association could sue for injunction as representative of its members).

203 *See, e.g.*, Southwest Suburban Board of Realtors, Inc., v. Beverly Area Planning Ass'n, 830 F.2d 1374, 1379–80 (7th Cir. 1987) (trade group denied standing because conduct aimed at its "member brokers"). Of course, members may assign their claims to the association. *See, e.g.*, Jefferson County Pharm. Ass'n, Inc. v. Abbott Lab., 460 U.S. 150 (1983).

204 *See* Commission of the European Communities, *White Paper on Damages Actions For reach Of The EC Antitrust Rules* (Apr. 2, 2008), at 4, *available at* http://ec.europa.eu/competition/antitrust/actionsdamages/files_white_paper/whitepaper_en.pdf; *see also* Laurence T. Sorkin, *International settlements, in* The International Handbook on Private Enforcement of Competition Law 575–89 (Albert A. Foer & Jonathan W. Cuneo eds., 2010).

4 Initiation of a private action

Michael D. Hausfeld[1]

§ 4.01 Introduction

Although the initiation of a private claim in the United States appears relatively straightforward – a plaintiff prepares, files, and serves a complaint – this process actually involves a number of important choices on the part of a litigant:

(1) Should the case be in court at all, or is some alternative forum preferable? This chapter discusses options such as complaining to the Federal Trade Commission or Department of Justice, pursuing arbitration, or attempting to negotiate a pre-litigation settlement.
(2) If the dispute or claim is to be in court, should it be filed in state or federal court? This chapter provides an overview of why one or the other might be more appropriate.
(3) What venue should be selected? This chapter explores requirements for jurisdiction and venue, the role of the multidistrict litigation process, and considerations about when to invoke the process and what factors to emphasize.
(4) Are U.S. courts even available? This chapter examines limitations on the right of foreign plaintiffs to take advantage of the U.S. court system.

[1] Chairman, Hausfeld LLP. Brent Landau, Faris Ghareeb, Carina Clark, Michael Doneson, and Jack Kitchen assisted in the preparation of this chapter.

(5) What are the procedural requirements for initiating a claim? This chapter concludes by summarizing the necessary contents of a complaint and the rules of service.

§ 4.02 Considering alternatives to courts

Before initiating a private claim, an injured party may consider several alternatives to filing suit in court. Possibilities include lodging complaints with the Federal Trade Commission, the Department of Justice or state regulators; or seeking arbitration or engaging in pre-litigation settlement negotiations.

4.02.1 Federal Trade Commission

The Federal Trade Commission was initially established for the purpose of addressing economically ambiguous conduct that could not be effectively regulated by conventional judicial procedures.[2] For this purpose the Commission has the power not only to seek injunctions and issue cease and desist orders, but also to use its rulemaking authority to address competitive problems on a more general basis.[3] This rulemaking authority is unique to the Commission in its role as a competition enforcer, as the Department of Justice does not possess this ability.

Since its establishment, the Commission has been granted the additional power to seek equitable remedies including restitution, rescission, or disgorgement of funds.[4] It still, however, lacks authority to impose criminal penalties or civil fines.[5]

The Commission is not a forum in which an aggrieved party can bring a private claim. Individuals or entities can make their competition concerns known to the Commission, but ultimately the decision whether to pursue the matter, and how to pursue it, is left with the Commission.[6] The appropriateness of using the Commission's powers to secure compensation for parties injured by competition violations has been a subject of controversy, with recent policy statements suggesting that it will be used sparingly in the future.[7] Factors that the Commission will consider prior to seeking such remedies include the blatancy of the violation and remedies available through other means such as private actions.[8]

---

[2] David Balto, *Returning to the Elman Vision of the Federal Trade Commission: Reassessing the Approach to FTC Remedies*, 72 ANTITRUST L.J. 1113 (2005).

[3] *Id.* at 1114–17; 15 U.S.C. §§ 46, 57a.

[4] Balto, *supra* note 2, at 1120; 15 U.S.C. § 53(b).

[5] Meghan K. Woodsome & Katherine S. Dumouchel, *Antitrust Violations*, 46 AM. CRIM. L. REV. 275, 305 (2009).

[6] PETER C. WARD, FEDERAL TRADE COMMISSION: LAW, PRACTICE AND PROCEDURE § 1.02[4], 1–9 (1986).

[7] FTC Policy Statement on Monetary Equitable Remedies in Competition Cases, 68 Fed. Reg. 45,820 (Aug. 4, 2003), *available at* http://www.ftc.gov/os/2003/07/disgorgementfrn.htm.

[8] Balto, *supra* note 2, at 1122; FTC Policy Statement on Monetary Equitable Remedies in Competition Cases, 68 Fed. Reg. 45,821 (Aug. 4, 2003), *available at* http://www.ftc.gov/os/2003/07/disgorgementfrn.htm.

4.02.2 Department of Justice

Unlike the Federal Trade Commission, the Antitrust Division of the Department of Justice is capable of bringing both civil and criminal actions against potential violators of competition laws.[9] Much like the Commission, however, the Division does not provide a forum for the resolution of private claims. While the Division may certainly act on information it receives from the general public, news stories, or other federal agencies, the ultimate decision on what cases to bring is left to its discretion.[10]

The Division's civil investigations are often resolved by entry of a consent decree.[11] In the criminal context, the Division will bring charges for those antitrust violations that courts have deemed to be *per se* illegal.[12] This includes violations for price fixing, bid rigging, or market allocation.[13] Charges can be brought against both the offending company and responsible persons in an individual capacity.[14] If convicted, both the company and its individual officers are subject to significant fines, and the individuals may also receive a prison sentence.[15]

As with the Federal Trade Commission, there is no guarantee that the Division will act on reports of anticompetitive activity. Even if the Division acts, the resolution may result in the cessation of harmful conduct but it will not directly lead to restitution for aggrieved consumers.[16] However, actions brought by the Federal Trade Commission or the Division could be used to bolster a private claim for civil damages. They could also lead to a quicker cessation of anticompetitive activity than may be accomplished through the courts.

4.02.3 State regulators

Like the federal government, states also have the ability to initiate actions under both federal and state antitrust law. These rights are typically exercised by state attorneys general on behalf of three constituencies: (1) consumers, using the state's *parens patriae*

---

9 *See* Ward, *supra* note 6, at 1.02[4], 1–9.

10 Mark R. Joelson, An International Antitrust Primer 31 (2006).

11 *See id.* at 31.

12 Edward Cavanagh, *Antitrust Remedies Revisited*, 84 Or. L. Rev. 147, 149 (Spring 2005); *see* Gary R. Spratling, Deputy Assistant Attorney General Antitrust Division, Transparency in Enforcement Maximizes Cooperation from Antitrust Offenders, Address Before the Fordham Corporate Law Institute 26th Annual Conference on International Antitrust Law & Policy (Oct. 15, 1999), *available at* http://www.usdoj.gov/atr/public/speeches/3952.htm.

13 U.S. Dept. of Justice, An Antitrust Primer for Federal Law Enforcement Personnel (Revised: April 2005), *available at* http://www.usdoj.gov/atr/public/guidelines/209114.

14 *See* Joelson, *supra* note 10, at 32; Anne K. Bingaman, Assistant Attorney General Antitrust Division, & Gary R. Spratling, Deputy Assistant Attorney General Antitrust Division, Criminal Antitrust Enforcement, Joint Address Before the Antitrust Section of the American Bar Association Criminal Antitrust Law and Procedure Workshop (Feb. 23, 1995), *available at* http://www.usdoj.gov/atr/public/speeches/95 02 23.txt.

15 *Id.*

16 The Division may also be able to obtain disgorgement, which is designed to divest a wrongdoer of its proceeds but not to compensate victims. *See* United States v. Keyspan Corporation, 763 F.Supp.2d 633, 638 (S.D.N.Y. 2011).

authority, (2) state agencies, divisions, and programs, which may have proprietary claims and (3) the state's general economy.[17] Additionally, states often work together to coordinate their antitrust enforcement efforts through the Multistate Antitrust Task Force of the National Association of Attorneys General.[18]

When bringing claims on behalf of consumers, states can pursue both injunctive relief and damages under either federal or state law. When bringing such suits, states exercise their *parens patriae* authority, which derives from different sources depending on whether or not the claims are brought under federal or state antitrust law. If a state brings a federal claim, then its *parens patriae* authority comes directly from Title III of the Hart-Scott-Rodino Act.[19] This authority, however, is limited to claims that fall under the purview of the Sherman Act.[20] As a result, due to the Supreme Court's decision in *Illinois Brick* giving only direct purchasers standing to bring Sherman Act claims, states may bring federal antitrust claims on behalf of direct purchasers but not indirect purchasers.[21] This limitation has a significant impact on a state's *parens patriae* authority because ultimate consumers are usually indirect purchasers. However, if the claims do satisfy the federal requirements, then the state's attorney general may seek treble damages on behalf of all natural persons who reside in the state.[22]

When bringing suit on behalf of natural persons, the state must notify all persons on whose behalf it is suing, and it must give them an opportunity to opt out of the case.[23] Individuals who are covered by the lawsuit and who elect not to opt out will be prohibited from suing for damages under § 4 of the Clayton Act.[24] While there is no requirement for class certification in a *parens patriae* lawsuit,[25] settlements still require court approval.[26]

As an alternative to bringing suit under federal law, most state attorneys general may sue to enforce state antitrust laws.[27] States that allow indirect purchasers to bring state law antitrust claims can also include such purchasers within the scope of their *parens patriae* state law actions.[28] State attorneys general may also act as *parens patriae* to prevent actual or threatened harm to a state's general economy.[29] As with federal regulators, however, whether and when to bring such a claim is at the discretion of each state's respective public officials.[30]

---

17 Jonathan M. Jacobson, American Bar Association, ANTITRUST LAW DEVELOPMENTS 723–24 (6th ed. 2007).

18 *Id.* at 724.

19 15 U.S.C. §§ 15c–15h.

20 *Id.*

21 Illinois Brick Co. v. Illinois, 431 U.S. 720, 733 n.14 (1977).

22 15 U.S.C. § 15c(a)(1).

23 15 U.S.C. §§ 15c(b)(1), (2).

24 15 U.S.C. § 15c(b)(3).

25 Pennsylvania v. Budget Fuel, 122 F.R.D. 184, 185 (E.D. Pa. 1988).

26 15 U.S.C. § 15c(c).

27 *See* Jacobson, *supra* note 17, at 729.

28 *Id.*

29 15 U.S.C. § 18a; State of Conn. ex rel. Blumenthal v. BPS Petroleum Distributors, Inc., No. 3:91-CV-00173(WWE) 1991 WL 177657 (D. Conn July 16, 1991).

30 For a discussion of the interplay between *parens patriae* actions and private class actions, see Chapter 11 of this Handbook.

4.02.4 Arbitration

Consent is necessary from both sides in order to arbitrate an antitrust dispute. This consent will often be found in the form of a pre-existing arbitration clause in a contract between the parties. Assuming such a clause exists, the process commences with the service of a notice of arbitration in the manner provided by the rules applicable to the contract.[31] Such notices usually include some detail regarding the claims being brought and the relevant facts.[32]

Arbitrations on behalf of a class, as opposed to individual plaintiffs, are only permitted when the parties have specifically agreed to a class arbitration. Thus, class arbitrations are not permitted if a contract is silent on the issue.[33] In addition, courts will strictly enforce contracts with provisions prohibiting class arbitrations.[34] As a practical matter, this means that in cases where there are binding arbitration clauses, effective classwide redress may be impossible, and only individual plaintiffs with substantial claims will have a real opportunity to recover.

If an opposing party refuses to arbitrate, the claimant must file a motion to compel arbitration in an appropriate forum, which might be a state or federal court.[35] If a respondent argues that an arbitration provision does not cover antitrust disputes, a court decides whether a particular claim is arbitrable unless the contract itself demonstrates a clear intent by the parties for the arbitrators to determine arbitrability.[36] When faced with broad arbitration clauses, courts often defer to the arbitrators on this issue.[37]

If some parties or claims are not subject to the arbitration agreement, they may not participate in the proceedings.[38] While courts may elect to stay related proceedings while an arbitration is underway, it is also possible that litigation in state or federal court could proceed simultaneously with arbitration.[39] This can be problematic in a large antitrust case in which allegations of a wider conspiracy involving several parties may implicate evidence from co-conspirators not subject to the arbitration.[40]

Because courts are split on the authority of arbitrators to order third-party production of evidence prior to an arbitral hearing, a claimant's ability to present a full case can be severely limited.[41] Some federal courts have acknowledged these issues and excused claimants from their obligation to arbitrate.[42]

---

[31] Elizabeth B. McCallum & R. Mark McCareins, *Arbitration Procedures: The Rules of the Road in Arbitrating Antitrust Disputes*, ANTITRUST, Fall 2004, at 15.

[32] *Id.*

[33] *See* Stolt Nielsen SA v. Animalfeeds International Corp., 130 S.Ct. 1758 (2010).

[34] *See* AT&T Mobility LLC v. Concepcion, 131 S.Ct. 1740 (2011).

[35] McCallum & McCareins, *supra* note 31.

[36] *Id.*

[37] *Id.* at 17.

[38] *Id.* at 16.

[39] *Id.*

[40] *Id.*

[41] *Id.* at 16, 18; *compare* Hay Group, Inc. v. E.B.S. Acquisition Corp., 360 F.3d 404, 412–13 (3d Cir. 2004) ("The power to require a non-party 'to bring' items 'with him' clearly applies only to situations in which the non-party accompanies the items to the arbitration proceeding"), *with In re* Security Life Ins. Co. of Am., 228 F.3d 865, 870–71 (8th Cir. 2000) ("implicit in an arbitration panel's power to subpoena relevant documents for production at a hearing is the power to order the production of relevant documents for review by a party prior to the hearing").

[42] Jung v. Ass'n of Am. Med. Colleges, 300 F. Supp.2d 119 (D.D.C. 2004).

The discovery process in arbitration is less formal and less structured than in court.[43] While some arbitration agreements will provide for more detailed discovery procedures, including those that will comport with the Federal Rules of Civil Procedure, most are more limited.[44]

Once an arbitral award is rendered, it will be set aside by a court only in "very unusual circumstances."[45] Judicial review of an arbitrator's findings of facts and conclusions of law is also very limited, and even a serious error will not be overturned if it appeared that the arbitrator was acting honestly and within the scope of his authority.[46] An example of an award that might be overturned is one that violates a well-defined and dominant public policy, or one that directs the parties to violate the antitrust laws.[47]

4.02.5 Pre-litigation settlement

Pre-litigation settlement is frequently a potential option for individual plaintiffs or a proposed class.[48] The motivation to settle on the part of a defendant will depend on a variety of factors, including the strength of the case of the party threatening litigation, the relationship between the parties, and the volume of business possibly affected by anticompetitive activity.

On behalf of a class, plaintiffs' lawyers can negotiate a potential agreement with defendants before any filings are made, and plaintiffs' lawyers can then file a settlement class action for certification.[49] Whether this is done at the same time as the filing of a complaint or subsequent to it, the parties ask the court for an order that simultaneously approves the settlement and certifies the class.[50] A court must review the terms of the settlement to ensure that it was fairly negotiated and is in the best interest of the class.[51] For certification of a settlement class, the class must satisfy all requirements set forth in Federal Rule of Civil Procedure 23 except for the manageability requirement.[52] However, according to the Supreme Court's ruling in *Amchem*, the remaining Rule 23 requirements, including predominance, typicality, and commonality, will demand "undiluted, even heightened, attention in the settlement context."[53]

Where a case is contemplated by individual plaintiffs, the parties can enter into a

---

43 McCallum & McCareins, *supra* note 31, at 17.

44 *Id.*

45 First Options, Inc. v. Kaplan, 514 U.S. 938, 942 (1995).

46 Associated Coal Corp. v. United Mine Workers of Am., Dist. 17, 531 U.S. 57, 62 (2000).

47 McCallum & McCareins, *supra* note 31, at 21.

48 For a full discussion of settlement practice and strategy, see Chapter 12 of this Handbook.

49 Martin H. Redish & Andrianna D. Kastanek, *Settlement Class Actions, The Case-or-Controversy Requirement, and the Nature of the Adjudicatory Process*, 73 U. CHI. L. REV. 545, 553 (2006).

50 *Id.*

51 FED. R. CIV. P. 23(e).

52 Amchem Products, Inc. v. Windsor, 521 U.S. 591 (1997). The prospect of unmanageable litigation, perhaps owing to variations in state laws or other obstacles, becomes less relevant in the settlement context.

53 *Id.* at 621. For further discussion of class action requirements under Federal Rule of Civil Procedure 23, see Chapter 5 of this Handbook.

pre-litigation settlement that is never seen by anyone and does not require judicial approval.[54] Parties negotiating such a settlement might consider entering into a tolling agreement during the course of the negotiations so that the statute of limitations does not run if the dispute cannot be resolved.

§ 4.03 Choosing between state and federal court

Once a potential litigant has decided to pursue a claim in court, it must choose between filing a complaint in state or federal court. Because federal courts have exclusive jurisdiction over Sherman Act claims, historically most antitrust cases were filed in federal court. However, some state laws allowed indirect purchasers to sue in cases where they do not have a federal claim, and state courts have sometimes been perceived as more friendly to plaintiffs.[55] With the recent passage of the Class Action Fairness Act, nearly all antitrust class actions, including indirect purchaser cases, are now heard in federal court, as discussed in more detail below.

4.03.1 Federal court

Federal courts have exclusive jurisdiction over private cases brought under federal antitrust law.[56] A federal claim, however, must involve conduct affecting interstate commerce.[57] The conduct itself need not constitute interstate commerce so long as there is a substantial and adverse effect on interstate commerce, or at least the potential for such harm.[58]

Because federal courts have exclusive jurisdiction, Sherman Act claims, even when accompanied by state law claims, may not be brought in state court, and if a plaintiff attempts to do so a defendant may either seek to remove the case from state to federal court or file a motion to dismiss for lack of subject matter jurisdiction.[59] But the reverse is not true: if a case presents both federal and state claims, a federal court can exercise supplemental jurisdiction over the state law claims.[60] In its discretion, the court may continue to do so even if the federal claims have been dismissed.[61]

Moreover, the Class Action Fairness Act (CAFA) provides for federal jurisdiction over many class actions based entirely on state law. CAFA was designed to address perceived

---

[54] Scott A. Moss, *Illuminating Secrecy: A New Economic Analysis of Confidential Settlements*, 105 Mich. L. Rev. 867, 883 (2007); *see also* Laurence T. Sorkin, *International settlements*, *in* The International Handbook on Private Enforcement of Competition Law 575–589 (Albert A. Foer & Jonathan W. Cuneo eds., 2010) (discussing pre-litigation settlements involving global cartel claims).

[55] *See generally* Thomas E. Willging & Shannon R. Wheatman, Fed. Judicial Ctr., An Empirical Examination of Attorneys' Choice of Forum in Class Action Litigation (2005).

[56] 15 U.S.C. § 4; 15 U.S.C. § 15(a).

[57] 15 U.S.C. § 1.

[58] McLain v. Real Estate Board of New Orleans, 444 U.S. 232 (1980).

[59] 28 U.S.C. § 1441; Dzik & Dzik, P.C. v. Vision Service Plan, C.A. 836, 1989 WL 3082 (Tenn. Ct. App. Jan. 20, 1989).

[60] 28 U.S.C. § 1367(a).

[61] 28 U.S.C. § 1367(c).

abuses associated with class actions filed in state courts, particularly suggestions that state courts were sometimes biased against out-of-state defendants and made judgments that imposed their view of the law on residents of other states in cases of national importance.[62]

Under CAFA, federal courts have jurisdiction if the amount in controversy exceeds $5 million and any member of the proposed class (A) is a citizen of a state different from any defendant; (B) is a foreign state or citizen or subject of a foreign state and any defendant is a citizen of a state; or (C) is a citizen of a state and any defendant is a foreign state or a citizen or subject of a foreign state.[63]

CAFA includes several exceptions. A federal court may decline to exercise jurisdiction if more than one-third but less than two-thirds of class members and the primary defendants are citizens of the forum state.[64] It also must decline to exercise jurisdiction if (A) more than two-thirds of class members are citizens of the forum state, at least one defendant from whom significant relief is sought and whose alleged conduct forms a significant basis for the claims is a citizen of the forum state, and principal injuries occur in the forum state, or (B) two-thirds or more of class members and the primary defendants are citizens of the forum state.[65]

4.03.2 State court

Provided that CAFA does not apply and that no federal claims are included, a plaintiff may elect to bring a claim in state court. State antitrust and consumer protection laws are generally similar to their federal counterparts, and many require harmonization with federal law.[66]

There are some differences, however, such as states that provide for full consideration damages, i.e. damages that account beyond the "actual damage" to the injured party, or states that require a showing of concerted conduct.[67] Significantly, some state laws allow indirect purchasers to seek antitrust damages, which is not permitted under the Supreme Court's interpretation of the Sherman Act in *Illinois Brick*.[68] Pre-CAFA, almost all indirect purchaser cases were brought in state court, resulting in similar claims pending in multiple courts. Today, a single federal court might handle pretrial proceedings for consolidated indirect purchaser claims arising entirely under the laws of various states.[69]

---

[62] P.L. 109-2, § 2(a)(4).

[63] 28 U.S.C. § 1332(d)(2).

[64] 28 U.S.C. § 1332(d)(3).

[65] 28 U.S.C. § 1332(d)(4). For further discussion of the Class Action Fairness Act, see Chapter 5 of this Handbook.

[66] *See, e.g.*, *In re* Relafen Antitrust Litig., 221 F.R.D. 260, 278 (D. Mass. 2004); D.R. Ward Construction Co. v. Rohm & Haas Co., 470 F. Supp. 2d 485 (E.D. Pa. 2006).

[67] *See, e.g.*, Kan. Stat. § 50-115 (allowing full consideration damages); Cal. Bus. & Prof. Code § 16720 (requiring concerted conduct). "Concerted conduct" means an agreement between two or more actors, as opposed to one firm's unilateral activities. *See, e.g.*, Apple, Inc. v. Psystar Corp., 586 F. Supp. 2d 1190, 1203 (N.D. Cal. 2008).

[68] Illinois Brick Co. v. Illinois, 431 U.S. 720 (1977); California v. ARC America Corp., 490 U.S. 93 (1983).

[69] *See, e.g.*, *In re* Intel Corp. Microprocessor Antitrust Litig., 496 F.Supp.2d 404 (D. Del. 2007).

§ 4.04 Selecting a venue

After determining to file in the federal system, a plaintiff must decide which federal court venue to select. A federal court must have jurisdiction over the defendants and it must be an appropriate venue.

Generally, a federal court has personal jurisdiction when a defendant has sufficient minimum contacts with that forum,[70] though all jurisdictions can and some do impose additional requirements.[71] Also, some federal courts have interpreted § 12 of the Clayton Act[72] to confer personal jurisdiction over an antitrust defendant anywhere in the United States, based on that defendant's contacts with the United States as a whole, rather than with any particular jurisdiction.[73]

If all defendants reside in the same state, then venue is proper in a federal court in that state.[74] If not, venue is proper where a substantial part of the events or omissions giving rise to the claim occurred or, if there is no district where the action may otherwise be brought, where any defendant may be found.[75] Additionally, an alien may be sued in any district in the United States.[76]

This means that for an antitrust claim involving a product sold throughout the United States, almost any federal district will be a potentially appropriate venue. Choosing one of these districts for filing involves consideration of the multidistrict litigation process and several other factors.[77]

4.04.1 Judicial Panel on Multidistrict Litigation

When similar cases are pending in multiple federal courts, the Judicial Panel on Multidistrict Litigation may transfer them to a single district for coordinated or consolidated pre-trial proceedings.[78] Generally, a party involved in one or more of the cases files a motion to transfer the actions to a particular district; other parties may support or oppose transfer or propose a different transferee court.[79] After a hearing, the Panel – which consists of seven district and appellate judges – renders its decision.[80] Subsequently filed, or "tag-along," cases are later transferred to the selected court as well.[81]

---

70 International Shoe Co. v. Washington, 326 U.S. 310 (1945).

71 *See, e.g.*, N.Y. C.P.L.R. § 302.

72 15 U.S.C. § 22.

73 *Compare In re* Auto. Refinishing Paint Antitrust Litig., 358 F.3d 288, 298 (3d Cir. 2004) (basing jurisdiction on nationwide contacts) *and* Action Embroidery Corp. v. Atlantic Embroidery, Inc., 368 F.3d 1174 (9th Cir. 2004) (same) *with* Daniel v. Am. Bd. of Emergency Med., 428 F.3d 408, 427 (2d Cir. 2005) (rejecting this interpretation) *and* GTE News Media Services, Inc. v. BellSouth Corp., 199 F.3d 1343 (D.C. Cir. 2000) (same).

74 28 U.S.C. § 1391(b)(1).

75 28 U.S.C. §§ 1391(b)(2), (b)(3).

76 28 U.S.C. § 1391(d).

77 For a discussion of procedural defenses challenging the legal sufficiency of a claim based on improper venue or lack of personal jurisdiction, see Chapter 6 of this Handbook.

78 28 U.S.C. § 1407(a).

79 *See* 28 U.S.C. § 1407(c)(ii); J.P.M.L. R. 7.2.

80 *See* 28 U.S.C. §§ 1407(c), (d).

81 J.P.M.L. R. 7.5.

When the cases are ready for trial, they are remanded to the courts in which they were originally filed; a transferee court does not have authority to assign a case to itself for trial.[82] Also, the filing of a consolidated complaint in the transferee court will not automatically waive remand rights.[83] However, there appears to be no case law addressing a situation where multiple nationwide class actions are filed in several jurisdictions and consolidated beyond pretrial proceedings – i.e., answering the question of whether duplicative class actions are each remanded to their transferor courts or whether they are tried together in some forum.

In any event, parties may consent to have the transferee court preside over trial.[84] This may be desirable because of the experience gained by the transferee court during pretrial proceedings, promoting efficiency, and possibly facilitating settlement.[85]

4.04.2 Considerations

Selecting a venue can involve considerations about applicable law, judges, and jury pools, among other factors. Different judicial circuits may have adopted different approaches on various legal issues, such as what type of conduct constitutes an antitrust violation, the proper tests to be used, or the standards for class certification.[86] If an action is based on state law but is heard by a federal court, state law governs substantive matters and federal law governs procedural matters.[87] If an action is transferred by the Judicial Panel on Multidistrict Litigation, the law of the transferee court governs pre-trial proceedings but the law of the transferor court will govern trial.[88]

Considering these factors when selecting a forum is both legal and ethical.[89] As Justice Harlan recognized in 1965, "litigants often choose a federal forum merely to obtain what they consider the advantages of the Federal Rules of Civil Procedure or to try their cases before a supposedly more favorable judge."[90] There are some limitations, however, such as a procedural rule allowing courts to impose costs on a plaintiff who withdraws a case in one forum or before one judge only to subsequently refile elsewhere.[91]

---

82 Lexecon Inc. v. Milberg Weiss Bershad Hynes & Lerach, 523 U.S. 26 (1998).

83 *In re* Propulsid Prod. Liab. Litig., 208 F.R.D. 133, 141–42 (E.D. La. 2002).

84 *In re* Carbon Dioxide Indus. Antitrust Litig., 229 F.3d 1321, 1326–27 (11th Cir. 2000).

85 *See* Fed. Judicial Ctr., Manual for Complex Litigation (Fourth) § 20.132 (2008). For further discussion of the Judicial Panel on Multidistrict Litigation, see Chapter 5 of this Handbook.

86 *Compare* Le Page's Inc. v. 3M, 324 F.3d 141 (3d Cir. 2003) *with* Cascade Health Solutions v. PeaceHealth, 502 F.3d 895 (9th Cir. 2007), to see contrasting treatments of bundled discounts.

87 *See* Erie v. Tompkins, 304 U.S. 64 (1938).

88 *See, e.g.*, *In re* Temporomandibular Joint (TMJ) Implants Prods. Liab. Litig., 97 F.3d 1050, 1055 (8th Cir. 1996).

89 *See* Alan B. Morrison, *Removing Class Actions to Federal Court: A Better Way to Handle The Problem of Overlapping Class Actions*, 57 Stan. L. Rev. 1521, 1521–22 (2005).

90 Hanna v. Plumer, 380 U.S. 460, 475 (1965) (Harlan, J., concurring).

91 *See* Fed. R. Civ. P. 41(d).

§ 4.05 Suits by foreign plaintiffs

Whether U.S. courts are open to a foreign antitrust plaintiff depends in part on whether U.S. or foreign law claims are being asserted.

4.05.1 U.S. law claims and the FTAIA

The Foreign Trade Antitrust Improvements Act (FTAIA) lays out the conditions under which conduct involving trade or commerce with foreign nations can fall under the authority of the Sherman Act. The FTAIA has two main requirements: first, that the conduct has a "direct, substantial, and reasonably foreseeable effect" on domestic commerce, and second, that the act rise to the level of a Sherman Act claim.[92] In *Empagran*, the Supreme Court expounded on this doctrine when it held that there is no subject matter jurisdiction under the FTAIA where a plaintiff's injury abroad is independent of anticompetitive effects in the United States.[93]

The Supreme Court ruled that the text and legislative history of the FTAIA demonstrate that only foreign conduct which has a direct, substantial, reasonably foreseeable, and harmful antitrust effect domestically may be subject to the Sherman Act.[94] The Sherman Act does not prevent American exporters or firms doing business abroad from "entering into business arrangements, however anticompetitive, as long as those arrangements adversely affect only foreign markets."[95]

The *Empagran* case was remanded to the D.C. Circuit, which held that a plaintiff's injury must be "proximately" caused by anti-competitive U.S. effects, and that "arbitrage effects" were not sufficient to meet this standard.[96]

Significantly, the FTAIA explicitly excludes domestic commerce and import commerce from its scope. As a result, the common law "effects test" still applies to foreign import commerce.[97] The effects test, as applied by the Supreme Court, holds as a "well established" principle that U.S. antitrust laws apply to "foreign conduct that was meant to produce and did in fact produce" substantial effects in the relevant U.S. market.[98]

4.05.2 Foreign law claims in U.S. courts

There are several hurdles that must be overcome by foreign claimants who wish to bring foreign law claims in U.S. courts. The ability of foreign plaintiffs to bring an EU-law claim was recently tested in the *Air Cargo* case pending in the United States District

---

92 15 U.S.C.A. § 6a.

93 F. Hoffmann-LaRoche Ltd. v. Empagran S.A., 542 U.S. 155 (2004).

94 *Id.* at 161–62.

95 *Id.* at 161.

96 Empagran S.A. v. Hoffmann LaRoche Ltd., 417 F.3d 1267 (D.C. Cir. 2005).

97 Daseul Kim, "*Perfectly Properly Triable" in the United States: Is Extradition a Real and Significant Threat to Foreign Antitrust Offenders?*, 28 Nw. J. Int'l L. & Bus. 583, 592 (2008).

98 Hartford Fire Ins. Co. v. California, 509 U.S. 764, 796 (1993). For further discussion of the FTAIA, see Chapter 6 of this Handbook; *see* Sorkin, *supra* note 54, at 577–80.

Court for the Eastern District of New York.[99] That court discussed several potential barriers to such claims, including the issues of *forum non conveniens* and international comity.

International comity is very case specific. Some examples of its application include situations where a foreign sovereign would bar a foreign claim, or where the adjudication of claims involves the application of unsettled foreign law.[100]

Analysis of *forum non conveniens* involves a three-step inquiry.[101] The first step involves "assess[ing] the amount of deference to be accorded to the plaintiffs' choice of forum."[102] There is usually a "strong presumption" in favor of the plaintiff's choice.[103] The greatest deference is typically afforded to a plaintiff's choice of its home forum.[104] "[L]ess deference" is afforded to a foreign plaintiff's choice of a United States forum.[105]

After completing this deference analysis, the second step is determining whether an adequate alternative forum exists. In *Air Cargo*, EU plaintiffs recognized that EU member state courts were empowered to hear their claims, but were concerned that these EU courts lacked the procedural mechanisms necessary to provide effective redress to individual plaintiffs in an antitrust suit.[106] The judge sympathized with these concerns, but ultimately ruled that the likelihood that a forum would grant a party the damages they sought was not relevant.[107] The mere "power" or ability of another court to award damages in such a case was sufficient to establish the existence of an adequate alternative forum, even if that power had never before been exercised.[108]

If the court determines that an adequate alternative forum does in fact exist, then its third step is to weigh a variety of public and private interest factors to determine the appropriateness of each forum. Such private factors include: (1) the interests of the litigants in having the case tried in a particular forum; (2) the relative ease of access to sources of proof; (3) the availability of compulsory process for attendance of unwilling witnesses; (4) the cost of obtaining attendance of willing witnesses; and (5) all other practical problems that make trial of a case easy, expeditious, and inexpensive.[109]

Issues of particular concern include the enforceability of a U.S. court's judgment applying foreign law or the enforceability of a class action judgment in forums that lack such a mechanism.[110] The relevant public interest factors include: (1) court congestion; (2) the interest of forums in having local disputes decided at home; and (3) the interest in having

---

99 *In re* Air Cargo Shipping Services Antitrust Litig., MD 06-1775JGVVP, 2008 WL 5958061 (E.D.N.Y. Sept. 26, 2008), *report and recommendation adopted in part*, 06-MD-1775(JG)(VVP), 2009 WL 3443405 (E.D.N.Y. Aug. 21, 2009).

100 *Id.* at *31.

101 *Id.*; Iragorri v. United Technologies Corporation, 274 F.3d 65 (2d Cir. 2001).

102 *Iragorri*, 274 F.3d at 70–73.

103 Piper Aircraft Co. v. Reyno, 454 U.S. 235, 255 (1981).

104 *Id.* at 255–56.

105 *Id.*

106 *Air Cargo*, 2008 WL 5958061 at *25.

107 *Id.*

108 Capital Currency Exch. v. Nat'l Westminster Bank PLC, 155 F.3d 603, 609 (2d Cir. 1998).

109 Gulf Oil Co. v. Gilbert, 330 U.S. 501, 508 (1947).

110 *Air Cargo*, 2008 WL 5958061 at *28.

the issues of law decided by courts of the nation whose law is involved.[111] One particular public interest concern raised by the magistrate judge in *Air Cargo* was the risk of being faced with undecided foreign law issues.[112]

It should also be noted that in the Supreme Court's *Empagran* decision, the Court frowned upon the possibility of analyzing foreign antitrust laws or comparing them to domestic policies to ensure that comity is upheld. The Court stated that such a process could "threaten interference with a foreign nation's ability to maintain the integrity of its own antitrust enforcement system."[113] The Court explained that even if U.S. and foreign laws were identical with respect to their views on an issue such as price fixing, they may still differ with respect to the type and scope of the appropriate remedy.[114] In the Court's view, this could result in an overall reduction of antitrust enforcement by decreasing the incentives for conspirators to enter into national amnesty programs.[115]

§ 4.06 Preparing and serving a complaint

Once a forum has been selected, a case is initiated by the filing of a complaint.[116] Particular courts may have individual rules about how complaints should look and what information they must contain, but generally complaints identify the parties, describe the bases for personal and subject matter jurisdiction, allege the relevant facts, set forth the legal claims for relief, and indicate whether a jury trial is demanded.[117]

Complaints in federal court must contain sufficient factual matter, accepted as true, to "state a claim to relief that is plausible on its face."[118] A claim has facial plausibility when the plaintiff pleads factual content that allows the court to draw the reasonable inference that the defendant is liable for the misconduct alleged.'[119] Thus, "[t]hreadbare recitals of the elements of a cause of action, supported by mere conclusory statements, do not suffice."[120]

After receiving a complaint, a federal court issues a summons, which a plaintiff must serve along with a copy of the complaint on each defendant within 120 days, though additional time is allowed for service on foreign defendants.[121] Then, a defendant has 20 days to answer or move to dismiss, or 60 days if it agrees to waive service.[122]

---

111 *Gilert*, 330 U.S. at 508–09.
112 *Air Cargo*, 2008 WL 5958061 at *29.
113 *LaRoche*, 42 U.S. at 168–69.
114 *Id.* at 169.
115 *Id.* For a discussion of procedural defenses challenging the legal sufficiency of a claim based on principles of international comity or *forum non conveniens*, see Chapter 6 of this Handbook.
116 FED. R. CIV. P. 3.
117 *See, e.g.*, N.D. Cal. Civ. Local R. 3-4 to 3-6.
118 Ashcroft v. Iqbal, 129 S.Ct. 1937, 1949 (2009) (quoting *Bell Atlantic Corp. v. Twombly*, 550 U.S. 544, 570 (2007)).
119 *Id.*
120 *Id.* (citing *Twombly*, 550 U.S. at 555).
121 FED. R. CIV. P. 4(c), (m).
122 FED. R. CIV. P. 12(a).

5 Class actions

J. Douglas Richards,[1] *Michael B. Eisenkraft,*[2] *and Abigail E. Shafroth*[3]

[1] J. Douglas Richards joined Cohen Milstein Sellers & Toll PLLC (Cohen Milstein) as the managing partner of its New York office in 2009. Prior to joining Cohen Milstein, he specialized in antitrust class actions for approximately 10 years as a partner at two other leading plaintiffs' class action firms, the Pomerantz firm and Milberg Weiss. Views expressed in this chapter are those of Mr. Richards, Mr. Eisenkraft, and Ms. Shafroth, and not necessarily those of Cohen Milstein.

[2] Michael B. Eisenkraft is an associate of Cohen Milstein and a former law clerk to Judge Barrington D. Parker of the United States Court of Appeals for the Second Circuit.

[3] Abigail E. Shafroth is an associate of Cohen Milstein and a former law clerk to Judge Richard A. Paez of the United States Court of Appeals for the Ninth Circuit.

§ 5.01 Introduction

Violations of the antitrust laws usually cause widespread injuries to many participants in a market. In cases brought by overcharged purchasers, injuries suffered by any one purchaser, standing alone, are usually too small to make independent pursuit of an individual damage claim cost-effective. It is therefore indispensable, if private civil damage claims are to vindicate the objectives of antitrust law effectively, that claims asserted in multiple courts on behalf of multiple plaintiffs are combined into one or more cases. Some form of orderly, consolidated leadership must also be established to prosecute the consolidated civil claims. In the absence of established procedures for such consolidation, the multiplicity of individual claims and duplicative costs of various kinds would overwhelm any possibility of feasible private antitrust enforcement in many cases.

In the United States, there are three basic procedural mechanisms for the consolidation of antitrust claims, pertaining, respectively, to: consolidation of cases into one court; establishment of common leadership of the consolidated cases; and common resolution of the consolidated claims in a class action. In the discussion below, we address each of those three basic components of the process for aggregation of antitrust claims into class actions.

§ 5.02 Consolidation of cases: The Judicial Panel and CAFA

There are a vast number of courts in which claimants can initiate antitrust cases in the United States, including all federal judicial districts and, under parallel state antitrust laws, state courts. The primary procedure in the United States for preventing judicial chaos stemming from parallel claims in different courts is the statutory mechanism for consolidation of multidistrict litigation (MDL) by the Judicial Panel on Multidistrict Litigation (the Judicial Panel), embodied in 28 U.S.C. § 1407 and in rules promulgated thereunder by the Judicial Panel. When cases that involve common questions of fact are pending in multiple federal districts, parties to those cases are entitled to make a motion under MDL procedures to have all of the cases transferred to a single judicial district for coordination of all pretrial proceedings. Such motions are heard by the Judicial Panel, which holds hearings periodically throughout the year at various locations, and then determines whether to transfer all related cases to a single district for pretrial proceedings. The United States Supreme Court has held that cases that survive pretrial proceedings must be sent back to the original transferor districts for trial.[4] In practice, however, the vast majority of cases are disposed of prior to being sent back to the transferor district, whether through pretrial proceedings or through settlement in those cases that survive pretrial proceedings.

Although some recent commentary attempts to make systematic sense of the criteria that have governed MDL decisions by the Judicial Panel,[5] the prevailing consensus

---

[4] Lexecon, Inc. v. Milberg Weiss Bershad Hynes & Lerach, 523 U.S. 26 (1998).

[5] *See* Daniel A. Richards, *Note, An Analysis of the Judicial Panel on Multidistrict Litigation's Selection of Transferee District and Judge,* 78 FORDHAM L. REV. 311 (Oct. 2009) (describing trends in the Judicial Panel's selection of transferee district and judge and arguing that factors that influence the Judicial Panel's decisions differ depending on the nature of the claims and the various other criteria).

among practicing class action attorneys is that the Judicial Panel's choice of transferee forum is often driven in part by opaque judicial politics and is highly unpredictable. Regardless of the criteria that determine Judicial Panel decisions, MDL procedures have been very effective in consolidating antitrust cases and avoiding duplication of effort, and the Judicial Panel is generally perceived among practicing attorneys to function smoothly and efficiently, and to eliminate undue complication very effectively when multiple federal cases are filed. When making arguments for tort reform in the United States, proponents of reform often cite the large number of class action cases filed against a defendant in the wake of an antitrust violation, in an effort to exaggerate an appearance of duplicative burdens from multiple class action cases. However, where multiple cases filed in federal court are concerned, Judicial Panel procedures function very well as the first step toward consolidation of large numbers of parallel class actions into a small number of related cases, heard at the same time by a single judge as to all pretrial matters. For example, although data gathered by the Federal Judicial Center for the years 2002–2006 showed an average of more than 78 antitrust class action cases filed each year, the bulk of that number was attributable to duplicative cases that were subsequently consolidated through Judicial Panel procedures into less than nine multidistrict class action cases per year.[6]

A more recent and controversial set of procedures applies to parallel federal and state cases under the Class Action Fairness Act (CAFA), enacted in 2005.[7] CAFA was enacted to provide that most class action cases may be removed, by either the plaintiffs or the defendants, from state court to federal court. The primary exceptions – "home state" and "local controversy" cases in which most or all parties reside in a single state – are seldom applicable, especially in antitrust class actions. After CAFA, nearly all antitrust class actions may successfully be removed to the federal courts, and may then be consolidated into a single forum pursuant to the Judicial Panel procedures discussed above.

§ 5.03 Common case leadership

Even with consolidation by the Judicial Panel under MDL procedures, multi-district litigation would remain chaotic if there were no procedural mechanism for the appointment of common leadership for closely related cases. Federal judges presiding in class action cases have broad authority under Rule 23(d) of the Federal Rules of Civil Procedure to prescribe measures to prevent undue repetition or complication in presenting evidence or argument, as well as authority under Rule 23(g) to appoint class counsel. Additionally, broader guidance to federal courts, concerning how and why to establish common leadership among class counsel, is set forth in § 21.27 of the Manual for Complex Litigation (Fourth) (the Manual), which, while not authoritative, is often cited as persuasive authority.

The policy cornerstone of common, court-appointed representation is that those who

---

[6] *See* American Antitrust Institute, The Next Antitrust Agenda: The American Antitrust Institute's Transition Report On Competition Policy To The 44th President 228–29 (Albert A. Foer ed., 2008).

[7] Pub. L. No. 109-2,119 Stat 4 (2005).

"represent" absent parties in litigation must "fairly and adequately represent the interests of the class." The Supreme Court elaborated on this basic principle in the class action context in *Amchem Prods., Inc. v. Windsor*.[8] Since *Amchem*, courts have recognized increasingly that inquiries concerning adequacy of representation also must be applied to class counsel, who often play the leading role in a class action, and not only to the named plaintiffs. Accordingly, in 2003, Rule 23 of the Federal Rules of Civil Procedure was amended to focus the inquiry concerning fairness and adequacy of representation on the attorneys appointed to represent the class, and not only the named party.

Rule 23 sets forth various criteria that "must" be applied by the court in appointing class counsel, including work done by candidate counsel in identifying or investigating potential claims, counsel's past experience in handling similar claims, counsel's knowledge of applicable law, and resources of counsel. Often, however, several firms that wish to be appointed by the court as lead counsel will be comparably qualified under those criteria. Courts are understandably reluctant to draw fine and sometimes unseemly distinctions based on such criteria, in what is sometimes referred to disparagingly as a "beauty contest" among fully qualified law firms. In practice, therefore, as the Manual recognizes, courts commonly follow a so-called "private ordering" approach toward selection of lead counsel for the class, in which "[t]he lawyers agree who should be lead class counsel and the court approves the selection after a review to ensure that the counsel selected is adequate to represent the class interests."[9]

§ 5.04 Common claim resolution

Once related cases have been consolidated, and once common attorney leadership has been established for a case under the procedures described above, it remains necessary to determine the circumstances under which named parties before the court may resolve claims asserted by others who have been injured by the same antitrust violation.

The primary procedural mechanism for resolving antitrust claims brought by overcharged purchasers is a class action under Rule 23 of the Federal Rules of Civil Procedure.[10] In this section we briefly address the following questions: (1) What is an antitrust class action? (2) What is required for a putative class to be certified under Rule 23? (3) How is the class certification decision made? (4) Which issues are resolved in the class action? (5) What special rules govern antitrust settlement classes? and (6) How do class actions and arbitration interact in antitrust cases?

---

[8] 521 U.S. 591 (1997).

[9] MANUAL FOR COMPLEX LITIGATION (FOURTH) § 21.272. For a discussion of "private ordering" in the context of class counsel's pre-complaint activities, see Chapter 2 of this Handbook.

[10] States have their own class-action procedural devices and their versions are often applied differently than Rule 23, even if the language of their rules is similar. See Smith v. Bayer Corp., 131 S. Ct. 2368, 2377–78 (2011) (observing that the West Virginia Supreme Court has declared "its independence from federal courts' interpretation of the Federal Rules – and particularly of Rule 23"). This is becoming less important, however, due to the ability to remove most class actions to federal court under CAFA. *See id.* at 2382 (CAFA allows defendants to remove most class actions to federal court where Rule 23 applies).

§ 5.05 What is an antitrust class action?

A class action is a procedural mechanism, governed in federal court by Rule 23 of the Federal Rules of Civil Procedure. Rule 23 allows claims of a large group of plaintiffs or defendants to be adjudicated efficiently through all stages of litigation: motion practice, discovery, trial, and potentially settlement. As a procedural device, the applicability of the class action mechanism is independent of the merits of the case.[11] However, class certification analysis frequently "will entail some overlap with the merits of the plaintiff's underlying claim," and when such overlap exists, a court must nonetheless determine whether Rule 23's requirements are in fact satisfied in order to determine whether to certify a class.[12] Classes can be certified where none, some, or all of the members of the class turn out to have meritorious claims.[13] The determination as to which members of a class have meritorious claims, if any, is left to the substantive adjudicatory process (via motions to dismiss, summary judgment, and trial before a finder of fact).[14] Once the adjudicatory process begins, it is not uncommon for classes to shrink in scope as the district court determines, at various stages of motion practice, that certain portions of the class do not have meritorious claims,[15] or cannot appropriately be represented by the named class representatives. Claims of certified classes are also often dismissed in their entirety for lack of merit either at summary judgment or trial. If, on the other hand, a class claim is deemed to be meritorious at trial, then damages should be awarded and distributed to

---

[11] *See* Miles v. Merrill Lynch & Co. (*In re* Initial Pub. Offering Sec. Litig., 471 F.3d 24, 41 (2d Cir. 2006) (Supreme Court precedent precludes consideration of the merits when a merits issue is unrelated to class certification); American Law Institute, Principles of the Law of Aggregate Litigation § 2.06(a) (2009) [hereinafter "ALI Principles"]. ALI Principles provides:

> If the suitability of multiple civil claims for class action treatment depends upon the resolution of an underlying question concerning the content of applicable substantive law or the factual situation presented, then the court must decide that question as part of its determination whether to certify the class. The obligation recognized in this subsection provides no authorization for the court ruling in the posture of a class-certification ruling to decide a question of law or fact or a mixed question of law and fact if determination of that question is not relevant to the suitability of class-action treatment.

Id.

[12] Wal-Mart Stores, Inc. v. Dukes, 131 S. Ct. 2541, 2551 (2011); *see also*, ALI Principles, *supra* note 11, at § 2.06(b) ("When deciding a question of fact pursuant to subsection (a), the court should apply a preponderance-of-the-evidence standard.").

[13] *See* Sullivan v. DB Invs., Inc., 667 F.3d 273, 2011 U.S. App. LEXIS 25185, *42 (3d Cir. 2011) ("Rule 23(6)(3) does not, as used by the objectors and the dissent, require individual class members to individually state a valid claim for relief.")

[14] *See id.* at *69 ("[P]laintiffs need not actually establish the validity of claims at the certification stage.").

[15] *See In re* Toyota Motor Corp. Unintended Acceleration Mktg., Sales Practices, & Prods. Liab. Litig., 2010 U.S. Dist. LEXIS 131330 (C.D. Cal. Nov. 30, 2010) (holding on motion to dismiss that "Plaintiffs who neither sought repairs pursuant to the recalls nor sought repairs for SUA-related issues may not pursue a claim for breach of express warranty based on the written warranty," while those who did may pursue such a claim); *In re* ARM Fin. Group, Inc. Sec. Litig., 2002 U.S. Dist. LEXIS 13451 (W.D. Ky. July 18, 2002) (plaintiffs with 1933 Act claims dismissed, while those with 1934 Act claims permitted to go forward).

class members either in the aggregate or according to a formula approved by the court. If, as is often the case, a class action settles before trial, then the settlement amount is generally distributed to individual class members by class counsel via a court-approved distribution plan. Regardless of whether the claims of a class are dismissed, settled, or prevail at trial, the class mechanism generally allows defendants, plaintiffs, and the courts to adjudicate a large number of similar claims far more efficiently and consistently than would be possible if the claims in question were adjudicated individually.

§ 5.06 What is required for a putative class to be certified under Rule 23?

5.06.1 Class actions principally seeking damages

5.06.1(A) Requirements embodied in Rule 23

The pertinent requirements for representation in a class action principally seeking damages are set forth comprehensively in Rule 23(a) and (b)(3). Those requirements are generally referred to as: (1) numerosity; (2) commonality; (3) typicality; (4) adequacy of representation; (5) predominance; and (6) superiority. If the requirements of Rule 23 are satisfied, then a class must be certified. This is not a discretionary determination, as Rule 23 "creates a categorical rule entitling a plaintiff whose suit meets the specified criteria to pursue his claim as a class action."[16]

5.06.1(A)(1) Numerosity

The first requirement is that "the class is so numerous that joinder of all members is impracticable."[17] In most antitrust class actions brought on behalf of overcharged purchasers, this requirement is easily satisfied. The class will generally consist of hundreds, thousands, or even millions of purchasers in a marketplace who were similarly affected during the class period. In some industries, however, the number of direct purchasers who are entitled to sue for antitrust law violations under federal antitrust law will be unusually small. For example, in some cases seeking to recover overcharges for prescription drugs, there may be as few as 30 true direct purchasers from defendant manufacturers.[18] This is somewhat smaller than the 40 plaintiffs conventionally referenced as a benchmark for numerosity.[19] Nevertheless, if smaller numbers of class members are widely dispersed geographically, they still may satisfy the numerosity requirement, since one element of the numerosity analysis involves considerations of judicial economy stemming from the consolidation of widely disparate individual actions into a single case.[20] Classes of as few as 30 plaintiffs have been held to satisfy the numerosity requirement when the plaintiffs have been geographically dispersed.[21]

Antitrust claims brought by persons other than overcharged purchasers, by contrast, often fail to satisfy the "numerosity" requirement of Rule 23. For instance, it is rare indeed

---

16 Shady Grove Orthopedic Assocs., P.A. v. Allstate Ins. Co., 130 S. Ct. 1431, 1437 (2010)

17 Fed. R. Civ. P. 23(a)(1).

18 *See* Meijer, Inc. v. Warner Chilcott Holdings Co., 246 F.R.D. 293, 305–07 & n.13 (D.D.C. 2007).

19 *See* Labauve v. Olin Corp., 231 F.R.D. 632, 665 (S.D. Ala. 2005) (citing cases).

20 *Meijer*, 246 F.R.D. at 306–07.

21 *See id.*

for the number of competitors who are excluded from a marketplace, and who can credibly claim that they otherwise would have met with competitive success in the marketplace, to be large enough to provide the requisite numerosity.

5.06.1(A)(2) COMMONALITY

The second requirement is that "there are questions of law or fact common to the class."[22] Because the same course of conduct in an antitrust case generally has broad effects on prices market-wide, this requirement is nearly always satisfied by the plaintiff's need to plausibly plead unlawful conduct. This requirement has therefore been non-controversial in the class certification context in nearly all antitrust class actions.

Some argue that the Supreme Court upset the status quo regarding commonality in its recent decision in *Wal-Mart Stores, Inc. v. Dukes*.[23] In *Dukes*, even while acknowledging that common questions abounded concerning whether the class members "have all suffered a violation of the same provision of law,"[24] the Court nonetheless surprisingly found that plaintiffs had not "established the existence of any common question."[25] What the court reasoned is necessary in order to present even one "common question" is that the validity of the class's claims "depend on a common contention" as to which "determination of its truth or falsity will resolve an issue that is central to the validity of each of the claims in one stroke."[26] What that signifies will surely be disputed in future cases.

Early indications from the courts suggest that in many cases the impact of *Dukes* will not upset prior case law on commonality (or in other respects) and may, in fact, be further limited by its unique fact-pattern, as plaintiffs sought to certify a class of 1.5 million female Wal-Mart employees working in approximately 3,500 stores nationwide in a pay and promotion gender discrimination suit. Indeed, a number of recent cases seem to have limited the precedential impact of *Dukes* to its anomalous facts.[27]

---

22 FED. R. CIV. P. 23(a)(2).

23 131 S. Ct. 2541 (2011).

24 *Id.* at 2551.

25 *Id.* at 2557.

26 *Id.* at 2551.

27 *See, e.g.*, Public Emples. Ret. Sys. of Miss. v. Merrill Lynch & Co., 2011 U.S. Dist. LEXIS 93222, 26–27 (S.D.N.Y. Aug. 22, 2011) (noting that "the Supreme Court's clarifying language in *Wal-Mart* has no effect on the commonality determination in this case" because "the facts in *Wal-Mart*, a case in which three named plaintiffs sought to represent a class of 1.5 million women in an employment discrimination suit, are entirely distinguishable from the facts of the instant securities class action."); Churchill v. Cigna Corp., 2011 U.S. Dist. LEXIS 90716, 11–13 (E.D. Pa. Aug. 12, 2011) (decision in *Dukes* "inapposite" because in *Dukes* the issue was local supervisor discretion while "Cigna indisputably has a national policy of denying coverage"); Ugas v. H&R Block Enters., LLC, 2011 U.S. Dist. LEXIS 86769 (C.D. Cal. Aug. 4, 2011) ("Unlike in *Wal-Mart*, here plaintiffs have shown that there was "a common mode of exercising discretion that pervades the entire company. . . ."); *In re* Aftermarket Auto. Lighting Prods. Antitrust Litig., 2011 U.S. Dist. LEXIS 82452, 11–12 (C.D. Cal. July 25, 2011) (analysis of *Dukes* did not affect case in which there was a "general policy" of price-fixing); Behrend v. Comcast Corp., No. 10-2865, 2011 U.S. App. LEXIS 17524, 56–57 n.12 (3d Cir. Aug. 23, 2011) ("The factual and legal underpinnings of [*Dukes*]–which involved a massive discrimination class action and different sections of Rule 23–are clearly distinct from those of this case. [*Dukes*] therefore neither guides nor governs the dispute before us.").

Defendants, however, will seek to isolate the weakest element of a plaintiff's claim, and argue that since the case "depends" on that element, commonality of questions as to other elements is insufficient to create commonality under Rule 23. Defendants may even propose to stipulate to questions that would otherwise be "common," in the hope of persuading a court that since those issues have been stipulated to, determination of their truth or falsity is not necessary and that they therefore cannot present "commonality." Defendants also will rely upon the language in the majority opinion in *Dukes* stating that "[w]hat matters is not the raising of common questions," but whether there are "[d]issimilarities within the proposed class" that "have the potential to impede the generation of common answers."[28] As the dissent in *Dukes* rightly points out, this "dissimilarities" analysis inherently "leads the Court to train its attention on what distinguishes individual class members, rather than on what unites them."[29] By focusing on that language, defendants will try to narrow the focus of district courts to questions that may not be common, and to argue that the existence of other, common questions does not "matter."

Plaintiffs, on the other hand, will point to elements as to which commonality is traditionally very clear – prototypically in antitrust cases, the presence or absence of a conspiracy among the defendants – and will argue that since the class claims logically "depend" upon the truth or falsity of those contentions, those issues establish commonality. In antitrust cases, plaintiffs should have the better of these arguments, since indisputably common questions like the presence or absence of unlawful conspiracy are issues on which liability "depends," and no comparably fundamental and clearly common questions were presented in *Dukes*.

5.06.1(a)(3) Typicality

The third requirement is that "the claims or defenses of the representative parties are typical of the claims or defenses of the class."[30] This requirement seeks to assure that those seeking to act as class representatives have no divergent interests that could cause them to sacrifice the interests of other class members in order to favor their own interests. In cases brought by classes of overcharged purchasers, all class members usually have been injured in the same way, as a result of increased price levels in the relevant market. Unlike in many other kinds of class actions, therefore, typicality usually is not a major obstacle to the pursuit of a class action in an antitrust case brought by overcharged purchasers.

Nevertheless, in some antitrust cases class members have been injured under different transactional circumstances, such as purchases under different types of contracts, or purchases in materially different markets. Such situations occasionally give rise to divergences of interest within the class, stemming from ways in which the claims of the class representative are atypical. For example, in *Deiter v. Microsoft Corp.*, the court excluded "Enterprise Purchasers" from the class on grounds of typicality because "Enterprise Purchasers," unlike the individual purchasers, purchased bundles of 250 or more software licenses at individually negotiated prices that were "unique to each transaction."[31]

---

28 *Dukes*, 131 S. Ct. at 2551 (internal citation omitted).
29 *Id.* at 2567 (Ginsburg, J., dissenting).
30 Fed. R. Civ. P. 23(a)(3).
31 436 F.3d 461 (4th Cir. 2006).

5.06.1(A)(4) ADEQUACY OF REPRESENTATION

The fourth requirement is that "the representative parties will fairly and adequately protect the interests of the class."[32] This requirement tends to overlap substantially with the "typicality" requirement discussed above, since divergent interests stemming from representation by an atypical class member are often the reason for any inadequacy of representation by that class member.[33]

As the Supreme Court pointed out in *Amchem*, however, adequacy of representation "also factors in competency and conflicts of class counsel."[34] For example, in the highly-publicized class actions against Christie's and Sotheby's for fixing auction commissions, counsel for clients in U.S. domestic auctions were found not to provide adequate representation to clients who made purchases in foreign auctions. The structure of their compensation as class counsel for U.S. auction clients gave rise to a "structural conflict" that ultimately led class counsel to attempt to compel class members to give up claims arising from foreign auctions for no compensation.[35] Other case law, similarly, has noted an inadequacy of representation in circumstances where class counsel found it expedient in a settlement to release claims of a portion of the class – thereby seemingly recognizing that those claims had substantial value – without providing any sort of consideration in exchange for the forfeiture of those claims.[36]

Another circumstance that may give rise to adequacy problems in antitrust class actions is when a substantial portion of the putative class benefited from the challenged conduct. For example, in *Valley Drug Co. v. Geneva Pharms., Inc.*,[37] the Eleventh Circuit concluded that three national wholesalers included in the plaintiff class, whose transactions collectively comprised more than 50 percent of the aggregate class claims, "experienced a net gain from the absence of generic drugs in the market for terazosin hydrochloride."[38] On that basis, the court in *Valley Drug* vacated a grant of class certification and remanded for consideration of whether a conflict of interest rendered representation of the class inadequate.[39]

---

32 FED. R. CIV. P. 23(a)(4).

33 *See* Amchem Prods. v. Windsor, 521 U.S. 591, 626 n.20 (1997) (adequacy of representation tends to "merge with" typicality analysis); *Dukes*, 131 S. Ct. at 2551 n.5 (commonality and typicality requirements "tend to merge with the adequacy-of-representation requirement, although the latter requirement also raises concerns about the competency of class counsel and conflicts of interest") (quoting Gen. Tel. Co. of Southwest v. Falcon, 457 U.S. 147, 157–58 n.13 (1982)).

34 *Amchem*, 521 U.S. at 626 n.20.

35 *In re* Auction Houses Antitrust Litig., 138 F. Supp. 2d 548, 551 (S.D.N.Y. 2001), *aff'd*, 2002 US App. LEXIS 15327 (2d Cir. 2002).

36 *See, e.g.*, National Super Spuds, Inc. v. New York Mercantile Exchange, 660 F.2d 9, 18 (2d Cir. 1981).

37 350 F.3d 1181 (11th Cir. 2003).

38 *Id.* at 1190.

39 *Id.* at 1192, 1196. The Eleventh Circuit did engage with plaintiffs' persuasive arguments that such analysis overlooked the fact that the degree to which costs are passed on in prices at the next stage of distribution is not properly considered in federal antitrust law under *Hanover Shoe v. United States Shoe Machinery Corp.*, 392 U.S. 481 (1968). *Valley Drug*, 350 F.3d at 1192–1194.

5.06.1(A)(5) PREDOMINANCE

The fifth requirement, that "questions of law or fact common to the members of the class predominate over any questions affecting only individual members,"[40] is usually the most controversial requirement for antitrust class actions seeking damages. In several prominent cases in recent years, some judges have begun to scale back on the scope of class actions, often by finding that the predominance requirement has not been met. As a result of this trend, counsel and courts have manifested widespread and deep confusion concerning basic principles governing predominance analysis. We discuss below six specific aspects of predominance analysis in which such confusion has been especially noteworthy and problematic.

(1) Any question that affects broad subgroups of plaintiffs is a common question and not an individual question: In recent years, a few courts and many defendants have questioned the predominance of common questions in antitrust cases not by arguing that truly "individual" issues predominate, but instead by arguing merely that the case includes questions not common to the class as a whole. For example, when confronted with state law antitrust claims from many different states, courts have sometimes viewed such differences in state law as weighing against a finding of predominance. To reason in that fashion, however, is inconsistent with the clear language of Rule 23(b)(3), which defines "individual" issues, for purposes of a predominance analysis, to be "questions affecting only individual members" of the class. A difference between the laws of multiple states clearly is not a question "affecting only individual members" of a class. On the contrary, each state's laws in such a case typically affect many thousands, if not millions, of class members. When engaging in a "predominance" analysis, it is important to recognize that questions that affect broad subgroups within the class – whether they are questions of law or of fact – should count on the "common" side of the balance, and not the "individual" side. Even though they may be questions that are not common to the entire class, they nonetheless are not questions "affecting only individual members" of the class.

(2) Predominance is a balancing test, which means that the presence of some individual issues does not necessarily defeat predominance: The plain language of Rule 23(b)(3) requires that "questions of law or fact common to the members of the class predominate over any questions affecting only individual members." A balancing test is thus inherent in the plain language of the statute. The word "predominate" means "to be the stronger or leading element or force"[41] – a phrase which assumes that countervailing, but weaker forces may be at play as well. As recognized in *In re Ford Motor Co. Ignition Switch Products Liability Litigation*, "[t]hat common issues must be shown to 'predominate' does not mean that individual issues need be non-existent. All class members need not be identically situated upon all issues, so long as their claims are not in conflict with each other. . . . The individual differences,

[40] FED. R. CIV. P. 23(b)(3).

[41] DICTIONARY.COM, http://dictionary.reference.com/browse/predominate (last visited Oct. 5, 2011).

however, must be of lesser overall significance and they must be manageable in a single class action. . . ."[42]

Despite the express text of Rule 23(b)(3), defendants often argue that the presence of even one individual issue precludes certification. This argument is perhaps most commonly advanced in the contexts of statutes of limitations and damages. Some courts have accepted the argument that, in the presence of any individualized questions regarding statutes of limitations or damages, classes cannot be certified.[43] However, such opinions often overlook other tools available to resolve these issues in an efficient manner, consistent with Rule 23(b)(3), and without compromising the fairness of a class verdict.[44] As the Second Circuit noted in *In re Visa Check/MasterMoney Antitrust Litigation*, "the predominance requirement calls only for predominance, not exclusivity, of common questions."[45] In the context of individualized damages issues, most courts have recognized the propriety of conducting a full predominance analysis.[46] The same can be said for cases involving individualized application of the statute of limitations.[47]

Rule 23(b)(3) clearly envisions a weighing and balancing of common and individual issues. It is antithetical to the language of the rule to consider any single or small number of issues, whether it be damages, statutes of limitations, or some other issue, to be so incompatible with class litigation that its mere presence would require denial of class certification.

(3) "Every" class member does not have to be injured for a class to be certified: Within many large antitrust classes, there may often be a small number of overcharged purchasers who, for idiosyncratic reasons, were not injured by the challenged conduct. For example, subjective preferences of some class members will sometimes cause

---

42 174 F.R.D. 332, 340 (D.N.J. 1997) (internal citations omitted).

43 *See, e.g.*, Emig v. Am. Tobacco Co., Inc., 184 F.R.D. 379, 391 (D. Kan. 1998) ("Even if the statute of limitations was tolled until relatively recently, the court will still have to determine when each class member learned of defendants' alleged concealment. . . . Such a determination involves an individual, fact intensive analysis that makes a class action suit an improper method of adjudicating these claims."); Owner-Operator Independent Drivers Ass'n, Inc. v. New Prime, Inc., 339 F.3d 1001, 1012 (8th Cir. 2003) (individual issues of damages alone predominated over common liability issues).

44 *In re* Visa Check/MasterMoney Antitrust Litig., 280 F. 3d 124, 140–41 (2d Cir. 2001) (noting district courts retain numerous tools to manage individual issues that might arise at later stages of the litigation, including: (1) bifurcating liability and damage trials, (2) appointing a Special Master to preside over individual damages or claims proceedings, (3) decertifying a class after the liability phase, (4) creating subclasses, or (5) altering the composition of the class).

45 280 F.3d 124, 140–41 (2d Cir. 2001).

46 *See, e.g.*, Seijas v. Republic of Arg., 606 F.3d 53, 58 (2d Cir. 2010) ("[I]t is well-established that the fact that damages may have to be ascertained on an individual basis is not sufficient to defeat class certification.").

47 *See, e.g., In re* Linerboard Antitrust Litig., 305 F.3d 145, 162 (3d Cir. 2002) ("[T]he mere fact that such concerns may arise and may affect different class members differently does not compel a finding that individual issues predominate over common ones."); Waste Mgmt. Holdings, Inc. v. Mowbray, 208 F.3d 288, 296 (1st Cir. 2000) (that such concerns may arise and may affect different class members differently does not compel a finding that individual issues predominate over common ones).

a small number of plaintiffs to pay a higher price for a product, even if the same product is available for a lower price elsewhere. Recent case law reveals stark disagreement concerning whether it is necessary to determine which class members may be subject to such idiosyncratic defenses and/or to exclude them from the class in order for a class to be certified.

Until recently, there was a broad judicial consensus that the presence within a class of a small proportion of class members who were not injured for idiosyncratic reasons would not preclude class certification.[48] Judge Richard Posner, one of the founders of the conservative "law and economics" movement at the University of Chicago and an influential voice in antitrust law circles, has continued to express strong support for this traditional view.[49]

However, in *New Motor Vehicles*, the First Circuit surprisingly held that the plaintiffs' methods of proof were required to "include some means of determining that each class member was in fact injured," and that the plaintiff was required to show "that *all* consumers would pay more" as a result of the challenged antitrust violation.[50] Pursuant to that holding, the district court subsequently granted a motion to dismiss the case, interpreting the First Circuit's ruling that the plaintiffs were required to "establish that *all* class members paid a higher price" to require such result.[51] However, under the First Circuit's opinion, at least as interpreted by the district court, it is difficult to see how one ever could have a successful antitrust class action, because, as Judge Posner recognizes in *Kohen*, it is "inevitable" that a few class members in any large class will not have been injured.

This view of First Circuit law, which could make class actions impossible in many cases, is inconsistent with basic principles concerning class actions and the burden of proof at the class certification stage. All that plaintiffs in an antitrust class action are required to prove with regard to the fact of injury is that it is more likely than not that each class member was injured. Such a showing establishes the requisite *prima facie* case of injury as to each class member. If that showing is based on common proof, then common issues predominate, and it is a question for trial whether the proof is persuasive. Even if some small number of unidentified class members could be shown by the defendants not to have been injured, plaintiffs, at class certification, need only offer common proof that carries the burden of establishing a *prima facie* case of injury as to all class members. In an individual case, it would suffice to establish a case of such *prima facie* injury if the plaintiff were to establish that the clear majority of persons in his position were injured. There is no reason why that

---

[48] For a thorough compilation of cases that have rejected a view that "all" class members must be injured in order to establish predominance, *see* J. Douglas Richards & Benjamin D. Brown, *Predominance of Common Questions – Common Mistakes in Applying the Class Action Standard*, 41 RUTGERS L. J. 163, 173–74 nn.52–53 (2009).

[49] *See*, e.g., Kohen v. Pacific Investment Management Co. LLC, No. 08-1075 (7th Cir. July 7, 2009) (Posner, J.) (stating that the "possibility or indeed inevitability" that a class "will often include persons who have not been injured by the defendant[']s" conduct does not preclude class certification).

[50] 522 F.3d 6, 27–29 (1st Cir. 2008) (emphasis in original).

[51] *In re* New Motor vehicles Canadian Export Antitrust Litig., MDL No. 1532, slip. op. at 22–23 (D. Me. July 2, 2009) (emphasis in original).

same proof should not be sufficient to establish a *prima facie* case of injury for all class members.

Fortunately, in its recent decision in *Dukes*, the Supreme Court appears to have consigned to the dustbin the few mistaken opinions, such as *New Motor Vehicles*, suggesting that "all" class members must be injured in order for the predominance requirement to be satisfied. In *Dukes*, the majority opinion states outright that whether something on the order of 0.5 percent or 95 percent of the employment decisions at Wal-Mart may have been determined on a discriminatory basis "is the essential question on which respondents' theory of commonality depends."[52] Although the Court likely did not mean to specify 95 percent as some sort of magic threshold, the Court's statement is logically irreconcilable with any view that 100 percent of the class must be impacted before a court can answer the question of common impact in the affirmative. Thus, consistent with the views expressed by Judge Posner in *Kohen*, as well as with the vast majority of prior precedent, common evidence need only establish by a preponderance of the evidence that the clear majority of class members were injured by common unlawful conduct.[53] Such proof would seem sufficient as a matter of law, under *Dukes*, to establish a predominance of common questions.

---

[52] 131 S. Ct. at 2554.

[53] While not advocating the extreme view that *all* class members need to be injured for class certification to be granted, at least one economist writing on the subject has opined that common proof of damages should be able to demonstrate "impact on all (or almost all) class members." Brett M. Dickey & Daniel L. Rubinfeld, *Antitrust Class Certification: Towards an Economic Framework*, 66 N.Y.U. Ann. Surv. Am. L. 459, 462 (2011). Respectfully, we assert that this approach runs contrary to the purposes of the antitrust laws as well as standard economic theory. The rationale often used to support the requirement that "almost all" class members must be damaged for a class to be certified is that it would be unjust for any significant number of uninjured class members to have a recovery. But as Judge Hornby recognized in *In re New Motor Vehicles Canadian Export Antitrust Litigation*, 235 F.R.D. 127, 143 n.55 (D. Me. 2006), *reversed in part, vacated in part and remanded*, 522 F.3d 6 (1st Cir. 2008), these arguments about uninjured class members have to be viewed with some skepticism because the transparent truth is that they want to avoid recovery for all plaintiffs. *See id.* ("If the plaintiffs have an adequate model to award aggregate damages, the defendants' concern that some class members may be overcompensated at the expense of other class members seems a little suspect. Under the guise of fairness, the defendants' real objective is to avoid recovery by anyone."). In reality, the key to fairness for negative value cases is to make sure that the *aggregate damages* paid by defendants is fair and proportionate to the harm they caused and the illegal benefits they reaped. This is the approach most in harmony with the antitrust laws whose "primary goal is to prevent wealth transfers from [antitrust] victims to firms with market power." Robert H. Lande & Joshua P. Davis, *Benefits from Private Antitrust Enforcement: An Analysis of Forty Cases*, 42 U.S.F. L. Rev. 879 (2008).

The public policy benefits to focusing on aggregate damages are recognized in 15 U.S.C. § 15(d), which makes proof of "common impact" unnecessary in *parens patriae* cases brought for price-fixing by state attorneys general. That statute provides that in *parens patriae* cases in which price-fixing is found:

> [D]amages may be proved and assessed in the aggregate by statistical or sampling methods, by the computation of illegal overcharges, or by such other reasonable system of estimating aggregate damages as the court in its discretion may permit without the necessity of separately proving the individual claim of, or amount of damage to, persons on whose behalf the suit was brought.

(4) Unique affirmative defenses that defendants may have against individual class members should not defeat class certification: Recently defendants have attempted to revive a flawed argument first rejected by the Ninth Circuit in 1975 – that defendants' right and potential ability to assert affirmative defenses like causation against individual plaintiffs can defeat class certification. In antitrust class actions, as mentioned above, a defendant can always assert that subjective preferences of some class members will sometimes cause a small number of plaintiffs to pay a higher price for a product, even if the same product is available for a lower price elsewhere. Likewise in securities class actions, a defendant can always argue that a few members of a large class may, in fact, have known about the challenged misstatements or omissions and purchased the security anyway. The danger is that defendants will try to use a possibility that a small number of individual class members may be vulnerable to individual affirmative defenses as an excuse to derail class certification entirely.

The most famous and influential case dealing with this argument is the Ninth Circuit decision in *Blackie v. Barrack*.[54] In *Blackie*, the Ninth Circuit rejected this argument, while recognizing its dangers, holding that:

> The right to disprove causation will not render the action unmanageable. A defendant does not have unlimited rights to discovery against unnamed class members, the suit remains a representative one. . . . We think procedures can be found and used which will provide fairness to the defendants and a genuine resolution of disputed issues while obviating the danger of subverting the class action with delaying and harassing tactics.[55]

Two recent decisions in the Southern District of New York addressing this same argument have followed the intellectual path blazed by *Blackie*. In *In re Monster Worldwide, Inc. Sec. Litig.*,[56] a backdating pay case, Judge Rakoff rejected defendants' arguments that many companies may have engaged in stock option backdating and that certain members of the class may have known about or suspected options backdating at Monster. The court ruled that "despite all of this speculation, Monster provides no direct evidence that any putative class member actually knew about option backdating at Monster before the scandal became public," and properly certified the class.[57] Similarly, in *Lapin v. Goldman Sachs & Co.*,[58] Judge Sullivan certified a class and found that defendants had offered no proof demonstrating "that any potential class plaintiff – including investment banks – had actual knowledge of, or participated in, any alleged fraud." Judge Sullivan concluded by pointing out that if

---

Id. We believe it would be appropriate to follow this approach in negative value antitrust actions. This approach would maximize Kaldor-Hicks efficiency, resulting in the greatest good. Even if the aggregate approach is not adopted, however, there is no justification in law, public policy, or economics for restricting class actions to situations where almost all of the class members have been damaged. A far lower threshold, perhaps a simple majority of class members, would be far more compatible with the purposes of the antitrust laws and bring the results much nearer to Kaldor-Hicks efficiency.

[54] 524 F.2d 891, 906 (9th Cir. 1975).

[55] Blackie v. Barrack, 524 F.2d 891, 906 (9th Cir. 1975).

[56] 251 F.R.D. 132 (S.D.N.Y. 2008).

[57] *Id.* at 137.

[58] 254 F.R.D. 168, 184 (S.D.N.Y. 2008).

this argument were permitted to succeed, defendants could "defeat class certification merely by citing comments by certain industry participants that note the potential for a type of fraud in the industry."[59]

This does not mean defendants are deprived of their right to bring affirmative defenses against individual class members. They retain their right to assert affirmative defenses against individual class members, but that right comes into play after common issues of liability are resolved in a class-wide trial. This happened recently, for example, in *In re Vivendi Universal, S.A. Sec. Litig.*,[60] a securities class action which went to trial and resulted in a jury verdict for the plaintiffs. The district court refused to enter final judgment for plaintiffs after the jury verdict, however, because defendants had the right to challenge individual issues of reliance against members of the class in individual trials if they chose.[61] That is the proper time to deal with potential affirmative defenses against individual class members – not at class certification.

(5) Because predominance of common questions means predominance at trial, issues of law that will be resolved without a trial do not affect predominance: Federal Rule of Civil Procedure 23(b)(3)(D) identifies "the likely difficulties in managing a class action" as one factor to be considered when deciding whether common issues predominate over individual ones. While Rule 23(b)(3)(D) does not define what "managing a class action" means, the Supreme Court has made it clear that "managing a class action," in the Rule 23(b)(3)(D) context, means managing a class action *at trial*.[62]

Since manageability at trial is the issue to be considered under Rule 23(b)(3)(D), issues that can be resolved prior to trial (e.g., issues which can be decided on summary judgment or a motion to dismiss) should not be considered when determining predominance on a motion for class certification. The First Circuit recognized this explicitly in *Waste Mgmt. Holdings, Inc. v. Mowbray*,[63] when it held:

> Rule 23(b)(3)(D) . . . states that "the difficulties likely to be encountered in the management of a class action" are pertinent to the predominance inquiry. Nonetheless, when "confronted with a request for settlement-only class certification, a district court need not inquire whether the case, if tried, would present intractable management problems, for the proposal is that there be no trial." *Amchem Prods., Inc. v. Windsor*, 521 U.S. 591, 620, 138 L. Ed. 2d 689, 117 S. Ct. 2231 (1997) (citation omitted). By like token, when the court supportably finds that an issue which, in theory, requires individualized factfinding is, in fact, highly unlikely to survive

59 *Id.*

60 2011 U.S. Dist. LEXIS 17514, 219–221 (S.D.N.Y. Feb. 17, 2011).

61 *Id.* at 219 ("For this reason, courts in securities fraud actions have consistently recognized that issues of individual reliance can and should be addressed after a class-wide trial, through separate jury trials if necessary.") (citing numerous cases).

62 *See* Amchem Prods. v. Windsor, 521 U.S. 591, 620 (1997) ("Confronted with a request for settlement-only class certification, a district court need not inquire whether the case, if tried, would present intractable management problems, *see* Fed. Rule Civ. Proc. 23(b)(3)(D), for the proposal is that there be no trial."); Eisen v. Carlisle & Jacquelin, 94 S. Ct. 2140, 2146 (1974) ("Commonly referred to as 'manageability,' this consideration encompasses the whole range of practical problems that may render the class action format inappropriate for a particular suit.").

63 208 F.3d 288, 298 (1st Cir. 2000).

> typical pretrial screening (such as a motion to strike or a motion for summary judgment), a concomitant finding that the issue neither renders the case unmanageable nor undermines the predominance of common issues generally will be in order.[64]

Despite the presence of Supreme Court and First Circuit precedent, defendants and even courts still occasionally cite to issues that can be dealt with pre-trial as evidence of a lack of predominance of common questions under Rule 23(b)(3)(D) for class certification purposes. For instance, in *Telecomm Tech. Servs. v. Siemens Rolm Communs., Inc.*,[65] the district court cited issues including whether "Rolm had copyright or patent protection on the product" and the "parameters of the numerous undefined markets" as obstacles to class certification – issues that seemingly could have been handled before trial. Similarly, in class actions brought under the laws of multiple states, defense counsel sometimes argue that common questions will not predominate due to differences among state laws that involve threshold legal issues, but which can be effectively resolved through a motion to dismiss or for summary judgment. As correctly recognized in *Waste Management*, such issues should not be considered when conducting a "predominance" analysis, since predominance contemplates the issues that will predominate at trial, not in pre-trial proceedings that are resolved as a matter of law.

(6) Predominance of common questions need not be established in order to certify a settlement class: As shown in the fifth aspect of predominance analysis discussed above, the First Circuit in *Waste Management* rightly recognized that predominance of common questions means predominance at trial. Where, by contrast, there is to be no trial due to settlement, a predominance analysis is unnecessary. This was recently recognized, for example, in *In re New Motor Vehicles Canadian Export Antitrust Litigation*,[66] where Judge Hornby, citing *Waste Management*, recognized that predominance concerns are no longer pertinent in the settlement context.[67] Similarly, the American Law Institute has recently recognized in its Principles of the Law of Aggregate Litigation that in determining whether to certify a settlement class, "[t]he court need not conclude that common issues predominate over individual issues"[68] and that "[s]o long as there is sufficient commonality to establish that the class is generally cohesive, the propriety of a settlement need not depend on satisfaction of a 'predominance requirement.'"[69] Although one occasionally sees arguments made that predominance must be established in order to certify a settlement class, such an argument would be contrary to these better reasoned authorities.[70]

---

[64] *See also* Sullivan v. DB Invs., Inc., 667 F.3d 273, 2011 U.S. App. LEXIS 25185, *61–62 (3d Cir 2011).

[65] 172 F.R.D. 532, 548 (N.D. Ga. 1997).

[66] 269 F.R.D. 92 & nn.88–89 (D. Me. 2010).

[67] *See also In re* New Motor Vehicle Canadian Exp. Antitrust Litig., 270 F.R.D. 30, 34–35 (D. Me 2011) (reiterating principle after First Circuit vacated and remanded original decision on other grounds).

[68] ALI PRINCIPLES, *supra* note 11, at § 3.06.

[69] *Id.* § 3.06, Comment A.

[70] For further discussion of settlement classes and settlement practice generally, see Chapter 12 of this Handbook.

5.06.1(A)(6) SUPERIORITY

The last requirement for class actions seeking to recover damages under Rule 23(b)(3) is that "a class action is superior to other available methods for fairly and efficiently adjudicating the controversy." Rule 23 identifies a number of criteria for a court to consider in making that determination. However, given the breadth of the superiority question, those criteria provide little concrete guidance for a court to consider. In substance, the "superiority" requirement functions as a catchall that permits a court to consider additional criteria that seem important to it in any particular case, without being rigidly bound by the more specific criteria that precede it. In practice, most U.S. courts tend to focus on the more specific criteria for class certification that are previously stated in Rule 23 and that are discussed above, rather than on a free-ranging "superiority" analysis.

One prominent exception, however, is Judge Easterbrook's opinion in *In re Bridgestone/Firestone, Inc. Tires Prods. Liability Litigation*, in which the Seventh Circuit prohibited class treatment of a nationwide case under state laws on policy bases having little, if any, grounding in specific Rule 23 requirements.[71] Specifically, Judge Easterbrook suggested that to consolidate all of the state law claims in a single federal class action reflected "the model of the central planner" and did violence to "principles of federalism" by "keep[ing] the litigation far away from state courts."[72] For a period of time, that decision and the principles articulated in it made it substantially more difficult to persuade federal judges to certify classes in cases arising under multiple state laws. However, such reasoning should be less viable in the wake of the Class Action Fairness Act of 2005 (CAFA), which reflects Congress' own policy determination that state law claims frequently should be consolidated into the federal courts regardless of federalism concerns.[73] It would hardly be fair or reasonable to require that nearly all state law class actions be removed to federal court for consolidation, pursuant to CAFA and the MDL procedures described above, and then to deny class certification on the basis that the case then involves multiple state laws that are better considered by state courts.

5.06.1(B) "STANDING" REQUIREMENTS OVER AND ABOVE THOSE OF RULE 23?

The Supreme Court has stated unequivocally that Rule 23 "creates a categorical rule entitling a plaintiff whose suit meets the specified criteria to pursue his claim as a class action."[74] Nevertheless, in apparent contradiction to that principle, some district courts in recent years have required that class representatives have the "standing" to represent absent class members.[75] This highly questionable determination has been most recently and prominently repeated in the specialized area of securities class actions brought on

---

[71] 288 F.3d 1012, 1020 (7th Cir. 2002).

[72] *Id.*

[73] For further discussion of CAFA, see Chapter 2 and Chapter 4 of this Handbook.

[74] Shady Grove Orthopedic Assocs., P.A. v. Allstate Ins. Co., 130 S. Ct. 1431, 1437 (2010).

[75] *See, e.g.*, *In re* Eaton Vance Corp. Secs. Litig., 220 F.R.D. 162, 165-171 (D. Mass. 2004) (plaintiffs lacked standing to bring claims for violations of the securities laws against four related mutual funds when the proposed lead plaintiffs purchased shares from two of the funds); *In re* Terazosin Hydrochloride Antitrust Litig., 160 F. Supp. 2d 1365, 1370–72 (S.D. Fla. 2001) (holding, in a multistate class action containing claims under state antitrust laws, that the class lacked standing to represent plaintiffs from certain states because there was no lead plaintiff from those states).

behalf of purchasers of mortgage backed securities. In those cases, some district courts have held that named plaintiffs who purchased certain mortgage backed securities cannot bring actions on behalf of purchasers of other mortgage backed securities issued under the same registration statement because they lack Article III standing to do so.[76]

A requirement that a named plaintiff have "standing" to represent absent class members constitutes a fundamental misconception about standing, Rule 23, and class actions. Normally, no party can litigate anyone else's claims. Class actions, however, constitute "an exception to the usual rule that litigation is conducted by and on behalf of the individual named parties only."[77] In the class action context, a named plaintiff must establish his own personal standing to bring a cause of action, but his ability to represent *other* claimants via a class action is governed by Rule 23. As the Supreme Court long ago explained, once the named plaintiff in a putative class action establishes that its injury is "real and immediate, not conjectural or hypothetical," it "shift[s] the focus of examination from the elements of justiciability to the ability of the named representative to 'fairly and adequately protect the interests of the class.'"[78]

The circuit courts have repeatedly and correctly reminded the district courts of the true relationship between Rule 23 and Article III standing and, on occasion, have provided corrective guidance to the district courts on this issue.[79] Leading

---

76 *See* Me. State Ret. Sys. v. Countrywide Fin. Corp., 722 F. Supp. 2d 1157, 1163 (C.D. Cal. 2010) ("Every court to address the issue in a [Mortgage-Backed Security (MBS)] class action has concluded that a plaintiff lacks standing under [] Article III of the U.S. Constitution . . . to represent the interests of investors in MBS offerings in which the plaintiffs did not themselves buy.") (citing *In re* IndyMac Mortgage-Backed Securities Litig., 718 F. Supp. 2d 495 (S.D.N.Y. 2010); Public Employees' Retirement System of Mississippi v. Merrill Lynch, 714 F. Supp. 2d 475 (S.D.N.Y. 2010)).

77 Gen.Tel. Co. of Sw. v. Falcon, 457 U.S. 147, 155 (1982).

78 Sosna v. Iowa, 419 U.S. 393 (1975) (quoting FED. R. CIV. P. 23(a)).

79 *See* Braden v. Wal-Mart Stores, Inc., 588 F.3d 585, 5912 (8th Cir. 2009) ("The district court erred by conflating the issue of Braden's Article III standing with his potential personal causes of action under ERISA."); Arreola v. Godinez, 546 F.3d 788 (7th Cir. 2008) (Article III standing concerns only whether the named plaintiff suffered an injury redressable by a lawsuit; questions regarding the plaintiff's ability to seek relief on behalf of a class should be answered in the context of Rule 23); Cent. States Se. & Sw. Areas Health & Welfare Fund v. Merck-Medco Managed Care, L.L.C., 504 F.3d 229, 241 (2d Cir. 2007) ("To establish Article III standing in a class action . . . for every named defendant there must be at least one named plaintiff who can assert a claim directly against that defendant, and at that point standing is satisfied and only then will the inquiry shift to a class action analysis."); Payton v. County of Kane, 308 F.3d 673, 677-82 (7th Cir. 2002) (permitting plaintiff class to sue 19 counties for similar violations even though the named plaintiffs did not include representatives from each of the 19 counties); Newton v. Merrill Lynch, Pierce, Fenner & Smith, Inc., 259 F.3d 154 (3d Cir. 2001) ("[W]hether an action presents a 'case or controversy' under Article III is determined vis-a-vis the named parties. . . . Once threshold individual standing by the class representative is met, a proper party to raise a particular issue is before the court, and there remains no further separate class standing requirement in the constitutional sense." (quoting 1 NEWBERG ON CLASS ACTIONS § 2.05 at 2–29 (3d ed., 1992)); *In re* Prudential Ins. Co. Am. Sales Practice Litig. Agent Actions, 148 F.3d 283, 307 (3d Cir. 1998) (once a representative plaintiff demonstrates a personal injury-in-fact traceable to the conduct of the defendant, "there remains no further separate class standing requirement in the constitutional sense . . . [;] the issue [becomes] one of compliance with the provisions of Rule 23, not one of Article III standing" (internal quotations omitted)); Piazza v. Ebsco Indus., 273 F.3d 1341, 1351 (11th Cir. 2001) ("Even though Piazza

commentators have also provided correct guidance on this point.[80] Despite this repeated and consistent guidance from the circuit courts, some district courts (as illustrated most vividly by the recent cases in the mortgage-backed securities context) have conflated the requirements of Article III standing and Rule 23. These decisions, in addition to being legally erroneous and logically flawed, decrease the efficiency of class actions as they require class representatives from each county, securitization offering, ERISA plan, or state when bringing a class action. This makes class actions "considerably more cumbersome to initiate, and in turn, less effective in overcoming a lack of incentives to prosecute individual rights and in "achiev[ing] economies of time, effort, and expense."[81]

An issue that has contributed further confusion to this question of "standing" to represent absent class members has been when decisions about standing should be made. In addressing whether a class representative has standing to assert its own claim, various courts and authorities have rightly focused on whether that issue should be decided before or after class certification.[82] In some courts, however, that focus on timing seems to have confused the courts into assuming, without carefully reasoned analysis, that a court has discretion to decline to certify a class based on whether the plaintiff would have standing

---

only has standing to assert this breach of fiduciary duty claim for the period of his participation in the [ERISA] Plan, he may still represent the class [which includes other periods] if his claim has the requisite *typicality*."); Goodman v. Lukens Steel Co., 777 F.2d 113, 122 (3d Cir. 1985) ("[C]ontrary to the defendants' contentions, the issue here is one of compliance with the provisions of Rule 23, not one of Article III standing. Each of the named plaintiffs has presented claims of injury to himself and has alleged facts which present a case or controversy under the Constitution."); Fallick v. Nationwide Mut. Ins. Co., 162 F.3d 410, 423 (6th Cir. 1998) ("[O]nce a potential ERISA class representative establishes his individual standing to sue his own ERISA-governed plan, there is no additional constitutional standing requirement related to his suitability to represent the putative class of members of other plans to which he does not belong.").

[80] 1 Newberg on Class Actions § 2:7 (4th ed. 2010) ("Whether or not the named plaintiff who meets individual standing requirements may assert the rights of absent class members is neither a standing issue nor an Article III case or controversy issue but depends rather on meeting the prerequisites of Rule 23 governing class actions."); *id.* at § 2.9 ("[W]hen a class plaintiff shows individual standing, the court should pass to Rule 23 criteria to determine whether, and to what extent, the plaintiff may serve in a representative capacity on behalf of the class."); 7AA Wright & Miller, Fed. Prac. & Proc. Civ. § 1785.1 (3d ed. 2010). Wright & Miller provide:

> Representative parties who have a direct and substantial interest have standing; the question whether they may be allowed to present claims on behalf of others who have similar, but not identical, interests depends not on standing, but on an assessment of typicality and adequacy of representation. . . . While a potential class representative must demonstrate individual standing vis-a-vis defendant, once standing has been established, whether he will be able to represent the putative class, including absent class members, depends solely on whether he is able to meet the additional criteria encompassed in Rule 23.

Id.

[81] *In re* Relafen Antitrust Litig., 221 F.R.D. 260, 268–70 (D. Mass. 2004) (quoting *Amchem*, 521 U.S. at 615–17).

[82] *See* Linda S. Mullenix, *Standing and Other Dispositive Motions after Amchem and Ortiz; The Problem of "Logically Antecedent" Inquiries*, 2004 Mich. St. L. Rev. 703, 729 (2004).

to assert on its own behalf the claims of absent class members.[83] Although the question whether a named plaintiff has standing to assert its own claims can properly be considered by a court either before or after class certification, that does not mean that "standing" to assert the claims of absent class members is a permissible element of a class certification analysis.

5.06.2 Class actions principally seeking equitable or declaratory relief

The first four criteria for damage class actions that are discussed above – numerosity, commonality, typicality and adequacy – are also applicable to classes seeking injunctive relief. Instead of predominance and superiority, however, the additional requirement for a class action seeking injunctive relief is that the defendant "has acted or refused to act on grounds that apply generally to the class, so that final injunctive relief or corresponding declaratory relief is appropriate with respect to the class as a whole."[84] In most antitrust class actions, if the substantive legal requirements for an injunction are satisfied in a case, this requirement that the class be generally affected will be satisfied as well. Thus, although there is frequent dispute in cases concerning whether the requirements for injunctive relief are satisfied as to any plaintiff, it is rare for the requirement of broader impact on the class to be separately disputed in the context of a class action for injunctive relief.

Outside the antitrust context, it had long been accepted practice to view various types of monetary relief, such as back pay in employment cases, as falling within the penumbra of injunctive or declaratory relief within the meaning of Rule 23(b)(2). Although such practices had little application in the antitrust field, they seem to have been significantly curtailed by the Supreme Court in its recent decision in *Dukes*. In *Dukes*, the Court unanimously held that plaintiffs' claims for back pay could not be certified in a Rule 23(b)(2) class because the damages sought were not merely "incidental to" injunctive or declaratory relief. Specifically, the Court reasoned that because Wal-Mart was entitled to assert individualized defenses to plaintiffs' Title VII backpay claims, these claims necessarily sought "individualized" relief, rather than relief that was merely incidental to the injunctive and declaratory relief. The Court further stated that, for a claim to be properly certified under Rule 23(b)(2), it is necessary that "a single injunction or declaratory judgment would provide relief to each member of the class."[85] According to the Court, even when a claim seeks injunctive or declaratory relief as distinguished from monetary relief, "[i]t does not authorize class certification when each individual class member would be entitled to a different injunction or declaratory judgment against the defendant."[86]

From the standpoint of antitrust class actions, the Supreme Court's delineation of the

---

83 *See, e.g.*, Smith v. Lawyers Title Ins. Corp., No. 07-12124, 2009 WL 514210 (E.D. Mich. Mar. 2, 2009) (citing Mullenix, *supra* note 82).

84 Fed. R. Civ. P. 23(b)(2).

85 131 S. Ct. at 2557.

86 *Id.* In this aspect, *Dukes* seems to mirror analytical principles adopted in ALI's Principles of the Law of Aggregate Litigation, which make the distinction between Rule 23(b)(2) classes, as to which no opt-out rights are necessary, and Rule 23(b)(2) classes, as to which opt-out rights are necessary, turn on whether the remedies sought in the case are "indivisible" or "divisible." ALI Principles, *supra* note 11, at § 2.04.

boundaries of Rule 23(b)(2) in *Dukes* may raise new issues to be resolved. In many antitrust cases, the antitrust claims that are asserted are coupled with additional claims for unjust enrichment. Those claims generally do not seek an individualized recovery for each unjust enrichment plaintiff. Instead, they seek to disgorge from the defendants a pool of unjust gains which, in equity and good conscience, the defendant should not be permitted to retain. Despite the fact that such disgorged profits would be monetary in nature, they would not seem to constitute "individualized" relief within the meaning of the legal standards established for Rule 23(b)(2) in *Dukes*. *Dukes* may therefore have opened the door to certification of unjust enrichment classes in antitrust cases, notwithstanding the monetary nature of the disgorgement remedy in question.

§ 5.07 How is the class certification decision made?

Whether a putative class satisfies Rule 23 and should be certified is determined solely by the district court after making findings of fact concerning the factors delineated in Rule 23. A decision on class certification is not final, and a judge can certify or decertify a class at any time in the proceedings, though Rule 23(c)(1) does recommend that a certification order should issue at "an early practicable time after a person sues or is sued as a class representative." A party who disagrees with a district court's decision on class certification may file a motion with the Court of Appeals requesting discretionary interlocutory appeal under Rule 23(f) of the Federal Rules of Civil Procedure.

A primary source of controversy in recent years has been the degree to which a court should resolve questions of fact in deciding questions of class certification. That controversy culminated in the Supreme Court's decision in *Dukes*, which gave the lower courts a clear holding that "[a] party seeking class certification must affirmatively demonstrate his compliance with the Rule – that is, he must be prepared to prove that there are in fact sufficiently numerous parties, common questions of law or fact, etc."[87] In other words, whether merits issues arise during the class certification inquiry is of no moment. The courts are obligated to conduct a "rigorous analysis," and "[f]requently that 'rigorous analysis' will entail some overlap with the merits of the plaintiffs' underlying claim. That cannot be helped."[88] With these phrases, the Supreme Court has eliminated any doubt that may still have remained, at least in some circuits, as to whether a court must find that the requirements of Rule 23 are in fact satisfied in order properly to certify a class.

Nevertheless, the Court does not hold that class certification requires a full trial on all merits questions. Nothing in the *Dukes* opinion or other Supreme Court cases so suggests. On the contrary, in another recent opinion, the Supreme Court confirmed that if an element of a claim does not relate to the Rule 23 factors, it should not be considered at all at class certification.[89] Instead, to determine whether the requirements of Rule 23(b)(3)

---

[87] 131 S. Ct. at 2551.

[88] *Id.*

[89] Erica P. John Fund, Inc. v. Halliburton Co., 180 L. Ed. 2d 24, 31–33 (2011) (loss causation, which is a required element of a private securities fraud claim based on violations of § 10(b) of the Securities and Exchange Act of 1934 and SEC Rule 10b-5, does not have to be shown for class certification); *see also* ALI PRINCIPLES, *supra* note 11, § 2.06(a) (The obligation to decide factual questions necessary to class certification "provides no authorization for the court to engage a

are met, all that a court must do is make factual findings that the factors of numerosity, commonality, typicality, adequacy, predominance, and superiority are met. In making the predominance determination, in particular, the court should identify the merits "questions" that are to be tried in a case, and should weigh those that are common to multiple class members against those that affect "only individual members" of the class. Rule 23 does not ask the court to resolve those questions on their merits, nor does it ask the court to determine which side of the disputed issues is correct. Language in the recent appellate case law prior to *Dukes* clearly recognized that to do so is inappropriate, and nothing in *Dukes* purports to change that aspect of the prior case law.

First, in *In re New Motor Vehicles Canadian Export Antitrust Litigation*, the First Circuit recognized that "the validity of plaintiffs' theory is a common disputed issue" and that "[i]t will be for the fact finder to decide whether this theory is persuasive."[90] The First Circuit explained that a court deciding class certification should not be making such "persuasiveness" determinations with regard to "hard factual proof," but instead should only scrutinize the plaintiffs' arguments for a satisfactory "explanation of how the pivotal evidence behind plaintiffs' theory can be established."[91]

Second, in *IPO*, the Second Circuit emphasized that in making determinations concerning whether the requirements of Rule 23 are satisfied, "a district judge should not assess any aspect of the merits unrelated to a Rule 23 requirement."[92] Nothing in *Dukes* suggests that merits questions that are unrelated to any of the requirements of Rule 23(b)(3) are appropriately to be resolved by a court in order to rule on a class certification motion.

Third, in *In re Hydrogen Peroxide Antitrust Litigation*, the Third Circuit stated that "Plaintiffs' burden at the class certification stage is not to prove" its case, but rather "the task for plaintiffs at class certification is to demonstrate that the element of antitrust impact is capable of proof through evidence that is common to the class rather than individual to its members."[93] Likewise, later in its *Hydrogen Peroxide* opinion, the Third Circuit stated that "the question at [the] class certification stage is whether, if such impact is plausible in theory, it is also *susceptible to proof* at trial through available evidence common to the class."[94] Thus, with regard to the key question of predominance, the

---

question of law or fact in the posture of a class-certification ruling if determination of that question does not bear upon the suitability of class-action treatment."); *id.* at comment (e) to § 2.06 ("Questions unrelated to the suitability of class-action treatment are appropriately engaged by the court through other procedural vehicles, such as summary judgment, or through pretrial rulings."); *id.* at Reporters' Notes to comment (e) to § 2.06. The Reporters' Notes to comment (e) of ALI Principles provide:

> Well-established principles for summary judgment call for the moving party to show that "there is no genuine issue as to any material fact and that the moving party is entitled to judgment as a matter of law." Fed. R. Civ. P. 56(c). Wholesale displacement of these principles by the lesser threshold of a mere preponderance of the evidence – the standard prescribed for the class-certification setting – threatens an unwarranted intrusion by the court upon the role of the factfinder at trial.

Id.

90 522 F.3d 6, 29 (1st Cir. 2008) [hereinafter *New Motor Vehicles*].

91 *Id.*

92 *Id.* at 41.

93 552 F.3d 305, 311–12 (3d Cir. 2008).

94 *Id.* at 325 (emphasis added).

question is only whether antitrust impact in the case is "capable of" or "susceptible to" proof through common evidence, not whether the element of antitrust impact has been proved on the merits or whether the court finds the plaintiff's evidence on that issue to be more persuasive than the defendants' opposing evidence. In determining whether impact is "capable of" or "susceptible to" proof through common evidence, *Hydrogen Peroxide* makes clear that the touchstone is to identify "the method or methods by which plaintiffs propose to use the evidence to prove impact at trial."[95] In that respect, the Third Circuit in *Hydrogen Peroxide* echoes the First Circuit's ruling, in *New Motor Vehicles,* that the court is required only to ascertain that there is a satisfactory "explanation of how the pivotal evidence behind plaintiff's theory can be established."[96]

For a period of time, other language in these decisions confused many attorneys and even some courts into believing that a court deciding class certification is now permitted to determine broadly whether it is persuaded by all of the plaintiffs' methods of common proof, thereby transforming the court's role from that of merely identifying common and individual questions in a case into the much more problematic role of determining the correct answers to key merits questions. Those who advocate this forced view of the case law emphasize language from *Hydrogen Peroxide*, for example, in which the Third Circuit states that "the court must resolve all factual and legal disputes relevant to class certification, even if they overlap with the merits." Those taking the radical view contend that such language requires a court, in effect, to determine at the time of class certification whether the plaintiffs' proposed common proof of their case is correct or incorrect, by a standard of the preponderance of the evidence. The effect of such an incorrect interpretation of recent case law would have been revolutionary. It would effectively have called for the court to stop class action cases from going to a jury even when there are "genuine issues of material fact" that would preclude summary judgment, in effect substituting a court's own evaluation of key merits questions for that of the jury.

Fortunately, the Third Circuit has now explicitly repudiated such incorrect interpretations of its *Hydrogen Peroxide* opinion in *Behrend v. Comcast Corp*.[97] In *Behrend*, the Third Circuit explicitly states that "nothing" in its *Hydrogen Peroxide* opinion "indicated that class certification hearings were to become actual trials in which factual disputes are to be resolved" or "requires plaintiffs to prove their case at the class certification stage."[98] Indeed, the *Behrend* opinion goes still further, correctly emphasizing that to interpret *Hydrogen Peroxide* to invite such mini-trials or proof of claims on class certification would run "dangerously close to stepping on the toes of the Seventh Amendment by preempting the jury's factual findings with our own."[99] The Third Circuit in *Behrend* also points out that such interpretation of *Hydrogen Peroxide* has been "uniformly" criticized in recent scholarship.[100]

---

95 *Id.* at 312.

96 *See also In re* Hydrogen Peroxide Antitrust Litig., 552 F.3d 305, 312 (3d Cir. 2008) (quoting *New Motor Vehicles* for proposition that "a district court must formulate some prediction as to how specific issues will play out in order to determine whether common or individual issues predominate . . . .").

97 2011 U.S. App. LEXIS 17524 (3d Cir. Aug. 23, 2011).

98 *Id.* at **45–46.

99 *Id.* at *46.

100 *Id.* One of the law review articles referenced by the Third Circuit in that regard was co-

The Third Circuit recently reaffirmed this view in *Sullivan* where it confirmed that "there is no 'claims' or 'merits' litmus test incorporated into the predominance inquiry beyond what is necessary to determine preliminarily whether certain elements will necessitate individual or common proof."[101]

The Third Circuit, and the scholarly commentary that it references in *Behrend*, are not the only recent authorities that have rejected a view that class certification should be a context for effective trial of all merits questions. Importantly, in its *Principles of the Law of Aggregate Litigation*, the American Law Institute has urged that:

> Well-established principles for summary judgment call for the moving party to show that "there is no genuine issue as to any material fact and that the moving party is entitled to judgment as a matter of law." Fed. R. Civ. P. 56(c). Wholesale displacement of these principles by the lesser threshold of a mere preponderance of the evidence – the standard prescribed for the class-certification setting – threatens an unwarranted intrusion by the court upon the role of the factfinder at trial.[102]

These statements by ALI strongly support the Third Circuit's opinion in *Behrend*, and should diminish the likelihood that other courts might make the errors that defense counsel were beginning to urge, routinely, based largely on the Third Circuit's confusing and unfortunate language in *Hydrogen Peroxide*.

Nothing in Supreme Court jurisprudence has ever conflicted with the Third Circuit's clarifying language in *Behrend* and the views expressed on this point in the ALI Principles. To be sure, like much of the recent Court of Appeals case law, the Supreme Court's decision in *Dukes* has stated definitively that in order to certify a class a court must make either "findings" or "determinations" that the prerequisites to class certification are satisfied. However, one must consider the substance of the specific class action requirements in question. In the *IPO* case, for example, the Second Circuit illustrated its statements with regard to the need for "determinations" by reference to the requirement of numerosity, stating that "in considering whether the numerosity requirement is met, a judge might need to resolve a factual dispute as to how many members are in a proposed class. Any dispute about the proposed class must be resolved. . . ."[103] This is true of the numerosity requirement, which on its face calls for the court to determine how numerous are the class members. Some other class action requirements, similarly, call for a court to make outright determinations of fact. For example, the requirement of adequacy of representation requires that the court find the representation to be in fact adequate.

By contrast, the key point, which is sometimes lost on those who wish to interpret recent Court of Appeals authority in a way that hinders class actions, is that, unlike Rule 23 requirements like numerosity or adequacy, the requirement of predominance does not

---

authored by one of the co-authors of this chapter. *See* J. Douglas Richards, *Heart of Darkness: A Satirical Commentary*, 66 N.Y.U. Ann. Surv. Am. L. 569 (2011) (criticizing a conceptually similar policy proposal, by former Antitrust Modernization Commission member Jonathan M. Jacobson, that before certifying a class, a court should require a plaintiff to establish a 40 percent probability of success on the merits of its claims).

101 Sullivan v. DB Invs., Inc., 667 F.3d 273, 2011 U.S. App. LEXIS 25185, *66 (3d Cir. 2011).

102 ALI Principles, *supra* note 11, Notes to comment (e) to § 2.06.

103 *IPO*, 471 F.3d at 40.

ask a court to determine whether proposed common methods of proof are correct or incorrect, persuasive or unpersuasive. Instead, all it asks the court to do is determine that common questions are presented that "predominate" and that the plaintiff genuinely has common methods of proof. Once that key point is grasped, it becomes clear that *Dukes* and recent Court of Appeals case law is far less radical than some have contended. Merits questions need not be answered in order for a court to determine that they are common questions. Accordingly, for a court in the context of the predominance inquiry to determine whether the plaintiffs' proposed common proof is correct or incorrect would violate the Second Circuit's admonition in *IPO* that "a district judge should not assess any aspect of the merits unrelated to a Rule 23 requirement."[104]

Most district courts that have been confronted with the more revolutionary interpretation of *IPO*, *Hydrogen Peroxide*, and *New Motor Vehicles* thus far have rejected the argument, thereby reaching conclusions consistent with the Third Circuit's opinion in *Behrend* and with corresponding views espoused in the ALI Principles.[105]

§ 5.08 Which issues are resolved in a class action?

Even in those antitrust cases where a class action cannot be certified as to all issues, Rule 23(c)(4) explicitly permits a class action to be maintained as to particular issues. For example, as the Advisory Committee Notes to Rule 23(c)(4) recognize, a class can be certified as to liability and "members of the class may thereafter be required to come in individually and prove amounts of their respective claims." Confronted with more "rigorous" scrutiny of questions of impact under *Dukes* and prior Courts of Appeals decisions, some plaintiffs' counsel will occasionally seek to establish key elements of liability such as unlawful conspiracy in a class action, and to leave impact on individual plaintiffs and the quantification of their damages to be resolved in later, individual proceedings. There has been a sharp controversy in class action case law, however, over whether such a process is appropriate.

On one hand, Rule 23(c)(4) provides on its face that "[w]hen appropriate, an action may be brought or maintained as a class action with respect to particular issues." In *Cordes & Co. Financial Services v. A.G. Edwards & Sons, Inc.*,[106] the Second Circuit reversed a denial of class certification and remanded the case to the district court to consider certification of part of the case under Rule 23(c)(4). In *Chiang v. Veneman*,[107] the Third Circuit observed that "courts commonly use Rule 23(c)(4) to certify some elements of liability for class determination, while leaving other elements to individual adjudication." Other case law similarly bears this out.[108] These cases reflect a strong consensus, which is also reflected in ALI's Principles of the Law of Aggregate Litigation, that the courts should

---

104 *Id.* at 41.

105 *See* Richards & Brown, *supra* note 48, at 171 n. 49 (citing and quoting from many cases).

106 502 F.3d 91 (2d Cir. 2007).

107 385 F.3d 256, 267 (3d Cir. 2004).

108 *See, e.g.*, Valentino v. Carter-Wallace, Inc., 97 F.3d 1227, 1234 (9th Cir. 1996); *In re* Nassau County Strip Search Cases, 461 F.3d 219, 221 (2d Cir. 2006) ("[A] court may employ Rule 23(c)(4)(A) to certify a class as to an issue regardless of whether the claim as a whole satisfies the predominance test.").

permit aggregate treatment of any common issue whenever "resolution of the common issue would (1) materially advance the resolution of multiple civil claims by addressing the core of the dispute in a manner superior to other realistic procedural alternatives . . . ."[109]

On the other hand, defendants seeking to oppose Rule 23(c)(4) certification primarily rely upon *Castano v. Am. Tobacco Co.*[110] In *Castano*, the Fifth Circuit took the view that Rule 23(c)(4) can be applied only when the predominance requirement of Rule 23(b)(3) has been met with regard to the claim as a whole, reasoning that "[r]eading rule 23(c)(4) as allowing a court to sever issues until the remaining common issue predominates over the remaining individual issues would eviscerate the predominance requirement of rule 23(b)(3); the result would be automatic certification in every case where there is a common issue, a result that could not have been intended." A few courts, particularly in the Eastern District of Pennsylvania, have agreed with this reasoning in *Castano.*[111] However, the majority of courts and commentators appear generally to disagree with *Castano*.[112] As the Second Circuit appropriately explains in *Nassau County*, the *Castano* court's view would inappropriately "render subsection (c)(4) virtually nil."[113]

§ 5.09 How do class actions and arbitration interact in antitrust cases?

In recent years, the rapid rise of arbitration agreements has raised novel and pressing questions regarding the availability of class proceedings when antitrust plaintiffs are subject to an arbitration agreement that either (a) is silent as to class procedures or (b) expressly bans such procedures. As discussed at the beginning of this chapter, antitrust claims that are small in absolute value or small in relation to the significant expenses of developing and prosecuting complex antitrust claims cannot feasibly be pursued absent class procedures, which allow for aggregation of claims and pooling of resources. Arbitration agreements that seek to bar class procedures and leave available only individual arbitration therefore pose a significant threat to private antitrust enforcement. The interpretation and enforceability of such agreements has been hotly disputed, and advocates for consumers, employees, and other likely class plaintiffs, as well as many state courts and lower federal courts concerned that arbitration agreements may be wielded to surreptitiously eliminate class action rights and exculpate corporate wrongdoers, have been engaged in a push-and-pull with corporate interests seeking to minimize class action exposure and with a Supreme Court enamoured of the Federal Arbitration Act (FAA) and skeptical of class arbitration. These issues have only become more urgent since the Supreme Court's decision in *AT&T Mobility LLC v. Concepcion*,[114] holding that states

---

109 ALI PRINCIPLES, § 2.02 (a).

110 84 F.3d 734 (5th Cir. 1996).

111 *See* Arch v. Am. Tobacco Co., 175 F.R.D. 469, 496 (E.D. Pa. 1997); Blain v. Smithkline Beecham Corp., 240 F.R.D. 179, 189–91 (E.D. Pa. 2007); Gates v. Rohm and Haas Co., 265 F.R.D. 208, 234 (E.D. Pa. 2010).

112 *See* 7A WRIGHT & MILLER, FED. PRAC. & PRO. § 1790 (3d ed. 2005); 2 ALBA CONTE & HERBERT NEWBERG, NEWBERG ON CLASS ACTIONS § 4:23 (2010); *id.* at § 18:7 (2002); Fleischman v. Albany Medical Center, 2010 WL 681992 (N.D.N.Y. July 28, 2009).

113 461 F.3d at 226–27.

114 No. 09-893, 563 U.S. ____, 131 S. Ct. 1740 (Apr. 27, 2011).

may not generally require the availability of class arbitration in consumer disputes consistently with the FAA.[115]

5.09.1 Background regarding arbitration and antitrust

Before discussing *Concepcion*, a brief history is in order. Although the Federal Arbitration Act was enacted in 1925,[116] arbitration is a relatively recent development in the realm of antitrust. Arbitration was originally conceived as an alternative forum for resolution of private – primarily contractual – disputes. In 1968, the Second Circuit held that antitrust claims are not arbitrable, reasoning that antitrust enforcement is a matter of strong public interest and that courts should not relinquish responsibility over legal matters of significant public concern and great complexity to private resolution.[117]

This understanding was uniformly held by the Courts of Appeals for nearly two decades until it was unsettled by the Supreme Court in *Mitsubishi Motors Corp. v. Soler Chrysler-Plymouth, Inc.*[118] The *Mitsubishi* Court held that a broad arbitration agreement between internationally diverse parties must be enforced under the FAA and the United Nations' Convention on the Recognition and Enforcement of Foreign Arbitral Awards, "even as to the antitrust claims."[119] Though the holding was limited to the international context presented, the Court "confessed some skepticism" toward *American Safety*'s conclusion that antitrust claims were generally not arbitrable, and rejected the argument that arbitrators were not sufficiently competent and neutral to conduct antitrust proceedings.[120] Most importantly, the Court explained that "without doubt, the private cause of action plays a central role in enforcing antitrust law and thus furthering the national interest in a competitive economy," but that "does not compel the conclusion" that parties may not agree to arbitration.[121] Rather, "so long as the prospective litigant effectively may vindicate its statutory cause of action in the arbitral forum, the statute will continue to serve both its remedial and deterrent function."[122]

Mitsubishi marked the changing of the tides on arbitration of statutory claims. Though the case concerned enforceability of an arbitration agreement between similarly sophisticated businesses, and some expected it to be limited to negotiated agreements between

---

[115] Congress thus far has not passed any laws addressing this dispute. However, several members reintroduced legislation that would specifically invalidate pre-dispute binding arbitration agreements requiring arbitration of consumer, employment, or civil rights disputes, and, on October 4, 2011, two senators introduced legislation which would ban mandatory arbitration clauses in cell phone and mobile service contracts – the type of contracts at issue in *Concepcion*. *See* Arbitration Fairness Act, H.R. 1873, S. 987, 112th Cong. (2011); Consumer Mobile Fairness Act, S. 1192 (2011).

[116] The FAA provides that arbitration agreements "shall be valid, irrevocable, and enforceable, save upon such grounds as exist at law or in equity for the revocation of any contract." 9 U.S.C. § 2 (2011).

[117] American Safety Equipment Corp. v. J. P. Maguire & Co, 391 F.2d 821, 826-28 (2d Cir. 1968).

[118] 473 U.S. 614 (1985).

[119] *Id.* at 620.

[120] *Id.* at 633–34.

[121] *Id.* at 634–35.

[122] *Id.* at 637.

sophisticated parties or to the international context, no such limitations took hold. In 1991, the Supreme Court observed in *Gilmer v. Interstate/Johnson Lane Corp.* that "it is by now clear that statutory claims may be the subject of an arbitration agreement" and that such agreements are enforceable in the absence of Congressional intent "to preclude a waiver of judicial remedies for the statutory rights at issue,"[123] "so long as the prospective litigant may effectively vindicate" the statutory cause of action consistent with the purpose of the statute.[124] Today, antitrust claims are generally subject to arbitration agreements.[125]

5.09.2 The emergence of arbitration agreements as a shield against class proceedings

In cementing the arbitrability of statutory claims in *Gilmer*, the Supreme Court also touched for the first time on the interplay between class proceedings and arbitration. The plaintiff in *Gilmer* opposed arbitration of his Age Discrimination in Employment Act (ADEA) claim partly on the ground that the arbitration agreement would deprive employees of the opportunity to proceed by way of a collective action, a proceeding similar to a class action that is specifically provided for by the ADEA. In rejecting plaintiff's argument, the Court noted that collective arbitration might be available under the relevant arbitration provisions.[126] The Court thus implied that class arbitration might be permissible and consistent with the FAA and Due Process.

Another decade passed with few courts or arbitrators addressing the availability of classwide arbitration, and few classwide arbitrations taking place.[127] Indeed, despite the *Gilmer* Court's suggestion that collective arbitration might have been available to employees in 1991, the major arbitration associations lacked any guidelines on how class arbitrations could proceed. Taking advantage of the general unavailability of class arbitration and the expansion of the FAA to allow for predispute agreements to arbitrate statutory claims, corporations increasingly introduced broad arbitration provisions into their contracts requiring plaintiffs to arbitrate any claims against them – and, by default, to do so in an individual capacity. Some even began to include language explicitly requiring that arbitration proceed on an individual rather than class basis.[128] Although proponents of

---

123 500 U.S. 20, 32 (1991).

124 *Id.* at 28 (quoting *Mitsubishi*, 473 U.S. at 637).

125 *See, e.g.*, Stolt-Nielsen S.A. v. AnimalFeeds Int'l Corp., 130 S. Ct. 1758 (2010); Seacoast Motors of Salisbury, Inc. v. DaimlerChrysler Motors Corp., 271 F.3d 6, 11 (1st Cir. 2001) ("We think time has passed by the *American Safety* doctrine and so hold."); Kotam Elec., Inc. v. JBL Consumer Prods., 93 F.3d 724, 728 (11th Cir. 1996) (en banc) ("In light of *Mitsubishi* and its progeny . . . we hold that . . . arbitration agreements concerning domestic antitrust claims are enforceable."); Nghiem v. NEC Elec., 25 F.3d 1437, 1441 (9th Cir. 1994) (Supreme Court decisions compel conclusion that domestic antitrust claims generally are arbitrable).

126 500 U.S. at 32.

127 *See* Jean R. Sternlight, *As Mandatory Binding Arbitration Meets the Class Action, Will the Class Action Survive?*, 42 Wm & Mary L. Rev. 1, 38 (2000) (few courts had ordered arbitration to proceed on a classwide basis and the author had found only one instance in which an arbitrator ordered class arbitration).

128 *See id.* at 5–6; *see also* Miriam Gilles, *Opting Out of Liability: The Forthcoming Near-Total Demise of the Modern Class Action*, 104 Mich. L. Rev. 373, 396–98 (2005).

arbitration focused publicly on arbitration's ability to deliver quicker results at lower cost, as compared to litigation, many advocates and attorneys encouraged corporations to use arbitration agreements specifically to reduce exposure to class actions, and the practice became increasingly commonplace.[129]

The Supreme Court finally addressed the intersection of class actions and arbitration head on in *Green Tree Financial Corp. v. Bazzle*.[130] In *Bazzle*, a plurality of the Court held that "whether the contracts forbid class arbitration" was for the arbitrator to decide, and remanded for the arbitrator to make that decision.[131] The opinion had two significant implications. First, it signalled the Court's approval of class arbitration. Accordingly, arbitration associations quickly leapt into action, developing rules for handling class arbitrations.[132] Second, by framing the question of class arbitrability as whether or not the agreement "forbid[s] class arbitration," the Court seemed to establish a presumption that broad arbitration provisions permit class arbitration absent express agreement otherwise. Indeed, as of 2009, only 5 percent of post-*Bazzle* putative class arbitrations before the American Arbitration Association (AAA) resulted in findings that the arbitration clause did not permit class arbitration.[133] Such reasoning is sound: if a broad arbitration clause sets forth an agreement to arbitrate all disputes and to make available all relief that would be available in the judicial forum, such a clause should not be read to silently exclude a significant class of disputes from arbitration. Thus, following *Bazzle*, class arbitrations finally commenced in significant numbers.

Because *Bazzle* substantially undermined the strategy of relying on broad arbitration agreements to reduce exposure to class claims that had taken shape following *Gilmer*, corporations have now changed tactics. They increasingly insert language waiving class procedures into arbitration agreements to better protect against class proceedings.[134] In turn, this has spurred class plaintiffs and advocates to focus on avenues to defeat enforcement of arbitration agreements with class waiver provisions, including asserting arguments – discussed further below – that such waivers are unconscionable as a matter of state contract law, or unenforceable as a matter of federal law because they would prevent vindication of statutory rights. And courts, sympathetic to claims that compelling individual arbitration of low-value or highly complex claims would

---

129 *See* Sternlight, *supra* note 127, at 5–12 (discussing trend); *see also* Edward Wood Dunham, *The Arbitration Clause as Class Action Shield*, 16 FRANCHISE L.J. 141, 142 (1997) (encouraging franchisors to adopt arbitration agreements because binding arbitration is "one of the strongest pieces of armor" in protecting against class actions).

130 539 U.S. 444 (2003).

131 *Id.* at 452–53.

132 *See* Brief of the American Arbitration Association as Amicus Curiae in Support of Neither Party, Stolt-Nielsen S.A. v. AnimalFeeds Int'l Corp., 130 S. Ct. 1758 (2010), at 3–4. *See also* AMERICAN ARBITRATION ASSOCIATION, SUPPLEMENTARY RULES FOR CLASS ARBITRATIONS (effective October 8, 2003), *available at* http://www.adr.org/sp.asp?id=21936 (last visited July 31, 2011); JAMS CLASS ACTION PROCEDURES, *available at* http://www.jamsadr.com/rules-class-action-procedures/ (last visited July 31, 2011).

133 *Id.* at 22.

134 *See* Gilles, *supra* note 128, at 410; Sarah Clasby Engel & Sherry Tropin, *Class Action Arbitration: A Plaintiff's Perspective*, 5 FLA. INT'L U. L. REV. 145, 148 (2009).

amount to precluding enforcement of such claims or enforcing exculpatory contracts, increasingly began invalidating class arbitration waivers or entire arbitration agreements.[135]

5.09.3 **Stolt-Nielson** ***and agreements that are "silent" as to class arbitration***

In 2010, the Supreme Court returned to the issues raised in *Bazzle* in *Stolt-Nielsen S.A. v. AnimalFeeds Int'l Corp.*,[136] and once again seemed to change the ground rules governing class arbitration. Like *Bazzle, Stolt-Nielsen* concerned a defendant's argument that class arbitration was improper where the arbitration agreement was silent as to class arbitration. This time, however, the Court held that the arbitrator exceeded his powers in determining that class arbitration was permitted under the agreement where it was unambiguously "silent" as to class arbitration.[137] Arguably, this represents a departure from the presumption previously gleaned from *Bazzle*, whereby class arbitration was presumed to be available when the agreement was silent on the issue. Some commentators considered this perceived turnabout to be the death knell for a class arbitration movement that had only just taken off, as arbitration agreements are rarely drafted explicitly to permit class arbitration.[138]

However, *Stolt-Nielsen*'s impact has proven to be less severe than many anticipated. As the Second Circuit explained, the Supreme Court simply held that "a party may not be compelled under the FAA to submit to class arbitration unless there is a contractual basis for concluding that the party agreed to do so."[139] This is hardly novel. Further, the *Stolt-Nielsen* court's decision that the arbitrator had exceeded its power in requiring class arbitration was premised on the unusual fact that the parties had assertedly stipulated that "their agreement was 'silent' in the sense that they *had not reached any agreement* on the issue of class arbitration," thus preventing the conclusion that the parties had agreed to class arbitration.[140] In contrast, the Second Circuit concluded that nothing was amiss where an arbitrator construed a broad arbitration agreement providing the rights and remedies available in courts, but not specifically mentioning class arbitration, to mean that the parties intended to include the right to proceed as a class and to seek class remedies.[141] Far from it, a contrary reading "would fail to give effect to the employees' contractual

---

[135] *See, e.g., In re* Am. Express Merch. Litig., 634 F.3d 187, 199 (2d Cir. 2011) (arbitration provision unenforceable because class waiver would preclude plaintiffs from enforcing their federal statutory antitrust rights).

[136] 130 S. Ct. 1758 (2010).

[137] 130 S. Ct. at 1768–74.

[138] *See* Keerthi Sugumaran, *Comment: Arbitration—United States Supreme Court Sounds the Death Knell for Class Arbitration—Stolt-Nielsen S.A. v. Animal Feeds Int'l Corp., 130 S. Ct. 1758 (2010)*, 16 Suffolk J. Trial & App. Adv. 147 (2011); Lea Haber Kuck & Gregory A. Litt, *Will Stolt-Nielsen Push Consumer, Employment and Franchise Disputes Back Into the Courts?*, 4 N.Y. Dispute Resolution Lawyer 16 (Spring 2011) (noting that the decision "has been widely heralded as a death knell for class arbitration").

[139] Jock v. Sterling Jewelers Inc., 646 F.3d 113, 121 (2d Cir. July 1, 2011) (quoting *Stolt-Nielsen*, 130 S. Ct. at 1775).

[140] *Id.* at 120 (quoting *Stolt-Nielsen*, 130 S. Ct. at 1768) (emphasis added).

[141] *Id.* at 127.

rights and expectations" under the agreement.[142] Thus, unless parties have specifically stipulated that they did not reach an agreement regarding the availability of class arbitration, arbitrators may continue to engage in contractual interpretation in assessing whether an arbitration agreement that does not specifically reference class procedures provides for class arbitration.[143]

5.09.4 **Concepcion** *and the road ahead*

Finally, in April 2011, the Supreme Court again returned to the intersection of class actions and arbitration in *AT&T Mobility LLC v. Concepcion*.[144] *Concepcion* concerned a putative consumer class action alleging that AT&T engaged in false advertising and fraud by charging customers $30.22 in sales tax on phones advertised as free.[145] Before the district court, AT&T moved to compel individual arbitration, and the court denied the motion, finding that the class waiver rendered the agreement unconscionable under California law pursuant to the "*Discover Bank*" rule.[146] The *Discover Bank* rule classifies as unconscionable class waivers whenever three factors are present: (1) a consumer contract of adhesion; (2) settings with predictably small damages; and (3) an allegation that defendant engaged in a scheme to cheat large numbers of people out of individually small sums. The Ninth Circuit affirmed, rejecting AT&T's argument that the FAA preempted the *Discover Bank* rule.

A split court reversed and remanded, holding that the FAA preempted the state *Discover Bank* rule because "requiring the availability of classwide arbitration interferes with fundamental attributes of arbitration and thus creates a scheme inconsistent with the FAA."[147] Stating that the purpose of the FAA is to "ensure that private arbitration agreements are enforced according to their terms" so that parties may design "efficient, streamlined procedures tailored to the type of dispute," the Court reasoned that this objective would be frustrated by the *Discover Bank* rule "allow[ing] any party to a consumer contract to demand [class arbitration] *ex post*" in circumvention of the arbitration agreement.[148] Notably, the Court described the three factors purporting to limit the *Discover Bank* rule as "toothless and malleable," resulting in a bright line rule that simply "classif[ies] most

---

142 *Id.*

143 *See* Smith & Wollensky Restaurant Group v. Passow, 2011 U.S. Dist. LEXIS 4495 (D. Mass. Jan. 18, 2011) (*Stolt-Nielson* did not compel conclusion that arbitration agreement not referencing class proceedings did not permit class arbitration); Louisiana Health Svc. Indemnity Co. v. Gambro, 756 F. Supp.2d 760, 2010 U.S. Dist. LEXIS 135579 (W.D. Louisiana December 2, 2010) (arbitrator's determination that class arbitration was available was not inconsistent with *Stolt-Nielson* because arbitrator applied appropriate legal principles rather than relying on own policy preferences).

144 131 S. Ct. 1740 (2011).

145 131 S. Ct. at 1744.

146 *Id.* at 1745 (citing Discover Bank v. Superior Court, 113 P.3d 1100 (2005)).

147 *Id.* at 1748. Notably, the opinion did not uphold the validity of AT&T's arbitration agreement or class ban, but simply held that the *Discover Bank* rule applied by the lower courts to invalidate the ban was preempted by the FAA, and remanded the case for further proceedings. *Id.* at 1753.

148 *Id.* at 1748, 1750.

collective-arbitration waivers in consumer contracts as unconscionable."[149] The Court also quickly dismissed the dissent's arguments that California acted within its authority to regulate contracts in setting forth circumstances in which it would be reasonable to believe that the terms of a contract might operate to insulate the author from liability by discouraging small dollar claims.[150] The Court stated that even if some claims "might . . . slip through the legal system" without class proceedings, such possibility does not allow states to "require a procedure that is inconsistent with the FAA," and further that the record before the Court indicated that the *Concepcion* plaintiffs would be more than able to resolve their claims pursuant to the arbitration agreement.[151]

Many of those who did not already believe that *Stolt-Nielsen* had killed the class action seem to be convinced that *Concepcion* will ultimately complete the job.[152] Certainly, the opinion evinces considerable suspicion regarding class arbitration.[153] Moreover, the *Discover Bank* rule the Court struck down had been frequently applied to invalidate class waivers in consumer cases and therefore prevent corporations from effectively exculpating themselves from liability for small value violations of the law. However, *Concepcion* neither fully insulated class waivers nor closed the door on class proceedings confronting potential arbitration agreements. Particularly in the antitrust context, there are at least seven bases on which antitrust class actions may continue to thrive.

First, as discussed above, arbitration agreements that do not contain class waivers remain open to constructions that allow for class arbitration.[154]

Second, as the Second Circuit has recognized, *Concepcion* does not foreclose the "vindication of statutory rights" analysis that has been applied to successfully invalidate class waivers in the antitrust context.[155] The Supreme Court has repeatedly explained that compelled arbitration of statutory claims is permissible and consistent with the statutes providing for the underlying cause of action "so long as the litigant effectively may vindicate its statutory cause of action in the arbitral forum,"[156] and that conversely, if the enforcement of a pre-dispute arbitration agreement would operate to "preclude a litigant . . . from effectively vindicating her federal statutory rights in the arbitral forum,"[157] plaintiff's showing of such preclusion would indeed constitute a defense to enforcement of the arbitration clause. Following this doctrine, as well as noting Supreme Court authority recognizing that class proceedings are frequently essential to make prosecution of certain claims feasible,[158] the First and Second Circuits have declined to compel class plaintiffs to

---

149 *Id.* at 1746, 1750.

150 *See id.* at 1753.

151 *Id.*

152 *See, e.g.*, Editorial, *Gutting Class Actions*, N.Y. TIMES, May 13, 2011, at A26.

153 *See Concepcion*, 131 S. Ct. at 1752 (critiquing class arbitration for "greatly increas[ing] risk to defendants," including "the risk of 'in terrorem' settlements that class actions entail" and class arbitrations would similarly invite).

154 *See, e.g.*, Jock v. Sterling Jewelers Inc., 646 F.3d 113 (2d Cir. July 1, 2011).

155 *In re* American Express Merchants' Litig., 667 F.3d 204 (2d Cir. 2012).

156 *Gilmer*, 500 U.S. at 28 (quoting *Mitsubishi Motors Corp.*, 473 U.S. at 637).

157 Green Tree Financial Corp. v. Randolph, 531 U.S. 79, 90–91 (2000).

158 *See, e.g.*, Amchem Products, Inc. v. Windsor, 521 U.S. 591, 617 (1997) ("The policy at the very core of the class action mechanism is to overcome the problem that small recoveries do not provide the incentive for any individual to bring a solo action prosecuting his or her rights. A class

arbitrate antitrust claims where plaintiffs demonstrated that the individual arbitrations required under the arbitration agreement would be cost-prohibitive, and thus would prevent vindication of plaintiffs' statutory rights under the Sherman Act.[159] Moreover, the Second Circuit has specifically recognized that this doctrine survives *Concepcion*. In *In re American Express Merchants' Litigation*,[160] the Second Circuit considered the Supreme Court's decision in *Concepcion*, and concluded that it did not address the issue of "whether a class-action arbitration waiver clause is enforceable even if the plaintiffs are able to demonstrate that the practical effect of enforcement would be to preclude their ability to vindicate their federal statutory rights."[161] Indeed in *Conception*, there was no reason to address whether a class arbitration ban would be enforceable if it operated to preclude vindication of plaintiffs' rights, as no evidence had been presented demonstrating that plaintiffs would *not* be able to vindicate their claims through individual arbitration. To the contrary, the Court noted that the record demonstrated that plaintiffs' claims were "most unlikely to go unresolved," as both the district and circuit courts had concluded that the particular terms of the arbitration provision at issue provided "sufficient . . . incentive" for prosecution of individual claims and ensured that individual customers were "essentially guarantee[d] to be made whole."[162] Thus, as recognized in *In re American Express Merchants' Litigation*, the Supreme Court's decision in *Concepcion* does not disturb the line of cases holding that arbitration agreements are not enforceable if they operate to preclude vindication of a plaintiff's statutory rights.

Relatedly, *Concepcion* addressed only the preemption of *state* law by the FAA, and does not require enforcement of a class waiver under the FAA where doing so would conflict with *federal* law, such as the Sherman Act. Thus, the District Court for the Southern District of New York denied a motion to reconsider in light of *Concepcion* its order declining to enforce an arbitration agreement with class waiver, explaining that because plaintiff could not pursue her Title VII pattern or practice discrimination claim in individual arbitration, enforcing the agreement would present a conflict with federal law.[163] The Supreme Court's application of preemption analysis to a state law conflict in

---

action solves this problem by aggregating the relatively paltry potential recoveries into something worth someone's (usually an attorney's) labor.").

[159] *See* Kristian v. Comcast Corp., 446 F.3d 25, 55–61 (1st Cir. 2006) (applying the vindication of statutory rights analysis in invalidating and severing a class ban in arbitration agreement in arbitration suit where expert expenses and attorney's fees would significantly outweigh individual recovery); *In re* American Express Merchants' Litig., 667 F.3d 204 (2d Cir. 2012) (holding that an arbitration agreement containing a class waiver was unenforceable in antitrust suit because "the evidence . . . . establishes, as a matter of law, that the costs of plaintiffs' individually arbitrating their dispute . . . . would be prohibitive, effectively depriving plaintiffs of the statutory protections of the antitrust laws"); *see also* Dale v. Comcast Corp, 498 F.3d 1216 (11th Cir. 2007) (applying Georgia unconscionability law in finding a class waiver unenforceable in Cable Act suit, but utilizing the vindication of statutory rights analysis and relying on findings that plaintiffs would "effectively be precluded" from vindicating their claims if limited to individual claims due to the high costs of bringing a claim relative to the potential recovery).

[160] 667 F.3d 204 (2d Cir. 2012).

[161] *Id.*

[162] *Concepcion*, 131 S. Ct. at 1753 (internal quotations omitted).

[163] Chen-Oster v. Goldman Sachs & Co, No. 1:10-cv-06950, 2011 U.S. Dist. LEXIS 73200 (S.D.N.Y. July 11, 2011). The United States Department of Labor and Equal Employment

Concepcion does not determine how potential conflicts between the FAA and federal law should be resolved.[164]

Third, *Concepcion*'s holding that the *Discover Bank* unconscionability rule adopted in California was preempted by the FAA certainly does not eliminate all unconscionability challenges to class arbitration waivers. Rather, the Court found that the *Discover Bank* rule was inconsistent with the purposes of the FAA because it understood the rule to broadly permit any party to a consumer contract to "ex post" reject the terms of an otherwise valid arbitration agreement and to unilaterally demand class arbitration. Unconscionability remains a valid defense to contracts and a basis for invalidation of an arbitration agreement under the FAA, and unconscionability determinations based on other considerations, including a demonstrated inability for a plaintiff to vindicate rights under a class arbitration waiver, should survive *Concepcion*.[165]

However, the scope of state challenges remaining after *Concepcion* clearly will be actively litigated for years to come throughout state and federal courts. Already, though some courts appear to be appropriately limiting *Concepcion* to the context of the mechanical state rule addressed, others have read the opinion to broadly preclude arguments that class waivers are unconscionable where they would deter large numbers of claims and act to exculpate the drafter – even where plaintiffs have introduced evidence of a strong exculpatory effect.[166] Such decisions are not mandated by *Concepcion*, which struck down a broad state rule that required no evidence of such exculpation, and where no such evidence was in the record.

Opportunities Commission have recently advanced the arguments adopted in *Chen-Oster*, and argued that class arbitration waivers are unenforceable if they would prevent vindication of statutory rights even after *Concepcion*. *See* Brief of the Secretary of Labor and EEOC as Amici Curiae, D.R. Horton, Inc. v. Cuda, No. 12-CA-25764 (filed before the National Labor Relations Board, July 27, 2011).

164 *See also In re* American Express Merchants' Litig., 667 F.3d 204 (2d Cir. 2012) ("*Concepcion* plainly offers a path for analyzing whether a state contract law is preempted by the FAA. Here, however, our holding rests squarely on a vindication of statutory rights analysis, which is part of the federal substantive law of arbitrablity.") (internal quotation omitted).

165 *See* Hamby v. Power Toyota Irvine, No. 11cv544-BTM (S.D. Cal. July 18, 2011) (allowing plaintiff to conduct discovery on issue of whether the arbitration agreement and class arbitration ban are unconscionable, and explaining that *Concepcion* "does not stand for the proposition that a party can never oppose arbitration on the ground that the arbitration clause is unconscionable"); *In re* Checking Account Overdraft Litig., No. 09-MD-02036-JLK (S.D. Fla. June 3, 2011) (permitting discovery pertaining to viability of individual arbitration before ruling on motion to compel arbitration). Similarly, where plaintiffs can show that significant procedural unconscionability infects the class waiver, particularly where other aspects of the arbitration agreement may combine to demonstrate substantive one-sidedness, unconscionability should remain a valid defense to individual arbitration. *See, e.g.*, Skirchak v. Dynamics Research Corp., 508 F.3d 49, 63 (1st Cir. 2007) (class action waiver buried in email attachment to employees was unconscionable where body of email indicated that the attachment did not limit or change employees legal rights and non-response was considered acceptance).

166 *See* Cruz v. Cingular Wireless, LCC, No. 07-00714-cv FTM 29 DNF, 2011 U.S. App. LEXIS 16811 (11th Cir. Aug. 11, 2011) (considering same arbitration agreement at issue in *Concepcion*, and concluding the plaintiffs' evidence that class waiver would cause most claims to slip through cracks, exculpating defendant, only provided support for the policy argument against enforcement rejected in *Concepcion*).

Still other courts also have misunderstood *Concepcion*'s scope. For example, a Colorado district court expressed sympathy for plaintiffs who asserted that they would not be able to pursue their claims at all if compelled to arbitrate individually, but reasoned that the *Concepcion* Court "considered the fact that the Concepcions and other class plaintiffs would be denied any recovery by its ruling, and ruled against the plaintiffs nonetheless," thus leaving the court "bound" to compel arbitration even where it would limit plaintiffs ability to recover.[167] However, *Concepcion* did not include such an analysis and does not bind courts to such a harsh rule; to the contrary, the *Concepcion* Court emphasized that the plaintiffs' claims "were most unlikely to go unresolved" and that both the district and circuit courts had found the arbitral scheme sufficient to ensure prosecution of plaintiffs' claims and permit full relief.

Fourth, although antitrust claims are generally arbitrable, in some cases plaintiffs' claims may not fall within the scope of the relevant arbitration agreement, thus allowing class action litigation to proceed. Arbitration agreements generally include broad language requiring arbitration of "all disputes arising out of" or "relating to" a contract or a relationship created through contract, and such language is generally construed liberally in accordance with the Supreme Court's repeated admonition that any doubts about the scope of arbitrable issues should be resolved in favor of arbitration.[168] However, in some instances antitrust claims have been found to fall outside the scope of the arbitration agreement. For example, in *AlliedSignal, Inc. v. B.F. Goodrich Co.*,[169] the Seventh Circuit held that a Clayton Act claim asserting injury from inflated prices was not within the scope of an arbitration provision because the underlying contract did not regulate pricing. Similarly, in *Coors Brewing Co. v. Molson Breweries*,[170] the Tenth Circuit held that while some of Coors' antitrust claims against licensee Molson were governed by an arbitration clause, others were not because they did not relate to the parties' underlying license agreement. The viability of such an argument in any given case will of course turn on the language of the arbitration provision setting forth its scope, as well as the relationship between the underlying contract and the claims asserted.

Fifth, though corporations will increasingly seek to include arbitration agreements with explicit class waivers in consumer, employment, franchise, supply, and other contracts likely to provide exposure to class actions following *Concepcion*, that process will take time. *Concepcion* will not work an instant change, and defendants generally may not impose a new class ban on members of a putative class after litigation has commenced.[171] Further, if litigation has already commenced and a defendant has not timely

---

167 Bernal v. Burnett, 2011 U.S. Dist. LEXIS 59829, at *20 (D. Colo. June 6, 2011).

168 *See* JLM Indus. v. Stolt-Nielsen *SA*, 387 F.3d 163, 171-76 (2d Cir. 2004) (price-fixing claims fell within scope of arbitration clause in standard contracts because injuries alleged resulted from entering into the contracts).

169 183 F.3d 568, 573 (7th Cir. 1999).

170 51 F.3d 1511, 1515-16 (10th Cir. 1995).

171 *See* Williams v. Securitas Sec. Servs. USA, Inc., No. 10-7181, 2011 U.S. Dist. LEXIS 75502, (July 13, 2011) (ordering defendant to rescind class and collective action waiver agreement sent to employees after some employees filed collective claims under the Fair Labor Standards Act, and concluding that *Concepcion* did not preclude determination that the agreement constituted an unfair and confusing communication to possible plaintiffs In violation of FLSA); *In re* Currency Conversion Fee Antitrust Litig., 361 F. Supp. 2d 237 (S.D.N.Y. 2005) (refusing enforcement of

asserted its right to arbitrate, such right may be forfeited.[172] That being said, defendants are now well aware of the value of compelling arbitration where doing so may prevent class proceedings, and businesses are fast incorporating arbitration clauses with class bans into their contracts and forms. The Wall Street Journal noted mere months after *Concepcion* that, "emboldened" by the Supreme Court's decision, "some small and regional U.S. banks are prohibiting unhappy customers from taking their complaints to court or joining class-action lawsuits, instead resolving them to resolve disputes through arbitration."[173]

Sixth, mandatory arbitration provisions may not be included in certain types of contracts, limiting corporations' ability to insert class waivers or other potentially exculpatory provisions. Federal law expressly prohibits inclusion of mandatory arbitration agreements in specific contract types, including franchise agreements between automobile manufacturers and dealers,[174] and residential mortgage loans.[175] Further, many courts have held that because the McCarran Ferguson Act[176] authorized states to regulate the business of insurance and bars application of federal law to supersede state law governing insurance, states may ban or limit the use of arbitration clauses in insurance agreements without running afoul of the FAA.[177] Many states have thus prohibited insurance companies from using mandatory arbitration clauses; *Concepcion* does not impact the validity of such state laws.[178]

Seventh and finally, in many putative antitrust class actions, there simply is no contractual relationship between plaintiffs and certain non-signatory defendants, and thus no opportunity to include an arbitration agreement banning class procedures.[179] For example, in *Ross v. Am. Express Co.*,[180] plaintiff holders of Visa, Mastercard, and Diners' Club credit cards filed suit against American Express and certain other defendants alleging participation in an antitrust conspiracy to charge inflated fees on certain transactions. The Second

---

class action bans mailed by defendant to members of putative class); H&R Block, Inc. v. Haese, 82 S.W.3d 331, 333, 336 (Tex. App. 2002) (refusing enforcement of class ban incorporated after class action was filed, as such action constituted "an unauthorized, impermissible, knowing and intentional communication with members of the plaintiff class" that would "obstruct the trial court in discharge of its duty to protect the plaintiff class"); Bilbrey v. Cingular Wireless LLC, 164 P.3d 131, 134 (Okla. 2007) (finding unconscionable and refusing to enforce retroactive arbitration clause banning class proceedings contained in a lengthy form contract of adhesion plaintiff signed long after initiating class action).

[172] *See* Zuckerman Spaeder, LLP v. Auffenberg, 646 F.3d 919, 2011 U.S. App. LEXIS 15661, 8-9 (D.C. Cir. July 29, 2011) (finding defendant forfeited right to compel arbitration by not asserting it "at the first available opportunity" and prejudicing opposing party). Nino v. Jewelry Exchange, Inc., 609 F.3d 191, 208 (3d Cir. 2010) (same); Lewallen v. Green Tree Serv. LLC, 487 F.3d 1085, 1090 (8th Cir. 2007) (same).

[173] Robin Sidell, *No Day in Court for Bank Clients*, The Wall Street Journal, August 2, 2011.

[174] 15 U.S.C. § 1226.

[175] 15 U.S.C. § 1639c(e)(1).

[176] 15 U.S.C. § 1012(b).

[177] *See* McKnight v. Chi. Title Ins. Co., 358 F.3d 854, 859 (11th Cir. 2004).

[178] *See, e.g.*, *Lawson v. Life of South*, No. 4:06-cv-00042, 2011 U.S. App. LEXIS 16412, *31 33 (11th Cir. Aug. 10, 2011) (Pryor, J. concurring).

[179] *See* National Consumer Law Center, *Life After Concepcion*, 29 NCLC Reports 21, 23 (March/April 2011).

[180] 547 F.3d 137 (2d Cir. 2008).

Circuit held that because defendants were not parties to the cardholder agreements and had no direct contractual relationship with the cardholders, defendants could not avail themselves of the arbitration clauses in plaintiffs' cardholder agreements or otherwise compel plaintiffs to arbitrate the dispute with them in the absence of plaintiffs' agreement.[181] Similarly, many states permit indirect purchaser suits under state antitrust law, and in such situations there may be no contractual relationship, and thus no arbitration agreement to bind the parties.[182]

---

[181] *See also* Lawson v. Life of South, No. 4:06-cv-00042, 2011 U.S. App. LEXIS 16412 (11th Cir. Aug. 10, 2011) (denying non-signatory defendant's motion to compel arbitration pursuant to arbitration agreement plaintiffs entered with third party, and rejecting defendant's argument that it could compel arbitration under equitable estoppel and third-party beneficiary theories); *but see In re* Wholesale Grocery Products Antitrust Litig., No. 0:09-cvi00983-ADM-AJB (D. Minn. July 5, 2011) (declining to follow *Ross v. Am. Express Co.*, and holding that plaintiffs were bound to arbitrate their claims against the non-signatory under the doctrine of equitable estoppel because (1) the claims allege "substantially interdependent and concerted misconduct between the non-signatory defendant and a signatory to the arbitration agreement"; and (2) the claims are "intimately founded in and intertwined with" the arbitration agreement).

[182] Only direct purchasers, who will be bound by a contract and likely an arbitration agreement, may bring claims based on federal antitrust laws under *Illinois Brick Co. v. Illinois*, 431 U.S. 720 (1976). There is continuing debate over whether *Illinois Brick* is good or bad policy. To the extent that the introduction of arbitration agreements into direct purchaser agreements will hinder private enforcement of antitrust laws, that may ultimately provide additional support for the viewpoint, expressed by the Antitrust Modernization Commission four years ago, that *Illinois Brick* should be overruled. *See* Antitrust Modernization Commission, Report and Recommendations 270 (April 2007).

6 Procedural defenses short of trial

Jonathan L. Rubin[1]

[1] Managing Member, Rubin PLLC, Washington, D.C. The author is an attorney and Ph.D economist specializing in antitrust litigation and counseling and is solely responsible for the contents of this chapter. He may be contacted at jr@rubinpllc.net.

§ 6.01 Introduction

Defendants in civil antitrust lawsuits brought in the U.S. federal courts have several opportunities short of a trial on the merits by which to dispose of claims against them. This chapter concerns three categories of defenses: (1) challenges to the court's subject matter jurisdiction, (2) defenses available by pre-answer motion, and (3) pre-trial summary proceedings and affirmative defenses. The next chapter in this Handbook deals with discovery issues under the Federal Rules of Civil Procedure.

Rule 12 of the Federal Rules of Civil Procedure[2] governs the presentment of defenses and the timing and nature of the responsive pleading required of a defendant after being legally notified of a suit filed against it (the "service of process"[3]). Rule 12(a) requires a defendant to serve a responsive pleading answering the allegations in the complaint and alleging the affirmative defenses the defendant intends to raise within 21 days after service of process. The time to respond to a complaint may be extended to 60 days (or 90 days for defendants not found in any U.S. judicial district) if the defendant acknowledges notice of the suit and waives objections to the form or manner of service of process.[4]

At a minimum the responsive pleading must answer the allegations in the complaint by either denying or admitting the truth of each allegation. In addition, certain defenses may be waived if not presented when the answer is due. Moreover, a defendant may waive compulsory or permissive counterclaims or cross-claims not pleaded when the answer is due.

Certain defenses, enumerated in Rules 12(b)(1)–(7), may be raised in a motion that extends the time for the responsive pleading until the expiration of 14 days after a ruling on the motion. Defendants frequently interpose a Rule 12(b) "pre-answer" motion precisely because it tolls the time in which to serve a responsive pleading. The list of defenses that may be raised in a pre-answer motion is non-exhaustive. Generally speaking, Rule 12(b) defenses require little or no inquiry beyond the pleadings, self-authenticating documents, or matters of public record.

---

2 The Federal Rules of Civil Procedure, which govern procedure, practice and evidence in the federal courts, are referred to hereinafter as the "Rules" or "Rule ___." The federal courts also promulgate "Local Rules" that codify the customary practice before that particular court for implementing the Rules. Congress authorizes the federal judiciary to promulgate the Rules in the Rules Enabling Act, 28 U.S.C. §§ 2071–77. Effective December 1, 2007, the Rules underwent a plenary revision in style and the sample forms were rewritten. Practitioners should be aware of numbering changes when conducting legal research on a particular Rule.

3 Service of process customarily consists of a summons issued by the court clerk and a complete copy of the complaint or petition personally delivered to an individual defendant or to the agent designated by a defendant business entity.

4 Rule 12(a)(1)(A)(ii).

The principal exception to this is found in the first of these defenses in Rule 12(b)(1), regarding lack of subject matter jurisdiction. Rule 12(b)(1) motions differ from motions based on the other pre-answer defenses in several important respects. First, because courts are never permitted to adjudicate claims for which subject matter jurisdiction is lacking, the court must dismiss an action at *any time* it is determined that it lacks subject matter jurisdiction, a principle embodied in Rule 12(h)(3). Thus, determinations of subject matter jurisdiction may arise not only on a Rule 12(b)(1) motion but at any stage of the litigation. Second, because courts cannot decide claims over which subject matter jurisdiction is lacking, dismissal on Rule 12(b)(1) grounds does not have the effect of a final decision on the merits of the claim, as does a final order of dismissal on other grounds, such as Rule 12(b)(6) grounds of failure to state a justiciable cause of action. Finally, the responsibility to establish subject matter jurisdiction lies with the plaintiff. Therefore, even though a challenge to jurisdiction may be raised by the defendant in a 12(b)(1) motion, the plaintiff will carry the burden of persuasion. Rule 12(b)(1) challenges to subject matter jurisdiction are the subject of Section 6.02 of this chapter.

Section 6.03 addresses the remaining procedural defenses permitted to be raised in a Rule 12(b) pre-answer motion. Two of these defenses – failure to state a claim upon which relief may be granted (Rule 12(b)(6)) and failure to join a required party to the lawsuit (Rule 12(b)(7)) – may, but need not be, raised in a Rule 12(b) pre-answer motion because they cannot be waived. A claim that the complaint fails to state a claim upon which relief may be granted is a demurrer, which tests the sufficiency of the pleaded allegations or challenges the plaintiff's legal right to prosecute the claim on the facts alleged. Rule 12(b)(6) and (7) defenses also may be raised for the first time later in the litigation, for example, in any pleading allowed by Rule 7(a), in a motion for judgment on the pleadings under Rule 12(c), or at trial, and may be heard and ruled upon at the court's discretion any time up to and including at trial.

The remaining defenses that may be raised in a pre-answer motion, listed in Rules 12(b)(2)–(5), are challenges to the court's jurisdiction over the defendant's "person,"[5] challenges concerning improper venue,[6] and challenges to the issuance of the court's summons or to the manner in which it was served upon the defendant.[7] These defenses may be waived if not raised in a timely manner, so they are customarily raised in a Rule 12(b) pre-answer motion.

Section 6.04 discusses the defensive use of summary proceedings for summary judgment or pretrial adjudication of affirmative defenses. A defendant can prevail on summary judgment if the parties' submissions demonstrate the absence of any disputed material issue of fact for determination at trial. A non-exhaustive list of affirmative defenses, which are also frequently determined on a motion for summary judgment, is set out in Rule 8(c).[8]

---

5 Rule 12(b)(2).

6 Rule 12(b)(3).

7 Rules 12(b)(4) and 12(b)(5).

8 The enumerated defenses are: accord and satisfaction; arbitration and award; assumption of risk; contributory negligence; discharge in bankruptcy; duress; estoppel; failure of consideration; fraud; illegality; injury by fellow servant; laches; license; payment; release; res judicata; statute of frauds; statute of limitations; and waiver.

§ 6.02 Dismissal for lack of subject matter jurisdiction

A federal court is a forum of limited jurisdiction with authority under Article III of the Constitution to hear only live "cases or controversies" involving specifically enumerated federal subject matter.[9] In addition, federal courts require statutory or common law authority to hear and decide the dispute before them, as they have only the authority granted to them by Article III and Acts of Congress. These requirements delineate the subject matter jurisdiction of the federal courts and suggest two types of subject matter jurisdictional challenges. The first type, discussed in Section 6.02.1, is a challenge to Article III jurisdiction, frequently couched in terms of the plaintiff's lack of "Article III standing" to bring the case.[10] The second type of challenge to subject matter jurisdiction is an attack on the common law or statutory basis upon which the action is brought. This type of challenge depends on the authority relied upon by the plaintiff to sue in federal court. Challenges to federal question jurisdiction are discussed in Section 6.02.1, to diversity jurisdiction in Section 6.02.2, and to supplemental jurisdiction in Section 6.02.3.

A lack of subject matter jurisdiction may never be waived by any party, nor may a party be estopped from asserting it or consent to submit to jurisdiction where none exists. Thus, while subject matter jurisdictional challenges may be raised by a Rule 12(b)(1) pre-answer motion well before trial, the defendants may also move for dismissal or suggest a lack of subject matter jurisdiction at any time the claim is pending, either before trial, at trial, or on appeal.

Rule 8(a)(1) specifies that a statement of a claim for relief must contain "a short and plain statement of the grounds for the court's jurisdiction . . . ." This jurisdictional pleading requirement applies only to subject matter jurisdiction, and not to jurisdiction over the person, or *in personam* jurisdiction.[11]

The plaintiff bears the burden of establishing subject matter jurisdiction, even though it may be challenged in the defendant's Rule 12(b)(1) pre-answer motion (or Rule 12(c) pre-trial motion for judgment on the pleadings).[12] In reviewing a *facial* challenge on a Rule 12(b)(1) or 12(c) motion, the court is limited to the allegations in the complaint (which are presumed to be true), the documents referred to in or attached to the complaint, and matters of public record.[13] In reviewing a *factual* challenge to subject matter jurisdiction, the court is not limited to the allegations in the complaint and the presumption of truthfulness does not attach to the complaint. The challenge is heard at an evidentiary hearing on a Rule 12(b)(1) motion or as an affirmative defense subject to proof on a Rule 56 motion for summary judgment or at trial. Where the subject matter jurisdiction challenge

---

[9] State trial courts, by contrast, are considered courts of "general jurisdiction," with presumptive common law jurisdiction to hear all civil disputes concerning persons, properties, or activities affecting the state.

[10] "Article III standing," which is necessary to establish subject matter jurisdiction, should not be confused with "antitrust standing," which is an element of a private antitrust cause of action. A challenge to the latter is properly raised in a Rule 12(b)(6) motion, *see* Section 6.03.1(d), below. For a full discussion of antitrust standing, see Chapter 3 of this Handbook.

[11] *See* Caribbean Broadcasting System, Ltd. v. Cable & Wireless PLC, 148 F.3d 1080, 1090 (D.C. Cir. 1998) (antitrust plaintiff not required to plead the basis of *in personam* jurisdiction).

[12] Kokkonen v. Guardian Life Ins. Co. of America, 511 U.S. 375 (1994).

[13] Gould Electronics Inc., v. U.S., 220 F.3d 169, 176 (3d Cir. 2000).

depends on significant issues of fact, the court may order the defendant to file a responsive pleading and defer a decision on the pre-answer Rule 12(b)(1) motion until later in the proceedings to allow a more fulsome factual record to develop.

6.02.1 Challenges to Article III jurisdiction

Article III of the U.S. Constitution confines the federal courts to adjudicating actual "cases" and "controversies."[14] Claims that do not satisfy the case-or-controversy requirement can be said to be "constitutionally non-justiciable." At its core, constitutional justiciability is a limitation of federal judicial power "to a role consistent with a system of separated powers and which are traditionally thought to be capable of resolution through the judicial process."[15] The courts have developed a series of justiciability doctrines to give meaning to the Article III case-or-controversy requirement, the most important of which is the doctrine that requires a litigant to have "standing" to invoke the jurisdiction of a federal court.

6.02.1(A) Constitutional standing

In order to demonstrate Article III standing a plaintiff must allege three elements. First, there must be a concrete and particularized injury and actual or imminent rather than conjectural or hypothetical harm (i.e., an "injury in fact"); second, the alleged injury must fairly be traceable to the defendant's conduct and not the result of the independent action of a third party; third, the plaintiff must allege that a favorable federal court decision is likely to redress the alleged injury.[16]

6.02.1(B) Ripeness

A second justiciability doctrine under Article III jurisprudence is ripeness. Ripeness separates those matters that are premature because the injury is speculative and may never occur from those that are appropriate for the court's review.[17]

An issue that sometimes arises in antitrust cases is whether the alleged economic injury is sufficiently actual to satisfy the injury-in-fact prong of Article III standing or is sufficiently ripe for adjudication. An allegation that the plaintiff paid supra-competitive prices in a market affected by anticompetitive conduct is generally sufficient to allege an injury in fact. An allegation that the plaintiff may be required to pay supra-competitive prices in the future may not be sufficient.

6.02.1(C) Fitness for judicial resolution and the political question doctrine

Article III jurisdiction is further limited to issues that are fit for judicial resolution. This requires that the plaintiff has suffered "an invasion of a legally protected interest,"[18] which is "traditionally thought to be capable of resolution through the judicial process."[19]

---

[14] U.S. CONST. art. III, § 2.

[15] Flast v. Cohen, 392 U.S. 83, 97 (1968).

[16] Lujan v. Defenders of Wildlife, 504 U.S. 555, 560–61 (1992).

[17] Abbott Laboratories v. Gardner, 387 U.S. 136, 148, (1967), *overruled on other grounds*, Califano v. Sanders, 430 U.S. 99 (1977).

[18] *Lujan*, 504 U.S. at 560.

[19] *Flast*, 392 U.S. at 97.

An example of an antitrust case determined recently to be constitutionally non-justiciable is *Spectrum Stores, Inc. v. Citgo Petroleum Corp.*,[20] in which U.S. domestic oil companies stood accused of participating with the Organization of Petroleum Exporting Countries (OPEC) in the planning and execution of output restrictions and other concerted conduct allegedly prohibited by § 1 of the Sherman Act. The defendants moved to dismiss under Rule 12(b)(1) for lack of subject matter jurisdiction on the grounds that the case presented a non-justiciable political question of foreign policy reserved to the Executive Branch and unfit for judicial resolution. The plaintiffs instead urged the court to treat the matter as a Rule 12(b)(6) motion to dismiss for failure to state a claim upon which relief may be granted.

The Fifth Circuit held that the "concept of justiciability, as embodied in the political question doctrine, expresses the jurisdictional limitations imposed upon federal courts by the 'case or controversy' requirement of Article III."[21] By contrast, the act of state doctrine, which the defendants also raised, provides foreign states with a substantive defense on the merits and does not implicate the court's power to hear the case. Accordingly, the political question doctrine is properly raised in a Rule 12(b)(1) motion, while a challenge based on the act of state doctrine is not.[22]

6.02.1(D) Rule 12(b)(1) and 12(b)(6) motions distinguished

It deserves emphasis that a Rule 12(b)(1) challenge to Article III jurisdiction based on a lack of constitutional standing, ripeness, or judicial fitness implicates the court's power to hear the case[23] and that these grounds for dismissal should be distinguished from the grounds of a lack of "antitrust standing" or "justiciability" that may be raised in a motion under Rule 12(b)(6), which challenges the sufficiency of the complaint. The Supreme Court in recent years has sought to disentangle the "two sometimes confused or conflated concepts: federal court 'subject-matter' jurisdiction over a controversy; and the essential ingredients of a federal claim for relief."[24] The difference can be consequential. Where subject matter jurisdiction is lacking, it cannot be waived, and a motion raising the issue may be brought by a party or by a court on its own initiative at any stage in the litigation, even after trial and the entry of judgment. Moreover, dismissal on subject matter grounds does not operate as a decision on the merits. The motion may or may not require a determination of facts and the plaintiff bears the burden of establishing subject matter jurisdiction in the first instance.

By contrast, raising a non-jurisdictional statutory deficiency in a Rule 12(b)(6) motion to dismiss challenges the sufficiency of the pleading, requiring an inquiry confined to the allegations in the complaint. The burden of establishing the deficiency rests with the movant. The difference, as one court has observed, stems from the distinction between two sources of congressional authority: "the constitutional authority to delineate the subject

---

20 632 F.3d 938 (5th Cir. 2011).

21 *Id.* at 948 (citation and alteration omitted); see also *id.* at 949 (citing the "six independent tests for the existence of a political question" described in Baker v. Carr, 369 U.S. 186, 217 (1962)) *and* Vieth v. Jubelirer, 541 U.S. 267, 277 (2004) (same).

22 *Spectrum Stores*, 632 F.3d at 948.

23 Morrison v. National Australia Bank, Ltd., 130 S.Ct. 2869, 2877 (2010).

24 Arbaugh v. Y&H Corp. 546 U.S. 500, 503 (2006).

matter jurisdiction of the lower courts" under Article III and "the constitutional authority to set forth the elements of a successful claim for relief."[25]

To differentiate between the two kinds of statutory limitations the Supreme Court in *Arbaugh v. Y&H Corp.*[26] adopted the "clear-statement rule:" a statutory provision establishes a jurisdictional limitation on the court only if the statutory text clearly says so. The *Arbaugh* Court held that unless the Legislature "clearly states that a threshold limitation on a statute's scope shall count as jurisdictional, . . . courts should treat the restriction as nonjurisdictional in character."[27]

An exception to the "clear-statement rule" arises in connection with the expiration of time limits in which to file suit or a notice of appeal. Procedural deadlines that customarily have been regarded as jurisdictional in nature by the Supreme Court (in contrast to lower federal courts) continue to be so.[28]

6.02.1(E) FTAIA NOT JURISDICTIONAL

One consequence of the line of jurisprudence that distinguishes subject matter jurisdictional challenges from non-jurisdictional defenses on the merits has been a clarification of the nature of a challenge to an antitrust action on the grounds that the violation alleged is removed from the purview of the antitrust laws by the Foreign Trade Antitrust Improvements Act of 1982 (FTAIA).[29] The FTAIA withdraws the right of a private antitrust action for "conduct involving trade or commerce (other than import trade or import commerce) with foreign nations" unless the domestic effects specified in the statute are established.

In *Animal Science Products, Inc. v. China Minmetals Corp.*[30] the Third Circuit held that "in enacting the FTAIA, Congress legislated pursuant to its Commerce Clause authority to articulate substantive elements that a plaintiff must satisfy to assert a meritorious claim for antitrust relief" and not "pursuant to its Article III powers to define the jurisdiction of the federal courts."[31] The court observed that "[t]he FTAIA neither speaks

---

[25] Animal Science Products, Inc. v. China Minmetals Corp., No. 10-2288, 2011 WL 3606995 (3d Cir. Aug.17, 2011). See also, *Baker v. Carr*, 369 U.S. 186, 198 (1962), distinguishing between these two categories of defenses:

> First: That the facts and injury alleged, the legal bases invoked as creating the rights and duties relied upon, and the relief sought, fail to come within that language of Article III of the Constitution and of the jurisdictional statutes which define those matters concerning which United States District Courts are empowered to act,
> Second: That, although the matter is cognizable and facts are alleged which establish infringement of appellants' rights . . . the court will not proceed because the matter is considered unsuited to judicial inquiry or adjustment.
> We treat the first ground of dismissal as "lack of jurisdiction of the subject matter." The second we consider to result in a failure to state a justiciable cause of action.

[26] 546 U.S. 500 (2006).

[27] *Id.* at 560–61.

[28] Bowles v. Russell, 551 U.S. 205 (2007); *see also* Reed Elsevier, Inc. v. Muchnick, 559 U.S., 130 S. Ct. 1237 (2010) (Ginsburg, J., concurring).

[29] § 7 of the Sherman Act, 15 U.S.C. § 6a.

[30] No. 10-2288, 2011 WL 3606995 (3rd Cir. Aug.17, 2011).

[31] *Id.* at *3.

in jurisdictional terms nor refers in any way to the jurisdiction of the district courts."[32] It seems likely that other federal Circuits will follow the Third Circuit.[33] Accordingly, a challenge on FTAIA grounds should be brought as a Rule 12(b)(6) motion to dismiss for failure to state a claim for which relief may be granted rather than as a Rule 12(b)(1) challenge to subject matter jurisdiction.

6.02.2 Challenges to federal question jurisdiction

In addition to challenges to the court's Article III jurisdiction a defendant may challenge the statutory basis for subject matter jurisdiction claimed by the plaintiff. There are four statutory grounds for subject matter jurisdiction:

- federal question jurisdiction;
- diversity of citizenship jurisdiction;
- admiralty jurisdiction; and
- supplemental jurisdiction.

Private federal civil antitrust claims are properly based on federal question jurisdiction, but in appropriate circumstances diversity jurisdiction may provide an additional statutory basis for jurisdiction, or establish federal jurisdiction over antitrust claims based on state law, including certain class actions. Antitrust claims do not arise in admiralty. This Subpart is devoted to challenges to federal question jurisdiction. Sections dealing with challenges to diversity and supplemental subject matter jurisdiction follow.

6.02.2 (A) Statutes authorizing a private right of action

Congress in 28 U.S.C. § 1331 authorizes the federal district courts to hear "all civil actions arising under the Constitution, laws, or treaties of the United States."[34] This jurisdiction also encompasses claims arising under federal common law, such as contract disputes with the federal government.[35] The broad grant of federal subject matter jurisdiction in § 1331 overlaps with other statutes, in which jurisdiction is granted to the district courts to hear particular private causes of action in specific areas of federal law. In the field of antitrust, 28 U.S.C. § 1337(a) authorizes the district courts to hear "any civil action or proceeding arising under any Act of Congress regulating commerce or protecting trade and commerce against restraints and monopolies. . . ."[36] In addition, § 4 of the Clayton Act, 15 U.S.C. § 15, provides that:

---

[32] *Id.*

[33] *See, e.g.*, Minn-Chem, Inc. v. Agrium Inc., 657 F. 3d 650 (2011) (recognizing the probable error in the *en banc* majority opinion in United Phosphorus Ltd. v. Angus Chemical Co., 322 F.3d 942 (7th Cir. 2003), but reserving overruling it for another day, seeing no need to remand "to apply 'a new Rule 12(b)(6) label [to] the same Rule 12(b)(1) conclusion'" that requires dismissal of the case on FTAIA grounds (quoting *Morrison*, 130 S.Ct. at 2877 (alteration in original))).

[34] 28 U.S.C. § 1331.

[35] Up State Federal Credit Union v. Walker, 198 F.3d 372, 375 n.4 (2d Cir. 1999).

[36] 28 U.S.C. § 1337(a).

> [A]ny person who shall be injured in his business or property by reason of anything forbidden in the antitrust laws may sue therefor in any district court of the United States in the district in which the defendant resides or is found or has an agent without respect to the amount in controversy, and shall recover threefold the damages by him sustained, and the cost of suit, including a reasonable attorney's fee . . . .

The statute thus grants an express private right of action in a district court for treble damages plus a reasonable attorney's fee to "any person" injured in his "business or property" by reason of conduct "forbidden in the antitrust laws." An antitrust treble damages complaint that states, "This court has subject matter jurisdiction over the federal antitrust claims asserted in this action under § 4 of the Clayton Act, 15 U.S.C. § 15, and Title 28 U.S.C. §§ 1331 and 1337," satisfies the pleading requirement of Rule 8(a)(1) for a "short and plain statement of the grounds for the court's jurisdiction," provided the balance of the pleading purports to set forth one or more claims based on conduct "forbidden in the antitrust laws."

Substantive antitrust violations include price fixing or cartelization, or the allocation of product lines, territories, customers, or market share, forbidden by § 1 of the Sherman Act, 15 U.S.C. § 1, or monopolization, monopoly maintenance, or attempted monopoly, forbidden by § 2, 15 U.S.C. § 2. Other substantive violations for which a private cause of action is available include price discrimination in the sale of goods in violation of § 2 of the Clayton Act, 15 U.S.C. § 13, commodity prices, discounts or rebates conditioned on an agreement not to deal with competitors in violation of § 3 of the Clayton Act, 15 U.S.C. § 14, or damages legally caused by an unlawful merger in violation of § 7 of the Clayton Act, 15 U.S.C. § 18.[37]

Plaintiffs sometimes seek an injunction to prevent a threatened antitrust injury. Section 16 of the Clayton Act, 15 U.S.C. § 26, authorizes private parties to "sue for and have injunctive relief . . . against threatened loss or damage by a violation of the antitrust laws. . . ." In the event of an emergency, a plaintiff may be heard on the need for an immediate court order to prevent some imminent, irreparable harm to persons or property due to a threatened antitrust violation.[38]

6.02.2(B) Statute of limitations

Several statutes limit federal question jurisdiction over private antitrust actions. For example, § 4B of the Clayton Act, 15 U.S.C. § 15b, provides that private antitrust causes of action "shall be forever barred unless commenced within four years after the cause of action accrued."

Rarely is a statute of limitations defense unambiguously borne out by the allegations pleaded in the complaint, so the defense is usually factual rather than facial. The defense may also be litigated as an affirmative defense and proven by admissions from the plaintiff or other evidence that the claim is time-barred.

---

[37] For further discussion of substantive antitrust violations, *see* Chapter 1 of this Handbook.

[38] 15 U.S.C. § 9; *see also* Rule 65. For further discussion of antitrust remedies, *see* Chapter 9 of this Handbook.

6.02.3 Challenges to diversity jurisdiction

Although federal question jurisdiction customarily provides the jurisdictional basis for antitrust matters, federal subject matter jurisdiction also exists for claims arising under state antitrust laws, including certain state antitrust class actions, if the applicable requirements of diversity of citizenship or supplemental jurisdiction are met. Plaintiffs may wish to plead a state cause of action because it affords them greater rights than are available under federal law. Diversity of citizenship jurisdiction is discussed in this subsection, and supplemental jurisdiction is discussed in the following subsection.

Under 28 U.S.C. § 1332(a) federal courts have original jurisdiction over state claims in four situations:

- a case between citizens of different U.S. states;
- between citizens of a state and a citizen or subject of a foreign state;
- between citizens of different states in which foreign citizens are additional parties; or,
- between a foreign state as plaintiff and citizens of a U.S. state.

The concept of "citizenship" for diversity purposes requires an individual to be domiciled in the state, amounting to physical presence with the intent to reside in the state indefinitely. A U.S. citizen domiciled abroad is not a "citizen of a state" nor a subject or citizen of a foreign state, so such an individual may not bring suit in the federal courts based on diversity jurisdiction.[39] On the other hand, Subsection 1332(a) provides that "an alien admitted to the United States for permanent residence shall be deemed a citizen of the State in which such alien is domiciled." A corporation is a citizen of each state in which it is incorporated plus the state in which it has its one principal place of business. Courts look either to the location of the corporation's headquarters (taking a corporate "nerve center" approach[40]), the place where the bulk of the corporate assets are found, or both.

All diversity claims must satisfy both the technical rules for diversity of citizenship and an amount in controversy requirement, which should be alleged as a "short and plain statement of the grounds for the court's jurisdiction," as required by Rule 8(a)(1). Diversity of citizenship requires "complete diversity," that is, all plaintiffs must have citizenship different from all defendants. Jurisdiction fails if any defendant shares citizenship with any plaintiff. The complaint should allege the citizenship of each individual party, the state of incorporation and principal place of business of each corporate party, and that the amount in controversy in each claim of each plaintiff exceeds $75,000, exclusive of interest and costs. A failure to allege jurisdictional facts in sufficient detail to establish complete diversity or the amount in controversy is grounds for a Rule 12(b)(1) pre-answer motion to dismiss for lack of subject matter jurisdiction.

Congress has made major changes in diversity jurisdiction for class actions commenced on or after February 18, 2005. A new Subsection 1332(d) provides more generous juris-

---

39 Coury v. Prot, 85 F.3d 244, 248 (5th Cir. 1996).

40 *See* Metropolitan Life Ins. Co. v. Estate of Cammon, 929 F.2d 1220, 1222 (7th Cir. 1991).

dictional standards for class actions that relax the complete diversity requirement and permit plaintiffs to aggregate their claims to meet a total amount in controversy threshold of $5 million. Sections 1332(d)(2)(A)–(C) provide that diversity for class actions is satisfied if any class member is a citizen of a different state from any defendant, any class member is a foreign state or a citizen of a foreign state and any defendant is a citizen of a U.S. state, or any class member is a citizen of a U.S. state and any defendant is a foreign state or citizen. However, Subsection 1332(d)(4) requires the court to decline jurisdiction where more than two-thirds of the class members are citizens of the forum state and any significant defendant is also a citizen of that state. Under Subsection 1332(d)(3) the court may decline to exercise jurisdiction where more than one-third but less than two-thirds of the class members and the primary defendants are citizens of the forum state, based on six factors enumerated in the statute. Subsection 1332(d)(9) excludes certain securities and corporate law class action claims. State law class actions based on diversity jurisdiction that do not satisfy all the standards of § 1332 may be challenged on subject matter jurisdiction grounds.

6.02.4 Challenges to supplemental jurisdiction

Supplemental jurisdiction is not an independent basis for subject matter jurisdiction, unlike federal question or diversity jurisdiction. It arises only when jurisdiction already exists for one or more of the other claims in the complaint, in which case the pleader is permitted to litigate non-federal claims related to the same "case or controversy."[41] Supplemental jurisdiction, authorized by Congress in 28 U.S.C. § 1367 in 1990, codifies the common law doctrines of pendant and ancillary jurisdiction.[42]

Supplemental jurisdiction will fail if the original action is based on diversity jurisdiction and the exercise of supplemental jurisdiction would contradict the requirements of diversity, except in exceptional circumstances.[43] Where the claims conferring original federal jurisdiction are dismissed, whether the claims based on supplemental jurisdiction may or must be dismissed depends on the reasons for dismissal. If the original federal subject matter jurisdiction was lacking, the supplemental claims must be dismissed. If dismissal relates to the merits of the federal claims, the district court has discretion to decline to continue to exercise jurisdiction.[44]

§ 6.03 Pre-answer defenses

This section begins by discussing challenges available to achieve dismissal of a complaint for failure to state a claim upon which relief may be granted, focusing on the significance of the *Bell Atlantic Corp. v. Twombly*[45] and *Ashcroft v. Iqbal*[46] decisions on the applicable

---

41 28 U.S.C. § 1337(a).

42 *See* Peacock v. Thomas, 516 U.S. 349, 355 n.5 (1996). Practitioners should be aware that some features of prior law in this area were abrogated by the statute.

43 28 U.S.C. § 1367(b).

44 28 U.S.C. § 1367(c)(3).

45 550 U.S. 544 (2007).

46 556 U.S. 662 (2009).

pleading standards for antitrust claims. The remainder of the section considers the other procedural defenses that may be raised in a pre-answer motion.

6.03.1 *Rule 12(b)(6) pre-answer motion to dismiss for failure to state a claim upon which relief may be granted*

As a practical matter, Rule 12(b)(6) pre-answer motions to dismiss for failure to state a claim arise in nearly every case. Rule 12(b)(6) codifies the common law plea of demurrer, that is, that the complaint fails "to state a claim upon which relief can be granted." It tests the legal sufficiency of the claim to screen out lawsuits "that are fatally flawed in their legal premises and destined to fail. . . ."[47] Dismissal on these grounds is warranted when a claim either (1) asserts a legal theory that is not cognizable as a matter of law, or (2) fails to allege sufficient facts to support a cognizable legal claim.

6.03.1(A) Non-cognizable claims and implied immunity

Some defenses that do not challenge subject matter jurisdiction are nonetheless based on a limitation of the applicability of the antitrust laws. In industries in which competitive conduct is regulated, defendants may claim an implied antitrust immunity (as distinct from an express statutory immunity or exemption) or, in a § 2 monopolization claim, the lack of any antitrust duty to deal.[48]

Implied antitrust immunity may arise where regulatory statutes are silent with respect to antitrust but where courts determine that application of the antitrust laws to conduct closely supervised by a regulatory body should be implicitly precluded. The Supreme Court re-formulated the standard for implied immunity in the 2007 case of *Credit Suisse Securities (USA) LLC v. Billing*.[49] The case involved a Sherman Act § 1 claim by a putative class of investors seeking to recover for injuries allegedly sustained as a result of anticompetitive agreements among major underwriters regarding the terms of sale for initial public offerings. Summarizing its view of prior securities industry cases, the Court identified the following factors as critical to finding sufficient incompatibility between the securities laws and the antitrust complaint in any given case:

> (1) the existence of regulatory authority under the securities law to supervise the activities in question; (2) evidence that the responsible regulatory entities exercise that authority; and (3) a resulting risk that the securities and antitrust laws, if both applicable, would produce conflicting guidance, requirements, duties, privileges, or standards of conduct.[50]

With respect to previous occasions on which the Court found an antitrust claim non-cognizable on the grounds of implied immunity by virtue of the securities laws, the Court

---

[47] Advanced Cardiovascular Systems, Inc. v. Scimed Life Systems, Inc., 988 F.2d 1157, 1160 (Fed. Cir. 1993).

[48] By an express statutory immunity, Congress divests the district courts of subject matter jurisdiction over immune activities or parties, so it is properly raised in a Rule 12(b)(1) motion. The resolution of an implied immunity defense, by contrast, requires, at a bare minimum, the factual background alleged in the complaint. If the facts alleged establish an implied immunity, the complaint should be dismissed under Rule 12(b)(6).

[49] 551 U.S. 264 (2007).

[50] 551 U.S. at 275–76.

noted that "the possible conflict [between antitrust and securities regulation] affected practices that lie squarely within an area of financial market activity that the securities law seeks to regulate."[51] As with other of its recent pronouncements in the field, the Supreme Court in *Credit Suisse* incrementally limited the reach of the antitrust laws by re-calibrating the standard applicable to the decision before it (in this case, the well-established "clear repugnancy" test governing antitrust immunity implied by a regulatory regime).

Implied immunity may be unavailable if an "antitrust savings clause" is enacted in the regulatory enabling legislation. But, at least four legal avenues other than implied immunity also may bar an antitrust claim against a regulated entity, even where Congress includes an antitrust savings clause. The first is the so-called "state action doctrine." This rule, originating in *Parker v. Brown*,[52] emerges from federalism to protect the activities of the states. The state action doctrine shields certain anticompetitive conduct when the conduct is (1) in furtherance of a clearly articulated state policy, and (2) actively supervised by the state. This protection is available to officials and agencies of the states and may be available to many lower-level functionaries and public–private activities.

The second defense is the "filed rate doctrine," adopted in *Keogh v. Chicago & N.W. Ry. Co.*,[53] and reaffirmed in *Square D Co. v. Niagara Frontier Tariff Bureau, Inc.*,[54] which bars antitrust claims which seek remedies that are incompatible with the rate approval process of a regulatory agency.

Third, the doctrine of primary jurisdiction directs a district court to defer an antitrust claim where the case "requires resolution of issues which, under a regulatory scheme, have been placed within the special competence of an administrative body."[55] "[I]n such a case the judicial process is suspended pending referral of such issues to the administrative body for its views."[56]

Finally, limitations on the cognizability of antitrust claims against regulated entities may arise from the alteration of the market environment induced by regulation or deregulation. Thus, in *Town of Concord v. Boston Edison Co.*,[57] the First Circuit did not say either that the antitrust laws did not apply to the electrical wholesale market or that they applied less stringently, but rather that the regulatory scheme itself made "a critical difference in terms of antitrust harms, benefits, and administrative considerations."[58]

In *Verizon Communications Inc. v. Law Offices of Curtis V. Trinko, LLP*,[59] the Supreme Court relied on this perspective to shield newly deregulated telephone companies from the application of § 2 of the Sherman Act. The deregulatory legislation imposed duties on regional monopoly telephone carriers to interconnect with rival firms. In the Court's

---

51 *Id.*
52 317 U.S. 341 (1943).
53 260 U.S. 156 (1922).
54 476 U.S. 409 (1986).
55 Ricci v. Chicago Merc. Exch., 409 U.S. 289 (1973).
56 United States v. Western Pacific R. Co, 352 U.S. 59, 64 (1956) (citing General American Tank Car Corp. v. El Dorado Terminal Co., 308 U.S. 422, 433 (1940)).
57 915 F.2d 17 (1st Cir. 1990), *cert. denied*, 499 U.S. 931 (1991).
58 915 F.2d, at 23.
59 540 U.S. 398 (2004).

view, this governmental scheme would have been "a good candidate for implication of antitrust immunity,"[60] but an antitrust savings clause prevented this. Nonetheless, the Court found that the investment disincentives of imposing an antitrust duty on telephone carriers to share their infrastructure were in tension with the underlying purposes of the antitrust laws. Moreover, regulatory redress was available and was obtained on the basis of the defendant's failure to abide by mandated interconnection duties. The Court also noted the prospect of inconsistent decisions in the area by antitrust courts throughout the country. Consequently, in a decision that appears to have narrowed the range of circumstances in which monopolists may be compelled by antitrust law to deal with rivals, the Court declined to recognize a cause of action for an incumbent telephone carrier's failure to fulfill its statutory duties. The Court concluded that the firms had not violated any duty to deal that was or should be imposed by the antitrust laws, rendering the plaintiff's claim non-cognizable.

6.03.1(B) Act of State Doctrine

Under the act of state doctrine "the courts of one country will not sit in judgment on the acts of the government of another, done within its own territory."[61] As a result, a private antitrust action brought against certain foreign actors may be subject to dismissal on a Rule 12(b)(6) pre-answer motion. For act of state purposes, the relevant acts are not merely those of the named defendants but any governmental acts whose validity would be called into question by adjudication of the suit.[62] "The burden lies on the proponent of the doctrine to establish the factual predicate for the doctrine's application."[63] In *Spectrum Stores, Inc. v. Citgo Petroleum Corp.*,[64] the Fifth Circuit affirmed dismissal of a private antitrust action against American subsidiaries of OPEC oil companies on the basis of the act of state doctrine, declining "to sit in judgment of the act of the foreign states that comprise OPEC."[65]

6.03.1(C) Failure to Allege Facts Sufficient to State a Cognizable Legal Claim

Two recent Supreme Court decisions, *Bell Atlantic Corp. v. Twombly*,[66] decided May 21, 2007, and *Ashcroft v. Iqbal*,[67] decided May 18, 2009, strengthened the interpretation of the pleading requirements of Rule 8(a)(2) for stating a claim in antitrust and other federal civil cases. As a consequence, private plaintiffs now bear a greater obligation at the inception of their lawsuit to allege facts reasonably confirmable by discoverable evidence and, based on a coherent antitrust and economic theory, reasonably sufficient, if proven, to establish the grounds for the plaintiffs' claimed right to compensatory and treble damages for an antitrust injury. Naturally, defendants in antitrust cases have been placing increas-

---

60 540 U.S. at 406.

61 Underhill v. Hernandez, 168 U.S. 250, 252 (1897).

62 Spectrum Stores, Inc. v. Citgo Petroleum Corp., 632 F.3d 938 (5th Cir. 2011); Callejo v. Bancomer, 764 F.2d 1101, 1116 (5th Cir. 1985).

63 *Spectrum Stores*, 632 F.3d at 954.

64 632 F.3d 938 (5th Cir. 2011).

65 *Id.* at 956.

66 550 U.S. 544 (2007).

67 556 U.S. 662 (2009).

ing emphasis on challenging the plaintiffs' right to seek relief on the basis of the facts alleged in the complaint.

In *Bell Atlantic Corp. v. Twombly*[68] the Court's stated intention was to "address the proper standard for pleading an antitrust conspiracy through allegations of parallel conduct,"[69] and to take a "fresh look at [the] adequacy of pleading when a claim rests on parallel conduct."[70] The plaintiffs were a putative class of consumers alleging that the defendants, the regional U.S. Bell telephone monopolies, had agreed to – and did – refrain from expanding into one another's service regions in order to maintain an anticompetitive market allocation and exclude competitive, third-party potential entrants, in violation of § 1. The plaintiffs also alleged that, in so doing, defendants acted against their individual economic self-interests. The Supreme Court in *Twombly* found that the allegations in the plaintiffs' amended complaint did not adequately establish grounds entitling plaintiffs to a claim for relief. An allegation of parallel conduct in a § 1 case, without more, the Court held, does not suffice to state a claim. "[S]uch a claim requires a complaint with enough factual matter (taken as true) to suggest that an agreement was made."[71]

The Court likened the plaintiffs' claim to a claim alleging parallel pricing, which by itself neither proves an unlawful § 1 agreement[72] nor is sufficient to overcome a defendant's motion for summary judgment.[73] Indeed, the amended complaint in *Twombly* was ideal for illustrating the principle that oligopolistic interdependence does not support an inference of agreement in the legal sense. Both before the 1996 deregulatory telecommunications legislation and afterward, the regional telephone companies each occupied in their own regions optimal, jointly profit-maximizing monopoly positions from which none of the companies would have had an economic incentive to deviate, and for the maintenance of which no prohibited agreement would have been necessary. To allege that the defendants had acted against their own self-interest after passage of the Act in circumstances where it appeared they had simply chosen to continue in a position upon which it was difficult or impossible to improve did not supply sufficient grounds to infer that the defendants had entered into an unlawful agreement.

Twombly was decided in light of settled precedent that to survive a defense motion for summary judgment in a parallel pricing case (and, perforce, to make out a *prima facie* case at trial), the plaintiff must present additional evidence beyond mere parallel conduct that

---

68 550 U.S. 544 (2007).

69 550 U.S. at 553.

70 *Id.* at 561, n.7.

71 *Id.* at 556.

72 Theatre Enterprises, Inc. v. Paramount Film Dist. Corp., 346 U.S. 537, 540 (1954) ("To be sure, business behavior is admissible circumstantial evidence from which the fact finder may infer agreement . . . [but the Court] . . . has never held that proof of parallel business behavior conclusively establishes agreement or, phrased differently, that such behavior itself constitutes a Sherman Act offense") (citing Interstate Circuit, Inc. v. United States, 306 U.S. 208 (1939); United States v. Masonite Corp. 316 U.S. 265 (1942); United States v. Bausch & Lomb Optical Co., 321 U.S. 707 (1944); American Tobacco Co. v. United States, 328 U.S. 781; United States v. Paramount Pictures, Inc., 334 U.S. 131 (1948)).

73 Matsushita Electric Industrial Co. v. Zenith Radio Corp., 475 U.S. 574, 588 (1986) ("[C]onduct as consistent with permissible competition as with illegal conspiracy does not, standing alone, support an inference of antitrust conspiracy.").

tends to contradict tacit, lawful oligopoly conduct in order to create a factual issue on whether there was an agreement. In connection with summary proceedings, ambiguous evidence of parallel conduct must be accompanied by what the courts have recognized as "plus factors," evidence "'that tends to exclude the possibility' that the alleged conspirators acted independently."[74] Although the question in *Twombly* of whether the pleaded allegations of parallel conduct in the amended complaint were sufficient to state a § 1 claim was decided against this background, the Court did not look to the plus factor paradigm to address what it framed as a separate issue here. Instead, it looked to the general requirements of Rule 8(a)(2), which calls for "a short and plain statement of the claim showing that the pleader is entitled to relief." Following a pattern seen in several recent decisions, the Court proceeded from first principles, modified the applicable standard, and then applied the modified standard to decide the case before it.

The plus factor paradigm in any case would have been inadequate for the Court's purposes of articulating pleading standards for § 1 driven by the evidentiary requirements for proving unlawful collusion. The plus factor approach treats all evidentiary factors more or less equally.[75] The Court's *Twombly* analysis, by contrast, distinguishes between four categories of evidence of agreement: (1) direct evidence of the agreement itself, (2) unambiguous circumstantial evidence of an agreement, (3) ambiguous evidence of an agreement, and, (4) "labels and conclusions" and formulaic recitations of the elements of a claim.

The *Twombly* Court held that "a plaintiff's obligation to provide the 'grounds' of his 'entitle[ment] to relief,' requires more than labels and conclusions, and a formulaic recitation of a cause of action's elements will not do."[76] Under the "Rule 8 entitlement requirement"[77] a complaint requires "[f]actual allegations . . . enough to raise a right to relief above the speculative level,"[78] and "something more . . . than . . . a statement of facts that merely creates a suspicion [of] a legally cognizable right of action."[79] The "threshold requirement [is] that the 'plain statement' possess enough heft to 'sho[w] that the pleader is entitled to relief.'"[80]

Thus, the Court explained that the Rule 8 entitlement requirement requires allegations

---

[74] *Id.* (quoting Monsanto Co. v. Spray-Rite Serv. Corp., 465 U.S. 752, 764 (1984)).

[75] *See* William E. Kovacic, *The identification and proof of horizontal agreements under the antitrust laws*, 38 Antitrust Bull. 5, 35 (Spring 1993) ("[C]ourts rarely attempt to rank plus factors according to their probative value or to specify the minimum critical mass of plus factors that must be established to sustain an inference that the observed market behavior resulted from concerted conduct rather than from 'consciously parallel' choices.").

[76] 550 U.S. at 555 (citation omitted, alteration in original).

[77] The Court cited Dura Pharmaceuticals, Inc. v. Broudo, 544 U.S. 336 (2005) for the "Rule 8 entitlement requirement." *Dura* involved securities fraud litigation in which the plaintiffs' alleged injury was having paid an inflated price for shares compared to what the price would have been in the absence of the fraud. The Supreme Court held that the purchase of shares, the market price of which fluctuates for a variety of reasons, does not cause injury, so the complaint lacked the required allegation of "loss causation." Reversing the Ninth Circuit, the Court held that a complaint lacking the necessary elements of a cause of action is insufficient under Rule 8, because it fails to give adequate notice of the grounds for the plaintiffs' entitlement to relief.

[78] 550 U.S. at 555.

[79] *Id.*

[80] *Id.* at 557 (citation omitted, second alteration in original).

Table 6.1 Summary of Twombly *standard*

	Nature of the allegation	Type of inference required	Applicable standard
1.	Direct evidence of agreement	No inference	Plausible
2.	Communications and other unambiguous circumstantial evidence of agreement	Ordinary inference from circumstantial evidence	Plausibly suggestive
3.	Parallel conduct and other ambiguous circumstantial evidence of agreement	Inference from economic data or market behavior	Plausibly suggestive when placed in context
4.	Labels and conclusions	No inference warranted	Not creditable

to be weighed in terms of plausibility, suggestiveness, and discoverability. Suggestiveness calls for allegations that cross the "boundary . . . between the factually neutral and the factually suggestive . . ." to enter "the realm of plausible liability."[81] Plausibility demands that grounds for entitlement be alleged with "enough facts to state a claim to relief that is plausible on its face."[82] And the discoverability component hinges entitlement to relief on a "reasonable expectation that discovery will reveal relevant evidence."[83]

With respect to allegations of conspiracy under § 1, the *Twombly* standard requires plausible direct evidence of agreement, circumstantial evidence "plausibly suggesting" agreement,[84] or parallel conduct "placed in a context that raises a suggestion of a preceding agreement."[85] "A blanket assertion of entitlement to relief" and "labels and conclusions" are not entitled to credit as well-pleaded facts. This flexible standard is summarized in Table 6.1.[86]

The most frequent forms of direct evidence of agreement in private § 1 claims are guilty pleas in criminal prosecutions and the admissions recited in deferred prosecution agreements. Unambiguous circumstantial evidence is indirect evidence, such as evidence of secret communications or clandestine meetings of the conspirators or of documents that appear to further a common scheme or purpose, which is probative of agreement and also tends to exclude the hypothesis of non-cooperation, justifying an inference of agreement. By contrast, evidence of parallel conduct or other economic data may be ambiguous on the issue of agreement, that is, as consistent with agreement as it is with oligopolistic interdependence.[87] In singling out this category of evidence for special treatment, the *Twombly* decision serves as the vehicle for the incorporation into antitrust of the principle that economic evidence of this kind often requires interpretation and factual

81 550 U.S. at 557 n.5. The word "plausible" appears 15 times in the opinion as a noun, adverb, and adjective, excluding quoted instances.

82 *Id.* at 570.

83 *Id.* at 556.

84 550 U.S. at 557.

85 *Id.*

86 Table 6.1 is a heuristic construct intended to summarize the author's analysis of the decision.

87 *See In re* High Fructose Corn Syrup Antitrust Litig., 295 F.3d 651, 655 (2002) ("The evidence upon which a plaintiff will rely will usually be . . . of two types – economic evidence suggesting that the defendants were not in fact competing, and noneconomic evidence suggesting that they were not competing because they had agreed not to compete.").

context to show that it rejects the hypothesis of a Nash non-cooperative equilibrium before an inference of agreement is justified. Standing apart from a sufficiently suggestive context, such evidence is what the *Twombly* court labeled "factually neutral" on the issue of agreement. The flexible plausibility standard, therefore, accommodates the practical distinction between allegations of non-economic, circumstantial evidence of agreement and economic evidence of a market outcome probative of agreement only if inconsistent with non-cooperation. Finally, allegations that are conclusions and labels do not constitute grounds for relief.

Under this standard, the *Twombly* plaintiffs' allegations that the defendants engaged in a "contract, combination or conspiracy" and "agreed not to compete with one another" were merely legal conclusions resting on the prior allegations or, in terms of the foregoing taxonomy, category 4 allegations not entitled to the presumption of truth.[88] "The nub of the complaint," the Court observed, "is the [defendants'] parallel behavior."[89] But, applying the standard for category 3 to those allegations, the *Twombly* Court concluded that the complaint had not "nudged [the] claims across the line from conceivable to plausible" by pleading a sufficiently suggestive context.

The alleged parallel conduct lacked a suggestive context even though the plaintiffs had alleged a widely recognized plus factor, that the defendants' conduct was contrary to their individual economic self-interests. Had the alleged plus factor been instead category 2 circumstantial evidence of agreement, the parallel conduct would have been more suggestive and plausible grounds for relief likely would have been stated. But, plaintiffs apparently knew of no category 2 evidence. The Court's implicit conclusion was that the complaint did not allege facts that were inconsistent with non-cooperative equilibrium in the U.S. telephone market, despite the alleged plus factor. Indeed, the defendants' *ex ante* occupancy of allocated monopolies fails to suggest that refraining from competition was necessarily against their individual economic self-interests. Under the circumstances, the Court deemed plaintiffs' assertion in this regard as conclusory and not entitled to the presumption of truth, placing it in category 4.

The Court cited three factual scenarios that might provide plausibly suggestive context for a claim based on parallel conduct. The first is "parallel behavior that would probably not result from chance, coincidence, independent responses to common stimuli, or mere interdependence unaided by an advance understanding among the parties."[90] The second is "conduct [that] indicates the sort of restricted freedom of action and sense of obligation that one generally associates with agreement."[91] Finally, "complex and historically unprecedented changes in pricing structure made at the very same time by multiple competitors, and made for no other discernible reason"[92] would also provide a suitable context. These allegations supporting a plausible inference of conspiracy are likely to

---

[88] 550 U.S. at 565.

[89] *Id.* at 566.

[90] 550 U.S. at 557 n.4 (quoting AREEDA & H. HOVENKAMP, ANTITRUST LAW ¶1425, at 167–85 (2d ed. 2003)).

[91] *Id.* (quoting Michael D. Blechman, *Conscious Parallelism, Signalling and Facilitating Devices: The Problem of Tacit Collusion Under the Antitrust Laws*, 24 N.Y.L. SCH. L. REV. 881, 899 (1979).

[92] *Id.* (quoting Brief for Respondent at 37, *Twombly*, 550 U.S. 544 (No. 05-1126)).

supplant plus factors as the focus of § 1 claims based on circumstantial evidence for the simple reason that what must be alleged also must be proven.

The *Twombly* decision adds significant precision to the analysis of proof of agreement in circumstantial § 1 cases and, as such, is an important antitrust precedent. But, the decision is also an important civil procedure precedent, in which the Court articulated a more granular pleading standard based on the character of the evidence being described. For complaints alleging direct evidence or unambiguous circumstantial evidence that possesses a reasonable hope of being discovered (i.e. category 1 and 2 allegations) the existing pleading standard remains largely unaffected. But, in complaints describing ambiguous circumstantial evidence and stating conclusory assertions of liability, that is, allegations in categories 3 and 4, grounds for entitlement to relief are unlikely to be stated unless the ambiguous evidence can be situated in a suggestive factual context.

It bears mention that, in spite of the Court's claim to the contrary, a pleading standard that differentiates conclusions and allegations of indeterminate evidence from allegations of standard direct and circumstantial evidence does not follow directly from the Court's precedent or the general standards of pleading. For half a century, the requirements of Rule 8(a)(2) have described a "notice pleading" standard based on "the accepted rule [of *Conley v. Gibson*] that a complaint should not be dismissed for failure to state a claim unless it appears beyond doubt that the plaintiff can prove no set of facts in support of his claim which would entitle him to relief."[93] By singling out for special treatment indeterminate and factually neutral circumstantial allegations, the *Twombly* standard is inconsistent with this part of the long-standing *Conley* rule. Repudiating this part of *Conley*, the Court declared that the "no set of facts" language "ha[d] earned its retirement,"[94] and observed that the language "ha[d] been questioned, criticized, and explained away long enough," and "[wa]s best forgotten as an incomplete, negative gloss on an accepted pleading standard. . . ."[95]

In *Erickson v. Pardus*,[96] decided two weeks after *Twombly*, however, the Court was quick to reaffirm the undisturbed portion of *Conley* and its continued fidelity to the concept of notice pleading. Quoting from *Twombly*, which in turn quoted from *Conley*, the Court's Per Curiam order reiterated that a pleading need only ". . . give the defendant fair notice of what . . . the claim is and the grounds upon which it rests." A more direct declaration of fidelity to the part of the *Conley* notice pleading standard that survived the Court's repudiation of the neighboring "no set of facts" formulation is difficult to imagine. Thus, rather than signaling a retreat from the essential standard of notice pleading, *Twombly* more profitably may be conceived as applying the notice pleading standard with greater rigor to the "short and plain statement . . . showing that

93 *Conley v. Gibson*, 355 U.S. 41, 45–46 (1957). For a discussion of bills introduced in the House and Senate to repeal *Twombly* and restore the *Conley* "no set of facts" standard, *e.g.*, Notice Pleading Restoration Act of 2009, S. 1504, 111th Cong. (1st Sess. 2009) ("A bill to provide that Federal courts shall not dismiss complaints under rule 12(b)(6) or (e) of the Federal Rules of Civil Procedure, except under the standards set forth by the Supreme Court of the United States in Conley v. Gibson, 355 U.S. 41 (1957)"), see Chapter 15 of this Handbook.

94 550 U.S at 563.

95 *Id.*

96 551 U.S. 89 (2007).

the plaintiff is entitled to relief" called for by Rule 8(a)(2). It does so using a plausibility standard with two effects. A substantive effect through the Rule 8 entitlement requirement calls for allegations that show a cognizable narrative of "loss causation" connecting a wrongful act by a defendant with a remediable injury to the plaintiff. A procedural effect is exerted through evidentiary standards that no longer tolerate complaints that describe facts merely consistent with a claim or allege more factually neutral evidence or conclusions of liability, requiring instead that a pleading allege suggestive and discoverable grounds for the plaintiff's entitlement to relief. The Court took up the subject of civil pleading standards again in *Ashcroft v. Iqbal*,[97] which confirmed that *Twombly*, as an "interpretation and application of Rule 8," "expounded the pleading standard for 'all civil actions.'"[98] The *Iqbal* Court offered the following guidance for implementing the *Twombly* standard:

> Determining whether a complaint states a plausible claim for relief will . . . be a context-specific task that requires the reviewing court to draw on its judicial experience and common sense. . . . [A] court considering a motion to dismiss can choose to begin by identifying pleadings that, because they are no more than conclusions, are not entitled to the assumption of truth. While legal conclusions can provide the framework of a complaint, they must be supported by factual allegations. When there are well-pleaded factual allegations, a court should assume their veracity and then determine whether they plausibly give rise to an entitlement to relief.[99]

Iqbal involved a civil claim against U.S. government officials for prisoner abuse and discrimination, which alleged that the Attorney General and FBI Director personally "knew of, condoned, and willfully and maliciously agreed to subject [the plaintiff]" to harsh conditions of confinement "as a matter of policy, solely on account of [his] religion, race, and/or national origin and for no legitimate penological interest."[100] The Court held that "[u]nder *Twombly*'s construction of Rule 8," these allegations "are conclusory and not entitled to be assumed true."[101] As to the remaining allegations describing the conduct of the officials inflicting the discrimination, while arguably consistent with an intent of the two named defendants to discriminate, the Court concluded that the plaintiff needed "to allege more by way of factual content to 'nudg[e]' his claim of purposeful discrimination 'across the line from conceivable to plausible.'"[102]

The *Twombly* plausibility standard suggests that Rule 12(b)(6) motions to dismiss claims based on circumstantial grounds for relief should identify and discredit conclusory allegations and then test whether the remaining allegations describe sufficiently suggestive facts to state grounds for relief. Facts that are equally as consistent with an entitlement

---

97 556 U.S. 662 (2009). The Court had already expanded the *Twombly* analysis to § 2 of the Sherman Act, *see* Pacific Bell Telephone Co. v LinkLine Comm'ns, Inc., 555 U.S. 438, 129 S.Ct. 1109, 1123 (2009) ("It is for the District Court on remand to consider whether the amended complaint states a claim [for predatory pricing] upon which relief may be granted in light of the new pleading standard we articulated in *Twombly*.").

98 129 S.Ct. at 1953 (quoting Rule 1).

99 *Id.* at 1950.

100 *Id.* at 1951.

101 *Id.*

102 *Id.* at 1952 (quoting *Twombly*, 550 U.S. at 570 (alteration in original)).

to relief as not, such as parallel conduct, state grounds for relief only if pleaded in a sufficiently suggestive factual context.[103]

Recently, a panel of the Seventh Circuit confirmed that the *Twombly* standard may indeed be satisfied even by a claim predicated solely on parallel conduct pleaded in a suggestive factual context, that is, in the terms of the framework provided in Table 6.1, a complaint devoid of either category 1 or category 2 allegations. In *In re Text Messaging Antitrust Litigation*,[104] Judge Richard Posner, writing for a three-judge panel, held that a complaint pleaded a sufficiently plausible case of price fixing in spite of the complete absence of any allegation of direct evidence of agreement (category 1) or even allegations of circumstantial evidence that would compel an inference of conspiracy (category 2). Not surprisingly, the set of category 3 allegations that nudged the complaint in *Text Messaging* over the line into the realm of plausibility involved the kinds of allegations described in footnote four of the *Twombly* opinion, allegations of what Judge Posner referred to as "the type of evidence that enables parallel conduct to be interpreted as collusive."[105]

The *Text Messaging* complaint alleged that the four national cellular telephone carriers – Verizon Wireless, AT&T Mobility, Sprint-Nextel, and T-Mobile – colluded to fix prices in the text messaging services market. The conclusory (category 4) allegation was that the defendants "entered into illicit agreements to increase prices of Text Messaging Services at some point prior to and during the period around July–December 2006 . . . and again at some point prior to and during the period around July–December 2007. . . ." The "factually neutral" (category 3) circumstantial economic evidence was the parallel movement of prices for text messaging services that occurred at the allegedly agreed to times. But, parallel behavior "of a sort anomalous in a competitive market," as Judge Posner observed, is "a symptom of price fixing; standing alone it is not proof of it."[106]

Although the defendants had pressed the court to require an allegation of direct evidence of agreement, i.e. a typical "smoking gun in a price fixing case," such as "an admission by an employee of one of the conspirators,"[107] *Twombly* does not require any category 1 allegations to state a claim. Accordingly, the Seventh Circuit flatly rejected any notion that an allegation of direct evidence is a "sine qua non" of a conspiracy claim. "Circumstantial evidence," the court declared, "can establish an antitrust conspiracy."[108]

But the real question raised by *Twombly* is not whether allegations of direct evidence are required but whether a claim is stated by allegations of *ambiguous* circumstantial evidence (in the sense that such allegations are no more consistent with agreement than with non-agreement, i.e., category 3). The *Text Messaging* decision answered affirmatively, holding that the complaint satisfied *Twombly* because it alleged "the type of evidence that enables parallel conduct to be interpreted as collusive."[109] Specifically, the complaint alleged an industrial context in which the allegations of agreement became suggestive, plausible, and

---

103 *Twombly* and *Iqbal* have been cited in tens of thousands of reported cases, including opinions issued by every Circuit Court of Appeal.

104 *In re* Text Messaging Antitrust Litig., 630 F.3d 622 (7th Cir. 2010).

105 *Id.* at 628.

106 *Id.* at 627.

107 *Id.* at 628.

108 *Id.* at 627.

109 *Id.* at 628.

discoverable: The four defendants sold 90 percent of text messaging services in the nation; they all belonged to a trade association through which prices and other information were exchanged; they all raised prices during periods of falling costs; and they all modified complex pricing policies simultaneously, circumstances unlikely to have arisen in the absence of cooperation. As Judge Posner explained, "an accusation that the thousands of children who set up makeshift lemonade stands all over the country on hot summer days were fixing prices would be laughed out of court because the retail sale of lemonade from lemonade stands constitutes so dispersed and heterogeneous and uncommercial a market as to make a nationwide conspiracy of the sellers utterly implausible."[110] By contrast, the context in which the parallel conduct alleged in *Text Messaging* occurred rendered a claim based on an illicit agreement sufficiently suggestive and plausible to state a cognizable claim under the pleading standards of *Twombly*.[111]

6.03.1(D) Dismissal for lack of antitrust standing

A Rule 12(b)(6) pre-answer motion may also seek dismissal on the grounds that the plaintiffs do not have "antitrust standing" to bring their claim. Antitrust standing is an element of a meritorious cause of action and should be distinguished from Article III constitutional standing. A challenge to the latter is properly brought in a Rule 12(b)(1) motion to dismiss for lack of subject matter jurisdiction.

Section 4 of the Clayton Act provides that "any person who shall be injured in his business or property by reason of anything forbidden in the antitrust laws may sue therefor."[112] The dual purpose of this provision is to deprive violators "of the fruits of their illegality and to compensate victims of antitrust violations for their injuries."[113] However, courts have never read § 4 to grant a private treble damage suit to every person to have incurred an economic loss as the result of an antitrust violation, nor does it "encompass every harm that can be attributed directly or indirectly to the consequences of an antitrust violation."[114]

A plaintiff may satisfy the constitutional requirement of injury in fact yet not necessarily be a proper party to bring a private antitrust action. "Harm to the antitrust plaintiff is sufficient to satisfy the constitutional standing requirement of injury in fact, but the court must make a further determination whether the plaintiff is a proper party to bring a private antitrust action."[115] The court evaluates a motion to dismiss for lack of antitrust standing under the same *Twombly-Iqbal* standards applied whenever the sufficiency of the pleaded facts to state a cause of action is challenged.[116]

---

110 *Id.*

111 See also West Penn Allegheny Health System, Inc. v. UPMC, 627 F.3d 85 (3d Cir. 2010) (complaint provided allegations sufficient to suggest that the conspiracy produced anticompetitive effects in the relevant markets).

112 15 U.S.C. § 15.

113 Pfizer Inc. v. Gov't. of India, 434 U.S. 308, 314 (1978) (internal quotation marks and citations omitted).

114 Associated General Contractors of California, Inc. v. California State Council of Carpenters, 459 U.S. 519, 529 (1983).

115 *Id.* at 535 n.31.

116 For further discussion of antitrust standing, see Chapter 3 of this Handbook.

6.03.1(E) Insufficient effect on U.S. domestic commerce or imports

A claim that the cause of action is barred by § 7 of the Sherman Act, 15 U.S.C. § 6a, also known as the Foreign Trade Antitrust Improvements Act of 1982 (FTAIA) is also a challenge to the sufficiency of the pleaded facts that may be determined on a defendant's Rule 12(b)(6) pre-answer motion to dismiss.[117] The FTAIA provides that the Sherman Act shall not apply to conduct involving trade or commerce with foreign nations, other than import transactions, unless (1) such conduct has "a direct, substantial, and reasonably foreseeable effect" on domestic or import commerce or on the export business of a domestic person and (2) the effect is of a kind that the antitrust laws consider harmful.

The FTAIA's domestic-injury requirement had been the subject of a split in authority among the Circuit Courts of Appeals,[118] but in a series of decisions arising out of the global vitamins cartel that came to light in the 1990s, the courts, including the U.S. Supreme Court, significantly clarified the pleading requirements for foreign parties suing for, or being sued for, a violation of U.S. antitrust law. The case was brought as a class action on behalf of both U.S. domestic and non-U.S. direct purchasers of vitamins against foreign and domestic vitamin manufacturers for injury caused by a global price-fixing conspiracy conducted largely outside the United States and for supra-competitive prices in the worldwide market. The defendants moved to dismiss the claims brought by non-U.S. purchasers, five vitamin distributors located in the Ukraine, Australia, Ecuador and Panama, on the grounds that the FTAIA makes the Sherman Act inapplicable to conduct involving non-import foreign trade or commerce. The defendants argued that, because the non-U.S. plaintiffs had not purchased vitamins in the United States, the conduct did not satisfy the domestic-injury requirement. The district court agreed, and dismissed the Sherman Act claim against them for lack of subject matter jurisdiction.

On appeal, the District of Columbia Circuit reversed, reinstating the foreign purchasers' claim, finding that the allegations of injurious anticompetitive effects of the foreign conduct in both U.S. and non-U.S. markets were sufficient to bring the claim within the domestic-injury requirement of the FTAIA. In *F. Hoffmann-LaRoche, Ltd. v. Empagran S.A.*,[119] the Supreme Court, on a limited set of facts, reversed, holding that the foreign purchasers' claims did not meet the domestic-injury requirement. The facts were limited to circumstances in which "[t]he price-fixing conduct significantly and adversely affected both customers outside the United States and customers within the United States, but the adverse foreign effect was independent of any adverse domestic effect."[120] The Court framed the basic question thus: "Why is it reasonable to apply this law to conduct that is significantly foreign *insofar as that conduct causes independent foreign harm and that foreign harm alone gives rise to the plaintiff's claim?*"[121]

Finding no good reason, the Court vacated the D.C. Circuit's order that reinstated the case. At the same time, however, the Court made note of its maintained assumption that the anticompetitive conduct "independently caused foreign injury; that is, the conduct's

117 *See, e.g.*, *In re* Elevator Antitrust Litig., 502 F.3d 47 (2nd Cir. 2007).

118 *See* F. Hoffmann-LaRoche, Ltd. v. Empagran S.A., 542 U.S. 155, 161 (2004) (citing cases).

119 542 U.S. 155 (2004).

120 *Id.* at 164.

121 *Id.* at 166 (emphasis in original).

domestic effects did not help to bring about that foreign injury."[122] Because it reviewed a limited set of facts, the Court did not consider the plaintiffs' related, alternative claim that the domestic U.S. effects were linked to the foreign injury, which could not have been inflicted but for the harm to the domestic U.S. economy. The plaintiffs contended that, because vitamins are fungible and readily transportable, cross-border price differentials would be arbitraged away, the defendants could not have maintained their international price-fixing arrangement, and the plaintiffs would not have suffered their foreign injury. The plaintiffs argued that such causation in fact was sufficient to bring their claim within the scope of the FTAIA domestic-injury exception.

The Supreme Court declined to consider this argument because the D.C. Circuit had not considered it. The Court instructed the D.C. Circuit on remand, however, to decide whether the plaintiff's alternative (and more economically realistic) scenario should bring the foreign conduct within the exception to the FTAIA's exclusion of non-import foreign trade from the Sherman Act.

On remand, the D.C. Circuit found that the plaintiffs had painted

> a plausible scenario under which maintaining super-competitive prices in the United States might well have been a "but-for" cause of the [plaintiff's] foreign injury. . . . [H]owever, "but-for" causation between the domestic effects and the foreign injury claim is simply not sufficient to bring anti-competitive conduct within the FTAIA exception. The statutory language – "gives rise to" – indicates a direct causal relationship, that is, proximate causation, and is not satisfied by the mere but for "nexus" the [plaintiffs] advanced in their brief. This interpretation of the statutory language accords with principles of "prescriptive comity" – "the respect sovereign nations afford each other by limiting the reach of their laws."[123]

The court held that while supra-competitive U.S. pricing may have facilitated the defendants' scheme, it was not alleged that U.S. domestic effects of the defendants' conduct proximately caused the foreign plaintiffs' injuries. As a consequence, the law in the D.C. Circuit provides that district courts have subject matter jurisdiction over foreign antitrust injury claims based on a Sherman Act violation only if the injury is alleged to have been proximately caused by the U.S. domestic anticompetitive effects.

The court distinguished its result from *Caribbean Broadcasting System, Ltd. v. Cable & Wireless PLC*,[124] in which the D.C. Circuit expressly found that the FTAIA exception applied to a non-U.S. plaintiff seeking redress against a non-U.S. defendant for economic harm occurring outside the United States. The defendant, a commercial radio station operator, stood accused of misrepresenting the reach of its signal for the purpose of monopolizing the U.S. and non-U.S. radio advertising markets for Caribbean-area advertisers. The court distinguished *Caribbean Broadcasting* from *Empagran* on the ground that the U.S. domestic effect, excessive prices paid by U.S. radio advertisers, was sufficient to bring the case within the scope of the FTAIA requirement. A more cogent basis on which to distinguish *Caribbean Broadcasting*, however, is that *Caribbean Broadcasting* involved a competing radio station that claimed injury from being excluded from business with U.S.

[122] 542 U.S. at 175.

[123] Empagran S.A. v. F. Hoffmann-LaRoche, Ltd., 417 F.3d 1267, 1270–71 (D.C. Cir. 2005), *cert. denied*, 546 U.S. 1092 (2006) (citations omitted).

[124] 148 F.3d 1080 (D.C. Cir. 1998).

domestic advertisers, so the U.S. domestic effects "gave rise to," or proximately caused, the non-U.S. harm. By contrast, *Empagran* involved a suit by non-U.S. direct purchasers in non-U.S. markets in transactions that can fairly be characterized as "wholly foreign."

The rule that an overlapping, global, or interrelated market, without more, does not satisfy the requirement that U.S. domestic effects "give rise to" the complained-of harm has since been followed in the Second,[125] Eighth,[126] and Ninth[127] Circuits.

Even where the plaintiff is a competitor in a global relevant geographical market in which worldwide anticompetitive conduct is alleged, jurisdiction over foreign antitrust injury is unlikely to lie on that basis alone. Thus, the district court in *Intel Corp. Microprocessor Antitrust Litigation*[128] found that harm occurring outside the United States was beyond the reach of the Sherman Act. The market in that case was the world supply of x-86 microprocessors, the brains of the personal computer, in which Intel and AMD constitute a duopoly. AMD fabricates its products in Germany and assembles them in Asia. In its complaint against Intel, AMD alleged that Intel's business practices throughout the world were designed to prevent AMD from expanding its worldwide market share or operating at efficient minimum scale.

Intel asserted that AMD was, in part, seeking relief for business practices that affected the sale of AMD's microprocessors in foreign countries, foreign claims outside of the domestic-injury requirement of the FTAIA. In response, AMD argued that the U.S. market was but an integral part of the world market, and that Intel had kept AMD from selling microprocessors in foreign markets with the purpose and effect of weakening AMD as a domestic rival. "Intel has necessarily had to cut AMD off from business opportunities throughout the market, including opportunities with foreign customers."[129]

The court, however, observed that the direct effects requirement meant that the effects in the U.S. had to be an immediate consequence of the alleged anticompetitive conduct abroad with no intervening developments. "AMD's chain of effects [was] full of twists and turns, which themselves [were] contingent upon numerous developments,"[130] including the use of profits from foreign sales to shore up U.S. domestic marketing. The court agreed with Intel that the "simultaneous, direct foreign and direct domestic effects, with the plaintiffs' antitrust claim arising from those direct domestic effects,"[131] that characterized *Caribbean Broadcasting* did not obtain where "the foreign harm . . . arises from the effects of the alleged foreign conduct and there is no direct link between the foreign conduct and the domestic antitrust injury."[132] The court then struck the allegations of AMD's complaint that claimed injury due to lost sales to European and Japanese computer manufacturers, the interference with product launches by those manufacturers, lost

125 Sniado v. Bank Austria AG, 378 F.3d 210 (2d Cir. 2004).

126 *In re* Monosodium Glutamate Antitrust Litig., 477 F.3d 535 (8th Cir. 2007).

127 *In re* Dynamic Random Access Memory (DRAM) Antitrust Litig., 546 F.3d 981 (9th Cir. 2008).

128 452 F.Supp. 2d 555 (D. Del. 2006).

129 *Id.* at 560 (citation omitted).

130 *Id.*

131 *Id.* at 562.

132 *Id.*

sales to non-U.S. distributors selling to non-U.S. markets, and interference with sales to European-based retailers.

It is worth noting that some FTAIA jurisdictional challenges may require a factual record. In *Sun Microsystems Inc. v. Hynix Semiconductor Inc.*, for example, where the defendants in a global DRAM chip price-fixing scheme moved to dismiss from U.S. litigation transactions made by the plaintiffs' foreign affiliates, the court ruled that "if plaintiffs can articulate and prove a legal theory that . . . they stand in the shoes of or are the alter ego of their foreign affiliates as well as a factual basis for such a claim, the court would be permitted to find that proximate cause under the FTAIA is necessarily satisfied, and that jurisdiction exists." The court denied the motion and moved the case into the discovery phase, without prejudice to a renewed defense motion on the same grounds after discovery. Ultimately, however, the plaintiff was unable to establish that it "stands in the shoes of its foreign subsidiaries," so the court viewed the foreign purchases "as foreign transactions made by independent subsidiary entities" that did not satisfy the jurisdictional requirements of the FTAIA.

A narrow interpretation by a panel of the 7th Circuit of the two exceptions to the FTAIA that brings foreign conduct back within the purview of the U.S. antitrust laws resulted in dismissal of an action against potash producers in Canada, Russia, and Belarus brought by U.S. direct and indirect purchasers in *Minn-Chem, Inc. v. Agrium Inc.*[133] The plaintiffs alleged that the defendants were engaged in a price-fixing conspiracy "to coordinate potash prices and price increases so as to fix, raise, maintain, and stabilize the price at which potash was sold in the United States at artificially inflated and anticompetitive levels." The court held this language to be "wholly conclusory" and insufficient under the standards of *Twombly* and *Iqbal* to satisfy the "import commerce" exception to the FTAIA.

Nor did the facts alleged in the *Minn-Chem* complaint satisfy the "direct effects" exception to the FTAIA. The court found in the general allegations of the complaint an

> absence of specific factual content to support the asserted proposition that prices in China, India, and Brazil serve as a "benchmark" for prices in the United States and that this benchmark, if it exists, has a strong enough relationship with the domestic potash market to raise a plausible inference that the defendants' foreign anticompetitive conduct has a "direct, substantial, and reasonably foreseeable effect" on domestic or import commerce. . . . Even taking into account "the nature of a global market," the allegations here amount to "nothing more than what courts have termed a 'ripple effect' on the United States domestic market, and the FTAIA prevents the Sherman Act from reaching such 'ripple effects.'"[134]

As of this writing a motion for a rehearing of the Seventh Circuit's decision in this case is pending.

6.03.1(F) Express antitrust immunities and exemptions

Numerous other statutes and common law doctrines limit the reach of the antitrust laws by providing an express immunity or exemption for particular industries or commercial activities, giving rise to additional potential challenges to an antitrust complaint.

---

[133] No. 10-1712 (7th Cir. Sept. 23, 2011).

[134] *Id.* (quoting *In re* Intel Corp. Microprocessor Antitrust Litig., 452 F.Supp.2d 555, 561 (D.Del. 2006)).

In the agricultural field, the Clayton Act § 6, 15 U.S.C. § 17, permits, among other things, the operation of non-profit, non-stock agricultural or horticultural mutual assistance organizations. The Capper-Volstead Agricultural Producers' Associations Act, 7 U.S.C. §§ 291–92, allows agricultural producers to act in concert for the purpose of "collectively processing, preparing for market, handling, and marketing" products, and to have "market agencies in common." The Capper-Volstead Cooperative Marketing Act of 1926, 7 U.S.C. §§ 451–57, authorizes the acquisition and exchange of past, present, and prospective pricing, production, and marketing data among agricultural producers and associations.

Similarly, under the Export Trading Company Act of 1982, 15 U.S.C. §§ 4001–03, a certificate of review issued by the Secretary of Commerce with the concurrence of the Attorney General provides limited antitrust immunity for specific export trade, export trade activities, and methods of operation. The Webb-Pomerene (Export Trade) Act, 15 U.S.C. §§ 61–66, immunizes the formation and operation of associations by competing businesses to engage in collective export sales, excluding anticompetitive effects within U.S. domestic commerce or injury to domestic competitors of the export trade association members.

Collective activity by employees relating to a dispute concerning terms or conditions of employment and legitimate objectives of labor organizations are immune from the antitrust laws by virtue of the Clayton Act § 20, 29 U.S.C. § 52. The Norris-LaGuardia Act of 1932, 29 U.S.C. §§ 101–15, provides that U.S. courts may not issue restraining orders or injunctions against certain labor union activities, for example, on the grounds of a threatened antitrust violation.

The McCarran-Ferguson Act, 15 U.S.C. §§ 1011–15 exempts the "business of insurance" from the antitrust laws to the extent "regulated by state law," except for acts of "boycott, coercion or intimidation." The Fishermens' Collective Marketing Act, 15 U.S.C. §§ 521–22, permits fishermen to act together for the purpose of catching, producing, and marketing their products. The Newspaper Preservation Act of 1970, 15 U.S.C. §§ 1801–04, provides a limited antitrust exemption for joint operating arrangements between newspapers that share production facilities and commercial operations. The Sports Broadcasting Act of 1961, 15 U.S.C. §§ 1291–95, exempts certain agreements among professional sports teams to negotiate through their leagues for the sale of television rights. Still other laws exempt certain joint research activities, local governments, and joint purchasing in national emergencies. These provisions, customarily pleaded as affirmative defenses in the responsive pleading, may also serve as the basis for a Rule 12(b)(6) pre-answer motion to dismiss.

6.03.2 Rule 12(b)(7) pre-answer motion to dismiss for failure to join a required party

Rule 19 covers certain circumstances in which a non-party to the litigation may be necessary and indispensable to the proper adjudication of the controversy. Rule 19(a)(1)(A) addresses a person in whose "absence, the court cannot accord complete relief among existing parties," and Rule 19(a)(1)(B) protects unrepresented interests in the subject of the action where adjudication would (1) "as a practical matter impair or impede the person's ability to protect the interest," or (2) leave the party "subject to a substantial risk of incurring double, multiple, or otherwise inconsistent obligations because of the interest."[135] The absence of a required party is typically raised by a Rule 12(b)(7) motion to dismiss for failure to join a party under Rule 19, but may also be raised in any responsive pleading. Although an objection that a required party has not been joined may be properly denied for lack of timeliness if it is raised too late in the proceedings, it is not among the Rule 12(b) defenses that is waived if not raised in a Rule 12(b) pre-answer motion (if one is filed) or in the responsive pleading (if a Rule 12 motion is not filed). The burden of persuasion lies with the party seeking dismissal to demonstrate that the non-party is a required party.

The Rule sets out a two-part analysis. First, the court will determine whether the person is essential to the litigation. If so, and joinder of the party is feasible, the court must issue an order joining the party. If the person is required but for some reason cannot be joined, the court must then use the factors outlined in Rule 19(b)(1)–(4) to "determine whether, in equity and good conscience, the action should proceed among the existing parties or should be dismissed." The application of Rule 19 is highly fact specific, and courts may examine both legal and factual elements of the court's ability to afford complete relief or the impairment of a non-party's interest in the litigation.

6.03.3 Rule 12 motions objecting to personal jurisdiction, venue, and service of process

The second category of procedural defenses are the three kinds of issues raised by pre-answer motions under Rules 12(b)(2)–(5), objections to personal jurisdiction, venue, and service of process. These defenses may be waived if not raised in a timely manner, or may be deemed waived by implication, if the defendant's conduct is inconsistent with the objection. These defenses must be raised in a Rule 12 motion if one is filed or in the responsive pleading if one is not.

6.03.3(A) Dismissal for lack of personal jurisdiction

Individual parties may be dismissed from a lawsuit if the exercise of the court's jurisdiction over the "person" of the defendant does not meet the due process standards of the Fifth and Fourteenth Amendments of the Constitution. However, when a case is dismissed for lack of personal jurisdiction, the plaintiff is not precluded from refiling the lawsuit in a forum where personal jurisdiction over the defendant lies. The practical consequence of the exercise of personal jurisdiction over a defendant is to require the defendant to travel to the court to defend the action. For most civil actions the limitations on the exercise of personal jurisdiction by state courts are guided by the same considerations of due process, so Rule 4(k) equates the territorial limits of effective service of process in the federal court with the limits of personal jurisdiction of the courts of the state in which the federal court sits, with a special provision for Rule 19 parties, third parties, and interpleaded parties, which may be served anywhere within one hundred miles of the federal court, irrespective of any limitation on the state courts. The Rule also allows for personal jurisdiction over certain parties that have sufficient contacts with the United States as a whole.[136]

---

[135] Rule 19(a)(1)(B)(i)–(ii).
[136] Rule 4(k)(2).

In the case of corporations, private antitrust suits present an exception to the general rules of personal jurisdiction by virtue of § 12 of the Clayton Act, 15 U.S.C. § 22, which permits private antitrust defendants to be sued and served in any judicial district "where it may be found or transacts business." The appellate courts are split on the extent to which federal "nationwide service of process" statutes obviate considerations of due process, with some courts holding that the plaintiffs' choice of forum must still be fair and reasonable even where Congress has authorized nationwide personal jurisdiction.[137] Service of process in non-U.S. jurisdictions ordinarily requires compliance with international treaties or service of process in accordance with the customs of the non-U.S. jurisdiction.

Objections to personal jurisdiction may be waived if not raised in a timely manner, that is, in a Rule 12(b)(2) motion to dismiss for lack of personal jurisdiction (if a Rule 12(b) motion is filed) or in the responsive pleading. The federal appellate courts are split as to whether a defendant contesting personal jurisdiction who simultaneously pleads a counterclaim is deemed to have waived objection to personal jurisdiction. The burden of persuasion lies with the party asserting that the court has jurisdiction. There is no required order for the court's determination as between an objection to subject matter jurisdiction and an objection to personal jurisdiction.[138]

The three kinds of jurisdiction over "persons or things" are: (1) personal, or *in personam*, jurisdiction, (2) attachment, or quasi *in rem*, jurisdiction, and (3) jurisdiction over an object or land, or *in rem* jurisdiction. At least one form of personal jurisdiction must be established over each defendant in the lawsuit. Private antitrust litigation ordinarily requires *in personam* jurisdiction over the defendant. If no form of jurisdiction has been acquired, the court will typically dismiss the action.

The due process analysis considers the contacts of the defendant with the forum state and the quality of the notice to the defendant. The most common means of satisfying the due process requirement are:

- the defendant's consent to personal jurisdiction;
- service of process on a defendant found within the state; and
- service of process on a defendant outside the state where the defendant has sufficient contacts with the forum state.

In general, parties to a contract may consent by agreement to personal jurisdiction in a specified forum. Parties that waive objection to personal jurisdiction because they fail to timely object may also be deemed to have consented. A defendant that objects to personal jurisdiction consents to be bound by the court's determination of whether personal jurisdiction exists.[139]

Because the Rules encourage waiver of service of process, they encourage defendants to consent to personal jurisdiction implicitly. Where a defendant submits a written waiver

---

137 *See, e.g.*, Peay v. BellSouth Medical Assistance Plan, 205 F.3d 1206, 1210 (10th Cir. 2000) (nationwide service of process proper where defendants "have adequate contacts [within] the United States as a whole").

138 Ruhrgas AG v. Marathon Oil Co., 526 U.S. 574 (1999).

139 Insurance Corp. of Ireland v. Compagnie des Bauxites di Guinee, 456 U.S. 694 (1982).

of service of process and, therewith, waives objections to personal jurisdiction, the time to respond to the complaint will be enlarged from 20 to 60 days.[140]

A defendant found within the state may be in transit and need not necessarily reside in the state or be regularly found there.[141] However, persons induced to travel to the forum state by coercion or fraud will not be subject to personal jurisdiction.[142] Defendants not found within the forum state may nonetheless be subject to the court's personal jurisdiction if the party has sufficient minimum contacts of such a nature so as not to offend "traditional notions of fair play and substantial justice."[143]

6.03.3(b) Motion to dismiss or to transfer for improper venue

Venue refers to the appropriate federal district in which to bring a lawsuit, and should be proper even where subject matter and personal jurisdiction are satisfied. The general criteria for federal court venue are set forth in 28 U.S.C. § 1391. Section 1391(a) covers cases in which federal jurisdiction is based on diversity of citizenship, and § 1391(b) covers non-diversity cases. Both provisions emphasize where the defendant resides, where the events giving rise to the lawsuit took place, and where a defendant is subject to personal jurisdiction.

Defendants have available two types of challenges to improper venue. A Rule 12(b)(3) motion to dismiss for improper venue invokes the common law principle of *forum non conveniens*, as described, for example, in *Gulf Oil Corp. v. Gilbert*.[144] The second kind of challenge to improper venue is a motion to transfer pursuant to the authority granted to the court by 28 U.S.C. § 1404, which provides that "[f]or the convenience of parties and witnesses, in the interest of justice, a district court may transfer any civil action to any other district or division where it might have been brought." However, 28 U.S.C. § 1406(a) provides that "a district court in which is filed a case laying venue in the wrong division or district shall dismiss, or if it be in the interest of justice, transfer such case to any district or division. . . ." Finally, § 1406(b) provides that "[n]othing . . . shall impair the jurisdiction of a district court of any matter involving a party who does not interpose timely and sufficient objection to the venue." That is, objections to venue, like objections to personal jurisdiction, may be waived if not timely raised. Courts are split on which party bears the burden of proof when venue is challenged, but the majority view is that the party that has chosen the forum bears the burden for establishing proper venue. The procedure for resolving objections to venue is the same as that for determining issues of personal jurisdiction.[145]

---

140 Rule 4(d)(1).

141 Rule 4(e)(2).

142 *See, e.g.*, Amusement Equipment, Inc. v. Mordelt, 779 F.2d 264, 271 (5th Cir. 1985). For further discussion of personal jurisdiction, see Chapter 4 of this Handbook.

143 International Shoe Co. v. Washington, 326 U.S. 310 (1945).

144 330 U.S. 501, 503 (1947) ("[T]he defendant, invoking the doctrine of *forum non conveniens*, claimed that the appropriate place for trial is Virginia, where the plaintiff lives and defendant does business, where all events in litigation took place, where most of the witnesses reside, and where both state and federal courts are available to plaintiff and are able to obtain jurisdiction of the defendant.").

145 *See* Gulf Ins. Co. v. Glasbrenner, 417 F.3d 353, 355 (2d Cir. 2005). For further discussion of venue, see Chapter 4 of this Handbook.

6.03.3(C) Dismissal for insufficient process or service

Rules 12(b)(4) and 12(b)(5) provide related but different procedures for objection to the basis on which the defendant was served with the court's process. Rule 12(b)(4) is used to challenge the sufficiency of the form of the process, rather than the manner or method by which it is served. By contrast, Rule 12(b)(5) challenges the mode of delivery or the lack of delivery of the summons and complaint.[146]

Service of process – i.e., the delivery of the summons and complaint – may be deficient if the forms are not properly issued or the summons sets forth the wrong name or is not sealed by the clerk of court. Such defects are challenged by way of a Rule 12(b)(5) motion to quash. Unless a party is able to demonstrate actual prejudice, however, courts will often overlook technical defects on the face of the service of process.

Similarly, the mode of delivery may be deficient if it is made at the wrong place, served on an incompetent, minor, or non-agent of the defendant, or not accomplished within 120 days after commencement of the action. Ordinarily, the appropriate defense is a Rule 12(b)(4) or (5) motion to quash for insufficient process or service, rather than a motion to dismiss. Mislabeling the motion under the wrong provision of the rules will ordinarily not be fatal to the defense. Where there is a reasonable chance that service of process is likely to be able to be accomplished on a second attempt, courts are more likely to quash service of process rather than dismiss the action.

In general, objections to service of process will be waived if not raised in a Rule 12(b) pre-answer motion (if one is filed) or else in the responsive pleading. However, where it is shown that the defendants never received actual notice of the complaint, defendants will be able to raise the failure of service of process in opposition to a motion for default. When service of process is challenged, the plaintiff has the burden to demonstrate proper service and process. An executed return of service constitutes *prima facie* evidence that service was properly effectuated, but it is not conclusive if the defendant can adduce evidence challenging the affidavit or return. A well-founded objection to service of process must be specific, must describe any prejudice suffered by the defendant, and must demonstrate how service of process was defective under the requirement of Rule 4. Dismissal for failure of service of process is usually without prejudice to permit the plaintiff to re-attempt service of process.

§ 6.04 Summary proceedings

Summary proceedings may be non-evidentiary or evidentiary. A defendant may move for dismissal or judgment through a Rule 12(c) motion for judgment on the pleadings, provided the pleadings are closed and the motion is based on admitted allegations or a facial infirmity in the pleadings.[147] The court may also consider matters of which it may take judicial notice, but without reference to any other extrinsic evidence. Where the pleadings

---

[146] Davies v. Jobs & Adverts Online, GMBH, 94 F.Supp. 2d 719 (E.D. Va. 2000).

[147] Rule 12(c). A motion for judgment on the pleadings, provided it is brought "early enough not to delay trial," is also the appropriate means by which to raise the defense of failure to state a claim on which relief may be granted, if that defense has not previously been raised in a pre-answer motion or in the pleadings. If a defendant's motion for judgment on the pleadings on these grounds is deemed untimely, the defendant may still raise the defense at trial.

must be supplemented by extrinsic evidence in order to demonstrate the defendant's entitlement to dismissal or judgment, such as through affidavits, discovery materials, and other evidence, the appropriate vehicle is a motion for summary judgment.[148]

Parties may seek through summary proceedings to have the court determine specific legal or factual issues, adjudicate a particular claim, or dispose of an entire case. Thus, defendants may raise the affirmative defenses generally not permitted to be raised in a Rule 12(b) pre-answer motion, but which must be alleged in a responsive pleading. Cases that survive a defendant's motion for summary judgment frequently stand considerably improved chances of being voluntarily settled.

6.04.1 Motion for judgment on the pleadings

A Rule 12(c) motion is appropriate any time after the pleadings are closed, even before discovery, but must be raised "early enough not to delay trial." However, a Rule 12(c) motion made before an answer is filed is premature, and will be treated as a Rule 12(b) pre-answer motion. A Rule 12(c) motion for judgment on the pleadings may not be used to raise defenses that have been waived because they were not raised in a pre-answer motion. The motion is well founded if the movant can demonstrate that no material facts remain for determination at trial based on the pleadings or matters of which the court may take judicial notice. If a Rule 12(c) motion is granted, the prevailing party is entitled to a judgment in its favor.

The legal standard applicable to a Rule 12(c) motion mirrors that of a Rule 12(b)(6) motion to dismiss. Thus, well-pleaded allegations of the non-moving party are accepted as true subject to the stipulations regarding conclusory or factually neutral allegations introduced by the Supreme Court in the *Twombly–Iqbal* modification to the federal civil pleading standards discussed above in connection with Rule 12(b) pre-trial motions.

6.04.2 Rule 56 Motions for summary judgment or adjudication of issues

A Rule 56 motion for summary judgment may be brought by either the plaintiffs or the defendants. Rule 56(b) provides that "[a] party against whom relief is sought may move at any time, with or without supporting affidavits, for summary judgment on all or part of the claim." Thus, defending parties may move for summary judgment at any time, although the Circuits are split as to whether a Rule 56 motion filed before an answer is filed tolls the time for filing an answer.[149] Rule 56 establishes the procedure by which a party may request or oppose judgment on one, some, or all of the issues in the case, and it allows for an interlocutory determination on liability even where only the amount of damages would remain as a genuine issue.

6.04.2(A) Standard of review

The legal standard for summary judgment is similar to the requirements for judgment as a matter of law under Rule 50 (the equivalent of a motion for a directed verdict), which

---

148 Rule 56; *see also* Rule 12(d).

149 *See, e.g.*, Rashidi v. Albright, 818 F. Supp. 1354 (D. Nev. 1993).

should be granted "if, under the governing law, there can be but one reasonable conclusion as to the verdict."[150] The test is whether a reasonable jury could return a verdict in the non-moving party's favor. While a Rule 50 motion is brought during trial and raises the question of whether the case should be submitted to the jury, a Rule 56 motion for summary judgment is brought before trial, and raises the question of whether there is a need to convene a trial at all.

The court may enter summary judgment when no genuine issue exists as to any material fact, entitling the moving party to judgment as a matter of law. In contrast to a Rule 12(b)(6) pre-answer motion, where the well-pleaded allegations are assumed true and evaluated for their legal sufficiency, the court on summary judgment may consult the pleadings, any affidavits, depositions, interrogatory answers, admissions, Rule 26 disclosures, or other material to determine whether a genuine issue exists for trial. The evidence of the non-moving party will be assumed to be true, and doubts about the evidence will be resolved against the moving party. In ruling on a Rule 56 motion for summary judgment, the court's role is never to weigh the evidence, the credibility of witnesses, or to resolve disputed issues of fact, and it should not venture beyond the threshold question of whether a genuine issue exists regarding a material fact that requires a trial.[151]

A "genuine issue" exists where the evidence submitted could support a finding by a rational factfinder in favor of the non-moving party.[152] A fact is "material" if, under the applicable substantive law, the fact might affect the outcome of the suit.[153]

6.04.2(B) Burden of production

A moving party may submit a written motion on its own, or supplement it with pleadings, affidavits, discovery materials, transcripts of oral testimony from other proceedings, or matters of which the court may take judicial notice. In general, the evidence must be of a character that is admissible at trial. However, parties frequently rely on affidavits that would not be admissible without the testimony of the affiant, although Rule 56(e)(1) requires that affidavits "set out facts that would be admissible in evidence." Similarly, a document referred to in an affidavit must be attached as "a sworn or certified copy."

Rule 56(e)(2) provides that a party opposing summary judgment may not rely on allegations or denials in its pleadings, but is required to produce affidavits or other evidence that "set out specific facts showing a genuine issue for trial." As the Supreme Court noted in *Matsushita Elec. Indus. Co. v. Zenith Radio Corp.*,[154] "[w]hen the moving party has carried its burden under Rule 56(c), its opponent must do more than simply show that there is some metaphysical doubt as to the material facts. . . . Where the record taken as a whole could not lead a rational trier of fact to find for the non-moving party, there is no genuine issue for trial. . . ."[155]

---

150 Anderson v. Liberty Lobby, Inc., 477 U.S. 242, 250–51 (1986).
151 *Id.*
152 Matsushita Elec. Indus. Co. v. Zenith Radio Corp., 475 U.S. 574, 586 (1986).
153 *Anderson*, 477 U.S. at 248.
154 475 U.S. 574, 585 (1986).
155 *Id.*

6.04.2(c) Summary judgment in antitrust cases

The Court's *Matsushita* decision in 1986 ushered in a period of more frequent use of summary judgment to dispose of antitrust cases. Prior to that, statements such as the Supreme Court's admonition in *Poller v. CBS*[156] that "summary judgment procedures should be used sparingly in complex antitrust litigation" led to considerable reluctance by courts to dispose of antitrust cases on summary judgment. But, the *Matsushita* Court's observation that "antitrust law limits the range of ambiguous evidence in a § 1 case," created a special burden for antitrust plaintiffs seeking to survive summary judgment, particularly in § 1 conspiracy cases based on circumstantial evidence. The Court stated that to survive a motion for summary judgment or for a directed verdict, a plaintiff seeking damages for violation of § 1 must present evidence "that tends to exclude the possibility" that the alleged conspirators acted independently.[157] It should be emphasized that *Matsushita's* "more likely than not" standard sets out a limited special rule for what is necessary in § 1 cases in addition to ambiguous evidence of conspiracy, such as parallel conduct, for a plaintiff to survive summary judgment, and it should not be read more broadly so as to impinge on the province of the jury or the preponderance of the evidence standard by which a private antitrust plaintiff ordinarily must prove its case. The *Matsushita* decision has given rise to the practice of producing evidence of "plus factors" in connection with summary judgment motions, evidence that tends to bolster the inference of conspiracy in light of inconclusive or ambiguous evidence of parallel conduct. As described by one court, a plus factor refers to "any showing . . . that 'tend[s] to exclude the possibility of independent action.'"[158]

In cases involving direct evidence of a § 1 conspiracy or concerning other kinds of antitrust violations, the effect of *Matsushita* is more limited, but it still imposes a requirement that "the non-moving party's inferences be reasonable in order to reach the jury."[159] *Matsushita* remains particularly relevant when there is a question regarding the plausibility of the plaintiff's economic theory. In addition to establishing plus factors to bolster ambiguous evidence, the *Matsushita* Court observed that where "the factual context renders [the] claim implausible – if the claim is simply one that makes no economic sense – [plaintiffs] must come forward with more persuasive evidence to support their claim than would otherwise be necessary."[160] Disclaiming any special burden on antitrust plaintiffs, the Supreme Court in *Kodak* observed that:

> *Matsushita* demands only that the nonmoving party's inferences be reasonable in order to reach the jury, a requirement that was not invented, but merely articulated, in that decision. If the plaintiff's theory is economically senseless, no reasonable jury could find in its favor, and summary judgment should be granted.[161]

---

156 368 U.S. 464, 473 (1962).

157 *Matsushita*, 475 U.S. at 588.

158 Williamson Oil Co., Inc. v. Philip Morris USA, 346 F.3d 1287, 1301 (11th Cir. 2003) (quoting City of Tuscaloosa v. Harcros Chems., Inc., 158 F.3d 548, 571 n.35 (11th Cir. 1998)).

159 Eastman Kodak Co. v. Image Tech. Servs., Inc., 504 U.S. 451, 468 (1992).

160 *Matsushita*, 475 U.S. at 589.

161 *Kodak*, 504 U.S. at 469.

Procedurally, the moving party carries its *prima facie* burden on summary judgment by demonstrating an absence of evidence supporting the non-moving party's claims or defenses. The burden of production then shifts to the non-moving party to show that a genuine issue of material fact remains for resolution by the jury.

7 Pretrial discovery in civil litigation

Joseph Goldberg[1] *and Dan E. Gustafson*[2]

[1] Joseph Goldberg is a partner in Freedman Boyd Daniels Hollander Goldberg Ives & Duncan, P.A., a law firm in Albuquerque, New Mexico. Mr. Goldberg practices in the area of antitrust law and complex commercial and class action litigation.

Mr. Goldberg and Mr. Gustafson wish to thank Karla Gluek for her invaluable assistance in writing this chapter.

[2] Dan E. Gustafson is a founding member of Gustafson Gluek PLLC, a law firm in Minneapolis, Minnesota. Mr. Gustafson practices in the areas of complex antitrust, patent, consumer protection, and class action litigation.

§ 7.01 Introduction

This chapter discusses the pretrial discovery process in civil litigation brought in federal court. Because most states model their rules governing civil litigation after the federal rules, the description of discovery in federal antitrust litigation provides substantial insight into the procedural rules applicable to many state antitrust lawsuits. Moreover, because the Class Action Fairness Act[3] requires many civil antitrust cases previously litigated in state courts to proceed in federal court, these cases are now often filed in or removed to federal court, and the state rules for discovery do not apply.

The nature of civil antitrust litigation makes pretrial discovery particularly important for several reasons. First, many of the acts that occur in the marketplace that give rise to antitrust concerns (for example, collusion) are usually covert. The civil discovery available in litigation is, therefore, a necessary tool for uncovering the details of those activities.[4]

Second, expert consultants and expert testimony are often utilized in antitrust litigation. For example, expert economists and statisticians often testify in antitrust litigation to assist in proving both liability and damages. Because of the extensive use of experts in civil antitrust litigation, the "expert" provisions of the federal pretrial discovery rules are often implicated in these cases.

Third, often civil antitrust litigation involves claims for very large damages amounts, which are subject to mandatory trebling under the Clayton Act.[5] Because of these high stakes, plaintiffs and defendants have an incentive to aggressively use pretrial discovery procedures to uncover all relevant information.

§ 7.02 Theory of the Federal Rules of Civil Procedure: Overview

The Federal Rules of Civil Procedure (the "Federal Rules" or the "Rules" or "Rule __") govern the procedure in all civil actions in the United States district courts, with a few exceptions. The stated purpose of the Federal Rules – the administration of a "speedy" or "inexpensive" determination reaching "justice"[6] – is the touchstone for the administration of the discovery process in federal court.

The disclosure of discoverable information by all parties to federal litigation is governed by the Federal Rules. The Rules provide for initial disclosures,[7] expert disclosures,[8] and pretrial disclosures.[9] Parties in civil litigation are required to make these disclosures without any formal discovery requests by the opposing party.

The Federal Rules also govern formal discovery requests, in which one party

---

3 28 U.S.C. § 1332(d) (2005).

4 Of course, public agencies involved in criminal antitrust enforcement also have powerful tools available for uncovering covert anticompetitive behavior, including the availability of federal and state investigative agencies. In addition, public enforcement agencies have civil discovery tools available (such as civil investigative demands).

5 15 U.S.C. § 15(a) (1982).

6 *See* FED. R. CIV. P. 1.

7 FED. R. CIV. P. 26(a)(1).

8 FED. R. CIV. P. 26(a)(2).

9 FED. R. CIV. P. 26(a)(3).

specifically requests certain information from another party to the litigation or from third parties. These formal discovery requests can be in the form of depositions,[10] written interrogatories,[11] and production of documents, including electronically stored information and tangible things.[12] Formal discovery requests can also seek entry onto land for inspection and other purposes,[13] physical and mental examinations,[14] and requests for admissions.[15] This chapter discusses each of these methods of discovery and their advantages or disadvantages to parties involved in civil litigation.

The discovery rules, which are found in Rules 26–37, are intended to provide the parties with the means to find the location of relevant information; to narrow the issues that are relevant to the litigation; and to obtain evidence for trial, thereby reinforcing the Rules' stated purpose of securing a "just, speedy and inexpensive determination."[16]

§ 7.03 Investigation/pre-filing discovery

7.03.1 Public enforcement agencies

Both the Antitrust Division of the United States Department of Justice (DOJ) and the Federal Trade Commission (FTC) have public enforcement responsibilities with respect to antitrust violations. Private antitrust litigation often follows public enforcement efforts and, occasionally, public enforcement is stimulated by private litigation.[17]

The federal public enforcement agencies are severely restricted in sharing information that they obtain through their investigative powers with private individuals (who are not the subject of the enforcement action).[18] However, that does not mean that no commu-

---

[10] FED. R. CIV. P. 27–32.

[11] FED. R. CIV. P. 33.

[12] FED. R. CIV. P. 34.

[13] *Id.*

[14] FED. R. CIV P. 35.

[15] FED. R. CIV P. 36.

[16] FED. R. CIV. P. 1. The enactment of Rules 26–37 changed pre-existing discovery practices in federal courts. *See* Hickman v. Taylor, 329 U.S. 495, 500–01 (1947); *see also* CHARLES ALAN WRIGHT, ARTHUR R. MILLER & RICHARD L. MARCUS, 8 FED. PRAC. & PROC. CIV. § 2001 (3d ed. 2010) (discussing the purposes and problems of discovery).

[17] For example, the consolidated private antitrust cases encaptioned *In re Nasdaq Market Makers Antitrust Litigation* were filed prior to any government investigation, and the information uncovered in the private litigation resulted in public enforcement that led to a substantial restructuring of the Nasdaq organization. *See generally, In re* Nasdaq Market Makers Antitrust Litig., 894 F. Supp. 703, 706 (S.D.N.Y. 1995); *see also* Arthur M. Kaplan, *Antitrust as a Public-Private Partnership: A Case Study of the NASDAQ Litigation*, 52 CASE WESTERN RES. L. REV. 111 (2001); *see also* Robert H. Lande & Joshua P. Davis, *Benefits from Private Antitrust Enforcement: Forty Individual Case Studies (2008), available at* http://papers.ssrn.com/abstract=1090661 (last visited Sept. 24, 2011) (listing a number of private suits not preceded by government actions).

[18] *See, e.g.*, FED. R. CRIM. P. 6(e) (generally prohibiting the disclosure of grand jury proceedings); 5 U.S.C. § 552(b)(7), which exempts from the Freedom of Information Act:

> records and information compiled for law enforcement purposes, but only to the extent that the production of such law enforcement records or information (A) could reasonably be expected to interfere with enforcement proceedings; . . . [or] (D) could reasonably be expected to disclose the identity of a confidential source, including a State, local or foreign agency or authority or

nication between public enforcement agencies and private litigants may occur. Private litigants often gain helpful information from publicly available information resulting from public investigations, through indictments, criminal plea agreements, allocutions, and proffers. Also, private litigants often voluntarily provide information to the DOJ or the FTC.[19]

7.03.2 Amnesty program

The Antitrust Division of the DOJ has a policy of providing leniency to corporations that report their illegal activity at an early stage, where certain conditions are met. In these situations, "leniency" means not charging such a firm criminally for the activity being reported, which is why the policy also is known as the "corporate amnesty" policy.

Although this "corporate amnesty" program encourages violators of the federal antitrust laws to reveal their illicit behavior to the DOJ, the threat of private antitrust litigation (and possibility of future treble damage judgments) that is likely to follow from any DOJ investigation may decrease incentives for early cooperation. In response to this concern, Congress passed the Antitrust Criminal Penalty Enhancement and Reform Act of 2004 (ACPERA), which provides that corporations that successfully enter the "corporate amnesty" program will have to pay only the actual damages (as opposed to treble damages) plus attorneys' fees, costs, and interest.[20] This limitation applies to antitrust violations litigated under both federal and state law and immunizes program participants from joint and several liability for the acts of their co-conspirators.[21] Significantly, the

---

> any private institution which furnished information on a confidential basis, and, in the case of a record or information compiled by criminal law enforcement authority in the course of a criminal investigation or by an agency conducting a lawful national security intelligence investigation, information furnished by a confidential source. . . .

Id.

[19] The public enforcement agencies occasionally will seek to delay discovery in private litigation on their claim that discovery in the private litigation will unduly interfere with the public agency's investigation. This claim will likely put the public agency and the private plaintiffs at odds with each other. *See In re* Air Cargo Shipping Servs., No. 06-1775, 2010 WL 5027536, at *1 (E.D.N.Y. Dec. 3, 2010) (recognizing that "courts in the Second Circuit have routinely granted motions made by prosecuting authorities seeking to intervene in civil actions for the purpose of obtaining stays of discovery"); *In re* Flash Memory Antitrust Litig., No. C 07-0086, 2007 WL 3119612 (N.D. Cal. Oct. 23, 2007) (recognizing that the government may intervene in a civil action for the purpose of limiting discovery when there is a parallel criminal proceeding involving a common question of law or fact).

[20] Antitrust Criminal Penalty Enhancement and Reform Act of 2004, Pub. L. No. 108-237, §§ 213(a)–(b), 118 Stat. 665, 66–67 (2004).

[21] "Joint and several liability" means that each member of a cartel or co-conspirator to an anticompetitive conspiracy is liable for the injured plaintiff's full damages. Although an injured plaintiff may not recover more than the judgment amount, joint and several liability can place added pressure on each of the co-conspirators, as each may be held liable for the acts of the other defendants in the litigation. For example, if there are three co conspirators and the plaintiff settles with two of them, each for $100,000, and the jury, after trial against the third co-conspirator, finds damages in the amount of $1,500,000, the remaining co-conspirator (because of joint and several liability) is liable for the full amount of the damages, trebled, minus the settlement amounts, or $1,300,000.

ACPERA requires the trial court to certify that corporations seeking to limit damages under the Act also have cooperated with the civil plaintiffs by providing them with documentation and reasonable access to potential witnesses.[22]

7.03.3 Talking with employees/former employees of possible antitrust violators

Prior to filing a lawsuit alleging antitrust violations, a lawyer for a plaintiff may wish to obtain more information regarding the potential antitrust activity by communicating with current or former employees of the companies that are suspected of committing antitrust violations. In some cases, the lawyer may have actually learned about the illegal activity from a current or former employee of one of the companies who came forward with information.

Many states have ethical rules governing lawyers' contact with current or former employees of an adverse party. Violations of those rules may result in disqualification of counsel to participate in the litigation against the company for which the current or former employees worked, and other possible sanctions.[23]

Rule 4.2 of the ABA Model Rules of Professional Conduct (Model Rules)[24] reads:

> In representing a client, a lawyer shall not communicate about the subject of the representation with a person the lawyer knows to be represented by another lawyer in the matter, unless the lawyer has the consent of the other lawyer or is authorized to do so by law or a court order.[25]

This Model Rule and similar rules adopted by individual states are concerned with counsel talking with a current or former employee of a corporation that may become a party to a lawsuit. Often, the propriety of such conversations under Model Rule 4.2 depends on the employee's role within the corporate structure.

---

22 *See* Antitrust Criminal Penalty Enhancement and Reform Act of 2004, Pub. L. No. 108-237, § 213(a)–(b), 118 Stat. 665, 66–67 (2004) (requiring that an amnesty applicant (1) must have a currently effective leniency agreement with the DOJ and (2) must cooperate with plaintiffs in the prosecution of the civil antitrust lawsuit). The Act does not apply to state attorney general lawsuits. In 2008, the DOJ clarified the leniency policy by establishing and answering a list of frequently asked questions. *See* U.S. Dep't of Justice, Frequently Asked Questions Regarding the Antitrust Div.'s Leniency Program & Model Leniency Letters, *available at* http://www.usdoj.gov/atr/public/criminal/239583.htm (last visited Sept. 24, 2011). On June 9, 2010, an amendment to ACPERA was passed, which, among other things, extends the operation of the statute until 2020. Pub. L. No. 111-190, § 211(a)(1), 124 Stat. 1275, 1275 (2010). The amendment also attempts to clarify what constitutes timely cooperation under the Act, a question that is often the subject of much dispute. Specifically, the amendment requires a leniency applicant to cooperate with civil plaintiffs "without unreasonable delay" following the expiration of a civil stay obtained by the Department of Justice. *Id.* at § 212(d).

23 *See, e.g., In re* Potash Antitrust Litig., No. 3-93-197, 1993 WL 543013, at *16–17 (D. Minn. Dec. 8, 1993); *compare* Camden v. Maryland, 910 F. Supp. 1115 (D. Md. 1996) (disqualifying counsel for ex parte contact with former employee) *with In re* EXDS, Inc., No. C05-0787, 2005 WL 2043020 (N.D. Cal. Aug. 24, 2005) (denying motion to disqualify counsel).

24 Since there is no single, federal rule governing this conduct and since the ABA Model Rules are widely adopted by the states, we use these Model Rules as the discussion reference.

25 Model Rules of Prof'l Conduct R. 4.2.

There are various tests that states apply to determine whether Model Rule 4.2 is violated by communications with an employee. The "control group" test operates to prevent opposing counsel from communicating with employees in the corporation's "control group" – i.e., the most senior corporate managers – without the corporate attorney's consent.[26] Under the "control group" test, only the employees with the power to control the corporation may properly be equated with the corporation itself.[27]

A second test has been described in official Comment [4] to Model Rule 4.2.[28] This test prohibits a lawyer for one party from communicating about the matter in dispute with persons having a managerial responsibility on behalf of the organization and with any person whose act or omission in connection with the matter may be imputed to the organization, or whose statement may constitute an admission on the part of the organization.[29] This test often turns on the meaning of "admission." Various courts have applied different meanings to the term "admission," thereby causing confusion as to what is permissible and what is not.[30]

In February 2002, the ABA revised Comment [4] to Model Rule 4.2 (now Comment [7] under the current Model Rules) to prohibit communications only with:

> [A] constituent of the organization who supervises, directs or regularly consults with the organization's lawyers concerning the matter or has authority to obligate the organization with respect to the matter or whose act or omission in connection with the matter may be imputed to the organization for purposes of civil or criminal liability.[31]

Several states have now adopted the ABA's 2002 changes to the Model Rules and Comments and have either adopted or proposed changes identical to or substantially similar to those in the new Comment [7].[32]

The question remains as to what limits apply to communications with former employees. The specific language quoted above does not appear to encompass former employees, and the 2002 version of Comment [7] to Model Rule 4.2 clearly states that "[c]onsent of the organization's lawyer is not required for communication with a former constituent."[33] The Comments caution, however, that a lawyer must not try to obtain any privileged communications or information from the former employee.[34]

---

26 *See* Ellen J. Messing & James S. Weliky, *Contacting Employees of an Adverse Corporate Party: A Plaintiff's Attorney's View*, 19 LAB. LAW. 353, 354–55 (2004).

27 *Id.*

28 MODEL RULES OF PROF'L CONDUCT R. 4.2 cmt.4 (1995).

29 Messing & Weliky, *supra* note 26, at 355–56 (citing MODEL RULES OF PROF'L CONDUCT R. 4.2 cmt.4 (1995)); *see also* MICH. RULES OF PROF'L. CONDUCT R. 4.2 cmt.

30 Messing & Weliky, *supra* note 26, at 356–57; *compare* Orlowski v. Dominick's Finer Foods, Inc., 937 F.Supp. 723, 730 (N.D. Ill. 1996) (prohibition should be read narrowly to permit broad access to witnesses), *with In re* Air Crash Disaster near Roselawn, 909 F.Supp. 1116, 1121 (N.D. Ill. 1995) (broad prohibition because "virtually every employee may conceivably make admissions binding on his or her employer").

31 *See* Messing & Weliky, *supra* note 26, at 357.

32 *Id.* at 358.

33 *Id.* at 363.

34 *Id.*; MODEL RULES OF PROF'L CONDUCT R. 4.2 cmt.7; *see also* Smith v. Kalamazoo Ophthalmology, 322 F. Supp. 2d 883, 888 (W.D. Mich. 2004) ("A majority of courts that have

When deciding whether to communicate with current or former employees of the opposing party, it is important for a lawyer to remember that whether a court will find the communication permissible is a fact-intensive determination, and the standard varies from state to state.[35] As such, it is difficult to generalize about what communications will be allowed and what communications will be prohibited. These concerns arise often as antitrust cases usually involve pre-filing investigations and often deal with information that emanates from a former employee of one of the companies in question.

7.03.4 Initial expert analysis

Prior to filing a lawsuit, the plaintiff may want to retain an expert consultant to do a preliminary analysis of the marketplace and an initial scope of damages.[36] This expert may or may not ultimately be disclosed as a "testifying expert" for the plaintiff. Unless the party has definitely determined at the outset that the expert consultant hired to do the initial analysis will not be the testifying expert, the party should treat this expert as a potential witness. The party must also remember that materials given to the expert may become discoverable by the opposing party in the litigation if the expert consultant is disclosed as a testifying expert or if the expert's analyses or opinions become part of the basis for allegations in the complaint.

Prior to filing the lawsuit, an expert in a potential antitrust action can provide various forms of useful information as to the relevant market. For example, an expert can define a relevant market and analyze the relevant market to determine: which products are within or outside the scope of the relevant market; the size of the relevant market and the amount of sales that may have been subject to the antitrust activity; the behavior of the actual and potential competitors in the relevant market; whether characteristics of the relevant market and the behavior of the firms in the relevant market are consistent or inconsistent with the exercise of market power; whether the pricing in the relevant market appears to reflect a competitive market; and whether the pricing in the relevant market supports a claim for antitrust violations. An expert can also analyze the possible overcharge that occurred to direct purchasers[37] as a result of the anticompetitive

---

considered the issue have held that Rule 4.2 does not bar *ex parte* communications with an adversary's former employees who are not themselves represented in the matter." (citations omitted)).

[35] *See, e.g.*, United States v. W.R. Grace, 401 F. Supp. 2d 1065, 1067 (D. Mont. 2005); *In re* Complaint of PMD Enters., Inc., 215 F. Supp. 2d 519, 526–27 (D.N.J. 2002) (applying New Jersey's version of Model Rule 4.2); Camden v. Maryland, 910 F. Supp. 1115, 1116 (D. Md. 1996); Clemons v. City of Detroit, 09-13480, 2010 WL 2089361 (E.D. Mich. May 24, 2010) (applying Michigan's version of Model Rule 4.2).

[36] For a full discussion of the role of expert witnesses in private antitrust actions, see Chapter 8 of this Handbook.

[37] A customer that does not purchase directly from a defendant lacks standing to sue for damages under the federal antitrust laws. *See* Hanover Shoe, Inc. v. United Shoe Machinery Corp., 392 U.S. 481 (1968) (prohibiting defendants from using a "pass on" defense against direct purchasers); Illinois Brick Co. v. Illinois, 431 U.S. 720 (1977) (finding that to allow standing to sue for indirect purchasers while refusing to allow a pass on defense would create a risk of double recovery against the defendants). For further discussion of antitrust standing, see Chapter 3 of this Handbook.

conduct and whether that overcharge was likely to be generally spread throughout the potential class.

Obtaining this type of information prior to filing an antitrust lawsuit may alert the plaintiff and plaintiff's counsel to possible pitfalls or problems, which might deter them from filing suit altogether or provide them with useful and important insight into the issues likely to arise during the litigation. Given the recent establishment of heightened pleading requirements in federal antitrust cases,[38] plaintiffs may wish to include information derived from any such expert analyses or opinions in support of the allegations in the complaint, keeping in mind the discovery obligations that might then arise.

7.03.5 FOIA requests/state law equivalent

Prior to initiating a lawsuit, the plaintiff or plaintiff's counsel may want to issue Freedom of Information Act requests to federal agencies seeking relevant public information.[39] The Freedom of Information Act[40] (FOIA or the Act) generally provides that any person has a right, enforceable in court, to obtain access to federal agency records, except to the extent that such records (or portions of them) are protected from public disclosure by one of nine exemptions or by one of three special law enforcement record exclusions.[41]

Obtaining certain records or information from a governmental agency may be a useful investigative tool. For example, if a party wants to assert that a company misused its patent to keep a generic manufacturer off the market in violation of the antitrust laws,[42] it may be beneficial to obtain the records that were submitted to the Patent Office by the company or the generic manufacturer.

However, not all records are accessible. For example, Exemption 4 of the Act protects "trade secrets and commercial or financial information obtained from a person [that is] privileged or confidential."[43] This exemption is intended to protect the interests of both the government and the individual or entity submitting the information by allowing the submitters to voluntarily provide the government with useful and reliable commercial or financial information with the assurance that the government will protect the information that is submitted from being released. This exemption, for example, may apply to a FOIA request to the Patent Office, if the information that a company submitted to the Patent Office is considered a "trade secret." It would then be excluded, under Exemption 4, from disclosures made pursuant to a FOIA request.

---

[38] *See* Bell Atlantic Corp. v. Twombly, 550 U.S. 544 (2007); Ashcroft v. Iqbal, 556 U.S. 662 (2009).

[39] Most states have some sort of Freedom of Information Act or Public Records Act that provides a method by which citizens may request access to government records. Again, these are subject to exemptions similar to the Federal FOIA and, therefore, have somewhat limited utility. *See, e.g.*, Minnesota Data Practices Act, Minn. Stat. § 13.03; New York State Freedom of Information Law, N.Y. Pub. Off. Law §§ 84–90 (2008).

[40] 5 U.S.C. § 552 (2000 & Supp. IV 2004).

[41] U.S. Dep't of Justice, Guide to the Freedom of Information Act Introduction, *available at* http://www.usdoj.gov/oip/foia_guide07/introduction.pdf (last visited Sept. 24, 2011).

[42] *See, e.g.*, *In re* Wellbutrin SR Antitrust Litig., Nos. 04-5525, 04-5898 & 05-396, 2006 WL 616292 (E.D. Pa. Mar. 9, 2006).

[43] 5 U.S.C. § 552(b)(4).

Another example of a useful FOIA request that may be made prior to filing a lawsuit is a request for documents related to the initiation of any enforcement action against the company that is the subject of the potential antitrust lawsuit. In this case, however, Exemption 7 of FOIA may come into play.

Exemption 7 of FOIA protects from disclosure "records or information compiled for law enforcement purposes." There are, however, several exceptions to this exemption that may permit the agency to produce documents in response to a FOIA request.[44]

An attorney representing a plaintiff or potential plaintiff in an antitrust case should consider utilizing these various resources to obtain information prior to even filing an antitrust complaint.

§ 7.04 Written discovery

Rule 26 sets forth the parties' duties to disclose and other general provisions governing discovery. The rule describes initial disclosures, expert disclosures, pretrial disclosures, and the timing for making those disclosures. It also identifies the scope of such discovery: "Parties may obtain discovery regarding any non-privileged matter that is relevant to any party's claim or defense – including the existence, description, nature, custody, condition, and location of any documents or other tangible things and the identity and location of persons who know of any discoverable matter."[45]

Rule 26 goes on to note that "[f]or good cause, the court may order discovery of any matter relevant to the subject matter involved in the action."[46] Relevant subject matter includes information that may not be admissible at trial but that may reasonably lead to the discovery of admissible evidence.[47]

7.04.1 Rule 26 initial disclosures

Rule 26(a)(1) requires that the parties make certain initial disclosures without waiting for a discovery request from the opposing side, unless exempted by Rule 26(a)(1)(B), or otherwise stipulated or ordered by the court. In the initial disclosures, a party must provide to the other parties early in the litigation, (1) the name and contact information (if known) of each individual that likely has discoverable information, along with a description of that information, that the party may use to support its claim or defenses; (2) a copy of, or description by category and location, of all documents that may be used to support the disclosing parties' claims or defenses; (3) a computation of each category of damages that the disclosing party is seeking and the documents upon which the computation is based;

---

[44] 5 U.S.C. § 552(b)(7); *see* U.S. Dep't of Justice, Guide to the Freedom of Information Act – Exemption 7, *available at* http://www.usdoj.gov/oip/foia_guide07/exemption7.pdf (last visited Sept. 24, 2011).

[45] Fed. R. Civ. P. 26(b)(1).

[46] *Id.*

[47] *Id.*

and (4) any insurance agreement which may satisfy all or part of a possible judgment in the action.[48]

The plaintiff in an antitrust action likely will not have a lot of information to disclose at the time of initial disclosures. Most of the relevant information is going to be in the hands of the defendants. Plaintiffs may be aware of names of company executives who have been indicted or charged with antitrust violations and, as such, would indicate those individuals as individuals likely to have discoverable information as required under Rule 26(a)(1)(A)(i). Plaintiffs also may be able to identify generally the types of documents that may be relevant. However, in antitrust cases, most of the relevant documents are likely to be in the possession of the defendant. In a price-fixing case, for example, plaintiffs often have invoices or other documents that demonstrate the fact of their purchase and the price they paid, but evidence of agreement and evidence tending to prove the amount of an overcharge is more likely to be found in defendants' records.

Part (iii) of Rule 26(a)(1)(A) asks for a computation of damages. Generally speaking, this information simply is not available at the time of initial disclosures. Computation of damages in antitrust cases often requires a statistical analysis of defendants' sales transaction data, usually by an economic expert, and, therefore, the damages usually cannot be computed without those records. As such, plaintiffs most often will respond in their initial disclosures that damages will be in the form of overcharges paid by the plaintiffs on the products that were the subject of the anticompetitive activity, and detailed computations will be provided pursuant to expert testimony.[49]

Finally, Part (iv) of Rule 26(a)(1)(A) also is not particularly relevant to plaintiffs in an antitrust action. As the plaintiff is the party seeking damages and is generally not subject to a judgment, there is no insurance coverage that is relevant to the plaintiff in these cases. Where the defendant has relevant insurance and that requirement is not waived or limited by court order, the policy must be made available for inspection or copying. Whether a corporation will have insurance that would pay for any damages that may arise from an antitrust case must be determined on a case by case basis by the defendants, who must decide whether their insurance policies would apply to any damages that may be awarded.

Pursuant to the Federal Rules, initial disclosures must be made within 14 days after the parties' Rule 26(f) conference.[50] The parties may stipulate or the court may order that initial disclosures be made at some other time. A party may also object during the Rule

---

[48] Fed. R. Civ. P. 26(a)(1)(A)(i)–(iv).

[49] The identity of or work performed by an initial expert does not have to be disclosed in the initial disclosures if the expert is going to be a non-testifying expert. *See* Crouse Cartage Co v. National Warehouse Investment Co., No. IP02-0072-C-T/K, 2003 WL 21254617 (S.D. Ind. 2003) (finding that the identity of a non-testifying expert is protected under Rule 26(b)(4)(B) and does not have to be included in initial disclosures).

[50] Rule 26(f) requires that the parties meet and confer as soon as practicable (but in no less than 21 days prior to the initial scheduling conference with the court) to discuss the nature of the claims and defenses, the possibility for settlement, the initial disclosures, and the development of a discovery plan. The discovery plan should include the parties' views and proposals on the timing of initial disclosures (if different from what is provided for by the rules), what discovery may be needed and when it should be completed, whether discovery should be conducted in phases, issues concerning electronically stored discovery, and issues relating to the privilege or work product protections, among other things.

26(f) conference that initial disclosures are not appropriate in the action, in which case the party must state the objection in the proposed discovery plan. "In ruling on the objection, the court must determine what disclosures, if any, are to be made and must set the time for disclosure."[51] Although the Federal Rules do require these initial disclosures, often courts do not strictly enforce these disclosure requirements in antitrust cases.

Initial disclosures pursuant to Rule 26(a)(1)(A) must be "based on information then reasonably available" to a party.[52] A party is "not excused from making its disclosures because it has not fully investigated the case or because it challenges the sufficiency of another party's disclosures or because another party has not made its disclosures."[53] That being said, the information available to an antitrust plaintiff will vary widely depending on the complexity of the issues, the number of defendants, and the number and location of witnesses and documents, among other things.

Under Rule 26(e), these initial disclosures must be supplemented or corrected during the litigation if the party learns that the disclosure is incomplete or incorrect. These corrections or supplementations must be made in a "timely manner."[54]

7.04.2 Interrogatories

Interrogatories are another method of discovery. These are formal, written requests by one party that require written responses from the opposing party. The answers to the interrogatories must be sworn to by the responding party and will constitute evidentiary admissions.[55] It is not sufficient for the attorney to sign the answers to interrogatories. Interrogatories must be answered by individuals that have the knowledge or information to provide the answer. Interrogatories that are directed to companies or other entities should be signed by an officer, agent, or employee who has the requisite knowledge.[56] A party may object to interrogatories, but must state the objection with specificity and must include all grounds to support the objection.[57] Typical objections include assertions that the interrogatory is vague, ambiguous, overly broad, unduly burdensome, seeks privileged information, or is outside the scope of Rule 26.

Rule 33 addresses interrogatories in specific detail. The rule limits the number of written interrogatories that any one party may serve on another party to no more than 25, unless the parties agree to a different number or a court order permits additional interrogatories.[58] This limitation includes subparts, so that a party may not circumvent the cap on interrogatories by way of clever labeling.[59] Rule 33 and Rule 26 together encourage parties to be discerning in both the amount and scope of information they seek through interrogatories. For this reason, interrogatories are best used to obtain specific, objective

---

51 Fed. R. Civ. P. 26(a)(1)(C).
52 Fed. R. Civ. P. 26(a)(1)(E).
53 *Id.*
54 Fed. R. Civ. P. 26(e).
55 Fed. R. Civ. P. 33(b)(5).
56 Fed. R. Civ. P. 33(b)(1)(B).
57 Fed. R. Civ. P. 33(b)(4).
58 Fed. R. Civ. P. 33(a)(1).
59 *Id.*

information. For example, interrogatories asking for names, titles, dates, or the identification of specific documents require a very specific and objective answer and, therefore, can be useful in tracking down additional relevant information. Interrogatories that are not as specific or narrowly focused can elicit vague answers that are usually qualified with so many objections that they become almost meaningless.

A party may ask "contention" interrogatories, which seek all facts that the opposing party possesses that support or refute any claims or defenses in the litigation. The requesting party may also ask for all documents that support the opposing party's response to that "contention" interrogatory. For example, a plaintiff may ask the defendants to "identify all facts that support the defendant's affirmative defense." The plaintiff then may also ask for all documents that support the defendant's affirmative defense. These interrogatories may be effective in forcing a party to identify the real claims or defenses at issue and the evidence the party has to support those claims or defenses. Often courts will set a deadline by which both parties have to respond to "contention" discovery. This deadline is frequently extended beyond the 30-day deadline set forth in Rule 33(b)(2) to a date that is further along in the discovery process (or even until the end of discovery) to allow the parties the benefit of that discovery when responding to the contention requests.

Rule 33(d) permits a party to produce business records in lieu of responding to interrogatories under certain conditions.[60] The production of documents or the identification of documents instead of a response to an interrogatory has advantages and disadvantages. On one hand, identifying or producing documents in response to an interrogatory puts the burden on the requestor to uncover the answer within those documents. This is not to say that a responding party can hide the answer among a mass of documents, most of which are not responsive to the interrogatory. Most courts in these circumstances will require the responder to identify the responsive documents.[61] Providing documents in lieu of a written answer also avoids providing the requesting party with an admission in the answering party's own words that may be damaging when read to a judge or a jury. On the other hand, merely identifying the documents or producing the documents rather than responding does not allow the responding party to craft the answer in the light most favorable to itself.

7.04.3 Requests for production of documents

Another means of obtaining discovery is through requests for the production of documents. Rule 34 permits a party to serve on another party a request to produce (or permit

---

[60] Fed. R. Civ. P. 33(d).

[61] Graske v. Auto Owners Ins. Co., 647 F. Supp. 2d 1105 (D. Neb. Aug. 13, 2009) (recognizing that "if a party responds to interrogatories pursuant to Rule 33(d), it must specify the documents from which the responses to the interrogatories can be derived in sufficient detail to enable the interrogating party to locate the documents as readily as the responding party could") (citing Fed. R. Civ. P. 33(d)); *see also In re* Sulfuric Acid Antitrust Litig., 231 F.R.D. 320, 326 (N.D. Ill. 2005) (finding that it is not sufficient for a responding party to simply direct the interrogating party to a mass of business records); Harry M. v. Pennsylvania Dept. of Public Welfare, No. 1:10-cv-922, 2011 WL 53047, at *1 (M.D. Pa. Jan. 7, 2011) (citing Fed. R. Civ. P. 33 advisory committee's notes to 1980 amendment noting that "directing the interrogating party to a mass of business records or . . . offering to make all . . . records available . . . [is] an abuse of" Rule 33(d)).

for inspection, copying, testing, or a sample) any designated documents or electronically stored information or any designated tangible thing.[62] In collusion cases, defendants' internal documents, obtained through discovery, are often the primary source of evidence of defendants' collusive behavior. Documents or electronically stored information include writings, drawings, graphs, charts, photographs, sound recordings, images, and other data or data compilations.[63] In antitrust litigation, document requests usually are a primary means of pretrial discovery and are typically served during the first wave of discovery. It is through these document requests that an antitrust plaintiff may obtain a defendant's transactional data that often provides key evidence in estimating damages. Again, the scope of documents or other information that may be sought by a party is limited by Rule 26.[64]

Rule 34 is limited to parties and itself does not require a non-party to respond to a request for production of documents. Rule 45, however, allows for such discovery from a non-party and will be discussed in more detail below.

The Federal Rules do not limit the number of document requests that a party can serve (although some courts place limits on the extent of discovery under Rule 34 in their local court rules), and a party responding to the request must state that no responsive documents exist, that inspection will be permitted, or that a copy will be produced, or else it must object to the request. If a party objects to one part of the request it must still produce documents in response to the non-objectionable portions of the request.[65]

Rule 34 requires only the production of those documents or information that is in the responding party's possession, custody, or control.[66] The question of what is meant by "possession, custody, or control" has been addressed by courts in various situations. Possession and custody includes both actual and constructive possession and custody. A party may also have "control" over responsive documents even if they do not have "possession" or "custody." For example, if the responding party has the legal right to obtain the documents, regardless of whether the document is actually in the party's possession, that party may be found to have "control" over the documents.[67] A party can be required to produce a document that is not in its direct possession but is in the possession of its legal counsel, its insurance company, or its other agents.[68]

In an antitrust case, the plaintiff is often suing large corporations that have many organizational divisions or entities. The question of whether the party has possession, custody, or control will often arise in the context of whether the duty to search and produce responsive documents extends beyond the accused organizational entity to its

---

[62] Fed. R. Civ. P. 34(a)(1)(A)–(B). As noted, Rule 34 also permits requests for items other than documents or electronically stored information. This is not as likely to come into play in an antitrust case as it would, for example, in a patent case, where the design of the product is at issue. Rule 34 also allows for the inspection, among other things, of land or other property. Fed. R. Civ. P. 34(a)(2). This is also an unlikely request in an antitrust case.

[63] Fed. R. Civ. P. 34(a)(1)(A).

[64] Rule 26 was amended in 2006 to provide additional guidance on electronically stored discovery, which will be discussed in more detail below.

[65] Fed. R. Civ. P. 34(b)(2)(B) & (C).

[66] Fed. R. Civ. P. 34(a)(1).

[67] 8A Wright, Miller & Marcus, *supra* note 16, § 2210.

[68] *Id.*

related entities. If the facts suggest that one of the corporate entities essentially controls the other, the court will likely find that the party is in "control" of the documents held at the related corporation for purposes of Rule 34 and require the responding party to produce those documents.[69]

Similarly, a question will often arise in antitrust cases with regard to documents of a former employee of a party corporation. Courts have generally found that corporations do not have control over former employees, but may require the corporations to make inquiries of former employees.[70]

A party responding to document requests may object to all or part of any request for production of documents. Common objections to document requests include an objection that the documents are not in the party's possession, custody, or control or are no longer in existence; that the request is unduly burdensome, overly broad, or vague; and that the documents requested are privileged. Again, these objections must specify which part of the request is objectionable. The responding party must reply within 30 days after service of the request, and must either produce the documents or identify a time and place for inspection and/or copying of the documents.[71] A responding party must also produce the documents in their native format or must organize and label them to correspond to the categories in the request.[72] The production of electronically stored documents is discussed below.

7.04.4 Electronic discovery

Electronic discovery or e-discovery is an area of discovery that is still developing. Much has been written and discussed about e-discovery in the last several years. Rule 34, as originally adopted, addressed discovery of "documents" and "things."[73] In 1970, in anticipation of the rise in the use of computerized technology, the Rule was amended to include discovery of "data compilations."[74] In 2006, Rule 34 was again amended to further take into account the issues raised by electronically stored information, including stored electronic data and stored electronic documents.[75] The 2006 amendments make clear that discovery of electronically stored information "stands on equal footing with discovery of paper documents."[76] The Comments state, "[t]he change clarifies that Rule 34 applies to information that is fixed in a tangible form and to information that is stored in a medium from which it can be retrieved and examined."[77] As such, requests for production of documents under Rule 34 should be understood to encompass, and responses should include, electronically stored information unless otherwise specified.

---

69 *Id.*
70 *Id.*
71 Fed. R. Civ. P. 34(b)(2)(A).
72 Fed. R. Civ. P. 34(b)(2)(E)(i).
73 Fed. R. Civ. P. 34 cmt. 2006 Amendment.
74 Fed. R. Civ. P. 34 cmt. 1970 Amendment.
75 *Id.*
76 *Id.*
77 *Id.*

Rule 26(f) was also amended to address the emergence of e-discovery. Rule 26(f) now directs the parties to meet and confer prior to a Rule 26(f) conference to discuss any issues about the disclosure or discovery of electronically stored information, including the form or forms in which it should be produced.[78]

In reality, and as the Comment states, the issues to be addressed during the Rule 26(f) conferences relating to e-discovery depend on the nature and extent of the contemplated discovery and the parties' information systems.[79] The Comment encourages parties to discuss those issues prior to the conference and become familiar with the systems at issue so the parties can develop a discovery plan that takes into account the capabilities of the various systems.[80] Such pre-conference meet-and-confers among the parties regarding e-discovery are especially helpful in antitrust cases where the parties often include large firms and where there will be extensive electronic information subject to discovery. Typically, issues discussed at these meet-and-confers include, among other things: (1) the nature, extent, and identification of information systems and databases; (2) the file formats in which electronic documents will be produced, such as "native," "tiff," "pdf," etc.; (3) the extent of "metadata"[81] produced with electronic documents and whether the documents will be "searchable;" (4) search parameters, including identification of document custodians and locations and electronic search terms; and (5) the medium of production (i.e., electronic files, disks, hard-drives, etc.).

Often, it is helpful for the parties to involve individuals who are familiar with the various computer systems utilized by the parties or who possess particular IT expertise in these early discussions.[82] Often, these discussions result in agreed upon protocols governing this facet of discovery. At least one state, Maryland, has adopted a suggested "Protocol for Discovery of Electronically Stored Information."[83]

In addition to meet-and-confers among the parties as to electronic document production (e.g. emails), it is also helpful to discuss production of the relevant parties' electronic transaction data. Often in antitrust cases, these data sets are large and can be complex and cryptic. Almost invariably, the electronic transaction data is provided to the parties' economic or statistical experts for analysis. Typically, parties discuss and try to reach agreement on issues with respect to transaction data, such as: (1) the existence of "data dictionaries" or other documents that would assist in identifying what information is in

---

78 FED. R. CIV. P. 26(f)(3)(C); *see also* FED. R. CIV. P. 26(f) cmt. 2006 Amendment.

79 FED. R. CIV. P. 26(f) cmt. 2006 Amendment.

80 *Id.*

81 Metadata is structured information about an electronic file that is embedded in the file but not normally visible when viewing a printed or on-screen rendition of the document, and which describes the characteristics, origins, usage, and validity of the electronic file. *See* The Sedona Conf. Working Group on Elec. Doc. Retention & Prod., *The Sedona Glossary: for E-Discovery & Digital Information Mgmt.*, 33 (Conor Crowley & Sherry Harris eds., 2d ed. 2007), *available at* http://www.thesedonaconference.org/dltForm?did=TSCGlossary_12_07.pdf.

82 In 2006, Rule 16(b) was also amended to alert the court to the possible need to address the handling of discovery of electronically stored information at the pretrial conference. FED. R. CIV. P. 16(b)(3)(B)(iii).

83 *See* D. Md., Suggested Protocol for Discovery of Electronically Stored Information ("ESI"), *available at* http://www.mdd.uscourts.gov/news/news/esiprotocol.pdf (last visited Sept. 24, 2011).

particular fields in the data; (2) the existence of "cross-walks" or other documents that would assist in identifying products, customers, and, locations; and (3) the availability of party IT personnel for informal consultation on data questions. Sometimes, such agreements are incorporated into an agreed upon protocol.

Rule 26(b)(2) was amended to address the specific limitations on e-discovery. Rule 26(b)(2)(B) states:

> A party need not provide discovery of electronically stored information from sources that the party identifies as not reasonably accessible because of undue burden or cost. On motion to compel discovery or for a protective order, the party from whom discovery is sought must show that the information is not reasonably accessible because of undue burden or cost. If that showing is made, the court may nonetheless order discovery from such sources if the requesting party shows good cause, considering the limitations of Rule 26(b)(2)(C).[84]

As the Comments make clear, the determination of whether the information is reasonably accessible or not is made on a case by case basis. "It is not possible to define in a rule the different types of technological features that may affect the burdens and costs of accessing electronically stored information."[85] The Comments also make clear that "[a] party's identification of sources of electronically stored information as not reasonably accessible does not relieve the party of its common law or statutory duties to preserve evidence."[86] Again, it is beneficial for the parties to discuss, at the outset of the case, whether a party believes the information sought will be reasonably accessible so those issues can either be agreed upon by the parties or brought before the court.

Finally, Rule 37(e) was amended in 2006 to protect a party from sanctions for failing to provide electronically stored information "lost as a result of the routine, good faith operation of an electronic information system."[87]

The Comments to the Rule confirm that "[t]he good faith requirement . . . means that a party is not permitted to exploit the routine operation of an information system to thwart discovery obligations by allowing that operation to continue in order to destroy specific stored information that it is required to preserve."[88]

For example, if a system has an automatic purge of information after 30 days, a party must take steps to disengage that feature if failure to do so would result in the loss of otherwise discoverable information. If a party is able to do so but does not, that party may be found to have not acted in good faith, and thus sanctions may be appropriate. As such, it may be beneficial for the parties to discuss, early in the litigation, what types of automatic purging of information or destruction of information occurs in a party's computer systems so it can be addressed either by agreement of the parties or by the court.

---

[84] FED. R. CIV. P. 26(b)(2)(B). For discussion of an antitrust plaintiff's ability to recover e-discovery costs pursuant to the Clayton Act, 15 U.S.C. § 15 (2009), see Chapter 9 and Chapter 10 of this Handbook.

[85] FED. R. CIV. P. 26(b)(2) cmt. 2006 Amendment.

[86] *Id.*

[87] FED. R. CIV. P. 37(e).

[88] FED. R. CIV. P. 37(f) cmt. 2006 Amendment.

7.04.5 Requests for admissions

Rule 36 governs requests for admissions. Rule 36 allows a party to serve on another party a written request to admit the truth of any matter that is otherwise discoverable under Rule 26(b)(1), and which relates to "(a) facts, the application of law to facts, or opinions about either; and (b) the genuineness of any described documents."[89]

Requests for admissions are not as commonly used as interrogatories, depositions, or requests for production of documents. However, requests for admission can be beneficial in narrowing the disputed issues for a hearing or trial.

Rule 36 states that if a party cannot admit the information set forth in the request, the party must "specifically deny it or state in detail why the answering party cannot truthfully admit or deny it."[90] Unlike interrogatories, which allow the responding party to craft the answer, requests for admission are closed-ended questions that are crafted by the requesting party. An admission in response to a request is conclusive, and that issue need not be proven any further at the hearing or trial.[91] As such, carefully propounded requests for admission can be a powerful tool for a litigant, if given a proper response.

Often, requests for admission are employed to establish foundation facts for important documents that a party anticipates using at trial, thereby avoiding detailed and repetitive evidentiary foundation testimony. The Federal Rules do not limit the number of requests to admit, although local rules or court orders may do so.

A party that does not respond to a request for admission is deemed to have admitted the request.[92] However, apart from admitting or denying, a responding party may object to the request for admission based on Rule 26(b) relevancy grounds; defective drafting grounds, such as overly broad, vague, or compound, among others; or based on a legal privilege. A party may also respond that he or she lacks the information or knowledge to admit or deny the request. The responding party, however, has to state that it made a reasonable inquiry and that the information it knows is insufficient to enable it to admit or deny.[93] A responding party may not object solely on the ground that the request presents a genuine issue for trial.[94]

7.04.6 Third party discovery

A party may also seek formal discovery from a non-party, or third party, to the litigation in the form of depositions or document requests. This can only be accomplished through the service of a subpoena on a third party, which is governed by Rule 45. A subpoena can command the person to whom it is directed to attend and testify at a deposition (or trial); to produce designated documents, electronically stored information, or tangible things in that person's possession, custody, or control; or to permit the inspection of premises.[95]

---

89 Fed. R. Civ. P. 36(a)(1).
90 Fed. R. Civ. P. 36(a)(4).
91 Fed. R. Civ. P. 36(b).
92 Fed. R. Civ. P. 36(a)(3); 8A Wright, Miller & Marcus, *supra* note 16, § 2259.
93 Fed. R. Civ. P. 36(a)(4).
94 Fed. R. Civ. P. 36(a)(5).
95 Fed. R. Civ. P. 45(a)(1)(A)(iii).

The Federal Rules do not provide a method for requiring a third party to respond to interrogatories or requests for admission.

A subpoena for attendance at a hearing or a trial must be issued from the court for the district where the hearing or trial will be held. A subpoena for attendance at a deposition must be issued from the court for the district where the deposition is going to take place. Finally, a subpoena for production or inspection of documents or tangible things must be issued from the court for the district where the production or inspection is to be made, unless the request is included on a subpoena to command attendance at a deposition, trial, or hearing.[96]

A subpoena must also be accompanied by one day of witness fees and mileage to cover the cost of travelling to the hearing or trial.[97]

The court that issued the subpoena must quash or modify the subpoena if: (1) the subpoena fails to allow a reasonable time to comply; (2) the subpoena requires a person who is not a party, nor a party's officer, to travel more than 100 miles from where the target of the subpoena resides, is employed, or regularly transacts business in person; (3) the subpoena requires disclosure of privileged or other protected matter, if no exception or waiver applies; or (4) the subpoena subjects a person to undue burden.[98]

Under Rule 45, as under Rule 34, a person responding to a subpoena that requests documents must produce the documents as they are kept in the ordinary course of business or must label them to correspond to the categories in the subpoena.[99] Similarly if the subpoena does not specify the form of production for electronic documents, the producing party must produce the information in the form in which it is ordinarily maintained or in a reasonably usable form.[100] Again, as under Rule 34, a person need not provide discovery of electronically stored information from sources that the person identifies as not reasonably accessible.[101]

7.04.7 Supplements to discovery

A party has a continuing obligation to supplement discovery responses in a timely manner as the litigation progresses.[102] This duty to supplement applies if the party learns that its disclosure or response is incomplete or incorrect in some material respect and if additional or corrective information has not otherwise been made known to the other party during the discovery process.[103] Under Rule 26(e)(2), expert disclosures must be supplemented no later than the pretrial disclosures called for under Rule 26(a)(3) – at least 30 days before trial, unless otherwise agreed or ordered by the court.

---

96 FED. R. CIV. P. 45(a)(2).
97 FED. R. CIV. P. 45(b)(1).
98 FED. R. CIV. P. 45(c)(3)(A).
99 FED. R. CIV. P. 45(d)(1)(A).
100 FED. R. CIV. P. 45(d)(1)(B).
101 FED. R. CIV. P. 45(d)(1)(D).
102 FED. R. CIV. P. 26(e).
103 FED. R. CIV. P. 26(e).

§ 7.05 Depositions

Rule 30 governs depositions by sworn oral examination.[104] Depositions by oral examination are a useful and often utilized discovery tool.[105] They allow a party to question individuals (and corporations, as is discussed below) to determine what information the deponent knows and does not know. Depositions provide a more spontaneous setting in which to elicit information during the discovery process. During a deposition, a witness must answer the questions posed in the deposition without consulting with his or her counsel or others. Depositions also allow the examiner to ask follow-up questions in response to any given answer. These are discovery techniques that are not available through interrogatories or requests for admissions. Through a deposition, the testimony of a witness is preserved so that it can later be used to impeach a party if they provide inconsistent testimony at trial, or in future depositions, or if the witness is unavailable to testify at trial. Depositions are the best way to discover the likely strengths and weaknesses of each party's case.[106]

The scope of depositions, like all discovery in civil cases, is limited by Rule 26(b). As such, deposition questions are limited to any non-privileged matter that is relevant to any party's claim or defense (or will lead to relevant evidence), and for good cause shown, the court may order discovery of any matter relevant to the subject matter involved in the action.[107] A party may take the deposition of any person, including a party, without

---

[104] *See* FED. R. CIV. P. 30. Rule 28 identifies persons before whom a deposition may be taken, distinguishing between depositions taken in the United States and outside the United States. Within the United States, a deposition must be taken before an officer authorized to administer oaths and take testimony either by federal law or by the law in the jurisdiction in which the deposition is taking place or a person appointed by the court where the action is pending. The term "officer" as defined in Rule 28, applies to Rules 30, 31, and 32. *See* FED. R. CIV. P. 28(a)(2).

[105] A party seeking to depose an individual or corporation must provide written notice to the deponent and all other parties to the litigation. The notice must state the time and place of the deposition and, if known, the deponent's name and address. FED. R. CIV. P. 30(b)(1). If a party wants a deponent to bring documents or other tangible items to a deposition, a subpoena *duces tecum* must be served on the deponent and a list of the documents or other items sought must be attached or, if the deponent is a party, the notice must include a Request for Production of Documents, pursuant to Rule 34. FED. R. CIV. P. 30(b)(2). The party issuing the notice of deposition may specify the location of the deposition (if the deposition is not of a non-party, and the location is not limited by the requirement of Rule 45, set out above). If, however, the deponent believes that the location of the deposition is unreasonable, the deponent may seek a protective order from the court pursuant to Rule 26(c). FED. R. CIV. P. 26(c)(2). Often, however, the issue of location of depositions will be discussed early in the litigation and may even be part of the Rule 26(f) conference, and the parties will reach agreement on where the deposition will occur. For example, the parties may agree that the depositions will occur where the deponent is located or they may agree that the depositions will occur where counsel is located.

[106] Another method of formal discovery is depositions upon written questions. *See* FED. R. CIV. P. 31. The difficulty with written depositions is that counsel propounding the written questions cannot ask follow-up questions based on answers given, as all of the questions have to be submitted ahead of time. Similarly, it is difficult to anticipate what areas would be fruitful for cross examination without knowing how the witness is going to answer the direct examination questions. For these reasons and given the efficacy of other means of discovery, depositions on written questions are rarely used.

[107] FED. R. CIV. P. 26(b)(1).

leave of court, except under certain limited situations. Leave of court is required if (1) the deposition would exceed the deposition limit established by the Rules or by agreement of the parties or order of the court; (2) the deponent has already been deposed; or (3) the deposition is sought before the parties have conferred pursuant to Rule 26(d).[108] A party must also seek leave of court to depose a person confined in prison.[109]

Because an individual generally can only be deposed once in his or her individual capacity, the deposing party must make a strategic decision as to when to take the deposition of an individual. Sometimes an early deposition can assist counsel in drafting more probing interrogatories or document requests, as the witness may be able to help solidify the facts. Early depositions may also provide more accurate testimony as they will occur closer in time to the events at issue. Also, depending on the answers to the deposition questions, an early deposition may help facilitate an early settlement.

Often in antitrust cases, however, the plaintiff will want to obtain documents requested from the defendants and others prior to taking depositions. This will allow the plaintiff to better identify the key employees or decision makers who may have participated in the antitrust conduct. In cartel cases, obtaining the documents will also assist the plaintiff in better understanding the methods used to implement any collusive agreements and thereby assist in framing the questions that should be asked during the depositions. Deposition timing is therefore a key strategic decision that must be made by the parties.

Depositions also allow plaintiffs to obtain, prior to trial, testimony by parties' witnesses on key documents that will be used at trial, as well as testimony to be used at trial by witnesses who cannot be compelled to appear at trial. The depositions may also help identify any weaknesses in the plaintiff's claims or the defendant's defenses. This allows the parties to then go back and make additional discovery requests to gather further evidentiary support to shore up their cases.

Rule 30 limits any party to a maximum of 10 depositions, unless the parties agree otherwise and the court so orders.[110] Often in complex antitrust cases, the parties enter into agreements that expand the number of depositions available to each side. Any limitation on the number of depositions may counsel in favor of waiting until after some written discovery is complete so as to not "waste" depositions on individuals that do not have relevant information. Rule 30(d)(1) limits a single deposition to one day of seven hours, unless otherwise stipulated or ordered by the court. However, the court can allow additional time if needed to fairly examine the witness or if the deposition has been impeded or delayed.[111]

§ 7.06 Rule 30(b)(6) depositions

Under Rule 30(b)(6), a party may also notice a deposition of an entity, such as a corporation. Obviously, a corporation itself cannot appear at a deposition, so the question

---

[108] Fed. R. Civ. P. 30(a)(1), (2).
[109] Fed. R. Civ. P. 30(a)(2)(B).
[110] Fed. R. Civ. P. 30(a)(2)(A)(i).
[111] Fed. R. Civ. P. 30(d)(1).

becomes what individual should appear on behalf of a corporation.[112] The rule provides that the notice naming an entity as the deponent must also describe with reasonable particularity the matters that are going to be the subject of the deposition questions.[113] The named entity must then designate one or more officers, directors, or managing agents, or other persons who consent to testify on its behalf about the specified subject matters.[114] The rule requires that the person designated must testify about information known or reasonably available to the organization, and such testimony is binding on the corporation.[115]

These Rule 30(b)(6) deponents therefore must be prepared to testify about the subject matters for which they are designated. There is no limit on the number of individuals a corporation can designate to testify on the subject matters identified in the notice. However, regardless of the number of individuals designated, a Rule 30(b)(6) deposition will only count as one deposition for purposes of the deposition limits.[116] Still, the deposition is limited to seven hours.[117] Courts have found that the Comments to Rule 30(b)(6) do not mean that each designated witness can be deposed for seven hours, as this would reward parties that issue very broad Rule 30(b)(6) notices requiring multiple designees.[118]

If, during the course of the deposition, it becomes clear that the designated witness is not knowledgeable about the subject matter for which he or she is designated, the party noticing the deposition may request that the deponent corporation produce a different witness and, if need be, may move to compel the production of a different witness.

The fact that a witness is designated as a Rule 30(b)(6) witness for a corporation does not preclude the parties from taking that person's deposition a second time in his or her individual capacity.[119] This situation may arise when an individual is designated for a single topic listed in the Rule 30(b)(6) deposition notice, but the plaintiff also wants to depose that individual as to his or her knowledge of other areas of the litigation as well. During the Rule 30(b)(6) deposition, the plaintiff is not permitted to ask questions beyond the subject matters for which that individual is designated under the Rule 30(b)(6) notice. The individual must be served with an individual deposition notice if plaintiff wishes to pursue different subject matters for which the individual is not the designated witness under Rule 30(b)(6). Often, counsel will try to work out a process in which the individual deposition of the person takes place at the same time or immediately following the Rule 30(b)(6) deposition so the individual does not have to appear more than once.

---

[112] Rule 30(b)(6) addresses depositions of corporations, partnerships, associations, governmental agencies, or other entities.

[113] FED. R. CIV. P. 30(b)(6).

[114] *Id.*

[115] *Id.*

[116] FED. R. CIV. P. 30 cmt. 1993 Amendments; *see also In re* Sulfuric Acid Antitrust Litig., No. 03-C-4576, 2005 WL 1994105, at *3 (N.D. Ill. Aug. 19, 2005).

[117] FED. R. CIV. P. 30(d)(1).

[118] *See In re* Rembrandt Techs., No. 09-CV-00691, 2009 WL 1258761, at *14 (D. Colo. May 4, 2009) (limiting the Rule 30(b)(6) deposition topics and expanding the seven hour limitation for the Rule 30(b)(6) deposition to ten hours regardless of the number of designees required to testify on those topics).

[119] *See* FED. R. CIV. P. 30(b)(6).

§ 7.07 Trial depositions

There are two types of depositions that may be used in trial. If counsel knows that a person is going to be unavailable to testify at trial, the party may take a trial deposition. Although the rules for discovery depositions still apply to trial depositions, the strategy is different. Unlike a deposition taken during discovery, where the purpose of the deposition is fact-finding, a trial deposition should mirror what would occur if that witness appeared live at the trial. As such, generally, neither counsel would typically ask questions where the answers were unknown, as they would not want to be surprised at trial. This type of deposition is less about fact-finding and more about eliciting facts that help support the claims or defenses for the party calling the witness. If the witness is hostile, the examiner will ask leading questions, as would occur at trial.

Rule 32 sets out the parameters for using a deposition in a court proceeding. The rule provides that a deposition may be used against a party when the party was present or represented at the deposition or had reasonable notice of the deposition.[120] Provisions (a)(2) through (a)(8) of Rule 32 delineate the permissible and impermissible uses of a deposition at trial. For example, a deposition may be used at a hearing or trial if the witness is unavailable to appear at the hearing or trial.[121] If the witness is unavailable, either a trial deposition or a previously taken discovery deposition may be used. If a party offers only parts of a deposition, the adverse party may offer other parts of that same deposition.[122] A deposition may also be used at a hearing or trial to contradict or impeach the testimony given by a deponent as a witness.[123]

Any objection that would be available if the witness were to testify at trial would also be available in response to deposition testimony.[124]

§ 7.08 Expert discovery

Parties often hire experts to assist them in the preparation of their cases or in the presentation of testimony at trial. There are different types of experts and the Federal Rules acknowledge these differences. One type of expert is a testifying expert. This expert will provide a report that includes the expert's opinions that will be served upon all other parties in the litigation.

In antitrust cases, experts in the fields of economics, statistics, and econometrics are often employed by the parties, along with experts in the industries or markets involved in the litigation. Often these experts are found in litigation consulting firms[125] or from

---

[120] Fed. R. Civ. P. 32(a)(1)–(8).

[121] Fed. R. Civ. P. 32(a)(4) explains when a witness may be considered unavailable, including because the witness is deceased, otherwise unable to attend for enumerated reasons, or, on motion and notice, in the interests of justice in exceptional circumstances.

[122] Fed. R. Civ. P. 32(a)(6).

[123] Fed. R. Civ. P. 32(a)(2).

[124] Fed. R. Civ. P. 32(b).

[125] There are large and small litigation consulting firms. The larger firms (such as LECG, CRA, and Compass/Lexecon) tend to be defense oriented, and the smaller firms (such as Nathan Associates, InfoTech, or ERS Group) often consult with plaintiffs or defendants. Most of the

academic ranks or from the industries involved. Since experts do not testify to percipient facts but rather to their expert opinions, they may be – and invariably are – paid for their testimony. Since expert opinions in antitrust cases often involve complex computer modeling employing large volumes of data, these expert fees – both for the testifying experts and the people who assist them – can amount to sizeable sums, often millions of dollars.

Parties also hire non-testifying consultants to assist in either the preparation of the case or the initial investigation of the case (as discussed above). Non-testifying consultants do not provide written reports or depositions, and their opinions and work product are not discoverable unless used by a testifying expert. In antitrust cases, the parties will often utilize testifying economic and statistical experts to opine on liability, causation, damages, and the industry and relevant markets. Often testifying experts utilize non-testifying consultants and assistants to help in preparing their analyses.

Sometimes a party will have employees that would be considered "experts" or could offer opinions in their field. Rule 702 of the Federal Rules of Evidence (FRE) defines what is considered "expert testimony." FRE 702 states:

> If scientific, technical, or other specialized knowledge will assist the trier of fact to understand the evidence or to determine a fact in issue, a witness qualified as an expert by knowledge, skill, experience, training, or education, may testify thereto in the form of an opinion or otherwise, if (1) the testimony is based upon sufficient facts or data, (2) the testimony is the product of reliable principles and methods, and (3) the witness has applied the principles and methods reliably to the facts of the case.[126]

FRE 701 states:

> If the witness is not testifying as an expert, the witness' testimony in the form of opinions or inferences is limited to those opinions or inferences which are (a) rationally based on the perception of the witness, (b) helpful to a clear understanding of the witness' testimony or the determination of a fact in issue, and (c) not based on scientific, technical, or other specialized knowledge within the scope of [FRE] 702.[127]

Therefore, FRE 701 and 702 should guide the determination of whether an employee's opinions fall within the definition of "expert testimony" that must be disclosed.

Rule 26(a)(2) sets out the requirements for disclosure of expert testimony and Rule 26(b)(4) discusses the discovery of information from either testifying or non-testifying experts. Both of these sections were recently amended to address concerns regarding expert discovery.[128]

Rule 26(a)(2) requires a party to disclose to the other parties the identity of any witnesses that may be used at trial to present evidence under FRE 702 (Testimony by Experts), 703 (Bases of Opinion Testimony by Experts), or 705 (Disclosure of Facts

---

litigation consulting firms have arrangements with college and university professors, who take on assignments as testifying experts on behalf of the consulting firms.

[126] Fed. R. Evid. 702.

[127] Fed. R. Evid. 701.

[128] Fed. R. Civ. P. 26 cmt. 2010 Amendment. For a discussion of precautions taken by experts with respect to expert discovery, see Chapter 8 of this Handbook.

or Data Underlying Expert Opinion).[129] Rule 26 requires that the disclosure be made through a written report that is prepared and signed by the expert, if the expert is going to provide expert testimony in the litigation. The written report must contain a complete statement of all opinions to which the witness will testify and the basis and reasons for those opinions. The report must also contain the facts or data considered by the expert in forming those opinions, any exhibits that the expert will use to summarize or support the opinions, the expert's qualifications (including a list of all publications authored in the previous ten years), a list of all other cases in which the expert has testified as an expert at trial or by deposition in the past four years, and a statement of the compensation to be paid for the study and testimony in the case.[130]

Rule 26 requires that these disclosures be made at the times and in the sequence that the court orders, or absent an order or stipulation, at least 90 days before the date set for trial or, if the evidence is solely to contradict or rebut evidence on the same subject matter identified by another party, then within 30 days after the other party's disclosure.[131] The timing and sequence of disclosing expert reports, pursuant to Rule 26(a)(2), are usually set out in the court's scheduling order. Often, the party with the burden of proof on any issue will be required to submit its expert disclosures first, usually shortly after the close of discovery, with response expert reports from the opposing side due sometime thereafter (for example, 30–60 days after the initial reports), and sometimes the courts will allow reply expert reports (for example, 30 days or so after the rebuttal reports). Parties usually discuss the timing and sequence of the expert disclosures and reports during their initial meet-and-confer prior to the Rule 26 conference and either will agree to a schedule or submit competing proposals to the court.

Rule 26(b)(4) addresses depositions of expert witnesses.[132] This rule permits the deposition of an expert that has been identified as one whose opinions may be presented at trial, but it requires that the deposition occur only after the report has been provided.[133]

A party may not discover facts known or opinions held by a consultant who has been retained by a party but who is not identified as an expert who will testify at trial. Rule 35(b) may provide the only limited exception to this limitation on discovery, allowing discovery from non-testifying consultants on a showing of exceptional circumstances under which the party cannot obtain facts or opinions on the same subject matter by other means.[134]

The schedule for deposing testifying experts is often set forth in the court's scheduling order. Often, the schedule will provide for the deposition of experts following submission of their expert reports, but prior to the scheduled submission of either the rebuttal or reply report. So, for example, the party with the burden of proof will submit the expert report and that expert will be deposed prior to the opposing party's submission of its rebuttal report. Once the expert rebuttal report is submitted, the rebuttal expert will be deposed prior to the submission of the initiating party's reply report. However, sometimes courts will defer all depositions until all reports are submitted.

---

[129] FED. R. CIV. P. 26(a)(2)(A); FED. R. EVID. 702–03, 705.

[130] FED. R. CIV. P. 26(a)(2)(B).

[131] FED. R. CIV. P. 26(a)(2)(C).

[132] FED. R. CIV. P. 26(b)(4).

[133] *Id.*

[134] FED. R. CIV. P. 26(b)(4)(B).

Finally, parties have a duty to supplement expert reports or testimony if appropriate.[135] For example, if the expert discovers or is told of new information or new facts that he or she considers in forming his or her opinions, then the party must disclose that new information or those new facts. If that new information changes the expert's opinion, the new opinion must also be disclosed. Rule 26(e)(2) sets a time limit on making such additions or changes, requiring that new information be disclosed by the time the party's pretrial disclosures are due under Rule 26(a)(3), and no later than 30 days prior to trial, unless otherwise agreed or ordered by the court.[136]

§ 7.09 *Daubert*

In *Daubert v. Merrell Dow Pharmaceuticals, Inc.*,[137] the United States Supreme Court replaced the pre-existing and restrictive "general acceptance" test of admissibility of expert testimony under *Frye v. United States*.[138] While still recognizing that the judge plays a "gatekeeper" role in ensuring that only expert opinions and testimony that will be of assistance to the jury will be admitted, the Supreme Court in *Daubert* liberalized the standards of admissibility.[139] In *Daubert,* the Supreme Court established a three-part test: (1) Is the expert qualified to testify competently on the matters at hand? (2) Is the methodology employed by the expert sufficiently reliable? (3) Will the testimony assist the trier of fact to determine a fact in issue?[140]

Because of the significance of expert testimony in antitrust cases and because antitrust plaintiffs often rely on expert testimony to establish essential elements of their claims (such as damages and causation, and sometimes liability), *Daubert* challenges to exclude expert testimony are common in antitrust cases. Despite the Supreme Court's clear indication that it was "liberalizing" the rules of admissibility of expert opinions, and the Advisory Committee to the Federal Rules of Evidence's explicit statement that "rejection of expert testimony is the exception rather than the rule,"[141] the increasing frequency of *Daubert* challenges appears to be having an adverse impact on the successful prosecution of private plaintiffs' civil antitrust actions.[142]

---

135 FED. R. CIV. P. 26(e)(2) ("For an expert whose report must be disclosed under Rule 26(a)(2)(B), the party's duty to supplement extends both to information included in the report and to information given during the expert's deposition.").

136 *Id.*; *see also* FED. R. CIV. P. 26(a)(3)(B).

137 509 U.S. 579 (1993).

138 293 F. 1013 (D.C. Cir. 1923). The *Frye* test limited admissibility of expert opinions to those that were accorded widespread acceptance within the relevant discipline. For further discussion of *Daubert*, see Chapter 8 of this Handbook.

139 *See* Daubert, 509 U.S. at 588. *See also* Estate of Bud Hill v. Conagra Poultry Co., No. 94-CV-0198, 1997 WL 538887 at *3 (D. Ga. 1997) (*Daubert* "relaxed the standard for admitting scientific evidence").

140 509 U.S. at 589.

141 FED. R. EVID. 702, Notes of Advisory Committee on 2000 Amendments; *In re* Gadolinium-Based Contrast Agents Products Liab. Litig., No. 1:08 GD 50000 (MDL-1909), 2010 WL 1796334, at *2 (N.D. Ohio), *modified*, 2010 WL 5173568 (N.D. Ohio).

142 *See* James Langenfeld & Chris Alexander, *Daubert Challenges of Antitrust Experts*, (American Antitrust Institute, Working Paper No. 08–06, Dec. 4, 2008) *available at* http://www.antitrustinstitute.org/node/11022. But, many courts have rejected *Daubert* challenges in antitrust

The trial judge's "gatekeeper" role under *Daubert* is not intended to replace the adversary system.[143] In its role as gatekeeper, the court's focus should be on the expert's methodology and not on the conclusions of the experts.[144] Therefore, so long as the experts' methodologies are reliable, the court need not resolve disputes between the experts as to their conclusions, which are for the jury to decide.

Where an expert's opinion on damages is challenged under *Daubert*, courts should be especially wary of excluding the expert's opinions. The Supreme Court has recognized a lenient standard for the admission of evidence estimating antitrust damages because the "wrongdoer is not entitled to complain that [damages] cannot be measured with the exactness and precision that would be possible if the case, which he alone is responsible for making, were otherwise."[145] This more lenient standard of proof may make a *Daubert* challenge as to expert opinions on damages more difficult.[146]

Daubert challenges are typically brought at the close of expert discovery. The trial judge will often hold an evidentiary hearing to evaluate the expert opinions, although such a hearing is not required. In class actions, *Daubert* challenges to expert opinions are occasionally brought at the class certification stage. Often, these *Daubert* challenges at class certification have been rejected as premature.[147] However, because of more recent decisions requiring district courts to resolve more factual controversies at class certification,[148]

---

cases. *See, e.g., In re* Ready Mixed Concrete Antitrust Litig., 261 F.R.D. 154, 164–65 (S.D. Ind. Sept. 9, 2009); *In re* Scrap Metal Antitrust Litig., No. 1:02 CV 0844, 2006 WL 2850453 at *16 (N.D. Ohio, Sept. 30, 2006). *See also In re* Linerboard Antitrust Litig., 497 F. Supp. 2d 666 (E.D. Pa. 2007); *In re* High Fructose Corn Syrup Antitrust Litig., 295 F.3d 652, 660–61 (7th Cir. 2002); *In re* Bulk Popcorn Antitrust Litig., 792 F.Supp. 650, 652 (D. Minn. 1992); *In re* High Pressure Laminates, No. 00 MDL 1368, 2006 WL 931692, at *1 (S.D.N.Y. April 7, 2006); *In re* Mercedez-Benz Antitrust Litig., No. 99-4311, 2006 WL 2129100, at *7–9 (D.N.J. July 26, 2006).

143 United States v. 14.38 Acres of Land, 80 F.3d 1074, 1078 (5th Cir. 1998).

144 *Daubert*, 509 U.S. at 595.

145 Story Parchment v. Pasterson Parchment Paper Co., 282 U.S. 555, 562 (1931); *see also* Bigelow v. RKO Pictures, Inc., 327 U.S. 251, 264 (1946); Matrix Warehouse, Inc. v. Daimler Benz AG, 825 F.2d 1033, 1043 (4th Cir. 1987).

146 *See In re* Polypropylene Carpet Antitrust Litig., 996 F. Supp. 18, 29 (1997).

147 *See, e.g.*, LaBauve v. Olin Corp., 231 F.R.D. 632, 644 (S.D. Ala. 2005) ("[A] full-blown *Daubert* investigation is premature at the class certification stage."); *In re* Monosodium Glutamate Antitrust Litig., 205 F.R.D. 229, 234–35 (D. Minn. 2001) ("Even assuming that there are problems with Dr. Beyer's methodology, however, Defendants' attack on that methodology is premature. The *Daubert* inquiry requires a more searching analysis than is appropriate at this preliminary stage.") (citations omitted); Bert v. AK Steel Corp., No. 1:02-CV-00467, 2006 WL 1071872, at *7 (S.D. Ohio Apr. 24, 2006) ("In ruling on Plaintiffs' class certification motion, the Court need not determine whether or not Dr. Bradley's opinion can survive a *Daubert* challenge."); Nichols v. Smithkline Beecham Corp., NO. CIV.A. 00-6622, 2003 WL 302352 (E.D. Pa. Jan. 29, 2003) ("At [the class certification] stage of the proceeding the Court does not consider whether an expert witness's opinion would be admissible pursuant to *Daubert*. . . .").

148 Walmart v. Dukes, 131 S. Ct. 2541, 2551–52 (2011) (holding that a court must conduct a "rigorous analysis" in determining whether Rule 23(a) is satisfied, including inquiry into the merits of underlying claims where merits issues overlap with class certification issues); *In re* Hydrogen Peroxide Antitrust Litig., 552 F.3d 305, 209 (3d Cir. 2008) (finding that class certification is proper only if the court is satisfied, after "a rigorous analysis" of the "factual and legal allegations" that Rule 23 is met) (citing Gen. Tel. Co. of Sw. v. Falcon, 457 U.S. 147, 161 (1982); Newton v. Merril

courts may now be more receptive to considering *Daubert* challenges at this early stage of the litigation.[149]

§ 7.10 Compelling discovery: Motion practice

Parties often disagree on what are appropriate discovery requests or responses. The Federal Rules set forth a mechanism for addressing these discovery disputes. If the responding party receives a discovery request that it believes to be overly broad or outside the scope of discovery or, alternatively, if the requesting party receives discovery responses that it believes are inadequate, the parties should attempt to resolve the dispute without formal motion practice, through a meet-and-confer process.

Indeed, the Federal Rules and many local rules require the parties to meet and confer prior to bringing a motion to compel or a motion for a protective order based on discovery requests or responses. If the moving party fails to do so the motion can be denied on that basis alone.[150] Even if the parties are not able to completely resolve the disputed issues, they may be able to narrow the issues of dispute prior to bringing a motion so that neither the parties nor the court will have to expend resources on discovery disputes that may easily be resolved through a meet-and-confer process.

If, however, the parties have attempted to resolve the discovery disputes but are unable to do so, then a party may move for an order compelling the disclosure of discovery requested.[151] Specifically, Rule 37 provides for motions to compel in situations where a party fails to make a disclosure required by Rule 26(a). It also provides that a party seeking discovery may move for an order compelling an answer, designation, production, or inspection if: (1) the deponent fails to answer a question during a deposition (either oral or written); (2) an entity fails to make a designation under Rule 30(b)(6) or 31(a)(4); (3) a party fails to answer an interrogatory; or (4) a party fails to respond that an inspection will be permitted or fails to permit an inspection requested under Rule 34.[152]

If the court grants the motion to compel, the court must, after giving the parties an opportunity to be heard, require the losing party, deponent, or attorney whose conduct or advice necessitated the motion, to pay the movant's reasonable expenses incurred in

---

Lynch, Pierce Fenner & Smith, Inc., 259 F.3d 154, 166 (3d Cir. 2001)); *In re* Initial Public Offering Securities Litig., 471 F.3d 24, 42 (2d Cir. 2006) (disavowing the suggestion that an expert's testimony may establish a component of a Rule 23 requirement simply by being not fatally flawed. A district judge is to assess all of the relevant evidence admitted at the class certification stage and determine whether each Rule 23 requirement has been met, just as the judge would resolve a dispute about any other threshold prerequisite for continuing a lawsuit.)

[149] *See Dukes*, 131 S. Ct. 2541, 2553–54 ("doubt[ing]" the district court's conclusion "that *Daubert* did not apply to expert testimony at the class-certification stage of class action proceedings"); *but see In re* Fed Ex Ground Package Sys., Inc. Employment Practices Litig., No. 3:05-MD-527RM (MDL-1700), 2007 WL 3027405, at *4 (N.D. Ind. 2007) (noting that a "more relaxed" Rule 702 standard may be appropriate at class certification stage).

[150] Fed. R. Civ. P. 37(a)(1); *see also, e.g.*, D. Minn. LR 37.1; Use Techno Corp. v. Kenko USA, Inc., No. 06-02754, 2007 WL 3045996, at *1 (N.D. Cal. Oct. 18, 2007) (denying motion to compel for failure to demonstrate good faith attempt to meet and confer).

[151] Fed. R. Civ. P. 37(a)(1).

[152] Fed. R. Civ. P. 37(a)(3)(A)–(B).

making the motion, including attorney's fees.[153] A party will not be awarded these costs if the movant did not in good faith try to obtain the discovery prior to making the motion or if the opposing party's non-disclosure, response, or objection was substantially justified or if other circumstances make the award unjust.[154]

If the party still refuses to provide the information after the court orders the party to respond or to produce the requested discovery, the court may impose sanctions on that party.[155] Rule 37(b)(2) sets out the various sanctions that a court may impose for failure to comply with an order compelling discovery, including: (1) directing that the matters or facts that were the subject of the order compelling discovery be taken as established for purposes of the litigation; (2) prohibiting the non-compliant party from supporting or opposing designated claims or defenses or from introducing designated matters into evidence; (3) striking pleadings in whole or in part; (4) staying further proceedings until the order is complied with; (5) dismissing the action or proceeding in whole or in part; (6) rendering a default judgment against the non-compliant party; or (7) treating the failure to comply with the order as contempt of court.[156] These sanctions can be imposed against the parties but can also be imposed against the parties' attorneys.[157]

§ 7.11 Limits on discovery

7.11.1 Protective/confidentiality orders

As indicated throughout this chapter, there are limits on discovery. The Federal Rules limit the scope of discovery, recognizing that discovery can be unduly burdensome and can be used to embarrass or harass the responding party. The Rules also recognize that discovery may seek the disclosure of trade secret information or other confidential or commercially sensitive information. In those situations, a party may seek a protective order to prevent the disclosure of the information or to at least protect the information from being disclosed publicly.

Rule 26 provides that a party from whom discovery is sought may move for a protective order in the court where the action is pending or, for a deposition, in the court for the district where the deposition will be taken.[158] Again, the motion must confirm that the parties have met and conferred in good faith in an effort to resolve the dispute.[159] The court may, for good cause shown, issue an order to protect a party from annoyances, embarrassment, oppression, or undue burden or expense by: (1) forbidding the disclosure

---

153 FED. R. CIV. P. 37(a)(5)(A); *see also* FED. R. CIV. P. 26(c)(3). Expenses awarded with regard to motions for protective orders are also governed by Rule 37(a)(5).

154 FED. R. CIV. P. 37(a)(5)(A).

155 FED. R. CIV. P. 37(b).

156 FED. R. CIV. P. 37(b)(2).

157 FED. R. CIV. P. 37(b)(2)(C) ("[T]he court must order the disobedient party, the attorney advising that party, or both to pay the reasonable expenses, including attorney's fees, caused by the failure. . . .").

158 FED. R. CIV. P. 26(c)(1).

159 *Id.*

or discovery; (2) specifying the terms, including the time and place, for disclosure or discovery; (3) prescribing a discovery method other than the one selected by the party seeking discovery; (4) forbidding inquiry into certain matters or limiting the scope of disclosure or discovery; (5) designating the persons who may be present while the discovery is conducted; (6) requiring that a deposition be sealed and opened only on a court order; (7) requiring that a trade secret or other confidential research, development, or commercial information not be revealed or be revealed only in a specified way; and (8) requiring that the parties simultaneously file specified documents or information in sealed envelopes, to be opened as the court directs.[160]

Often, the parties will discuss and try to stipulate to the entry of a protective order or confidentiality order prior to the initiation of discovery. These types of protective orders or confidentiality orders address the parties' interest in protecting trade secret and other confidential commercial information. If the parties can agree on a proposed order, courts will often enter it prior to the start of discovery. If the parties do not agree on the language of a proposed protective order, often the parties will submit competing proposed protective orders and the court will enter one or the other or its own protective order. The entrance of a protective order prior to the start of discovery will expedite the discovery process at the outset, as it will provide comfort to the parties that their trade secrets or confidential information will be protected.

7.11.2 Privilege logs

The Federal Rules also recognize that certain information is subject to privileges and as such, does not have to be produced. Rule 26(b)(1) states that discovery is limited to "nonprivileged matter." The laws of evidence have determined what information is considered privileged.[161] Generally, privileges may apply to communications that occur in furtherance of certain relationships (e.g., doctor and patient, lawyer and client) that have been found to warrant various forms of protection.[162]

Among the common privileges asserted in litigation are the attorney–client privilege and work product protection. If a party has communications with his or her attorney that are intended to be confidential, those communications are privileged and do not need to be produced or disclosed during discovery, except under very limited circumstances. Similarly, if counsel for a party creates a document as part of the litigation that contains the mental thoughts or impressions of the attorney, then that document or portions of the document may be protected from disclosure by the work product exception to discovery.[163]

A party that is claiming privilege to withhold information that would otherwise be discoverable must expressly make the claim and describe the nature of the documents,

---

160 Fed. R. Civ. P. 26(c)(1)(A)–(H).

161 *See* Fed. R. Evid. 501.

162 *See* Perrigon v. Bergen Brunswig Corp., 77 F.R.D. 455, 458 (D.C. Cal. 1978) ("The law of privilege is not just a rule governing the admissibility of evidence. Its primary purpose is to protect the confidentiality of certain communications where such confidentiality serves broad societal goals.").

163 *See generally* Fed. R. Evid. 502 (setting forth the provisions that apply when information protected by the attorney–client privilege or work product doctrine is disclosed).

communications, or tangible things not produced or disclosed, and must do so in a manner that will enable the other party to assess the claim.[164]

The parties will usually exchange a "privilege log" which will identify the type of documents being withheld and the stated privilege. Typically the logs will include the types of documents withheld, the names of the author and recipients of those documents, the dates of the documents, and a general description of the nature of information that is contained on each of the withheld documents.

The issue of whether or not a privilege log complies with Rule 26(b)(5) often is the subject of meet-and-confers among the parties and may result in motions to compel a more complete privilege log to allow the requesting party to assess whether the claim of privilege should be challenged.

7.11.3 Expert stipulations

Another limitation that may be agreed upon by the parties is the scope of discovery relating to expert witnesses. Parties often agree to stipulate to limiting the materials that each will produce with respect to their opposing expert witnesses. For example, the parties may agree that they will not have to produce drafts of written expert reports or that they will not have to produce communications between the attorneys and the testifying experts. Although historically this information arguably had to be produced under Rule 26(a)(2), the parties would often agree not to require its production in order to facilitate communication between the attorneys and their respective expert witnesses.

To at least partially address this issue, Rule 26(b)(4) was amended in 2010 to "provide work-product protection against discovery regarding draft expert disclosures or reports and – with three specific exceptions – communications between expert witnesses and counsel."[165] Under the amended rule, drafts of any report or disclosure under Rule 26(a)(2), regardless of the form in which the draft is recorded, is protected from disclosure.[166] Communications between the party's attorney and any witness required to provide a report are also protected subject to three specific exceptions: (1) where the communication is related to compensation for the expert's study or testimony; (2) where the communication identifies facts or data that the party's attorney provided and that the expert considered in forming the opinions expressed; or (3) where the communication identifies assumptions that the party's attorney provided and that the expert relied on in forming the opinions expressed.[167] The amendments to Rule 26(a)(2) require disclosures regarding expected expert testimony of those expert witnesses not required to provide expert reports.[168]

7.11.4 In camera proceedings

Occasionally, the court may decide that it needs to see the documents that are at issue either with respect to whether or not they are properly the subject of a motion to compel

---

164 Fed. R. Civ. P. 26(b)(5).
165 Fed. R. Civ. P. 26 cmt. 2010 Amendment.
166 Fed. R. Civ. P. 26(b)(4)(B).
167 Fed. R. Civ. P. 26(b)(4)(C).
168 Fed. R. Civ. P. 26(b)(2)(A).

(i.e., they truly do fit within the scope of discovery) or to assess whether or not the documents should be withheld on privilege grounds. The court may issue an order that the party opposing production of certain information or documents produce those documents to the court *in camera*, which means the court and only the court will review the documents initially to assess whether the documents should be produced or whether the documents are privileged. The court may also have the parties pay for a special master to review the documents and make a recommendation to the court as to whether the documents should be produced. Generally, the more often the parties come before the court on discovery disputes, the more frustrated the court gets with the parties' inability to work through these issues. As a practical matter, this may play a role in whether a court decides to appoint a special master at cost to the parties. If the parties are constantly before the court on discovery disputes and the court believes that they are not trying hard enough to resolve these issues on their own, the court may believe that the parties will be more likely to resolve the disputes if they are required to pay a special master to resolve them. Parties should generally try to resolve discovery disputes and only resort to motion practice on those issues that are critical to the case; otherwise, the parties will lose credibility with the court.

§ 7.12 Conclusion

Given the stakes and nature of antitrust litigation, pretrial discovery plays a significant role for both parties. The formal categories of discovery are established by the Federal Rules. And although this regime relies heavily on lawyer initiative, the discovery and discovery disputes are subject to court supervision and control. While the object of the Federal Rules is to encourage full pretrial disclosure of relevant information or information that likely will lead to relevant evidence, the recent trend is for courts to be more restrictive in applying the discovery rules. This may have an adverse impact on plaintiffs, who rely substantially on discovery to get at the evidence that will reveal covert anticompetitive activity.

8 Economic experts

James Langenfeld, Gregory G. Wrobel, and Michael J. Waters[1]

[1] James Langenfeld is a Managing Director at Navigant Economics, adjunct professor at Loyola University Chicago School of Law, and former Director for Antitrust in the Bureau of Economics of the Federal Trade Commission. Gregory G. Wrobel is a shareholder, head of the Antitrust Practice Group and member of the Litigation Practice Group of Vedder Price P.C. Michael J. Waters is a shareholder and member of the Litigation and Antitrust Practice Groups of Vedder Price P.C.

§ 8.01 Introduction

Antitrust statutes focus on restraints of trade, monopoly, competition, markets, and consumer welfare. These concepts are grounded in economic principles, so economic experts have an important role in explaining how economic theory applies to antitrust claims and defenses. Courts have held that expert economic evidence is admissible and even necessary for plaintiffs to prove antitrust claims, and both plaintiffs and defendants offer such evidence as a matter of course on a variety of liability elements, such as the existence of a conspiracy, definition of relevant markets, defendants' market power or monopoly power, competitive effects of challenged conduct, competitive injury to the plaintiff, and damages and other remedies. In class action cases, economic experts offer evidence on whether the claims are suitable for treatment as a class action, in particular whether the element of antitrust injury can be proven with evidence and analytical techniques that are common to members of the proposed class. Moreover, the role of experts has expanded due to court rulings that limit the claims subject to the per se standard of illegality and thereby expand the need for analysis of actual competitive effects.[2] The higher pleading standard under *Twombly*[3] has likewise increased the role of experts, especially early in a potential case.

The central role of expert economic evidence is reflected by the prevalence of challenges to the admissibility of such evidence before trial, in particular by defendants.[4] Plaintiffs have the burden of proof, and their economic experts may need to apply complex economic theories and models to support key elements of antitrust claims. Moreover, summary judgment proceedings and gatekeeper challenges are critical hurdles for plaintiffs' economic experts, because antitrust claims may be rejected before trial if the court rules that their evidence is not sufficiently reliable to be admissible at trial. The converse may not be true for defendants' economic experts, because the plaintiff still must satisfy its burden of proof at trial even if the defendant's expert is not permitted to testify. In addition, the plaintiff's expert typically offers affirmative evidence intended to carry the plaintiff's burden of proof, while the defendant's expert may take a rebuttal posture focused on perceived flaws in the plaintiff's proof.

These differences in the parties' procedural posture and the role of their experts may explain why pretrial challenges to plaintiffs' economic experts have been much more common. Nevertheless, economic experts on both sides of antitrust cases play a critical role in the outcome of antitrust cases at these and later stages of litigation. Not only do plaintiffs need experts to assist in carrying their burden, defendants typically need an economist to help shape their arguments and develop information for challenging the opinions of the plaintiff's expert.

The discussion below proceeds as follows. Sections 8.02 and 8.03 provide an overview

---

[2] Commentators have observed that parties and courts in antitrust cases have increasingly relied on economic authority as the application of per se illegality has declined, requiring economic experts to analyze and testify about detailed factual issues. *See, e.g.*, John E. Lopatka & William H. Page, *Economic Authority and the Limits of Expertise in Antitrust Cases*, 90 Cornell L. Rev. 617 (2005).

[3] 550 U.S. 544, 570 (2007); *Ashcroft v. Iqbal*, 129 S. Ct. 1937 (2009).

[4] *See* James Langenfeld & Christopher Alexander, Daubert *and Other Gatekeeper Challenges of Antitrust Experts*, Antitrust, Summer 2011, at 21.

of how to select an economic expert and frame issues for which the expert will provide evidence. Sections 8.04 to 8.14 describe the role of economic experts at various stages of a case, with particular emphasis in Section 8.11 on pretrial gatekeeper motions to exclude economic experts from testifying at trial. Section 8.15 describes key elements of antitrust claims on which economic experts typically provide evidence, and the common analytical techniques that experts use in antitrust cases. Section 8.16 concludes.

§ 8.02 Selecting economic experts

Given the key role of economic experts in antitrust cases, parties and counsel often weigh several key factors in selecting an expert. First, parties and counsel consider whether an expert has suitable education, training, and experience to perform the needed analyses and withstand any challenge to the expert's qualifications. Depending on the exact nature of the testimony, the expert will benefit from having (1) a graduate-level degree in economics or a closely related field, (2) testimonial experience and publications in professional journals on relevant topics, (3) relevant experience in government, and/or (4) teaching experience at a university. Second, it will be an advantage for the expert to be well versed in the particular type of case or related antitrust matters. Third, the expert should have appropriate technical skills and staff support to evaluate and analyze various types of important evidence, including potentially large and complex data sets that may be pertinent to the case. Fourth, it is helpful for the expert to have knowledge of the industry and market in question, if for no other reason than that it will take the expert less time to develop and support opinions. Fifth, the economist should have sufficient objectivity to provide an independent expert opinion that the finder of fact will perceive as useful and unbiased. If an expert has given testimony only for plaintiffs or defendants, has previously taken positions contradictory to those that would be needed in the case, or has testified repeatedly for a particular party, then the expert's objectivity might be questioned. Nevertheless, many experts and some consulting firms tend to specialize in defendant or plaintiff work, due to working relationships that develop with counsel and perhaps to avoid conflicts. Sixth, the most effective experts have the ability to explain complex economic analyses clearly and simply in writing and speech, so the court and the finder of fact can understand and evaluate the merits of the expert's opinions.

More subjective judgment is required to assess whether an expert has communications skills suitable to explain potentially complex economic theories, methodology, and data in an understandable and convincing way, but these skills are vital for the expert to be effective not only at trial, but in pretrial proceedings where the expert's written report and deposition testimony often play a very important role. Even courts and jurors with some intuitive understanding of basic economic principles of supply and demand, market concentration, and competitive prices may not readily grasp the more advanced economic theories, assumptions, and analytical methods that economic experts use in antitrust cases. Indeed, the majority of trial judges and most jurors do not have formal education or prior experience with economics.

Economic expert testimony can involve substantial costs, and the costs can vary, not only according to the areas covered in the testimony but also by the economist and the support staff. Counsel is frequently faced with trying to evaluate the added benefit of a more expensive economist and staff when choosing an expert. In addition, economic experts and their staff typically bill by the hour plus expenses. Their payments are not contingent on the outcome of the case to avoid the appearance that their opinions may be unduly influenced by an interest in the litigation, even if such arrangements are not expressly prohibited by court rules or case law.

Counsel also should consider whether a single expert or multiple experts are best suited to provide the expert economic evidence needed for the case. A single economic expert may be qualified and well suited to testify on both liability and damages issues, but in some cases a separate expert with accounting or other expertise may be better suited to analyze detailed business records and then testify on damages. For cases with complex market structures or government regulation, an economic expert with deep experience in the industry may be needed to testify on issues of relevant market definition and market power, but a second expert with broader experience in antitrust cases may be better suited to analyze data on injury and damages.

§ 8.03 Framing the issues

Counsel and the expert often reach a preliminary understanding of how economic analyses will be used to shape and test the key aspects of the legal theory of the case. This process entails an assessment of the elements of claims and defenses to identify issues for which economic expert testimony is needed. The expert has an important role at this early stage: to identify and explain relevant economic theories and models that apply to the case and the market in question.[5] In these initial proceedings, counsel generally verify that: (1) the expert identifies economic theories that are accepted in the field and provide theoretical support for the position of the party; (2) discovery and/or independent investigation are reasonably likely to yield information and data needed to apply these general theories to the facts of the case; (3) the expert has the requisite knowledge, experience, and credentials to perform these tasks and explain the expert's analysis and opinions convincingly to the finder of fact. Moreover, antitrust cases are inherently dynamic with shifts occurring in claims, defenses, and issues as the case evolves, so counsel will have to work with experts to make adjustments in how economic issues and evidence are framed as the case progresses.

§ 8.04 Complaint and motion to dismiss

One area where expert economic analysis can be brought to bear early in the litigation process is crafting and supporting the complaint. In *Bell Atlantic Corp. v. Twombly*, the Supreme Court altered long-standing notice pleading precedent and increased the burden on antitrust plaintiffs to allege "enough facts to state a claim to relief that is plausible on its face."[6] Given this standard, and because plaintiffs in civil antitrust actions often lack knowledge regarding the specifics of alleged antitrust violations prior to discovery,

---

[5] *See generally* ABA Section of Antitrust Law, Econometrics 1–14 (2005) (describing general considerations for issue selection and specification of models for econometric analysis).

[6] 550 U.S. 544, 570 (2007). In *Ashcroft v. Iqbal*, 129 S. Ct. 1937 (2009), the Supreme Court clarified that this pleading standard extends beyond antitrust claims. For an analysis of notice pleading standards after *Twombly* and *Iqbal*, see Chapter 6 of this Handbook.

a consulting economist may assist in preparing complaint allegations that are consistent with economic theory, supported by market facts, and that provide a plausible explanation of anticompetitive conduct and effects. The plaintiff also may attach a preliminary report of an economic expert to the complaint to support the plausibility of antitrust claims. Similarly, the defendant may submit a preliminary report of an economic expert with a motion to dismiss to show that antitrust claims are not plausible under the pleading standard set forth in *Twombly*, and the plaintiff may be forced to hire its own expert to respond to the motion.

§ 8.05 Discovery

The economic expert needs access to specific information and data on the parties and the market in question to conduct a proper analysis, including information available only through discovery in the case. An expert retained early in litigation therefore can be very useful in developing an effective discovery plan. In particular, the expert can help identify documents and data needed for relevant economic and statistical analyses, develop deposition strategies to obtain information relevant to economic principles that the expert may use as a basis for opinions, and explain why particular information and data are needed if discovery disputes must be resolved by the court. Parties who defer the retention of an economic expert until late in the discovery process or after the close of fact discovery may fail to request and obtain essential information and data that the economic expert requires for a comprehensive analysis.

Experts in antitrust cases usually are required to agree in writing to comply with a protective order agreed to by the parties and approved by the court to preserve the confidentiality of sensitive information disclosed during discovery. In some cases, each party will keep copies of such written agreements for its own experts and consultants, but in other cases the parties are required to provide a copy to opposing counsel. The exchange of these written agreements, if required in the case, may be the first occasion to learn the identity of adverse experts, so counsel may want to consider the timing of disclosures to the expert of discovery materials that are covered by the protective order.

In the past, counsel and testifying experts were circumspect in communications and work product on expert testimony due to the possibility that the party might be obligated to produce the expert's communications with counsel, draft reports, summaries of documents and evidence from the case, and other similar materials. To limit such disclosures, counsel and experts favored oral communication, shared work product at face-to-face or web-based meetings, and used drafting techniques that avoid the preservation of draft work product. Rule 26 of the Federal Rules of Civil Procedure was amended as of December 2010 to protect from disclosure required under Rule 26(a)(2) any draft expert report, regardless of the form in which the draft is recorded, and communications between the party's attorney and any witness required to provide a report under Rule 26(a)(2)(B), regardless of the form of the communications. The amendment enhances counsel's ability to communicate with experts and participate in the review and preparation of expert reports. Rule 26, however, includes important exceptions to the general rule protecting communications between counsel and an expert, and counsel is likely to benefit from reviewing and considering the Rule in determining the form and content of communications on expert reports and testimony.

§ 8.06 Class certification

To obtain class certification, plaintiffs must satisfy the prerequisites set forth in Rule 23(a) of the Federal Rules of Civil Procedure: numerosity, commonality, typicality, and adequacy of representation.[7] In addition, plaintiffs must satisfy one of the three criteria set forth in Rule 23(b), which in summary are: (1) the prosecution of separate actions by or against individual members of the class would create a risk of inconsistent or varying adjudications or adjudications that would impair or impede the ability of members not party to the adjudication to protect their interests; (2) the party opposing the class acted or refused to act on grounds generally applicable to the class; or (3) the court finds that the questions of law or fact common to the members of the class predominate over any questions affecting only individual members, and that a class action is superior to other available methods for the fair and efficient adjudication of the controversy. Economic experts can assist in demonstrating that one of these prerequisites is satisfied, in particular whether questions of law or fact common to the members of the class predominate over any questions affecting only individual members, which is often the operative criterion for antitrust plaintiffs arguing in favor of class certification. This may include economic evidence on the lack of conflict within the class, class-wide impact demonstrable through common proof, and the existence of a feasible and formulaic approach to measuring damages.[8]

Courts increasingly are requiring that the plaintiff provide detailed economic evidence in support of the class certification motion to show that the element of antitrust injury, or common impact, can be proven at trial with evidence and analytical methods that are common to members of the class, rather than through individualized proof for each class member. In addition, courts are requiring not only a description of the general economic theory and econometric methods that may be used to demonstrate common impact at trial, but also that the economic expert actually apply these techniques to evidence for the case to show that such proof is feasible.

The Supreme Court in *Wal-Mart Stores, Inc. v. Dukes*, stated that Rule 23 is not "a mere pleading standard"; rather, a party seeking class certification "must affirmatively demonstrate his compliance with the Rule—that is, he must be prepared to prove that there are *in fact* sufficiently numerous parties, common questions of law or fact, etc."[9] This

---

[7] For a detailed discussion of class certification and the requirements of Rule 23, see Chapter 5 of this Handbook.

[8] Paul E. Godek & Janusz A. Ordover, *Economic Analysis in Antitrust Class Certification: Hydrogen Peroxide*, ANTITRUST, Fall 2009, at 62.

[9] Wal-Mart Stores, Inc. v. Dukes, 131 S. Ct. 2541, 2551 (2011) (emphasis in original); *see also* Behrend v. Comcast Corp., No. 10-2865, 2011 WL 3678805 (3d Cir. Aug. 23, 2011) (affirming class certification where lower court conducted a rigorous certification analysis and weighed experts' competing positions on certification issues); *In re* Hydrogen Peroxide Antitrust Litig., 552 F.3d 305, 316 (3d Cir. 2008) (indicating that it is incumbent upon court to conduct a "rigorous" certification analysis, including an analysis of all expert testimony, whether offered by the party seeking or by the party opposing class certification); *In re* New Motor Vehicles Canadian Export Antitrust Litig., 522 F.3d 6 (1st Cir. 2008) (remanding certification decision for additional analysis of plaintiffs' damages model and theory for proving common impact); Cordes & Co. v. A.G. Edwards & Sons, Inc., 502 F.3d 91 (2d Cir. 2007) (remanding class certification ruling for, among other things, dis-

developing trend of analyzing expert testimony in depth at the class certification stage has required parties to engage in detailed discovery at the class certification stage so that economic experts can refine and actually apply econometric techniques to show whether the predominance and other requirements of Rule 23(b) are satisfied.

Courts have used varying standards in ruling on *Daubert* challenges to expert economic evidence at the class certification stage.[10] For example, in *In re Ready-Mixed Concrete Antitrust Litigation*, the court applied a substantially relaxed Rule 702 analysis[11] and accepted the expert's evidence because the methodology used was widely accepted.[12] Similarly in *In re Evanston Northwestern Healthcare Corp. Antitrust Litigation*,[13] while noting that the report of the defendant's expert "contains some misleading information and analysis," the court refused to "undertake a *Daubert* analysis at this procedural juncture" and instead stated it would give the report the weight it was due.[14] In *Dukes*, however, the Supreme Court, without directly ruling on the issue, expressed doubt that *Daubert* did not apply to expert testimony at the certification stage of class proceedings.[15]

§ 8.07 Report of testifying expert

Reports of economic experts must satisfy the content requirements of Rule 26(a)(2)(B) of the Federal Rules of Civil Procedure. This includes: (1) a complete statement of all opinions the witness will express and the basis and reasons for them; (2) the data or other information considered; (3) any exhibits that will be used to summarize or support the opinions; (4) the witness's qualifications; (5) a list of all other cases in which, during the previous four years, the witness testified as an expert at trial or by deposition; and (6) a statement of the expert's compensation.

The scope and timing of expert discovery is determined initially by Rule 26, but also by the terms of pretrial discovery orders negotiated and entered in the case. The expert will often include all information required by Rule 26(a)(2) in the expert's report, to avoid the need for submission of other documents or work product. The parties may agree or the district court may order that other materials will be produced with respect to expert testimony and reports. For example, opposing experts may seek electronic copies of database econometric models used for analysis, so the party's own expert can seek to replicate the opposing expert's results, or modify terms of a model to show how such changes affect

---

trict court determination as to which expert presented correct injury-in-fact analysis); *In re* Initial Public Offering Securities Litig., 471 F.3d 24 (2d Cir. 2006) (holding district judge cannot certify class without first assessing all evidence related to Rule 23 requirements, including expert evidence); Blades v. Monsanto, 400 F.3d 562 (8th Cir. 2005) (at class certification stage, plaintiffs must show that expert evidence could prove claims with common evidence).

[10] *Daubert v. Merrell Dow Pharm., Inc.*, 509 U.S. 579 (1993), interprets Federal Rule of Evidence 702 and sets for the standard for the admission of expert testimony.

[11] *See* discussion *infra* § 8.11.

[12] *In re* Ready-Mixed Concrete Antitrust Litig., 261 F.R.D. 154 (S.D. Ind. 2009).

[13] 268 F.R.D. 56 (N.D. Ill. 2010).

[14] 268 F.R.D. at 77.

[15] *Dukes*, 131 S. Ct. at 2553–54; *see also* American Honda Motor Co. v. Allen, 600 F.3d 813, 815–16 (7th Cir. 2010) (requiring full *Daubert* analysis when expert report or testimony is critical to class certification).

results. Even if parties are not required to produce such materials as part of the mandatory disclosures required by Rule 26(a)(2), the parties may derive mutual benefit from reaching agreement on exchange of such documents and information.

In the absence of a stipulation or a court order, Rule 26(a)(2)(D) provides that Rule 26(a)(2) expert disclosures must be made: (1) at least 90 days before the date set for trial or for the case to be ready for trial; or (2) if the evidence is intended solely to contradict or rebut evidence on the same subject matter identified by another party under Rule 26(a)(2)(B) or (C), within 30 days after the other party's disclosure. Given that expert discovery is often complex in antitrust cases, and may involve multiple experts and the generation of multiple reports, counsel may wish to stipulate to a discovery schedule that provides for Rule 26(a)(2) disclosures further in advance of trial than provided for in Rule 26(a)(2)(D), and that provides more than 30 days for rebuttal reports.

Experts often receive documents and information on a piecemeal basis from counsel and from independent market research. Counsel may provide the expert with certain documents or deposition transcripts at the onset of work, and counsel may supplement with additional information, often at the request of the expert, over the duration of the engagement. Counsel should make sure that the opposing party supplements required disclosures under Rule 26 if the expert modifies opinions or the grounds for opinions, and may seek to take a supplemental deposition of the expert if the changes are material.

The content of the expert report will vary greatly depending on the type of claims asserted (e.g., litigation involving mergers and acquisitions, anticompetitive horizontal agreements, vertical restraints, or unilateral anticompetitive conduct) and whether the plaintiff's claims will be analyzed under the per se, rule of reason, or quick look standard.[16] The expert will normally provide a concise but complete statement of each opinion the expert will offer at trial, explaining the economic principles, econometric techniques, and case facts used as a basis for analysis and opinions. Developing the expert report typically entails close cooperation between the expert and counsel to ensure that the expert's opinions, supporting economic methodology, and case facts are consistent with the party's positions on liability and damages. The report is typically prepared by the expert using the expert's own language to ensure that the report accurately reflects the expert's analysis and opinions. Counsel may work with the expert on edits to ensure that the report is cogent and understandable to a layperson, and accounts for all relevant information submitted to or obtained by the expert. The opinions of the economic expert will usually focus on the allegations and defenses framed by the pleadings in the case, and not on claims of alleged anticompetitive conduct that are not raised by the pleadings.[17]

The expert's report will be most useful if it clearly delineates the scope of expected testimony and shows how the testimony supports or addresses particular elements of claims and defenses in the case. Care in structuring the expert's report may assist counsel and

---

[16] For a discussion of antitrust standards of illegality, see Chapter 1 of this Handbook.

[17] In *Behrend v. Comcast Corp.*, 626 F. Supp. 2d 495 (E.D. Pa. 2009), the plaintiffs' expert submitted a report with opinions that Comcast had engaged in multiple forms of exclusionary conduct, including one that was not specifically alleged in the complaint. The defendants sought to bar the expert's opinion or any claim for damages based on this conduct. The court acknowledged that the opinion was new and that the conduct in question was not emphasized in the complaint, but held that the complaint allegations sufficiently put the defendants on notice of the claim.

the court in using the report during summary judgment proceedings, and avoid disputes over the scope of expected testimony at trial. This is particularly important where expert opinions are not offered on ultimate issues of liability or particular elements of a claim or defense, or where the opinions will be used in conjunction with other expert testimony. If the party does not provide a clear statement of the scope of the expert's opinion, the court may infer a broader scope than the party intends and address issues of admissibility based on this misconception.[18]

§ 8.08 Rebuttal expert and report

Parties in antitrust litigation often submit a rebuttal report of a new or existing economic expert to respond to evidence offered by the opposing party's expert. Counsel should be cognizant of this possibility when preparing the discovery schedule.[19] Counsel also should consider whether expert depositions should occur before or after rebuttal reports are submitted, and whether experts who submit such reports should be deposed again. Experts may benefit from review of the opposing expert's deposition before preparing a rebuttal report, but this approach may entail a second round of depositions with attendant cost and burden, as parties normally wish to examine opposing experts after all reports have been submitted to avoid surprise during summary judgment briefing or at trial.

As the name suggests, rebuttal reports are meant to rebut the report of the opposing party's expert and are not intended to serve as an extension of the expert designation and report production deadline. Thus, courts may strike rebuttal reports if they believe a party is using the rebuttal to sandbag the opposition with claims and issues that should have been included in the initial expert report.[20]

§ 8.09 Expert depositions

Expert depositions are permitted by Rule 26 and are commonplace in antitrust cases. Counsel examining an opposing party's economic expert may wish to cover basic topics as follows, and engage in other examination as time permits: (1) determine that the expert

[18] Such was the case in *City of Tuscaloosa v. Harcros Chems., Inc.*, 158 F.3d 548 (11th Cir. 1998). The plaintiffs in this price-fixing case attempted to introduce expert testimony from multiple witnesses, including a certified public accountant and a statistician. The district court excluded the testimony of plaintiffs' certified public accountant on the basis that the accountant was not qualified to render opinions based on economic theory, and excluded the testimony of plaintiffs' statistician because his data and testimony were insufficient to show a successful conspiracy. The Eleventh Circuit overruled the district court and held that the majority of the excluded testimony should not have been withheld. The court observed that the accountant was not rendering opinions based on economic theory, but was testifying within his realm of expertise, and that the statistician's analysis was helpful and admissible under Federal Rule of Evidence 702 even if it did not by itself demonstrate a successful conspiracy

[19] *See, e.g.*, Congressional Air, Ltd. v. Beech Aircraft Corp., 176 F.R.D. 513, 516–17 (D. Md. 1997) (excluding rebuttal expert report that was produced after close of discovery and less than one month prior to trial).

[20] *See, e.g.*, *In re* Ready-Mixed Concrete Antitrust Litig., 261 F.R.D. 154, 159 (S.D. Ind. 2009). For a discussion of expert reports in the context of evidence gathering generally, see Chapter 7 of this Handbook.

fully complied with disclosures required by Rule 26; (2) identify all documents, information, and data that the expert considered and how the information was used for the expert's analysis and opinions; (3) identify all assumptions that the expert used (or decided not to use) in deriving opinions, and the basis for the assumptions in economic theory and practice; (4) identify how the expert's methodology differs from that used in previous engagements and publications, or by other experts, in particular by experts for the party that counsel represents; (5) identify follow-up work that the expert intends to complete and the reasons for the same; (6) seek admissions on flaws, limitations, or factual inconsistencies in the expert's opinions and data analysis; and (7) seek admissions favorable to the methodologies, data, and conclusions of counsel's own expert.

Experts, like all witnesses, should listen carefully to questions and give direct and complete answers, but many questions posed to experts do not have simple "yes" or "no" answers. The expert will usually want to respond to open-ended and hypothetical questions with answers that help to explain the expert's opinions, but avoid unnecessary digressions and answers that could be taken out of context in a manner that does not reflect the expert's actual opinions and analyses. In any event, the expert should avoid giving answers that can be taken out of context and used against the expert and the party who retained the expert in later proceedings in the case.

Expert depositions are important in preparing and positioning the case for summary judgment and trial. Cross-examination may expose potential flaws in the expert's use of economic theory, methodology, and case facts. However, the expert may be able to mitigate the impact of such exposures before summary judgment briefing or trial. Depositions also may reveal how the opposing party will seek to rebut the expert's opinions and data analysis, which may aid the expert in preparing to testify at trial. Transcripts of expert depositions will be used for summary judgment briefing, and may be used at trial for impeachment, so the expert should be thoroughly prepared to explain and defend the opinions, analysis, and factual and theoretical grounds set forth in the expert's reports. Moreover, due to the importance of expert testimony in summary judgment proceedings and at trial, a successful expert deposition can make the opposing party question its likelihood of prevailing and help facilitate settlement.

§ 8.10 Summary judgment motions

The plausibility of the plaintiff's claims, which may initially be addressed at the pleading stage, is an issue that again arises on a motion for summary judgment. In *Matsushita Electric Industrial Co. v. Zenith Radio Corp.*, the Supreme Court held that a defendant is entitled to summary judgment if the evidence is "as consistent with permissible competition as with illegal conspiracy" unless the plaintiff can "present evidence 'that tends to exclude the possibility' that the alleged conspirators acted independently."[21] Parties seeking or opposing summary judgment can present evidence through expert affidavits.

Although Rule 705 of the Federal Rules of Evidence allows an expert to give opinions without prior disclosure of underlying facts, an affidavit submitted by an expert still must

---

21 475 U.S. 574, 588 (1986) (quoting Monsanto Co. v. Spray-Rite Service Corp., 465 U.S. 752, 764 (1984)).

comply with Rule 56(e) of the Federal Rules of Civil Procedure, which requires that affidavits submitted in summary judgment proceedings set forth specific facts.[22] An expert affidavit that is conclusory and devoid of reasoning does not comply with Rule 56(e).[23] Given the importance of expert evidence in summary judgment proceedings, parties often desire and courts typically require complete disclosure by experts, including supporting data, prior to summary judgment briefing.

§ 8.11 *Daubert* and other gatekeeper motions

The exclusion of expert testimony in an antitrust case can have a profound impact on the plaintiff's ability to prevail, and in some circumstances can result in entry of summary judgment against the plaintiff.[24] In addition, unlike motions for summary judgment, which are reviewed on appeal under a de novo standard, rulings on *Daubert* and other gatekeeper motions are reviewed under an abuse of discretion standard.[25] Thus, parties and experts must conduct briefing and argument on *Daubert* motions with significant care.

Daubert and Rule 702 are the most common bases for challenging antitrust experts. Federal Rule of Evidence 702 mandates that testimony by experts (1) is based upon sufficient facts and data, (2) is the product of reliable principles and methods, and (3) applies the principles and methods reliably to the facts of the case. Other non-*Daubert* gatekeeper challenges to expert evidence may arise under Rule 703 (typically concerning the type of evidence relied on by the expert), and Rule 704 (typically concerning the expert improperly usurping the role of the ultimate finder of fact).[26]

Daubert directs a court analyzing the admissibility of expert testimony to make a "preliminary assessment of whether the reasoning and methodology underlying the testimony is scientifically valid and of whether that reasoning or methodology properly can be applied to the facts in issue."[27] In conducting this analysis, courts consider whether the expert's testimony is sufficiently tied to the facts of the case such that it will aid the jury

---

22 M&M Med. Supplies & Serv. v. Pleasant Valley Hosp., 981 F.2d 160, 164–65 (4th Cir. 1992) (en banc); City of Chanute, Kan. v. Williams Natural Gas Co., 743 F. Supp. 1437 (D. Kan. 1990).

23 *Id.*; *see also* Major League Baseball Props., Inc. v. Salvino, Inc., 542 F.3d 290, 311–12 (2d Cir. 2008) (expert's conclusory disagreement with opposing expert's detailed report insufficient to overcome summary judgment); Lamb's Patio Theatre, Inc. v. Universal Film Exchs., Inc., 582 F.2d 1068, 1070 (7th Cir. 1978) (affirming summary judgment in favor of defendant and stating that in face of "sworn denial of the existence of conspiracy, it was up to plaintiff to produce significant probative evidence by affidavit or deposition that conspiracy existed if summary judgment was to be avoided").

24 *See, e.g.*, *In re* Fresh Del Monte Pineapples Antitrust Litig., No. 04-md-1628, 2009 WL 3241401 (S.D.N.Y. Sept. 30, 2009).

25 United States v. Gabaldon, 389 F.3d 1090, 1098 (10th Cir. 2004); United States v. Bahena, 223 F.3d 797, 809 (8th Cir. 2000).

26 *See* Langenfeld & Alexander, *supra* note 4, at 23 (excluding non-*Daubert* challenges from study, including challenges under FRE 703 for expert's reliance on statements made out of court, other data that should not be admitted, or testimony of another expert that was excluded, and challenges under FRE 702 or FRE 704 for expert opinions that usurp role of finder of fact or seek to interpret subjective motivations of parties).

27 *Daubert*, 509 U.S. at 592–93.

in resolving the factual dispute.[28] In other words, the expert's testimony must not only meet the various *Daubert* reliability factors, such as peer review and publication, testing, known or potential error rate, and general acceptance, but must also "fit" the particular facts of the case.[29] Counsel and the economic expert must assure that the expert's opinions and economic analysis incorporate all relevant facts about the parties, industry, and market. If the expert fails to account for pertinent facts, the court may deem the expert's opinion inadmissible even if the expert is qualified and has otherwise applied a reliable methodology.[30]

Defendants are highly motivated to make *Daubert* motions as part of summary judgment efforts. If the defendant can successfully exclude plaintiff's expert, then the effect on plaintiff's case is likely devastating.[31] The same may not be true for a plaintiff that successfully challenges the defendant's expert, because the plaintiff may still lose at summary judgment or trial by failing to carry its burden of proof. Plaintiffs also may forgo *Daubert* challenges due to expense and uncertain upside.[32] If the plaintiff's experts survive a *Daubert* challenge, then the case will usually settle or go to trial, and either outcome is often acceptable to the plaintiff. Courts, as a practical matter, also may be reluctant to bar the defendant's expert from testifying when permitting the plaintiff an opportunity to present expert testimony.

The importance of experts in antitrust cases means that preparing for *Daubert* and other challenges to experts is critical for both plaintiffs' and defendants' counsel. These preparations require more than selecting a well-qualified economist, since successful challenges are most often tied to whether the expert has applied methodologies recognized by the courts as appropriate and based on reliable data.

The expert and counsel will usually need to demonstrate that economic models and methodologies used by the expert are based on sound economic principles, even for models that are well established, standard, and widely recognized.[33]

---

28 *Id.* at 591 (citing United States v. Downing, 753 F.2d 1224, 1242 (3d Cir. 1985)).

29 Concord Boat Corp. v. Brunswick Corp., 207 F.3d 1039, 1055 (8th Cir. 2000) (citing *Daubert*, 509 U.S. at 591).

30 *See, e.g.*, ZF Meritor LLC v. Eaton Corp., 646 F. Supp. 2d 663 (D. Del. 2009) (excluding expert opinion based on projections from business plan because source unknown and untested by expert); Corey Airport Services v. City of Atlanta, 632 F. Supp. 2d 1246 (N.D. Ga. 2008) (ruling that, even if expert's methodology was reliable, there was "too great an analytical gap between the data and the opinion" offered by expert); U.S. Information Systems v. International Brotherhood of Electrical Workers Local Union No. 3, 313 F. Supp. 2d 213 (S.D.N.Y. 2006) (excluding expert testimony after determining expert's data sample was biased); *In re* Polypropylene Carpet Antitrust Litig., 93 F. Supp. 2d 1348 (N.D. Ga. 2000) (barring expert from offering evidence based on census data that was used to estimate changes in market share and determine whether defendants restricted output, because data did not accurately represent defendants' sales and would thus be misleading).

31 Christopher B. Hockett, Geraldine M. Alexis & Christina M. Wheeler, Daubert *Redux: Revisiting the Admissibility of Expert Testimony in Antitrust Cases*, ANTITRUST, Summer 2001, at 7.

32 *See* Langenfeld & Alexander, *supra* note 4, at 23, 25 (economists testifying for plaintiffs are subject to 85 percent of all *Daubert* motions in antitrust cases, and approximately 50 percent of such challenges are successful in whole or in part (excluding challenges at the class certification stage when courts may apply a more relaxed standard for admissibility); defendants' economic experts in antitrust cases have rarely been barred from testifying).

33 Concord Boat Corp. v. Brunswick Corp., 207 F.3d 1039 (8th Cir. 2000) (excluding plain-

The expert will usually want to explain the methodology used for data analysis, show that it is a good fit for the case facts, and perform thorough due diligence to verify the accuracy and completeness of data and other information sources. Expert opinions have been excluded in many cases due to flaws in data reliability and applicability even where the expert's methodology may be accepted.[34] The expert often will also explicitly address information that may be interpreted as contradictory to the expert's opinions or data analysis, to avert claims that the expert inappropriately cherry-picked facts.

Courts have excluded expert evidence under Rule 704 where the expert offered opinions that improperly took the place of the ultimate finder of fact. Counsel and experts need to have a clear understanding of limits the court will place on the expert's evidence and frame proposed opinions in a manner that avoids this concern, particularly where those opinions relate to issues for which the finder of fact must weigh conflicting evidence from fact witnesses and documents. Similarly, counsel and experts often take steps to avoid issues under Rule 703, in particular where the expert relies on opinions or analysis of another expert, so a successful challenge to one expert does not result in exclusion of both. Where possible, each expert may provide alternative and independent grounds for opinions and analysis, and review and approve of the methodology and supporting materials of the other expert.

§ 8.12 Expert witness trial preparation

Counsel often work closely with the expert to prepare for testimony at trial. The expert and/or counsel typically prepare demonstrative exhibits to assist in presenting opinions and data analysis, recognizing that courts and juries may need simple explanations of complex models and data analysis to grasp the expert's reasoning and see how it supports the party's positions in the case. Counsel and the expert typically prepare an outline of examination with specific questions to elicit a complete statement of the expert's opinions and supporting analysis. Where possible, counsel may wish to conduct a practice examination with an audience representative of the court or jury who will hear the case, and adjust testimony based on feedback to ensure that the expert uses terms and explanations that are understandable and persuasive.

---

tiff's economic expert in part because court did not find references in case law to Cournot economic model, even though model is widely used and recognized in economics literature and by antitrust practitioners); *see also* American Banana Co. v. J. Bonafede Co., No. 09-4561-cv, 2010 WL 4342217 (2d Cir. Nov. 3, 2010) (ruling expert testimony inadmissible because, among other reasons, expert failed to sufficiently explain the "reasoned economic analysis" underlying conclusions); Worldwide Basketball & Sports Tours, Inc. v. National Collegiate Athletic Ass'n, 273 F. Supp. 2d 933 (S.D. Ohio 2003) (barring expert on definition of "submarkets" and opining that NCAA rule would reduce quality of games because expert failed to explain economic basis of opinions).

[34] *See, e.g.*, Kentucky Speedway v. National Ass'n of Stock Car Auto Racing, 588 F.3d 908 (6th Cir. 2009) (excluding expert who employed recognized "SSNIP" test for market definition because court believed the expert had "used his own version" of the test); Nilavar v. Mercy Health System–Western Ohio, No. 06-3819, 2007 WL 2264439 (6th Cir. Aug. 7, 2007) (affirming exclusion of expert testimony on relevant market definition where expert used recognized Elzinga-Hogarty and critical loss tests but made assumptions that contradicted the proposed definition of the relevant product market).

The expert should prepare for cross-examination at trial. Counsel often conduct a practice examination using the expert's deposition(s), summary judgment briefs, court rulings, pre-trial order, and testimony and documents actually admitted (or excluded) at trial before the expert testifies. Counsel may be less familiar with economic theory and analysis than the expert, but may have a greater command of the overall factual record in the case and the opposing party's positions. The expert will typically identify potential weaknesses in the economic theories, models, and data analysis that will be presented on direct examination, and work with counsel on how to rebut these issues. The expert may also review key evidence that opposing counsel may use on cross-examination and prepare responses that show why the evidence does not detract from the expert's opinions and analysis.

The expert will have less control over the flow of testimony during cross-examination, but a well-prepared expert will still focus the finder of fact on expert's opinions and supporting grounds, and show that points raised by opposing counsel do not contradict or undermine the expert's opinions and direct testimony. Opposing counsel may seek to show that the expert's assumptions are not supported by or consistent with the evidence. Effective experts are typically prepared to respond in a clear, forthright, and direct manner, but without making unwarranted concessions that may undermine the weight accorded to the expert's opinions. At the same time, the expert will often prepare responses that would not cause the finder of fact to see the expert as overly dogmatic, combative, or unwilling to accept legitimate weaknesses and alternative hypotheses directed at the expert's opinions.

§ 8.13 Trial testimony

The expert's trial testimony should be within the scope of opinions, supporting grounds, and fact evidence disclosed in the expert's report and deposition. The expert and counsel often consider whether the expert needs to reconsider reliance on any case facts due to court rulings on admissibility or use of evidence made during trial or pretrial hearings. In addition, experts who offer rebuttal evidence often attend the trial testimony of the opposing expert if permitted by the court, given that the opposing expert may make similar adjustments in trial testimony.

Direct testimony usually proceeds with a presentation of the expert's qualifications and experience, followed by an offer of the witness as an expert qualified to testify on a particular field of expertise, unless qualifications are covered by a pretrial stipulation. The expert then will present a summary of main opinions, describe pertinent economic theories and models, present data analysis and other case facts that support the opinions, and explain how these opinions and analysis support the party's position on elements of claims and defenses. The expert also may testify to some potential criticisms and perceived flaws in these opinions and analysis, in anticipation of rebuttal. The expert typically concludes direct examination with a recap of main opinions.

The expert will often use demonstrative exhibits to aid direct testimony, including bullet point slides, charts, tables, time lines, and key documents and excerpts of testimony. The expert should present opinions and supporting grounds in simple terms with minimal use of technical jargon, and explain key economic terms, theories, analytical methods, and data. The expert may use simple examples to explain complex methods such as regression analysis and game theory, and where possible use a narrative story line to tie the expert's opinions and supporting grounds together. At the same time, the expert should not completely forgo discussion of technical concepts and analysis, to avoid unwarranted criticism by the opposing expert and provide a complete evidentiary record in the event of an appeal. The expert will typically tie all opinions and supporting analysis to the key issues in the case to which they relate, and not assume that these relationships will be obvious to the finder of fact.

During cross-examination, the expert should listen carefully to questions and respond directly and succinctly, using narrative responses only where a detailed explanation is necessary to rebut the focus of the cross-examination. Even with thorough trial preparation, opposing counsel may confront the expert with new and unforeseen evidence and questions. Counsel often work with the expert on how to respond to such circumstances, so the expert does not make unwarranted concessions, engage in speculation, or appear evasive or ill-prepared, all of which may undermine the expert's credibility.

§ 8.14 Post-trial briefing and argument

Parties in antitrust cases often submit post-trial motions for a permanent injunction, judgment as a matter of law, or a new trial, which may examine whether the evidence admitted at trial supports a jury verdict or judgment entered by the court. For example, Rule 50(a)(1) of the Federal Rules of Civil Procedure provides that a party may obtain judgment as a matter of law if substantial evidence does not support the jury's factual findings, or if those factual findings cannot support the legal conclusions implied from the jury's verdict.[35] Similarly, the court may grant a new trial if the verdict is contrary to the clear weight of the evidence or is based on evidence that is false.[36] In briefing these post-trial motions, the economic expert typically is not permitted to submit a new report or testimony, but can assist counsel to analyze the evidence admitted at trial and explain why, from an economic perspective, the evidence does or does not support the jury's verdict. If the court reserves issues of damages or injunctive relief for a separate trial, the expert may engage in further data analysis, discovery, and testimony after the liability trial.

§ 8.15 Types of economic analyses

Economic experts provide evidence on several key elements of antitrust claims under §§ 1 and 2 of the Sherman Act (conspiracy and monopolization, respectively), § 7 of the Clayton Act (mergers), and the Robinson Patman Act (price discrimination), among others.[37] Economic experts also provide evidence on liability issues (market definition, market power and monopoly power, inference of conspiracy, anticompetitive effect, and antitrust injury), damages and equitable relief, and class certification. In addressing these

---

[35] Masimo Corp. v. Tyco Health Care Group, L.P., No. CV 02-4770, 2006 WL 1236666 (C.D. Cal. Mar. 22, 2006) (citing Chiron Corp. v. Genentech, Inc., 363 F.3d 1247, 1252 53 (Fed. Cir. 2004)).

[36] *Id.* (citing Hangarter v. Provident Life & Accident Ins. Co., 373 F.3d 998, 1005 (9th Cir. 2004)).

[37] For an overview of antitrust claims and their elements, see Chapter 1 of this Handbook.

issues, economists use a variety of different economic theories, models, and statistical analyses as grounds for their opinions.

In evaluating antitrust liability or damages, economists use a variety of methods to analyze market structure and the nature of competition within the market, and to attempt to directly measure the impact of alleged anticompetitive acts. Analysis of market definition often is based on methods outlined in the Horizontal Merger Guidelines,[38] and calculation of market shares and other measures of market concentration are used as a starting point for analysis of market power and monopoly power. Analysis of direct evidence of anticompetitive effects, which some argue may obviate the need to define relevant markets and analyze market concentration, typically entails a comparison of prices, output, and quality of products or services before and after the alleged anticompetitive conduct, or with similar geographic areas or market sectors that are not affected by the alleged conduct, while attempting to control for other normal factors that influence markets. The discussion that follows is an overview of some of the common elements of antitrust claims on which economic experts offer opinions, and the general types of analytical methods used to support these opinions.

8.15.1 Elements of antitrust claims and defenses

8.15.1(A) Inference of cartel conduct

Economic theory has established certain market conditions that are in general necessary for a horizontal conspiracy among suppliers or customers in a market to operate successfully. Typically, a conspiracy not to compete involves parallel action occurring at similar times, such as price increases, decisions not to expand output, and decisions not to expand sales or marketing into other firms' territories or customers. Decisions of this type may occur on a unilateral basis due to normal market conditions and competition, so evidence of such parallel conduct by itself may not be considered sufficient to show a conspiracy. Also, in general, conspiracies are more likely to be successful, and thus attempted, in markets with fewer competitors, such as in an oligopoly.[39] In an oligopoly, however, economics teaches us that firms are more likely to anticipate and take account of the actions of their competitors in determining their strategies, such as pricing and where to focus sales and marketing efforts, in the absence of an agreement to fix prices or not to compete.[40]

For example, assume that firms A and B each dominate different regions of the United States. The firms may agree not to expand into each other's territories, expecting that this agreement will enable each firm to increase and maintain prices above competitive market levels. Alternatively, firm A may decide unilaterally, without any agreement, not to expand into the territory dominated by firm B. Why? Firm A may anticipate that, if it did so, firm B would retaliate by expanding into firm A's territory. Firm B may reach the same

---

38 *See* U.S. Dep't of Justice & Fed. Trade Comm'n, Horizontal Merger Guidelines (2010), *available at* http://www.justice.gov/atr/public/guidelines/hmg-2010.pdf.

39 *See, e.g.*, George J. Stigler, *A Theory of Oligopoly*, 72 J. Pol. Econ. 44 (1964).

40 For a discussion that highlights the difficulties economics encounters in evaluating conspiracies in an oligopoly setting, see Michael D. Whinston, Lectures on Antitrust Economics 20 (2006).

conclusion, again without any agreement with firm A. Thus, for oligopoly markets where collusion is more likely to be successful, parties in antitrust cases may find it is difficult to distinguish anticompetitive collusion from normal competitive actions that are not part of a conspiracy to restrain trade.

Economic experts may analyze whether an inference of conspiratorial agreement is plausible in market settings where economic theory predicts that competing suppliers may take their rivals' actions into consideration without the rivals entering into an explicit agreement. As the Supreme Court decision in *Matsushita* illustrates, analysis of economic incentives and competitive market forces may show that it would not be economically rational to infer that suppliers acted in furtherance of an anticompetitive conspiracy.[41] Thus, expert economic analysis may be offered as a "minus" factor to rebut an inference of conspiracy.

Expert economic evidence also is frequently used to show that "plus factors" exist to support the inference that defendants' interdependent or parallel conduct is circumstantial evidence of a conspiracy to restrain trade.[42] For example, the plaintiff's expert may provide evidence that the market in question is sufficiently concentrated with high barriers to entry such that it would be plausible for a conspiracy to be successful. The expert also may show that suppliers engaged in behavior that would be profitable with a conspiracy, but not profitable without conspiracy.[43] The typical example is where rivals quickly adopted a price increase that would not be profitable unless each rival did so, because the rivals otherwise had the ability to keep their prices low and a strong profit incentive to do so. Another example is where rivals had a strong profit incentive to expand sales into other territories, even considering the potential for unilateral retaliation, but did not expand.

Economic analysis of cartels presents some inherent limitations. There may not be sufficient information available to determine whether suppliers engaged in behavior that would be profitable with a conspiracy, but not profitable without conspiracy. Moreover, it is difficult to infer a conspiracy only from market information of parallel conduct in an oligopoly market setting, because economic theory also may provide a plausible explanation for why rivals would engage in parallel but independent conduct. Thus, the economic expert may be able to show that market conditions are conducive to an economically rational conspiracy, but not necessarily that a conspiratorial agreement is the sole or most plausible explanation for parallel conduct that is observed.[44]

8.15.1(b) Market definition and market power

Economic experts offer opinions on the definition of relevant markets using economic principles such as cross-elasticity of demand and supply, barriers to entry, and other well-established, standard, and widely recognized economic principles, such as reasonable interchangeability of products in use, and the geographic area of effective competition

---

41 Matsushita Elec. Indus. Co. v. Zenith Radios Corp., 475 U.S. 574, 587 (1986).

42 The Sedona Conference, Working Group on the Role of Economics in Antitrust, The Sedona Conference Commentary on the Role of Economics in Antitrust Law (Feb. 2006), *available at* http://www.thesedonaconference.org.

43 *See* Gregory Werden, *Economic Evidence on the Existence of Collusion: Reconciling Antitrust Law with Oligopoly Theory*, 71 Antitrust L.J. 719, 767 (2004).

44 Whinston, *supra* note 40, at 20.

in which sellers operate and to which purchasers can turn for supplies. Experts also offer opinions on the defendant's market power or monopoly power, using economic principles based on the degree of market concentration among suppliers or purchasers, and in some cases based on direct evidence of anticompetitive effects. Evidence on these elements is required, for example, for § 1 rule-of-reason claims, § 2 monopoly claims, and challenges to mergers and acquisitions under § 7 of the Clayton Act.

Economic experts select methodologies for analysis based on the claims at issue and data available for the case, which may include natural experiments, statistical analysis, evidence on the cost structure of suppliers, and historical evidence on trends in market information, as discussed below. Experts also apply the analytical methods and standards on market definition and market power contained in the Horizontal Merger Guidelines, not only for government merger investigations and court challenges, but also for private antitrust cases.

8.15.1(c) Anticompetitive effects

Economic experts offer opinions and supporting analysis on whether the defendant's challenged conduct caused anticompetitive effects, such as reduced output, price increases above competitive market levels, and reduced quality, or a substantial increase in market concentration that enabled the defendant to achieve and exercise market power. Experts also offer opinions on whether the defendant's conduct produced efficiencies and other procompetitive effects, and whether on balance the conduct has a net procompetitive effect. Experts use a variety of analytical methods to support such opinions, not only to show the nature and magnitude of competitive effects, but also to show that the effects were caused by the defendant's anticompetitive conduct and not by other factors, including other market forces.

8.15.1(d) Antitrust injury

Economic experts offer opinions and supporting analysis on whether the plaintiff suffered an injury that is causally linked to the anticompetitive effect in the market, and is the type of injury that the antitrust laws were intended to prevent and that flows from what makes the defendant's challenged conduct unlawful.[45] In class action cases, economic experts also offer opinions on whether substantially all members of the proposed class suffered such injury, and whether the fact of injury can be proven with evidence common to members of the class. As discussed below, experts often use statistical methods such as regression analysis to demonstrate that the plaintiff's injury is linked to the defendant's conduct and not to other factors, including normal market forces.

8.15.1(e) Damages[46]

Measurement of damages typically proceeds from the improper acts at issue in the case. Damages experts typically assume that such bad acts did occur. The primary areas of

---

[45] For further discussion of antitrust injury and antitrust standing, see Chapter 3 of this Handbook.

[46] For further discussion of damages awards, as well as alternative remedies for plaintiffs, see Chapter 9 of this Handbook.

focus then become: (1) the impact of the acts on the plaintiff; and (2) the quantification of damages based on the impact. Accordingly, the damages expert typically assesses the likely effects of the defendant's allegedly improper acts by reconstructing what would likely have happened "but for" the acts.[47] Determining the relevant market characteristics in the actual and "but for" worlds is important to damage analysis, because damages to the plaintiff are estimated by the difference in actual and "but for" outcomes. For example, in a price-fixing case, damages analyses typically compare actual prices paid by customers during the period of the price-fixing conspiracy against estimates of "but for" prices that would have been paid during that same period absent the conspiracy. A similar type of analysis can be applied to other types of antitrust claims.

The determination of "but for" prices to quantify antitrust damages typically entails a combination of economic reasoning and analysis of available financial data to generate an economically reasonable estimate.[48] There are a variety of economic techniques that can be used to estimate "but for" prices.

One technique is the "before and after" (or "before and during") approach, which uses information on economic behavior before the allegedly improper acts to make inferences about likely economic behavior in the "but for" world that excludes the allegedly improper acts.[49] In an antitrust case involving an allegation of reduced competition and higher prices, the damages expert may use historical prices or historical price trends in the market prior to the alleged reduction in competition as a benchmark to estimate prices "but for" the allegedly anticompetitive actions, controlling for other market influences as appropriate. Similarly, economists may use "during and after" or "before, during, and after" tests, using the period after the alleged illegal behavior as a benchmark to estimate "but for" prices. The "during and after" approach can be particularly useful when data on the period before the alleged anticompetitive behavior is not available.

Another technique is the "yardstick" approach, in which the damages expert makes use of potential comparable markets or industries in estimating "but for" outcomes. For example, in an antitrust case alleging reduced competition and higher prices, the damages expert could potentially use prices or price trends in comparable "competitive markets" to estimate prices "but for" the allegedly anticompetitive actions.[50]

One important consideration in making comparisons using either a "before and after" approach or a "yardstick" approach is to ensure that the market outcomes in the market of comparison are economically reasonable predictors of the likely outcomes in the "but for" market at the time of the allegedly improper acts. For that reason, it can be important that the damages expert analyze and compare the economic characteristics of the

---

[47] *See* Stephen H. Kalos, *Antitrust*, *in* LITIGATION SERVICES HANDBOOK: THE ROLE OF THE FINANCIAL EXPERT 24-11 to 24-13 (Roman L. Weil et al. eds., 4th ed. 2007) ("The courts use a but-for standard to calculate both overcharge and lost profits damages; this standard compares actual prices or profits and the prices or profits that would have occurred but for the anticompetitive acts."); *see also* ABA SECTION OF ANTITRUST LAW, PROVING ANTITRUST DAMAGES: LEGAL AND ECONOMIC ISSUES 53, 125–26 (2d ed. 2010).

[48] *See* ABA SECTION OF ANTITRUST LAW, *supra* note 47, at 125–26.

[49] *See* Kalos, *supra* note 47, at 24-11 to 24-12; *see also* ABA SECTION OF ANTITRUST LAW, *supra* note 47, at 57, 126–27.

[50] *See* Kalos, *supra* note 47, 24-12 to 24-13; *see also Econometrics and Regression Analysis, in* ABA SECTION OF ANTITRUST LAW 127, *supra* note 47; *see also Quantifying Damages, in id.* at 57–58.

comparison market with the economic characteristics in the market in which the allegedly improper acts occurred. In particular, damages analysis must reasonably account for factors other than the allegedly improper acts that may be causing market outcomes in the market of concern (e.g., relatively high prices).

Various economic and statistical techniques are described below that can be used to hold these types of factors constant and thus isolate the economic impact of the allegedly improper acts. One technique involves regression analysis, which is a formal statistical technique used to isolate the impact of different independent variables on a dependent variable.[51] However, the data are not always available for regression analysis, and there are other reliable techniques that can effectively isolate the potential impact of the allegedly improper acts. Another commonly used technique to isolate the impact of allegedly improper acts involves using so-called "natural experiments" as a benchmark to estimate "but for" market outcomes.

8.15.2 Analytical methods

8.15.2(A) NATURAL EXPERIMENTS AND BENCHMARKING

Economists use "benchmarks" or comparables in antitrust cases to provide evidence on liability or damages for allegedly anticompetitive actions. These analyses usually compare the market outcomes from the alleged behavior to outcomes that are not affected by that behavior. The use of comparables is intended to control for many of the influences on a market that are not related to the actions at issue, and is referred to as "natural experiment" analysis. That is, a natural experiment compares market outcomes associated with the firm or market of interest with those of other similar firms or markets that serve as a control group (unaffected by the behavior of interest). When properly done, natural experiments can provide important insights and allow economists to draw relevant conclusions.

For example, in price-fixing cases, prices have often been studied to see if they increase at the time of the alleged unlawful agreement, compared to prices in unaffected geographic areas or for similar (but unaffected) products. If prices increase more in the area or products of interest than the benchmarks, then economists may infer that the excess price increase is due to the alleged agreement. In damages analyses, prices and sales are frequently compared to appropriate benchmarks to estimate what they likely would have been "but for" the challenged conduct.[52]

Use of natural experiment analysis in government merger cases came to the forefront in *FTC v. Staples, Inc.*,[53] in which the Federal Trade Commission (FTC) successfully challenged the proposed merger of Staples and Office Depot. An important part of the FTC's

---

[51] *See Econometrics and Regression Analysis, in* SECTION OF ANTITRUST LAW 132–36, *supra* note 47.

[52] *See* WILLIAM H. PAGE, PROVING ANTITRUST DAMAGES: LEGAL AND ECONOMIC ISSUES 36–39 (1996); SHANNON P. PRATT, ROBERT F. REILLY & ROBERT P. SCHWEIHS, VALUING A BUSINESS: THE ANALYSIS AND APPRAISAL OF CLOSELY HELD COMPANIES 869–70 (4th ed. 2000); ABA SECTION OF ANTITRUST LAW, ANTITRUST LAW DEVELOPMENTS 838–44 (6th ed. 2007); Robert H. Lande & James Langenfeld, *The Perfect Caper? Private Damages and the* Microsoft *Case*, 69 GEO. WASH. L. REV. 902 (2001).

[53] 970 F. Supp. 1066 (D.D.C. 1997).

evidence for both market definition and competitive effects was pricing data of the two firms that arguably showed lower prices where the firms were in direct competition in a local area, compared to areas or times when they were not.[54] These analyses are natural experiments, since they look at the impact of prior changes in, or contemporaneous differences in, the number and identity of competitors before the merger to draw conclusions about what would happen if the merger occurred. The FTC's evidence included company documents describing lower pricing in areas where more office superstores were in direct competition. The FTC also submitted econometric analyses that estimated the impact of changes in the number and identity of office superstore competitors (and other office supply competitors) in a local area, while attempting to control for important differences across local areas that could also influence prices. The FTC argued that competition between the two firms caused Staples to reduce its prices in local areas where Office Depot also had stores, and that eliminating that competition would lead to higher prices.

This type of analysis is reliable provided (1) the natural experiment (or benchmark) is sufficiently similar to the market or time period at issue, and (2) the existence of the allegedly anticompetitive acts is a major difference between the benchmark and the market or time period at issue.[55] As in other economic analyses, natural experiment analyses are only useful if (1) they reasonably fit the facts of the case, (2) they employ sound economic methodologies that are based on reliable information, and (3) the inferences are accurately drawn from an appropriate economic model and given other available evidence.

8.15.2(B) STATISTICAL AND ECONOMETRIC ANALYSES

Most econometric models that economic experts use in antitrust cases require the expert to identify and account for the effect of major influences other than the alleged unlawful acts that affect prices or other important variables. Statistical and econometric techniques, including in particular regression analyses, are particularly useful in separating the impact of an alleged anticompetitive act on market outcomes (such as pricing) from the impact of several other influences.[56] That is, when correctly implemented, econometric techniques can isolate and measure the effect of a single explanatory factor on the economic outcomes that are relevant to the analysis.[57]

Econometric analyses may have inherent limitations, depending on the nature of the alleged anticompetitive conduct, what else is occurring in the market or industry

---

54 *See* Jonathan B. Baker, *Econometric Analysis in* FTC v. Staples, 18 J. PUB. POL'Y & MARKETING 11 (1999); Serdar Dalkir & Frederick R. Warren Boulton, *Prices, Market Definition, and the Effects of Mergers*: Staples–Office Depot, *in* THE ANTITRUST REVOLUTION 52 (John E. Kwoka, Jr. & Lawrence J. White eds., 4th ed. 2004); Alan Frankel & James Langenfeld, *Sea Change or Submarkets?* Federal Trade Commission v. Staples, Inc. and Office Depot, Inc., GLOBAL COMPETITION REV., June/July 1997, at 29.

55 James Langenfeld & Mary Coleman, *Natural Experiments, in* ABA SECTION OF ANTITRUST LAW, ISSUES IN COMPETITION LAW AND POLICY 743 (2008).

56 *See* Jonathan B. Baker & Daniel L. Rubinfeld, *Empirical Methods in Antitrust: Review and Critique*, 1 AMER. L. & ECON. REV. 386, 388 (1999); ABA SECTION OF ANTITRUST LAW, *Econometrics and Regression Analysis, in* PROVING ANTITRUST DAMAGES: LEGAL AND ECONOMIC ISSUES ch. 6 (2d ed. 2010).

57 *See* JEFFREY M. WOOLDRIDGE, ECONOMETRIC ANALYSIS OF CROSS SECTION AND PANEL DATA 3–4 (2002).

in question during the period of the conduct, and data availability. Accordingly, the economic expert must perform analyses in a manner that avoids or accounts for these considerations. For example, even sophisticated econometric techniques may not yield reliable results if the particular effect of interest cannot be distinguished from the effect of other factors.[58] Successful identification typically requires that pricing and other data for the case reflect variations for the transactions, products, geographic area, or time period affected by alleged unlawful conduct, that are not substantially mirrored by ("correlated" with) other explanatory variables that are unrelated to alleged unlawful conduct or effects. If such data exist and there are adequate controls for the effects of other economic factors, identification generally will be possible.[59]

8.15.2(c) Critical loss

The U.S. Department of Justice and the FTC use critical loss analysis to evaluate the potential competitive effects of proposed merger transactions, and this analysis is often used in some form in other antitrust cases. The agencies define a relevant market as a geographic area and group of products in which a hypothetical monopolist of the relevant market could profitably impose a small but significant and nontransitory price increase. If this hypothetical monopolist were to increase price, it would sell fewer units but also earn a higher profit on those units that it continued to sell. Thus, a price increase would be profitable only if the additional profit that the merged firm would earn on continued unit sales exceeds the profit that it would lose on units that it no longer sells.

Critical loss analysis entails an estimate of unit sales that must be lost before a given price increase would be unprofitable, and an assessment of whether the price increase would lead to this loss of unit sales.[60] The methodology involves three steps: (1) estimating the hypothetical monopolist's per-unit margin before the price increase; (2) estimating the percentage of unit sales the hypothetical monopolist could lose before a price increase becomes unprofitable; and (3) estimating whether the hypothetical monopolist would actually lose this percentage of sales if it increased price. Critical loss is intended to create a benchmark for market definition analysis, and not to create a presumption of anticompetitive effects.

Critical loss analysis typically uses historical data that shows how customers have shifted or considered shifting purchases between products or locations in response to relative changes in prices or other competitive variables, and data on margins that rival suppliers can earn on sales. A higher margin suggests a smaller break-even critical loss (i.e., lost profits on each unit of lost sales is higher for a given price increase), but economic theory also implies that a firm with high margins may face more elastic demand compared to firms with lower margins (i.e., the actual unit sales loss will be greater for a given price increase).[61] Thus, a high margin implies that a given price increase is less likely to be profitable, which may be consistent with a broader market, but also will result in lower unit sales

58 *Id.* at 52–53.

59 *Id.*

60 *See, e.g.*, James Langenfeld & Wenqing Li, *Critical Loss Analysis in Evaluating Mergers*, 46 Antitrust Bull. 299 (2001).

61 *See, e.g.*, Kenneth Danger & H.F. Frech III, *Critical Thinking about "Critical Loss" in Antitrust*, 46 Antitrust Bull. 339 (2001).

loss, which would be consistent with narrower markets. These two implications of critical loss can create tensions in the analysis. Accordingly, economists must take particular care in applying critical loss, and typically will need to find empirical evidence of consumers' sensitivity to pricing.

8.15.2(D) Diversion analysis and upward pricing pressure

Economic experts may use diversion analysis and upward pricing pressure (UPP) to analyze unilateral price effects of horizontal mergers among suppliers of differentiated products.[62] This type of analysis also may be applied to analyze monopolization, attempted monopolization, and certain conspiracy claims, and on issues of market definition, monopoly power, and competitive effects.

Economic models used to analyze markets with differentiated products proceed from standard economic theory that a firm will set its prices at a level that maximizes profits, following a merger or in connection with other challenged conduct, and that market power resulting from such conduct may lead to higher prices that are profitable for the firm. Diversion analysis is a method to quantify the extent to which customers substitute purchases of differentiated products in response to changes in their relative prices. As applied to a merger, UPP extends diversion analysis by recognizing that a merging firm would lose some sales to the other party if it increased its prices, but due to the merger those sales may be captured by the merged firm. The profits on these captured sales may make a price increase profitable even though neither party to the merger would have found price increases to be profitable prior to the merger. This rational profit opportunity is referred to as "upward pricing pressure" and takes the form of a simple mathematical test for whether UPP will arise.

The economic models for UPP generate a positive result if there is any meaningful sales diversion between products of the merging firms. Some UPP models use a standard offset to account for downward price pressure due to efficiencies that reduce the merged firm's operating costs and thus provide a rational incentive to reduce prices. These UPP models signal concern with a merger only if net UPP is positive after applying an offset (e.g., 10 percent efficiency credit), to account for variable operating cost efficiencies produced by the merger.

Diversion analysis and UPP have been used as of mid-2011 primarily for government investigations of proposed mergers, but economic experts may begin to offer opinions and analysis based on these methods for other antitrust cases in court. However, the admissibility in court of diversion and UPP analyses is largely untested.[63]

---

[62] UPP simplifies full computer simulation of the impact of mergers by using minimal data metrics. *See, e.g.*, Joseph Farrell & Carl Shapiro, *Antitrust Evaluation of Horizontal Mergers: An Economic Alternative to Market Definition*, 10 B.E. J. Theoretical Econ., No. 2, art. 9, at 28–29 (2010), *available at* http://www.bepress.com/bejte/vol10/iss1/art9; Joseph Simons & Malcolm Coate, *Upward Pressure on Price Analysis: Issues and Implications for Merger Policy*, 6 Euro. Competition J. 378 (2010). For a general discussion of UPP, see James Langenfeld & Gregory Wrobel, *Upward Pricing Pressure Analysis Under the 2010 Horizontal Merger Guidelines*, Antitrust, Fall 2010, at 21.

[63] *See, e.g.*, City of New York v. Group Health Inc., No. 06 Civ. 13122 (S.D.N.Y. May 11, 2010) (entering summary judgment for defendants due to plaintiffs' failure to allege a proper relevant product market for claims seeking to unwind consummated merger of two health plans; denying

§ 8.16 Conclusion

Economic experts are an integral part of almost all antitrust cases, providing critical opinions and supporting analysis on various aspects of liability and damages in § 1 conspiracy cases, § 2 monopoly cases, merger challenges under § 7 of the Clayton Act, and other types of cases. Expert economic evidence also is key to class certification proceedings, and to prove antitrust injury and damages in per se conspiracy cases.

The expert needs strong credentials and analytical skills, and should be skilled in describing opinions and data analysis in terms that are understandable and persuasive to the court and finder of fact. The stakes in gatekeeper challenges to expert testimony are high. To limit the risk that the entire case may be decided by the successful exclusion of expert testimony, counsel must work closely with the expert to ensure that the expert bases opinions on sound and pertinent economic theory, obtains reliable information and data needed to support opinions, and applies sound economic models and analytical methods in a manner that accounts for pertinent case facts. Once the expert is selected, the expert usually works closely with counsel throughout the course of antitrust cases to: (1) shape allegations in pleadings, (2) identify key information and data to obtain in discovery, (3) prepare and defend the expert's report and opinions, (4) assist with examination and rebuttal of opposing experts, (5) structure evidence provided through fact witnesses and documents, (6) assist the briefing of motions to dismiss, class certification, and summary judgment, (7) testify at trial, and (8) assist with any post-trial briefing.

---

motion to amend complaint that was based in part on UPP analysis, noting that court found no court decision adopting UPP to determine the likely effects of a merger).

9 Plaintiffs' remedies

W. Joseph Bruckner and Matthew R. Salzwedel[1]

§ 9.01 Introduction

Unlike most of the world, the United States has long maintained that private victims of anticompetitive conduct are entitled to seek private redress for violations of the

[1] W. Joseph Bruckner is a Partner at Lockridge Grindal Nauen PLLP in Minneapolis, Minnesota. Matthew R. Salzwedel is Corporate Counsel at HomeServices of America, Inc. in Minneapolis, Minnesota. The authors thank Devona Wells for her able research assistance in preparing this chapter.

antitrust laws. Indeed, the array of relief available to private plaintiffs, both monetary and injunctive, is designed to encourage plaintiffs to bring private actions. This has the benefit of, first, remedying wrongs done to the plaintiffs themselves and, second, leveling a given competitive playing field. The deterrence value of private antitrust enforcement is discussed throughout this Handbook, but the incentivizing force behind that deterrence – plaintiffs' remedies – is discussed here.

This chapter begins by discussing the linchpin of private antitrust remedies, namely, the treble-damages award. The chapter then discusses attendant considerations: joint-and-several liability; measurement and distribution of damages; and the availability of prejudgment and postjudgment interest, attorneys' fees, and costs. The chapter concludes by discussing various equitable remedies and related issues.

§ 9.02 Single versus treble damages

One of the primary economic deterrents of the American antitrust laws is the ability of successful plaintiffs to recover statutorily mandated awards of treble (three times) actual damages, in addition to whatever other legal or equitable relief they may receive under the law. Section 4 of the Clayton Antitrust Act of 1914[2] establishes both a private right of action and an award of treble damages. It states: "Any person who shall be injured in his business or property by reason of anything forbidden in the antitrust laws may sue therefor . . . and shall recover threefold the damages by him sustained, and the cost of suit, including a reasonable attorney's fee."[3]

The United States Supreme Court has acknowledged two primary goals for awarding civil plaintiffs treble damages under the Clayton Act: (1) to punish past violations of the law; and (2) to deter future antitrust violations.[4] Because Congress intended treble-damages awards to serve a quasi-punitive function, a number of federal courts have concluded that parties cannot – even knowingly and voluntarily – contractually waive their ability to pursue awards of treble damages.[5] In addition, a jury in an antitrust case is not told that its award of damages will be trebled; instead, a court automatically multiplies a damages award by three.[6]

---

[2] The entirety of the Clayton Antitrust Act of 1914 is codified at 15 U.S.C. §§ 12–27 (2009). Section 4 of the Clayton Act is codified at 15 U.S.C. § 15 (2009).

[3] Clayton Act, 15 U.S.C. § 15(a) (2009); *see also* Volvo Trucks N. Am., Inc. v. Reeder-Simco GMC, Inc., 546 U.S. 164, 176 (2006) (treble damages may be recovered for violations of the Robinson Patman Act); Kristian v. Comcast Corp., 446 F.3d 25, 47 (1st Cir. 2006).

[4] Agency Holding Corp. v. Malley-Duff & Assocs., Inc., 483 U.S. 143, 151 (1987); Mitsubishi Motors Corp. v. Soler Chrysler-Plymouth, Inc., 473 U.S. 614, 635 (1985) ("The treble-damages provision wielded by the private litigant is a chief tool in the antitrust enforcement scheme, posing a crucial deterrent to potential violators.") (citing Perma Life Mufflers, Inc. v. Int'l Parts Corp., 392 U.S. 134, 138–39 (1968)), *overruled on other grounds*, Copperweld Corp. v. Independence Tube Corp., 467 U.S. 752 (1984)). *But cf.* Atl. Richfield Co. v. USA Petroleum Co., 495 U.S. 328, 331 n.1 (1990) (stating that the treble-damages provision of the Clayton Act is a "remedial provision").

[5] Kristian v. Comcast Corp., 466 F.3d 25, 47–48 (1st Cir. 2006) (citing Mitsubishi Motors Corp. v. Soler Chrysler-Plymouth, Inc., 473 U.S. 614, 637 n.19 (1985)) (noting that other circuit courts also have disapproved of waiver of statutory remedies for antitrust violations (citing Gaines v. Carrollton Tobacco Bd. of Trade, Inc., 386 F.2d 757, 759 (6th Cir. 1967))).

[6] Pollock & Riley, Inc. v. Pearl Brewing Co., 498 F.2d 1240, 1242 (5th Cir. 1974).

Because of the availability of treble damages under the Clayton Act, punitive damages are not otherwise available under the Sherman or Clayton Acts.[7] In addition, plaintiffs generally are only entitled to treble damages for *either* (1) overcharges paid[8] or lost profits attributable to the antitrust violation; or (2) the diminution in the value of the plaintiff's business as the result of the anticompetitive conduct, but not both.[9]

§ 9.03 Joint-and-several liability

In cases where multiple defendants have engaged in a conspiracy with anticompetitive effects, it is well established that each defendant is liable not only for the injury caused by its own conduct, but also is jointly and severally liable for the injuries caused by the illegal acts of its coconspirators.[10] An antitrust action is a tort action, and, as such, coconspiring joint tortfeasors are jointly and severally liable for the entire amount of damages caused by their acts.[11] Thus, joint-and-several liability helps to ensure that a plaintiff receives the

---

[7] Brown v. Presbyterian Healthcare Servs., 101 F.3d 1324, 1332 (10th Cir. 1996) (citing McDonald v. Johnson & Johnson, 722 F.2d 1370, 1381 (8th Cir. 1983)); *see also* Hawaii v. Standard Oil Co., 405 U.S. 251, 263–64 (1972) (holding that although a state may sue to recover three times the actual damages it has suffered from an alleged antitrust violation, the same as any citizen, it cannot also recover antitrust damages for harm to "its general economy" because such recovery "would open the door to duplicative recoveries."). If "general economy" damages under the antitrust laws were allowed, "we should insist upon a clear expression of a congressional purpose to make it so, and no such expression is to be found in § 4 of the Clayton Act." Hawaii v. Standard Oil Co., 405 U.S. 251, 264 (1972). (Four years later, Congress authorized states to sue on behalf of their general economies by including an express grant of *parens patriae* authority in the Hart Scott Rodino Act, 15 U.S.C. § 15c (1976).)

[8] S. Pac. Co. v. Darnell-Taenzer Lumber Co., 245 U.S. 531 (1918); *In re* Linerboard Antitrust Litig., 305 F.3d 145, 159–60 (3d Cir. 2002); Paper Sys. Inc. v. Nippon Paper Indus. Co., 281 F.3d 629, 631–32 (7th Cir. 2002); Hasbrouck v. Texaco, Inc., 842 F.2d 1034, 1043 (9th Cir. 1988).

[9] L.A. Mem'l Coliseum Comm'n v. Nat'l Football League, 791 F.2d 1356, 1374 (9th Cir. 1986). In addition, the Supreme Court has held that, with limited exceptions, only direct purchasers may recover monetary damages under the Clayton Act for violations of the Sherman Act. Ill. Brick Co. v. Illinois, 431 U.S. 720, 735 (1977) ("[T]he antitrust laws will be more effectively enforced by concentrating the full recovery for the overcharge in the direct purchasers rather than by allowing every plaintiff potentially affected by the overcharge to sue only for the amount it could show was absorbed by it."). Similarly, the Court has held that a defendant may not defend such a claim by demonstrating that the plaintiff had passed on any overcharges to indirect purchasers and consumers. Hanover Shoe, Inc. v. United Shoe Mach. Corp., 392 U.S. 481, 494 (1968). Indirect purchasers still may sue for injunctive relief under the Clayton Act. In addition, several states allow monetary recovery by indirect purchasers for violations of the states' antitrust and unfair trade-practices statutes. For further discussion of direct- and indirect-purchaser standing, see Chapter 3 of this Handbook.

[10] *In re* Cotton Yarn Antitrust Litig., 505 F.3d 274, 284 (4th Cir. 2007) (quoting Wilson P. Abraham Constr. Corp. v. Tex. Indus., Inc., 604 F.2d 897, 904 n.15 (5th Cir. 1979)); *In re* Uranium Antitrust Litig., 617 F.2d 1248, 1257 (7th Cir. 1980); *see also* Paper Sys. Inc. v. Nippon Paper Indus. Co., 281 F.3d 629, 632–33 (7th Cir. 2002).

[11] *E.g.*, Wainwright v. Kraftco Corp., 58 F.R.D. 9, 11–12 (N.D. Ga. 1973). Soon after Congress enacted the Sherman Act, courts "treated antitrust violations as akin to torts" and applied joint-and-several liability as a remedy for plaintiffs. Burlington Indus. v. Milliken & Co., 690 F.2d 380, 391 (4th Cir. 1982). The Antitrust Modernization Commission also supported continuing joint-and-several liability in antitrust cases with some modifications. *See* ANTITRUST MODERNIZATION COMM'N, REPORT & RECOMMENDATIONS 44 (Apr. 2007).

full damages due. Like treble damages, imposing joint-and-several liability for collusive antitrust violations is intended to deter anticompetitive conduct.[12]

§ 9.04 Damages measured

In most large antitrust cases, it is nearly impossible to determine with precision the exact amount of damages resulting from antitrust violations. As a result, federal courts permit antitrust plaintiffs substantial leeway in calculating and showing their damages.[13]

"An antitrust plaintiff seeking treble damages under section 4 of the Clayton Act must prove an antitrust violation, fact of damage or injury, and measurable damages."[14] A plaintiff's damages calculation, therefore, consists of two related damage components – the fact of injury or damage, and the measure of damage.[15]

First, a plaintiff must show "the fact of damage." That is, the antitrust plaintiff must show injury, which courts sometimes deem to be the predicate "injury in fact."[16] "The fact of damage requirement is one of causation; the plaintiff must show that the defendant's unlawful conduct was a material cause of injury to its business."[17] "The fact of injury may be established by inference or circumstantial evidence."[18]

Second, the plaintiff must establish the "measure of damage,"[19] which is the amount of damages directly flowing from the predicate fact of damage.[20] Once a plaintiff shows "fact of damage," his burden of persuasion in proving the amount of damages is relaxed,[21] and he must only satisfy a relatively lower just-and-reasonable-inference standard in measuring damages (discussed below).[22] To this end, a plaintiff is entitled to offer evidence

---

12 *See* Paper Sys. Inc. v. Nippon Paper Indus. Co., 281 F.3d 629, 631–33 (7th Cir. 2002).

13 Eleven Line, Inc. v. N. Tex. State Soccer Ass'n, Inc., 213 F.3d 198, 207 (5th Cir. 2000). For a discussion of the role of economic experts in calculating and showing damages, see Chapter 8 of this Handbook.

14 Danny Kresky Enter. Corp. v. Magid, 716 F.2d 206, 209 (3d Cir. 1983).

15 *In re* New Motor Vehicles Canadian Exp. Antitrust Litig., 522 F.3d 6, 19 n.18 (1st Cir. 2008); Nichols v. Mobile Bd. of Realtors, Inc., 675 F.2d 671, 675–76 (5th Cir. 1982).

16 Zenith Radio Corp. v. Hazeltine Research, Inc., 395 U.S. 100, 114 n.9 (1969); Am. Seed Co. v. Monsanto Co., 271 Fed. Appx. 138, 140 (3d Cir. 2008) (citing Bogosian v. Gulf Oil Corp., 561 F.2d 434, 454 (3d Cir. 1977)); *In re* New Motor Vehicles Canadian Exp. Antitrust Litig., 522 F.3d 6, 19 n.18 (1st Cir. 2008); Robinson v. Tex. Auto. Dealers Ass'n, 387 F.3d 416, 422 (5th Cir. 2004); *In re* Cardizem CD Antitrust Litig., 200 F.R.D. 326, 339 (E.D. Mich. 2001).

17 El Aguila Food Prods., Inc. v. Gruma Corp., 131 Fed. Appx. 450, 452 (5th Cir. 2005).

18 *In re* Cardizem CD Antitrust Litig., 200 F.R.D. 326, 339 (E.D. Mich. 2001); *see also* Cont'l Ore Co. v. Union & Carbon Corp., 370 U.S. 690, 700 (1962).

19 Blades v. Monsanto Co., 400 F.3d 562, 566 (8th Cir. 2005) (citing Amerinet, Inc. v. Xerox Corp., 972 F.2d 1483, 1490 (8th Cir. 1992)).

20 *Zenith Radio Corp.*, 395 U.S. at 114 n.9 (stating that an antitrust plaintiff's "burden of proving the fact of damage under § 4 of the Clayton Act is satisfied by its proof of *some* damage flowing from the unlawful conspiracy; inquiry beyond this minimum point goes only to the amount and not the fact of damage").

21 El Aguila Food Prods., Inc. v. Gruma Corp., 131 Fed. Appx. 450, 452 (5th Cir. 2005); Eleven Line, Inc. v. N. Tex. State Soccer Ass'n, Inc., 213 F.3d 198, 206–07 (5th Cir. 2000); Pierce v. Ramsey Winch Co., 753 F.2d 416, 435 (5th Cir. 1985); In re Plywood Antitrust Litig., 655 F.2d 627, 635 (5th Cir. 1981).

22 *Plywood*, 655 F.2d at 635 (quoting Malcolm v. Marathon Oil Co., 642 F.2d 845, 858 (5th Cir. 1981) (citing Terrell v. Household Goods Carriers' Bureau, 494 F.2d 16, 23–24 (5th Cir. 1974)));

of damages, and, after hearing such evidence, a "jury is entitled to award damages in an antitrust case based on expert testimony."[23]

§ 9.05 Just-and-reasonable-measurement standard[24]

Courts substantially relax the precision of proof required for showing the measure of plaintiff's damages "to facilitate the policy of the antitrust laws."[25] According to the Supreme Court, "[a]ny other rule would enable the wrongdoer to profit by his wrongdoing at the expense of his victim."[26]

In *J. Truett Payne Co. v. Chrysler Motors Corp.*, for example, the Supreme Court, in explaining its "traditional rule excusing antitrust plaintiffs from an unduly rigorous standard of proving antitrust injury," articulated the reasons for its willingness to accept a degree of uncertainty in proving a plaintiff's measure of damages.[27] The Court recognized the difficulty in determining actual damages in antitrust cases compared to other civil matters:

Lehrman v. Gulf Oil Corp., 464 F.2d 26, 46 (5th Cir. 1972); *see also* Eleven Line, Inc. v. N. Tex. State Soccer Ass'n, Inc., 213 F.3d 198, 207 (5th Cir. 2000) (highlighting that once the fact of antitrust damage is shown, plaintiff's burden of proof in showing the amount of damages is more relaxed than the showing needed to justify an award in other civil cases) (citing Pierce v. Ramsey Winch Co., 753 F.2d 416, 434 (5th Cir. 1985)); Allied Accessories & Auto Parts Co. v. Gen. Motors Corp., 901 F.2d 1322, 1326 (6th Cir. 1990) ("While the damages may not be determined by merely speculation or guess, it will be enough if the evidence show[s] the extent of the damages as a matter of just and reasonable inference, although the result be only approximate. The wrongdoer is not entitled to complain that they cannot be measured with the exactness and precision that would be possible if the case, which he alone is responsible for making, were otherwise.") (quoting Allied Accessories & Auto Parts Co. v. Gen. Motors Corp., 825 F.2d 971, 974 (6th Cir. 1987) (quoting Story Parchment Co. v. Paterson Parchment Paper Co., 282 U.S. 555, 563 (1931))).

[23] *In re* Scrap Metal Antitrust Litig., 527 F.3d 517, 533 (6th Cir. 2008) (citing Texaco Inc. v. Hasbrouck, 496 U.S. 543, 572 (1990)). Expert testimony and analysis is not required as a matter of law to support a plaintiff's proof of damages, but it is almost universally offered in practice. For further discussion of the role of experts in calculating damages, see Chapter 8 of this Handbook.

[24] In addition to the relaxed standard for measuring antitrust damages, a plaintiff need only show that the antitrust violation was a *material* cause of the plaintiff's injury and resulting damages; the antitrust violation need not have been the *sole* cause. *See, e.g.*, L.A. Mem'l Coliseum Comm'n v. Nat'l Football League, 791 F.2d 1356, 1366 (9th Cir. 1986) (citing Zenith Radio Corp. v. Hazeltine Research, Inc., 395 U.S. 100, 114 n.9 (1969); William Inglis & Sons Baking Co. v. ITT Cont'l Baking Co., 668 F.2d 1014, 1051 (9th Cir. 1981)). Finally, a plaintiff's profitability does not preclude a damages award. *See* Image Tech. Servs., Inc. v. Eastman Kodak Co., 125 F.3d 1195, 1222 (9th Cir. 1997) (holding that plaintiffs demonstrated that, although plaintiffs remained profitable, defendants' anticompetitive replacement-parts policy handicapped plaintiffs' growth) (citation omitted)); Pierce v. Ramsey Winch Co., 753 F.2d 416, 436–37 (5th Cir. 1985) (noting that a plaintiff can establish antitrust injury by showing that it would have earned an even higher profit but for the antitrust injury).

[25] Malcolm v. Marathon Oil Co., 642 F.2d 845, 858 (5th Cir. 1981) (citing Ford Motor Co. v. Webster's Auto Sales, Inc., 361 F.2d 874, 887 (1st Cir. 1966)); J. Truett Payne Co. v. Chrysler Motors Corp., 451 U.S. 557, 566 (1981); Hobart Bros. Co. v. Malcolm T. Gilliland, Inc., 471 F.2d 894, 903 (5th Cir. 1973); *In re* Scrap Metal Antitrust Litig., 527 F.3d 517, 533 (6th Cir. 2008).

[26] Bigelow v. RKO Radio Pictures, Inc., 327 U.S. 251, 264 (1946).

[27] J. Truett Payne Co. v. Chrysler Motors Corp., 451 U.S. 557, 565 (1981); *see also* Texaco Inc. v. Hasbrouck, 496 U.S. 543, 572–73 (1990).

> The vagaries of the marketplace usually deny us sure knowledge of what the plaintiff's situation would have been in the absence of the defendant's antitrust violation. But our willingness also rests on the principle articulated in cases such as *Bigelow* [*v. RKO Radio Pictures*], that it does not "come with very good grace" for the wrongdoer to insist upon specific and certain proof of the injury which it has itself inflicted.[28]

In *Bigelow*, the Court concluded that not allowing a jury to make "a just and reasonable estimate" of damages based on direct, as well as inferential, proof could preclude recovery for an antitrust plaintiff, and thereby incentivize future antitrust wrongdoing by defendants.[29]

Courts will affirm an award of damages based "on a plaintiff's estimate of sales it could have made absent the antitrust violation,"[30] despite the inherent imperfections in such an estimate. Indeed, "[t]he antitrust cases are legion which reiterate the proposition that, if the fact of damages is proven, the actual computation of damages may suffer from minor imperfections."[31] Additionally, "[a] plaintiff need not calculate a specific damage figure so long as he proposes an acceptable method for calculating damages."[32] The amount of damages, however, must not be a product of "speculation or guess work."[33]

In determining whether the amount of a plaintiff's claimed damages are just and reasonable, federal courts generally apply one or more of four measure-of-damage tests: (1) the yardstick method; (2) the violation-free-market method; (3) regression analysis; and (4) the before-and-after method. Each is discussed below.

---

[28] *J. Truett Payne Co.*, 451 U.S. at 566–67 (quoting Hetzel v. Balt. & Ohio R.R. Co., 169 U.S. 26, 39 (1898) (quoting U.S. Trust Co. v. O'Brien, 143 N.Y. 284, 289, 38 N.E. 266, 267 (1894)); Story Parchment Co. v. Paterson Parchment Paper Co., 282 U.S. 555, 563 (1931).

In *Bigelow*, the Supreme Court permitted an award of damages based on the difference in movie-theater receipts before the defendant unlawfully distributed films and fixed admission prices and the receipts after the plaintiff could no longer show certain new films. *See* Bigelow v. RKO Radio Pictures, Inc., 327 U.S. 251, 261–63 (1946); *see also* Zenith Radio Corp. v. Hazeltine Research, Inc., 395 U.S. 100, 123 (1969) (stating that "[t]rial and appellate courts alike must also observe the practical limits of the burden of proof which may be demanded of a treble-damage plaintiff who seeks recovery for injuries from a partial or total exclusion from a market; damage issues in these cases are rarely susceptible of the kind of concrete, detailed proof of injury which is available in other contexts.").

[29] Bigelow v. RKO Radio Pictures, 327 U.S. 251, 264 (1946); *see also* Pac. Coast Agric. Exp. Ass'n v. Sunkist Growers, Inc., 526 F.2d 1196, 1207 (9th Cir. 1975).

[30] Conwood Co. v. U.S. Tobacco Co., 290 F.3d 768, 794 (6th Cir. 2002) (citation omitted).

[31] *In re* Scrap Metal Antitrust Litig., 527 F.3d 517, 533 (6th Cir. 2008); Conwood Co. v. U.S. Tobacco Co., 290 F.3d 768, 795 (6th Cir. 2002) (quoting Se. Coal Co. v. Consol. Coal Co., 434 F.2d 767, 794 (6th Cir. 1970)).

[32] Rodney v. N.W. Airlines, Inc., 146 Fed. Appx. 783, 791 (6th Cir. 2005).

[33] *In re* Linerboard Antitrust Litig., 497 F. Supp. 2d 666, 675 (E.D. Pa. 2007) (quoting *In re* Lower Lake Erie Iron Ore Antitrust Litig., 998 F.2d 1144, 1176 (3d Cir. 1993)); *see also* Blanton v. Mobil Oil Corp., 721 F.2d 1207, 1216 (9th Cir. 1983); MCI Commc'ns Corp. v. Am. Tel. & Tel. Co., 708 F.2d 1081, 1161 (7th Cir. 1983)).

9.05.1 Yardstick method

The yardstick method attempts to calculate the profits of businesses in an industry closely comparable to the plaintiff's industry, or prices charged for products comparable to the affected products, but in markets or industries not affected by the anticompetitive conduct.[34] But the plaintiff "bears the burden to demonstrate the reasonable similarity of the business whose earning experience he would borrow."[35]

9.05.2 Violation-free-market method

The violation-free-market method attempts to estimate the amount of sales the plaintiff could have made (or what prices would have been for a particular product) absent the defendant's antitrust violation[36] by (1) constructing an "offense-free" world; and (2) using and evaluating that "offense-free" world to determine what would have happened in the particular market "but for" the defendant's anticompetitive conduct.[37]

9.05.3 Regression analysis

Another way to measure antitrust damages is a statistical analysis known as multiple- or variable-regression analysis.[38] Regression analysis attempts to estimate a plaintiff's damages by determining the effect that two or more independent variables have on a single dependent variable.[39] According to one court:

> Multiple regression analysis is a statistical tool for understanding the relationship between two or more variables . . . . [It] is sometimes well suited to the analysis of data about competing

---

[34] Conwood Co. v. U.S. Tobacco Co., 290 F.3d 768, 793 n.8 (6th Cir. 2002); Eleven Line, Inc. v. N. Tex. State Soccer Ass'n, Inc., 213 F.3d 198, 207 n.17 (5th Cir. 2000); Lehrman v. Gulf Oil Corp., 500 F.2d 659, 667 (5th Cir. 1974).

[35] Eleven Line, Inc. v. N. Tex. State Soccer Ass'n, Inc., 213 F.3d 198, 208 (5th Cir. 2000); *see also* Lehrman v. Gulf Oil Corp., 500 F.2d 659, 667 (5th Cir. 1974).

[36] Conwood Co. v. U.S. Tobacco Co., 290 F.3d 768, 794 (6th Cir. 2002) (citing J. Truett Payne Co. v. Chrysler Motors Corp., 451 U.S. 557, 565 (1981)).

[37] LePage's Inc. v. 3M, 324 F.3d 141, 165 (3d Cir. 2003) (citing Callahan v. A.E.V., Inc., 182 F.3d 237, 254–58 (3d Cir. 1999); Rossi v. Standard Roofing, Inc., 156 F.3d 452, 484–87 (3d Cir. 1998)); Conwood Co. v. U.S. Tobacco Co., 290 F.3d 768, 793 n.8 (6th Cir. 2002); Eleven Line, Inc. v. N. Tex State Soccer Ass'n, Inc., 213 F.3d 198, 207 n.17 (5th Cir. 2000).

[38] Conwood Co., v. U.S. Tobacco Co., 290 F.3d 768, 793 (6th Cir. 2002); Petruzzi's IGA Supermarkets, Inc. v. Darling-Delaware Co., 998 F.2d 1224, 1238 (3d Cir. 1993); *In re* Flat Glass Antitrust Litig., 191 F.R.D. 472, 485–86 (W.D. Pa. 1999) (discussing multiple-regression analysis), *cited in In re* Linerboard Antitrust Litig., 305 F.3d 145, 153 (3d Cir. 2002).

[39] Eng'g Contractors Ass'n of S. Fla. Inc. v. Metro. Dade Cnty, 122 F.3d 895, 917 (11th Cir. 1997); *see also* Piggly Wiggly Clarksville, Inc. v. Interstate Brands Corp., 100 Fed. Appx. 296, 299 (5th Cir. 2004); Conwood Co. v. U.S. Tobacco Co., 290 F.3d 768, 793 n.8 (6th Cir. 2002); Gutierrez v. Johnson & Johnson, 2006 WL 3246605, *5 (D.N.J. Nov. 6, 2006); *In re* Polypropylene Carpet Antitrust Litig., 93 F. Supp. 2d 1348, 1359 (N.D. Ga. 2000); *In re* Flat Glass Antitrust Litig., 191 F.R.D. 472, 486 (W.D. Pa. 1999) (citing Daniel L. Rubinfeld, *Reference Guide On Multiple Regression*, REFERENCE MANUAL ON SCIENTIFIC EVIDENCE at 419 (1994)); *In re* Aluminum Phosphide Antitrust Litig., 893 F. Supp. 1497, 1504 (D. Kan. 1995).

> theories in which there are several possible explanations for the relationship among a number of explanatory variables . . . . [It] may also be useful (1) in determining whether a particular effect is present; (2) in measuring the magnitude of a particular effect; and (3) in forecasting what a particular effect would be, but for an intervening event.[40]

Regression analysis can be used to estimate the effect of an antitrust violation on prices charged during the violation period by attempting to hold constant all other material "non-violation" variables that also affected prices during the same period. In 1993, the United States Court of Appeals for the Third Circuit observed that multiple-regression analysis is considered a reliable method to measure antitrust damages.[41]

9.05.4 Before-and-after method

The before-and-after method of measuring antitrust damages (sometimes called the "before-during-after" method) attempts to measure damages by comparing the plaintiff's profits or defendant's prices charged during some period shown to be free of the antitrust violation (perhaps before the violation commenced, after its cessation, or during a breakdown in the midst of an otherwise ongoing violation) to prices charged or profits earned during the violation period.[42] But the before-and-after method is not easily applied to a plaintiff who is driven out of business by anticompetitive conduct because it often cannot easily compile a subsequent earnings history to estimate its lost profits. In such circumstances, a yardstick lost-profits method sometimes is used.[43]

§ 9.06 Distribution of damages

When multiple antitrust plaintiffs sue, the distribution of damages (whether through settlement or jury verdict) depends on the number of plaintiffs and the degree to which each plaintiff was damaged by defendants' conduct in relation to the other plaintiffs. In antitrust class or mass[44] actions, for example, total damages may be distributed to the

---

40 *In re* Linerboard Antitrust Litig., 497 F. Supp. 2d 666, 670 n.8 (E.D. Pa. 2007) (quoting *In re* Linerboard Antitrust Litig., 203 F.R.D. 197, 219 (E.D. Pa. 2001)).

41 Petruzzi's IGA Supermarkets, Inc. v. Darling-Delaware Co., 998 F.2d 1224, 1238 (3d Cir. 1993); *see also* Conwood Co. v. U.S. Tobacco Co., 290 F.3d 768, 793 (6th Cir. 2002); City of Tuscaloosa v. Harcros Chems., Inc., 158 F.3d 548, 566 (11th Cir. 1998) (citing Askew v. City of Rome, 127 F.3d 1355, 1365 n.2 (11th Cir. 1997)).

42 *In re* Scrap Metal Antitrust Litig., 527 F.3d 517, 529 (6th Cir. 2008); Conwood Co. v. U.S. Tobacco Co., 290 F.3d 768, 793 n.8 (6th Cir. 2002); Eleven Line, Inc. v. N. Tex. State Soccer Ass'n, Inc., 213 F.3d 198, 207 n.17 (5th Cir. 2000) (quoting Lehrman v. Gulf Oil Corp., 500 F.2d 659, 667 (5th Cir. 1974)).

43 Eleven Line, Inc. v. N. Tex. State Soccer Ass'n, Inc., 213 F.3d 198, 207 n.17 (5th Cir. 2000) (quoting Lehrman v. Gulf Oil Corp., 500 F.2d 659, 667 (5th Cir. 1974)). In *Eleven Line, Inc.*, the court observed that, although the before-and-after method and the yardstick lost-profits method are common ways to quantify antitrust damages, different damages measures may be appropriate depending on the facts of the particular case "so long as the estimates and assumptions used [in the chosen method of showing antitrust damages] rest on adequate data." 213 F.3d at 207.

44 When the class-action mechanism is not available, perhaps because a class could not be certified for failing to meet the requirements of Rule 23, sometimes various cases will nonetheless be

various class members or individual plaintiffs based on matrices comparing a given class member's or plaintiff's total purchases or sales to the total of all qualified class members or plaintiffs.

But courts usually do not permit "fluid recovery" distribution, which is the "distribution of unclaimed or unclaimable funds to persons not found to be injured but who have interests similar to those of the class."[45] The Second Circuit has banned fluid recovery, while the Ninth Circuit has greatly limited it to situations "where conventional methods of proof are unavailable and, even then, only in an extraordinary circumstance."[46]

But the concept of fluid recovery as a method for *distributing* damages, which generally is not allowed, should not be confused with the concept of a court or jury finding class-wide impact from an antitrust violation and *awarding* "aggregate" or class-wide damages as a result. The United States Court of Appeals for the Sixth Circuit has held that "[d]amages in an antitrust class action may be determined on a classwide, or aggregate, basis, without resorting to fluid recovery where the [evidence] . . . provide[s] a means to distribute damages to injured class members in the amount of their respective damages."[47]

In a class action recovering damages for victims of a price-fixing conspiracy, class members claiming against a recovery fund must be qualified – i.e., they must show (initially to class plaintiffs' class counsel or claims administrator, and then ultimately to the court) that they purchased a product or products whose price is shown to have been affected by the antitrust violation, and that they purchased the product during the violation period. Such a showing is typically established by purchase or other transaction information provided by the class member or the selling defendant.

§ 9.07 Prejudgment interest allowed only on a finding of defendants' bad faith and material delay

In addition to authorizing awards of treble damages, the Clayton Act, as amended in 1982, allows successful plaintiffs to recover prejudgment interest. But plaintiffs qualify for

---

consolidated according to Judicial Panel procedures, with only named plaintiffs participating. *See* Fed. Judicial Ctr., *Manual for Complex Litigation* (Fourth) § 22 (2008).

[45] *In re* Scrap Metal Antitrust Litig., 527 F.3d 517, 534 (6th Cir. 2008) (quoting *In re* NASDAQ Market-Makers Antitrust Litig., 169 F.R.D. 493, 525 (S.D.N.Y. 1996) (citing Schwab v. Philip Morris USA, Inc., 2005 WL 3032556, *1 (E.D.N.Y. Nov. 14, 2005))). Fluid recovery is conceptually distinct from a *cy pres* distribution. A *cy pres* distribution may be used to distribute damages that for one reason or another have not been claimed by class members. *See* Six (6) Mexican Workers v. Ariz. Citrus Growers, 904 F.2d 1301, 1307 (9th Cir. 1990) (holding "that the district court properly considered cy pres distribution for the limited purpose of distributing the unclaimed funds"). For further discussion of *cy pres*, see Chapter 14 of this Handbook.

[46] Gutierrez v. Wells Fargo & Co., 2009 WL 1247040, *3 (N.D. Cal. May 5, 2009) (citing *In re* Hotel Tel. Charges, 500 F.2d 86, 89–90 (9th Cir. 1974)). In *Gutierrez*, the district court pointed out that such an extraordinary circumstance would be "where a defendant has not preserved its records so as to allow a more precise calculation of damages." *Id.*

[47] *In re* Scrap Metal Antitrust Litig., 527 F.3d 517, 534 (6th Cir. 2008) (quoting *In re* NASDAQ Market-Makers Antitrust Litig., 169 F.R.D. 493, 526 (S.D.N.Y. 1996)).

this relief only if there is a finding that the defendants engaged in bad faith that caused a material delay in the litigation.

In these limited circumstances, the court may award prejudgment interest "on actual damages for the period beginning on the date of service [of the complaint] . . . and ending on the date of judgment, or for any shorter period therein, if the court finds that the award of such interest for such period is just in the circumstances."[48] Because plaintiffs must overcome such a high bar, apparently there are no reported cases where a court has awarded prejudgment interest to a successful antitrust plaintiff.[49]

§ 9.08 Postjudgment interest

In addition to prejudgment interest, a successful antitrust plaintiff may recover postjudgment interest. Postjudgment interest compensates a successful antitrust plaintiff for being deprived of compensation between the entry of judgment and the subsequent payment of the judgment by the defendant.[50] Postjudgment interest generally runs from the date judgment is entered by the court, rather than the date of the jury's verdict.[51]

§ 9.09 Indemnification or contribution

The Clayton Act does not provide for contribution, i.e., the right of a joint tortfeasor to recover from other joint tortfeasors. Nor does the common law provide a right of contribution among joint tortfeasors in such circumstances. The Supreme Court has held that it will not find such a right by statutory implication or under common law in cases arising under the Sherman and Clayton Acts.[52]

---

48 Clayton Act, 15 U.S.C. § 15(a)(1–3) (2009). *See* Masters v. Wilhelmina Model Agency, Inc., 473 F.3d 423, 435–36 (2d Cir. 2007); Fishman v. Estate of Wirtz, 807 F.2d 520, 561 (7th Cir. 1986); *In re* Linerboard Antitrust Litig., 504 F. Supp. 2d 38, 64–66 (E.D. Pa. 2007) (court found plaintiffs' damages claim for "opportunity costs" akin to prejudgment interest and therefore did not allow it absent a finding of bad faith and material delay).

49 *See* Zapata Gulf Marine Corp. v. P.R. Mar. Shipping Auth., 133 F.R.D. 481, 487 n.4 (E.D. La. 1990) (noting that neither the court nor the parties cited any case where a court awarded prejudgment interest under 15 U.S.C. § 15(a)).

50 H.J. Inc. v. Flygt Corp., 925 F.2d 257, 261 (8th Cir. 1991) (citation omitted).

51 Kaiser Aluminum & Chem. Corp. v. Bonjorno, 494 U.S. 827, 835 (1990). The postjudgment interest rate is set by statute. It is calculated from the date of judgment, and the rate is "equal to the weekly average 1-year constant maturity Treasury yield" as set by the Federal Reserve System. 28 U.S.C. § 1961.

52 Tex. Indus., Inc. v. Radcliff Materials, Inc., 451 U.S. 630, 639–46 (1981). *See generally* Chemung Canal Trust Co. v. Sovran Bank/Md., 939 F.2d 12, 17 (2d Cir. 1991). In 2007, the congressionally chartered Antitrust Modernization Commission recommended that Congress enact legislation allowing non-settling defendants to seek contribution from other non-settling defendants to the extent a plaintiff has collected a disproportionate share of its judgment from one or more of the non-settling defendants. Two of the 12 commissioners declined to join the Commission's recommendation; one commissioner believed that current policy better furthers the goal of deterrence by destabilizing cartels and discouraging their formation. ANTITRUST MODERNIZATION COMMISSION, REPORT & RECOMMENDATIONS 252–55 (Apr. 2007). To date, Congress has enacted no such legislation, and the rule barring a right of contribution among co-defendants in antitrust cases remains

§ 9.10 Fees[53]

Many antitrust attorneys representing plaintiffs seek their fees on a contingency-fee basis. Under a contingency-fee arrangement, the plaintiffs' attorneys offer their time and pay the cost of prosecuting the litigation. If they succeed, the lawyers receive a percentage of the settlement or damages award.

Some larger single-plaintiff cases, however, may be brought under an hourly-fee or other attorney-fee arrangement. For example, a large plaintiff that opts out of a class action and files its own lawsuit may decide to pay its attorneys on an hourly basis to prosecute its tag-along action.

The general "American Rule" for attorneys' fees provides that, absent statutory or other similar authority, each party pays its own costs, no matter who wins in the litigation.[54]

In private antitrust civil litigation, the Clayton Act provides such statutory authority and specifically mandates[55] that a losing defendant must pay the attorneys' fees of a successful plaintiff: "Any person who shall be injured in his business or property by reason of anything forbidden in the antitrust laws may sue therefor . . . and shall recover threefold the damages by him sustained, and the cost of suit, *including a reasonable attorney's fee*."[56] Like awards of treble damages, parties may not agree to waive their rights to recover attorneys' fees (for example, through agreements to arbitrate their antitrust claims).[57] Also as with treble-damages awards, the jury is not told that a successful plaintiff may recover attorneys' fees.[58]

Additionally, an antitrust plaintiff need not entirely or even substantially succeed in the litigation to obtain an award of attorneys' fees. In 1990, for example, the Fifth Circuit concluded that a successful plaintiff need only show (1) defendant's violation of the

---

the law. For further discussion of the Commission's proposal, along with other recent reform proposals, see Chapter 15 of this Handbook.

53 For further discussion of attorneys' fees in the context of financing private enforcement, see Chapter 10 of this Handbook.

54 Alyeska Pipeline Serv. Co. v. Wilderness Soc'y, 421 U.S. 240, 247 (1975); Fleischmann Distilling Corp. v. Maier Brewing Co., 386 U.S. 714, 718 (1967); Arcambel v. Wiseman, 3 U.S. (3 Dall.) 306 (1796); Goldberger v. Integrated Res., Inc., 209 F.3d 43, 47 (2d Cir. 2000); Kelco Disposal, Inc. v. Browning-Ferris Indus., 845 F.2d 404, 410 (2d Cir. 1988).

55 Hasbrouck v. Texaco, Inc., 879 F.2d 632, 635 (9th Cir. 1989) (citing Twin City Sportservice, Inc. v. Charles O. Finley & Co., 676 F.2d 1291, 1312 (9th Cir. 1982)).

56 Clayton Act, 15 U.S.C. § 15 (2009) (emphasis added). This provision is *not* a "loser pays" statute; instead, it mandates an award of fees only to a successful *plaintiff*, not to a successful defendant.

57 Kristian v. Comcast Corp., 466 F.3d 25, 53, 64 (1st Cir. 2006). *But cf.* AT&T Mobility LLC v. Concepcion, No. 09-893, 563 U.S. __, 131 S. Ct. 1740 (2011) (holding that a California state common law rule declaring the unconscionability of class action waivers in arbitration agreements was preempted by the Federal Arbitration Act, and thus the waiver was enforceable against plaintiff). However, the Court in *Concepcion* did not disturb precedent requiring arbitration agreements to allow for the effective vindication of federal statutory rights. *See, e.g.*, Green Tree Financial Corp v. Randolph, 531 U.S. 79 (2000) ("It may well be that the existence of large arbitration costs could preclude a litigant . . . from effectively vindicating her federal statutory rights in the arbitral forum."). For more on *Concepcion*, see Chapter 5 of this Handbook.

58 Insignia Sys. Inc. v. News Am. Mktg. In-Store, Inc., 2011 WL 382964, *1 (D. Minn. Feb. 3, 2011) (citing cases).

antitrust laws; and (2) the predicate "fact of damage" to recover attorneys' fees from the losing defendant.[59] Therefore, "the actual recovery of compensatory damages [is] irrelevant to the recoverability of attorneys' fees."[60] The Supreme Court has similarly held that the Clayton Act authorizes fees "for legal services performed at the appellate stages of a successfully prosecuted private antitrust action."[61]

The Ninth Circuit has pointed out that the general public receives a substantial benefit when courts award fees to a successful plaintiff: The purpose of requiring an award of attorneys' fees under the Clayton Act "is to insulate treble damage recovery from expenditures for legal fees, consistent with Section [4 of the Clayton Act's] purpose to encourage private persons to undertake enforcement of antitrust laws."[62] Shifting the payment of attorneys' fees from a successful plaintiff to a losing defendant also serves to deter future antitrust violations.[63]

Awarding attorneys' fees to a successful plaintiff, however, should not result in a windfall to successful plaintiffs' counsel.[64] To guard against the potential for excessive attorneys' fee awards, federal courts assess the amount of "reasonable"[65] fees requested by plaintiffs' counsel based not on the actual amount paid by a plaintiff to his attorneys, but instead on the market rate for similarly situated attorneys in the particular legal market, however defined.[66]

In *Hasbrouck v. Texaco*, the Ninth Circuit noted that in certain cases reasonable attorneys' fees could exceed the agreed-on contingency-fee arrangement between the plaintiff and his attorneys.[67]

---

[59] Sciambra v. Graham News, 892 F.2d 411, 415 (5th Cir. 1990) (citing Ala. v. Blue Bird Body Co., 573 F.2d 309, 317 (5th Cir. 1978)); Terrell v. Household Goods Carriers' Bureau, 494 F.2d 16, 20–22 (5th Cir. 1974).

[60] Sciambra v. Graham News, 892 F.2d 411, 415–16 (5th Cir. 1990).

[61] Aspen Highlands Skiing Corp. v. Aspen Skiing Co., 738 F.2d 1509, 1527 (10th Cir. 1984) (quoting Perkins v. Standard Oil Co., 399 U.S. 222, 223 (1970)) (citing Alexander v. Nat'l Farmers Org., 696 F.2d 1210, 1211–12 (8th Cir. 1982)); Moore v. James H. Matthews & Co., 682 F.2d 830, 839 & n.11 (9th Cir. 1982); Carpa, Inc. v. Ward Foods, Inc., 536 F.2d 39, 55–56 (5th Cir. 1976); 2 Stuart M. Speiser, Attorneys' Fees § 14:6 (1973)).

[62] Hasbrouck v. Texaco, Inc., 879 F.2d 632, 639 (9th Cir. 1989) (quoting Twin City Sportservice, Inc. v. Charles O. Finley & Co., 676 F.2d 1291, 1312 (9th Cir. 1982)).

[63] Sciambra v. Graham News, 892 F.2d 411, 416 (5th Cir. 1990) (quoting Farmington Dowel Prods. Co. v. Forster Mfg. Co., 421 F.2d 61, 90 (1st Cir. 1970)) (citing Tic-X-Press, Inc. v. Omni Promotions Co., 815 F.2d 1407, 1423–24 (11th Cir. 1987)); Illinois v. Sangamo Constr. Co., 657 F.2d 855, 859–60 (7th Cir. 1981) (quoting Farmington Dowel Prods. Co. v. Forster Mfg. Co., 421 F.2d 61, 90 (1st Cir. 1970)).

[64] La. Power & Light Co. v. Kellstrom, 50 F.3d 319, 328 (5th Cir. 1995) (citing Hensley v. Eckerhart 461 U.S. 424, 430 n.4 (1983)); *see also* City of Riverside v. Rivera, 477 U.S. 561, 580 (1986) (quoting S. Rep. No. 94-1011 (1976), *reprinted in* 1976 U.S.C.C.A.N. 5908, 5913)).

[65] The hourly fee of only the senior-most partners of a law firm does not constitute a reasonable hourly billing rate. *See In re* Rite Aid Corp. Sec. Litig., 396 F.3d 294, 306 n.14 (3d Cir. 2005) (citing Gunter v. Ridgewood Energy Corp., 223 F.3d 190, 195 n.1 (3d Cir. 2000); *In re* Cendant Corp. PRIDES Litig., 243 F.3d 722, 732 n.11 (3d Cir. 2001)).

[66] La. Power & Light Co. v. Kellstrom, 50 F.3d 319, 328 (5th Cir. 1995) (citing Blum v. Stenson, 465 U.S. 886, 895–96 (1984); Blanchard v. Bergeron, 489 U.S. 87, 93 (1989) (stating that "[s]hould a[n] [attorney's] fee agreement provide less than a reasonable fee . . ., the defendant should nevertheless be required to pay the higher [market-based] amount")).

[67] Hasbrouck v. Texaco, Inc, 879 F.2d 632, 639 (9th Cir. 1989).

Courts have employed several methods to calculate a reasonable attorneys' fee to be awarded to a successful plaintiff, including: (1) the percentage-of-the-fund method; (2) the lodestar method; (3) the lodestar cross-check method; and (4) the *Johnson-Kerr* method. These methods are discussed more fully in Chapter 10 of this *Handbook*, which addresses the funding of private antitrust litigation.

§ 9.11 Costs

In addition to authorizing an award of attorneys' fees, the Clayton Act also authorizes recovery of a successful antitrust plaintiff's costs: "[A]ny person who shall be injured in his business or property by reason of anything forbidden in the antitrust laws may sue therefore . . . and shall recover threefold the damages by him sustained, *and the cost of suit*, including a reasonable attorneys' fee."[68] The recovery of costs also is discussed more fully in Chapter 10 of this Handbook.

§ 9.12 Equitable remedies

9.12.1 Injunctive relief

9.12.1(A) Permanent injunctive relief

Section 16 of the Clayton Act specifically authorizes awards of injunctive relief: "Any person, firm, corporation, or association shall be entitled to *sue for and have injunctive relief*, in any court of the United States having jurisdiction over the parties, against *threatened loss or damage* by a violation of the antitrust laws . . . ."[69]

Injunctive relief, therefore, is available to an antitrust plaintiff as an equitable remedy, even if the plaintiff has not yet suffered any actual antitrust damages.[70] Where a plaintiff has not yet suffered any damages, a plaintiff "need only demonstrate a significant threat of injury from an impending violation of the antitrust laws or from a contemporary violation likely to continue to recur."[71]

An injunction is intended to provide a private plaintiff with important non-monetary

---

68 Clayton Act, 15 U.S.C. § 15 (2009) (emphasis added).

69 Clayton Act, 15 U.S.C. § 26 (2009) (emphasis added); *see also* Cargill, Inc. v. Monfort of Colo., Inc., 479 U.S. 104, 110–11 (1986); *In re* New Motor Vehicles Canadian Exp. Antitrust Litig., 522 F.3d 6, 12 (1st Cir. 2008); Rosebrough Monument Co. v. Mem'l Park Cemetery Ass'n, 666 F.2d 1130, 1147 (8th Cir. 1981).

70 Cargill, Inc. v. Monfort of Colo., Inc., 479 U.S. 104, 111 (1986); Zenith Radio Corp. v. Hazeltine Research, Inc., 395 U.S. 100, 130 (1969); *In re* New Motor Vehicles Canadian Exp. Antitrust Litig., 522 F.3d 6, 12 (1st Cir. 2008) (citations omitted).

71 Zenith Radio Corp. v. Hazeltine Research, Inc., 395 U.S. 100, 130 (1969) (citing Swift & Co. v. United States, 196 U.S. 375, 396 (1905)); Bedford Cut Stone Co. v. Journeymen Stone Cutters' Ass'n, 274 U.S. 37, 54 (1927); United States v. Or. State Med. Soc'y, 343 U.S. 326, 333 (1952); United States v. W. T. Grant Co., 345 U.S. 629, 633 (1953)); *see also* Cargill, Inc. v. Monfort of Colo., Inc., 479 U.S. 104, 111 (1986); *In re* New Motor Vehicles Canadian Export Antitrust Litig., 522 F.3d 6, 13 (1st Cir. 2008) (quoting Mid-West Paper Prods. Co. v. Cont'l Group, Inc., 596 F.2d 573, 591 (3d Cir. 1979)); Rosebrough Monument Co. v. Mem'l Park Cemetery Ass'n, 666 F.2d 1130, 1147 (8th Cir. 1981).

relief. But like awards of treble damages, it also is vital to enforcing the antitrust laws and deterring future antitrust violations. As such, courts are flexible in granting injunctive relief, with "adjustment and reconciliation between the public interest and private needs as well as between competing private claims."[72]

The plaintiff has the burden to show the presence of the threat of injury sufficient for an award of injunctive relief.[73] A plaintiff seeking injunctive relief must demonstrate "a 'cognizable danger' of injury, not just a 'mere possibility.'"[74]

The broader range of anticompetitive conduct subject to injunctive relief was recognized by the First Circuit in *Cia. Petrolera Caribe, Inc. v. Arco Caribbean, Inc.* There, the court concluded that Congress intended courts to grant antitrust relief even to plaintiffs who do not qualify for money damages, and that the law establishes lower standards for injunctive relief than for damages.[75] According to the First Circuit, a plaintiff seeking injunctive relief must only show "a threat of injury rather than an accrued injury."[76]

The distinction between the proof required for injunctions versus damages also took center stage in *Ocean State Physicians Health Plan, Inc. v. Blue Cross & Blue Shield.* There, the United States Court of Appeals for the First Circuit held that although a jury could permissibly find no damages on an antitrust claim, that jury finding still "arguably requires the lower court to [independently] consider awarding injunctive relief."[77]

9.12.1(B) Preliminary injunctive relief

As opposed to permanent injunctive relief, which a court typically awards at the end of the litigation, courts also may grant requests for preliminary injunctions. A preliminary injunction is an extraordinary equitable remedy, and therefore the antitrust plaintiff's "right to relief must be clear and unequivocal."[78]

Courts in antitrust cases have recognized different elements necessary to obtain a pre-

---

72 Zenith Radio Corp. v. Hazeltine Research, Inc., 395 U.S. 100, 131 (1969) (citing Hecht Co. v. Bowles, 321 U.S. 321, 329–30 (1944)); *see also* Ginsburg v. INBEV NV/SA, 623 F.3d 1229, 1235 (8th Cir. 2010) ("Fashioning appropriate equitable antitrust relief requires that courts balance the benefit to competition against the hardship or competitive disadvantage the remedy may cause.").

73 *In re* New Motor Vehicles Canadian Exp. Antitrust Litig., 522 F.3d 6, 14 (1st Cir. 2008) (citations omitted).

74 Datagate, Inc. v. Hewlett-Packard Co., 941 F.2d 864, 870 (9th Cir. 1991) (quoting TRW, Inc. v. FTC, 647 F.2d 942, 954 (9th Cir. 1981)); *see also* Lake Hill Motors, Inc. v. Jim Bennett Yacht Sales, Inc., 246 F.3d 752, 755 (5th Cir. 2001) ("Likewise, a plaintiff seeking injunctive relief under § 16 of the Clayton Act can only obtain that relief when they show a significant threat of some injury to their business or property from a violation of the antitrust laws." (citing McCormack v. Nat'l Collegiate Athletic Ass'n, 845 F.2d 1338, 1341 (5th Cir. 1988); Cargill, Inc. v. Monfort of Colo., Inc., 479 U.S. 104, 113 (1986) (same))). When assessing a plaintiff's right to injunctive relief, a court may consider "the effect of another injunction on the plaintiff's showing of injury." Howard Hess Dental Labs. Inc. v. Dentsply Int'l, Inc., 602 F.3d 237, 250 (3d Cir. 2010).

75 Cia. Petrolera Caribe, Inc. v. Arco Caribbean, Inc., 754 F.2d 404, 407–08 (1st Cir. 1985); *see also In re* New Motor Vehicles Canadian Export Antitrust Litig., 522 F.3d 6, 13 (1st Cir. 2008).

76 Cia. Petrolera Caribe, Inc. v. Arco Caribbean, Inc., 754 F.2d 404, 408 (1st Cir. 1985).

77 Ocean State Physicians Health Plan, Inc. v. Blue Cross & Blue Shield, 883 F.2d 1101, 1106 (1st Cir. 1989).

78 SCFC ILC, Inc. v. Visa USA, Inc., 936 F.2d 1096, 1098 (10th Cir. 1991) (citing GTE Corp. v. Williams, 731 F.2d 676, 678 (10th Cir. 1984)); Penn v. San Juan Hosp., Inc., 528 F.2d 1181, 1185 (10th Cir. 1975); Matzke v. Block, 542 F. Supp. 1107, 1112–13 (D. Kan. 1982); *see also* Grand River

liminary injunction, and have also specified different levels of necessary proof. In 1986, the Supreme Court concluded that to obtain preliminary injunctive relief, a plaintiff must allege a threatened loss or damage of the type the antitrust laws were designed to prevent, which in turn flows from what makes defendants' acts unlawful.[79] Twenty-one years later, however, the Second Circuit appeared to apply a relaxed standard for preliminary injunctive relief. It concluded that an antitrust plaintiff must merely show that, without a preliminary injunction, it is likely to suffer irreparable harm as a result of the defendants' conduct[80] (in addition to showing a likelihood of success on the merits of the litigation[81]).

The Seventh Circuit, in contrast, has varied its treatment of requests for preliminary injunctive relief. In 1999, in *Allied Signal v. B.F. Goodrich Co.*, the Seventh Circuit held that a plaintiff seeking a preliminary injunction first must show that he is likely to prevail on the merits of the litigation and had suffered irreparable harm for which there was no adequate remedy.[82] If the plaintiff makes that preliminary showing, the court then

---

Enter. Six Nations, Ltd. v. Pryor, 481 F.3d 60, 66 (2d Cir. 2007) (citing Moore v. Consol. Edison Co., 409 F.3d 506, 510 (2d Cir. 2005)).

[79] Cargill Inc. v. Monfort of Colo., Inc., 479 U.S. 104, 109 (1986) (citing Brunswick Corp. v. Pueblo Bowl-O-Mat, Inc., 429 U.S. 477, 489 (1977)).

[80] Grand River Enter. Six Nations, Ltd. v. Pryor, 481 F.3d 60, 66 (2d Cir. 2007) (explaining that, to satisfy the irreparable-harm requirement, an antitrust plaintiff must demonstrate that, absent a preliminary injunction, it will suffer "'an injury that is neither remote nor speculative, but actual and imminent,' and one that cannot be remedied 'if a court waits until the end of trial to resolve the harm'" (quoting Freedom Holdings, Inc. v. Spitzer, 408 F.3d 112, 114 (2d Cir. 2005) (quoting Rodriguez v. DeBuono, 175 F.3d 227, 234 (2d Cir. 1999))).

[81] *Grand River*, 481 F.3d at 66 (quoting Brooklyn Legal Servs. Corp. v. Legal Servs. Corp., 462 F.3d 219, 225 (2d Cir. 2006)).

[82] Allied Signal, Inc. v. B.F. Goodrich Co., 183 F.3d 568, 573 (7th Cir. 1999) (citing Doran v. Salem Inn, Inc., 422 U.S. 922, 931 (1975)); Roth v. Lutheran Gen. Hosp., 57 F.3d 1446, 1453 (7th Cir. 1995). Previously, Judge Richard Posner introduced a mathematical formula to guide the analysis of whether or not to grant a preliminary injunction: $P \times Hp > (1 - P) \times Hd$. Under this formula, a preliminary injunction should be granted only if the harm to the P (plaintiff) if the injunction is denied multiplied by the probability that the denial would be an error (so that P would win at trial) exceeds the harm to the defendants if the injunction is granted, multiplied by the probability that granting the injunction would be an error. Judge Posner said that this formula was not offered as a new legal standard but was intended to assist with the analysis of a preliminary injunction by presenting succinctly the factors that the court must consider in making its decision and by articulating the relationship among the factors. *See* Am. Hosp. Supply Corp. v. Hosp. Prods. Ltd., 780 F.2d 589, 593 (7th Cir. 1986); *see also* Gen. Leaseways, Inc. v. Nat'l Truck Leasing Ass'n, 744 F.2d 588, 590 (7th Cir. 1984) (citing Libertarian Party v. Packard, 741 F.2d 981, 984–85 (7th Cir. 1984) (holding that a preliminary injunction requires analysis of the harm to the plaintiff and the harm to the defendant from denial or grant of the injunction, respectively, the likelihood of the plaintiff prevailing on the merits when the case is tried, and the effect on the public of granting or denying the preliminary injunction)); Roland Mach. Co. v. Dresser Indus. Inc., 749 F.2d 380, 386–87 (7th Cir. 1984) (holding that an antitrust plaintiff must show that (1) he has no adequate remedy at law; (2) he will suffer irreparable harm if the preliminary injunction is not granted; and (3) he has some likelihood of succeeding on the merits; then, the court will determine the likelihood of success on the merits in determining whether to grant a preliminary injunction).

In contrast, the United States Court of Appeals for the Sixth Circuit has held that a preliminary-injunction analysis weighs whether (1) the plaintiff is likely to prevail on the merits; (2) whether the plaintiff would suffer irreparable injury if the court does not grant the injunction; (3) whether a preliminary injunction would cause substantial harm to others; and (4) whether a preliminary

applies a sliding-scale analysis that balances the harms to the parties with the public's interest.[83]

In 1988, however, the Ninth Circuit held that a party seeking a preliminary injunction must show either (1) a likelihood of success on the merits and the possibility of irreparable injury; or (2) the existence of serious questions going to the merits and the balance of hardships tipping in its favor.[84] According to the Ninth Circuit, either test requires a plaintiff to show a significant threat of irreparable harm.[85]

9.12.2 Declaratory relief

Although a plaintiff may not always recover money damages for allegedly anticompetitive conduct, he may be entitled to declaratory relief to determine his rights in relation to another party.[86]

In 1980, for example, the Ninth Circuit said in dicta that the strong policy favoring enforcement of the antitrust laws may entitle a plaintiff to injunctive or declaratory relief even if it is not entitled to damages.[87] In *Beacon Theatres, Inc. v. Westover*, the Supreme Court recognized that plaintiffs could bring an action for declaratory judgment under the antitrust laws; however, the defendant was still entitled to a jury trial on the issue of antitrust liability.[88]

§ 9.13 Limitation periods

The Clayton Act provides for a four-year statute of limitations for claims under the several civilly enforceable antitrust laws: "[A]ny action to enforce any cause of action under [15 U.S.C. § 15, 15a, or 15c] shall be forever barred unless commenced within four years after the cause of action accrued."[89]

Because Congress in the Clayton Act provided for a four-year statute of limitations in civil antitrust actions, that limitations period provides the exclusive limitations period for civil antitrust claims and is subject to very limited exceptions.[90] The Fourth Circuit,

---

injunction would be in the public interest. See Samuel v. Herrick Mem'l Hosp., 201 F.3d 830, 833 (6th Cir. 2000) (citing Glover v. Johnson, 855 F.2d 277, 282 (6th Cir. 1988)).

83 Am. Hosp. Supply Corp. v. Hosp. Prods. Ltd., 780 F.2d 589, 593–94 (7th Cir. 1986).

84 U.S. v. BNS Inc., 858 F.2d 456, 464 (9th Cir. 1988) (citing Apple Computer, Inc. v. Formula Int'l Inc., 725 F.2d 521, 523 (9th Cir. 1984)). In its balance of hardships, the Ninth Circuit considers whether a critical public interest would be injured by granting a preliminary injunction. Malaney v. UAL Corp., 2010 WL 3790296, *10–11 (N.D. Cal. Sept. 27, 2010) (citation omitted).

85 *BNS Inc.*, 858 F.2d at 464 (citing Oakland Tribune, Inc. v. Chronicle Pub. Co., 762 F.2d 1374, 1376 (9th Cir. 1985)).

86 THI-Hawaii, Inc. v. First Commerce Fin. Corp., 627 F.2d 991, 996 (9th Cir. 1980); *see also* Am. Safety Equip. V.J. P. Maguire & Co., 391 F.2d 821, 824 (2nd Cir. 1968).

87 *THI-Hawaii, Inc.*, 627 F.2d at 996 (citing Phillip E. Areeda & Donald E. Turner, Antitrust Law ¶ 348a (1978)); *cf.* Florists' Nationwide Tel. Delivery Network v. Florists' Tel. Delivery Ass'n, 371 F.2d 263 (7th Cir. 1967).

88 359 U.S. 500, 504 (1959).

89 Clayton Act, 15 U.S.C. § 15(b) (2009); Zenith Radio Corp. v. Hazeltine Research, Inc., 401 U.S. 321, 338 (1971).

90 Holmberg v. Armbrecht, 327 U.S. 392, 395 (1946) (citing Herget v. Cent. Nat. Bank & Trust Co., 324 U.S. 4 (1945)).

for example, has held that an arbitration agreement between the parties may reduce the four-year limitations period to as short as one year, noting that the Clayton Act does not prevent parties from agreeing to a contractually shortened limitations period.[91] That is because courts generally consider this four-year limitations period to be procedural, not substantive, which means that it can be varied by agreement of the parties.[92]

9.13.1 Accrual

Given the statute of limitations, a key question is: when does a civil antitrust cause of action accrue, thereby triggering the limitation period?

The Supreme Court has held that an antitrust claim accrues "when a defendant commits an act that injures a plaintiff's business"[93] and when the injured plaintiff is aware, or should be aware, of the existence and source of her injury.[94] Generally, this means an antitrust plaintiff must file its claim within four years following the defendant's injurious act, where the plaintiff was or should have been aware of the existence and source of the injury.[95] Important exceptions to this general rule are discussed more fully below.

9.13.2 Laches

The equitable doctrine of laches is similar to, but legally and factually distinct from, a statute of limitations. Laches can bar an antitrust claim where it would be inequitable to permit a claim to be enforced because of a change in the condition or relations of the property or parties. It is possible, but not likely, that laches could bar an antitrust claim even though the statute of limitations for the claim has not yet expired.[96] For example, in *Kloth v. Microsoft Corporation*, the Fourth Circuit concluded that the district court did not abuse its discretion in dismissing plaintiffs' claims for injunctive relief based on the doctrine of laches, noting that plaintiffs did not pursue their equitable claims for injunctive relief with diligence.[97]

---

[91] *In re* Cotton Yarn Antitrust Litig., 505 F.3d 274, 287–88 (4th Cir. 2007). For a discussion of defendants raising limitation periods as a procedural defense, see Chapter 6 of this Handbook.

[92] *Cotton Yarn*, 505 F.3d at 287–89.

[93] Rotella v. Wood, 528 U.S. 549, 554 (2000); Zenith Radio Corp. v. Hazeltine Research, Inc., 401 U.S. 321, 338 (1971); Morton's Mkt., Inc. v. Gustafson's Dairy, Inc., 198 F.3d 823, 827 (11th Cir. 1999) (quoting Zenith Radio Corp. v. Hazeltine Research, Inc., 401 U.S. 321, 338 (1971)), *amended in part*, 211 F.3d 1224 (2000); *In re* Cotton Yarn Antitrust Litig., 505 F.3d 274, 287–90 (4th Cir. 2007); *In re* Nine West Shoes Antitrust Litig., 80 F. Supp. 2d 181, 191 (S.D.N.Y. 2000); Sanderson v. Spectrum Labs, Inc., 227 F. Supp. 2d 1001, 1011 (N.D. Ind. 2000).

[94] Oshiver v. Levin, Fishbein, Sedran & Berman, 38 F.3d 1380, 1386 (3d Cir. 1994) (noting that a different rule for determining the time of accrual for a cause of action would require an insufficient degree of diligence on the part of the potential claimant).

[95] Morton's Mkt., Inc. v. Gustafson's Dairy, Inc., 198 F.3d 823, 827 (11th Cir. 1999) (citing Clayton Act 15 U.S.C. § 15(b)).

[96] Holmberg v. Armbrecht, 327 U.S. 392, 396 (1946) (citing Galliher v. Cadwell, 145 U.S. 368, 373 (1892)); *see also* S. Pac. Co. v. Bogert, 250 U.S. 483, 488–89 (1919).

[97] 444 F.3d 312, 325–26 (4th Cir. 2006).

9.13.3 Tolling

9.13.3(A) Pendency of government action

The Clayton Act authorizes the tolling of a civil antitrust action while the United States (typically the Department of Justice or the Federal Trade Commission) pursues a criminal or civil cause of action against the targeted defendants.[98] The Clayton Act provides:

> Whenever any civil or criminal proceeding is instituted by the United States to prevent, restrain, or punish violations of any of the antitrust laws, but not including an action under section 15a of this title, the running of the statute of limitations . . . *shall be suspended during the pendency thereof and for one year thereafter* . . . .[99]

This tolling provision applies to "all proceedings in the government action until its termination in a final decree disposing of all issues."[100]

In 1970, the Second Circuit determined that the pendency of a government action continues until the time that a judgment or decree becomes final so that the government and defendants are satisfied (to the extent possible) with the result of the litigation and have decided not to appeal.[101] Consequently, according to the Second Circuit, "only after the time to appeal has expired can private litigants rely on the irrevocability of determinations made in the [pendent] government action."[102] Finally, a plaintiff's right to toll the statute of limitations during the pendency of a government action does not depend on the government's success (or lack thereof) in proving its allegations.[103]

There are several reasons why the statute of limitations for a civil antitrust claim is tolled during the pendency of a government criminal or civil enforcement action. Tolling during the pendency of a government action seeks to balance competing policy objectives of the antitrust laws, namely (1) retaining private antitrust litigation as a tool for effective enforcement of the antitrust laws;[104] and (2) providing certainty in applying the statute's tolling provision to avoid overly prolonged antitrust litigation.[105]

Tolling during the pendency of a government action, however, is not without limits.

---

98 Clayton Act, 15 U.S.C. § 16(i) (2009); *see also In re* Scrap Metal Antitrust Litig., 527 F.3d 517, 536–37 (6th Cir. 2008).

99 Clayton Act, 15 U.S.C. § 16(i) (2009) (emphasis added). Congress intended the pendency-of-government-action provision in the Clayton Act to replace "diverse state laws with a uniform federal rule requiring that private antitrust actions be brought within four years of accrual or within one year after a government enforcement action ceased to pend." Russ Togs, Inc. v. Grinnell Corp., 426 F.2d 850, 853 (2d Cir. 1970) (citing S. Rep. No. 619 (1955), *reprinted in* 1955 U.S. Code Cong. & Admin. News, pp. 2332–33)).

100 Russ Togs, Inc. v. Grinnell Corp., 426 F.2d 850, 854 (2d Cir. 1970).

101 *Id.* at 857.

102 *Id.* at 857 (citing Twentieth Century-Fox Film Corp. v. Brookside Theatre Corp., 194 F.2d 846, 857–58 (8th Cir. 1952)).

103 Leh v. Gen. Petroleum Corp., 382 U.S. 54, 65–66 (1965) (citing Minn. Mining & Mfg. Co. v. N.J. Wood Finishing Co., 381 U.S. 311, 316 (1965)).

104 Novell, Inc. v. Microsoft Corp., 505 F.3d 302, 320 (4th Cir. 2007), *cert. denied* 552 U.S. 1276 (2008) (quoting Minn. Mining & Mfg. Co. v. N.J. Wood Finishing Co., 381 U.S. 311, 318, 320 (1965)).

105 *Novell, Inc.*, 505 F.3d at 320 (citing Greyhound Corp. v. Mt. Hood Stages, Inc. 437 U.S. 322, 335 (1978)).

In 2007, for example, the Fourth Circuit stated that plaintiffs cannot "'sit on their rights' and assert, years after the traditional statute of limitations has run, 'claims so much broader than those asserted by the government that they open entirely new vistas of litigation.'"[106]

9.13.3(B) EQUITABLE TOLLING AND THE FRAUDULENT-CONCEALMENT DOCTRINE

The equitable tolling doctrine extends the Clayton Act's four-year statute of limitations starting from the date the operable facts supporting plaintiff's claims either *actually* become apparent to the plaintiff, or the date where the operable facts *should have* become apparent to a reasonably prudent person in the plaintiff's position.[107] Equitable tolling[108] prevents the statute of limitations for an antitrust claim from barring a claim even if a plaintiff fails to bring the claim within four years after the date the claim accrued.[109]

Equitable tolling may toll the statute of limitations in several circumstances: where the defendant actively misled plaintiffs by fraudulently concealing its unlawful conduct; where the plaintiff in an extraordinary circumstance has been prevented from asserting its rights; and where the plaintiff timely asserted its rights but mistakenly did so in the wrong judicial forum.[110]

The first of these, the fraudulent concealment doctrine, generally seeks "to prevent a defendant from 'concealing a fraud, or . . . committing a fraud in a manner that it concealed itself until such time as the party committing the fraud could plead the statute of limitations to protect it.'"[111] Significantly, the doctrine is read into every federal statute

[106] *Id.* at 322 (quoting *In re* Microsoft Corp. Antitrust Litig., 2005 WL 1398643, *5 (D. Md. June 10, 2005)).

[107] Zenith Radio Corp. v. Hazeltine Research, Inc., 401 U.S. 321, 338 (1971); *In re* Scrap Metal Antitrust Litig., 527 F.3d 517, 536 (6th Cir. 2008); Forbes v. Eagleson, 228 F.3d 471, 486 (3d Cir. 2000) (noting that equitable tolling differs from the discovery rule in that equitable tolling centers on a plaintiff's cognizance of the facts supporting the plaintiff's cause of action rather than the plaintiff's cognizance of actual injury. Equitable tolling, therefore, presumes accrual while the discovery rule is meant to determine the accrual date of a claim to determine when the statute of limitations begins to run) (quoting Oshiver v. Levin, Fishbein, Sedran & Berman, 38 F.3d 1380, 1390 (3d Cir. 1994)).

[108] In 1998, the United States Court of Appeals for the Tenth Circuit stated that "'tolling' means 'to suspend or stop temporarily,' whereas the phrase, 'a cause of action accrues' refers to 'when a suit may be maintained thereon.' Also, the federal equitable tolling doctrine 'is at times misnamed because it often provides a rule for determining when the limitation period accrues.'" Sterlin v. Biomune Sys., 154 F.3d 1191, 1195 n.8 (10th Cir. 1998) (quoting Ebrahimi v. E.F. Hutton & Co., 852 F.2d 516, 520 n.6 (10th Cir. 1988)).

[109] Forbes v. Eagleson, 228 F.3d 471, 486 (3d Cir. 2000) (citing Oshiver v. Levin, Fishbein, Sedran & Berman, 38 F.3d 1380, 1387 (3d Cir. 1994)).

[110] Oshiver v. Levin, Fishbein, Sedran & Berman, 38 F.3d 1380, 1387 (3d Cir. 1994) (citing Sch. Dist. of City of Allentown v. Marshall, 657 F.2d 16, 19–20 (3d Cir. 1981)); *see also* Miller v. Beneficial Mgmt. Corp., 977 F.2d 834, 845 (3d Cir. 1992); Smith v. Am. President Lines, Ltd., 571 F.2d 102, 109 (2d Cir. 1978).

[111] New York v. Hendrickson Bros., Inc., 840 F.2d 1065, 1083 (2d Cir. 1988) (quoting Bailey v. Glover, 88 U.S. (21 Wall.) 342, 349 (1874)); *see also In re* Cotton Yarn Antitrust Litig., 505 F.3d 274, 287–91 (4th Cir. 2007) (citing Holmberg v. Ambrecht, 327 U.S. 392, 397 (1946)); Supermarket of Marlinton, Inc. v. Meadow Gold Dairies, Inc., 71 F.3d 119, 122 (4th Cir. 1995)).

of limitations.[112] The test varies by circuit and sometimes even within the same circuit.[113] But in general, "acts of fraudulent concealment by the [antitrust] defendant toll the limitations period for as long as the concealment continues."[114] In the Sixth Circuit, "a plaintiff seeking to invoke the doctrine of fraudulent concealment in order to toll the statute of limitations in an antitrust case must prove 'affirmative acts' of concealment; 'concealment by mere silence is not enough.'"[115]

In the Sixth and Fourth Circuits, an antitrust plaintiff must show that (1) the defendant concealed from him the existence of his cause of action;[116] (2) he remained ignorant of his potential claim within the four years before he filed his claim; and (3) his continuing ignorance was not attributable to any lack of diligence on his part.[117] In the Second Circuit, the test is slightly different. The plaintiff must show that (1) the defendant concealed the existence of the cause of action; (2) the plaintiff sued within the applicable limitations period after learning about the cause of action; and (3) the plaintiff's ignorance of the cause of action did not result from a lack of diligence.[118]

---

112 *See* Holmberg v. Armbrecht, 327 U.S. 392, 396 (1946).

113 Nat'l Group for Commc'ns & Computers, Ltd. v. Lucent Techs. Inc., 420 F. Supp. 2d 253, 265, 265 n.15 (S.D.N.Y. 2006) (stating that "[t]here has been some variation in the way that the three [fraudulent-concealment] elements have been articulated in the [Second] Circuit").

114 *In re* Scrap Metal Antitrust Litig., 527 F.3d 517, 536 (6th Cir. 2008) (citing Norton-Children's Hosps., Inc. v. James E. Smith & Sons, Inc., 658 F.2d 440, 443 (6th Cir. 1981)).

115 *In re* Scrap Metal Antitrust Litig., 527 F.3d 517, 538 (6th Cir. 2008) (quoting Pinney Dock & Transp. Co. v. Penn Cent. Corp., 838 F.2d 1445, 1467 (6th Cir. 1988)).

116 In 1995, the Fourth Circuit observed that different federal circuit courts of appeals apply different standards to determine if antitrust plaintiffs have satisfied the first element of the fraudulent-concealment doctrine. *See* Supermarket of Marlinton v. Meadow Gold Dairies, 71 F.3d 119, 122 (4th Cir. 1995). These differing standards are: (1) the self-concealing standard; (2) the separate-and-apart standard; and (3) the affirmative-acts standard. *Id.* The self-concealing standard is satisfied simply by showing that a self-concealing antitrust violation has occurred. *Id.* (citing New York v. Hendrickson Bros., Inc., 840 F.2d 1065, 1084 (2d Cir. 1988)). The separate-and-apart standard, however, requires the plaintiff to provide evidence separate and apart from the acts of concealment involved in the defendants' antitrust violation, namely, that defendants affirmatively acted to conceal the plaintiff's claim. *Id.* (citation omitted). Finally, the affirmative-acts standard requires the plaintiff to show that the defendant affirmatively acted to conceal its antitrust violation, but the plaintiff's proof may include acts of concealment involved in the antitrust violation itself. *Id.* (citing Texas v. Allan Constr. Co., 851 F.2d 1526, 1532 (5th Cir. 1988)). *See also* Conmar Corp. v. Mitsui & Co. (U.S.A.), 858 F.2d 499, 505 (9th Cir. 1988) (holding that more than passive concealment is required to toll the statute of limitations unless the defendant had a fiduciary duty to disclose information to the plaintiff (citing Volk v. D.A. Davidson & Co., 816 F.2d 1406, 1416 (9th Cir. 1987); Rutledge v. Bos. Woven Hose & Rubber Co., 576 F.2d 248, 250 (9th Cir. 1978))).

117 Hamilton Cnty. Bd. of Comm'rs v. Nat'l Football League, 491 F.3d 310, 315 (6th Cir. 2007) (quoting Dayco Corp. v. Goodyear Tire & Rubber Co., 523 F.2d 389, 394 (6th Cir. 1975)) (citing Pinney Dock & Transp. Co. v. Penn Cent. Corp., 838 F.2d 1445, 1465 (6th Cir. 1988)); Supermarket of Marlinton v. Meadow Gold Dairies, 71 F.3d 119, 122 (4th Cir. 1995) (citing Weinberger v. Retail Credit Co., 498 F.2d 552, 555 (4th Cir. 1974)); *see also* Pinney Dock & Transp. Co. v. Penn Cent. Corp., 838 F.2d 1445, 1465 (6th Cir. 1988); *In re* Beef Indus. Antitrust Litig., 600 F.2d 1148, 1169 (5th Cir. 1979).

118 New York v. Hendrickson Bros., Inc., 840 F.2d 1065, 1083 (2d Cir. 1988); Cerbone v. Int'l Ladies' Garment Workers' Union, 768 F.2d 45, 48 (2d Cir. 1985); City of Detroit v. Grinnell Corp., 495 F.2d 448, 460 (2d Cir. 1974). In the Second Circuit, to satisfy the first prong of the fraudulent-

The last element – the plaintiff's due diligence – is particularly important. In 1997, the Supreme Court held, citing a litany of cases, that a plaintiff who is not reasonably diligent cannot rely on the fraudulent-concealment doctrine to equitably toll the statute of limitations.[119]

9.13.3(C) CONTINUING-VIOLATION INJURY

In addition to tolling during the pendency of a government action and equitable tolling (including the fraudulent-concealment doctrine), the statute of limitations for a civil antitrust claim may be tolled if the defendant has engaged in a continuing antitrust violation.

In 1997, in *Klehr v. A.O. Smith*, the Supreme Court observed that:

> Antitrust law provides that, in the case of a "continuing violation," say, a price-fixing conspiracy that brings about a series of unlawfully high priced sales over a period of years, "each overt act that is part of the violation and that injures the plaintiff," e.g., each sale to the plaintiff, "starts the statutory period running again, regardless of the plaintiff's knowledge of the alleged illegality at much earlier times."[120]

---

concealment test, the plaintiff must show either that (1) "the defendant took affirmative steps to prevent the plaintiff's discovery of his claim or injury"; or (2) "that the wrong itself was of such a nature as to be self-concealing." New York v. Hendrickson Bros., Inc., 840 F.2d 1065, 1083 (2d Cir. 1988); *see also* Hinds County v. Wachovia Bank N.A., 620 F. Supp. 2d 499, 521 (S.D.N.Y. 2009) ("Allegations of bid-rigging and price-fixing conspiracies . . . are self-concealing such that 'a plaintiff is not required to show defendants took affirmative steps to conceal their conduct.'") (quoting *In re* Nine West Shoes Antitrust Litig., 80 F. Supp. 2d 181, 193 (S.D.N.Y. 2000)). The Second Circuit's self-concealing-conspiracy prong is more lenient than the strict tests in the Fifth and Sixth Circuits. There, concealment by silence is not enough. RX.com v. Meco Health Solutions, Inc., 2009 WL 1067954, *2–3 (5th Cir. Apr. 22, 2009); *In re* Packaged Ice Antitrust Litig., 2010 WL 2671306, *21 (E.D. Mich. July 1, 2010) (stating that the Sixth Circuit requires "affirmative acts" of concealment). It is unclear which test applies in the Eighth Circuit. *In re* Wholesale Grocers Prods. Antitrust Litig., 723 F. Supp. 2d 1079, 1084–85 (D. Minn. 2010) (declining to decide whether fraudulent concealment requires an "affirmative act" of concealment or whether it is sufficient to plead the self-concealing nature of the violation).

[119] Klehr v. A.O. Smith Corp., 521 U.S. 179, 194–95 (1997) (noting that many antitrust cases require due diligence by the plaintiff or that the plaintiff could reasonably have known of the offense, and that none state to the contrary) (quoting 2 PHILLIP E. AREEDA & HERBERT HOVENCAMP, ANTITRUST LAW ¶ 338 at 152 (1995)) (citing IRVING SCHER, ANTITRUST ADVISER § 10.27, p. 10–62 (4th ed. 1995)); Conmar Corp. v. Mitsui & Co., 858 F.2d 499, 502 (9th Cir. 1988); Texas v. Allan Constr. Co., 851 F.2d 1526, 1533 (5th Cir. 1988); Pinney Dock & Transp. Co. v. Penn Cent. Corp., 838 F.2d 1445, 1465 (6th Cir. 1988); New York v. Hendrickson Bros., Inc., 840 F.2d 1065, 1083 (2d Cir. 1988); Berkson v. Del Monte Corp., 743 F.2d 53, 56 (1st Cir. 1984); Charlotte Telecasters, Inc. v. Jefferson-Pilot Corp., 546 F.2d 570, 574 (4th Cir. 1976). In *Hinds County v. Wachovia Bank N.A.*, 620 F. Supp. 2d 499, 521 (S.D.N.Y. 2009), the court surveyed the disagreement among the courts regarding whether the due-diligence prong required the plaintiff to show that its ignorance was not a result of lack of diligence, or whether, instead, the plaintiff had to show its due diligence in pursuing the discovery of its claim.

[120] Klehr v. A.O. Smith Corp., 521 U.S. 179, 189 (1997) (quoting 2 PHILLIP E. AREEDA & HERBERT HOVENCAMP, ANTITRUST LAW ¶ 338b at 145 (1995) (footnote omitted)) (citing Zenith Radio Corp. v. Hazeltine Research, Inc., 401 U.S. 321, 338 (1971)); Hanover Shoe, Inc. v. United Shoe Mach. Corp., 392 U.S. 481, 502 n.15 (1968); DXS, Inc. v. Siemens Med. Sys., Inc., 100 F.3d 462, 467 (6th Cir. 1996); *see also In re* Cotton Yarn Antitrust Litig., 505 F.3d 274, 287–91 (4th Cir. 2007); Midwestern Mach. v. N.W. Airlines, 392 F.3d 265, 269 (8th Cir. 2004).

The Supreme Court also has distinguished a continuing antitrust violation from a distinctly new violation, stating that "the commission of a separate new overt act generally does not permit the plaintiff to recover for the injury caused by old overt acts outside the limitations period."[121]

In 2006, the Tenth Circuit set forth the requirements in that circuit for extending the statute of limitations as the result of a continuing antitrust violation: "1) It must be a new and independent act that is not merely a reaffirmation of a previous act; and 2) it must inflict new and accumulating injury on the plaintiff." [122] Similarly, in 1999, the Eleventh Circuit pointed out that:

> [A]n act constitutes a "continuing violation," if it injures the plaintiff over a period of time. Even though the illegal act occurs at a specific point in time, if it inflicts "continuing and accumulating harm" on a plaintiff, an antitrust violation occurs each time the plaintiff is injured by the act.[123]

For the purpose of determining the point when the running of the statute of limitations recommences, the focus should generally be on the timing of the defendant's overt acts, rather than the effects of the overt acts.[124] In 2004, the Eighth Circuit, for example, concluded that the continuing-violation theory can apply only where the violator "actively reinitiates the anti-competitive policy and enjoys benefits from that action."[125] The Eighth Circuit further noted that the distinction between a new and a continuing violation "allows the statute of limitations to have effect and discourages private parties from sleeping on their rights."[126]

---

[121] Klehr v. A.O. Smith Corp., 521 U.S. 179, 189 (1997) (citing Zenith Radio Corp. v. Hazeltine Research, Inc., 401 U.S. 321, 338 (1971); Pa. Dental Ass'n v. Med. Serv. Ass'n, 815 F.2d 270, 278 (3d Cir. 1987); Hennegan v. Pacifico Creative Serv., Inc., 787 F.2d 1299, 1300 (9th Cir. 1986); Nat'l Souvenir Cent., Inc. v. Historic Figures, Inc., 728 F.2d 503, 509 (D.C. Cir. 1984)); Imperial Point Colonnades Condo., Inc. v. Mangurian, 549 F.2d 1029, 1034–35 (5th Cir. 1977); Crummer Co. v. Du Pont, 223 F.2d 238, 247–48 (5th Cir. 1955)); *In re* Nine West Shoes Antitrust Litig., 80 F. Supp. 2d 181, 192 (S.D.N.Y. 2000). *Cf.* 2 Phillip E. Areeda & Herbert Hovencamp, Antitrust Law ¶ 338b at 149 (1995).

[122] Champagne Metals v. Ken-Mac Metals, Inc., 458 F.3d 1073, 1088 (10th Cir. 2006) (quoting Kaw Valley Elec. Coop. Co. v. Kan. Elec. Power Coop., Inc., 872 F.2d 931, 933 (10th Cir. 1989)).

[123] Morton's Mkt., Inc. v. Gustafson's Dairy, Inc., 198 F.3d 823, 828 (11th Cir. 1999) (quoting Hanover Shoe, Inc. v. United Shoe Mach. Corp., 392 U.S. 481, 502 n.15 (1968)).

[124] Varner v. Peterson Farms, 371 F.3d 1011, 1019 (8th Cir. 2004) (quoting DXS, Inc. v. Siemens Med. Sys., Inc., 100 F.3d 462, 467 (6th Cir. 1996) (citing Peck v. Gen. Motors Corp., 894 F.2d 844, 849 (6th Cir. 1990))).

[125] Midwestern Mach. v. N.W. Airlines, 392 F.3d 265, 271 (8th Cir. 2004).

[126] Midwestern Mach., 392 F.3d at 271.

10 Funding litigation

K. Craig Wildfang and Stacey P. Slaughter[1]

§ 10.01 Introduction

Private litigation in the United States is financed through a variety of attorney fee arrangements, including contingency fees, hourly fees, and alternative billing arrangements. Behind the scenes, these agreements between attorneys and clients are the lifeblood of private claims, as all such claims require adequate funding at each stage of

[1] K. Craig Wildfang is a partner at the law firm of Robins, Kaplan, Miller & Ciresi L.L.P. in their Minneapolis, Minnesota office. Before joining the firm's antitrust practice, Mr. Wildfang served as Special Counsel to the Assistant Attorney General for Antitrust, United States Department of Justice in Washington, D.C. from 1993 to 1996. Stacey P. Slaughter is also a partner at the law firm of Robins, Kaplan, Miller & Ciresi L.L.P. in Minneapolis, MN and admitted to practice in Minnesota and New York.

the litigation process to proceed. This chapter discusses the attorney fee arrangements commonly employed in private antitrust litigation in the United States. Although all such arrangements are addressed, the authors place particular emphasis on contingency fees, which have evolved to become a convention of our system's primary tool for the private redress of the widespread harm that can be caused by antitrust violations: the class action. This chapter also discusses the typical costs associated with antitrust litigation, which are likewise significant in funding private antitrust claims in the United States. Costs play a role in budget considerations and vary depending on the stage of the litigation. Finally, this chapter discusses some of the noteworthy antitrust damage recoveries from the previous two decades and the funding arrangements that have accompanied them.

§ 10.02 A history of contingent fees in the United States

The modern contingent fee system is traceable to early English prohibitions preventing a claimant from selling speculative judgment proceeds to a disinterested party in consideration for funding the claimant's underlying claim.[2] Commonly known as "champerty," this common law prohibition existed as early as the thirteenth century, when English feudal lords and magnates could take advantage of the poor by abusing the legal system in furtherance of their own power or property.[3] As the American colonies separated from England and began forming a distinct legal system, access to the courts and assistance of counsel for poor and rich alike became prominent concerns.[4] Acceptance of the attorney contingency fee grew from the need to foster this access and assistance.[5]

Although the formal prohibition on champerty would remain, a drastic departure from traditional English common law foundations, which forbade any such "contingency fees," began in earnest during the late colonial period in America.[6] In the early and mid-nineteenth century, the need for such a departure had been validated by title disputes concerning land ownership, which had caused many settlers to be removed from their properties by the true landowners for not being able to afford to defend themselves.[7] Likewise, during the Industrial Revolution, workers who were the victims of increasing transportation and work-related accidents found that they too needed legal representation they could ill-afford.[8] Over time, the increase in such claims forced the American Bar Association to accept the contingency fee as a valid

---

[2] Stephen Landsman, *The History of Contingency and the Contingency of History*, 47 DePaul L. Rev. 261, 262 (1998).

[3] *Id.* at 263.

[4] *Id.*

[5] David A. Root, *Attorney Fee-Shifting in America: Comparing, Contrasting, and Combining the "American Rule" and "English Rule"*, 15 Ind. Int'l & Comp. L. Rev. 583, 593 (2005).

[6] Peter Karsten, *Enabling the Poor to Have Their Day in Court: The Sanctioning of Contingency Fee Contracts, A History to 1940*, 47 DePaul L. Rev. 231, 232 (1998).

[7] Kristin Porcu, *Protecting the Poor: The Dangers of Altering the Contingency Fee System*, 5 Suffolk J. Trial & App. Advoc. 149, 152–53 (2000).

[8] Angela Wennihan, *Let's Put the Contingency Back in the Contingency Fee*, 49 SMU L. Rev. 1639, 1645–46 (1996).

system for attorney compensation.[9] By the late nineteenth century, contingency fees were well-accepted.[10]

During the late nineteenth and early twentieth centuries, contingency fees grew in popularity. Professor Peter Karsten notes that even before "some of their high courts had sanctioned contingency fees, the American public was putting them to increasing numbers of use."[11] For example, contingency fee contracts could be found among:

> [M]inority stockholders and dissident stock subscribers suing corporations, importers and customs brokers suing the federal government, depositors suing banks, creditors suing insolvent railroads and manufacturing firms, merchants and traders reporting depredations and losses at the hands of either Indian tribes or others before federal Claims Commissions, passengers and crews suing steamship companies, urban park commissioners seeking to clear title to park land, county commissioners and state auditors suing for title to land from those without proper title, subordinate government entities suing higher ones over tax revenues, towns and counties suing to halt the issuance or transfer of railroad bonds, as well as bondholders suing counties and municipalities to collect on these bonds.[12]

Such contracts thus began to garner widespread use and binding recognition even before their official sanctioning.[13] However, despite increasingly broad approval, certain forms of legal representation were deemed unfit for contingency fees, including the pursuit of alimony as part of a divorce, criminal matters,[14] the securing of "a discharge for one who had been drafted during the Civil War," and the lobbying of legislators for purely private interests.[15] Nevertheless, Congressional attempts to limit contingency fees were met with resistance from the courts. When a 1915 law purported to "[limit] the contingency fees of attorneys representing Southerners claiming damages for depredations or uncompensated takings" that occurred during the Civil War,[16] many high courts found the limitations unconstitutional. By this time there was "clear evidence of the propensity of jurists . . . to treat [contingency] arrangements as part of the legal landscape and as the bread and butter of a large segment of the profession, to be defended when contravened by either the client or the defendant."[17]

Not all courts were willing to sanction contingency fee agreements as written, and legal fictions were sometimes used to work around such restrictions. For example, some courts voided clauses containing an "attorney's promise to pay all of the costs associated with the suit."[18] In Massachusetts, contingency fee arrangements were only tolerated if the

---

9 Root, *supra* note 5, at 593.
10 Karsten, *supra* note 6, at 249. (Supreme Court Chief Justice Morrison once called a contingency fee arrangement "a legitimate and honorable professional assistance").
11 *Id.* at 248.
12 *Id.*
13 *Id.* at 249.
14 Porcu, *supra* note 7, at 154.
15 Karsten, *supra* note 6, at 249.
16 *Id.*
17 *Id.* at 250.
18 *Id.* at 253.

agreement did not contain a "no-win, no-fee" clause (even though all parties understood that the client would not pay if the action was unsuccessful).[19]

Today, contingency fee agreements have the official sanction of the American Bar Association. Rule 1.5 of the ABA's Model Rules of Professional Conduct allows for contingency fee arrangements, provided that they are reasonable and placed in writing. However, courts retain discretion in making a final determination of reasonableness.[20] Judges may require attorneys to provide detailed justifications for their fees, or risk the court reducing the fee proportionally to the amount the court determines the attorney has proven reasonable.[21] For example, when determining the reasonableness of attorney fees drawn from a common class fund, the Third Circuit has held that courts should consider (1) the size of the fund created and the number of persons benefitted; (2) the presence or absence of substantial objections by members of the class to the settlement terms and/or fees requested by counsel; (3) the skill and efficiency of the attorneys involved; (4) the complexity and duration of the litigation; (5) the risk of nonpayment; (6) the amount of time devoted to the case by plaintiff's counsel; and (7) the awards in similar cases. [22]

Contingency fee advocates often defend the contingency fee structure on the basis of freedom of contract,[23] and the economic notion that freedom to contract for services enables a market to function most efficiently.[24] Some courts have been reluctant to lower attorneys' contingency fees on the grounds that, "absent fraud or overreaching, the attorney-client contract for legal services should not be intruded upon by the State."[25] Nevertheless, courts routinely do reduce contingency fees. Attorneys and judges alike recognize the equitable power of the court to reduce a contingency fee when it seems excessive, or as a means to administer justice or discipline an unscrupulous attorney.[26]

§ 10.03 Considerations before funding a contingent fee case

In the modern era, antitrust fee arrangements have seen many different shapes, forms, and sizes. Indeed, differences among funding arrangements in private antitrust cases are often found among opposing parties. A defendant in an antitrust case usually pays attorneys'

---

19 *Id.*

20 Porcu, *supra* note 7, at 155–56; *see also In re* Relafen Antitrust Litig., 231 F.R.D. 52 (D. Mass. 2005).

21 Porcu, *supra* note 7, at 153.

22 *In re* Rite Aid Corp. Sec. Litig., 396 F.3d 294, 301 (3d Cir. 2005) (citing Gunter v. Ridgewood Energy Corp., 223 F. 3d 190, 195 (3d Cir. 2000)); *see also* Segen v. Optionsxpress Holdings, Inc., 631 F.Supp. 2d 465, 466 (D. Del. 2009) (reducing requested attorney fees from 33 percent to 8 percent of the recovery).

23 Angela Wennihan, *Let's Put the Contingency Back in the Contingency Fee*, 49 SMU L. REV. 1639, 1650; *see also* Stephen D. Annand & Roberta F. Green, *Legislative and Judicial Controls of Contingency Fees in Tort Cases*, 99 W. VA. L. REV. 81, 94 (1996) (citing Henry H. Drummonds, *The Law and Ethics of Percentage Contingent Fees in Oregon*, 72 OR. L. REV. 859, 872 n.56 (discussing the enforcement of contingent fees under contract theory)).

24 Wennihan, *supra* note 23, at 1650.

25 *Id.*

26 *Id.* at 1665.

fees on a per diem, or billable hour, basis. Although plaintiffs also pay attorneys' fees by the hour in some circumstances, more often plaintiffs fund antitrust litigation using some form of contingent fee arrangement in which the attorney's fees are paid only if the plaintiff ultimately prevails in the lawsuit. If the plaintiff does not prevail, then the plaintiff does not pay the attorney's fees (or the defendants' expenses).[27]

When a law firm agrees to represent a client on some type of contingent or alternative fee arrangement, it will consider several factors. These factors include "(1) the likelihood of a favorable outcome, (2) the time frame in which the recovery is likely to occur, (3) the probable amount of recovery, and (4) the percentage contracted for."[28] In reality, these factors may vary and other considerations may come into play, including a weighing of a particular attorney or firm's expertise, the other cases that the firm or attorney is handling, and the needs of the particular client. Due to the professional expertise such weighing involves, often the attorney is better positioned than the client to make a determination.[29]

Certain fixed costs and expenses are associated with litigating a private antitrust case. As part of its retainer agreement with the client, the law firm will address how such costs will be paid. The litigation costs typically range from small expenses such as photocopying and mail service, to larger expenses such as expert fees and travel. These expenses are "out of pocket." In other words, the law firm will have to pay the expenses as they come due, regardless of whether or when there will be a favorable recovery in the case.

When a law firm considers whether to accept a case on an alternative fee basis, it must evaluate what the estimated costs of the case will be. The following items are merely examples, not an exhaustive list, of the larger costs typically associated with litigating a case: electronic document retrieval, storage (or hosting), and production; expert fees; deposition stenographer hourly reporting fees; deposition transcript costs; travel expenses; and legal research using electronic search services.[30]

In cases in which multiple law firms agree to represent a plaintiff – or more typically, several plaintiffs – on an alternative fee basis, the firms divide the costs of the litigation and the attorneys' fees ultimately recovered.[31] This assessment is sometimes based on a lodestar value, which is discussed in more detail below. Simply put, the costs and fees are

---

[27] Root, *supra* note 5, at 583, 589, 597–98; Virginia G. Maurer, Robert E. Thomas & Pamela A. DeBooth, *Attorney Fee Arrangements: The U.S. And Western European Perspectives*, 19 Nw. J. Int'l L. & Bus. 272, 293, 306 (1999).

[28] Drew C. Phillips, *Contingency Fees: Rules & Ethical Guidelines*, 11 Geo. J. Legal Ethics 233, 237 (1998) (citing Stephen Gillers, Regulation of Lawyers: Problems of Law and Ethics 140 (1995)).

[29] Phillips, *supra* note 28, at 238 ("[I]n most cases, the lawyer is far better equipped than the client to evaluate the criteria that should determine whether or not to take a case on a contingent basis.").

[30] The federal tax laws impose an additional hurdle by treating expenses and costs that a plaintiffs' attorney advances as "loans" to the client or putative class of clients. These expenditures are therefore not deductible from income as business expenses for the attorney when they are incurred. In complex cases, these expenses can run into the millions of dollars and financing them can pose a formidable challenge.

[31] For a discussion of recovery of attorneys' fees and costs in the context of plaintiffs' remedies, see Chapter 9 of this Handbook.

assessed and distributed equitably, based upon the number of hours that each law firm works on the case. Thus, at the end of the case, the attorneys' fees would be distributed to the various law firms based upon the lodestar value.

According to a recent study of class action settlements spanning 1993 to 2008, costs and expenses were a small percentage of the average class recovery.[32] In fact, costs and expenses remained a constant percentage over this 15-year period.[33] From 1993 to 2002, the mean costs were 2.8 percent of recovery, and they actually decreased to 2.7 percent during 2003 to 2008.[34] The median costs remained at 1.7 percent for the entire time period.[35]

Finally, in some cases, insurance policies may cover the attorney's fees and expenses for litigation.[36] Generally, if a business has purchased a general liability insurance policy, part of the policy's coverage may go towards attorneys' fees. Individuals, unless they have the risk of suit in a professional capacity, do not often purchase general liability insurance in the United States.

§ 10.04 E-Discovery costs

The cost of electronic discovery is another consideration for attorneys in antitrust, indeed any, litigation.[37] We live in a digital age where the use of electronically-stored information (ESI) is the norm. Instead of requesting a collection of paper documents, lawyers who deal with discovery in today's environment must be able to identify the key custodians who have responsive information, determine what type of electronic documents exist, establish where the information is stored, and copy the ESI into a useable format. Despite the prevalent use of ESI, courts still wrestle with what aspects of e-discovery are "taxable court costs" that are recoverable.

Generally, the costs of actually producing the electronic documents are taxable, but various other costs associated with electronic discovery may not be. Recoverable e-discovery costs include the copying of files in their native format and the conversion to a standardized file format.[38] One court described this process as the "21st century equivalent of making copies."[39] In *Neutrino Dev. Corp. v. Sonosite, Inc.*, for example, the court found that the costs of removing metadata from files to be redacted and

---

32 Theodore Eisenberg & Geoffrey P. Miller, *Attorneys' Fees and Expenses in Class Action Settlements: 1993–2008*, 26 (Cornell Law Faculty Working Papers, NYU Center for Law, Economics and Organization, Law & Economics Research Paper Series Working Paper No. 09-50, Draft of October 30, 2009).

33 *Id.*

34 *Id.*

35 *Id.*

36 This subject is worthy of its own separate article and will not be discussed at great length here.

37 This subject is likewise worthy of its own separate article and will not be discussed at great length here.

38 *See* CBT Flint Partners, LLC v. Return Path, Inc., 676 F. Supp. 2d 1376, 1381 (N. D. Ga. 2009). *See also* BDT Prods. V. Lexmark Int'l, Inc., 405 F.3d 415, 420 (6th Cir. 2005); Fast Memory Erase, LLC v. Spansion, Inc., 2010 U.S. Dist. LEXIS 132025, at *18–19 (N.D. Tex. Nov. 10, 2010).

39 *Id.*

produced electronically are recoverable.[40] Other courts have placed limits on the idea that copying electronic files is equivalent to making paper copies, finding that only costs associated with the copying and conversion of "necessary" ESI are recoverable but copying and conversion for counsel's convenience is not.[41] Some courts do not allow the cost of searching and extracting information because that process is "more like the work of an attorney or legal assistant in locating and segregating documents that may be responsive to discovery than it is like copying those documents for use in a case."[42] For example, in *Zenith Elecs. Corp. v. WH-TV Broad. Corp.*, the Northern District of Illinois held that costs such as computer time and costs of a computer consultant to search through electronic documents are not recoverable under 28 U.S.C. § 1920 (the bill of costs statute).[43]

§ 10.05 Types of fee arrangements

The most common fee arrangement in a private antitrust action is the contingency fee.[44] As fee arrangements are often privately negotiated in the United States, public data on this subject is scarce. In the American Antitrust Institute's Private Enforcement Project study,[45] 30 of the 40 cases analyzed are included in tables describing the percentage of plaintiffs' recovery awarded as attorneys' fees.[46] These cases are all contingent-based; the remaining cases' fee structures are not otherwise discussed or disclosed. In addition to the contingent fee arrangement, the incentive-based fee arrangement, the "billable hour," the task-based arrangement, the flat fee arrangement, mixed arrangements, and the attorney investment arrangement have all been utilized in some form in antitrust cases. These arrangements are discussed below.

10.05.1 100 percent contingent agreements

The 100 percent contingent arrangement is the commonly understood "no-win, no-pay" system. This arrangement is common in large, class-action lawsuits, including antitrust lawsuits.[47] The attorneys accept the case in return for "a percentage of any award or

---

40 Civil Action No. H-01-2484, 2007 U.S. Dist. LEXIS 23464, at *12 (S.D. Tex. Mar. 30, 2007).

41 *See* Race Tires Am., Inc. v. Hoosier Racing Tire Corp., 2011 U.S. Dist. LEXIS 48847 *at 11–12 (W.D. Pa. May 6, 2011) (discussing the dividing line between "necessary" and "for the convenience of counsel").

42 Kellogg Brown & Root, Int'l Inc. v. Altanmia Comm. Mktg. Col. W.L.L., 2009 U.S. Dist. LEXIS 44137, at *15 (S.D. Tex. May 26, 2009); *see also* Klaymin v. Freedom's Watch, Inc., 2008 WL 5111293, at *2 (S.D. Fla. Dec. 4, 2008); Windy City Innovations, LLC v. AOL, Inc., 2006 WL 2224057, at *3 (N.D. Ill. July 31, 2006).

43 No. 01 C 4366, 2004 U.S. Dist. LEXIS 13657, at *19–20 (N.D. Ill. July 19, 2004).

44 Sarah Northway, *Non-Traditional Class Action Financing and Traditional Rules of Ethics: Time for A Compromise*, 14 Geo. J. Legal Ethics 241, 245 n.30 (2000).

45 Robert H. Lande & Joshua P. Davis, *Benefits from Private Antitrust Enforcement: An Analysis of Forty Cases*, 42 U.S.F. L. Rev. 879 (2007).

46 *Id.* at Tables 6A–6C.

47 Paula Batt Wilson, *Attorney Investment in Class Action Litigation: The Agent Orange Example*, 45 Case W. Res. L. Rev. 291, 291(1994).

settlement."[48] ABA Model Rule of Professional Conduct 1.5 allows for these types of arrangements, provided that:

> A contingent fee agreement shall be in a writing signed by the client and shall state the method by which the fee is to be determined, including the percentage or percentages that shall accrue to the lawyer in the event of settlement, trial or appeal; litigation and other expenses to be deducted from the recovery; and whether such expenses are to be deducted before or after the contingent fee is calculated. The agreement must clearly notify the client of any expenses for which the client will be liable whether or not the client is the prevailing party. Upon conclusion of a contingent fee matter, the lawyer shall provide the client with a written statement stating the outcome of the matter and, if there is a recovery, showing the remittance to the client and the method of its determination.[49]

This type of arrangement creates several advantages. First, and most importantly, this arrangement provides disadvantaged plaintiffs with the opportunity for greater access to justice.[50] Plaintiffs can pursue worthy cases without a large, up-front fee arrangement. Second, contingency fee agreements promote progressive litigation.[51] The Supreme Court identified this advantage in *Deposit Guar. Nat'l Bank of Jackson, Miss. v. Roper,* where the Court described the role of the contingency fee agreement as an effective tool in vindicating smaller aggregated claims unremedied by the regulatory action of government, likening the role of plaintiffs and plaintiffs' counsel to a "private attorney general."[52] Examples of other progressive litigation include the abolition of government immunity in some states, the right of parents to recover for the wrongful death of an unborn child, and liability lawsuits which have removed harmful products such as flammable children's pajamas, cars that explode on impact, and harmful contraceptive devices.[53] Third, contingency fee agreements help align the interests of the attorney and client by providing shared incentives and shared risks.[54] Fourth, contingency fee agreements that are based upon a percentage of recovery are easier to compute than other common alternative fee arrangements.[55]

Although contingency fees open the justice system for many people, some critics have identified disadvantages of the traditional contingency fee agreement. First, while the client and attorney share a similar end goal of a successful action, their interests are not completely aligned. For instance, "the attorney may want to settle early for a guaranteed fee rather than invest additional hours in the case. Those hours might result in a marginally greater recovery for the client, or alternatively, in the loss of the case altogether."[56] However, professional responsibility requirements to the client must ultimately motivate the litigation.

---

48 *Id.* at 297.

49 ABA Model Rules of Prof'l Conduct R. 1.5(c) (2004).

50 Wennihan, *supra* note 23, at 1649–51.

51 *Id.* at 1651.

52 445 U.S. 326, 338 (1980).

53 Wennihan, *supra* note 23, at 1651.

54 Michael McKee, Rudy Santore & Joel Shelton, *Contingent Fees, Moral Hazard, and Attorney Rents: A Laboratory Experiment*, 36 J. Legal Stud. 253, 269–71 (2007).

55 Wilson, *supra* note 47, at 308.

56 *Id.* at 300.

Second, as the critics note, contingency fees may result in windfall profits for the attorney. For example, an attorney may accept a case with very little risk and very little work required, but with a large potential damage amount. In such a situation, the attorney may collect a "windfall" amount.[57] Nevertheless, such fee arrangements are subject to checks and balances. Courts often act as gatekeepers to ensure that attorneys do not recover "windfall" amounts. In the *In re Visa Check/MasterMoney Antitrust Litigation*, for example, Judge Gleeson concluded that the plaintiff attorneys' fee request was "excessive" and "absurd."[58] Plaintiffs' counsel had requested fees at 18 percent of the clients' monetary relief, or around $609,012,000.[59] After applying a six-factor test to determine an appropriate fee, Judge Gleeson awarded $220,290,160.44 in reduced fees.[60]

Nevertheless, the largest number of cases in which a court awards reduced contingency fees to an individual plaintiff are personal injury cases. These are difficult to compare in size, scope, and damages award amounts to even a small antitrust claim. The similarity that exists is that in either type of case, the court retains the authority to reduce a fee that it believes is excessive. Attorneys may pre-empt this problem by asking the court at the outset for a reduced contingency percentage when the higher-than-expected recovery is returned. In 2007, a report by the American Antitrust Institute's Private Enforcement Project found that attorneys' contingency fees in antitrust cases tend to reach the standard one-third amount only in suits resulting in smaller recoveries.[61] In cases where the recovery is between $100 and $500 million, the percentage of attorneys' fees drops proportionally.[62] Of the five cases with recoveries greater than $500 million included in the study, four had attorney's fee percentages between 5.2 and 13 percent. The perceived (and proportional) fairness of the fees guides the court in its determination, whether plaintiffs are injured individuals or members of a large class. Professional associations also recommend limits on such recoveries. The ABA Rules attempt to regulate contingent recoveries by requiring all fees to be "reasonable."[63]

A third criticism of the contingency fee model is the increase in litigation that it may engender.[64] However, such criticism is largely unfounded.[65] In fact, as discussed later, the

---

57 *Id.* at 309.

58 *In re* Visa Check/MasterMoney Antitrust Litig., 297 F. Supp.2d 503, 522 (2003). In his book about the lawsuit, attorney Lloyd Constantine argues that his fee request for the attorneys on the case was justified. LLOYD CONSTANTINE, PRICELESS 224–27 (2009). Mr. Constantine recounts the measures that he and colleagues took to present the attorneys' fees to Judge Gleeson, including cutting attorney hours that were billed for excessively long days. "In this exercise, my hours were cut for numerous days when I traveled to San Francisco and worked through the night; that is, after my drink in the Redwood Room of the Clift Hotel." *Id.* at 225.

59 *In re* Visa Check/MasterMoney Antitrust Litig., 297 F. Supp.2d at 522.

60 Mr. Constantine, who disagreed with the Court's fee calculation, argues that Judge Gleeson actually awarded a 3.5 multiplier of the $62,940,045.84 submitted as the lodestar in the fee application. *Id.* at 232.

61 Lande & Davis, *supra* note 45, Table 6A (2007).

62 *Id.* at Table 6B.

63 ABA MODEL RULES OF PROF'L CONDUCT R. 1.5(a) (2004).

64 Wennihan, *supra* note 23, at 1658.

65 Wennihan, *supra* note 23, at 1659 (citing Stephen Budiansky, et al., *How Lawyers Abuse the Law*, U.S. NEWS & WORLD REP., Jan. 30, 1995, at 50–56, for the fact that personal injury contingency litigation remained constant from 1975 to 1990, and has fallen since 1990).

process that attorneys undertake to evaluate a case, as well as the costs associated with litigating a case, often serve as an inherent check on unfettered litigation.[66]

Despite the criticism, a percentage-based contingency fee model has become a widely-used and accepted method for funding private antitrust litigation. As the court commented in *Wal-Mart Stores, Inc. v. Visa U.S.A. Inc. and MasterCard Int'l, Inc.*, the trend has been towards applying the percentage-based method because "it directly aligns the interests of the [party] and its counsel and provides a powerful incentive for the efficient prosecution and early resolution of litigation."[67]

10.05.2 Incentive-based fee arrangement

The incentive-based fee arrangement "creates an incentive for the attorney to obtain a favorable result at a lower cost to all clients in a manner not unlike the contingent fee arrangements for plaintiff clients."[68] Under an incentive-based fee arrangement, an attorney's fees are dependent upon the result – the more favorable the settlement or judgment, the more fees collected by the attorney.[69] Thus, in this type of arrangement, an "attorney is given an incentive to resolve the lawsuit for the lowest possible cost to the client."[70] Furthermore, the "client benefits either from low fees and/or settlement costs due to a favorable resolution of the case or from reduced fees if the settlement or judgment is not favorable."[71]

10.05.3 The "billable hour"

The traditional "billable hour" method gained popularity in the mid-1960s.[72] This method is the simplest to calculate. The fee is computed by taking the number of hours worked multiplied by the attorney's hourly billing rate. It was originally thought to improve "fairness." Calculating a fee based on "the hours of work that a lawyer put[s] into a task was an objective way to measure the amount a client should owe."[73] Thus, this hourly rate is perceived as the "fair value" of services provided to a client.

---

66 *Id.* at 1659 ("[T]he lawyer acts as a buffer between the plaintiff and defendant by not accepting baseless claims because it is not in her own economic best interest to do so.") (citing Philip H. Corboy, *Contingency Fees: The Individual's Key to the Courthouse Door*, 1976 LITIGATION 27 (1975–1976); Root, *supra* note 5, at 596 ("[T]he lawyer who takes a certain percentage of the proceeds from a victorious case will screen out those cases lacking sufficient merit to avoid the opportunity cost of wasting his time and resources. Coinciding with this 'screening out' argument, others argue that contingency fees actually decrease the amount of frivolous litigation by changing the lawyer's incentives.").

67 396 F.3d 96, 121 (2nd Cir. 2005); *see also In re* Lease Oil Antitrust Litig. (No. II), 186 F.R.D. 403, 444 (S.D. Tex. 1999) (commenting upon the strong trend toward the percentage method).

68 Stephen W. Jones & Melissa Beard Glover, *The Attack on Traditional Billing Practices*, 20 U. ARK. LITTLE ROCK L.J. 293, 304 (1998).

69 *Id.* at 304–05.

70 *Id.* at 305.

71 *Id.*

72 *Id.* at 293–99.

73 *Id.* at 294.

In reality, one of the biggest disadvantages of this billing system is the potential for unnecessary increases in litigation costs. The billable hour method rewards inefficiency, because "the more hours worked, the more fees are generated."[74] Furthermore, the method lacks a mechanism to control costs, which can be a serious flaw given the unpredictability of litigation. It also fails to solve some of the problems identified earlier in this chapter. People who may not otherwise have access to the court system because they cannot afford it will not be able to fund litigation this way. Moreover, even people who have the funds may not be willing to pursue viable but nevertheless high-stakes, cutting edge legal issues.

10.05.4 Task-based and flat fee arrangements

Task-based fee systems are based on the completion of various tasks instead of an hourly or contingent agreement. Tasks may be "defined as narrowly as a specific deposition or as broadly as completion of fact research and case analysis."[75] Fees for each task can be negotiated, "creating an incentive for the attorney to perform efficiently."[76]

Flat fee agreements are exactly that – a fee is "charged for handling a matter from beginning to end."[77]

10.05.5 Mixed arrangements

While the above fee arrangements can be used as the sole type of fee agreement for a specific matter, many fee arrangements in complex litigation are a blending of various types of arrangements. A common "blend" is the partial contingent agreement. In such an agreement, the attorney will be paid a reduced hourly fee, in exchange for an amount from the final judgment. In such a system, for example, an attorney may charge reduced fees in exchange for 10 percent of the final settlement or judgment.

10.05.6 Attorney investment

An attorney investment arrangement involves an attorney advancing a share of the litigation expenses in exchange for a specified return on investment to be allocated from the amount approved for attorneys' fees following judgment or settlement.[78] However, the setting of attorneys' fees by fixing a rate of return on an initial investment is uncommon, perhaps as a result of professional responsibility rules dictating that fees must be "reasonable."[79] Setting a fixed rate of return on an investment before any recovery is realized may obstruct fairness, as compared to a contingency fee, which may have a greater

---

74 *Id.* at 295.
75 *Id.* at 306.
76 *Id.*
77 *Id.*
78 Wilson, *supra* note 47, at 311–12.
79 *See* ABA Model Rules of Prof'l Conduct R. 1.8(i) (2004) ("A lawyer shall not acquire a proprietary interest in the cause of action or subject matter of litigation the lawyer is conducting

claim to reasonableness due to its proportionality, whether or not a recovery ultimately covers the expenses advanced. Though the attorney-investment model exists, attorneys have been wary of utilizing it. This is partly due to some high-profile difficulties that arose during the *Agent Orange* litigation,[80] but primarily due to the availability of the contingency fee method, which is accepted as the norm in class action litigation.

10.05.6(A) The Agent Orange example

The *Agent Orange* cases have become famous for their association with attorney investment. The plaintiffs in the *Agent Orange* cases adopted an attorney investment fee model after lengthy and "tortuous" attempts to finance the massive, complex litigation.[81] This case was initiated in 1979 by plaintiff Edward J. Gorman and his attorney Victor J. Yannacone, Jr.[82] Eventually, Yannacone was replaced by a three-member Plaintiffs' Management Committee ('PMC').[83] After the court "threw the plaintiffs' camp into a 'near-panic' by setting a trial date which gave the parties less than seven months to complete pre-trial investigation and preparation of the case," the PMC sought help.[84] Nine members of a new PMC "executed an agreement requiring six members to advance $200,000 each for litigation expenses."[85] These six "investor-attorneys," in exchange for the investment, would receive $600,000 each from the amount of approved attorneys' fees if the case was successful, and also 50 percent of the remaining amount, which the six were to divide equally.[86] Of the other 50 percent of the remaining amount, 30 percent would be divided according to hours expended on the case, and 20 percent would be divided based on majority vote.[87]

After the court expressed "serious doubt about its legality and propriety," the PMC members executed a new agreement.[88] The new agreement left unchanged the percentage on the return on investment (300 percent), but allowed for an increase of $50,000 per contributing investor-attorney.[89] The new agreement, however, eliminated the earlier provisions giving the six investor attorneys 50 percent of the remaining amount, and substituted "division among all PMC members 'in the proportion the individual's and/or firm's fee award bears to the total fees awarded.'"[90]

10.05.6(B) Ethical considerations of attorney-investors

One of the biggest ethical issues raised by attorney investment concerns litigation objectives. A primary premise of American law is that the client defines the objectives of the

---

for a client except that the lawyer may: (1) acquire a lien granted by law to secure the lawyer's fee or expenses; and (2) contract with a client for a reasonable contingent fee in a civil case.")

[80] Wilson, *supra* note 47.
[81] *Id.* at 311.
[82] *Id.*
[83] *Id.*
[84] *Id.*
[85] Wilson, *supra* note 47, at 312.
[86] *Id.*
[87] *Id.*
[88] *Id.*
[89] *Id.*
[90] Wilson, *supra* note 47, at 312.

litigation. In a situation where the attorney holds a financial investment in a case, and in class actions in general, the attorneys "function essentially as entrepreneurs who bear a substantial amount of the litigation risk and exercise nearly plenary control over all important decisions in the lawsuit."[91]

Other conflicts may also arise in attorney-investor agreements. Financial conflicts may arise in cases where an attorney has a financial investment in a case and exercises such great control over day-to-day litigation decisions. These problems may be further exacerbated when a client has difficulty getting information from the attorney about a case or has difficulty dismissing an attorney.[92] Specifically, the attorney may be guided by his financial considerations instead of the client's wishes. The Fifth Circuit phrased the issue as follows: "Whenever an attorney is confronted with a potential for choosing between actions which may benefit himself financially and an action which may benefit the class which he represents there is a reasonable possibility that some specifically identifiable impropriety will occur."[93] In *Agent Orange*, the Second Circuit stated:

> Given the size and complexity of the litigation, it seems apparent that the potential for abuse was real and should have been discouraged. . . . The conflict obviously lies in the incentive provided to an investor-attorney to settle early and thereby avoid work for which full payment may not be authorized by the district court. Moreover, as soon as an offer of settlement to cover the promised return on investment is made, the investor-attorney will be disinclined to undertake the risks associated with continuing the litigation.[94]

Thus, the investor-attorney model leads to serious potential conflicts. In *Agent Orange*, the Second Circuit refused to accept the PMC's attorney-investment agreement. Nevertheless, some legal scholars essentially have suggested that the PMC fee arrangement used in *Agent Orange* should be institutionalized, insofar as it creates a risk multiplier for expenses.[95] "Giving attorneys a risk premium for expenses advanced, as well as for fees, would increase the attorney's recovery and theoretically minimize the effect of champerty in inducing settlement."[96]

10.05.7 Other investors

In recent years, the litigation funding industry has grown, especially with regard to plaintiffs' personal injury cases.[97] There are now companies that exist to invest money in litigation, by advancing those funds to the attorney or plaintiff involved in the contingency fee case and negotiating the type of return on that investment.[98] It appears that, though

---

91 *Id.* at 316.

92 *Id.*

93 Zylestra v. Safeway Stores, Inc., 578 F.2d 102, 104 (5th Cir. 1978).

94 *In re* "Agent Orange" Prod. Liab. Litig., 818 F.2d 216, 224 (2d Cir.), *cert. denied*, 484 U.S. 926 (1987).

95 Wilson, *supra* note 47, at 318.

96 *Id.*

97 *See* Susan Lorde Martin, *The Litigation Financing Industry: The Wild West of Finance Should Be Tamed Not Outlawed*, 10 Fordham J. Corp. & Fin. L. 55, 55 (2004).

98 Douglas R. Richmond, *Other People's Money: The Ethics of Litigation Funding*, 56 Mercer L. Rev. 649, 650 (2005).

the majority of such investments are also structured on a percentage-based contingency fee recovery,[99] some negotiate a flat fee, based on the specific rate of return on that initial investment.[100] For example, a litigation funding company may loan an attorney money for costs of the litigation, and the attorney, upon recovery, will repay the amount loaned, plus a fee.[101] Some companies attach a high interest rate, such as 50 percent, on the money that was initially loaned to the plaintiff.[102] If the plaintiff does not recover any damages from the litigation, the investor recovers nothing, thus participating in the risk involved.[103]

The increase in funding arrangements such as these is more common in the personal injury arena now, probably due to the much smaller amount of money needed to advance the costs of such a lawsuit. If companies such as these continue to grow, non-lawyer investors may be able to fund large antitrust class action cases. Proponents of the increase in litigation funding point to the fact that it increases legal access and thereby "evens the playing field on an economic level in a way that traditional banking institutions cannot."[104] Most banks regard litigation, with its accompanying uncertainties, as too risky a venture for investment.[105] Additionally, attorneys have been unable in most instances to borrow money to fund a lawsuit from a bank, due to the ethical restrictions on the division of fees and the possibility of accidental partnership formation with non-lawyers.[106]

§ 10.06 Court factors in awarding attorneys' fees

Historically, courts employed a multi-factor test to calculate fee awards in class action cases.[107] Those factors included time and labor, customary fee, whether the fee was fixed or contingent, reputation and ability of the attorneys, awards in similar cases, the professional nature of the relationship between attorney and client, preclusion of other employment, the novelty and difficulty of the case, the skill required to render the legal services, and the undesirability of the case.[108] Today, some courts still utilize factors to determine appropriate attorneys' fees in class action cases.[109] More typically, courts now employ the percentage method, the lodestar method, or a combination of the two to calculate attorneys' fees.

---

99 Martin, *supra* note 97, at 55.
100 Richmond, *supra* note 98, at 650.
101 *Id.*
102 Martin, *supra* note 97, at 56.
103 *Id.*
104 Christy B. Bushnell, *Champerty Is Still No Excuse in Texas: Why Texas Courts (And The Legislature) Should Uphold Litigation Funding Agreements*, 7 HOUS. BUS. & TAX. L.J. 358, 364 (2007).
105 *Id.* at note 43.
106 Wilson, *supra* note 47, at 342.
107 Johnson v. Georgia Highway Express, 488 F.2d 714, 717–19 (5th Cir. 1974).
108 *Id.*
109 *See* Thompson v. Connick, 553 F.3d 836 (5th Cir. 2008); Gunter v. Ridgewood Energy Corp., 223 F.3d 190, 195 n. 1 (3d Cir. 2000).

10.06.1 The percentage method

Under the percentage method, courts multiply the amount that the class recovers by a percentage factor. The Ninth Circuit employs a 25 percent benchmark fee in common fund cases but allows departures based on individual case factors.[110] The Eleventh Circuit has recognized that its district courts also employ a 25 percent benchmark.[111]

10.06.2 The "lodestar" method

Other courts utilize the lodestar method. The lodestar method was developed in the Third Circuit, and has now been approved by most circuit courts in the United States.[112] In using this method, the court "multipl[ies] the number of hours reasonably worked on a client's case by a reasonable hourly billing rate for such services based on a given geographical area, the nature of services provided, and the experience of the attorneys" to create an objective "lodestar."[113] Courts then utilize multipliers to adjust the fee subjectively for various situations, such as high-risk litigation.[114]

Despite the popularity of the lodestar method, some critics cite drawbacks to this system. Criticisms of this method include:

> its [creation of] . . . incentives to pad billable hours, its burden on the parties and the court, and the fact that its guarantee of fees in successful cases may cause attorneys to reject a favorable settlement for the class. In 1985, the Third Circuit . . . formed a Task Force to address the "widespread belief that the deficiencies of the current system either offset or exceed its benefits." Specifically, the Third Circuit Task Force "concluded that the lodestar formula increases the use of judicial resources, encourages attorneys to bill excessive hours, and discourages early settlement."[115]

Other commentators have noted the drawbacks from a different perspective:

> In some cases, plaintiffs' attorneys can be tempted to negotiate early with the defense counsel about settlement. The ensuing pre-litigation work becomes merely a "meaningless exercise" to bill additional hours after a settlement has been agreed upon in actuality. In this way, the lodestar approach can produce structural, de facto collusion between the plaintiff's attorney and defendants. In this scenario, the defendant makes a low settlement offer and then cooperates with the plaintiff's attorney to allow the latter to accumulate hours, which are deducted from the class recovery at no additional cost to the defendant. "At no point must either side actually link the fee award and the settlement size in their negotiations – the law does this for them by tying fee awards to hours billed rather than settlement size."[116]

Thus, the lodestar method can "award a settling attorney the same fee award she would receive if she litigated a much higher recovery for the plaintiffs at trial."[117] As a

---

110 *See, e.g.*, Torrisi v. Tucson Elec. Power Co., 8 F.3d 1370, 1376 (9th Cir. 1993).
111 Camden I Condominium Ass'n v. Dunkle, 946 F.2d 768, 774 (11th Cir. 1991).
112 *Id.* at 305.
113 *In re* Rite Aid Corp. Sec. Litig., 396 F.3d 294, 305–06 (3d Cir. 2005).
114 Wilson, *supra* note 47, at 305–06.
115 *Id.* at 307.
116 *Id.* at 307–08 (citations omitted).
117 *Id.* at 308.

consequence, the lodestar approach of setting fees can be "too vulnerable to collusive settlements."[118] Attorneys get no compensation for accepting additional risk by litigating the case, and instead are encouraged to accept large settlements, even if a litigated recovery could be greater.[119]

Nevertheless, these criticisms have not deterred courts from applying the lodestar method in a number of cases. For example, in *Kenny A. ex rel. Winn v. Perdue*, the court awarded $10.5 million in attorney's fees which included an upward adjustment under the lodestar method.[120] In support of the 75 percent upward adjustment from the requested fees, the court praised the plaintiff's counsel for their skill, expertise, and professionalism, stating:

> [T]he evidence establishes that the quality of service rendered by class counsel, including their extraordinary commitment of capital resources, was far superior to what consumers of legal services . . . could reasonably expect to receive for the rates used in the lodestar calculation. . . .[121] [T]he Court is unaware of any other case in which a plaintiff class has achieved such a favorable result on such a comprehensive scale.[122]

10.06.3 Combined method

Often in antitrust cases, courts will also utilize the lodestar method in order to verify the reasonableness of the percentage-based attorney fee request.[123] For example, the court in *In re Relafen Antitrust Litigation* granted $22.3 million in attorneys' fees (one-third of the recovery) after conducting a lodestar crosscheck.[124] The court, citing precedent granting percentage-based fees in excess of four times the lodestar value, stated that the fee request was reasonable as a matter of law.[125] A court may utilize both the percentage method and the lodestar method as a "check" on the reasonableness of the attorneys' fees.

10.06.4 The Goldberger *factors*

Although the Second Circuit has approved both the percentage and lodestar methods for calculating attorneys' fees, the court cautions against the use of "benchmarks" and instead promotes a traditional fact-specific inquiry to determine what amount is reason-

---

[118] *Id.*

[119] *Id.*

[120] 454 F.Supp. 2d 1260 (N.D. Ga. 2006), *aff'd by* 532 F.3d 1209 (11th Cir. 2008).

[121] *Id.* at 1288.

[122] *Id.* at 1290; *see also* Rodriguez v. West Publishing Corp., 563 F.3d 948 (9th Cir. 2009) (antitrust suit appropriately applying the lodestar method was remanded for consideration of attorney fees in light of conflict of interest resulting from incentive agreements).

[123] *In re* Insurance Brokerage Antitrust Litig., 2009 WL 411856, *4 (D.N.J. Feb. 17, 2009) ("While either the lodestar or percentage-of-recovery method should ordinarily serve as the primary basis for determining the fee, the Third Circuit has instructed that it is sensible to use the alternative method to double check the reasonableness of the fee.").

[124] *In re* Relafen Antitrust Litig., 231 F.R.D. 52, 81–82 (D. Mass. 2005).

[125] *Id.* at 82; *see also* Wal-Mart Stores, Inc. v. Visa U.S.A. Inc. and MasterCard Int'l, Inc., 396 F.3d 96, 123 (2nd Cir. 2005) (approving a percentage-based fee 3.5 times the lodestar value as reasonable).

able under the circumstances.[126] The Second Circuit's six-factor *Goldberger* test includes (1) the time and labor expended by counsel; (2) the magnitude and complexities of the litigation; (3) the risk of the litigation; (4) the quality of the representation; (5) the requested fee in relation to the settlement; and (6) public policy considerations.[127]

In 2003, the court in *In re Visa Check/MasterMoney Antitrust Litigation* applied the *Goldberger* test to determine the appropriate amount of attorneys' fees, after rejecting counsel's "excessive" requested fee.[128] The court found that although the suit went on for many years,[129] was of a significant size and complexity,[130] involved substantial risk,[131] and was excellently represented by plaintiffs' counsel,[132] the request for fees was "excessive."[133] Nevertheless, despite counsel's fee request, which the Court found was "fundamentally unreasonable" and "absurd," the *Goldberger* factors "compel[led]" the court to an "award of an extraordinary fee."[134] The court emphasized that the size of the settlement obtained made "even the exorbitant fee . . . award[ed] seem[] small in comparison."[135] Finally, the public policy considerations merited a "substantial fee award,"[136] due to the "significant and lasting benefits for America's merchants and consumers"[137] arising out of the litigation. The court's ultimate award of $220,290,160.44 in fees represented 6.511 percent of the settlement fund.[138]

The United States Supreme Court, however, has been critical of courts applying tests similar to the *Goldberger* factors. In reference to the *Johnson-Kerr* method of calculating attorney's fees, an approach originating in the Fifth Circuit in which courts generally consider the following non-exclusive factors: (1) the time and labor required;[139] (2) the novelty and difficulty of the questions involved;[140] (3) the skill requisite to perform the legal service properly;[141] (4) the preclusion of other employment by the attorney due

---

126 Goldberger v. Integrated Resources, Inc., 209 F.3d 43 (2d Cir. 2000).

127 *Id.* at 50.

128 *In re* VISA Check/MasterMoney Antitrust Litig., 297 F. Supp. 2d 503, 521–22 (E.D.N.Y. 2003) (citing *Goldberger*).

129 *Id.* at 523.

130 *Id.*

131 *Id.*

132 *Id.* at 524.

133 *In re VISA Check/MasterMoney Antitrust Litig.*, *supra* note 128 at 522.

134 *Id.* at 523.

135 *Id.* at 524.

136 *Id.*

137 *Id.* at 524.

138 *In re VISA Check/MasterMoney Antitrust Litig.*, *supra* note 128 at 522.

139 The major consideration in determining the amount of a fee award is the result achieved. *See* Hensley v. Eckerhart, 461 U.S. 424, 436 (1983) ("most critical factor is the degree of success obtained").

140 *See, e.g.*, *In re* Linerboard Antitrust Litig., 2004 WL 1221350, *10 (E.D. Pa. June 2, 2004) (finding an antitrust class action "is arguably the most complex action to prosecute") (quotation omitted); *In re* Motorsports Merch. Antitrust Litig., 112 F. Supp. 2d 1329, 1337 (N.D. Ga. 2000); *In re* Shopping Carts Antitrust Litig., 1983 WL 1950, *7 (S.D.N.Y. Nov. 18, 1983) ("antitrust price fixing actions are generally complex, expensive and lengthy").

141 The caliber of opposing counsel is relevant in assessing the quality of counsel's work. *See, e.g.*, *In re* Equity Funding Corp. Sec. Litig., 438 F. Supp. 1303, 1337 (C.D. Cal. 1977); J.N. Futia Co. v. Phelps Dodge Indus., Inc., 1982 WL 1892 (S.D.N.Y. Sept. 17, 1982).

to acceptance of the case; (5) the customary attorney fee;[142] (6) whether the fee is fixed or contingent; (7) time limitations imposed by the client or the circumstances; (8) the amount involved and the results obtained; (9) the experience, reputation, and ability of the attorneys;[143] (10) the "undesirability" of the case; (11) the nature and length of the professional relationship with the client; and (12) awards in similar cases,[144] the Court noted that this method gives little guidance to federal district courts in setting attorneys' fees with "sometimes subjective factors [that] place unlimited discretion in trial judges and [produce] disparate results."[145]

In a recent study of fee recoveries in class actions from 1993 to 2002, researchers found that courts' use of the lodestar method had declined, with only 9.6 percent of cases utilizing this method solely.[146] The study concluded that the percentage method was the primary method that courts used to calculate fees, with many courts performing the lodestar calculation as a check on that fee amount.[147] Another study of all class action settlements in federal court in 2006 and 2007 supported this finding, and revealed that most judges utilized a percentage of the settlement method for calculating attorneys' fees.[148] The median and mean fee amount was 25 percent of the recovery.[149] The pure lodestar method was used most often in consumer and debt collection cases.[150]

§ 10.07 Recovery awarded as attorneys' fees in antitrust cases

With respect to class actions generally, one study of attorneys' fees and settlements from 1993 to 2008 confirmed that courts granted the attorneys' fees requested in more than 70 percent of the cases.[151] The Second Circuit granted such requests the least often, particularly compared to the Third Circuit and the Ninth Circuit.[152] When the courts did not award the requested attorneys' fees, the mean fee amount actually awarded was 68 percent

---

142 The customary fees paid in contingent fee, non-class actions are also a factor in this analysis. *See, e.g., In re* Remeron Direct Purchaser Antitrust Litig., 2005 WL 3008808, *16 (D.N.J. Nov. 9, 2005). Some private contingent cases (*i.e.*, non-class action cases, and therefore not subject to court approval) provide for fees equaling 30-40 percent of the recovery. *See, e.g., In re* M.D.C. Holdings Sec. Litig., 1990 WL 454747, *7 (S.D. Cal. Aug. 30, 1990); Phemister v. Harcourt Brace Jovanovich, Inc., 1984 WL 21981, *15 (N.D. Ill. Sept. 14, 1984).

143 *In re* Agent Orange Prod. Liab. Litig., 611 F. Supp. 1296, 1313 (E.D.N.Y. 1985); *In re* Ashanti Goldfields, 2005 WL 3050284, *4 (E.D.N.Y. Nov. 15, 2005).

144 Brown v. Phillips Petroleum Co., 838 F.2d 451, 454–55 (10th Cir. 1988); Kerr v. Screen Extras Guild, Inc., 526 F.2d 67, 69–70 (9th Cir. 1975) (citing Johnson v. Ga. Highway Express, Inc., 488 F.2d 714, 717–719 (5th Cir. 1974)); *cf.* United Steelworkers of Am. v. Phelps Dodge Corp., 896 F.2d 403, 406 & n.3 (9th Cir. 1990) (noting that the factors from *Kerr* are used in preliminary determinations of the lodestar).

145 Pennsylvania v. Del. Valley Citizens' Council for Clean Air, 478 U.S. 546, 563, (1986).

146 Eisenberg & Miller, *supra* note 32, at 20.

147 *Id.*

148 Brian T. Fitzpatrick, *An Empirical Study of Class Action Settlements and Their Fee Awards*, (Vanderbilt University Law School, Public Law & Legal Theory, Working Paper Number 10-10, Law & Economics, Working Paper Number 10-06 (draft of July 7, 2010)).

149 *Id.* at 25, 27.

150 *Id.* at 25.

151 Eisenberg & Miller, *supra* note 32, at 3, 23.

152 *Id.*

of the requested amount.[153] All in all, the mean class recovery calculated under the study during this time period was $116 million, with a mean fee of $12.8 million.[154] The median class recovery was $12.5 million, with a mean fee of $2.3 million.[155]

This study showed that class action litigation in federal court is concentrated heavily in only a few jurisdictions, with more than half of all class action lawsuits occurring in five courts: Southern District of New York, Eastern District of Pennsylvania, Northern District of California, District of New Jersey, and Northern District of Illinois.[156] The Eastern District of New York came in at a close sixth.[157] The researchers also suggested that the jurisdiction depended largely on the type of class action matter, with the Eastern District of Pennsylvania being the leading federal jurisdiction for antitrust and consumer cases.[158]

The factor that most determined what fee amount courts awarded was the size of the classes' recovery.[159] Other factors, though not as significant, included the fee method used and the riskiness of the case at issue.[160] Generally, courts awarded an increased fee for cases with greater risk.[161] Except for "Antitrust and Other cases," the mean fee percentages were higher in high-risk cases.[162] The study found that cases with objectors had higher fee percentages than cases without objectors.[163] Also, cases with more than one class member who opted out had lower fee percentages than cases with one or fewer class members who opted out.[164]

In the Fitzpatrick study, during the 2006–2007 period, there were $33 billion in class action settlements, 15 percent of which, or $5 billion, was awarded to attorneys.[165] Fitzpatrick also found that fee percentages were inversely related to the size of the settlement.[166]

In 2007, a report of the American Antitrust Institute's (AAI) Private Enforcement Project analyzed 40 recent private antitrust cases and the results obtained in the cases. Table 1 of the Report indicates that the recoveries in private cases for the 40 cases analyzed ranged from $36 million to $5.6 billion.[167] Attorneys' fees recoveries ranged from 5.2 percent of the recovered amount in a case with a $552 million recovery, to 33.3 percent of the recovered amount in several cases with recoveries ranging from $50 million to $220 million.[168]

---

153 *Id.*
154 *Id.* at 11.
155 *Id.*
156 Eisenberg & Miller, *supra* note 32, at 3, 23.
157 *Id.*
158 *Id.* at 10–11.
159 *Id.* at 3.
160 *Id.*
161 Eisenberg & Miller, *supra* note 32, at 3, 23.
162 *Id.*
163 *Id.* at 19.
164 *Id.*
165 *Id.* at 19, 31.
166 *Id.* at 32.
167 Lande & Davis, *supra* note 45, at Table 1.
168 *Id.* at Tables 6A–6C.

10.07.1 Recoveries exceeding $500 million

In five of the antitrust cases in the AAI study where recoveries exceeded $500 million, the authors of the study reported the attorneys' fees as a percentage of recovery as follows:[169] *In re Visa/MasterMoney:* 6.5 percent of $3.383 billion;[170] *Auction Houses:* 5.2 percent of $552 million;[171] *El Paso:* 6 percent of $1.427 billion;[172] *Fructose:* 25 percent of $531 million;[173] *In re NASDAQ:* 13 percent of $1.027 billion.[174] *Fructose* and *In re NASDAQ* had the highest percentages.[175] In *Fructose*, the attorneys received attorneys' fees that equaled 25 percent of the recovery amount.[176] *In re Fructose* involved allegations of price fixing among the major manufactures of fructose. No indictments were ever brought, even though the government convened a grand jury. The private enforcement class action lasted for 10 years before finally settling for $531 million. Of this damages recovery, $100 million was paid by a foreign entity, A.E. Staley Manufacturing.[177] The payments to the class members themselves were larger than average – over $10 million per class member in some cases – due to the relatively small number of fructose purchasers.[178] The case established important precedent in antitrust and civil conspiracy, and the court may have awarded the higher percentage of the fund to class counsel due to the ability of counsel, which the court frequently praised.[179] In *In re NASDAQ*, the attorneys recovered fees that equaled 13 percent of the recovery amount.[180] Here, the class received aggregate settlements of approximately $1.027 billion, all in cash.[181] Because the size of the attorneys' fees was a modest percentage of the settlement, class members received $896,233,301.[182]

---

169 *Id.* at Table 6C.

170 *In re* Visa Check/MasterMoney Antitrust Litig., 297 F. Supp.2d 503, 522 (E.D.N.Y. 2003).

171 *In re* Auction Houses Antitrust Litig., 164 F. Supp.2d 345 (S.D.N.Y. 200), *aff'd*, 2002 US App. LEXIS 15327 (2d Cir., July 30, 2002) *and* Kruman v. Christie's Int'l PLC, 284 F.3d 384 (2d Cir. 2002).

172 Sweetie's v. El Paso Corp., No. 319840 (S.F. Super. Ct.); Continental Forge Co. v. Southern Ca. Gas Co., No. BC237336 (L.A. Super. Ct.); Berg v. Southern Ca. Gas Co., No. BC241951 (L.A. Super. Ct.); City of Long Beach v. Southern Ca. Gas Co., No. BC247114 (L.A. Super. Ct.); Phillip v. El Paso Merchant Energy *L.P.*, No. BC265905 (L.A. Super. Ct.); Phillip v. El Paso Merchant Energy LP, No. GIC 759425 (S.D. Super. Ct.); Phillip v. El Paso Merchant Energy LP, No. GIC 759426 (S.D. Super. Ct.).

173 *In re* Fructose Antitrust Litig., MDL No. 1087, Master File No. 94-1577 (C.D. Ill.).

174 *In re* NASDAQ Market-Makers Antitrust Litig., MDL No. 1023, No. 94 Civ. 3996 (S.D.N.Y. 1998).

175 Lande & Davis, *supra* note 45, at Table 6C.

176 *Id.*

177 *Id.* at Case 14 Summary.

178 *Id.*

179 *Id.*

180 *Id.* at Table 6C.

181 *Id.* at Case 21 Summary.

182 *Id.*

10.07.2 Recoveries between $100 million and $500 million

In the eight antitrust cases in the AAI study in which the damages recovered ranged from $100 million to $500 million, the percentage of attorneys' fees recovered ranged from 20 percent to 33.3 percent.[183] These cases include *Buspirone* (33.3 percent of $220 million);[184] *Cardizem* (30 percent of $110 million);[185] *DRAM* (25 percent of $326 million);[186] *Flat Glass* (32 percent of $122 million);[187] *Linerboard* (30 percent of $202 million);[188] *Lease Oil* (25 percent of $193 million);[189] *Paxil* (20 and 30 percent of $165 million);[190] and *Relafen* (33 percent of $250 million).[191] In *Paxil*, the plaintiffs received a "megafund" settlement of over $165 million, on behalf of direct and indirect purchasers of Paxil, with a claim that the defendant Smithkline Beecham Corporation had abused its patent approval process in order to maintain its monopoly over the drug.[192] Because plaintiffs in the two cases were able to coordinate discovery, plaintiffs were able to achieve both a timely result and the favor of the court.[193] The court awarded 20 and 30 percent of the respective settlements to counsel, due to the case's complexity and the attorneys' skill and efficiency.[194] In *Linerboard*, the class received a cash settlement of $202.5 million, representing approximately 42–55 percent of plaintiffs' alleged damages.[195] Counsel received 30 percent of that settlement in fees.[196] In determining the fee award, the court emphasized both the "superb" lawyering demonstrated and the groundbreaking nature of this private enforcement action, as the class did not benefit from an earlier government investigation in its case.[197]

10.07.3 Recoveries less than $100 million

In the 17 antitrust cases in the study in which the damages recovered were less than $100 million, the attorneys' fees ranged from 7 percent to 33.3 percent of recovery.[198] These cases are *Airline Ticket Commission* (33.3 percent of $86 million);[199] *Augmentin*

---

183 *Id.* at Table 6C.
184 *In re* Busiprone Antitrust Litig., MDL Docket No. 1413, 85 F.Supp. 2d 340 (S.D.N.Y. 2002).
185 *In re* Cardizem CD Antitrust Litig., MDL No. 1278, 105 F.Supp. 2d 682 (E.D. Mich. 2000).
186 *In re* Dynamic Random Access Memory Antitrust Litig., Master File No. M-02-1486PJH, MDL No. 1486 (N.D. Ca.).
187 *In re* Flat Glass Antitrust Litig., DL 1200, Master Dkt. No. 97-0550 (W.D. Pa.).
188 *In re* Linerboard Antitrust Litig., 2005 WL 1221350 (E.D. Pa. June 2, 2004).
189 *In re* Lease Oil Antitrust Litig. *No. II*, 186 F.R.D. 403 (S.D. Tex. 1999).
190 Stop & Shop Supermarket Co., et. al. v. SmithKline Beecham Corp., 2005 WL 1213926, at *17–18 (E.D. pa. May 19, 2005); Nichols v. SmithKline Beecham Corp., 2005 WL 950616, at *20 (E.D. Pa. Apr. 22, 2005).
191 *In re* Relafen Antitrust Litig., Civ. Action No. 01-12239, 231 F.R.D. 52 (D. Mass. 2005).
192 Lande & Davis, *supra* note 45, at Case 27 Summary.
193 *Id.*
194 *Id.*
195 *Id.* at Case 18 Summary.
196 *Id.*
197 *Id.*
198 Lande & Davis, *supra* note 45, at Table 6C.
199 *In re* Airline Ticket Comm'n Litig., 1996 US Dist. LEXIS 20361.

(20 percent and 25 percent of $91 million);[200] *Automotive Refinishing Paint* (32 percent of $67 million);[201] *NCAA* (26.8 percent of $74 million);[202] *Remeron* (33.3 percent of $75 million);[203] *Platinol* (33.3 percent of $50 million);[204] *Taxol* (30 percent of $66 million);[205] *Drill Bits* (30.8 percent of $53 million);[206] *Polypropylene Carpet* (33.3 percent of $50 million);[207] *Sorbates* (22–33 percent of $96 million);[208] *Terazosin* (33.3 percent of $74 million);[209] *Microcrystalline Cellulose* (33.3 percent of $50 million);[210] *Specialty Steel* (30 percent of $50 million);[211] *Lysine* (7 percent of $65 million);[212] *Commercial Explosives* (30 percent of $77 million);[213] *Graphite Electrodes* (15 percent of $47 million).[214]

10.07.4 Tax implications

Finally, brief mention of tax considerations is appropriate. A circuit court split exists regarding the appropriate tax treatment of contingent attorneys' fees contained within a recovery.[215] Some of the circuits have held that contingent attorneys' fees contained within a recovery are part of a recovering party's taxable gross income, while others have determined that these fees are not part of gross income.[216] Whether contingent attorneys'

---

200 Ryan-House et al. v. GlaxoSmithKline PLC, C.A. Doc. No. 2:02cv442 (E.D. Va. 2004) and SAJ Distributors, Inc. and Stephen L. LaFrance Holdings, Inc. v. SmithKline Beecham Corp., Doc. No. 2:04cv23 (E.D. Va. 2004).

201 *In re* Automotive Refinishing Paint Antitrust Litig., 2004 US Dist. 29162 (E.D. Pa. Oct. 13, 2004).

202 Law v. National Collegiate Athletic Assoc., 902 F. Supp. 1394 (D. Kan. 1995); *aff'd*, 134 F. 3d 1010 (10th Cir. 1998).

203 *In re* Remeron Antitrust Litig., 2005 US Dist. LEXIS 27013 (D.N.J. 2005)

204 North Shore Hematology & Oncology Assoc. v. Bristol-Myers Squibb Co., Civil Action No.:04cv248 (2004).

205 Oncology & Radiation Associates v. Bristol-Meyers Squibb Co., Case No. 1:04CV00248 (D.C.C.).

206 Eagle Resources, et. al., v. Baker Hughes Inc., et. al., No. 4:91cv00627 (Docket) (S.D.Tex. Mar. 11, 1991).

207 *In re* Polypropylene Carpet Antitrust Litig., 93 F.Supp. 2d 1348 (N.D. Ga. 2000).

208 *In re* Sorbates Direct Purchaser Antitrust Litig., 2002 WL 31655191 (N.D. Cal. Nov. 15, 2002).

209 *In re* Terazosin Hydrochloride Antitrust Litig., 2005 U.S. Dist. LEXIS 13992 (S.D. Fla. July 8 2005).

210 *In re* Microcrystalline Cellulose Antitrust Litig., 218 F.R.D. 79 (2003).

211 Transamerican Refining Corp. v. Dravo Corp., et. al, No. 4:88CV00789 (S.D.Tex. 1988) (settlement 1992).

212 *In re* Amino Acid Lysine Antitrust Litig., 918 F. Supp. 1190 (N.D. Ill. 1996).

213 *In re* Commercial Explosives Litig., 945 F. Supp. 1489 (D. Utah 1996).

214 *In re* Graphite Electrodes Antitrust Litig., 2003 WL 22358491 (E.D. Pa. Apr. 24, 2003).

215 Kristina Maynard, *The Fruit Does Not Fall far from the Tree: the Unresolved Tax Treatment of Contingent Attorney's Fees*, 33 Loy. U. Chi. L.J. 991, 993 (2002) (explaining that the Seventh Circuit held that contingent attorneys' fees incurred in obtaining a taxable recovery must be included in taxpayer's gross income. The Third, Fourth, Ninth, Tenth, and Federal Circuits all have held that a taxpayer's gross income includes contingent legal fees paid to obtain a taxable recovery. The Fifth, Sixth, and Eleventh Circuits have held that such fees are not gross income to the taxpayer).

216 Lande & Davis, *supra* note 45, at Table 6C.

fees recovered by a party will be included in that party's gross income will depend on the jurisdiction. An attorney and client could take the tax treatment of their jurisdiction into account when structuring a settlement, although timing may matter in that calculation.[217] Litigation, especially large-scale litigation, can take several years. This fact alone can significantly impact tax liability and should be considered when assessing fees, expenses, and the ultimate recovery.[218]

§ 10.08 Conclusion

Although contingent and other alternative fee arrangements have their detractors and critics, such arrangements permit important antitrust work to proceed in private enforcement actions, which might not occur otherwise. Moreover, courts have typically embraced alternative fee arrangements in antitrust cases, where the issues are complex and require skilled attorneys.

---

[217] *See* Edward A. Morse, *Taxing Plaintiffs: a Look at Tax Accounting for Attorney's Fees and Litigation Costs*, 107 Dick. L. Rev. 405, 424 (2003).

[218] *Id.* at 431.

11 Interaction of public and private enforcement

Kevin J.L. O'Connor, Anthony J. Gaughan, Hannah L. Renfro, Adam C. Briggs, and Wendy K. Arends[1]

§ 11.01 Introduction

One of the unique features of antitrust enforcement is the multiplicity of potential plaintiffs, governmental and private, authorized to challenge allegedly unlawful conduct under

[1] Kevin J. O'Connor is a shareholder with Godfrey & Kahn, S.C., and chairs the firm's Antitrust and Trade Regulation Practice Group. Before joining Godfrey & Kahn, O'Connor headed the Wisconsin Department of Justice's Office of Consumer Protection and Antitrust. While an Assistant Attorney General in Wisconsin DOJ, O'Connor also chaired the National Association of Attorneys General's Multistate Antitrust Task Force. He has exhaustive experience in private and public antitrust actions. Hannah L. Renfro is an attorney with the Wisconsin Department of Commerce, Adam C. Briggs is an attorney in Singapore, and Anthony J. Gaughan is a law professor at Drake University, all formerly lawyers at Godfrey & Kahn, S.C. Wendy K. Arends is currently an associate attorney at Godfrey & Kahn, S.C.

federal and state antitrust law.[2] Not only do the United States Department of Justice (DOJ) and Federal Trade Commission (FTC) maintain overlapping antitrust enforcement authority,[3] but other federal agencies also possess the authority to block business transactions in certain industrial sectors.[4] In addition, state attorneys general and private plaintiffs are empowered to sue under federal and state antitrust law. Although similar to their federal equivalent, state antitrust laws often present potential plaintiffs with remedies beyond those obtainable under federal law.[5]

In short, the antitrust enforcement system has evolved into a system including multiple enforcers, each possessing concurrent enforcement authority: two federal antitrust agencies, other federal agencies reviewing industry-specific transactions, 50 state attorneys general, and thousands of private parties. However, except for certain non-antitrust federal agencies, all federal litigants operate in an integrated federal court system under a single body of federal precedent.[6] Even most state antitrust laws are guided by federal precedent either by statute or state decisional law.[7] Consequently, while American antitrust law has not evolved linearly, the decisional law of the past century guides virtually all antitrust actions, regardless of the identity of the plaintiff in a particular action. Simply put, it was not apparent in 1890 that this degree of convergence would be possible over 100 years later. This chapter explores that convergence from a practical perspective.

11.01.1 Varying remedies

In general, each category of antitrust enforcers can seek various remedies unavailable to other enforcers. For example, the DOJ has criminal enforcement authority and civil authority to seek injunctions and forfeitures, but not damages on behalf of injured parties.[8] The FTC may seek injunctive relief, administrative relief, and, more recently,

---

[2] *See* International Competition Policy Advisory Committee, U.S. Dep't of Justice, Final Report 146 (Feb. 28, 2000), http://www.justice.gov/atr/Icpac/finalreport.html [hereinafter ICPAC]. (No other legal system in the world distributes decision-making power for competition policy issues so widely.)

[3] The DOJ has exclusive federal governmental authority to enforce the Sherman Act and shares federal authority to enforce the Clayton Act with the FTC. *See* ABA Section of Antitrust Law, Antitrust Law Developments 691–92 (6th ed. 2007) [hereinafter ALD VI].

[4] 15 U.S.C. § 21(a) provides the Federal Communications Commission (FCC), the Secretary of Transportation, and the Federal Reserve Board with limited Clayton Act authority. *See generally* ALD VI, *supra* note 3, at 691. The ICPAC report focused its discussion on several agencies including the Surface Transportation Board (STB) (railroads), the FCC (telephone), and the U.S. Department of Transportation (airlines). ICPAC, *supra* note 2, at 148–51.

[5] *See* ALD VI, *supra* note 3, ch. 7.

[6] For example, the FCC and the STB review mergers in their respective industry sectors under "public interest" standards subject to little or no oversight by the federal antitrust agencies. 47 U.S.C. § 214(a); 47 U.S.C. § 310(d); 49 C.F.R. § 1180.1 (2010). The benchmark for the FCC in 47 U.S.C. § 214(a) for license transfers and acquisitions is "the present or future public convenience and necessity." The FCC test in 47 U.S.C. § 310(d) is the "public interest, convenience, and necessity." The STB in 49 C.F.R. § 1180.1 interprets the "public interest" standard as a balancing test that weighs the potential benefits to applicants and the public against the potential harm to the public.

[7] *See* ALD VI, *supra* note 3, at 624.

[8] For a detailed discussion of the DOJ's civil and criminal remedies, *see id.* at 687–724.

disgorgement of profits.[9] State attorneys general as *parens patriae* may seek direct damages on behalf of "natural persons" and injunctive relief under federal law.[10] Forty-seven states and the District of Columbia also have authority under state laws to seek some form of criminal penalty;[11] at least 21 states and the District of Columbia permit indirect purchasers to recover damages for state antitrust violations;[12] and virtually all states have the authority to recover direct damages on behalf of state agencies.[13]

11.01.2 Varying incentives and concerns

In addition to varying remedies, prospective plaintiffs often have varying incentives and concerns. Private plaintiffs and their counsel are often most interested in obtaining monetary damages and related, usually contingent, fee awards. State antitrust enforcers may be particularly sensitive to the effects of antitrust violations on the local and state level. Bid-rigging on state and local contracts, for example, may not only impose costs on local government but also have more macro-level implications by undermining the government's competitive bidding process. Similarly, a merger of large companies that operate in a local market is likely to be of acute concern to state antitrust enforcers because of the direct impact on the community.[14] Finally, states are particularly attentive to recovering

---

9 *See id.* at 656–64. An example of the FTC seeking disgorgement of profits can be found in the case of *In Re Lorazepam & Clorazepate Antitrust Litig.*, 205 F.R.D. 369, 2002–1 Trade Cas. (CCH) ¶73,649 (D.D.C. 2002), where the FTC, along with several states, agreed to settle with drug manufacturer Mylan Laboratories, Inc. in litigation where Mylan was accused of attempting to monopolize the markets for generic anti-anxiety drugs. The settlement provided over $71 million to consumers who purchased the drugs during the relevant period and a total of $100 million in disgorgement of Mylan's profits. Disgorgement can complicate damages awards and a disgorgement may mean that plaintiffs' lawyers do not receive the portion of the damages they would otherwise receive.

10 *See* ALD VI, *supra* note 3, at 724–25. For a detailed discussion of state *parens patriae* power, *see* Pennsylvania v. Playmobil USA, 1995–2 Trade Cas. (CCH) ¶71,215 (M.D. Pa. 1995); New York v. Reebok Int'l, 903 F. Supp. 532 (S.D.N.Y. 1995); *In re* Mid-Atlantic Toyota Antitrust Litig., 560 F. Supp. 760 (D. Md. 1983).

11 *See* ABA Section of Antitrust Law, State Antitrust Practice and Statutes, introduction (4th ed. 2009).

12 *See id.*

13 *See* ALD VI, *supra* note 3, at 725–26. For further discussion of remedies, see Chapter 9 of this Handbook.

14 In 1998, several states worked closely with the DOJ Antitrust Division in reviewing the proposed merger of Waste Management, Inc. and United Waste Services, Inc. The merger ultimately was cleared, but only after divestiture relating to numerous local solid waste disposal markets. *See* DOJ Antitrust Division, Antitrust Division Annual Report, Appendix B: Antitrust Merger Challenges, *United States and Commonwealth of Pennsylvania v. USA Waste Services, Inc., United Waste Systems, Inc., and Riviera Acquisition Corp. (8/22/97)* (1999), *available at* http://www.justice.gov/atr/public/4523h.htm (last visited Sept. 20, 2011) (merger challenge by United States and States of Ohio, Arizona, California, Colorado, Florida, Commonwealth of Kentucky, States of Maryland, Michigan, New York, Commonwealth of Pennsylvania, States of Texas, Washington, and Wisconsin). At one point in the review of this merger, the federal enforcers were prepared to resolve the case with divestitures affecting only the largest local markets. States not in those markets insisted that additional divestitures be discussed because of the likely impact on other local markets.

damages for their own citizens, especially in cases involving indirect purchasers who cannot recover damages under federal law.

Of course, when state attorneys general seek damages on behalf of their citizens or attempt to block a merger in federal court, their actions are governed by federal antitrust statutes and decisional law.[15] But when state attorneys general or private plaintiffs seek remedies under state antitrust law or state law applies to an action removed to federal court,[16] the same principles generally apply. Virtually all state antitrust provisions are patterned after or analogous to the Sherman Act, and many state statutes provide that the state antitrust provisions shall be interpreted consistently with federal precedent.[17] Therefore, the decisional law of the past century guides virtually all antitrust actions, regardless of the identity of the plaintiff in a particular action.

§ 11.02 Public enforcers often initiate cases before private plaintiffs

A common pattern for the interaction of private and public cases begins where a government enforcement agency initiates an investigation or even obtains indictments or guilty pleas. When the fact of the investigation or preliminary outcome becomes public in some form, "follow on" class actions are often filed in federal and state courts seeking damages for direct and indirect purchasers.[18] In many cases, these follow on actions are filed as soon as possible after a government investigation is made public, which may maximize an opportunity to act as lead counsel for the lawyers who file suit first.[19] This rush occurs even though plaintiffs are generally protected from the running of the statute of limitations in such cases.[20]

Follow-on private plaintiffs may be able to take advantage of factual developments and legal judgments established in government actions without having to expend the resources to duplicate the government's investigative and enforcement efforts. Section 5 of the Clayton Act provides that certain final judgments or decrees entered against a defendant in a government criminal or civil proceeding brought under the antitrust laws may be used in a subsequent private antitrust action as "*prima facie* evidence against such defendant . . . as to all matters respecting which said judgment or decree would be an estoppel as

---

[15] Even in the seminal case establishing the state attorneys general's authority to seek divestiture in merger cases notwithstanding a decision by the federal agencies to not challenge the merger, the states were held to be governed by the same substantive merger law. *See generally* California v. American Stores Co., 495 U.S. 271 (1990).

[16] Barry E. Hawk & Laraine L. Laudati, *Antitrust Federalism in the United States and Decentralization of Competition Law Enforcement in the European Union: A Comparison*, 20 Fordham Int'l L.J. 18, 21 (1996).

[17] ALD VI, *supra* note 3, at 623–24.

[18] *But see* discussion *infra* § 11.03 (private plaintiffs also may take the lead in initiating cases, with or without the government "following on").

[19] Some critics of this rush to the courthouse have argued that plaintiffs file baseless, duplicative actions as soon as the investigation is announced regardless of whether the private plaintiff has obtained anything more "than the fact of the investigation and conclusory allegations of collusive conduct." Steven F. Cherry & Gordon Pearson, *Why* Twombly *Does (and Should) Apply to All Private Antitrust Actions, Including Alleged Hard-Core Cartels*, 7 Antitrust Source 1, 6 (2007).

[20] Section 5(i) of the Clayton Act tolls the statute of limitations while some government suits are pending.

between the parties in the government suit."[21] Moreover, even though a judgment under a federal antitrust law is not proof of a violation under a parallel state antitrust law, the factual development from a federal action (based on federal law) can be employed in a subsequent state action.

At the same time that private plaintiffs may rely on judgments from governmental actions, the defendants' liability in a follow-on private action is generally unaffected by amounts paid out to government enforcers through civil forfeitures, damages, or criminal fines. Moreover, private plaintiffs can obtain treble damages awards and often attorneys' fees, and rarely face any real risk of paying defendants' attorneys fees.[22]

Perhaps in part because of these advantages of a follow-on or private suit, a very active plaintiffs' antitrust bar has emerged. The bar is comprised of large firms and solo practitioners specializing in private-plaintiff antitrust claims and, in many cases, the individual firm or attorney represents various plaintiffs in massive nationwide class actions.[23] There are firms that represent both plaintiffs and defendants in antitrust cases, but some of these must deal with the concomitant difficulties associated with practicing under two different business models. Perhaps most notably, it is typical for members of the plaintiffs' antitrust bar to represent clients on a contingency fee basis while members of the defense bar charge hourly fees.

The *DRAM* case exemplifies how a large-scale, privately-initiated antitrust suit can follow closely in the tracks of a government-led enforcement effort. In that case,[24] the DOJ obtained criminal indictments and guilty pleas against several dynamic random access memory (DRAM) producers and their executives.[25] A number of private class actions on behalf of indirect purchasers quickly followed, attempting to rely on the early groundwork completed by the federal enforcers. Almost three years later, 41 states filed antitrust claims for civil damages against a cartel of DRAM manufacturers for price-fixing over a period of several years.

While the inception of the private claims in the *DRAM* case demonstrates how the plaintiffs' bar can coalesce around a national assortment of direct and indirect purchasers, the difficulties these private plaintiffs have encountered demonstrate that private enforcers face their own unique legal challenges. In *DRAM*, in fact, the federal judge presiding over the consolidated multidistrict litigation concluded that indirect purchasers, who had purchased products *containing* DRAM but had not purchased DRAM itself, could not survive a motion for judgment on the pleadings under a number of state-based *Illinois Brick* repealer statutes because they did not "participate" in the DRAM market at issue in the case.[26] (The trial court's decision, not incidentally, is contrary to substantial author-

---

[21] ALD VI, *supra* note 3, at 977–78.

[22] *See* Robert H. Lande & Joshua P. Davis, *Benefits from Private Antitrust Enforcement: An Analysis of Forty Cases*, 42 U.S.F. L. Rev. 879 (2008).

[23] *See, e.g.*, California v. Infineon Technologies AG, No. 06-4333 (N.D. Cal. filed July 14, 2006) (involving 21 law firms representing over 21 parties).

[24] *Id.*

[25] Press Release, U.S. Dept. of Justice, Infineon Technologies AG Agrees to Plead Guilty to Participating in DRAM Price-Fixing Conspiracy (Sept. 15, 2008), *available at* http://www.usdoj.gov/atr/public/press_releases/2004/205437.pdf (last visited Oct. 6, 2011).

[26] *In re* Dynamic Random Access Memory (DRAM) Antitrust Litig., 536 F. Supp. 2d 1139 (N.D. Cal. 2008).

ity that an indirect purchaser can recover for damages stemming from overcharges for incorporated products.[27])

In addition, in the *Vitamins* indirect purchaser litigation, the DOJ similarly led the enforcement effort followed by a number of private indirect purchaser actions. Only after the DOJ obtained guilty pleas, and while the private actions were still pending, did a collection of state attorneys general eventually join with private plaintiffs' counsel in negotiating a comprehensive settlement. Despite the significant "overlap" among federal, state, and private enforcement actions, government and private enforcers coordinated on litigation strategies and settlement negotiations. Coordination between private plaintiffs and state attorneys general was particularly extensive and effective.[28] Indeed this state–private cooperation yielded $305 million dollars in settlement agreements for indirect, private purchasers.[29]

11.02.1 Applicability of rulings in prior government cases

Follow-on private-plaintiff lawsuits are facilitated by the applicability of rulings in prior government cases, which is provided for under federal law. Section 5(a) of the Clayton Act essentially allows private plaintiffs to shorten the relative distance between filing and collecting on an antitrust claim by "piggyback[ing] on public enforcement outcomes and work product."[30] Even those commentators seemingly opposed to private plaintiffs' "parasitic" or "piggyback" use of prior rulings in government antitrust cases will not deny its "obvious efficiency" for private plaintiffs and for the antitrust enforcement system as a whole.[31] As one critic – Professor Richard Epstein – concedes, the current policy allows plaintiffs and their counsel to review the content of prior rulings before committing their own resources to the task of private recovery. Regardless of whether, as some argue, this policy creates negative externalities,[32] the availability of the "piggyback" option remains a key part of antitrust enforcement in the United States.

In most cases, § 5(a) allows prior rulings to have conclusive and controlling effects over subsequent private actions under the collateral estoppel doctrine.[33] Under the collateral estoppel doctrine, a judgment in one case is conclusive on the issues litigated in that case

---

[27] *See, e.g., In re* Linerboard Antitrust Litig., 305 F.3d 145 (3d Cir. 2002); Holder v. Archer Daniels Midland Co., No. 96-2975, 1998 WL 1469620 (D.C. Super. Nov. 4, 1998); Comes v. Microsoft Corp., 646 N.W.2d 440 (Iowa 2002).

[28] Kevin O'Connor, *Is the* Ilinois Brick *Wall Crumbling?*, 15 ANTITRUST 34, 37 (2001).

[29] *Id.*

[30] David Rosenberg & James P. Sullivan, *Coordinating Private Class Action and Public Agency Enforcement of Antitrust Law*, 2 JNL. COMPETITION L. & ECON. 159, 161 (2006).

[31] Richard Epstein, *The Coordination of Public and Private Antitrust Actions, in* OECD POLICY ROUNDTABLES: PRIVATE REMEDIES 2007 (2008), http://www.oecd.org/dataoecd/24/62/39892177.pdf.

[32] Ilya R. Segal & Michael D. Whinston, *Public vs. Private Enforcement of Antitrust Law: A Survey, available at* http://ssrn.com/abstract=952067, p. 12.

[33] JULIAN O. VON KALINOWSKI, ANTITRUST LAWS AND TRADE REGULATION § 169 (2d ed. 2006) [hereinafter VON KALINOWSKI]. Section 5(a) was legislatively expanded in 1980 to recognize, by statute, that virtually all government antitrust rulings other than FTC rulings can have a collateral estoppel effect over privately-initiated antitrust actions. *Id.*

between those parties, and a party from that earlier case is precluded from re-litigating the issues from that case in a different, subsequent legal action, provided certain fairness criteria are met. A plaintiff's successful "offensive" use of collateral estoppel can obviate the need for virtually any fact-finding or judgments on the merits.[34] Where the same underlying facts are at issue, federal courts give the preclusive effect to a state court judgment to the extent permitted by that state's law.[35]

Moreover, even where the requirements of collateral estoppel are not satisfied, § 5(a) still offers an invaluable advantage to private antitrust plaintiffs. Specifically, antitrust plaintiffs may use prior government rulings to establish their *prima facie* case, essentially arriving at the courthouse steps with a rebuttable presumption of having proved their case.[36] The ready-made *prima facie* case dramatically reduces the amount of resources that a plaintiff or a group of plaintiffs must commit to survive initial dispositive motions. While such plaintiffs still carry a heavy burden of proving that they were specifically injured by the anticompetitive conduct alleged, it is cheaper and easier to prove one has been injured by an anticompetitive scheme when the existence of that scheme is assumed from the start.

Generally, consent judgments and *nolo contendere* pleas[37] arising from federal government antitrust actions will not shift burdens or otherwise reduce plaintiffs' burdens in private antitrust actions.[38] For any other government decision or decree exhibiting key criteria, however, private plaintiffs can take full advantage of the collateral estoppel or *prima facie* effect.

"Under the doctrine of non-mutual offensive collateral estoppel, 'a litigant who was not a party to a prior judgment may nevertheless use that judgment "offensively" to prevent a defendant from re-litigating issues resolved in the earlier proceeding.'"[39] For collateral estoppel to apply, several factors must be met. First, the judgment in favor of the government on which the private plaintiff wants to rely must be "final." This means the judgment must be fully litigated and completed at the trial court and appellate levels.[40] In other words, no aspect of the government's case may remain unresolved for the judgment to be "final."[41]

Second, the judgment must have been obtained in a suit brought by the United States via the DOJ or FTC. However, "[i]t has also been held that an appellate court judgment affirming and enforcing an FTC order is not admissible as prima facie evidence in

---

34 Collateral estoppel may also be employed to defend against an antitrust claim. "Defensive use [of collateral estoppel] occurs when a defendant seeks to prevent a plaintiff from asserting a claim the plaintiff has previously litigated and lost against another defendant." Parklane Hosiery Co. v. Shore, 439 U.S. 322, 326 n.4 (1979).

35 VON KALINOWSKI, *supra* note 33, § 169.05.

36 *Id.*

37 A *nolo contendre* plea is a "no contest" plea in which the defendant declines to contest or admit that he or she is guilty of the charges against him or her.

38 Some FTC decisions may carry a *prima facie* effect for purposes of § 5(a), however.

39 Discover Financial Services v. Visa USA. Inc., 598 F. Supp. 2d 394, 398 (S.D.N.Y. 2008) (quoting Parklane Hosiery Co. v. Shore, 439 U.S. 322, 326 (1979)).

40 VON KALINOWSKI, *supra* note 33, § 169.02.

41 Fifth & Walnut, Inc. v. Loew's Inc., 176 F.2d 587, 593 (2d Cir. 1949); VON KALINOWSKI, *supra* note 33, § 169.02.

a private suit since appellate review is instituted by the defendant, a private party, and accordingly is not a proceeding brought by the United States."[42]

Third, the judgment must have been obtained in an action arising under federal antitrust laws. This requirement is generally construed to include actions arising under the Sherman Act, Clayton Act, and Wilson Tariff Act, but the FTC Act is not included.[43]

Fourth, as noted above, the judgment cannot be a consent decree entered prior to taking testimony. This provision applies to *nolo contendere* pleas as well. If some testimony has been taken in a case, however, any resulting consent decree may have *prima facie* effect. In other words, the consent decree can be used as evidence that the defendant violated the antitrust laws. Similarly, defendants' guilty pleas are excluded from this provision.[44] The law is less clear on whether judgments arising from stipulated facts are also considered consent decrees and thus excluded from the *prima facie* effect.[45]

Fifth, the government judgment must assert an antitrust violation. In *Wendkos v. ABC Consolidated Corp.*, an FTC judgment that did not specify whether it related to violations of the FTC Act or one of the enumerated "antitrust laws" was not given any *prima facie* effect in a subsequent private action.[46]

While not an enumerated criterion, it also bears noting that government judgments will only carry a *prima facie* or collateral estoppel effect in a subsequent private plaintiff's favor as to issues that have been fully addressed by the adjudging court.[47] Issues that might have been adjudicated but were not cannot give rise to any outcome-determinative effect in a follow on action.[48] In addition, temporal and geographical limitations on prior judgments may limit their applicability to future plaintiffs.[49]

11.02.2 Limits on private plaintiffs' use of materials and information acquired in the government's suit

While the availability of collateral estoppel and *prima facie* treatment affords advantages to plaintiffs, these procedural advantages are not limitless in their value. In follow on actions attempting to rely on prior criminal proceedings, for example, plaintiffs may have limited access to key information and may not even be able to review key judgments and decrees because of secrecy relating to ongoing investigation of other criminal activities.

A full transcript of grand jury testimony in a federal government antitrust investigation might be of immense value to a civil plaintiff, but few plaintiffs attempting to obtain such testimony for follow on actions are able to meet the stringent "particularized need" standard required to obtain it.[50] Since grand jury testimony is presumptively secret, follow

---

42 Von Kalinowski, *supra* note 33, § 169.02[b][1].
43 *Id.*; Lawrence A. Sullivan & Warren S. Grimes, Law of Antitrust: An Integrated Handbook § 17.8 (2d ed. 2006).
44 Thomas V. Vakerics, Antitrust Basics § 3.03[3][a] (2009).
45 Von Kalinowski, *supra* note 33, § 169.02.
46 379 F. Supp. 15, 21 (E.D. Pa. 1974).
47 Von Kalinowski, *supra* note 33, § 169.04.
48 *Id.*
49 *Id.*
50 *See* Douglas Oil Co. v. Petrol Stops Northwest, 441 U.S. 211 (1979).

on private plaintiffs rarely have the benefit of any such testimony when pursuing their own claims.[51] Since private plaintiffs also face increasingly demanding standards for detailed notice pleading (pursuant to the Supreme Court's *Twombly* decision, which is discussed below), grand jury secrecy constitutes a more significant hurdle for private enforcers than their government counterparts.

Furthermore, guilty pleas in the antitrust context often relate only to narrow pieces of larger conspiracies, and accordingly represent only a portion of a plaintiff's overall case.

To be sure, government antitrust defendants are well aware of the risks that await them after government proceedings conclude. Nothing prevents government defendants from negotiating for settlements that are of as little value as possible to any other private party. Still, as Von Kalinowski notes, the very threat of follow on plaintiffs' lawyers opportunistically cashing in on the government's work serves an important social purpose: taxpayers save money on antitrust enforcement when government defendants feel compelled to negotiate consent decrees that carry collateral estoppel or *prima facie* effects.[52]

§ 11.03 Private plaintiffs take the lead in initiating some cases

"The genius of the U.S. legal system is that it allows private parties to remedy wrongs, hold tortfeasors accountable, and deter future violations without government action. Congress intended no less in enacting the Sherman and Clayton Acts. . . ."[53] Among critics of the private enforcement model, the stereotypical follow on plaintiff is merely a disgruntled competitor incapable of competing with the defendant in a free market and resorting to opportunistic but meritless private antitrust claims against a government-penalized competitor to secure a windfall or more favorable market conditions.[54] Another popular archetype is the indirect purchaser seemingly happy with, for example, her computer, and indifferent to anyone's litigation costs until a clever plaintiff's attorney convinces her

---

[51] FED. R. CRIM. P. 6(e)(2)(B) (imposing secrecy on grand jury testimony and proceedings).

[52] VON KALINOWSKI, *supra* note 33, § 169.01.

[53] William J. Blechman, *Why Twombly Does Not (And Should Not) Apply to Hard Core Cartels*, 7 ANTITRUST SOURCE 1, 7 (2007).

[54] Cherry & Pearson, *supra* note 19, at 6 (criticizing private plaintiffs who race to the courthouse to file what turn out to be entirely baseless complaints based on "vague press reports" immediately following the heels of a government action against the same defendants); Lande & Davis, *supra* note 22, at 883–89 (summarizing criticisms of private antitrust enforcement); *see also* Interview with J. Thomas Rosch, Commissioner, Federal Trade Commission, 23 ANTITRUST 32, 43 (2009). In this interview, FTC Commissioner Rosch noted that while he witnessed abuses in treble damages class actions, the private bar also can play an important role in protecting consumers, and courts should consider the most effective way of curing the abuses without adversely affecting private antitrust actions that curb anticompetitive conduct. He stated:

> What happens is that by shrinking substantive antitrust principles, which we've seen in *Credit Suisse* and *Trinko* for example, out of a concern about private litigation, that can slop over into public enforcement and it can hobble public enforcement as well. I don't think that's a sound way to address concerns about private treble class action abuses. Rather, I think a much sounder way is for the Supreme Court to consider remedying those abuses directly, head on.

Id.

that she can get some easy money by putting her name on a complaint against a foreign electronics supplier already prosecuted by a government agency.

In many cases, however, private plaintiffs have superior or timelier information by virtue of being direct market participants. "Private parties have superior information about potential violations and the resulting harm" thanks to their crucial possession of "decentralized knowledge" unavailable to the government.[55] Because they are sometimes better positioned to uncover antitrust violations, private plaintiffs are not always relegated to follow on status. As recent research has demonstrated, private plaintiffs have led the way more frequently than previously realized. Professors Robert Lande and Joshua Davis discovered in their 2008 research that more than one-third of 40 large, privately-initiated antitrust suits studied were not preceded by government action.[56] While "piggybacking" remains common, it is far from the only type of private action that is brought.

Indeed, in some cases it may be the government itself "piggybacking" on private investigative and enforcement efforts. As Lande, Davis, and other commentators have noted, the *Visa/MasterMoney* case involved private-plaintiff efforts upon which government enforcers subsequently relied.[57]

11.03.1 Advantages of private enforcement

Whether subsequently used by the government or not, these private actions represent a sizeable component of government enforcement policy. Focusing on 40 large, successful antitrust actions between 1998 and 2008, Lande and Davis found that private plaintiffs recovered between $7.631 and $8.981 billion from the 15 cases that did not follow or arise simultaneously with a government action.[58] Instead, the government followed the private plaintiffs' suit or the government did not commence an action at all. By enabling these actions to proceed from inception to completion, federal and state governments effectively achieved billions of dollars in recovery in just a 10-year period, along with some measure of accompanying deterrence, without spending any taxpayer dollars.[59] By including a "private" component, U.S. antitrust policy effectively outsourced a portion of its enforcement role and gave taxpayers a massive return on essentially no investment. As Lande and Davis assert, these cases "have saved the United States taxpayer tremendous sums in enforcement costs by shifting the enormous burdens and risks of litigating against sophisticated, well-financed lawbreakers to private plaintiffs' counsel."[60] Moreover, the authors found that fines resulting from private actions are a greater deterrent than fines or criminal prosecutions imposed by the DOJ.[61]

---

55 Segal & Whinston, *supra* note 32, at 4.

56 Lande & Davis, *supra* note 22, at 898, Table 3. The 40 cases were merely representative of large cases won by or settled to the benefit of the plaintiffs bringing the action.

57 *See, e.g., In re* Visa Check/MasterMoney Antitrust Litig., 297 F. Supp. 2d 503, 524 n.31 (E.D.N.Y. 2003) (noting that the "government piggybacked on Class Counsel's efforts").

58 Lande & Davis, *supra* note 22, at 897–99. That amount is cash and does not include "products, services, discounts, coupons, [or] injunctive relief." *Id.* at 891.

59 *Id.* at 898.

60 *Id.* at 905.

61 *Id.* at 895.

However, it deserves noting that participants in the DOJ Antitrust Division's Corporate Leniency Program are eligible for relief from the full amount of damages which a private plaintiff would otherwise be entitled to recover. The leniency program grants amnesty from criminal prosecution to the first member of an illegal conspiracy that reports the illegal conduct to the government and cooperates with the ensuing investigation. The Antitrust Criminal Penalty Enhancement and Reform Act (ACPERA) of 2004 limits the civil liability of the amnesty program's participants.[62] Participants' damages in a follow-on private lawsuit are limited to the actual damages incurred by the antitrust plaintiff. This means that under ACPERA, the plaintiff cannot recover treble damages from a participant in the leniency program, which is intended to incentivize those involved in illegal activity to report the criminal activity.[63]

The vast availability of "private attorneys general" able to take the lead on antitrust enforcement prevents the dilution of public enforcement through budgetary constraints and electoral politics. Government enforcers operate on fixed budgets and have strong normative and pragmatic disincentives to pursue cases they are unlikely to win.[64] State and federal prosecutors shy away from hard-to-prove cases not only because they have fewer resources, but also because they often have rational but "selfish" motives to "bring cases that the agency will win" and burnish their own credentials accordingly.[65] To "pick and choose" the low hanging fruit makes too much sense for an agency and its individual attorneys.[66]

Nor can these government officials be expected to be impervious to political pressures. As many legal commentators and historians have long noted, government-led antitrust enforcement came to a standstill during the presidency of Ronald Reagan, did not approach the pre-Reagan level until the second term of the Clinton presidency, and has arguably never risen all the way to its pre-Reagan levels.[67] Turnover among state attorneys general (who are sometimes referred to as "governors in training") can similarly affect state-level enforcement.

Finally, no discussion of this subject would be complete without noting that the interest of some states in the Microsoft litigation originated in the perceived weakness of the decree negotiated by DOJ and Microsoft in 1994–95.[68] In 1998, several states began

---

62 Pub. L. 108–237 (2004), 118 Stat. 665 (2004). ACPERA was reauthorized in 2010 and will remain in effect until at least 2020 pursuant to the Antitrust Criminal Penalty Enhancement and Reform Act of 2004 Extension Act. Pub. L. No. 111-190 (2010).

63 For a discussion of how the leniency program and ACPERA can assist a private plaintiff in deciding whether to bring a case, see Chapter 2 of this *Handbook*; for a discussion of the utility of the leniency program and ACPERA as evidence gathering tools for private plaintiffs, see Chapter 7 of this Handbook.

64 Lande & Davis, *supra* note 22, at 906.

65 Sullivan and Grimes, *supra* note 43, § 17.1c.

66 *Id.*

67 *See* Ernest Gelhorn, William E. Kovacic & Stephen Calkins, Antitrust Law and Economics in a Nutshell Section XIII.A.1 (5th ed. 2004); Lande & Davis, *supra* note 22, at 915.

68 *See* United States v. Microsoft Corp., 159 F.R.D. 318, 330–38 (D.D.C.) (finding proposed consent decree was not in the public interest because it failed to address all of Microsoft's alleged anticompetitive behavior and did not have an effective monitoring mechanism), *rev'd and remanded,* 56 F.3d 1448 (D.C. Cir. 1995).

investigating Microsoft shortly after the entry of the federal decree and eventually began pressing the DOJ to join them in bringing a broader case against Microsoft that would address a wide array of conduct. Although the remedy obtained was not wholly effective, the D.C. Circuit's decision on liability is an important statement of the applicability of the antitrust laws to a significant industry.[69] The *Microsoft* case is illustrative of the manner in which an intermixing of state enforcers, private enforcers, and federal enforcers, in service of diverse constituencies, can collectively shape enforcement outcomes, a subject that is further discussed *infra* in § 11.04.

11.03.2 Difficulties faced by private plaintiffs

While private plaintiffs have been a part of national and state-level antitrust enforcement for over a century, and can derive advantages from the collateral estoppel and *prima facie* effects of prior rulings, they also bear their own unique difficulties.

First, while the government possesses the statutory standing to enforce its own laws, private antitrust plaintiffs must prove that they have standing to sue based on their actual connection to the alleged wrongdoing. Antitrust standing is among the most debated but least settled areas of antitrust law, and the hurdles imposed by this amorphous standing doctrine have limited the access of competitor plaintiffs to legal relief.[70] Among the most slippery elements required to prove antitrust standing is proving antitrust injury.

Antitrust injury is "injury of the type the antitrust laws were intended to prevent and that flows from that which makes defendants' acts unlawful."[71] This means the alleged injury must be proximately caused by the anticompetitive conduct that is the subject of the lawsuit. In *Blue Shield of Virginia, v. McCready*, the U.S. Supreme Court explained that the standard did not require fixed indicia on price or output.[72] But a plaintiff must show that its injury-in-fact was "inextricably intertwined with the injury" the defendants sought to cause.[73]

While this discussion does not attempt to recapture the entire history of the antitrust injury doctrine, the key limitation preventing many private plaintiffs from reaching trial is the requirement that a plaintiff show injury not just to itself, but to competition in the relevant market.[74] Accordingly, mere allegations of lost profits or constrained production are not sufficient to establish standing.[75] While individual plaintiffs may have superior information about the harms they themselves have sustained, demonstrating harm to the market through discovery but before trial can sometimes prevent otherwise viable antitrust claims from being asserted.[76]

In addition, the U.S. Supreme Court's controversial *Twombly* opinion and its progeny

---

69 United States v. Microsoft Corp., 253 F.3d 34 (D.C. Cir.), *cert. denied*, 534 U.S. 952 (2001).

70 SULLIVAN & GRIMES, *supra* note 43, § 17.1a.

71 Atlantic Richfield Co. v. USA Petroleum Co., 495 U.S. 328, 334 (1990).

72 457 U.S. 465, 482 (1982).

73 *Id.* at 484.

74 *See* Brunswick Corp. v. Pueblo Bowl-O-Mat, 429 U.S. 477 (1977).

75 *Id.*

76 For further discussion of antitrust standing and antitrust injury, see Chapter 3 of this Handbook.

further raise the bar for private plaintiffs.[77] Under *Twombly*, private antitrust plaintiffs bringing § 1 claims must plead the conspiratorial activity in sufficient detail just to survive a motion to dismiss.[78] This recent holding represents a key victory for defendants who can now effectively subject any private plaintiff to a more stringent notice-pleading requirement through a motion to dismiss before such a plaintiff can even obtain basic discovery.

Accordingly, even as private plaintiffs can avoid some of the burdens carried by government enforcers, they must satisfy a range of other requirements before presenting their claims to a jury, much less obtaining discovery.

§ 11.04 Coordinated action among private and public plaintiffs

Given the multiplicity of enforcers and the varying incentives each is given under federal and state antitrust laws, it is unlikely that any serious antitrust violation will not be the subject of at least one, and probably several, overlapping lawsuits. For example, after the members of the vitamin price-fixing cartel were prosecuted criminally by the DOJ, they were subsequently subjected to follow on private civil suits in federal court for damages incurred by direct purchasers in addition to private and state suits for damages incurred by indirect purchasers.[79] This pattern of litigation raises issues about litigation costs and optimal procedures for resolving overlapping claims.[80] On the other hand, the multiplicity of antitrust enforcers does minimize the possibility that valuable cases will be overlooked. To the extent the system encourages the filing of cases with little or no merit (something the authors do not concede),[81] the courts are given an opportunity to dismiss those cases at various stages of the litigation, thereby creating precedents that enhance the transparency of antitrust law. Professor Jean Burns takes the argument even further and asserts

---

[77] Bell Atlantic Corp. v. Twombly, 550 U.S. 544 (2007).

[78] *Id.* at 555–57.

[79] Harry First, *The Vitamins Case: Cartel Prosecutions and the Coming of International Competition Law*, 68 Antitrust L. J. 711, 712–19 (2001); Joel M. Cohen & Trisha Lawson, *Navigating Multistate Indirect Purchaser Lawsuits*, 15 Antitrust 29, 31 (2001); Michael L. Denger & D. Jarrett Arp, *Does Our Multifaceted Enforcement System Promote Sound Competition Policy?*, 15 Antitrust 41, 41 (2001).

[80] *See, e.g.*, Cohen & Lawson, *supra* note 79, at 33.

[81] The American Antitrust Institute has found:

> The frivolous litigation myth is premised on the idea that plaintiffs will bring weak claims in order to obtain settlements and that defendants will settle such claims in order to avoid the costs of discovery . . . or the small risk of "massive exposure" that may accompany class actions as a result of treble damages, joint and several liability, and fee shifting . . . Both theories are seriously flawed.
>
> * * *
>
> Beyond the flawed theory, the claim of widespread frivolous antitrust litigation is unsupported in fact. It is not simply that there are no empirical studies to support the claim; there are apparently no good examples of settlements of frivolous antitrust suits. And absent such settlements, class action plaintiffs have nothing to gain by bringing such suits. The evidence suggests that if there is a problem with class action settlements in antitrust cases, it is that plaintiffs sometimes settle strong cases for too little, not weak cases for too much. In sum, there is simply no basis to believe that frivolous antitrust class actions are a significant problem.

that "by bringing inconsistency, unpredictability, and flat-out contradictions into the law, federalism enhances antitrust jurisprudence," reminding us that we do not yet have all the answers about appropriate antitrust policy and that reasonable minds can and do differ about the appropriate goals of antitrust policies.[82]

Overlapping representation results in part from the interplay of *parens patriae* authority and private class actions. Some of the differences between the states and private plaintiffs' ability and incentive to bring cases are discussed here.

11.04.1 Parens patriae *actions*

Federal law allows the federal government and certain private plaintiffs to sue for violations of antitrust law, but also allows state attorneys general to file antitrust claims for monetary damages on behalf of "natural persons" under *parens patriae* authority found in § 4(c) of the Clayton Act.[83]

Under this authority, a state attorney general acts much like a class representative in a private class action suit, but need not obtain "certification," nor prove that she is a proper representative for a class of aggrieved consumers.[84] State attorneys general also have authority to initiate actions on behalf of the state as a purchaser of goods and services.[85]

When undertaken in conjunction with private class actions, this federally derived *parens patriae* authority allows for the overlap of concurrently pending cases, ostensibly pursued on behalf of many of the same consumers. While defendants face additional challenges in this "overlap" environment, state attorneys general and private plaintiffs often find that coordinating two overlapping actions poses challenges of its own.

Unlike private plaintiff actions, for example, federally-initiated *parens* actions are limited to damages to natural persons (not businesses) who were direct purchasers, arising from Sherman Act violations.[86] However, should plaintiffs falling within the permitted scope of such a *parens* action obtain relief through the attorney general, they may not separately seek duplicative relief as private plaintiffs.[87] The recovery is essentially the same for plaintiffs in a *parens* action and a private action. The main distinction is that private plaintiffs' attorneys usually take a contingency fee out of the total damages awarded while attorneys general will receive their attorney fees as a separate damages award from the defendant(s). Likewise, plaintiffs who have already obtained private relief may not be

---

AMERICAN ANTITRUST INSTITUTE, THE NEXT ANTITRUST AGENDA: THE AMERICAN ANTITRUST INSTITUTE'S TRANSITION REPORT ON COMPETITION POLICY TO THE 44TH PRESIDENT OF THE UNITED STATES 231–34 (ALBERT A. FOER ED., 2008).

[82] Jean Wegman Burns, *Embracing Both Faces of Antitrust Federalism:* Parker *and* ARC America Corp., 68 ANTITRUST L. J., 29, 41–42 (2000). A debate on the role of concentration in antitrust analysis was the focus of a proceeding under the auspices of the ABA Antitrust Section. REPORT OF THE TASK FORCE ON FUNDAMENTAL THEORY (July 2001).

[83] 15 U.S.C. § 15(c). For an introduction and explanation of the *parens patriae* authority generally, see Chapter 4 of this Handbook.

[84] New York v. Reebok Int'l, 96 F.3d 44, 46 (2d Cir. 1996).

[85] Georgia v. Pennsylvania R.R. Co., 324 U.S. 439 (1945).

[86] *See* 15 U.S.C. § 15(c); *see also* Illinois Brick Co. v. Illinois, 431 U.S. 720 (1977).

[87] 15 U.S.C. § 15c(b)(3).

included in damages calculations in a *parens* action.[88] States can also seek civil penalties through *parens* actions, which are unavailable to private plaintiffs.

While these *parens* actions sometimes precede private class actions, in other cases a private class will be certified before the filing of a federally-derived *parens* claim, effectively making the *parens* action subordinate to the private class as a potential judgment creditor. While this diminished stature as a potential creditor might seem to remove the largest incentive to bring a *parens* action, a state attorney general electing to proceed with such a case may simply conclude that the certified class is not sufficiently representative of the full population of injured parties, and may also be responding to political incentives.

Notably, nearly half of all states also provide statutory authority for their attorneys general to initiate *parens* actions in state court, in some instances with fewer restrictions than the federal *parens* authority.[89] While such state-derived *parens* actions may still be removed to a multi-district litigation (MDL) forum under the preemptive federal procedural code,[90] these state *parens* actions are not subject to the Class Action Fairness Act of 2005 (CAFA).[91] In instances in which state *parens* actions come first, private plaintiffs may view the existence of a state-driven action as a source of additional leverage to obtain a more favorable settlement upon attaining certification.

A practical example of the ways in which overlapping private and *parens* actions can add complexity is settlement. When a private class action and a state *parens* action addressing the same anticompetitive conduct proceed to settlement, states may assert that their *parens* claims are separate and superior to the claims of the private class.[92]

Twombly may alter the nature of private enforcement's interactions with state *parens* enforcers. *Twombly*, discussed *supra*, holds antitrust plaintiffs to a more stringent standard of articulating details about an alleged anticompetitive act before being permitted to proceed to discovery.[93] As private plaintiffs may be less equipped than before to survive preliminary motions to dismiss and obtain discovery, states may play a greater role in coordinating pre-complaint investigations with private plaintiffs.

11.04.2 Private class actions

A recent study of private antitrust enforcement found that the "growth [of private antitrust cases] is fuelled by extraordinary increases in the number of antitrust class action

---

[88] *Id.* at § 15c(a)(1)(A).

[89] *See, e.g.,* Conn. Gen. Stat. § 35-32(c) (2011) (allowing attorney general to initiate *parens* actions on behalf of "persons," not just "natural persons").

[90] *Parens* actions may also be removed to federal court on diversity grounds, depending on a court's determination of whether diversity exists among the defendants and the real parties in interest. *See* Hood v. F. Hoffmann-La Roche, Ltd., 639 F. Supp. 2d 25, 31–34 (D.D.C. 2009).

[91] The Fifth Circuit recently cautioned, however, that a state *parens* case may not avoid CAFA's reach if it were not "truly" a *parens* action but something else in disguise. Louisiana *ex rel.* Caldwell v. Allstate Ins. Co., 536 F.3d 418 (5th Cir. 2008).

[92] *See In re* Compact Disc, No. 00-1361 (D. Me. Oct. 21, 2002) (class definition in settlement agreement excluded natural persons in plaintiff states). For further discussion of settlement practice and strategy in private antitrust cases, see Chapter 12 of this Handbook.

[93] *See Twombly*, 550 U.S. at 544.

lawsuits filed in recent years."[94] The authors of this study found that class actions now constitute 70 percent of antitrust cases, while they constituted only 15 percent of antitrust cases 10 years ago.[95] While many class actions are duplicative (i.e., not each case represents different anticompetitive conduct engaged in by a different defendant), this trend is significant.

To maintain an antitrust class action, a plaintiff must meet the same requirements of any class action brought under Federal Rule of Civil Procedure 23 or a state equivalent. Most states have laws allowing class actions and most of them track Rule 23 of the Federal Rules.[96]

> Careful application of Rule 23 accords with the pivotal status of class certification in large-scale litigation because "denying or granting class certification is often the defining moment in class actions (for it may sound the 'death knell' of the litigation on the part of the plaintiffs, or create unwarranted pressure to settle nonmeritorious claims on the part of the defendants)."[97]

To satisfy the requirements under Rule 23(a): (1) the class must be sufficiently numerous that joinder of all the class members is impracticable; (2) there must be questions of law or fact common to the class; (3) the claims of the party or parties representing the class must be typical of the class claims; and (4) the representative party or parties must adequately represent the interests of the class. In addition to the numerosity, commonality, typicality, and adequacy of representation requirements, Rule 23(b) also requires the plaintiff to show that (1) requiring individual suits by the putative class members would create the risk of inconsistent rulings, or that a ruling on one individual class member's claim may be dispositive of other class members' claims and thus "substantially impair[ing] or imped[ing] their ability to protect their interests"; (2) the party against whom the putative class seeks relief has acted or refused to act on grounds generally applicable to the class, "so that final injunctive relief or corresponding declaratory relief is appropriate respecting the class as a whole"; or (3) common questions of law or fact predominate over individual questions, and that proceeding by way of class action would be "superior to other available methods for fairly and efficiently adjudicating the controversy." In analyzing whether the class action is superior to alternative legal routes of remedying the anticompetitive conduct at issue, some courts have deferred to pending *parens patriae* actions.[98]

CAFA decreased the likelihood that private parties can maintain a class action in state court. Now defendants can remove to federal court a class action based on state law claims if: "(1) minimal diversity exists between members of the plaintiff class and the defendants;

---

[94] Joseph Ostoyich, David Emanuelson, & Parker Normann, *More of the Same: Growth in Private Antitrust Litigation and Cutbacks by the US Supreme Court* 46, *in* The Antitrust Review of the Americas (2009), *available at* http://www.globalcompetitionreview.com/reviews/9/sections/27/chapters/351/more-same-growth-private-antitrust-litigation-cutbacks-us-supreme-court/.

[95] *Id.*

[96] The nuances of state class action law, of which there are many, are beyond the scope of this chapter.

[97] *In re* Hydrogen Peroxide Antitrust Litig., 552 F.3d 305, 310 (3d Cir. 2008) (quoting Newton v. Merrill Lynch, Pierce, Fenner & Smith, Inc., 259 F.3d 154, 162 (3d Cir. 2001).

[98] ALD VI, *supra* note 3, at 906. For a detailed discussion of class actions generally and the Rule 23 requirements in particular, see Chapter 5 of this Handbook.

(2) the aggregate value of the individual class members' claims exceeds $5 million dollars; (3) the number of putative class members exceeds 100; and (4) the defendants are not 'States, State officials, or other government entities.'"[99] CAFA does not, in practice, apply to *parens patriae* actions brought by state enforcers. This means that these cases can stay in state court while (perhaps overlapping) private class actions may be removed to federal court.[100]

Since states' *parens patriae* authority generally extends only to natural persons, and does not include businesses, only private lawyers can ordinarily bring actions on behalf of direct purchasers or intermediate indirect purchasers. It is not just state attorneys general who can represent government entities in class actions. In most states, private class actions could include state agencies as part of the class, although most plaintiffs' lawyers simply exclude all governmental entities. With respect to cases representing consumer indirect purchasers, state *parens* actions generally take priority over private actions. States can seek certain remedies, such as civil penalties, that private plaintiffs cannot.

11.04.3 Overlapping lawsuits: Case examples

The issues surrounding overlapping private–public lawsuits are best illustrated through actual examples of concurrent, or even competing, enforcers choosing alternative paths.

Hartford Fire Insurance Co. v. California[101] is an example of a case which the DOJ Antitrust Division declined to investigate despite a direct request to do so by several states.[102] In the face of federal inaction, 19 states sued 32 insurers, reinsurers, and an important trade association of insurers, alleging boycotts of certain types of business and municipal insurance. The states were particularly sensitive to these violations because their own municipalities and governmental agencies were unable to obtain liability insurance from the domestic commercial property and casualty insurers, allegedly due to a conspiracy among domestic insurers, domestic and foreign reinsurers, and the trade association representing the domestic industry. In other words, although the conspiracy was international in scope, the effects of the conspiracy were felt most acutely at the local level. Ultimately, the states prevailed on three important issues in the Supreme Court, including the issue concerning the ability of U.S. courts to reach the conduct of foreign reinsurers operating largely outside of the United States. The case settled for important structural relief.[103]

---

99 ALD VI, *supra* note 3, at 882.

100 For further discussion of CAFA, see Chapters 4 and 5 of this Handbook.

101 509 U.S. 764 (1993). There are numerous additional examples that could be cited in industries as diverse as national debit cards, cable television, and retail grocery. *See generally* ALD VI, *supra* note 3, ch. 15.

102 In 1987, several states asked the DOJ Antitrust Division to investigate the property and casualty insurance industry, including several syndicates of Lloyd's of London. The Division declined to do so. *See* Michael F. Brockmeyer, *State Antitrust Enforcement*, 57 Antitrust L. J. 169, 170 n.4 (1988).

103 The structural relief included transforming the Insurance Services Office, the principle trade association of commercial insurers, from an organization dominated by the industry into one controlled by non-industry board members. Also, two independent organizations were created from resources contributed by the defendant insurers and reinsurers to provide key services to

Many of the international cartel cases now resulting in antitrust enforcement by the DOJ Antitrust Division are premised on the precedent established by *Hartford Fire Insurance*.[104] Had the system not provided concurrent authority to the states (and private plaintiffs who represented various affected classes of injured parties), not only would the conspiracy have continued, but an important piece of decisional authority would not have been created.

Similarly, *In Re NASDAQ Market-Makers Antitrust Litigation* is another high-profile example where private plaintiffs acted despite the inaction of federal enforcers.[105] In this litigation, private plaintiffs sued several NASDAQ market-makers after learning about a potential bid-rigging activity first exposed in a business journal.[106] The activity essentially involved a "rounding up" of specific bid/ask spreads, which resulted in substantially higher spreads (and higher broker/dealer profits) than with comparable securities traded on other markets.[107] At the time, the settlement ($1.027 billion) was apparently the largest antitrust recovery in history. Both the DOJ and the Securities and Exchange Commission began formal investigations of the activity only after the private suits had already been filed, and not without questioning whether collusion could have occurred as a matter of economic theory.[108] In fact, the federal district court approving the settlement emphasized that the private plaintiffs "[awoke] the federal government to . . . price collusion that the government had previously ignored," and "pulled the laboring oar in advancing this case."[109]

These examples illustrate how the role of private plaintiffs can generate opportunities for the courts to develop important precedents even where the national enforcers choose not to act. This constant testing of facts against theory facilitates the emergence of a meaningful consensus or, at least, a sharpening of the antitrust dialogue. The various circuit courts of appeal rely on reported decisions from each other as persuasive but not controlling precedent, facilitating a convergence of national antitrust enforcement policy and highlighting the outstanding areas of doctrinal differences. The concurrent enforcement system in the United States allows the United States to assume a leadership role globally not only because it is a leader in governmental enforcement,[110] but because its system generates a wide range of decisional law and allows most parties entitled to relief under the antitrust laws to commence an action for recovery.

---

governmental entities seeking to insure outside of the commercial market. *See* Michael L. Weiner, *Developments at the Division, in the Court, and in Congress: The Increasing Internationalization of Antitrust*, 8 ANTITRUST 31, 31 (1993) (discussing the case and settlement).

[104] Hartford Fire Insurance Co. v. California, 509 U.S. 764 (1993). *See* O'Connor, *supra* note 28, at 34, 38. *See also* Robert Skitol & James Meyers, *Ten Milestones In Twentieth Century Antitrust Law and Their Importance to the Decade Ahead*, 1 ANTITRUST REPORT 6 (2000) (listing *Hartford Fire Insurance* as a "milestone case" in the field of antitrust law).

[105] 184 F.R.D. 506 (S.D.N.Y. 1999).

[106] Arthur M. Kaplan, *Antitrust as a Public-Private Partnership: A Case Study of the NASDAQ Litigation*, 21 CASE W. RES. L. REV. 111 (2001).

[107] *Id.*

[108] *Id.* at 116 n.17 and accompanying text.

[109] *Id.* at 112 n.4 and accompanying text (citing Affidavit of Columbia Professor John C. Coffee, Jr., ¶24). In more colorful language, the private parties' role was described as "not a case where plaintiffs' counsel can be cast as jackals to the government's lion, arriving on the scene after some enforcement or administrative agency has made the kill." *Id.* at 112.

[110] *See* First, *supra* note 79, at 731–32.

None of this is meant to assume away the relative merits of more centralized enforcement systems: less complexity, greater predictability due to fewer decisionmakers, more uniformity, and lower compliance/litigation costs. However, decentralized systems tend to generate more case law and fewer false negative enforcement decisions because there is no monopolization of the enforcement decision-making apparatus. While it is not possible to quantify these costs and benefits in a meaningful manner, it is possible to appreciate the dynamic nature of the American system even while we attempt to minimize the costs associated with it.

11.04.4 Coordination problems and solutions

Private plaintiffs and public enforcers practice under and are guided by substantially the same substantive law, and frequently represent, or at least attempt to represent, overlapping groups of individuals, businesses, and other entities that claim to be injured by violations of the antitrust laws. But, as discussed throughout this chapter, private plaintiffs and public enforcers operate according to varying incentives, are subject to varying constraints, and are entitled to varying remedies. As a result of these differences, there may be tensions between the private plaintiffs and public enforcers. To best achieve the overarching objective of stopping the alleged anticompetitive conduct and providing relief to victims of the conduct, private plaintiffs and public enforcers should coordinate their efforts as much as possible. At the very least, they should communicate on a consistent basis and determine at what points and for what litigation tasks the private plaintiffs and public enforcers can coordinate.

Generally, there are three phases to a civil lawsuit in which issues arise about coordination between private plaintiffs and public enforcers: (1) investigative and precomplaint case strategy; (2) litigation; and (3) settlement or arbitration. What follows is a description of best practices for coordination between private plaintiffs and public enforcers.

11.04.4(A) The investigative and precomplaint case strategy phase

An issue that arises in this phase is whether public enforcers, when in the process of investigating or developing enforcement actions, should encourage private class counsel to represent parties not represented by the government. Where the investigation is confidential, the government will be precluded from sharing information with private parties. But where there are no confidentiality concerns, the government may find it beneficial to encourage the involvement of private parties, especially if the governmental entity is facing budget constraints. Not only does a private lawsuit mean that the anticompetitive conduct with which the government is concerned may be stopped, but private counsel may be able to identify for the government additional cases for investigation. As discussed in Chapter 6 of this Handbook, *Twombly* and its progeny pose challenges to private parties who may be unable to meet the stricter pleading standard set forth in that case. After *Twombly*, there may be cases in which private plaintiffs should, or must, cede to the government, as the *Twombly* standard does not apply to governmental actions.

Another issue that arises in this initial, investigative phase is whether state enforcers should bring overlapping actions where there is no concern about the quality of representation in the private action and there is no specific need for governmental involvement (for example, where specific injunctive relief – conduct or structural – which is more likely to be sought and obtained by government plaintiffs, is not at issue). In such cases, the governmental entity considering suit should determine whether an overlapping suit – even an investigation – is worth the resources. State attorneys general must consider public finance and budgetary constraints. Of course this is not to suggest that private plaintiffs all have access to unlimited resources – they too may be constrained with limited funds to devote to an antitrust lawsuit that will likely require retaining experts, reviewing enormous amounts of discovery, taking and defending numerous depositions, and engaging in extensive briefing on complex matters. But the source of and method of addressing financial constraints differ in the private and public realms.[111]

There are distinct advantages to overlapping suits, and there are circumstances under which they should be pursued. The government can add credibility to an action while the private bar can perhaps bring greater resources. In addition, the parties can avoid future potential conflicts in class actions involving both direct and indirect purchasers.

In practice, governmental agencies may want to reserve the initiation of an overlapping suit for compelling cases. State enforcers may also wish to adopt selection criteria for bringing indirect purchaser cases. In addition, state enforcers may assign highest priority to cases in which there is a need for specific injunctive relief; there are insufficient – if any – private plaintiff or adequate class counsel; the anticompetitive conduct at issue is egregious; or no other governmental entity has dealt with the conduct.

In the event the government decides to pursue an investigation in anticipation of bringing suit, the public and private parties should discuss how to proceed most efficiently, including at settlement. Private plaintiffs and public enforcers should discuss as soon as practicable a case management strategy.

11.04.4(B) LITIGATION PHASE

There are several principles that private plaintiffs and public enforcers may employ to guide a coordinated action. First, private plaintiffs and public enforcers should enter into common interest agreements as soon as practicable to protect joint work product.[112] This should be completed as soon as possible to allow the maximum confidentiality protection. Second, counsel for the class and the government should, if they have not already, adopt a litigation strategy that will maximize the recovery for injured parties they are representing. That litigation strategy should include an optimal combination of cases to file in federal and state courts, which should consider limitations imposed by CAFA, state indirect purchaser and class certification law, among a host of other issues that invariably affect any litigation and complex antitrust litigation suits in particular.

Third, private plaintiffs and public enforcers should coordinate discovery as much as

---

[111] For further discussion of the funding of private antitrust litigation, see Chapter 10 of this Handbook.

[112] Parties involved in the same or a related case who share a common interest in the litigation may enter into a common interest agreement, which can be a useful tool. Assuming all of the particular elements required by the applicable state law are met, a common interest agreement allows parties represented by separate counsel to exchange verbal and written information in furtherance of the parties' common interest without waiving the attorney–client privilege or work product protection.

practicable. Discovery can be enormously expensive and time consuming.[113] Without coordination, these efforts may be unnecessarily duplicated by the public and private plaintiffs.

Fourth, private plaintiffs and public enforcers should communicate with each other about litigation schedules, significant deadlines, and components of the case in which each can utilize the other's assistance. For example, the public and private plaintiffs should be prepared to assist each other with amicus briefs on matters in which they have a mutual interest.

Fifth, the parties should consider and discuss any other time saving measures. The parties should not hesitate to raise these issues as they arise over the course of litigation.

11.04.4(C) Settlement/arbitration phase

As with the other phases discussed above, coordination is essential during settlement or arbitration. Where the private and public lawsuits represent overlapping classes or groups of injured parties, the private plaintiffs and public enforcers should coordinate to the extent possible a settlement or arbitration negotiation strategy. In private actions in which government enforcers are able to get involved but have not done so, class counsel should consider inviting the government to become part of the settlement or arbitration process. According to David Rosenberg and James Sullivan, "[c]oordinating public and private litigation and settlement decisions is . . . crucial to the effective enforcement of antitrust laws" to ameliorate the "overbearing litigation costs and excessive sanctions" that, according to the authors, accompany private antitrust class actions.[114]

A final aspect of this third phase is the cy pres doctrine. This doctrine is applied in antitrust class actions "where direct distribution of the damages awarded to all the class members is not feasible, permitting funds to be distributed in the next best fashion in order to benefit the intended class as closely as possible and to avoid retention of ill-gotten gains by defendants."[115]

Where cy pres is part of a settlement agreement, the private and public plaintiffs should consider several guiding principles:

(1) the first priority in a damages award in an antitrust case is to return the damages to the injured class members;

---

[113] In *Twombly*, the Supreme Court emphasized the expensive discovery costs associated with litigating an antitrust suit. 550 U.S. at 558–59 (citing the following: William H. Wagener, *Modeling the Effect of One-Way Fee Shifting on Discovery Abuse in Private Antitrust Litigation*, 78 N.Y.U. L. Rev. 1887, 1898–99 (2003) (discussing the unusually high cost of discovery in antitrust cases); Federal Judicial Center, Manual for Complex Litigation § 30, (4th ed. 2004) (describing extensive scope of discovery in antitrust cases); Memorandum from Paul V. Niemeyer, Chair, Advisory Committee on Civil Rules, to Hon. Anthony J. Scirica, Chair, Committee on Rules of Practice and Procedure (May 11, 1999), 192 F.R.D. 354, 357 (2000) (reporting that discovery accounts for as much as 90 percent of litigation costs when discovery is actively employed)).

[114] Rosenberg & Sullivan, *supra* note 30, at 162.

[115] Albert Foer, *Enhancing Competition Through the Cy Pres Remedy: Suggested Best Practices*, (AAI Working Paper No. 07-11, 2007) (internal quotation omitted), *available at* http://www.antitrustinstitute.org/Archives/WP07-11.ashx). For a full discussion of cy pres, see Chapter 14 of this Handbook.

(2) cy pres should be used only if the class is so large compared to the size of the fund that the transaction costs render a distribution of cash infeasible;
(3) if a cy pres award is made, there must be an adequate nexus between the nature of the claim and the uses to which the cy pres funds will be put;
(4) where the fund is sufficiently large, a foundation-like process should be used to oversee the selection of the recipients and their expenditures; and
(5) if the fund is not sufficiently large, plaintiffs should present one or more candidates for the court to select based on *detailed* proposals by the candidates.

The United States' model of private and public enforcement maximizes the opportunities for injured parties to recover from anticompetitive conduct.

11.04.5 Qualitative and quantitative results of multiple layers of enforcement

It is precisely the concurrent enforcement system that allows time-honored theories to be tested against the facts of particular cases (which carries qualitative and quantitative elements). Qualitatively, the concurrent enforcement system allows private parties, through litigation, to test theories adopted by the federal government in previous cases[116] or in guidelines.[117] Even bedrock doctrine, such as the per se illegality of horizontal price-fixing,[118] has subsequently been "clarified" in private litigation.[119] Perhaps the most prominent example of an attempt to test theories adopted by the federal government is the attempt by a number of states to obtain injunctive relief against Microsoft beyond what had already been obtained by the DOJ and several other states through negotiation. Whatever one thinks of the merits of the litigating states' position, their persistence is likely to generate significant decisional law on the appropriate antitrust remedies in an ever-evolving and expanding industry.[120]

Quantitatively, in 2010, the DOJ Antitrust Division filed 14 civil cases in federal courts: 10 merger challenges, three pursuant to Sherman Act § 1, and one "other" civil case.[121] The Antitrust Division also filed 60 criminal cases in 2010.[122] Additionally, the FTC filed

---

[116] *Compare* United States v. Arnold, Schwinn & Co., 388 U.S. 365 (1967), *with* Continental T.V. v. GTE Sylvania, 433 U.S. 36 (1977). *GTE Sylvania* is, of course, viewed as a seminal case in antitrust jurisprudence. *See, e.g.,* Thomas B. Leary, *The Essential Stability of Merger Policy in the United States*, 70 ANTITRUST L. J.105, 110 (2002).

[117] *See, e.g.*, United States v. Baker Hughes Inc., 908 F.2d 981 (D.C. Cir. 1990) (citing, some what critically, the FTC/DOJ Horizontal Merger Guidelines with respect to the importance of entry in merger analysis).

[118] *See, e.g.*, United States v. Socony-Vacuum Oil Co., 310 U.S. 150 (1940).

[119] *See, e.g.*, Broadcast Music, Inc. v. Columbia Broadcasting System, Inc., 441 U.S. 1 (1979).

[120] *See generally* Robert Pitofsky, *Antitrust Remedies in the 21st Century: Too Many Actions? Too Much – or Still Too Little – Recovery?*, 1 ANTITRUST SOURCE 1, 11 (2002) (indicating a judicial decision would be useful regarding appropriate relief given the governments' victory in the Court of Appeals).

[121] *See* U.S. DEP'T OF JUSTICE, ANTITRUST DIV. WORKLOAD STATISTICS FY 2001–2010, *available at* http://www.justice.gov/atr/public/workload-statistics.html (district court antitrust cases).

[122] *Id.*

seven non-merger and 22 merger challenges.[123] State antitrust enforcers account for a large percentage of antitrust cases filed (in state and federal courts) in an average year.[124] As the Antitrust Modernization Commission pointed out in its 2007 report, there are both vocal critics and proponents of state enforcement.[125] However, the Commission concluded that the benefits of state enforcement outweigh the costs:

> State antitrust enforcement can benefit consumers by obtaining treble damages for consumers and supplementing federal enforcement. The states have unique authority to recover antitrust damages for their consumers and local government purchasers. The vast majority of state enforcement activity over the past fifteen years has involved areas in which state enforcers may have a comparative advantage in terms of knowledge – that is, with respect to local markets, local competitive effects, and local government purchasers. During the same time period, the states' enforcement efforts have targeted most frequently those antitrust violations most likely to cause significant consumer harm, such as price-fixing, bid-rigging, and market allocation.[126]

As a result, the Commission did not recommend elimination of state enforcement but instead recommended mechanisms for state and federal enforcers to coordinate their efforts to best protect competition without imposing unnecessary costs on businesses and taxpayers.[127]

Aside from governmental enforcement of the antitrust laws, there were 523 private antitrust actions in federal court in 2010, accounting for 91.8 percent of the total number of antitrust cases filed.[128] Since 1975, private antitrust actions have accounted for 83.4 percent to 96.6 percent of all antitrust actions filed.[129] The number of antitrust actions filed by private parties in state courts is not tabulated, although it appears that private plaintiffs increasingly are using state fora to obtain damages in indirect purchaser cases.[130]

Although this volume of antitrust filings is somewhat misleading (in that separate cases brought by various enforcers often allege overlapping violations as they seek varying remedies), it does indicate that the system produces numerous opportunities for courts to apply the general precepts of competition law to particularized facts.

---

[123] FTC Competition Enforcement Database, *available at* http://www.ftc.gov/bc/caselist/index.shtml (accessed Oct. 6, 2011).

[124] Although state antitrust cases are more difficult to track, a review of the ALD Annual Supplements and various NAAG publications supports this assertion, even counting multistate complaints filed in federal court as one complaint, though such complaints may assert claims under state law that alternatively could have been filed in multiple state courts. *See generally* ABA Section of Antitrust Law, Annual Review of Antitrust Law Developments 183–90 (2008) (previous issues offer similar discussions of the annual number of state enforcement actions).

[125] Antitrust Modernization Comm'n, Report and Recommendations 185–87 (2007).

[126] *Id.* at 186.

[127] *Id.* at 186–203.

[128] Bureau of Justice Statistics, Sourcebook of Justice Statistics Online: Antitrust Cases Filed in U.S. District Courts by Type of Case, 1975–2010, *available at* www.albany.edu/sourcebook/pdf/t5412010.pdf.

[129] *Id.*

[130] *See generally* O'Connor, *supra* note 28, at 34; First, *supra* note 79 (discussing *Vitamins* indirect purchaser litigation).

11.04.6 The multiple layers create a unique antitrust enforcement landscape

It is undoubtedly true that this diversity of potential enforcers motivated by varying incentives has resulted in an active antitrust litigation environment in the United States. Whether this environment results in a greater degree of enforcement than would be optimal from some perspectives is a valid concern.[131] It certainly is not the case that the optimal number of enforcers approaches infinity. Some commentators have suggested eliminating the competition enforcement authority of a number of federal agencies because they apply "soft" competition standards to mergers in specific industry sectors and have only limited expertise in competition analysis. The ICPAC report singles out the overlapping authority of these sectoral agencies and the federal antitrust agencies as a "defect" of the American system.[132] In addition to the increased transaction costs and the relative lack of antitrust expertise in the sectoral agencies, critics of the current system point to the broad "public interest" standard that governs agency review of these transactions.[133] This standard imports non-competition criteria into the analysis, thereby allowing some transactions to be evaluated on grounds inconsistent with those governing other industries. These criticisms are well taken, and underscore that in any system of concurrent enforcement, the potential enforcers ought to be governed by a single set of competition standards, preferably reviewable in an integrated court system.

Moreover, a system of multiple potential enforcers applying the same law has produced numerous opportunities for federal and state courts to rule on antitrust questions, creating a rich trove of antitrust decisional law, at least in comparison to other enforcement regimes. Even in those instances where a state or private enforcer unsuccessfully litigates an alleged violation, the end result can be the development of useful or even significant case law.[134]

§ 11.05 Conclusion

Antitrust enforcement is strengthened by concurrent enforcement. Antitrust litigation in multiple jurisdictions and by numerous plaintiffs produces tangible benefits in the number of reported decisions and facilitates the continual and transparent evolution of the law. There are several benefits to an enforcement system that produces a wealth of litigation. One premier benefit is that litigation requires parties and courts to apply the broad

---

[131] *See* Douglas H. Ginsburg & Scott H. Angstreich, *Multinational Merger Review. Lessons from Our Federalism*, 68 Antitrust L. J., 219, 220 (2000). *See also* Ky P. Ewing, Jr., Speech at the Fourth Annual Competition Conference, The European University Institute, Fiesole, Italy: Suggestions for a Framework for Governmental Discussion About Antitrust Procedures and Principles, (Oct. 27, 2000).

[132] ICPAC, *supra* note 2, at 144.

[133] *See, e.g.*, Milton A. Marquis, *DOJ, FTC and FERC Electric Power Merger Enforcement: Are There Too Many Cooks in the Merger Review Kitchen?*, 33 Loy. U. Chi. L. J. 783, 788–89 (2002).

[134] *See, e.g.*, New York v. Kraft Gen. Foods, 862 F. Supp. 1030 (S.D.N.Y. 1993) (New York unsuccessfully challenged Nabisco acquisition after DOJ chose not to act); Continental T.V. v. GTE Sylvania, 433 U.S. 36 (1977) (private plaintiff's unsuccessful challenge to location clause resulted in precedent virtually eliminating the applicability of the per se rule to non-price vertical restraints).

language of the antitrust laws to the specific facts at issue. As case law develops, parties are provided more guidance on the contours of what constitutes illegal anticompetitive conduct. This guidance assists firms, and individuals avoid liability with knowledge of what conduct violates the antitrust laws. It also assists litigating plaintiffs because they have a more specific framework on which to base their claims.

12 Settlement practice from both a plaintiff and defense perspective

Joseph Tabacco[1] *and Scott Martin*[2]

[1] Joseph Tabacco is managing partner of the San Francisco office of Berman DeValerio. He is grateful for the very substantial contributions of his colleague Matthew Pearson to this chapter.

[2] Scott Martin is a shareholder in the New York office of Greenberg Traurig, LLP.

§ 12.01 Introduction: A unique landscape for settlement

To paraphrase Winston Churchill, a negotiated settlement may be the worst form of resolving a significant private antitrust dispute, except for all of the others that have been tried from time to time. Trials occur, to be sure, but only for parties prepared for substantial expense and risk, often with a singularly perverse mix of uncertainty for future business practices and reputations, and for courts that are left with no alternative but the sacrifice of an extended block of trial time and other court resources.

Additionally, antitrust cases often involve fact-swollen issues of market definition and antitrust injury, among others, that are ill-suited for disposition on summary judgment – and the discovery path leading there can be so expensive and intrusive that it was noted by the Supreme Court as a consideration in the watershed *Twombly* opinion that raised the bar in pleading requirements.[3] Accordingly, familiar incentives for settlement of a major litigation are often more pronounced, for both sides, in the context of a private antitrust case.

However, the antitrust context also presents special complications. The seasoned litigator is well-prepared for the client's usual threshold questions, such as "Will it be perceived as weakness if we broach the idea of settlement?" Discussing dispute resolution in an antitrust case, however, raises thornier issues. Consider, for example, an action brought by a competitor challenging alleged exclusionary conduct under § 2 of the Sherman Act.

---

[3] *See* Bell Atlantic Corp. v. Twombly, 550 U.S. 544, 558 (2007) ("[I]t is one thing to be cautious about dismissing an antitrust case in advance of discovery, but quite another to forget that proceeding to antitrust discovery can be expensive." (citations omitted)).

The plaintiff likely seeks declaratory and injunctive relief concerning the defendant's conduct. If such relief is an essential part of a resolution, then the parties' settlement discussions will require scrupulous antitrust counseling. Even though the discussions themselves should be immunized from potential antitrust liability under the *Noerr-Pennington* doctrine,[4] there is no such assurance of protection for the substance and effect of any agreement reached between competitors (or potential competitors) concerning conduct in the market post-litigation. Fortunately, the focus of both sides' counsel should be aligned in this regard, at least insofar as they not invite a potential § 1 claim against their respective clients based upon the settlement.

These same concerns also generally augur for confidentiality clauses concerning the terms of antitrust settlements reached between private parties (an option not available, but also generally not needed, in the class action context). Indeed, careful practitioners may choose an "off-the-record" agreement before proceeding with discussions – i.e., that none of the participants will refer to the substance, or even the fact, of such discussions in any other forum (except under compulsion). Confidentiality also can take on special significance in the settlement dialogue itself, as it may be necessary to exchange highly sensitive price, cost, customer, market analysis, and business method information in order for the parties, their counsel, and perhaps even experts retained for the purpose of evaluating the claims to make a meaningful assessment. Businesspersons almost never are completely sanguine about the parameters of such an exchange, the restrictions on access to such information, and the prohibition against its use for any other purpose.

Overlaid on these special considerations are the complexities of an antitrust case, such as damages valuations, which may depend upon mountains of data subject to multiple interpretations, reduced (at great expense) to graphical summaries; parallel regulatory actions; legal and economic analyses of concepts like relevant markets, interchangeability, and exclusionary conduct; and, in cartel cases, complications associated with criminal investigations. Strategic questions also abound, including:

(1) when and how to initiate (and re-initiate) settlement talks;
(2) whom to involve in the discussions;
(3) how to address joint defense agreement obligations, joint and several liability, third-party releasees, and issues implicating any co-defendants;
(4) whether to coordinate with other actions or jurisdictions to obtain a "lasting" or "global" litigation peace; and
(5) if the case is a class action, how to prepare a battle plan for successful settlement class certification, preliminary and final approval of the proposed settlement as fair and adequate, effective notice, and provisions for potential opt-outs, among other considerations.

The answers to those questions vary from one antitrust case to the next. And a survey of the relevant case law and documentation is well beyond the scope of a single handbook

---

[4] *See, e.g.*, Columbia Pictures Indus., Inc. v. Professional Real Estate Investors, Inc., 944 F.2d 1525, 1528 (9th Cir. 1991) (settlement discussions, including offers of settlement, constitute "conduct incidental to the prosecution of the suit" protected under *Noerr-Pennington*).

chapter.[5] In the pages that follow, though, we hope to provide some practical and generally applicable insights to reaching the "correct" settlement solutions.[6]

§ 12.02 Windows of opportunity: When to engage in settlement discussions

Most antitrust cases are both complex and prolix, usually measured in years rather than months. Typically, these cases involve sophisticated and experienced attorneys on both sides who vigorously and competently represent their clients' respective interests. Nonetheless, even these talented attorneys sometimes overlook opportunities to achieve settlement, in whole or in part, at the earlier and mid-stages of litigation. For plaintiffs, an early settlement, even if partial, can help achieve some part of the litigation goal and advance the case as to remaining claims or defendants. For a settling defendant, an early resolution relieves it of the costs of protracted litigation and exposure to treble damages.

These "windows" of settlement opportunity generally occur at various inflection points in the litigation, which we review chronologically below.

12.02.1 Pre-complaint settlements

In special circumstances, antitrust disputes may be susceptible to settlement prior to the filing of a judicial complaint. This is particularly so in individual actions where the attendant publicity and disclosure obligations triggered by an antitrust complaint may serve as settlement catalysts, but not so much in class actions, which present special complications and considerations due to their representative nature. In individual antitrust actions, plaintiffs' counsel often have a good idea of the harm attributable to the defendants' conduct and the nature of relief that would effectively restore competition, and they will have an early assessment of their likelihood of prevailing at trial. When sophisticated defense counsel are involved and can evaluate risk and exposure, a meaningful dialogue may ensue.

In one scenario that arises from time to time, the potential defendants in a civil antitrust action are under investigation by the U.S. Department of Justice ("DOJ") or state attorneys general for anticompetitive conduct, typically conspiratorial in nature. In these circumstances, the DOJ's "amnesty program," which will remain in effect until at least 2020 pursuant to a recent extension of the Antitrust Criminal Penalty Enhancement and Reform Act ("ACPERA"), incentivizes conspirators to "turn state's evidence" and cooperate with the governmental investigation.[7] In exchange, the first self-reporting defendant

---

[5] Prefaced by the disclosure that both of the authors of this chapter were deeply involved on both sides of these matters, the decision in Judge Brock Hornby's orders in *In re Compact Disc Minimum Advertised Price Antitrust Litig.*, 216 F.R.D. 197 (D. Me. 2003) and *In re New Motor Vehicles Canadian Export Antitrust Litigation*, No. MDL 1532, 2006 WL 623591 (D.Me. 2006), together with the briefing and settlement documentation in the cases, are an excellent educational starting point for virtually any issue in complex antitrust class action settlements.

[6] The authors' objective is to provide practical insights from their respective positions on, principally, the plaintiff and defense sides of the bar. Unless specifically noted, individual statements herein should not be assumed to represent a consensus perspective.

[7] *See* Antitrust Criminal Penalties Enforcement & Reform Act of 2004, Pub. L. 108–237, 118 Stat. 666 (codified as a note to 15 U.S.C. § 1). For further discussion of ACPERA as an evidence gathering tool, see Chapter 7 of this Handbook.

receives amnesty from prosecution and reduced exposure to any subsequently filed civil antitrust suits, whether they be individual or class actions. In this scenario, the company procuring amnesty may be enticed to seek an early settlement of civil litigation, including any threatened litigation.

Pre-filing settlements in class actions, however, are particularly complicated. Courts have heightened concerns about possible settlement collusion, or that an early settlement may not have been reached through completely arms' length negotiations.[8] Objectors to the settlement often exacerbate such concerns by alleging collusion formally, or by alleging that the plaintiffs were not fully informed. Objections may also come from other plaintiffs asserting that the settling plaintiffs are not empowered to release claims and have no authority to enter into a settlement on behalf of a class where no court has previously approved the appointment of "Lead Counsel" to act on behalf of even a putative class.

Nonetheless, in the right circumstances, particularly large multi-defendant conspiracy cases, the monetary and non-monetary benefits that an early settlement affords class plaintiffs, including discovery cooperation, could outweigh the above considerations. An early partial settlement providing for discovery cooperation or voluntary disclosures could benefit the class down the road because it could advance, at an early stage, a plaintiff's comprehension of the scope and facts of the underlying case. For the defendant, a pre-filing settlement may make smart business sense despite the obstacles to court approval, particularly where that defendant may be cooperating with governmental officials in any parallel investigation.

12.02.2 Settlement at the pre- and post-motion to dismiss or class certification stage

In light of the Supreme Court's decision in *Twombly*, defendants' motions to dismiss are no longer the long shots they once were perceived to be in many antitrust cases. Accordingly, sophisticated counsel now recognize that the uncertainties inherent in a motion to dismiss or the class certification process may also open a settlement "window."

From a plaintiff's perspective, motions to dismiss are no longer viewed as risk-free, nor can class certification motions appropriately be taken for granted. Defendants have increasingly used both *Twombly* motions and opposition to class certification to highlight deficiencies in case theory or problems in the application of Rule 23 treatment to particular cases. Obviously, the success of these attacks is directly tied to the facts of each case. Where there are numerous indictments in multi-defendant conspiracy cases, plaintiffs can likely take more comfort in their chances for success. By contrast, where private actions are brought without aid of a parallel governmental investigation or there are serious questions of market definition or measuring impact, defendants may feel more secure in their prospects of prevailing than plaintiffs' counsel.

---

[8] The Supreme Court's seminal decision in the *Amchem* case illustrates the uncertainty of pre-litigation settlements in class actions. In that case, the parties reached a massive settlement of actual and potential asbestos claims prior to filing the complaint. The same day the complaint was filed in federal district court, the case settled. While the case ultimately turned on the appropriateness of class certification where released claims and claimants were not known or determinable, the Supreme Court highlighted the fact that the settlement was achieved before a case was actually filed. Amchem Prods., Inc. v. Windsor, 521 U.S. 591 (1997).

Accordingly, there is no "magic" time when the parties should consider initiating settlement discussions with the other side. When one party believes strongly that it will succeed in its motion or its opposition to a motion, a realistic settlement dialogue may not be possible. Conversely, where predicting an outcome of a motion to dismiss or for certification is more of a "coin toss," all sides in a multi-party litigation should strongly consider engaging in settlement discussions.

Often, litigators are afraid that to even broach the subject of settlement with their opponent is a sign of weakness, which creates great reluctance to initiate such discussions. The plaintiff may be concerned about a perception that their case is somehow weak. Conversely, defendants may view even the act of raising settlement as a capitulation that will unrealistically raise plaintiffs expectations and "whet the appetite."

12.02.3 Breaking the ice

As described elsewhere in this chapter, it is de rigueur for counsel and their clients to call upon the services of the extensive network of excellent professional mediators who have national reputations for helping parties settle complex litigation such as antitrust disputes. However, some members of the bar recall that, not so long ago, lawyer opponents could and would easily engage in settlement dialogue directly, without third parties.

It does not take much to "test the settlement waters." Often, particularly if opposing counsel have a civil dialogue, inquiries can be made of the other side as to whether there is an interest in exploring settlement. One generally accepted approach is to start the dialogue by surveying the current litigation landscape and, importantly, acknowledging the uncertainties that both sides face. Often, these discussions will attempt to set a framework, or a general ballpark range of settlement terms, to see if the parties can get in the same "zip code" for starters. Other topics include whether to engage the services of a mediator, which parties should or could be included or excluded in discussions, and the role that clients should and will play in such discussions, including in-house counsel.

Uncertainty often informs a party's determination of when to "break the ice." Settlement dialogues sometimes begin when motions to dismiss are submitted but pending, motions for class certification with the attendant discovery are underway or submitted, or other moments of uncertainty have evolved in the existing litigation climate. For example, settlement dialogues can be triggered by developments in a parallel governmental investigation, or other relevant cases or matters.

In the context of class actions, decisions about initiating settlement discussions can be complicated by the requirement of Rule 23 approval. Courts in all federal circuits look to a shopping list of factors in considering whether to grant or deny final approval to a class action settlement under Rule 23. Antitrust class actions are particularly susceptible to analysis under the *Grinnell* factors or the *Girsh* factors.[9] One factor that is easily satisfied,

---

[9] *See* City of Detroit v. Grinnell Corp., 495 F.2d 448 (2d Cir. 1974); Girsh v. Jepson, 521 F.2d 153, 157 (3d Cir. 1975); *In re* Jiffy Lube Sec. Litig., 927 F.2d 155 (4th Cir. 1991); Reed v. General Motors Corp., 703 F.2d 170, 172 (5th Cir. 1983); Mirfashi v. Fleet Mortgage Corp., 450 F.3d 745, 748 (7th Cir. 2006); Synfuel Tech., Inc. v. DHL Express (USA), Inc., 463 F.3d 646, 653 (7th Cir. 2006); Grunin v. Int'l House of Pancakes, 513 F.2d 114, 124 (8th Cir. 1975); Molski v. Gleich, 318 F.3d 937, 953 (9th Cir. 2003) (listing factors); *In re* New Motor Vehicles Canadian Exp. Antitrust

even with respect to settlements occurring at early stages of litigation, is that enough of the merits are "laid bare" for the parties to represent that they have made informed decisions about the propriety of settlement. Both parties must simply perform due diligence to satisfy themselves and the court, often through the use of informal or even formal discovery. The settling parties also should have little trouble demonstrating that they are reasonably knowledgeable about the risks of litigation and the rewards to the class for a resolution at a stage in the litigation where perhaps not a single deposition has been taken or even a single document produced.

One trend that seems to be emerging, however, is more careful consideration of the scope of settlements, particularly after passage of the Class Action Fairness Act of 2005 (CAFA). CAFA tends to put federal courts in the position of having to evaluate the settlement of multistate antitrust claims in addition to, or separate and apart from, the settlement of federal antitrust claims. Accordingly, courts seem more willing to allow settlements to proceed, even if reached at an early stage in the litigation, if other aspects of the settlement such as class definitions and scope of release are justified, and if the compensation bears a reasonable relationship to the risks of litigation and collectability.

12.02.4 Last call: Settlements after close of discovery but before trial

It has been said that there is no easier time, yet no harder time, to settle cases than after the parties have completed discovery and are staring at a trial. Settlement should be more easily obtained at this stage because the parties and their lawyers have become fully educated on the strengths and weaknesses of their case and thus can recognize the risks of trial. In reality, however, settlements sometimes become more difficult to obtain at this phase because of the "emotional" disconnect between reality and inflated perceptions of a case's strength.

Where experienced lawyers are able to make a reasonable evaluation of their respective cases, and are also able to engage in frank discussions with their counterparts, it is still possible (in this day and age of Alternative Dispute Resolution (ADR)) for lawyers or parties to come together and reach a settlement. It seems, however, that the trend in settlement is for parties to engage professional mediators to facilitate discussions and, hopefully, a resolution of the case.

Finally, one "wild card" in the late stage settlement process is the trial judge. Fundamentally, most courts try to encourage settlement. Some courts become fixated with settlement to avoid their scarce resources being tied up in long trials of complex matters. Practitioners should try to determine their respective courts' approaches to settlement and whether the parties can realistically expect the opportunity to actually try their case on a reasonable schedule. This valuable information will certainly help guide and inform the settlement process.

Litig., MDL Docket No. 1532, 2011 U.S. Dist. LEXIS 40843 (D. Me. Apr. 13, 2011) (applying list of factors, but noting that First Circuit has not adopted a list). *See also* Jonathan R. Macey & Geoffrey P. Miller, *Judicial Review of Class Action Settlements*, N.Y.U. Law and Econ. Working Papers, Paper 104, Sept. 26, 2007.

§ 12.03 The players involved: Shaping the table and filling the seats

Laying the groundwork for settlement discussions in an antitrust dispute should not unnecessarily delay or impede the discussions themselves, but it does require care. For example, the parties need to consider whether they are adequately protected by the assurance of non-admissibility of settlement statements and conduct for purposes of liability, damages, and impeachment, as provided by Rule 408 of the Federal Rules of Evidence. In order to avoid any potential mischaracterization of the discussions (especially if they are occurring between competitors or potential competitors), it may be desirable to agree that the content and even the fact of the discussions will be "off the record" except insofar as disclosure may be required by law or in response to an inquiry by the court.

Antitrust cases also may involve the voluminous exchange of granular pricing and other sensitive data and information in order to advance such discussions. Limitations on access to and use of such materials must be clearly negotiated up front. Because the objective is settlement, the parties are likely to be more forthcoming and expeditious in production, forgiving in definitions and objections, and sometimes even accommodating in preparing special data runs, than they would be during formal discovery. For those reasons, more often than not the information produced in connection with settlement discussions will not be usable in litigation or for any other purpose, and direct access may be limited to lawyers, experts, and perhaps a mediator. Even so, participants are sometimes wary of demonstrating to the other side, in the event the discussions collapse, what information "can" be provided given sufficient motivation to do so.

12.03.1 Businesspersons and experts

Certain dynamics of settlement discussions in significant civil matters are familiar. There will be divergent perspectives, or at least posturing, on liability and exposure. Negotiations are likely to occur on two or more fronts – not only between adverse parties, but perhaps between a party and a mediator, and even between parties and their respective counsel. And consideration may be given to an agreement staying the litigation proceedings to focus efforts and expenses on the settlement front.

Other dynamics, however, may be singular to antitrust actions, including the involvement of a number of players around the negotiating table. Because a substantial check may be written and/or significant modifications made to business activities, the persons involved in negotiations, directly or indirectly (as it may be advisable not to have them in the room with one another), likely will extend beyond outside and in-house counsel, potentially to the CEO or CFO, as well as to persons who "own" the key conduct issues. Additionally, economic experts may be needed to assess market structure and dynamics, class size and allocation (if a class action), and damages (through one or more statistical models). If a party, for strategic reasons, chooses not to disclose its testifying expert of choice, to test certain models with the other side, or to involve special settlement counsel (discussed below), a back-up economist may be employed for this purpose.

Antitrust cases can also be unique for involving challenges to fundamental ways in which a company maximizes its profitability, exploits its intellectual property, or otherwise conducts its business and maintains its competitive edge. Even though leading antitrust lawyers are often specialists who are well-known to one another and in near-complete agreement on the legal principles at issue, a rule of reason case in particular lends itself to varying applications of law to facts (even where facts are undisputed), as well as myriad potential remedies to dissipate anticompetitive effects and restore free competition. And cases involving per se unlawful conduct are not immune from complication: the antitrust "pocketbook" issues of damages theories, ability to pay, non-cash compensation, and joint and several liability can be among the most hotly debated points.

12.03.2 Facilitators

Mediation as an ADR method has become commonplace in antitrust litigation, regardless of whether ADR is required or actively encouraged by the court. Consequently, there are a number of private mediators, including retired judges and magistrates, who are familiar with antitrust issues and experienced in such disputes. These individuals not only can serve the usual mediator's function of facilitating a dialogue, but also may provide a "reality check" for clients concerning the strength of their cases and uncertainties of litigation. And the best of them may actually help to fashion creative business solutions (e.g., future supply arrangements), mindful of antitrust concerns, that provide relief that could never be awarded through a mandatory injunction in litigation, thereby maximizing the settlement's value for each side.

12.03.3 Settlement counsel

So-called "settlement counsel," attorneys brought in specifically to seek to resolve claims, are sometimes employed in antitrust litigation. Although antitrust plaintiffs were at the forefront of the use of settlement counsel, by now the practice is by no means exclusive to one side. Such counsel may spend very little time actually litigating, and may never enter a formal appearance in a case, but they may appear in discussions at any of the potential settlement windows discussed above.

A potential advantage in the use of settlement counsel is that they are *not directly involved in the litigation*; they are unencumbered by the aggressive history of motion practice and discovery disputes and the perceptions of the other side's litigators. A potential disadvantage, too, is that settlement counsel are *not directly involved in the litigation*: to be most effective, they should be among the most experienced at their craft in terms of both antitrust jurisprudence and creativity in settlement negotiations; be quick studies of both facts and legal arguments; possess an appreciation of business objectives; and, ideally, be involved well in advance of settlement discussions, as they may wish to consult with economists in valuation exercises.

§ 12.04 Multi-party and multi-jurisdictional cases: Strategic complications

12.04.1 For the plaintiffs: "Picking from" and "picking off" multiple defendants

The minority of antitrust cases, at least in the class action context, involve a single defendant; those cases typically concern claims of monopolization or attempted monopolization. More often than not, some type of horizontal conspiracy or concerted action is implicated, and multi-defendant antitrust cases raise a number of special issues for initiating and approaching settlement discussions.

12.04.1(A) Cases arising from DOJ investigations

In situations where the DOJ has brought a criminal indictment, or there is public information about an ongoing grand jury investigation with allegations of market collusion, early settlement strategies are easier to formulate. In that circumstance, often there is a cooperating defendant that has come forward to assist the government in its investigation in exchange for amnesty, provided there is cooperation with plaintiffs. The amnesty recipient is often a ripe candidate for early settlement discussions, because the guilty plea typically will carry a collateral estoppel effect on liability as to the timing and products alleged by the DOJ. The trick for plaintiffs' counsel is figuring out which defendant is the "stoolie." The answer is not hard to determine. Nothing beats picking up the phone and asking counsel for defendants, in the context of Federal Rule of Evidence 408, if they represent the cooperating defendant. If yes, or the more likely response, "I can't say. . .," this should prompt the next question: Does their client have an interest in an early resolution of the civil cases? Under ACPERA, an amnesty recipient is also given immunity from the treble damages provisions of the federal antitrust laws. Accordingly, the "threat" of a large treble judgment as leverage to engage in settlement negotiations is somewhat lessened. However, the negative value of this diminished leverage, along with a potentially lower monetary recoupment, is usually more than offset by the tremendous advantages that can be obtained from cooperation by an early settling defendant. Indeed, the main value of an early settlement with an amnesty applicant is usually the information provided to lay out a roadmap of whatever conspiracy or violation is alleged. This cooperation can include keys to inculpatory evidence as well as more mundane assistance, such as hints as to where to target discovery and explanations of industry players and nomenclature.

12.04.1(B) Cases where there is no pending governmental proceeding or investigation

When there is no pending governmental investigation in a private, multi-defendant action, and none of the conspirators have heightened settlement incentives stemming from the collateral estoppel effects of a guilty plea, initiating early settlement discussions with any particular defendant might seem less straightforward. However, experience has shown that the same rules of engagement usually apply in this circumstance.

Within any multi-defendant conspiracy case, there are typically major and minor players, measured both in relative market share and relative culpability. Strategically, plaintiffs should consider the advantages of arriving at an early resolution with either major or minor defendants. As might be expected, it is typically easier to initiate discussions with minor defendants. Early settlements, particularly before challenges to the pleadings are settled, can be of significance to plaintiffs, as much for the value of cooperation as for any monetary recovery.

As class actions progress, particularly antitrust class actions, the developing trend over the past several years has been for defendants to vigorously contest class certification. Recent case law has only encouraged litigating class certification issues, particularly in cases not involving straightforward horizontal price fixing.[10] Plaintiffs may find it to their strategic advantage to reach agreement with one or more defendants, pre-class certification, for a variety of reasons. First, there is a certain psychological advantage to having a stipulated settlement class agreed to in advance of a contested class certification motion. Second, should the class motion fail and class certification not be obtainable in the litigation context, a stipulated settlement class may nonetheless survive Rule 23 approval because the court would not have to confront trial manageability issues.[11]

Finally, as cases approach trial, partial settlements provide many significant advantages to the plaintiffs as long as the remaining defendants have the culpability and financial resources to reasonably ensure plaintiffs' prospects for success at trial and collection of any judgment. In this context, picking the appropriate defendants with which to initiate discussions and reach agreement is an important strategy. Once again, it is usually to the plaintiffs' advantage to initiate such discussions rather than wait for a defendant to "knock on the door." For the same reasons that partial settlements can provide psychological and financial comfort prior to resolution of class certification issues, partial settlements before a trial verdict likewise provide a level of "insurance" that all will not be lost should the trial be unsuccessful.

12.04.2 For the defendants: Breaking up can be hard to do

Regardless of who initiates the settlement approach, the participants can find themselves confronted with special contractual and strategic complications in a multi-defendant antitrust case.

12.04.2(A) Joint defense and judgment sharing agreements

It is commonplace for antitrust defendants to have a joint defense agreement ("JDA"), particularly in a cartel case.[12] In the context of a settlement discussion, both sides must be scrupulous to ensure that the agreement is not breached, which could imperil a potential settlement or result in disqualification of counsel, among other things. This means not only that no joint work product or information shared in the joint defense efforts can be utilized by a participating defendant in separate settlement discussions (or in furtherance of commitments to cooperate with a plaintiff), but also that the participating defendant may be required to give notice of the settlement negotiations to other defendants. Often, defendants draft such notice provisions to be triggered only when an agreement in principle is reached, since prior to sharing information with co-defendants, each defendant's counsel has an incomplete view of the landscape and its own client's role or potential culpability – and thus wishes to preserve maximum flexibility to potentially explore settlement options. However, that is not always the case, so the counsel should have a clear

---

[10] *See, e.g.*, *In re* Hydrogen Peroxide Antitrust Litig., 552 F.3d 305 (3d Cir. 2008).

[11] *See, e.g.*, *In re* New Motor Vehicles Canadian Exp. Antitrust Litig., 269 F.R.D. 80 (D. Me. 2010) (certifying settlement classes despite the First Circuit vacating earlier order certifying litigated class). It should be remembered however, that as currently drafted, Rule 23 does not differentiate between settlement and litigation class certification.

[12] There may, of course, be multiple agreements or special provisions when a leniency applicant is involved.

understanding of what they can say and how far they can proceed before certain obligations may be triggered under the JDA.

In some instances, joint defense participants may also have covenants concerning "judgment sharing" that can factor into settlement negotiations. Joint and several liability under the Sherman Act can potentially leave one defendant "holding the bag" for the sales of other defendants. And unsettled law concerning contribution rights under certain state antitrust statutes in indirect purchaser cases (as well as accepted contribution rights in foreign jurisdictions) can potentially expose a settling defendant to contribution claims from other defendants. To address these issues and ensure that a settlement can afford some closure, defendants may agree among themselves to each "remove their sales" in the event of a separate settlement of the action – *i.e.*, obtain plaintiffs' agreements not to seek damages against the other defendants based upon the settlor's sales – or else face potential sharing obligations with their contracting co-defendants. The arithmetic implications for the plaintiff are clear: in entering into a settlement dependent on that condition, there may be no other source of recovery for damages flowing from that defendant's sales, and the settlement truly must stand on its own. More than once, particularly in class actions, such a provision has prolonged and complicated settlement discussions.

12.04.2(B) Most favored nation ("MFN") provisions

A frequent debate in partial settlements of multi-defendant cases is whether it is strategically advantageous for plaintiffs to agree to a so-called "most favored nation" clause (or MFN), which typically provides that the plaintiffs will not settle in the future on terms less favorable than those agreed to with the earlier settling defendant (or will give the first settlor the benefit of the later bargain). Early-settling defendants, of course, are incentivized to seek an MFN to ensure that they do not lose face (counsel with clients, and client management with shareholders) by paying too much too soon. Plaintiff practitioners, by contrast, generally seek to avoid MFNs because the restrictions can impair their ability to negotiate future settlements when circumstances of the litigation change, sometimes unexpectedly.

Nevertheless, the parties may see eye-to-eye on an MFN in principle. The provision can be useful to plaintiffs in some circumstances, particularly where the liability potential of the non-settling defendants is strong and ability to pay is not an issue. If one or more of those defendants is motivated to settle, the plaintiff will be heard to say "my hands are tied" by the MFN in demanding a richer deal from the later-settling defendant.

If an MFN is included, definitional questions are crucial. What is an appropriate benchmark for measuring a "better" deal? Is it based on relative market share? Does the MFN contemplate a "first out discount" that requires a premium for future settlements? Can there be exceptions for settlors with impaired abilities to pay, and if so, how is that measured? Should an MFN have a sunset provision (for example, expiring upon a class certification decision or at the beginning of trial)? Especially in the MFN context, addressing all possible issues with careful drafting can avoid potentially embarrassing disputes later.

12.04.3 Multiple jurisdictions and "global peace"

Antitrust actions often span multiple jurisdictions, particularly in the price-fixing context, in which effects may be alleged at both the direct and indirect purchaser levels, and potential plaintiffs come from around the country if not the world. More often than not, a settling defendant seeks "global peace" – an end to the time and expense of litigation (except to the extent it is subject to third-party discovery or continuing cooperation obligations), releases from all claims and claimants, and a return to business as usual. That concept is aspirational and often elusive.

A single settlement, or even a coordinated series of negotiations, may not bring a defendant truly global peace because not all parties are at the table, especially in the form of absent class members who may elect not to participate.[13] Global peace also may not be achieved because truly "global" (that is, worldwide) settlements have been hobbled by effective means of collective redress for civil claims arising outside of the United States. Attempts to pursue and settle such claims in U.S. courts are restricted by the Supreme Court's decision in *Empagran*,[14] and, with the exception of Parker ITR's private settlement of foreign claims in the *Marine Hose* matter through an opt-in procedure, no model for settlement of cartel claims worldwide on a collective basis has emerged.[15]

For U.S. claims, at least, some progress has been made toward achieving more complete resolutions. Where multiple federal cases are filed, consolidation, or at least coordination, is normally ordered by the Judicial Panel on Multi-District Litigation. And with the enactment of CAFA, many of the complications of multi-jurisdictional state court or state/federal cases have started to dissipate.[16] However, pre-CAFA cases and those cases that fall outside CAFA raise interesting questions when the cases arise out of the same facts pending in both state and federal court and involve the same or related classes of plaintiffs and defendants.

While it is true that Supreme Court cases such as *Matsushita* and *Phillips Petroleum* have cleared the way for global resolutions by settlement in courts that might not even have jurisdiction over all of the underlying settled causes of action, the law remains murky in other respects. *Matsushita* involved securities cases that were brought about the same time, one in the Chancery Court in Delaware under state and federal law, and the other in federal court in California under federal securities laws, which provide for exclusive federal jurisdiction.[17] In the California case, the district court declined to certify the class and entered summary judgment in favor of Matsushita.[18] Plaintiffs appealed to the Ninth Circuit. While the California case was on appeal, the parties in the Delaware action settled globally and purported to release all state and federal claims arising out of the transaction at issue.[19] Matsushita argued to the Ninth Circuit that the settlement in Delaware

---

[13] Strategies for addressing opt-out plaintiffs are discussed later in this chapter.

[14] Empagran S.A. v. F. Hoffman-LaRoche, Ltd., 542 U.S. 155 (2004).

[15] Open issues remain under the *Marine Hose* model, including the prospects of further litigation and exposure to potential plaintiffs who did not opt in to the settlement and possible contribution claims from co-defendants concerning foreign direct and indirect purchaser claims. Laurence T. Sorkin provides an excellent review of the foreign settlement frontier in Chapter 37 ("International Settlements") of The International Handbook on Private Enforcement of Competition Law (Albert A. Foer & Jonathan W. Cuneo eds., 2010).

[16] For further discussion of CAFA and Judicial Panel procedures, see Chapter 4 and Chapter 5 of this Handbook.

[17] Matsushita Elec. Indus. Co., Ltd. v. Epstein, 516 U.S. 367, 370–72 (1996).

[18] *Id.* at 370.

[19] *Id.* at 370–71.

precluded the California claims. The Ninth Circuit, however, disagreed, finding that the Delaware settlement could not "extinguish exclusively federal claims which it could not have extinguished through adjudication."[20]

In reversing the Ninth Circuit, the U.S. Supreme Court held that the Delaware court had the power to approve the settlement, and the Delaware court's judgment and dismissal were entitled to full faith and credit by the federal district court in California, even though the Delaware court would not have had jurisdiction to litigate the federal claims that it dismissed.

In *Phillips Petroleum v. Shutts* the high court upheld the power of one state court in Kansas to approve a settlement that released claims of residents of other states, in a limited partnership class action involving oil royalties. Even though few of the class members and oil leases at issue were located in Kansas, the Supreme Court held that the Kansas state court properly asserted jurisdiction over absent class members because they were provided notice, the opportunity to opt out, and adequate representation.[21] The Kansas court erred, however, in applying Kansas law to all claims.[22]

Multi-jurisdictional cases present unique challenges. Defendants typically bargain for total peace. Plaintiffs as well want to enter settlement agreements that are enforceable. The simplest approach, but one that is not always achievable in multi-jurisdictional cases, is to reach agreement with all plaintiffs on terms that all plaintiffs agree are in everyone's best interest. This is easier said than done as, inevitably, disputes about the relative strength and weakness of particular jurisdictions' laws complicate such negotiations. It is in the multi-jurisdictional context that parties often benefit from experienced mediators if such mediations bring all interested parties together.

The path to settlement often depends on whether one court has appropriate jurisdiction over all the cases filed and whether the court is willing to exercise jurisdiction to consider approval of a single, multi-jurisdictional class action settlement. This is a problem particularly when state court actions are pending in multiple states. It is less of a problem in federal courts because multidistrict procedures provide for consolidation of cases filed in various federal courts into one MDL proceeding presided over by one federal district judge. In these MDL proceedings, the courts clearly have authority to consider and approve global settlements of multi-jurisdictional cases.

Of course, even where circumstances would allow for resolution of the jurisdictional quandaries associated with multidistrict settlements, the class action's procedural progenitor, Rule 23, still requires that we ask: are there unifying facts and law that allow for the appropriate definition of a settlement class or classes? Debate rages today following Third Circuit decisions in *Warfarin* and *Prudential* involving settlements of multi-state state law claims in one class or one or more sub-classes.[23] An instructive ruling of note is that by

---

20 Epstein v. MCA, Inc., 50 F.3d 644, 666 (9th Cir. 1995), *rev'd* 516 U.S. 367 (1996).

21 472 U.S. 797, 811 ("In this case we hold that a forum State may exercise jurisdiction over the claim of an absent class-action plaintiff, even though that plaintiff may not possess the minimum contacts with the forum which would support personal jurisdiction over a defendant.").

22 *Id.* at 821–22.

23 The Third Circuit may shortly set forth certain parameters for such settlements as it recently heard en banc argument in *Sullivan v. De Beers*, where the district court had approved a 50-state settlement class.

Judge Hornby from the District of Maine, approving a federal antitrust settlement class even though the underlying Sherman Act claims were dismissed on *Illinois Brick* grounds where the right of appeal of that order had been preserved at the time of settlement.[24] Suffice it to say that multi-jurisdictional cases, including those pending in both state and federal courts concurrently and those pending in various state courts, present challenges for settlement beyond those typically confronted in a case that has been consolidated for all purposes before one court.

§ 12.05 Class settlement considerations

Settlements in antitrust class actions raise the additional complication of court approval, to protect the rights of the absent class members whose claims may be resolved. The process for approval of a class settlement is generally well-established. There is a presentation of the proposed settlement to the court, generally on the plaintiffs' motion, with a request for preliminary approval and certification of a settlement class as to the settling defendant(s); if that request is granted, appropriate notice is provided to class members of the terms of the proposed settlement, the timing of a final approval hearing, and the class members' opportunity to object to or opt out of the proposed settlement; and, if final approval is granted, submitted claims are processed and any settlement proceeds disbursed according to a plan of distribution (generally, along with an award of attorneys' fees and costs). The issues that arise along that road, however, are numerous.

12.05.1 Scope of claims settled and released

As noted, settling defendants want the broadest possible release to ensure that they will not have to face litigation of tangential claims in the future,[25] but that desire must be tempered by the rights of absent class members whose claims will be extinguished. These competing interests raise substantive, procedural and practical issues, addressed below. How broad may a settlement release be without violating the due process rights of absent class members? What are the prospects of obtaining settlement class certification when the release covers a variety of claims under a number of jurisdictions' laws? Will a defendant even be willing to settle for something less than "global peace"?

12.05.1(A) Due process concerns

Substantively, the scope of a settlement release may be quite broad. Several federal courts have held that settlements may release the claims that were actually brought in the litigation, those that were not brought, and even claims that *could not have been* brought. As discussed, the Supreme Court in *Matsushita* observed that "[i]n order to

---

[24] *New Motor Vehicles*, 269 F.R.D. 80, 93 (D. Me. 2010).

[25] *See* Joseph M. McLaughlin, McLaughlin on Class Actions: Law & Practice § 6.28, at 141 (5th ed. 2009) ("[A] settlement is ordinarily impractical unless it covers all claims, actual and potential, state and federal, arising out of the same transaction or conduct at issue."); Wal-Mart Stores, Inc. v. Visa U.S.A. Inc., 396 F.3d 96, 106 (2d Cir. 2005) ("Broad class action settlements are common, since defendants and their cohorts would otherwise face nearly limitless liability from related lawsuits in jurisdictions throughout the country.").

achieve a comprehensive settlement that would prevent litigation of settled questions at the core of a class action, a court may permit the release of a claim based on the identical factual predicate as that underlying the claims in the settled class action even though the claim was not presented and might not even have been presentable in the class action."[26] Accordingly, the Court held that a class settlement in state court may release claims within the exclusive jurisdiction of federal courts.[27] Courts have widely followed this rule of law.[28]

Courts do not permit the scope of a release in a representative class action, however, to be limitless. The settlement release must be limited to claims arising under the same set of facts as the instant action.[29] This has been referred to as the "identical factual predicate" doctrine.[30] Thus, a settlement release in a price-fixing case may release any actual or potential antitrust-related claims of class members who bought the price-fixed product, including claims under federal and state antitrust statutes and state consumer protection and unjust enrichment laws – claims which, in essence, could have been pled in the action. But the release generally should not and could not, for example, extinguish a class member's product liability claims associated with a defect in the product.

Some courts also add a second limitation. Even if a particular claim arose from the identical factual predicate, the claim "will not be precluded where class plaintiffs have not adequately represented the interests of class members."[31] This does not mean that named plaintiffs have to bring every conceivable claim in order for that claim to be released through settlement. Instead, "adequate representation of a particular claim is determined by the alignment of interests of class members, not proof of vigorous pursuit of that claim."[32]

Thus, it is important for class counsel to consider the scope of claims that may be asserted by the class when negotiating the settlement, including whether some members

---

[26] Matsushita Elec. Indus. Co. v. Epstein, 516 U.S. 367, 377 (1996) (quoting TBK Partners, Ltd. v. Western Union Corp., 675 F.2d 456, 460 (2d Cir. 1982) (internal quotation marks omitted)).

[27] *Matsushita*, 516 U.S. at 369.

[28] *See, e.g.*, Grimes v. Vitalink Comm. Corp., 17 F.3d 1553, 1563 (2d Cir. 1994) ("[I]t is widely recognized that courts without jurisdiction to hear certain claims have the power to release those claims as part of a judgment."); Reppert v. Marvin Lumber & Cedar Co., 359 F.3d 53 (1st Cir. 2004); *but see In re* New Motor Vehicles Canadian Exp. Antitrust Litig., MDL Docket No. 1532, 2011 U.S. Dist. LEXIS 40843, at *49–50 (D. Me. Apr. 13, 2011) (refusing to approve class action settlement that purported to release Hawaii state law antitrust claims arising under the same facts as the certified nationwide Sherman Act claim because the plaintiffs could not pursue the Hawaii claim without involvement of the Hawaii Attorney General).

[29] *See* Nat'l Super Spuds, Inc. v. N.Y. Mercantile Exch., 660 F.2d 9 (2d Cir. 1981). In reversing the district court's order approving a settlement that purported to release claims of class members holding certain contracts that were not at issue in the litigated action, the Second Circuit stated:

> We assume that a settlement could properly be framed so as to prevent class members from subsequently asserting claims relying on a legal theory different from that relied upon in the class action complaint but depending upon the very same set of facts. This is not such a case.

Id. at 18 n.7. The release in *National Super Spuds* covered claims "which depend not only upon a different legal theory but upon proof of further facts," making the release impermissibly broad. *Id.*

[30] *See Wal-Mart Stores*, 396 F.3d at 106–07.

[31] *Id.* at 109.

[32] *Id.* at 113.

of the class may be able to assert different or additional claims than other class members. And defendants seeking a broad release are well-advised to include a provision in the settlement agreement by which the class members expressly waive their rights under laws that prevent a general release from extending to unknown or unsuspected claims in favor of the releasor that, if known at the time of execution, would have materially affected the settlement.[33] Adequacy of representation concerns therefore can arise in the course of determining the scope of the release or the fairness of the settlement as a whole, and not just in determining whether Rule 23(a)(4) is satisfied.[34]

12.05.1(B) Prospects of certifying a settlement class

Even if the substantive law permits a broad release, the scope of the settlement class may pose procedural hurdles. In particular, the litigants must consider how the scope of the class and the claims settled will affect the prospects of certifying a settlement class under Federal Rule of Civil Procedure 23. Under *Amchem*, a settlement class must meet all requirements of Rule 23, with the exception of manageability.[35] Thus, when seeking certification of a settlement class under Rule 23(b)(3), for example, the class must meet the numerosity, commonality, typicality and adequacy of representation requirements of Rule 23(a), as well as the predominance and superiority requirements of Rule 23(b)(3). Indeed, as the *Amchem* court noted, "other specifications of [Rule 23] – those designed to protect absentees by blocking unwarranted or overbroad class definitions – demand undiluted, even heightened, attention in the settlement context."[36]

On one hand, certification of settlement classes in antitrust cases would seem fairly straightforward compared to other substantive areas of law. As the U.S. Supreme Court has noted, antitrust cases generally are prime candidates for class treatment.[37] This is because much of the focus in these cases is on the defendant's monopolistic or conspiratorial conduct, which is often commonly felt by all members of the class. Even so, settlement classes comprised of members having diverse claims under more than one jurisdiction's laws and varied rights to relief will pose greater challenges to settlement class certification.

12.05.1(B)(1) Direct purchaser vs. indirect purchaser classes

As a threshold matter, the prospect of meeting Rule 23's requirements varies greatly by the type of antitrust case brought. In particular, a key factor is whether the class is comprised of direct purchasers, indirect purchasers, or both. A class comprised of only direct purchasers is the simplest case, because it does not pose the challenges concerning state law variations that may hinder certification of indirect purchaser classes. Each direct purchaser

---

33 *See, e.g.*, Cal. Civ. Code § 1542.

34 *See, e.g., In re* Cmty. Bank of N. Va. & Guaranty Nat'l Bank of Tallahassee Second Mortgage Loan Litig., 622 F.3d 275 (3d Cir. 2010) (questioning the adequacy of representation of the class when strong claims held by one-third of the class were not asserted or considered in negotiating the settlement).

35 Amchem Prods., Inc. v. Windsor, 521 U.S. 591 (1997). For further discussion of the class certification requirements under Rule 23, see Chapter 5 of this Handbook.

36 *Amchem*, 521 U.S. at 620.

37 *See id.* at 625 ("Predominance is a test readily met in certain cases alleging consumer or securities fraud or violations of the antitrust laws.").

class member shares a single common claim that arises out of the same course of anticompetitive conduct undertaken by defendants. Thus, there are rarely problems associated with a nationwide direct purchaser settlement class, unless the overcharge resulting from the alleged unlawful conduct affects one geographic region differently from another.

Settlement classes of indirect purchasers are a different story. Indirect purchasers are barred from recovering damages under federal antitrust law by reason of the Supreme Court's *Illinois Brick* decision.[38] They must instead bring claims under antitrust and consumer protection laws of various states.[39] At the same time, defendants, seeking "global peace" will typically want the settlement class to be nationwide. Since not all states allow indirect purchasers to sue for damages, class members may be differently situated depending on the state in which they reside.

As we will see, this distinction between direct and indirect purchasers plays a role throughout the settlement class certification analysis.

12.05.1(B)(2) RULE 23(a): NUMEROSITY, COMMONALITY, TYPICALITY AND ADEQUACY

In most complex antitrust class actions, numerosity is not an issue. It is not uncommon to see settlement classes with millions or even tens of millions of class members.

Likewise, commonality is often satisfied in antitrust class settlements. Rule 23(a)(2) requires that there be "questions of law or fact common to the class." The language of Rule 23(a)(2), as courts and commentators have noted, only requires the existence of a single question of law or fact common to the class.[40] Given the focus on the defendant's conduct in antitrust cases – e.g., whether competitor defendants conspired to fix prices, or whether a defendant unlawfully monopolized a market – it is usually not difficult to find one common issue of fact or law common to the class. The more difficult issue is whether the common questions *predominate* over individual questions; this requirement of Rule 23(b)(3) is discussed below.[41]

---

38 *See* Illinois Brick Co. v. Illinois, 431, U.S. 720 (1977). For further discussion of indirect purchaser standing, see Chapter 3 of this Handbook.

39 After *Illinois Brick*, a number of states have permitted indirect purchasers to sue and recover damages under state antitrust or consumer protection laws. *See generally* ERIC J. MCCARTHY ET AL., INDIRECT PURCHASER LAWSUITS: A STATE-BY-STATE SURVEY (2010); Daniel R. Karon, *"Your Honor, Tear Down that Illinois Brick Wall!" The National Movement Toward Indirect Purchaser Antitrust Standing and Consumer Justice*, 30 WM. MITCHELL L. REV. 1351 (2004).

40 *See, e.g., In re* Insurance Brokerage Antitrust Litig., 579 F.3d 241, 276 (3d Cir. 2009) ("[T]he commonality requirement is 'satisfied if the named plaintiffs share at least one question of fact or law with the grievances of the prospective class' . . . .") (quoting Newton v. Merrill Lynch, Pierce, Fenner & Smith, Inc., 259 F.3d 154, 183 (3d Cir. 2001)); ALBA CONTE & HERBERT NEWBERG, NEWBERG ON CLASS ACTIONS § 3.12 at 314 (4th ed. 2002) [hereinafter NEWBERG] ("The Rule 23(a)(2) prerequisite requires only a single issue common to the class.").

41 The Supreme Court's recent opinion in *Wal-Mart Stores, Inc. v. Dukes*, 564 U.S. ___ (2011), has the potential to make the commonality requirement a higher hurdle to certification, depending on how *Dukes* is applied in other contexts. In *Dukes*, the 5-4 majority Court considered dissimilarities among class members to determine whether commonality under Rule 23(a)(2) was satisfied. In responding to the dissent's criticism that the majority had blended the 23(b)(3) predominance requirement with the commonality requirement, the Court stated: "We consider dissimilarities not in order to determine (as Rule 23(b)(3) requires) whether common questions *predominate*, but in order to determine (as Rule 23(a)(2) requires) whether there *is* '[e]ven a single [common] question.'"

Typicality is satisfied according to the language of Rule 23(a)(3) when "the claims or defenses of the representative parties are typical of the claims or defenses of the class." This can be a higher hurdle when the settlement class includes indirect purchasers in various states. But the typicality requirement overlaps with many of the other requirements of Rule 23,[42] and courts often consider potential differences among class members as to indirect purchaser standing when considering predominance. The typicality inquiry, then, is focused on ensuring that the *nature* of the class representative's claims is typical of the class's claims.[43] Irrespective of rights to relief, the class representative's claims are typical of the class's claim if both concern the same type of injury suffered, caused by the same conduct of defendants. Factual circumstances may vary to some degree between the named plaintiff and the class – e.g., the amount of product purchased or the prices paid – without destroying typicality.[44] In the ordinary price-fixing case, for example, class members all claim to have paid a higher price due to an illegal agreement to fix prices among defendants. In this sense, courts often agree, the claims of the class representatives are typical of those of the class.[45]

12.05.1(B)(3) PREDOMINANCE

Rule 23(b)(3) requires that "the questions of law or fact common to class members predominate over any questions affecting only individual members, and that a class action is superior to other available methods for fairly and efficiently adjudicating the controversy." Predominance is a key battleground in the litigation context, and it can be an obstacle to certification of a settlement class, too. The standards for judging predominance in the settlement context are hotly debated, especially when plaintiffs seek certification of indirect purchaser settlement classes, and courts vary widely in their approaches.

For direct purchaser settlement classes, the question of predominance often hinges on whether the element of antitrust impact can be established with proof common to the class. Expert testimony is often necessary to opine on how the defendants' conduct affected the price in the market. Although direct purchasers may have paid different prices in different regions, many courts have relied on the presumption of common impact set forth in *Bogosian v. Gulf Oil Corp.*, which permits class certification regardless of whether conspiratorially affected prices were universally elevated to the same degree.[46] But even

---

Slip op. at 19 (emphasis and alteration in original). The Court made clear that not all common questions will do. Instead, class members' claims must share a "common contention," and that contention "must be of such a nature that it is capable of classwide resolution – which means that determination of its truth or falsity will resolve an issue that is central to the validity of each one of the claims in one stroke." *Id.* at 9. For further discussion of the potential effects of *Dukes* on class certification analysis, see Chapter 5 of this Handbook.

What remains to be seen is whether *Dukes* will be applied beyond its particular facts and disturb the abundant case law finding commonality easily satisfied in most antitrust cases.

42 *See* NEWBERG § 3.13 at 317–24.

43 NEWBERG § 18:9 at 30; *id.* § 18:8 at 26.

44 NEWBERG § 18:9 at 30–35.

45 *See* NEWBERG § 18:9 at 35 n.6 (listing cases).

46 561 F.2d 434, 448 (3d Cir. 1977). In *Bogosian*, the Third Circuit stated:

> If the price structure in the industry is such that nationwide the conspiratorially affected prices at the wholesale level fluctuated within a range which, though different in different

if the *Bogosian* presumption applies, it may be advisable to present economic analysis to buttress the presumption. Such a "belt and suspenders" approach has been successful for plaintiffs, and with greater emphasis on merits inquiry at class certification, the approach may become the norm.[47]

Establishing predominance when seeking certification of indirect purchaser classes likewise requires presentation of common proof of impact. Further economic analysis showing the pass-through of the illegal overcharge from direct purchasers to indirect purchasers may also be necessary. Additionally, unlike direct purchaser classes, indirect purchaser classes may find that varying rights to relief under different states' laws pose challenges to establishing predominance. Settlement objectors will often argue that predominance is destroyed by the lumping together of class members from *Illinois Brick*-repealer states with those in states that do not permit indirect purchaser standing. But several courts have certified nationwide settlement classes despite these state law differences. In *In re Warfarin Sodium Antitrust Litigation*, for example, the Third Circuit upheld the district court's certification of a nationwide settlement class of indirect purchasers who had brought a variety of federal and state antitrust and consumer protection claims.[48] Plaintiffs complained that the defendant, Dupont, had engaged in an anticompetitive and misleading campaign to lead consumers into believing Dupont's product, Coumadin, was superior to the generic equivalent.[49] In determining whether differences in state law defeated predominance, the Third Circuit found that settlement classes were different than litigation classes, and "[t]he difference is key."[50] In particular, the district court did not need to "determine whether variations in state laws present the types of insuperable obstacles which render class litigation unmanageable," because such variations and manageability concerns "are irrelevant to certification of a settlement class."[51] Further, although variations among states' laws may defeat predominance in some circumstances, the Third Circuit agreed that "the fact that there may be variations in the rights and remedies available to injured class members under the various laws of the fifty states in this

---

> regions, was higher in all regions than the range which would have existed in all regions under competitive conditions, it would be clear that all members of the class suffered some damage, notwithstanding that there would be variations among all dealers as to the extent of their damage.

Id. at 455; *see also In re* Linerboard Antitrust Litig., 305 F.3d 145 (3d Cir. 2002) (relying on *Bogosian*); *In re* New Motor Vehicles Canadian Exp. Antitrust Litig., 235 F.R.D. 127, 139 n.35 (D. Me. 2006) (recognizing that courts continue to approve of the *Bogosian* presumption).

[47] *See Linerboard*, 305 F.3d at 153, 155 (applying "belt and suspenders" approach); *In re* Pressure Sensitive Labelstock Antitrust Litig., MDL No. 1556, 2007 U.S. Dist. LEXIS 85466, at *49 n.8 (M.D. Pa. Nov. 19, 2007) (noting that courts and litigants often rely on *Bogosian* coupled with economic analysis); *In re* Bulk [extruded] Graphite Prods. Antitrust Litig., No. 02-6030, 2006 U.S. Dist. LEXIS 16619, at *35 (D.N.J. Apr. 4, 2006) (unpublished) (approving of "belt and suspenders" approach). For a discussion of the role of economic experts in proving common impact, see Chapter 8 of this Handbook.

[48] *In re* Warfarin Sodium Antitrust Litig., 391 F.3d 516 (3d Cir. 2004).

[49] *Id.* at 522–23.

[50] *Id.* at 529.

[51] *Id.* (citing *Amchem*, 521 U.S. at 620).

matter does not defeat commonality and predominance."[52] Other courts have similarly certified nationwide indirect purchaser settlement classes, despite differences in state law.[53]

Although class members need not have identical claims in order to satisfy commonality or predominance,[54] indirect purchaser plaintiffs still may find it advantageous to assert a common claim, such as a nationwide Sherman Act claim for damages or injunctive relief, even if the claim has been dismissed or is subject to dismissal on *Illinois Brick* grounds. Plaintiffs should continue to assert the claim and maintain a right of appeal throughout the litigation. At least one district court has found the existence of a dismissed, but appealable, claim shared by all class members to be helpful in finding commonality and predominance in certifying a settlement class.[55]

12.05.2 Allocation among disparate groups and subclasses

When some class members are situated differently from others, settling parties and courts must come up with creative ways to fairly allocate settlement proceeds to account for these differences. These differences often fall into two main categories: (1) the class includes members who have purchased at different levels of the distribution chain, which may affect the amount of damage suffered by each class member; and (2) the class includes members who reside or purchased in different states, which may affect the right to relief available to class members.

12.05.2(A) ALLOCATING AMONG DIFFERENT LEVELS OF THE DISTRIBUTION CHAIN

Cases are not often cleanly categorized as direct purchaser cases and indirect purchaser cases. Related direct and indirect purchaser cases are commonly consolidated into a single action, either through Rule 42(a) or via proceedings before the Judicial Panel on Multidistrict Litigation. In such cases, courts often define separate classes of direct purchasers and indirect purchasers, and assign separate counsel to each. Further, given the realities of the marketplace, where indirect purchasers – be they wholesalers, retailers or consumers – may buy at various levels in a distribution chain, courts may further divide an indirect purchaser class into subclasses to account for the different interests of each group.

The use of settlement subclasses in this context puts the issue of "pass on" before the court. In other words, parties will argue as to how and to what degree an overcharge resulting from defendants' unlawful conduct is passed down the distribution chain from direct purchasers to the various levels of indirect purchasers. For example, purchasers higher up the chain at the wholesale level may absorb some of the overcharge, lessening the effect

---

52 *Id.* at 530.

53 *See, e.g.*, *In re* Cardizem CD Antitrust Litig., 218 F.R.D. 508 (E.D. Mich. 2003); *In re* New Motor Vehicles Canadian Exp. Antitrust Litig., 269 F.R.D. 80 (D. Me. 2010).

54 *See Warfarin*, 391 F.3d at 530 ("In *Prudential*, we noted that 'a finding of commonality does not require all class members share identical claims,' 148 F.3d at 310, and we rejected an objector's contention that predominance was defeated because claims were subject to the laws of fifty states, *id.* at 315.") (citing *In re* Prudential Ins. Co. Am. Sales Practice Litig. Agent Actions, 148 F.3d 283 (3d Cir. 1998)).

55 *See New Motor Vehicles*, 269 F.R.D. at 88 (noting the propriety of settling a nationwide Sherman Act claim subject to appeal); *see also* Ramirez v. DeCoster, 142 F. Supp. 2d 104 (D. Me. 2001).

on those purchasing further down the chain, such as consumers. Counsel for each class or subclass will advocate for a fair allocation and ensure that all voices are heard.

Although subclasses may be necessary to avoid conflicts of interest, they also place considerable cost and timing demands on class counsel, who must devise an allocation plan. Determining the proper allocation for each type of purchaser often involves complex economic analysis provided by expert witnesses, including competing expert witnesses who may submit reports on behalf of each class or subclass. In addition, if the settlement is reached prior to formal discovery, counsel for various classes or subclasses may require the defendant to agree to provide discovery in order to enable this expert analysis. Nonparty discovery may also be necessary.

The *Sullivan v. De Beers* case illustrates the use of subclasses in determining a fair allocation of settlement proceeds. There, the district court certified a direct purchaser class and an indirect purchaser class.[56] The indirect purchaser class was further divided into a "consumer" subclass and a "reseller" subclass, with the latter consisting of diamond wholesalers and retailers that did not buy directly from De Beers. Each class and subclass was represented by separate counsel. The settlement called for $22.5 million to be allocated to the direct purchaser class, and $272.5 million to the indirect purchaser class. To determine the apportionment between the reseller and consumer subclasses, the district court appointed a special master to consider extensive briefing and expert reports concerning the diamond industry, diamond prices, and other issues relevant to allocating settlement proceeds. The process involved enormous time and effort by class counsel and the special master, but such an effort may be necessary to ensure the adequate representation of differently situated class members.

12.05.2(B) Allocating among class members in different states

When the settlement class is comprised of indirect purchasers across the country asserting various state antitrust and consumer protection law claims, courts take a number of different approaches in determining how to fairly allocate settlement money across the class. First, some courts approve allocation plans that do not differentiate between class members of various states. This streamlines administration of claims, ensures that all those releasing claims are compensated, and assists class members in comprehending their rights by simplifying the settlement notice. But such plans are subject to objections from class members in *Illinois Brick*-repealer states who may argue that they deserve a greater share of the settlement money than those class members residing in states whose laws do not permit indirect purchasers to sue for damages.

Second, courts may require that class counsel weigh the various claims of class members and provide greater recovery to those with the strongest claims. In some instances, courts

---

[56] In *Sullivan*, the district court certified nationwide direct and indirect purchaser classes and granted final approval of the settlement. Sullivan v. DB Investments, Inc., 2008 U.S. Dist. LEXIS 81146 (D.N.J. May 22, 2008). Objectors appealed, and a three-judge panel of the Third Circuit, in a 2-1 decision, questioned whether the case could be certified for settlement purposes as drawn and remanded to the district court. Sullivan v. DB Investments, Inc., 613 F.3d 134 (3d Cir. 2010). On plaintiffs' motion, shortly thereafter, the Third Circuit vacated the panel's decision and granted rehearing en banc. Sullivan v. DB Investments, Inc., 619 F.3d 287 (3d Cir. 2010). The en banc rehearing occurred in early 2011, but as of this writing, the court has not filed its opinion.

will employ subclasses to ensure that the various competing interests are adequately represented in this respect.[57] But weighing what are often only hypothetical claims is inherently imprecise, and courts have not articulated the criteria that should be used to determine if, and by how much, the claims of a class member in one state are stronger than the claims of a class member in another state. For example, state antitrust and consumer protection laws not only vary by whether indirect purchasers have standing to sue for damages, they may also vary as to (1) the remedy available (e.g., single versus treble damages); (2) whether the claim may be asserted on behalf of a class; (3) whether the claim is limited to intrastate commerce or conduct; and (4) whether there is a presumption of antitrust impact from a showing of unlawful conspiracy. Still other factors may also vary among states' laws, and given this complexity, class members confronted with a settlement notice may have difficulty understanding why they will receive less money than others, which may inform their determination of whether to object or opt-out.

Unsurprisingly, the added complexity associated with subclasses also leads to added costs. In fact, subclasses can require significant extra attorney time, from a greater number of attorneys, who will ultimately seek and be entitled to recompense from the settlement proceeds, thereby diminishing the total amount of cash distributed to class members. Expert reports submitted on behalf of each subclass may further drive up expenses and diminish the amount of settlement proceeds distributed to class members. These costs should be carefully considered, especially when recovery is limited, and weighed against concerns about adequacy of representation.

Finally, it is important to note that perfection is not the standard when judging an allocation plan. "An allocation formula need only have a reasonable, rational basis, particularly if recommended by experienced and competent class counsel."[58] Significant differences among class members should be considered, but other considerations like fairness and efficiency need not yield entirely to a perfect, precise allocation plan.

12.05.3 Coupon settlements, claims-made settlements, and non-monetary consideration

12.05.3(A) Coupon settlements

Settlements that provide compensation to class members in the form of coupons, discounts, credits, or other non-monetary consideration have been criticized over the years.[59] Professor Leslie has identified three main problems with coupon settlements: (1) with low redemption rates, coupon settlements offer little meaningful compensation to class members; (2) when a coupon is not redeemed, the defendant does not give up any money, making it likely that the defendant will retain ill-gotten gains; and (3) coupon settlements require class members to do future business with the defendant.[60]

Congress listened and included in CAFA specific provisions concerning coupon settlements that are aimed at reigning in abuse. CAFA provides two main safeguards. First, attorney fee awards must be based on the "value to class members of the coupons that are

---

57 *See, e.g.*, *In re* Relafen Antitrust Litig., 231 F.R.D. 52, 62–63 (D. Mass. 2005).
58 *In re* WorldCom, Inc. Sec. Litig., 388 F. Supp. 2d 319, 344 (S.D.N.Y. 2005).
59 *See, e.g.*, Christopher R. Leslie, *The Need to Study Coupon Settlements in Class Action Litigation*, 18 Geo. J. Legal Ethics 1395 (2005).
60 *Id.* at 1396–97.

redeemed."[61] Second, approval of a coupon settlement may only be made after the court has conducted a fairness hearing and made written findings that the settlement is fair, reasonable, and adequate.[62] Although this second provision mirrors prior law applicable to all settlements, some courts have interpreted the inclusion of these provisions in CAFA to suggest that coupon settlements are subject to heightened scrutiny at final approval.[63]

Does this mean coupon settlements are out of the question in federal court? No, but practitioners should realize that seeking approval of coupon settlements presents unique challenges. The settling parties can take several steps to put the settlement in the best possible position for approval. First, the coupon settlement needs to be structured carefully. The closer the degree to which coupons may be used like cash, the better. The parties should consider including the following components:

(1) The coupons should be freely transferrable.[64] The parties should consider creating a secondary market for the coupons, through market makers or eBay, to enhance transferability.
(2) Class members should be able to aggregate coupons (i.e., combine settlement coupons, and also combine settlement coupons with other discounts).[65]
(3) The redemption period should be sufficiently long such that class members can realistically use the coupons.[66] Some settling defendants will refuse to honor coupons until final approval is granted and all appeals are resolved, which can take months or years. In such cases, coupons that expire prior to any appeals being resolved provide little or no value to class members.
(4) The coupons should not be limited to specific products or services.[67]

The parties should also consider adding a cash component to the coupon settlement.[68] Or, if possible, providing class members with gift cards instead of coupons may be preferred. Gift cards alleviate many of the concerns associated with coupon settlements – they can be freely transferred, used for any product or service, and aggregated with other gift cards, coupons or discounts. Such gift cards may also, depending on the structure of the settlement, be convertible to cash.

Second, since many of the problems with coupon settlements are linked with low redemption rates, plaintiffs need to employ a robust notice plan to get the coupons into the hands of as many class members as possible. If the coupons are transferable within

---

61 28 U.S.C. § 1712(e).

62 *Id.*

63 *See, e.g.*, Figueroa v. Garner, 517 F. Supp. 2d 1292, 1320–21 (S.D. Fla. 2007).

64 David Martinez & Rebecka Biejo, *Coupon Settlements Under Seige*, Los Angeles Lawyer (Feb. 2009), *available at* http://rkmc.com/Coupon-Settlements-Under-Siege.htm.

65 *Id.*

66 Leslie, *supra*, note 59 at 1404–05; Martinez & Biejo, *supra*, note 64.

67 Martinez & Biejo, *supra* note 64; Leslie, *supra* note 59 at 1406–07. As Professor Leslie notes, some defendants want settlement coupons to increase sales of secondary products. He cites, for example, *In re Cuisinart Food Processor Antitrust Litigation*, 1983-2 Trade Cas. (CCH) P 65,680 (D. Conn. Oct. 24, 1983), an antitrust case concerning food processors in which the settlement coupons could not be redeemed to purchase food processors. Leslie, *supra* note 59 at 1406.

68 Martinez & Biejo, *supra* note 64.

a secondary market, the notice plan must clearly explain how this works so that class members can obtain as much value out of the coupons as possible.

Third, since the key to final approval is maximizing value to class members, plaintiffs must be able to provide the district court with as much reliable information as possible about how the coupons will bring value to class members and not just enrich class counsel.[69] For example, plaintiffs may employ experts to estimate likely redemption rates,[70] which will be higher if the coupons come with the fewest restrictions, as discussed above. Plaintiffs also need to have conducted sufficient discovery into the merits of the case so that the judge can weigh the coupon value versus the risks of continuing litigation.[71] Coupon settlements achieved in a case in which the defendant is very likely to win on the merits will have a greater chance of being approved than a coupon settlement entered prior to discovery or litigation of any major issues. Finally, a coupon settlement reached through the use of a mediator may have a greater chance of success.[72] Using a mediator may give the judge comfort that the parties are fully informed of the strengths and weaknesses of the case and that the coupon settlement was reached under the guiding hand of a neutral.

12.05.3(B) Claims-made settlements

Another form of settlement that may be employed, but has been subject to criticism, is the "claims-made" settlement.[73] In these settlements, defendants pay based on the actual claims filed by class members, and the total amount paid is usually capped at a maximum amount. In the antitrust context, for example, a defendant may set aside a fund and agree to pay the estimated overcharge suffered to class members who file a claim. Any amount remaining in the fund after claims are processed is returned to the defendant.

Antitrust cases pose some additional challenges not found in other types of cases when claims-made settlements are proposed. First, if the claim is based on estimates of damages suffered by class members, some expert analysis may be necessary, and it may require significant discovery from the defendant. Thus, a claims-made settlement is more likely to be employed near the end of a case when the damages analysis is already complete. Second, if the product at issue is sold to unidentifiable consumers, notice efforts will be restricted to publishing notice in newspapers, magazines, and the Internet. Although publication notice plans are often effective, they may not be able to reach all class members.[74] Consequently, class members not viewing the notice will not make a claim, and they will receive nothing from the settlement. A robust notice plan is necessary to reach as many class members as possible.

---

[69] *See id.*

[70] *Id.*

[71] *Id.*

[72] *Id.*

[73] *See, e.g.*, Kakani v. Oracle Corp., No. C 06-06493 WHA, 2007 U.S. Dist. LEXIS 47515 (N.D. Cal. June 19, 2007) (rejecting claims-made settlement).

[74] For a discussion of how to effectively pursue publication notice, see Chapter 13 of this Handbook.

12.05.4 Injunctive relief

Plaintiffs will often seek some form of injunctive relief as part of a settlement. The relief may take a number of forms, depending on the particular facts of the case. Whatever the form, the parties should consider two factors on which courts have recently focused.

First, an important factor in determining whether an injunctive class will be certified is whether the threat of injury from defendants' conduct is imminent. The trend today is for courts to deny certification of injunctive classes – settlement or otherwise – under Rule 23(b)(2) if defendants have already ceased the offending conduct or other factors have intervened to reduce or eliminate the likelihood of injury. For example, in *In re New Motor Vehicles Canadian Export Antitrust Litigation*, the First Circuit, in considering defendants' challenge to the district court's order certifying a nationwide class under Rule 23(b)(2), dismissed outright plaintiffs' Clayton Act claim for injunctive relief. In the appellate court's view, an outside factor – in this case, the exchange rate between Canada and the United States – had so changed since the filing of the case that no imminent threat of injury to class members existed. Although decided in the context of litigation and not settlement, the First Circuit's opinion was later relied on by the district court to deny certification of a settlement class under Rule 23(b)(2).[75] Thus, class counsel must consider whether the injunctive relief they seek is necessary to prevent imminent harm. If not, the Rule 23(b)(2) class will likely be denied certification.

Second, the type of injunctive relief sought may be key to the certification prospects. As the Supreme Court's recent decision in *Wal-Mart v. Dukes* made clear, certification of a Rule 23(b)(2) class may not be appropriate if the injunctive relief sought is primarily monetary in character.[76]

12.05.4(A) Cooperation agreements

Often, plaintiffs will seek promises of cooperation from defendants as part of the injunctive class settlement. These cooperation agreements are matters of contract and should not be affected by whether the court certifies a Rule 23(b)(2) class. But plaintiffs should be aware that, in the case of a partial settlement, cooperation agreements may give nonsettling defendants standing to object to the settlement when they otherwise would have no such standing. Nonsettling defendants will want assurances that they, too, will receive any discovery promised to plaintiffs by a settling defendant.

12.05.5 Cy pres

In some cases, settlements will propose distributing all or a part of the settlement proceeds to one or more nonprofit or charitable organizations instead of directly to class members. Such a distribution is called a "cy pres" distribution, a term that originated in trust and estates law.[77] In the class action context, cy pres distributions are used in two

---

[75] *See In re* New Motor Vehicles Canadian Exp. Antitrust Litig., 269 F.R.D. 80, 87 (D. Me. 2010).

[76] *See* Wal-Mart, Inc. v. Dukes, 131 S.Ct. 2541 (2011).

[77] *See In re* Pharm. Indus. Average Wholesale Price Litig., 588 F.3d 24, 33 (1st Cir. 2009) [hereinafter *AWP*]. For a full discussion of cy pres remedies, see Chapter 14 of this Handbook.

main situations. First, a cy pres distribution is proposed when distributing money to class members is not feasible.[78] For example, class members may be so difficult to find, or the number of class members may be so large compared to the recovery, that notice costs coupled with the costs of cutting checks may not justify the disbursement of proceeds to class members.[79] Sometimes, direct distribution of funds will only be feasible for part of the class, and the parties will propose making a cy pres distribution of part of the settlement proceeds for the indirect benefit of those not receiving a direct payment. Whether such a cy pres component will be approved depends on the circumstances of each particular case.[80]

Second, parties may propose to make a cy pres distribution of any settlement proceeds that remain after checks have been sent to eligible claimants. A residual may remain because some class members simply do not cash their checks.[81] Or, the allocation may be based on the claims actually made by class members, but the settlement contemplates a cy pres distribution instead of a reversion to the defendant.[82] When a residual remains, the trend is to first require a second distribution to class members, if feasible, even if that risks giving class members a windfall.[83]

Although courts have approved cy pres awards on a number of occasions, practitioners should heed the following guidelines. First, make every effort to identify and distribute direct payment to class members. Courts will be skeptical of cy pres awards, especially when the parties propose a cy pres distribution of the entire settlement fund. Second, ensure that cy pres awards are made to organizations whose interests closely match those of class members not receiving direct payment. Plaintiffs may consider sending out requests for proposals from various charitable organizations or even employing consultants to find appropriate cy pres recipients. Making the extra effort will ensure that the cy pres distribution provides a benefit to the class.[84]

---

[78] *AWP*, 588 F.3d at 34.

[79] *See id.*

[80] *Compare In re* Agent Orange Prod. Liab. Litig., 818 F.2d 179, 184–85 (2d Cir. 1987) (approving use of a portion of the settlement fund to fund assistance programs for the class as a whole where distribution to individuals was not feasible), *and In re* Relafen Antitrust Litig., 231 F.R.D. 52, 82–83 (D. Mass. 2005) (approving partial cy pres award for the indirect benefit of a subset of the class with the weakest claims and highest chance of receiving no recovery), *with In re* New Motor Vehicles Canadian Exp. Antitrust Litig., MDL Docket No. 1532, 2011 U.S. Dist. LEXIS 40843, at *36–39 (D. Me. Apr. 13, 2011) (rejecting cy pres award proposed for the indirect benefit of a subset of the class with the weakest claims when distribution to such class members was not feasible). The Fifth Circuit in Klier v. Elf Atochem, 2011 U.S. App Lexis 19650 (September 26, 2011), recently rejected a proposed cy pres award of the residual funds in a medical monitoring class action settled several years earlier. The Court's ruling, although limited to the specific provisions of the settlement agreement which provided that residual funds from one subclass should be paid over to the other subclass, was generally critical of cy pres where class members could be found and funds distributed in a practical manner. The Court observed that the settlement agreement ". . . preserved for the class something akin to a reversionary interest in funds unused for a particular subclass." *Id.*

[81] *AWP*, 588 F.3d at 34.

[82] *Id.*

[83] *See* Principles of Aggregate Litig. § 3.07 at 218–19.

[84] *See also* Albert A. Foer, *Enhancing Competition Through the Cy Pres Remedy: Suggested Best Practices*, 24 Antitrust 86 (Spring 2010) (suggesting best practices for the invocation of cy pres).

§12.06 Approval of class settlements

In a matter as significant and public as settlement of an antitrust class action, failure is expensive, in terms of wasted resources, credibility with the court, and reputation of the counsel involved. Nonetheless, the same motivations that can bring the parties together – plaintiffs' desire to create an opening in prosecuting or resolving the action, and defendants' desire for an early and economical resolution – create temptations that can doom antitrust class settlements.

When a settlement fails to win final approval in court (or in the "court of public opinion" among class members, i.e., a significant number of class members opt-out), the failure is often attributable to a shortfall in the information provided to justify the fairness and adequacy of the settlement. The preliminary approval stage, after all, represents merely a determination that the terms of the proposed settlement merit consideration by class members, the court having concluded that such terms are the product of arms' length negotiations conducted by experienced counsel with sufficient discovery to act intelligently (and that they face few known objectors, or relatively few compared to the size of the class). At final approval, however, Rule 23(e) provides for approval only "after a hearing and on finding that [the settlement] is fair, reasonable, and adequate." In addition to the negotiation history, the factors relevant to such a finding include the likelihood of success on the merits and the costs of continued litigation.[85] Here, the parties are well-served to include specifics concerning the issues raised in the litigation, particularly any unsettled ones, even though some plaintiffs may do so reluctantly.

In the final analysis, though, because the adequacy of a class settlement is partly determined by a somewhat amorphous criterion (i.e., the "uncertainty" of continued litigation), class members' approval and acceptance of a settlement can depend more on "optics" than precise mathematics. The court likely will expect some estimation of damages attributable to the alleged conduct, of course, but plaintiffs may be wary of potentially tying themselves to a too-conservative damages theory if litigation against other defendants is continuing. The result may be a need to justify as adequate a number that represents a very small percentage of damages. To illustrate, a rule-of-thumb among many antitrust practitioners is that cartel conduct may result in overcharges on the order of 10 percent of the affected commerce (before trebling of damages). Yet, that being at best an order-of-magnitude estimation, class settlements have been approved that concededly provided cash compensation of less than two or three percent of the allegedly affected sales.[86]

When presenting such a settlement for approval, plaintiffs must be prepared to accept significant hurdles to the continued prosecution of the action, including, obviously, the lost prospect of recovery against the settling defendant, but also, more abstractly, the loss of a defendant with the ability to pay. At the same time, plaintiffs must make a convincing case for the substantial value of the settling defendant's cooperation and any injunctive relief provided by the settlement. Even if a settlement is approved by the court, in the

---

[85] *In re* Cardizem CD Antitrust Litig., 218 F.R.D. 508, 522 (E.D. Mich. 2003) (discussing approval factors).

[86] *In re* GMC Pickup Truck Fuel Tank Prods. Liability Litig., 55 F.3d 768 (3d Cir. 1995)

absence of such a well-documented analysis, it may be subject to additional scrutiny by objectors[87] and potential collateral attack or skepticism by class members, who then deign to opt out.

Finally, an antitrust class settlement is generally too important to risk dooming for a failure of administration, such as an inadequate notice plan. Experienced claims administration professionals should be utilized both to design an adequate notice plan and assist in preparation of an appropriate "plain English" notice. (In addition to processing claims, administrators are often well-versed in the mechanics and tax reporting associated with escrow accounts for settlement proceeds properly set up in a "Qualified Settlement Fund" pursuant to Treasury regulations.)[88]

§ 12.07 The negotiation and award of plaintiffs' attorneys fees and expenses[89]

Virtually without exception, plaintiffs' attorneys work on some form of contingent fee arrangement in civil antitrust cases. This is particularly true in the class action arena. Typically, the award of fees and reimbursement of expenses are made under the common fund doctrine. In common fund cases, courts award and pay fees and expenses from the gross recovery. Increasingly, particularly in federal antitrust litigation, courts award a percentage-of-recovery fee rather than a fee based strictly on the lodestars of the plaintiffs' attorneys.

12.07.1 Common fund cases

One of the perennial issues that arise in settlement negotiations of antitrust class actions is the timing and negotiation of fees and expenses. Simply put, in common fund cases this should be a non-issue. There is no need for negotiation. The settling defendant pays an "all in" dollar amount. Plaintiffs' attorneys apply to the court for an award of fees and expenses to be paid from the gross settlement proceeds before payments are made to eligible class claimants.

Plaintiffs' attorneys would be well-advised not to negotiate for what is commonly referred to as a "clear sailing" provision. Such a provision typically compels the defendant to refrain from objecting or requires a settling defendant to affirmatively support a fee application. In recent years, some courts have been critical of such provisions. The better practice is for the defendant to take no position on fees and expenses, because once the "all in" amount has been paid in settlement, the settling defendants should

---

87 Whether objectors are drawn to a class settlement can be impacted by a number of factors addressed herein (e.g., avoiding any suggestion of collusion through appropriate confirmatory discovery and use of experts, employing third-party mediators if appropriate, and retaining a respected notice expert), as well as the prospect for attorneys fees for an objector's counsel, which are allowable under Fed. R. Civ. P. 23, depending upon the ultimately viability of the objection.

88 For further discussion of the importance of employing notice and claims administration experts, see Chapter 13 of this Handbook.

89 For further discussion of awards for attorney fees and expenses, see Chapter 9 and Chapter 10 of this Handbook.

have no interest in the disbursement of such funds, as long as the plaintiffs' requests for an award of fees and expenses do not jeopardize the court granting preliminary or final settlement approval.

12.07.2 Mixed compensation settlements

Plaintiffs' attorney fees become a more complicated issue when settlements are structured to include significant non-cash benefits. For example, a settlement can include cash compensation in a common fund amount but also include significant injunctive relief providing tangible benefits to class members. In that circumstance, plaintiffs' attorneys may believe, and correctly so, that they have conferred a benefit on the class beyond the monetary recovery, for which they should be fairly compensated. In these circumstances, experience has shown that applications for such compensation are more likely to attract objections from class members who contest the value placed upon such non-monetary settlement benefits. Typically, since they are not class members and work for cash compensation, attorneys cannot share in the benefits obtained by injunctive relief that, for instance, may require a settling defendant to undertake future affirmative acts such as offering product discounts, etc. Therefore, plaintiffs' attorneys usually seek additional compensation from the cash component of the settlement, potentially setting the stage for a battle on the value of any such non-cash compensation and the appropriate amount to be paid from the common fund. Plaintiffs' counsel are well advised to carefully and conservatively value any such compensation sought and should be prepared to defend such valuation with appropriate demonstration, including well grounded opinions by those with expertise in valuing such benefits.

12.07.3 When to negotiate

As mentioned above, common fund settlements do not require a separate negotiation on attorneys' fees. When the settlement structure involves non-monetary compensation or mixed cash and non-cash compensation, the parties should be attuned to important ethical issues concerning negotiations over the amount of attorneys' fees to be paid by the settling defendant. More than one settlement has been derailed because the parties did not sufficiently separate settlement negotiations from fee negotiations. Over the past few decades, the majority of court decisions seem to hold that, where the settling defendant is paying fees on top of settlement consideration, the parties need to reach an agreement in principal on all essential terms of the settlement benefits for class members before negotiations on the subject of attorneys' fees and expenses may begin.

Tension for the parties with regard to the ethical need to separate negotiations usually comes from the settling defendant wanting to know the whole cost of the settlement. If the parties first reach agreement on the essential terms of a non-monetary or mixed compensation settlement without any negotiation or agreement on the amount of attorneys' fees, defendants usually do not have complete knowledge of the total costs of settlement. This "timing" problem can usually be handled in a variety of ways. Experienced counsel have a general idea as to the amount of a reasonable fee that is likely to be approved by the court. Thus, counsel should be able to advise the settling defendant as to the likely parameters of a reasonable fee. Often an experienced mediator who is familiar with the general range of accepted fee awards can advise the parties as well. Finally, when all else fails, the parties may agree to disagree and, having preserved the terms of the settlement for the benefit of the class, submit the question of appropriate fees to the court with both parties advocating for what they deem to be an appropriate award. Some creative solutions in this scenario include asking the settling court to appoint a special master to hear, report, and recommend an award of fees and expenses, or having the parties stipulate to a "high/low," depending on the award approved by the court. In other words, plaintiffs will cap their request if defendants agree not to object to a request as long as it is below a certain ceiling.

12.07.4 What is a reasonable fee request?

For the past 15 years or more, courts have migrated away from fee awards based strictly on the lodestar approach. Well-founded criticism of the lodestar method usually focused on the very intensive effort required by the approving court in scrutinizing the fee submissions of petitioning plaintiffs' counsel in determining the appropriate lodestar. Among the common issues confronting courts determining an appropriate lodestar are (1) whether the hourly rates charged are reasonable; (2) whether the time expended for individual tasks, often in multi-year litigation, was reasonable; and (3) whether staffing was efficient, i.e. whether attorneys with the requisite level of experience were assigned to tasks commensurate with their skill level and hourly rates.[90]

Most federal courts follow a percentage of recovery approach. Under this methodology, courts look at the settlement achieved and award a percentage of such a recovery as fees. In this circumstance, most courts will apply what is referred to as a "lodestar cross-check." In other words, courts will look at the total reported lodestar (although without diving into the minutiae of such reports) to see if the lodestar bears a reasonable relationship to the percentage fee requested. Unless the recovery is unusually large, fees in the neighborhood of 25–33 percent of the gross settlement recovery and that equate to no more than three-to-four times the lodestar will typically pass muster with most approving courts. Most circuits have guidelines for trial court approval of fees and expenses. These multi-part tests usually look at the results obtained compared with potential damages, the stage of the litigation at the time of settlement, the percentage fee request relative to the lodestar, the assessment of risk in the case, and the overall quality of work and representation by petitioning counsel.[91]

12.07.5 Incentive awards to named plaintiffs

In complex antitrust cases, which often pit customer victims against their suppliers in market allocation or price fixing cases, courts generally recognize the sacrifice that named plaintiffs have to make to step forward on behalf of the class members. Most courts will recognize the benefits conferred on the class when settlements are achieved by the named

---

[90] Gunter v. Ridgewood Energy Corp., 223 F.3d 190 (3d Cir. 2000).

[91] *In re* ATT Corp. Sec. Litig., 455 F.3d 160 (3d Cir. 2006).

plaintiff.[92] Although not a completely settled area of the law, courts generally will approve reasonable and modest special payments to named plaintiffs.[93] Depending on the circumstance, such awards can range from a few hundred dollars, where there are many individual consumer plaintiffs, to tens of thousands of dollars in cases where there are very few named plaintiffs who have taken on the next level of distribution in industries where they engage in commerce. These plaintiffs risk "retaliation," which is hard to measure, as well as the burdens of discovery that absent class members avoid. Of course, under Rule 23, named plaintiffs also are entitled to no greater treatment than absent class members when it comes to sharing in the distribution of settlement proceeds. For these reasons, courts will generally look favorably upon an application for an incentive award as long as it is proportional to awards in other similar cases and does not materially prejudice absent class members.

§ 12.08 Dealing with class settlement opt-outs

In terms of both unresolved exposure and potential for continuing litigation, opt-outs from an antitrust settlement class are a trap for the unprepared. From the perspective of class plaintiffs' counsel, opt-outs are by definition not their clients, but they still present a concern insofar as they impede a settlement's consummation or reduce its absolute or relative value. For defendants, significant opt-outs not only eviscerate the concept of global peace, but in some instances they are indicative of important customers' dissatisfaction with what the defendant has done to "make things right." And because the opt-outs are no longer members of a putative class suing the settling defendant(s), they no longer benefit from a toll on the statute of limitations provided by the pendency of the class action. As a result, they face pressures to promptly sue, settle, or enter into a separate tolling agreement (depending upon the risk tolerances and leverage possessed by the opt-out and the defendant).

For these reasons, defense counsel in particular are well-advised to assess and address the potential opt-out landscape as accurately and as far in advance as possible.[94] In recent years, significant purchasers of allegedly price-fixed goods have begun joining forces (in joint negotiations, through joint prosecution arrangements, and sometimes through common representation) to leverage their ability to acquire more information about the fairness of a proposed class settlement and, commonly, to demand a premium for

---

92 *See, e.g., In re* Relafen Antitrust Litig., 231 F.R.D. 52, 82 (D. Mass. 2005) (noting that incentive awards "serv[e] an important function in promoting class action settlements, particularly where . . . the named plaintiffs participated actively in the litigation").

93 *See, e.g., id.* at 82; *In re* Compact Disc Minimum Advertised Price Antitrust Litig., 292 F. Supp. 2d 184, 189 (D. Me. 2003); *In re* Lupron Mktg. & Sales Practices Litig., MDL Docket No. 1430, 2005 U.S. Dist. LEXIS 17456, at *25 (D. Mass. Aug. 17, 2005); *In re* Electrical Carbon Products Antitrust Litig., 447 F.Supp.2d 389 (D.N.J. 2006).

94 Opt-outs are singled out here because their impact on a settlement that is thought to be a "done deal" can be so significant if not properly anticipated. Significant eleventh-hour problems also can arise in the form of responding to class settlement objectors, negotiating acceptable media statements, and taking appropriate measures to establish a Qualified Settlement Fund, among others. The wide-ranging settlements identified in note 5, *supra*, are tools that can be utilized in planning ahead for such issues.

releasing their claims. Information about such large potential opt-outs may be forthcoming prior to a class settlement being reached, even if no separate lawsuits actually have been filed. If the potential opt-outs are current customers, for example, they might make inquiries about the litigation through businesspersons. Their counsel might also be seen monitoring court proceedings from the gallery. And their counsel might make themselves known to the defendants, as neither an opt-out nor a settling defendant is well-served if a defendant's limited settlement resources are imprudently allocated to a class resolution that would resolve less than the defendant anticipated.

The calculus for resolving opt-out claims is complex and fact-dependent. If important ongoing business relationships are involved, non-cash components can enrich the value. The significance of cooperation provisions may be quite different for an opt-out (or opt-out group) than for class counsel, depending upon the opt-out's strategy for negotiations and plans, if any, to actually litigate. The opt-out may have the availability of a friendlier venue in which to pursue an action, if filed. In some instances, even on a dollar-to-dollar cash comparison basis, the opt-out may seek exactly what the class is receiving, because it expects to net more owing to an advantageous fee agreement with its own separate, independent counsel. Thus, even in instances in which class counsel may try to negotiate their own MFN for the class with respect to separate settlements (a tactic likely to be dismissed by any defendant not utterly desperate to settle), there is plenty of drafting room for a defendant to deal with opt-outs.

To protect itself from as yet unknown opt-outs and to accommodate a known or unknown opt-out risk, a defendant can seek to include: (1) a provision to "blow" (or "blow up") the settlement, to wit, a one-way option to rescind the agreement if the number of opt-outs (sometimes the measure in a consumer class action), and/or the percentage of purchases represented by opt-outs, reaches a defined threshold; and/or (2) a provision for reduction(s) of its settlement payment according to defined level(s) of opt-outs. These provisions can be subject to substantial negotiations, as a number of plaintiffs' attorneys have expressed concern that the terms encourage others to free-ride on their efforts and opt out to avoid paying class counsel's fees. To address opt-out groups that may seek to game the process at the preliminary approval stage, class counsel now often file the numerical threshold for the "blow" provision under seal with court approval.

In the event that a defendant has not appropriately planned for the opt-out issue in advance, it can be extremely difficult to address later. Because class members are generally not to be treated unequally, opt-outs generally cannot participate in a class settlement that class counsel has crafted (by negotiating broad releases and requiring that claimants represent that they have not received other compensation for released claims). In rare and appropriate circumstances, it may be possible for certain opt-outs to participate in the class and receive compensation for a broader release than that granted in the class action, but the timing of such negotiations and the legitimacy of the claims may be scrutinized and challenged. Accordingly, in confronting potential opt-out issues, as with most aspects of antitrust settlements, careful planning is critical.

13 Class notice and claims administration

Katherine Kinsella and Shannon Wheatman[1]

§ 13.01 Introduction

Much has been written and discussed about the negative aspects of class action litigation, both in antitrust and in other areas of law.[2] To be sure, the class action device is far from perfect. Of the many concerns raised by critics, perhaps the most serious involves the threat posed to fundamental due process rights. The opportunity to be heard is a pillar of our due process guarantees, but in class action litigation, rank-and-file class members do not control the litigation; they leave their legal fate in the hands of lead plaintiffs. At least in theory, therefore, class actions may present a problem. In practice, however, since modern class action litigation emerged over 70 years ago, federal and state laws have evolved safeguards to protect the due process rights of class members. They do this most prominently by requiring lead plaintiffs and their lawyers to notify potential members of the class that litigation concerning their rights is proceeding, and that individual members are free to opt out. This chapter discusses the contours of those notice rules.

[1] Katherine Kinsella is the President and Shannon Wheatman, Ph.D. is a Vice President of Kinsella Media. They are leading, nationally and internationally recognized experts in the design, preparation, and dissemination of legal notice in class actions and bankruptcies.

[2] For a response to some of these negative critiques, see the Introduction to this Handbook.

§ 13.02 Overview

Notification has played a prominent role in class action litigation since Rule 23 of the Federal Rules of Civil Procedure was established in 1938. The role of notice in class actions was expanded in 1966 when Rule 23 was modified to require lead plaintiffs to give the "best notice practicable."[3] Class action notice provisions advanced even further in 2003, when Rule 23 was amended to require that notifications use plain language to make it easier for potential class members to recognize when class litigation might affect their rights.[4] Additionally, Rule 23 requires close judicial scrutiny over the entire class action process, and it provides an explicit standard ("fair, reasonable, and adequate") for approving a settlement.[5] In addition, for class actions brought in federal court, the Class Action Fairness Act of 2005 (CAFA) allows federal and state attorneys general and regulators to scrutinize settlements, thereby enhancing due process protections for class members.[6]

Notifying potential class members about a lawsuit, and giving them an opportunity to be heard, solves many problems inherent in class actions. Beginning with the landmark ruling by the U.S. Supreme Court in *Mullane v. Central Hanover & Trust Company*,[7] class action jurisprudence has repeatedly affirmed that notice plays a critical role in due process. There, the Court stated:

> [A]n elementary and fundamental requirement of due process in any proceeding which is to be accorded finality is notice reasonably calculated, under all the circumstances, to apprise interested parties of the pendency of the action and afford them an opportunity to present their objection.[8] It has been said that notice helps to "democratize" the class action procedure.[9]

Notice provides the mechanism for class members to act. Every class member has an equal right to participate in the class action, but those rights have value only when individuals receive notification. Notice in Rule 23(b)(1) and (b)(2) classes, where money damages are not involved, does not include a right to exclude oneself (opt-out) and is given at the court's discretion when appropriate under the circumstances of the case. However, notice is mandatory in Rule 23(b)(3) classes where money damages are involved.[10] Where the litigation is moving towards trial, the notice typically is disseminated at least 30 days

---

3 FED. R. CIV. P. 23(c)(2)

4 *Id.*

5 FED. R. CIV. P. 23(e).

6 The Class Action Fairness Act of 2005, 28 U.S.C. §§ 1712–1715 (2005).

7 339 U.S. 306 (1950)

8 *Mullane*, 339 U.S. at 315.

9 *See* Benjamin K. Kaplan, *Continuing Work of the Civil Committee: 1966 Amendment of the Federal Rules of Civil Procedure (1)*, 81 HARV. L. REV. 356, 392 (1967).

10 Rule 23(b)(1) prevents inconsistent adjudication that might occur if individual actions were allowed. Rule 23(b)(2) is used when plaintiffs are seeking declaratory or injunctive relief. Rule 23(b)(3) is suitable when a class action is superior to other available methods and common questions predominate over individual ones. Herbert B. Newberg & Alba Conte, 2 NEWBERG ON CLASS ACTIONS § 4:1 (4th ed., West 2002). For further discussion of Rule 23 requirements, see Chapter 5 of this Handbook.

before the start of the trial. If the litigation is being settled, the notice will be disseminated shortly after the court grants preliminary approval to the settlement.

The remainder of this chapter provides an overview of the notification requirements under Rule 23; suggests ways that lawyers and judges can evaluate a notice program to ensure that potential class members receive notices and can easily understand and act upon them; and explains how to design and execute a notice program. The chapter concludes with a discussion about administering class action litigation.

§13.03 Individual notice

Individual notice is sent directly to the class member, via first class mail (in the form of a letter or postcard) or electronic mail. The Supreme Court, in *Eisen v. Jacquelin,* made clear that individual notice must be provided to all class members who are identifiable through reasonable efforts, regardless of the cost.[11] "[W]hat is 'the best notice practicable under the circumstances' and what constitutes 'reasonable effort' is a determination of fact to be made in the individual litigation."[12] In *Jones v. Flowers,* the Court held that due process dictates that reasonable steps be taken to deal with undelivered mail.[13]

In referencing the notice requirements of Rule 23, the court in *In re Nissan Motor Corporation Antitrust Litigation* stated, "The United States Supreme Court has declared that subdivision (c)(2) expresses an 'unambiguous requirement' that 'individual notice must be provided to those class members who are identifiable through reasonable effort.'"[14] The Court in *Nissan* went on to explain, "[o]bviously, the word 'reasonable' cannot be ignored. In every case, reasonableness is a function of anticipated results, costs, and amount involved."[15] Generally, the cost of providing notice to a class certified for trial falls on the plaintiffs.[16] However, the court can order that the defendant bear some of the costs of identifying potential class members.[17] When a class action is being certified for settlement purposes only, typically the defendants will either separately pay for the costs of notice, or the money will be deducted from the settlement fund.[18]

§ 13.04 Paid media notice

The key question in any notice program is what constitutes "the best notice practicable"? When comprehensive mailing lists of class members exist, direct mail (by post or email) should be the primary method used for notification. When comprehensive mailing lists are unavailable or cannot be compiled through reasonable effort, then "notice by publication

---

[11] Eisen v. Jacquelin, 417 U.S. 156, 173 (1974).

[12] *In re* "Agent Orange" Prod. Liab. Litig., 100 F.R.D. 718, 729 (E.D.N.Y. 1983) (internal citations omitted).

[13] Jones v. Flowers, 547 U.S. 220, 225 (2006).

[14] *In re* Nissan Motor Corp. Antitrust Litig., 552 F.2d 1088, 1097 (5th Cir. 1977) (internal citations omitted).

[15] *Id.* at 1099.

[16] *Eisen*, 417 U.S. at 177.

[17] Oppenheimer Fund, Inc. v. Sanders, 437 U.S. 340, 350, 355–56, 358 (1978).

[18] For further discussion of settlement practice, see Chapter 12 of this Handbook.

will suffice under Rule 23(c)(2) and under the due process clause."[19] In *In Re Domestic Air Transportation Antitrust Litigation* the court held, "[i]f class members . . . cannot be identified, there is no other requirement of mandatory individual notice, and the Court must exercise its discretion to provide the best notice practicable under the circumstances."[20]

The overarching goal of any notice program is to effectively reach the members of the class so that they have a "meaningful" opportunity to be heard.[21] Rule 23 can "comport with constitutional standards of due process only if there is a maximum opportunity of notice to the absentee class members . . . ."[22] Each class action requires a notice program tailored to the specifics of the case. Factors such as the distribution or consumption of a product or service, the number of readily identifiable class members, the anticipated class size, the demographics of class members, and the geographic location of class members influence the direction and scope of a notice program.

For instance, direct and indirect purchasers form distinct classes in many antitrust cases. Direct purchasers, which are often businesses that may have registered agents authorized to receive notice, are usually "readily identifiable" and can be reached through direct mailed notice. The names and addresses of indirect purchasers, who are typically consumers of a particular product or service, whether an individual or entity, are not usually known. While there are many ways to communicate information, paid media is usually the basic component of a notice plan intended to reach unidentifiable class members. Lawyers for the class can target paid media to specific demographic groups. Accredited marketing research firms can help to ensure that the notice has sufficient reach and is published frequently enough. Paid media also has the advantage of affording class lawyers a contractual guarantee that notices will be published on specific dates.

To select which publication will run the notice, it is important to rely on an expert to analyze demographics and media usage. Lawyers are not trained in this analysis and usually lack the requisite skills. An expert can help ensure that the notice program uses the optimal media or mixture of media to ensure that the notice does not cost too much money, and that it reaches the proper audience. Cost efficiency is critical in any large media campaign. Of course, the overall cost of class notice depends on the size and geographic location of class members. For example, a national notice program relying entirely on paid media is expensive – costs frequently run to over a million dollars.

13.04.1 Identifying a target demographic and selecting media

Demographics of class members guide the selection of media in a class action notice program. Individuals within the general population consume media differently based on income, gender, age, education, and other factors. Notice programs therefore must establish a clear demographic target or targets in order to select media to reach a specific audience. How a product or service was used or how a product exposure occurred, by or

---

[19] Carlough v. Amchem Prods., Inc., 158 F.R.D. 314, 325 (E.D. Pa. 1993) (citing *Mullane*, 339 U.S. 306, 317–18 (1950)).

[20] *In re* Domestic Air Transp. Antitrust Litig., 141 F.R.D. 534, 555 (N.D. Ga. 1992).

[21] Armstrong v. Manzo, 380 U.S. 545, 552 (1965) (due process requires an opportunity to be heard "at a meaningful time and in a meaningful manner").

[22] Greenfield v. Villager Indus., Inc., 483 F.2d 824, 831 (3d Cir. 1973).

to whom, where and over what period of time, provides critical information in identifying key demographic and geographic characteristics of potential class members. This research establishes the parameters for identifying and locating class members and shapes the notice program.

This profile of the class is developed from accredited media and marketing research firms, which provide data on audience size, composition, and other factors pertaining to major media, including broadcast, print, and outdoor advertising. In particular, the Survey of the American Consumer, conducted on an ongoing basis by Gfk MRI (MRI)[23] provides a single source measurement of major media, products, services, and in-depth consumer demographic and lifestyle or psychographic characteristics. These surveys are conducted nationally through in-person interviews and questionnaires. Other sources may also be consulted. These include, for example, the Nielsen Company, which provides measurement of television and Internet audiences.[24]

Demographic profiles of individuals who use a specific service or product can be constructed from these surveys. For example, the data allow notice and media experts to identify the demographics of consumers who are cell-phone users, homeowners, cigarette smokers, insurance policyholders, or prescription drug purchasers. In many instances, product usage by brand or type is available.

In addition, it is possible to evaluate the media habits of sets of product users or demographics. It is possible to determine if groups of people are light newspaper readers, heavy television viewers, moderate Internet users, and so forth. A media expert can compare different types of media for audience penetration and cost. For example, TV penetration of a particular target audience can be compared to that of radio, magazines, and newspapers. In addition, the data is indexed by media vehicle – a specific television show, radio program, or magazine – with respect to its penetration of the target audience. This information provides direction to the media selections and ensures that the media used actually reaches the target audience.

For example, in the class action *In Re Pharmaceutical Industry Average Wholesale Price Litigation*, the classes involved residents of Massachusetts and other states who made co-payments for Zoladex, a drug manufactured for cancer treatment, especially prostate cancer.[25] Kinsella Media consulted several research sources in order to determine the appropriate vehicles to carry the notice. The Gfk MRI survey provided the demographic characteristics and media usage of people who have taken a branded prescription drug for a prostate ailment. This was shown to be predominantly males, age 50 years and older. Data from Nielsen Media Research provided information on the television and cable programs watched by this group. ComScore, a provider of digital marketing data, provided rankings and audiences for websites visited by class members.[26] This audience data revealed which media vehicles provided the most efficient means of reaching class members (in this case newspapers and television), as well as how many insertions were necessary to adequately reach a substantial number of them.

---

23 *See* GFK MRI, http://www.mediamark.com (last visited Sept. 2, 2011).

24 *See* NIELSEN, http://www.nielsen.com/us/en.html (last visited Sept. 2, 2011).

25 Declaration of Katherine Kinsella, *In Re* Pharmaceutical Ind. Average Wholesale Price Litig., No. 01-CV-12257-PBS (D. Mass. Dec. 14, 2010) (on file with the authors).

26 *See* COMSCORE, http://www.comscore.com (last visited Sept. 2, 2011).

13.04.2 Measuring media-based notice

There are a number of ways to measure media penetration. Two aspects mentioned above, reach and frequency, are especially important. Reach is the estimated percentage of a target audience reached through a specific media vehicle or combination of media vehicles. Frequency is the estimated average number of times an audience is exposed to an advertising vehicle carrying the message. Reach and frequency calculations are estimates within a standard margin of error that provide the advertiser with a reliable basis upon which to judge penetration of target audiences by media.

Software programs created by the media industry allow media planners to calculate reach and frequency estimates. Statistical formulas factor out duplication of readership or viewership among the target audience and allow calculation of reach and frequency as well as other media measurements. This allows determination of the net audience reach of a media schedule using various kinds of print, online, and broadcast media.

Reach and frequency targets depend upon a number of factors, which help lawyers determine whether a notification program is reasonable and practicable. In a tort settlement, for instance, relevant considerations might include the type of relief sought (injunctive relief or damages), the seriousness of the tort, the size of the settlement, and the percentage of the class to be reached through media versus direct mail.

13.04.3 Determining the adequacy of notice

Rule 23 and the relevant case law do not define what constitutes adequate notice. However, the guarantee of due process that is inherent in the Fifth and Fourteenth Amendments of the U.S. Constitution provides valuable information on the minimum notice required.[27] As the Fifth Circuit has explained, "[t]he essence of due process is that 'deprivation of life, liberty, or property by adjudication be preceded by notice and opportunity for hearing appropriate to the nature of the case.'"[28] The Seventh Circuit has added that "due process requires notice reasonably calculated to provide actual notice of the proceeding and a meaningful opportunity to be heard."[29]

To demonstrate to a court that a notice program satisfies due process, the program should provide certain objective and quantifiable elements. These include, for example, the size of the class and the percentage of class members reached through direct notice. In particular, a notice program directed to unidentified class members should: (1) identify the demographics of class members and establish a target audience, (2) outline the methodology for selecting the media and other plan elements and how they relate to product usage or exposure, and (3) provide results that quantify for the court the adequacy of the notice based upon recognized tools of media measurement.

Where there is a measurable demographic target available through survey data, and where the reach and frequency can be accurately measured, the notice expert can

27 *See* Zadvydas v. Davis, 533 U.S. 678, 693 (2001).

28 *In re* Nissan Motor Corp. Antitrust Litig., 552 F.2d 1088, 1103–04 (5th Cir. 1997) (citing Mullane v. Central Hanover Bank & Trust Co., 339 U.S. 306, 313 (1950)).

29 Nazarova v. INS, 171 F.3d 478, 482–83 (7th Cir. 1999).

demonstrate to the court what percentage of a target audience was reached and how many opportunities class members had to see the notice. In situations where a measurable target demographic is not available (for instance, because of limitations on survey data) the notice expert must demonstrate to the court the rationale for selecting the media and why it is effective in reaching class members. A demographic analysis can provide reasonable guidance to a notice expert in determining what media is best to reach the class. For example, in a class composed of highly educated people, without any other discerning demographic characteristics, such an analysis might show that newspapers would likely be the best choice.

In the class action in *Cobell v. Salazar*, it was not possible to measure the effectiveness of media with regard to Native Americans, the principal target audience.[30] However, Kinsella Media constructed a multi-faceted program that included extensive radio, television, online, and print notice as well as third-party outreach to federally recognized Native American tribes and Alaska Native villages. The notice program included translation of outreach materials into ten Native American languages. Using an outreach team, a plan of layered community outreach was constructed with over 2,200 tribal governments, nonprofit organizations, and commercial enterprises participating. Reports to the court chronicled all aspects of the notice program, quantifying efforts and results that demonstrated its success.

13.04.4 Content and design of notice

According to one court, "[i]t is in the government's interest that class members meaningfully understand their rights and make knowing, intelligent and voluntary choices."[31] The 2003 plain language amendment to Rule 23 stems from the same impulse, namely, a desire to ensure that class members are fully informed of their rights.[32] During the rule-making process, the U.S. judicial branch's Advisory Committee on the Federal Rules of Civil Procedure asked the Federal Judicial Center (FJC) to conduct research and develop model plain language notices.[33] The Advisory Committee notes accompanying the revised rules discuss the importance of plain language:

> The direction that class-certification notice be couched in plain, easily understood language is a reminder of the need to work unremittingly at the difficult task of communicating with class members. It is difficult to provide information about most class actions that is both accurate and easily understood by class members who are not themselves lawyers. Factual

---

[30] Declaration of Katherine Kinsella, Cobell v. Salazar, No. 1:96 CV 01285 (D.D.C. May 16, 2011) (on file with the authors).

[31] Orantes-Hernandez v. Meese, 685 F.Supp. 1488, 1499 (C.D. Cal. 1988).

[32] *See* Kinsella Media, LLC & Rust Consulting, Inc., *Plain Language Primer for Class Action Notice*, http://www.kinsellamedia.com (last visited Sept. 2, 2011).

[33] The FJC is the research and education agency of the federal judicial system. More information on the research that was done by the FJC on the model notice project can be found at http://www.fjc.gov. *See also* Shannon R. Wheatman, *The Effects of Plain Language Drafting on Layperson's Comprehension of Class Action Notices* (2001) (Ph.D. dissertation, University of Georgia) (on file with the authors). This dissertation was based on research that was done at the FJC on the model notice project.

> uncertainty, legal complexity, and the complication of class-action procedure raise the barriers high.[34]

According to the FJC, the first impression of any notice must "persuade the readers that they have a stake in the class action and that they will be able to comprehend the notice."[35] The notice must clearly describe all of the rights and options available to class members (such as filing a claim, appearing in court, objecting to the settlement, or opting out of the class[36]), as well as the binding nature of any judgment on anyone who fails to opt out of the class.[37] Rule 23 also requires that class members be notified of an attorney fee motion by class counsel and be given an opportunity to object to it.[38] This transparency of attorneys' fees is also recommended by *The Manual for Complex Litigation, Fourth*, a reference guide for judges and practitioners.[39]

§ 13.05 Class Action Fairness Act

In 2005, CAFA imposed new notice requirements and increased judicial scrutiny of coupon settlements (which usually give class members a coupon for future services or products with the defendant's company) and attorneys' fees.[40] CAFA requires defendants in federal court to give notice of a proposed class action settlement to certain state and federal government officials. Attorneys general and regulatory agencies now have a chance to comment on class action settlements, providing yet another opportunity to safeguard the rights of class members. CAFA provides very detailed and comprehensive requirements to give notice to regulating authorities, which must be undertaken within 10 days of filing a proposed settlement. CAFA prohibits the governing court from approving the settlement for 90 days after this notice has been given.

§ 13.06 Administering a class action

Every class action settlement requires the terms of the settlement to be carried out, which involves disseminating class notice via mail, email, or other means to class members; answering class members' questions via phone, email, website, or other correspondence; receiving and processing claims, with whatever specific parameters each settlement requires; calculating awards; distributing settlement benefits; and reporting to the parties. The parties can retain a settlement administrator to manage some or all of these processes. Notice experts also may be retained by the parties to work closely with the settlement

---

34 Fed. R. Civ. P. 23(c)(2)(B) advisory committee notes.

35 *See* Federal Judicial Center, http://www.fjc.gov/ (last visited Sept. 2, 2011)

36 Rule 23(e)(4) allows the court to condition settlement approval on the defendant's willingness to provide a second opportunity to opt out.

37 "Surely 'the best notice practicable under the circumstances' cannot stop with . . . generalities. It must also contain an adequate description of the proceedings written in objective, neutral terms, that . . . may be understood by the average absentee class member." *In re* Nissan Motor Corp. Antitrust Litig., 552 F.2d 1088, 1104 (5th Cir. 1977).

38 Fed. R. Civ. P. 23(h).

39 Manual for Complex Litigation (Fourth) § 21.312 (2004).

40 The Class Action Fairness Act of 2005, 28 U.S.C. §§ 1712–1715 (2005).

administrator to ensure that the court-approved notice program is properly implemented.[41] While hired by one or more of the parties to the lawsuit, the settlement administrator generally works according to the terms of the settlement agreement, accepting only the joint direction of the parties to resolve matters not made clear by the settlement agreement. At one or more key points in the administration of the settlement, the settlement administrator typically provides a detailed summary of its actions to the court and the parties in the form of one or more affidavits or declarations. Such reporting is most often submitted prior to the hearing at which the court determines whether to grant the class action final approval, but may also be done after each phase of administration or as a final accounting.

The basic methods of administering a class action settlement require the parties and administrator to consider how best to provide the class with clear and easily understandable information, and to minimize the risk of objections. These safeguards, of course, help to ensure the settlement receives its strongest chance of approval by the court.

13.06.1 Data concerns

Data management is crucial to every successful class action notification program. This includes strict adherence to relevant (sometimes industry-specific) privacy laws and best practices. An administrator often receives class member data, sometimes to create (and maintain) mailing lists. Administrators can also receive more sensitive financial or medical information to use to prepare personalized notice materials, score or verify claims, or calculate settlement benefits.

The lawyers, parties, and an administrator of a settlement must consider strategies to avoid violating any privacy laws. Sometimes third parties can minimize potential privacy concerns. For example, in the administration of the *Authors Guild, Inc. v. Google Inc.* settlement, hundreds of copyright organizations, publisher associations, and author groups worldwide were contacted to ask for assistance with giving direct notice to the class. This eliminated the need to release any personal information to the administrator.[42]

13.06.2 Communicating with class members

Using the Internet and websites can expand the reach of class action notifications. For instance, a class action administrator can use a website to communicate information, in a way that allows class members to view the site whenever is convenient for them. And websites do not merely broadcast information; class members can use them to communicate back to the class administrator or lawyers. Approximately 30 times as many class members filed claims online as filed through traditional paper claims in the *Google* settlement.[43]

A typical settlement website includes a summary of the case information including the terms of the settlement, answers to frequently asked questions, links to settlement

---

[41] The notice expert firm may or may not be affiliated with the claims administration firm.

[42] Declaration of Katherine Kinsella, Authors Guild, Inc. v. Google Inc., No. 05-8136 (S.D.N.Y. Feb. 10, 2010) (on file with the authors). This settlement was not granted final approval; however, the court applauded the notice effort.

[43] *Id.*

documents such as the long-form notice, claim form, and settlement agreement, and, increasingly, the functionality to submit questions or claim forms online. By utilizing these features, many of the cost-prohibitive and time-consuming aspects of settlement administration are bypassed.

Despite this increasingly online experience, an administrator must continue to work with more traditional methods of communication, including Interactive Voice Response (IVR) systems and regular mail. Once callers dial the administrator's office, an IVR system – that is, a pre-recorded messaging system set up in a series of menus – allows for cost-effective administration. Because many callers' questions or needs are satisfied through this automated messaging, the need for live operators in many languages is greatly reduced or eliminated. Voicemail can allow operators to call back potential class members at a later time, rather than sit available for extended periods of time awaiting calls.

13.06.3 Claims processing

The administrator also facilitates the processing of claims. Settlement structures and funds vary greatly, so this process can be as simple as logging receipt of a claim, or as complex as reviewing claim information such as receipts, proof of ownership documents, and financial transaction records. Similarly, benefits may be pre-determined awards (i.e., $5 per claimant) or require complex calculations based on pre-existing and/or class member-provided documentation.

Once the settlement has received final approval and the calculation of awards is completed, an administrator disseminates the settlement benefits to eligible class members. Most often, benefits are paid in the form of checks, but they can take the forms of coupons, vouchers, or even products, depending on the settlement. The distribution phase of administration includes both the printing and mailing of checks and follow-up processing including handling of undelivered checks, re-mailing of checks to better addresses, reissuing checks when necessary, and distribution account management. Typically, this process lasts 180 days, at which point any remaining, unused or unclaimed funds are handled in accordance with the settlement agreement or the parties' joint instruction.

§ 13.07 Conclusion

Notice "provides the structural assurance of fairness that permits representative parties to bind absent class members."[44] The "assurance of fairness" can only be achieved if the class is adequately reached with a notice that is easy to understand and act upon. The ability to act upon the notice requires proper administration of the class action. Administrators have the important task of ensuring that the voices of class members are heard, by answering class member inquiries and by processing claims, objections, and opt-outs.

Careful planning has to take place to fully satisfy Rule 23's notice requirements. The notices must reach the intended audience in the most efficient and cost-effective manner possible. Failure to communicate in accordance with Rule 23 can have far-reaching,

---

44 Amchem Prods., Inc. v. Windsor, 521 U.S. 591, 627 (1997).

expensive consequences. Drafting materials in plain language, working to meet CAFA requirements, and providing notice that reaches your intended audience will satisfy due process, silence objectors, prevent collateral attack, and ensure judicial approval of the notice program.

14 Cy pres as a remedy in private antitrust litigation

Albert A. Foer[1]

§ 14.01 Introduction

The normal remedies in a private antitrust case are a combination of injunctions and treble damages that are paid to the victim or victims of the anticompetitive activity. When an aggregate amount of damages is established, the primary objective is to distribute the damages to those who were injured. In antitrust class action litigation, however, it is often impossible or impracticable to compensate all victims. Administrative concerns may work against payments to individual plaintiffs, as in the case of an extremely large class where the fund is not sufficient to justify the transaction costs of distribution to individual claimants. Consequently, in some cases, there is money left over in the form of unclaimed funds. In such cases, courts sometimes employ the doctrine of "cy pres" to put the unclaimed funds to "the next best use," which may include awarding funds to public interest organizations or charities for purposes related to the case. There is increasing interest in utilizing the cy pres doctrine as part of an antitrust remedy because of its potential to enhance competition.[2] At the same time, cy pres opens up possibilities of corruption, waste, and public criticism.[3]

---

[1] The author is President of the American Antitrust Institute. This chapter is based on previously published work including Albert A. Foer, *Enhancing Competition Through the Cy Pres Remedy: Suggested Best Practices*, 24 ANTITRUST 86 (2010). The author thanks AAI Research Fellow Kevin Kim, for updating and enlarging aspects of the earlier works.

[2] By "competition" the author refers not only to the possibility of usages of cy pres funds that may directly enhance the competitive process within a particular market that was the subject of an antitrust violation. More generally, it may also refer to usages that indirectly benefit the class by contributing to enhancement of the competitive process through such projects as education of consumers, training of judges or regulators, or the support of enforcement activities related to the underlying antitrust violation in the case.

[3] Cy pres has its critics. *See* Adam Liptak, *Doling Out Other People's Money*, N.Y. TIMES, Nov. 26, 2007, at A12; Ted Frank, *Cy Pres Settlements* (2008), http://www.aei.org/article/27789 (last visited Aug. 27, 2011); Amanda Bronstad, *Cy Pres Awards Under Scrutiny*, NAT'L J. ONLINE,

This chapter provides background on the law of cy pres and suggests "best practices" for its invocation.

§ 14.02 The cy pres doctrine in antitrust class action litigation

The cy pres remedy has evolved into a workable device that often fits well into an antitrust class action settlement. The cy pres doctrine originated as a rule in the law of trusts and estates, allowing courts to provide for the "next-best use" of gifts or fair disposition of charitable trusts or wills that would otherwise fail.[4] By analogy, courts began to apply the cy pres doctrine in class actions in the 1970s, after the 1966 amendments to Federal Rule of Civil Procedure 23 expanded the class action procedure.[5] The process known as aggregate cy pres distribution permits unclaimed or residual class action funds to be put to their next best use for the aggregate, indirect, prospective benefit of class members. Examples described later in this chapter include the *Diamond Chemical* case and the *California Vitamins Cartel* litigation.[6] Although Rule 23 does not directly address remedies,[7] nearly all modern jurisdictions apply the cy pres doctrine in a broad variety of cases.[8] In class actions brought under Rule 23, a court's order approving a class action settlement – including one that involves a cy pres award – is reversible only upon an abuse of discretion.[9]

Aug. 11, 2008, http://www.nlj.com; Martin H. Redish, Peter Julian & Samantha Zyontz, *Cy Pres Relief and the Pathologies of the Modern Class Action: A Normative & Empirical Analysis*, 62 FLA. L. REV. 617 (2010); U.S. CHAMBER INSTITUTE FOR LEGAL REFORM, CY PRES: A NOT SO CHARITABLE CONTRIBUTION TO CLASS ACTION PRACTICE (2010). These articles, probably overstating the problems inherent in current cy pres situations, constitute one reason why it is now appropriate to adopt "best practices" in this area.

4 The cy pres doctrine is sometimes known as the fluid recovery rule, although fluid recovery more precisely applies to an effort to approximate the injured class of consumers through the provision of relief to future consumers, for example, by discounting the price in future sales.

5 *See* S.R. Shepherd, *Damage Distribution in Class Actions: The Cy Pres Remedy*, 39 U. CHI. L. REV. 448 (1972). With rare exceptions, cy pres will be a possibility only in indirect purchaser (consumer) class actions that are settled. In practice, very few antitrust class actions proceed all the way to adjudication. Class actions by direct purchasers (usually businesses) will contain well-defined members whose individual damages can be calculated with fairly high precision. Therefore, a settlement fund will usually be exhausted by the claimants. In consumer class actions, there may be millions of class members, with little predictability of how many will file valid claims. Accordingly, there is a much stronger potential for cy pres distribution in these cases.

6 *See infra* text at notes 35 and 63.

7 A federal court may approve a proposed settlement of a class action only after a hearing and on a finding that it is "fair, reasonable, and adequate." FED. R. CIV. P. 23(e)(2). The authority for federal courts to fashion equitable remedies may also lie within FED. R. CIV. P. 54(c) (equitable remedies). *See also* Natalie A. Dejarlais, *The Consumer Trust Fund: A Cy Pres Solution to Undistributed Funds in Consumer Class Actions*, 38 HASTINGS L.J. 729 (1987) (citing Note, *Managing the Large Class Action*: Eisen v. Carlisle & Jacquelin, 87 HARV. L. REV. 426, 447 & n.120 (1973)); FED. R. CIV. P. 54(c) ("[E]very other final judgment should grant the relief to which each party is entitled, even if the party has not demanded such relief in its pleadings.").

8 *See, e.g.*, Susan B. Farmer, *More Lessons From the Laboratories: Cy Pres Distributions in Parens Patriae Antitrust Actions Brought by State Attorneys General*, 68 FORDHAM L. REV. 361, 404 (1999).

9 *See In re* Airline Ticket Comm'n 2001, 268 F.3d 619, 625 (8th Cir. 2001) ("We review a district court's cy pres distribution for an abuse of discretion.") (citing Powell v. Georgia-Pac. Corp.

Class actions may be brought as suits by private plaintiffs or as *parens patriae* actions pursuant to Section 4C of the Clayton Act,[10] under which state attorneys general may bring antitrust actions for damages on behalf of natural person citizens of the state. As in private litigation, courts adjudicating *parens patriae* antitrust actions must determine how to distribute damages, whether ascertained through a trial or settlement. In performing this task, such courts are given vast discretion to approve the distribution of damages.

§ 14.03 When cy pres is appropriate

The use of the cy pres remedy has been limited to situations where distribution to individual class members is economically infeasible, or where funds remain after class members are given a full opportunity to raise a claim.[11] A distribution to class members is considered economically infeasible in situations where there are a large number of class members but only a small individual recovery per person. Under such circumstances, the cost of separately proving and distributing damages to each class member would outweigh the potential recovery.[12] The cost of distribution is often considered economically infeasible in cases where it is difficult to identify or locate class members.[13] The cy pres remedy in this case would act in lieu of a distribution to class members.

A cy pres distribution can also be made using the funds remaining after an initial distribution to class members. Such a situation can occur when some members of the class fail to claim their share of the settlement fund. The settlement agreement can conditionally create such a cy pres distribution if there are funds remaining after a distribution to class members.[14] Consistent with the standard governing cy pres distributions in lieu

---

119 F.3d 703, 706 (8th Cir. 1997); *see also In re* Gen. Motors Corp. Pick-Up Truck Fuel Tank Prod. Liab. Litig., 55 F.3d 768 (3d Cir. 1995) (finding and discussing abuse of discretion in a class action case).

[10] 15 U.S.C. § 15c(b)(2) & (3). *See also* Hart Scott Rodino Antitrust Improvements Act, Pub. L. No. 94-435, sec. 301, 4C, 90 Stat. 1383, 1394 (codified at 15 U.S.C. 15c (1994)).

[11] *See* Herbert B. Newberg & Alba Conte, Newberg on Class Actions 10:16 (4th ed. 2002); *see also* American Law Institute, Principles of the Law of Aggregate Litigation § 3.07 (2010).

[12] Six Mexican Workers v. Ariz. Citrus Growers, 904 F.2d 1301, 1305 (9th Cir. 1990).

[13] *See In re* Metlife Demutalization Litig., 689 F. Supp. 2d 297, 343 (E.D.N.Y. 2010) ("The administrative burden is aggravated by the fact that the non-closed-block portion of the class includes former policyholders whose policies went out of force after the demutualization. Because Metlife does not maintain current addresses for the former policyholders, determining their present location (assuming they were alive), and mailing individual small checks to them would be substantially more burdensome than a mailing to current policyholders"); Masters v. Wilhelmina Model Agency, Inc., 473 F.3d 423, 436 (2d Cir. 2007) (vacating a cy pres distribution and explaining, "In the case before us, neither side contends that Cy Pres distribution is appropriate because it would be onerous or impossible to locate class members or because each class member's recovery would be so small as to make an individual distribution economically impracticable").

[14] *See, e.g.*, Rodriguez v. West Publishing Corp., 563 F.3d 948, 957 (9th Cir. 2009); Radosti v. Envision EMI, LLC, 717 F. Supp.2d 37, 58 (D.C. 2010); Garner v. State Farm Mut. Auto Ins. Co., No. CV 08 1365 CW (EMC) 2010 U.S. Dist. LEXIS 49477 (N.D. Cal., Apr. 22, 2010); Nickel v. Bank of Am. Nat. Trust and Savings Ass'n, No. CV 08 1365 CW (EMC) 2010 U.S. Dist. LEXIS 49491 (N.D. Cal., Apr. 22, 2010); *In re* Janney Montgomery Scott LLC Financial Consultant Litig., No. 06-3202 2009 U.S Dist. LEXIS 60790 (E.D. Pa., Apr. 26, 2007).

of a distribution to class members, a cy pres distribution may be used as an adjunct to a payment to class members where the amount remaining after the initial distribution is small relative to the administrative costs of distribution.[15]

Many courts have expressed a preference to distribute as much of the settlement fund to the class members as possible, only then using the remainder for a cy pres distribution.[16] In *Park v. Thomson Corp.*, for example, the court agreed with objectors to the initial proposed settlement that a cap on recovery for each class member would risk overwhelming "the purpose for the lawsuit-payment to the class."[17] The initial proposed settlement would have set aside a greater proportion of the fund for cy pres than for distribution, a result which the objectors feared would cause the fund to be "destined for a cy pres abyss."[18] The court approved an amended settlement, which eliminated the proposed cap and allowed only for the remainder of uncashed claimants' checks and unused funds set aside for administrative costs to "devolve to a cy pres fund."[19]

Conversely, some courts do not automatically require redistribution in situations where it is still feasible.[20] For example, the court in *Hall v. AT&T Mobility LLC* chose not to order a second pro rata distribution of unclaimed settlement funds.[21] In this case, the objector and class counsel both argued that a distribution of the remaining funds to the class members was not an "insurmountable task." While the court accepted the argument as true, it nevertheless found the risk for potential fraudulent claims and the potential of a windfall to certain class members weighed against granting a second distribution.[22] The court was also concerned with providing fairness to class members who opted out or failed to file a claim, "since such individuals might have decided to file a claim had they known that their recovery would be increased by excess funds."[23]

---

15 *In re Metlife Demutualization Litig.*, 689 F. Supp. 2d at 343; Powell v. Georgia Pacific Corp., 119 F.3d 703, 706–07 (8th Cir., 1997); *Garner*, 2010 U.S. Dist. LEXIS 49477; *Nickel*, 2010 U.S. Dist. LEXIS 49491. *See also* Park v. Thomson Corp., No. 05 Civ. 2931 (WHP) 2008 U.S. Dist. LEXIS 84551 (S.D.N.Y., Oct. 22, 2008) (approving an amended settlement that removed the previous $40 cap for damages and provided that the class would receive the entirety of the fund, and only any remaining unclaimed funds would be administered to a cy pres distribution).

16 *See e.g.*, *Masters*, 473 F.3d at 436 (vacating the proposed cy pres distribution and remanding because the court was "confident that the district court, fully aware of the breadth of its discretion, will see to an appropriate distribution of the funds remaining after the [class members] have been compensated for their actual losses").

17 Park v. Thomson Corp., No. 05 Civ. 2931 (WHP) 2008 U.S. Dist. LEXIS 84551 at *4 (S.D.N.Y. Oct. 22, 2008).

18 *Id.*

19 *Id.* at *5.

20 *See, e.g.*, *In re* Pharm. Indus. Average Wholesale Price Litig., 588 F.3d 24, 35–36 (1st Cir. 2009).

21 Hall v. AT&T Mobility LLC, No. 07-5325 (JLL) 2010 U.S. Dist. LEXIS 109355 (D.N.J. Oct. 13, 2010).

22 *Id.* at *38–39 (the risk of fraudulent claims also comes with the administrative costs of investigation; the windfall would be to certain members who suffered no initial out of pocket expenses prior to the litigation).

23 *Id.* at *39.

§ 14.04 The importance of a nexus between the case and the remedy

The purpose of a remedy in an antitrust case is threefold: (1) to protect or restore competition in the market; (2) to deter anticompetitive behavior; and (3) to compensate victims of illegal conduct.[24] Given these purposes, allowing courts to formulate broad cy pres distributions of damages has several significant benefits. First, deterrence is served because, an amount of damages having been determined, the unclaimed funds do not return to the defendant. Second, the defendant is not unjustly enriched if all potential plaintiffs do not assert a claim. Third, because the funds will be used to promote competition or dissuade the kinds of actions that constituted an antitrust violation, or will benefit society in general, class members who did not assert a claim benefit indirectly. The essence of the cy pres doctrine, however, is that distributions should be made "for a purpose as near as possible to the legitimate objectives underlying the lawsuit."[25] While some cy pres distributions have adequately reflected this "nexus" between the injured class and the cy pres distribution,[26] the nexus has been remote[27] or completely absent[28] in other cases.

Most courts correctly insist that a nexus not be absent. But what constitutes an adequate nexus? It is not necessary for the nexus between injured consumers and cy pres recipients to be direct in order to be adequate. When courts distribute funds to support public interest programs, for example, the nexus between those directly harmed and the distribution of damages may be indirect, although not altogether absent.[29] Moreover, the nexus is generally deemed sufficient when a proposed use of cy pres funds would benefit the industry in which an antitrust violation occurred, despite the absence of any relationship to the particular product involved in the case.

Another measure of nexus adequacy is the geographical overlap between the area served by the cy pres recipient and the class members. Where the case involves a nationwide class, some courts will favor cy pres recipients that benefit people throughout the country.[30] By contrast, where a case involves a smaller class in a more specific geographic

---

[24] *See* United States v. Microsoft Corp., 253 F.3d 34, 103 (D.C. Cir. 2001) (citing cases).

[25] *In re* Airline Ticket Comm'n Antitrust Litig., 307 F.3d 679, 682 (8th Cir. 2002).

[26] *See, e.g.*, Mkt. St. Ry. Co. v. R.R. Comm'n, 28 Cal. 2d 363, 371, 171 P.2d 875, 881 (Cal. 1946) (stating that "inasmuch as the people of the city paid the excess fares they are the natural beneficiaries thereof").

[27] *See* Jeffrey G. Casurella & John R. Bevis, *Class Action Law in Georgia: Emerging Trends in Litigation, Certification, and Settlement*, 49 Mercer L. Rev. 39, 67 n.158 (1997) (discussing a case involving predatory lending, where the court approved cy pres funds for a legal aid society that provides legal assistance to low income homeowners who are victims of predatory lending).

[28] *See, e.g.*, Six Mexican Workers v. Ariz. Citrus Growers, 904 F.2d 1301, 1308 (9th Cir. 1990) ("Even where cy pres is considered, it will be rejected when the proposed distribution fails to provide the 'next best' distribution."); *In re* Matzo Food Prods. Litig., 156 F.R.D. 600, 607 (D.N.J. 1994) ("Thus, plaintiffs' rationale for approval of a settlement pursuant to which the class members themselves receive nothing is simply inadequate.")

[29] *See* West Virginia v. Chas. Pfizer & Co., 314 F. Supp. 710, 728 (S.D.N.Y. 1970); Superior Beverage Co. v. Owens-Illinois, Inc., 827 F. Supp. 477, 479 (N.D. Ill. 1993) (public health programs to benefit both damaged and undamaged consumers granted cy pres funds).

[30] *See e.g.*, Schwartz v. Dallas Cowboys Football Club Ltd., 362 F.Supp. 2d 574, 577 (E.D. Pa. 2005) ("[W]hile the class and geographic scope of the law suit is nationwide, the relief proposed by plaintiffs would be limited to organizations based in the Philadelphia area. On the other hand, . . .

area, courts may favor a cy pres distribution to an organization with a more limited geographic outreach.[31] But courts do not always require a geographic nexus.[32]

Some courts in *parens patriae* cases have ordered the entire damage award to be used for public interest purposes, such as education with respect to the industry in which liability was established,[33] even though the consumers on whose behalf the case was brought did not recover their actual damages. In other instances, cy pres distributions have been ordered to be used by state attorneys general to fund antitrust enforcement.[34] This use, while not addressing the consumers or the industry specifically affected by the defendant's conduct, has a nexus with an antitrust case insofar as it seeks to promote compliance with antitrust laws.

Courts have also found an adequate nexus outside the *parens patriae* context when cy pres funds would be used to further enforcement and education concerning the types of violations undergirding the plaintiffs' claims. Judge Kollar-Kotelly's 2007 *Diamond Chemical* opinion provides one of the most interesting discussions of this type of antitrust cy pres award.[35] In *Diamond Chemical*, class plaintiff sought distribution of the undistributed settlement funds, which amounted to more than $5 million, to The George Washington University Law School for the purpose of establishing an endowment for a new Center for Competition Law. In approving the distribution over the objection of the defendant chemical companies, the court noted that the award would be closely related to the underlying action (price-fixing by an international cartel) and would benefit members of the injured class because the new Center would focus on problems of globalization and private antitrust enforcement. In other words, in this price-fixing case, a cy pres grant aimed at improving competition through education and advocacy satisfied the test for an adequate nexus. Moreover, the court was convinced by the plaintiff's detailed plans, which demonstrated that the Center had been carefully contemplated and had a good chance of success. Even the fact that some of the Center's work would involve foreign jurisdictions was found to support the proposal because the Center could deter foreign cartels from actions that would harm U.S. consumers. The nexus to the underlying suit was satisfied

the ultimate beneficiaries [in the defendants' competing cy pres distribution proposal] are located throughout the country."); *see also* Coppolino v. Total Call Intern., Inc., 588 F.Supp. 2d 594, 605 (D.N.J. 2008) (criticizing the approval of a cy pres distribution to two churches and Pepperdine University where the case involved a nationwide class).

[31] *See e.g.*, *In re* Linerboard Antitrust Litig., No. 98-5055, 99-1341 2008 U.S. Dist. LEXIS 77739, at *12–14 (E.D. Pa. Oct. 3, 2008) (awarding a cy pres distribution to the Philadelphia Bar Foundation, which gives grants to legal services organizations dedicated to protecting the rights of the poor and indigent in the Philadelphia area).

[32] *See e.g.*, *In re* Motorsports Merchandise Antitrust Litig., 112 F.Supp. 2d 1329 (N.D. Ga. 2000) (approving a settlement of a nationwide class action, with a cy pres distribution where seven of the ten beneficiaries were Georgia charities or Georgia branches of national charities).

[33] *See* New York v. Dairlylea Coop., No. 81 Civ. 1891 (RO), 1985 U.S. Dist. LEXIS 18501, at *4–5 (S.D.N.Y. Jun. 26, 1985); *see also* New York *ex rel.* Koppell v. Keds Corp., No. 93 Civ. 6708 (CSH), 1994 U.S. Dist. LEXIS 3362, at *8 (S.D.N.Y. Mar. 21, 1994).

[34] *See* Farmer, *supra* note 8.

[35] Diamond Chem. Co. v. Akzo Nobel Chems. B.V., No. 01-2118 2007 U.S. Dist. LEXIS 49406 (July 10, 2007); Press Release, The George Washington University, Leading the Way in Competition Law: Law School Receives $5.1 Million for New Center (July 11, 2007), *available at* http://www.gwu.edu/~magazine/archive/2007_law_fall/docs/dept_philanthropy.html.

because the suit involved an international cartel to fix prices. It was not necessary that the funds be used with respect to the chemical industry. Accordingly, the implications for a public interest organization seem relatively clear. A class action cy pres settlement may be approved, even over defendants' objection, where the proposed expenditure will support pro-enforcement activity aimed at the type of violation that occurred, even without connection to the specific industry involved.

By way of contrast, consider the unique decision in *Motorsports Merchandise Antitrust Litigation*,[36] involving price fixing of NASCAR souvenirs. The court approved distribution of excess settlement funds to 10 charities. In its cy pres order, the court described each charity chosen to receive funds, defined the use that the charity would make of the funds, and assessed its impact on the community. Any funds remaining after all distributions were made and all costs paid were to be given to two legal aid organizations.[37] The court stated that it "attempted to identify charitable organizations that may at least indirectly benefit the members of the class of NASCAR racing fans."[38] In reality, while the class and geographic scope of the lawsuit was nationwide, funds were distributed mainly to local organizations having relatively little to do with either class members or the issues of the case.[39]

The result in the aforementioned case raises the following question: what limits, if any, should there be on distributions of funds to charitable or public interest organizations in antitrust cases? Everyone agrees the best cy pres distribution would be one in which the connection between the cy pres benefit and the injured consumer is clear. But such a clear nexus is not always possible under the circumstances of the case.[40] Support for the class action mechanism, not to mention for the institution of antitrust itself, can be undermined if the public comes to see the outcome of class litigation as having too tenuous a connection to the underlying cause of action.

Critics of cy pres distributions often allege that the awards create the mere "illusion of compensation."[41] The U.S. Chamber Institute for Legal Reform has criticized cy pres

---

[36] *See In re* Motorsports Merch. Antitrust Litig., 160 F. Supp. 2d 1392 (N.D. Ga. 2001). The court solicited proposals from charitable organizations proposed by the parties. The American Antitrust Institute was invited by the judge, at the request of one of the parties, to submit a proposal. AAI proposed a detailed two-year project to benefit the class of automobile racing spectators as well as other consumers by studying how meaningful remedies can be provided to indirect purchasers who are injured by antitrust violations. AAI was not selected for an award.

[37] *Id.*; *see generally* Robert E. Draba, *Motorsports Merchandise: A Cy Pres Distribution Not Quite "As Near as Possible,"* 16 LOY. CONSUMER L. REV. 121 (2004); *see also* Linda Zazove, *The Cy Pres Doctrine and Legal Service for the Poor: Using Undistributed Class Action Funds to Improve Access to Justice*, ABA NATIONAL INSTITUTE ON CLASS ACTIONS (2001).

[38] *See Motorsports*, 160 F. Supp. 2d 1392.

[39] The *Motorsports* court approved the distribution of $250,000 each to The Make-a-Wish Foundation, The American Red Cross, Race Against Drugs, Children's Healthcare of Atlanta, The Atlanta Legal Aid Society, The Georgia Legal Services Program, Kids' Chance, Duke Children's Hospital and Health Center, and The Lawyers Foundation of Georgia. The court also ordered $100,000 of the settlement proceeds distributed to the Susan G. Komen Breast Cancer Foundation.

[40] *See* Jones v. Nat'l Distillers, 56 F. Supp. 2d 355, 358 (S.D.N.Y. 1999) ("there is no obvious use for the money that provides a particular benefit to class members").

[41] Martin H. Redish, Peter Julian & Samatha Zyontz, *Cy Pres Relief and the Pathologies of the Modern Class Action: A Normative and Empirical Analysis*, 62 FLA. L. REV. 617, 649 (2010).

distributions, stating "[t]he bedrock of our system of civil justice is that a plaintiff who is injured can seek compensation for his or her injuries; using civil litigation to redistribute wealth to charities turns that fundamental goal on its head."[42] Maintaining a nexus between the cy pres award and the litigation addresses such criticism by maintaining consistency with the principles of cy pres; namely, that the distribution is in fact a "next best" use of the funds, that the class members will receive indirect benefits, and that the cy pres award is not merely a redistribution of wealth to charities.

§ 14.05 Conflicts within the nexus

Courts will also often look for a conflict existing within the nexus. A conflict can arise where the proposed cy pres remedy directly or indirectly benefits the defendant, or where the recipient has ties to class counsel.[43] Where such a conflict arises, the court will often look upon the proposal with skepticism and may even reject the settlement.[44] The existence of such a conflict will not necessarily result in the settlement being rejected.[45] It is still possible that a conflict can exist in a settlement that meets the "near as possible" purpose requirement.[46]

The court in *Radosti v. Envision EMI, LLC* was presented with a proposed settlement that would conditionally create a scholarship fund if the amount distributed to class members did not exceed a certain amount. The proposed scholarship fund would be administered by the defendant with nearly complete discretion.[47] The court expressed concerns that if the amount in the scholarship fund was substantial, the defendant would use the scholarships as a promotional tool to its own benefit. Despite these concerns, the court conditionally approved the settlement until the amount distributed to class members was determined, at which point the parties could submit a more detailed plan regarding the administration of the fund.[48]

The liaison counsel for the class in *In re Linerboard Antitrust Litigation* recommended that a part of the cy pres distribution to the Philadelphia Bar Foundation be directed to two other public interest legal organizations. Although the court agreed that both were deserving recipients of cy pres funds, it refused to order a distribution to these organiza-

---

42 U.S. Chamber Institute for Legal Reform, *Cy Pres: A Not So Charitable Contribution to Class Action Practice* 12 (2010), *available at* www.instituteforlegalreform.com/sites/default/files/cypres_0.pdf.

43 The existence of such conflicts is another frequent point of public criticism. *Id.* at 12–14; Adam Liptak, *Doling Out Other People's Money*, N.Y. Times, Nov. 26, 2007, *available at* http:/www.nytimes.com/2007/11/26/washington/26bar.html (last visited Aug. 27, 2011) ("the specter of judges and outside entities dealing in the distribution and solicitation of large sums of money creates an appearance of impropriety").

44 *See, e.g.*, SEC v. Bear Stearns & Co., Inc., 626 F. Supp. 2d 297, 343–44 (S.D.N.Y. 2009) (rejecting a proposal that the remaining funds in a settlement be put towards settling another of the defendant's claims).

45 Schwartz v. Dallas Cowboys Football Club Ltd., 362 F. Supp. 2d 574, 577 (E.D. Pa. 2005) (approving a cy pres distribution to a non-profit group which bears the defendant's name and was funded in part by it prior to the suit).

46 *Id.*

47 *Radosti v. Envision EMI, LLC*, 717 F. Supp. 2d 37, 47–48 (D.C. 2010).

48 *Id.* at 64.

tions. One of the organizations employed an attorney who was once associated with the case, while the other was founded by a former partner of liaison counsel. Because of the ties to class counsel, the court left it to the Philadelphia Bar Foundation to decide whether or not any funds should be directed to these groups.[49] This case suggests that if counsel has ties with the proposed cy pres recipients, an independent organization or committee can be recommended to participate in the cy pres distribution process to alleviate concerns over potential conflicts of interest.

The U.S. Chamber Institute for Legal Reform also criticizes cy pres awards on the grounds that they allow class counsel to collect "exorbitant" fees, regardless of how much absent class members get out of the settlement.[50] "[C]y pres provides class counsel with an easy mechanism to generate high legal fees without having to devise settlements that confer actual benefits on the absent class members. It also diminishes any incentive to identify class members since the lawyer will receive the same amount of fees even if participation is negligible."[51] These arguments fail to consider how attorney's fees are calculated and the checks courts hold on such abuses. Courts can choose from a variety of methods in determining how much to award attorneys.[52] Fee awards are typically a reflection of what the attorney accomplished, and are subject to court approval under Rule 23(h).[53] Concerns about a lack of incentive to identify class members are also overstated; Rule 23(e)(1) holds that "[t]he court must direct notice in a reasonable manner to all class members who would be bound by the proposal."[54]

§ 14.06 Review standard for cy pres proposals

In *Six Mexican Workers v. Arizona Citrus Growers*, the Ninth Circuit held that a cy pres distribution must be rejected "when the proposed distribution fails to provide the 'next best' distribution."[55] In general, the approval by a district court of a class action settlement will only be reversed by an appellate court upon a showing of an abuse of discretion.[56] The "abuse of discretion" standard of review is notoriously unclear,[57] but it is generally considered deferential.[58] Consequently, appellate courts frequently grant deference to

49 *In re* Linerboard Antitrust Litig., at *12–14.

50 U.S. Chamber Institute for Legal Reform, *supra* note 42, at 13.

51 *Id.*

52 For a discussion of the various methods by which courts award attorneys' fees, see Chapter 9 and Chapter 10 of this Handbook. *See also* Eisenberg & Geoffrey P. Miller, *Attorney Fees in Class Action Settlements, An Empirical Study*, 1 J. Empirical Legal Studies 27, 30–32 (2004) (summarizing the multifactor approach, the lodestar method, and percentage fee awards for attorneys fees).

53 Fed R. Civ. P. 23(h) ("In a certified class action, the court may award reasonable attorney's fees and nontaxable costs that are authorized by law or by the parties' agreement.").

54 Fed R. Civ. P. 23(e)(1).

55 Six Mexican Workers v. Ariz. Citrus Growers, 904 F.2d 1301, 1308 (9th Cir. 1990).

56 *In re* Agent Orange Prod. Liab. Litig., MDL No. 381, 818 F.2d 179, 181 (2d Cir. 1987).

57 *See* Zervos v. Verizon New York, Inc., 252 F.3d 163, 168–69 n.4(2d Cir. 2001) ("In explicating this term, we are mindful of the need to tread lightly. Abuse of discretion is famously slippery – its meaning can vary between contexts . . . ." (quotations omitted)).

58 *See, e.g.*, Zervos v. Verizon N.Y., Inc., 252 F.3d 163, 169 (2d Cir. 2001) (a district court abuses its discretion when its decision rests on an error of law or a clearly erroneous factual finding, or when its decision cannot be located within the range of permissible decisions); *In re* Warfarin

district courts when reviewing settlements involving cy pres distributions. Nevertheless, courts have under limited circumstances reversed the approval of cy pres distributions, and remanded with new instructions.[59]

In *Masters v. Wilhelmina Model Agency, Inc.*, the Second Circuit remanded the settlement approval, which distributed the funds remaining after distribution to class members to cy pres recipients.[60] The Second Circuit held that in approving the proposed cy pres distribution, the District Court "was not aware of the extent of its discretion, failing to recognize that it was empowered to allocate the funds to the members of the class as treble damages."[61] At the same time, the Second Circuit stated that the lower court had not committed an abuse of discretion, but that a treble damages award using the funds remaining after the initial distribution should be considered on remand.[62]

§ 14.07 Cy pres as a competition-enhancing remedy

In situations where the nexus is not direct and immediate, it should be necessary to link the distribution to the underlying purposes of the statute that was violated. In cases brought under the antitrust laws, the allegations will concern anticompetitive conduct that has deprived the public of freely functioning markets. Most often, the violation will involve horizontal collusion and the class will consist of indirect purchasers who overpaid as a consequence. Thus, a cy pres distribution would have a suitable nexus if it were directed at any of the following: (1) compensating the class; (2) restoring competition within the particular market where the violation occurred; and/or (3) maintaining competition more generally.

In the *California Vitamin Cases*, a California court reviewed a proposed cy pres settlement of $38 million related to a vitamin price-fixing scheme.[63] The vitamins involved in the scheme were used as supplements, included in food products, and even added to pet foods. Almost any adult citizen of California could have been a class member. Due to the sheer size of this class, the amount of any individual damages would have been so small that transaction costs associated with the processing and payment of individual consumers rendered that remedy untenable. The court instead upheld the distribution of all

---

Sodium Antitrust Litig., 391 F.3d 516, 527 (3d. Cir. 2004) ("An abuse of discretion may be found where the district court's decision rests upon a clearly erroneous finding of fact, an errant conclusion of law or an improper application of law to fact."); Langbecker v. Elec. Data Sys. Corp., 476 F.3d 299, 306 (5th Cir. 2007) (a district court abuses its discretion when it "rests its legal analysis on an erroneous understanding of governing law"); *In re* Mego Fin. Corp. Sec. Litig., 213 F.3d 454, 458 (9th Cir. 2000) ("[W]e will affirm if the district court judge applies the proper legal standard and his findings of fact are not clearly erroneous." (citation omitted)).

59 *See, e.g.*, *In re* Airline Ticket Comm'n Antitrust Litig., 268 F.3d 619, 624–26 (8th Cir., 2001) (remanding the case to the district court for consideration of distribution to cy pres recipients with a more national scope).

60 Masters v. Wilhelmina Model Agency, Inc., 473 F.3d 423, 423 (2d Cir. 2007).

61 *Id.* at 435.

62 The issue of awarding treble damages before cy pres awards is discussed below. *See* discussion *infra* § 14.08.

63 *In re* Vitamin Cases, 107 Cal. App. 4th 820, 824 (Cal. Ct. App. 2003).

$38 million to charitable, governmental, and nonprofit organizations for the purpose of promoting the health and nutrition of the consumer class members or otherwise furthering "the purposes underlying the lawsuit."[64] The settlement also established a system for cy pres distribution, which included employment of a funds administrator who operated much like a foundation, generating highly detailed applications that were reviewed by a staff and presented to a committee that would make recommendations to the court. The administrator was also charged with monitoring grantees for compliance with the grant documents.

The American Antitrust Institute was one such grantee, receiving approximately $500,000 to undertake a two-year antitrust education project focused largely on California. In the first phase, a TV video was produced, demonstrating the value of antitrust laws for consumers and businesses. The video was subsequently reedited for classroom use and made part of a package of classroom materials and additional web based resources for introduction into California high school curricula.[65] Although money did not go directly to individual consumers, one can read into the approval of this use of cy pres funding that there was a clear nexus between the antitrust statute that was violated and the intended use of the funds, i.e., the law is more likely to be followed if more members of the public are familiar with it.[66] As the *Diamond Chemical* distribution demonstrates,[67] a grant to a foundation or center for research on complex antitrust litigation could be structured with a clear nexus to the public interest in enforcing the applicable statute and could reasonably lead to fewer violations or better administration of the antitrust laws. Put differently, education, research, and advocacy involving the enhancement of the antitrust enterprise can be appropriate "next best" uses of a class action remedial fund in an antitrust case.

---

[64] *Id.*; *see also* Catherine M. Sharkey, *Punitive Damages as Societal Damages*, 113 YALE L.J. 347, 453 n. 243 (2003).

[65] The educational website is www.fairfightfilm.org. The video was produced under the supervision of the AAI by Filmmakers Collaborative. It received two national awards for documentaries and was aired on public television stations first in California and then around the country. The video, with its segments each introduced by a California prosecutor, was fully viewable on the website for several years and is now distributed via catalog to educators. The curriculum materials available on the website were produced under the supervision of the AAI by Street Law, an organization experienced in the development of law related materials for schools. Street Law also conducted training of teachers in California to encourage the introduction of the materials into the classroom.

[66] *Cf. In re* Folding Carton Antitrust Litig., 744 F.2d 1252, 1254 (7th Cir. 1984) (creating a committee for the reserve fund's administration and the subsequent establishment of the National Public Interest Fellowship Program); Houck v. Folding Carton Admin. Comm., 881 F.2d 494, 502 (7th Cir. 1989) (not excluding law schools from "being the beneficiaries of some new appropriate *cy pres* use"); *see also In re* Folding Carton Antitrust Litig., MDL No. 250, 1991 U.S. Dist. LEXIS 2553 (N.D. Ill. Mar. 6, 1991).

[67] Diamond Chem. Co. v. Akzo Nobel Chems. B.V. No. 01-2118 2007 U.S. Dist. LEXIS 49406 (July 10, 2007).

§ 14.08 The ALI principles of the law of aggregate litigation

The cy pres remedy today is coming under closer public and legal scrutiny than at any previous time.[68] The American Law Institute (ALI) on November 18, 2008 issued Council Draft No. 2 of the Principles of the Law of Aggregate Litigation. Section 3.07, previously approved by the membership, deals with cy pres settlements. It provides that a court may approve a settlement that proposes a cy pres distribution subject to the following three criteria:

> a) If individual class members can be identified through reasonable effort, and the distributions are sufficiently large to make individual distributions economically viable, settlement proceeds should be distributed directly to individual class members.
> b) If the settlement involves individual distributions to class members and funds remain after distributions (because some class members could not be identified or chose not to participate), the settlement should presumptively provide for further distributions to participating class members unless the amounts involved are too small to make individual distributions economically viable or other specific reasons exist that would make such further distributions impossible or unfair.
> c) If the court finds that individual distributions are not viable based upon the criteria set forth in subsections (a) and (b), the settlement may utilize a cy pres approach. If, and only if, no recipient whose interests reasonably approximate those being pursued by the class can be identified, after thorough investigation and analysis, a court may approve a recipient that does not reasonably approximate the interests being pursued by the class.[69]

Subsection (a) is a traditional and unobjectionable restatement of the law. Subsection (b), however, could in some situations substantially reduce the funds available for cy pres distribution, and requires further discussion, some of which is provided by the ALI's commentary:

> This Section rejects the position urged by a few commentators that a cy pres remedy is preferable to further distributions to class members. Those commentators reason that further direct distributions would constitute a "windfall" to those class members. However, few settlements award 100 percent of a class member's losses, and thus it is unlikely in most

---

[68] A number of states have adopted rules relating to how courts may exercise their discretion in cy pres distributions. For example, Massachusetts' Rule 23 was amended, effective January 1, 2009, to provide that, "in matters where the claims process has been exhausted and residual funds remain, the residual funds shall be disbursed to one or more nonprofit organizations or foundations (which may include nonprofit organizations that provide legal services to low income persons) which support projects that will benefit the class or similarly situated persons consistent with the objectives and purposes of the underlying causes of action on which relief was based, or to the Massachusetts IOLTA Committee to support activities and programs that promote access to the civil justice system for low income residents of the Commonwealth of Massachusetts." *See* Danny Van Horn & Daniel Clayton, *It Adds Up: Class Action Residual Funds Support Pro Bono Efforts*, 45 TENN. B.J. 12 (2009).

[69] AMERICAN LAW INSTITUTE, PRINCIPLES OF THE LAW OF AGGREGATE LITIGATION § 3.07 (2010). The draft version of Section 3.07(c) said that the settlement may utilize a cy pres approach, "only if the parties can identify a recipient involving the same subject matter as the lawsuit that reasonably approximates the interests being pursued by the class." American Law Institute, Principles of the Law of Aggregate Litigation § 3.07, at 225 (Nov. 18, 2008) (Counsel Draft No. 2) (on file with the author).

> cases that further distributions to class members would result in more than 100 percent recovery for those class members. In any event, this Section takes the view that in most circumstances distributions to class members better approximate the goals of the substantive laws than distributions to third parties that were not directly injured by the defendant's conduct.[70]

Although it may be more correct with regard to other types of cases, there is neither an empirical nor a theoretical basis for the ALI's statement that few settlements award 100 percent of a class member's loss in an antitrust case. It is certainly true that settlements never obtain treble damages to which a plaintiff would be entitled in a trial victory, but we can only hypothesize as to what the outcome of the trial would have been and the amount of actual damages that would have been established as the basis for trebling. In other words, the precise damages to which an individual class member is entitled in a settled antitrust class action case is a fiction. A settlement represents a compromise between two estimates for the damages that might be determined in a future trial for a class whose size and makeup are rarely foreseeable on a precise basis, taking into account conflicting discounts for predicted trial outcomes and collection risk, in a context where the trebling of actual damages is a factor intended to provide deterrence and an incentive for plaintiffs to come forward. Although we can doubt (without the possibility of empirical evidence) that actual damages, as opposed to negotiated damages, are often obtained, there is no reason to conclude that a class member is entitled to recover actual damages in a settled case. Rather, what the court finds to be a "fair, reasonable, and adequate" basis for damages after a Rule 23 hearing should be taken as a reasonable approximation for what should be distributed to individual qualified claimants within the overall context of the litigation, taking both the compensation and deterrence goals of antitrust into account. A supplemental distribution to the same claimants who have already received what the court found adequate is unlikely to make these claimants "whole," since "whole" cannot be determined in this context with anything approaching precision. Moreover, distributing excess funds to those who filed valid claims ignores both remaining class members who, for whatever reasons, did not file qualified claims as well as the overall purpose of the case, which is to provide a remedy not only to those who were directly injured but also to those who were indirectly injured or who would likely be injured in the future but for the efforts of the litigants (the deterrence factor).

The ALI's commentary to Subsection (c), which finally authorizes cy pres, properly rejects the option of returning the remaining funds to the defendant, as this would reward the wrongdoer.[71] It also rejects escheat to the state because this would benefit all citizens equally, even those who were not harmed by the defendant's alleged conduct.[72] The commentary continues:

---

[70] *Id.* at 219.

[71] *Id.*

[72] *Id.* A cy pres remedy that enhances the competitive process in an antitrust case would presumably benefit the public at large as well as members of the class, because of the statutory determination that antitrust serves the public interest. There is no reason to think the ALI would rule out such a grant on the basis that its benefits extend beyond the class, however.

> Section 3.07(c) provides that if an award to a recipient whose interests reasonably approximate the interests of the class is not practicable, the court may designate an alternative recipient. . .. A cy pres remedy should not be ordered if the court or any party has a significant prior affiliation with the intended recipient that would raise substantial questions about whether the selection of the recipient was made on the merits.[73]

The ALI's concern about conflicts of interest is well grounded, although judgment will be called for in determining what kinds of prior affiliations are significant enough to create a substantial question.[74] The more difficult question is whether the ALI would sanction cy pres distributions to third parties whose mission is to enhance the purposes of the law under which the litigation was conducted. The ALI commentary explains circumstances in which a cy pres payment to the NAACP Legal Defense Fund would be "appropriate."[75] In the example, the Legal Defense Fund was not a party, but the case involved enforcement of the civil rights statutes, the special cause of the fund. A parallel understanding of antitrust would hold it appropriate to award cy pres funds to a non-profit organization for the enhancement of the purposes of the antitrust laws.

§ 14.09 Recommended best practices

As the frequency of cy pres distribution has increased, problems relating to the fairness of distributions, such as the possible close relationship between plaintiffs' attorney and grant recipients, as well as the accountability and evaluation of proposals, are presented. In most of the cases, a list of recommended recipients was offered by plaintiffs' lead counsel in a stipulated or unopposed order and the court generally accepted them. On occasion, a court has requested proposed recipients to elaborate on how they would utilize the funds or to appear before the court to make a presentation. Plaintiffs' attorneys may be helpful by proposing a procedure for selecting the beneficiaries instead of specifying the particular cy pres distribution recipients in the settlement. In any event, fair and clear selection procedures should be established to serve the best interests of absent class members and minimize disputes over the settlement. The following are proposed best practices for courts, plaintiffs' lawyers, defense counsel, and state enforcement officials:[76]

1. The first priority of an antitrust class action remedy is to assure that as many members of the injured class as possible are aware of their opportunity to file a claim and that the claims process is as simple and fair as possible, consistent with the need to deter fraud and achieve transactional efficiency.
2. If there are funds remaining after qualified claims have been met or if the class is so large compared to the size of the fund that transaction costs render a distribution of cash infea-

---

[73] *Id.* at 228.

[74] *See* discussion *supra* § 14.05.

[75] *Id.* at 220.

[76] These recommendations were discussed extensively in two joint meetings with class action plaintiffs' attorneys and state assistant attorneys general for antitrust and reflect an apparent consensus of those present. See Summary of Second Meeting on Private/State Antitrust Enforcement (Dec. 18, 2007), *available at* http://www.antitrustinstitute.org/Archives/states2.ashx.

sible, then a cy pres alternative should be designed as an essential part of the settlement or adjudicated order.

3. Where funds are not distributed directly to injured consumers, there must be a nexus between the nature of the claim and the uses to which the cy pres funds will be put. Class counsel (or parens patriae counsel, if applicable) must come forward with a plan for distribution, and other counsel should evaluate the proposal and inform the court of any objections or proposed revisions. After notice to the class and an opportunity for objections, the court can then hold a hearing to determine if the remedy is equitable, administrable, and consistent with the requirements of the cy pres doctrine.
4. The benefit to the class may be direct or indirect and may be related to the industry in which the antitrust violation occurred, the type of harm that occurred, or the restoration or enhancement of competition.
5. All things equal, proposals for direct benefit to the class are to be preferred to proposals for indirect benefit, and proposals that relate to the geographic scope of the harm are preferred to proposals that relate only to a segment of the geographic market in which the harm occurred.
6. Proposals entailing possible anticompetitive effects, such as providing a marketplace advantage to a defendant, should be rejected.
7. Where the fund is sufficiently large, the court should establish a grant-making process not only for awarding and distributing the money but also for overseeing the expenditures by cy pres recipients. In this case, a percentage of the fund should be set aside for administration, and the order should specify general objectives of the distribution, which could include different percentages targeted at different objectives. The administrator should have experience in analyzing, evaluating, and supervising grant proposals and their implementation.
8. Where the fund is not sufficiently large to encompass a formal grant-making process, the plaintiffs should present multiple candidates for awards and describe how the candidates were selected (e.g., transparently explaining any conflict or bias on the recommenders' part). The candidates should provide the court with their background, their proposal for how an award would be utilized, a justification for the award in terms of benefit to the class, and a commitment to provide one or more reports to the court in the future on how the money was expended.
9. Types of cy pres remedies appropriate in an antitrust case could include education, research, and/or advocacy with respect to the improvement of antitrust enforcement or compliance in the industry where the violation occurred. In parens patriae cases, if relief focused on consumer payments is not feasible, the remedy could include carefully constructed grants to encourage entry or otherwise improve the state of competition within the industry.
10. States should adopt cy pres guidelines, and ad hoc policies and procedures should be minimized.

There may be ways in which the transaction costs associated with cy pres could be reduced through cooperative action. An example would be to establish a national administrative entity which, at the court's discretion, would help administer cy pres funds. Under such a system, the forum court should retain the power to determine who will receive funds, the amounts, and for what purposes. The central administrator, funded through a percentage of cy pres moneys, should complement this function, investigating applicants as an agent for the court and administering the funds, including monitoring expenditures. In discharging this duty, the central administrator would provide economies of scale and a level of expertise and oversight that rarely occurs in today's cy pres distributions.

§ 14.10 Conclusion

The doctrine of cy pres has a proper role to play in the context of antitrust class actions, but there is a danger of abuse that has been recognized in the media and must be addressed by the bar and the judiciary. A variety of "best practices" can help avoid the pitfalls while assuring that cy pres is part of a remedy for competitive problems that brought the class into the courtroom.

15 Proposals for reform

Pamela Gilbert[1] *and Victoria Romanenko*[2]

§ 15.01 Introduction

The private enforcement scheme of the U.S. antitrust laws has stood the test of time for almost a century. That scheme, as established by § 4 of the Clayton Act in 1914, provides for treble damages and costs, including attorneys' fees, for any person "injured in his business or property by reason of anything forbidden in the antitrust laws."[3]

The Supreme Court has repeatedly found that private actions play a critical role in the enforcement of the antitrust laws and the protection of a fair marketplace. It explained in *Mitsubishi Motors Corp. v. Soler Chrysler-Plymouth, Inc.* that "[t]he treble-damages provision wielded by the private litigant is a chief tool in the antitrust enforcement scheme, posing a crucial deterrent to potential violators."[4]

Over time, some Supreme Court rulings have narrowed the scope of the private right of action and others have expanded it. Congress has also stepped in with legislation that has affected the rules governing private enforcement of the antitrust laws. But throughout the many decades of litigation and legislation, the core enforcement scheme has remained intact.

In Congress, the Judiciary Committees in the House of Representatives and the Senate have responsibility for antitrust legislation and oversight. The committees hold hearings,

---

[1] Pamela Gilbert is a partner at Cuneo Gilbert & LaDuca and a member of the board of directors of the American Antitrust Institute. Ms. Gilbert focuses her practice on government relations matters and has testified before the U.S. Congress over 50 times. Ms. Gilbert can be reached at Pamelag@cuneolaw.com.

[2] Victoria Romanenko is an associate at Cuneo Gilbert & LaDuca, working primarily in the area of antitrust class action litigation. Ms. Romanenko can be reached at Vicky@cuneolaw.com.

[3] Clayton Act, 15 U.S.C. § 15 (1914).

[4] 473 U.S. 614, 635 (1985).

commission reports, vote on legislation, and oversee the Antitrust Division of the Department of Justice. The Senate Judiciary Committee is also responsible for considering and voting on the President's nominee to head the Antitrust Division. On a number of occasions through the years, Congress has, instead of conducting its own study and analysis of the complex area of antitrust law, created blue ribbon commissions to study the antitrust laws and make recommendations for change.[5] In 2002, Congress created the Antitrust Modernization Commission (AMC)[6] to analyze the state of the antitrust laws and recommend changes to fortify them.

This chapter discusses proposals for reform contemplated by Congress or the AMC in eight areas that affect private antitrust enforcement. Three of the areas – pleading standards, class action waivers, and the rights of indirect purchasers – involve the ability to bring a private action in the first place. One area – claims reduction and contribution – concerns the treble damage remedy and joint and several liability. The remaining topics – reverse payments, resale price maintenance, the Robinson-Patman Act, and the Railroad Antitrust Enhancement Act – address specific antitrust-related conduct. The chapter also discusses one piece of legislation that was recently amended, the Antitrust Criminal Penalty Enforcement and Reform Act (ACPERA).

With the exception of the ACPERA amendments, none of the proposed legislation discussed in this chapter has been enacted as of this writing.

§ 15.02 *Twombly* and *Iqbal*: Federal pleading standards

The U.S. Supreme Court substantially altered pleading standards in federal civil litigation through two cases decided in 2007 and 2009.[7] The 2007 case, *Bell Atlantic v. Twombly*,[8]

---

[5] Prior to the most recent such commission in 2002, Congress established five blue ribbon antitrust commissions: the Temporary National Economic Committee (1938–41) (created to evaluate the state of the antitrust laws after the Great Depression and credited with contributing to the Celler-Kefauver Act); the Attorney General's National Committee to Study the Antitrust Laws (1955) (focused on distribution issues and recommended that the rule of reason be used to evaluate non-*per se* offenses); the White House Task Force on Antitrust Policy (1967–69) (recommended legislation to contend with high market concentrations); the National Commission for Review of Antitrust Laws and Procedures (1977–79) (created to evaluate antitrust immunities and exemptions and to analyze the procedures governing litigation of complex cases); and the International Competition Advisory Committee (1998–2000) (assembled to respond to the growth of new markets around the world and the increase in international trade). None of these commissions directly gave rise to legislation, though some of them exerted considerable influence on antitrust policy. For a full description of these blue ribbon study commissions, see Albert A. Foer, *Putting the Antitrust Modernization Commission into Perspective*, 51 BUFF. L. REV. 1029, 1032 (2003).

[6] Congress created the AMC through the Antitrust Modernization Commission Act of 2002, Pub. L. No. 107–273, §§ 11051–60, 116 Stat. 1856. Around the same time, the American Antitrust Institute and the American Bar Association Section of Antitrust Law also produced reform proposals. For an interesting comparative summary of these proposals, see AMERICAN ANTITRUST INSTITUTE, COMPARISON OF AMC, AAI, AND ABA ANTITRUST SECTION RECOMMENDATIONS (compiled by BK Lee, Dec. 12, 2008), *available at* http://www.antitrustinstitute.org (search site for "AMC AAI ABA"; follow "Side-by-side Comparison of Antitrust Agendas . . ." hyperlink; follow "View the matrix" hyperlink).

[7] For a more detailed description of the cases, see Chapter 6 of this Handbook.

[8] 550 U.S. 544 (2007).

was an antitrust case alleging that regional telephone companies had conspired to limit competition in local telephone markets. The Court reversed the Second Circuit, which had overturned the district court's dismissal of the case, finding that the plaintiffs' complaint had failed to state a claim for relief because it did not state enough facts to persuade the court that the claim was "plausible on its face."[9] Prior to *Twombly*, the pleading standard in federal courts had been based on a 1957 Supreme Court decision entitled *Conley v. Gibson*.[10] In *Conley*, the Court had ruled that civil cases in federal courts should not be dismissed "unless it appears beyond doubt that the plaintiff can prove no set of facts in support of his claim that would entitle him to relief."[11] The *Twombly* court expressly "retired" the *Conley* "no set of facts" language.[12]

Two years later, the Court expanded on the *Twombly* standard in *Ashcroft v. Iqbal*, explaining that "a claim has facial plausibility when the pleaded factual content allows the court to draw the reasonable inference that the defendant is liable for the misconduct alleged,"[13] and that in making that determination, a court is to "draw on its judicial experience and common sense."[14] While conceding that "well-pleaded factual allegations" should be assumed to be true at the motion to dismiss stage, the Court made a distinction between "factual allegations" and "conclusory allegations." Without clearly defining the difference between the two, the Court ruled that conclusory allegations are not entitled to the assumption of truth for purposes of a motion to dismiss.[15] In *Iqbal*, the Court also made clear that the plausibility standard established in *Twombly* was not confined to antitrust cases, but rather, was meant to apply to all federal civil litigation.[16]

Within antitrust circles, the *Twombly* ruling made a substantial impact. Plaintiffs in antitrust cases were unclear as to the factual specificity required in drafting complaints to meet the new "plausibility" standard. Moreover, without the benefit of discovery beforehand, it was unclear how those facts would be learned. Many in the antitrust plaintiffs' bar called for some kind of congressional response to the ruling, but, standing alone, they lacked the political heft to move legislation.

The ruling in *Iqbal*, however, expanded these concerns to all federal litigants. As such, it was instantly controversial throughout the legal establishment. Academics criticized the Court for unilaterally changing the pleading standards without going through the procedures established by the Rules Enabling Act[17] or through Congress. Public interest groups and many litigators claimed that, by overturning half a century of notice pleading in the federal courts, the decisions would close the courthouse doors to many civil litigants. Others noted that the heightened pleading standards would likely have the greatest

---

9 *Twombly*, 550 U.S. at 570.
10 355 U.S. 41 (1957).
11 *Conley*, 355 U.S. at 45–46.
12 *Twombly*, 550 U.S. at 563.
13 129 S. Ct. 1937, 1949 (2009).
14 *Iqbal*, 129 S. Ct. at 1949–50.
15 *Id.* at 1950.
16 *Id.* at 1953.
17 28 U.S.C.A. § 2072 (1990). The Rules Enabling Act gives the judicial branch the power to promulgate federal rules of procedure. Under the Act, the creation and revision of rules is supposed to be carried out by the Judicial Conference of the United States, the policymaking body of the United States federal courts.

adverse impact on complex litigation, such as antitrust cases, where the information about the details of the wrongful conduct is often in the possession of the defendant and will not be known until after discovery commences.

Professor Arthur R. Miller of the New York University School of Law, author of the multivolume treatise *Federal Practice and Procedure*, testified:

> *Twombly* and *Iqbal* have swung the pendulum away from the prior emphasis on access for potentially meritorious claims; it probably will affect litigants bringing complex claims the hardest. Those cases – many involving Constitutional and statutory rights that seek the enforcement of important national policies and often affecting large numbers of people – include claims in which factual sufficiency is most difficult to achieve at the pleading stage and tend to be resource consumptive. Already, recent decisions suggest that complex cases, such as those involving claims of discrimination, conspiracy, and antitrust violations, have been treated as if they were disfavored actions.[18]

Congressional legislation was introduced to overturn *Twombly* and *Iqbal*. On July 22, 2009, Senator Arlen Specter (D-PA) introduced a bill known as the Notice Pleading Restoration Act of 2009. The bill consisted of one simple paragraph:

> Except as otherwise expressly provided by an Act of Congress or by an amendment to the Federal Rules of Civil Procedure which takes effect after the date of enactment of this Act, a Federal court shall not dismiss a complaint under rule 12(b)(6) or (e) of the Federal Rules of Civil Procedure, except under the standards set forth by the Supreme Court of the United States in *Conley v. Gibson*, 355 U.S. 41 (1957).[19]

On November 19, 2009, Representative Jerrold Nadler (D-NY) introduced a bill called the Open Access to Courts Act of 2009. Representative Nadler's bill had the same goal as Senator Specter's bill, but instead of referring to *Conley* by name, Representative Nadler's bill established the standard articulated in *Conley* as the correct standard for dismissal under Rule 12(b) of the Federal Rules of Civil Procedure. In addition, Representative Nadler's bill specifically prohibited courts from granting motions to dismiss based on he standards enunciated in *Twombly* and *Iqbal*. The relevant portion of the bill states:

> A court shall not dismiss a complaint under subdivision (b)(6), (c) or (e) of Rule 12 of the Federal Rules of Civil Procedure unless it appears beyond doubt that the plaintiff can prove no set of facts in support of the claim which would entitle the plaintiff to relief. A court shall not dismiss a complaint under one of those subdivisions on the basis of a determination by the judge that the factual contents of the complaint do not show the plaintiff's claim to be plausible or are insufficient to warrant a reasonable inference that the defendant is liable for the misconduct alleged.[20]

A coalition of civil rights, women's, seniors', environmental, consumer, and legal groups formed to support legislation to overturn the two cases, although the coalition never formally endorsed either the Specter bill or the Nadler bill. The U.S. Chamber of Commerce

---

[18] *Access to Justice Denied: Ashcroft v. Iqbal: Hearing Before the Subcomm. on Constitution, Civil Rights and Civil Liberties of the H. Comm. on the Judiciary*, 111th Cong. 17–18 (2009) (statement of Arthur R. Miller, Professor of Law, New York University School of Law).

[19] Notice Pleading Restoration Act of 2009, S. 1504, 111th Cong. (2009).

[20] Open Access to Courts Act of 2009, H.R. 4115, 111th Cong. (2009).

and over three dozen companies and trade associations came out strongly in opposition to the measures. In a letter to the House Judiciary Committee, the business groups wrote:

> This legislation . . . would produce a revolutionary change in pleading rules, cause tremendous confusion over the applicable legal standards, and make it impossible for defendants to obtain dismissal of complaints that are legally insufficient under decades of well-settled law. This drastic change in standards would impose enormous costs on already struggling businesses and further impede economic recovery.[21]

Hearings were held in the House and the Senate, but neither bill came up for a vote in either house of Congress during the congressional session. No legislation addressing *Twombly* or *Iqbal* has been introduced since that time.

The Civil Rules Advisory Committee for the Judicial Conference Committee on the Rules of Practice and Procedure has been studying the impact of *Twombly* and *Iqbal* on federal litigation by reviewing opinions in which the cases are discussed and applied. A staff memorandum discussing the case law was released in March 2011.[22] This memorandum found that, so far, there is no indication that "*Iqbal* has dramatically changed the application of the standards used to determine pleading sufficiency."[23] The staff did find, however, that some courts have stated that "*Twombly* and *Iqbal* have raised the bar for defeating a motion to dismiss based on failure to state a claim."[24] To date, the Advisory Committee has not made any proposals to change or modify pleading standards under the Federal Rules. The American Antitrust Institute (AAI) has recommended to President Obama that an investigation be conducted to determine the "extent to which [*Twombly*] has impaired Rule 8's notice pleading standard, and possible remedial measures."[25] The administration has not responded to this recommendation.

§ 15.03 Class action waivers

Controversy over class action waivers has arisen from a perceived conflict between the Federal Arbitration Act (FAA)[26] and Rule 23 of the Federal Rules of Civil Procedure, which allows for the aggregation of private claims meeting certain criteria.[27] The FAA requires that arbitration agreements be placed on equal footing with other contracts,[28] and that they be enforced according to their terms.[29] However, the terms of many arbitration

---

[21] Letter from AEGON USA LLC et al. to the Hon. Jerrold Nadler and the Hon. James Sensenbrenner 1 (Oct. 26, 2009).

[22] Memorandum from Andrea Kuperman on Review of Case Law Applying *Bell Atlantic Corp v. Twombly* and *Ashcroft v. Iqbal* (March 29, 2011).

[23] *Id.* at 3.

[24] *Id.* at 4.

[25] American Antitrust Institute, The Next Antitrust Agenda: The American Antitrust Institute's Transition Report on Competition Policy to the 44th President 220 (Albert A. Foer ed., 2008).

[26] 9 U.S.C. § 1 *et seq.* (1947).

[27] *See* Fed. R. Civ. P. 23.

[28] Buckeye Check Cashing, Inc. v. Cardegna, 546 U.S. 440, 443 (2006).

[29] Volt Information Sciences, Inc. v. Board of Trustees of Leland Stanford Junior Univ., 489 U.S. 468, 469 (1989).

agreements include a waiver of the signer's right to adjudicate his or her claims as part of a class, a right that may be essential for the efficient redress of harm done to various types of litigants, such as a large number of consumers who have been deprived of small sums. Some arbitration clauses preclude claimants from effectively pursuing class action lawsuits. Others prevent claimants from effectively pursuing any form of class adjudication, including class arbitration. However, plaintiffs often bring putative class actions seeking to challenge class waivers contained in arbitration clauses, either on "such grounds as exist at law or in equity for the revocation of any contract,"[30] such as "fraud, duress, or unconscionability,"[31] or under the federal substantive law of arbitrability. These arguments have been explored by several courts.

In 2011, in *AT&T Mobility v. Concepcion*, the Supreme Court reviewed a Ninth Circuit decision approving a California state court's application of California's common law "*Discover Bank* rule," which operates as a bar to certain class waivers on unconscionability grounds.[32] The rule, which was formulated in *Discover Bank v. Superior Court*,[33] provided specifically for the unconscionability of all arbitration clauses prohibiting class adjudication of low-value disputes regarding schemes to defraud large numbers of consumers. The Supreme Court held that the state law was preempted by the FAA, as its enforcement would effectively eviscerate the federal statute. The Court explained:

> The overarching purpose of the FAA, evident in the text of §§ 2, 3, and 4, is to ensure the enforcement of arbitration agreements according to their terms so as to facilitate streamlined proceedings. Requiring the availability of classwide arbitration interferes with fundamental attributes of arbitration and thus creates a scheme inconsistent with the FAA.[34]

With regard to defenses raised under the federal substantive law of arbitrability, the Supreme Court has stated, in *Gilmer v. Interstate/Johnson Lane Corp.*, that an arbitration clause is still valid, even if it prevents plaintiffs from exercising their rights to bring a judicial action called for by a federal statute, so long as the plaintiffs are able to effectively vindicate their federal rights through arbitration.[35] Thus, the Court held that an Age Discrimination in Employment Act (ADEA) claim could be arbitrated in a proceeding allowing for collective actions, but stated that "even if the arbitration could not go forward as a class action or class relief could not be granted by the arbitrator, the fact that the ADEA provides for the possibility of bringing a collective action does not mean that individual attempts at conciliation were intended to be barred."[36]

A number of courts of appeal have interpreted this decision to mean that an arbitration agreement prohibiting class actions is valid and does not deprive a litigant of his ability to vindicate his federal rights. The Third Circuit, for instance, has stated that it "[does] not agree that compelling arbitration of the claim of a prospective class action plaintiff irrec-

---

[30] 9 U.S.C. § 2.

[31] Doctor's Associates, Inc. v. Casarotto, 517 U.S. 681, 687 (1996).

[32] 131 S. Ct. 1740 (2011). For further discussion of *Concepcion* and the intersection of arbitration and class actions, see Chapter 5 of this Handbook.

[33] Discover Bank v. Superior Court, 113 P.3d 1100, 36 Cal. 4th 148, 162–63 (2005).

[34] *Concepcion*, 131 S. Ct. at 1748.

[35] 500 U.S. 20 (1991).

[36] *Id.* at 32.

oncilably conflicts with TILA's [the Truth in Lending Act's] goal of encouraging private actions to deter violations of the Act."[37]

Other courts of appeal have disagreed. In *Kristian v. Comcast Corp.*, the First Circuit, evaluating a claim that plaintiffs had relinquished their rights to obtain a classwide resolution of their dispute by signing an arbitration clause with a class mechanism waiver, held that "[i]f the class mechanism prohibition here is enforced, Comcast will be essentially shielded from private consumer antitrust enforcement liability, even in cases where it has violated the law[;] [p]laintiffs will be unable to vindicate their statutory rights."[38] The First Circuit further stated that, given the expense of bringing an antitrust case, preventing the plaintiffs from distributing that expense precluded them from benefitting from their statutory rights to initiate such a proceeding.[39]

In addition to determining that, in some instances, plaintiffs can effectively waive their rights to a class lawsuit, the Supreme Court has also decided that classwide arbitration cannot be read into an arbitration agreement that is otherwise silent on the issue. In *Stolt-Nielsen S.A. v. AnimalFeeds International Corp.*, a case alleging a price-fixing conspiracy among a cartel of shipping companies, the Supreme Court held that an arbitration agreement which did not mention classwide arbitration could not be construed as allowing it.[40] The Court stated that "a party may not be compelled under the FAA to submit to class arbitration unless there is a contractual basis for concluding that the party *agreed* to do so."[41]

Many corporate advocates suggest that parties to arbitration agreements should not be entitled to any class-based mechanism. They argue that class resolution should be waivable in an arbitration agreement. The basis for this argument is that arbitration was concocted as a simplified and more expedient way of allowing corporations to resolve consumers' and employees' disputes, and that requiring arbitration to proceed on a class basis, or invalidating an arbitration agreement because it prevents class actions, deprives the mechanism of its utility. As one supporter explained, "[b]y permitting class arbitration, with its attendant discovery, class certification, and class settlement formalities, the parties essentially forgo the advantages of arbitration."[42] Proponents of arbitration clauses also argue that, in many cases, claimants involved in individual arbitration are put in no worse a position than plaintiffs who are positioned as class members.

---

37 Johnson v. West Suburban Bank, 225 F.3d 366, 374 (3d Cir. 2000). *See also* Gay v. CreditInform, 511 F.3d 369, 382 (3d Cir. 2007) (holding that language in the Credit Repair Organizations Act stating that an injured party was entitled to bring a class action did not demonstrate Congress' intent to preclude arbitration of claims brought under that act and therefore, the arbitration provision in the defendant's contract was properly enforceable).

38 Kristian v. Comcast Corp., 446 F.3d 25, 62 (1st Cir. 2006).

39 *Id.* at 58. *See also In re* American Express Merchants Litig., 634 F.3d 187, 194 (2d Cir. 2011) (forcing plaintiffs to arbitrate would have the effect of "depriving plaintiffs of the statutory protections of the antitrust laws.").

40 130 S. Ct. 1758, 1775 (2010).

41 *Id.* at 1775 (emphasis in original).

42 Ramona Lampley, *Is Arbitration Under Attack?: Exploring the Recent Judicial Skepticism of the Class Arbitration Waiver and Innovative Solutions to the Unsettled Legal Landscape*, 18 Cornell J.L. & Pub. Pol'y 477, 509 (2009).

Many consumer advocates, on the other hand, oppose such waivers, suggesting that "even a cursory review of the FAA's legislative history reveals that Congress did not intend for the statute to apply to contracts between parties with unequal bargaining power."[43] These opponents argue that the Act was only meant to apply to disputes between corporations, and that it is unreasonable to apply the FAA to bar an action brought by an unsophisticated consumer against a powerful corporation, given that most consumers do not read or comprehend arbitration clauses attached to the adhesion contracts they enter into with companies in superior bargaining positions.[44] Class waivers in arbitration clauses are said to essentially allow corporations to take advantage of consumers who are not savvy enough to understand the significance of the rights they are foregoing.

Opponents of class waivers argue further that by depriving plaintiffs of the ability to bring class actions or even obtain classwide arbitration, such waivers completely deprive victims of any ability to obtain a remedy for the wrongs they have suffered. For practical purposes, no lawyer will be willing to represent individual clients in the species of small claims that are often subject to such agreements (e.g., consumer claims for as little as $5 or $10). As Professor David Horton stated, prior to the Supreme Court's decision in *Concepcion*:

> Indeed, "[t]he realistic alternative to a class action is not 17 million individual suits, but zero individual suits, as only a lunatic or a fanatic sues for $30." And when statutory rights are at issue, the problem is not simply that class arbitration waivers are unfair. It is that, in the aggregate, they "write private enforcement out of the underlying statute." Allowing the FAA to swallow the class action device would thus allow private parties to rewrite substantive laws. The Court should hold that the FAA does not preclude class arbitration of low-value consumer and employment disputes.[45]

Justice Breyer, in his dissent in *Concepcion*, echoed Professor Horton's concerns that depriving plaintiffs with small claims of class action mechanisms results in a bar on their ability to seek redress for their injuries.[46]

Congress has responded to concerns about arbitration clauses and the waivers contained in them with a series of bills aimed at promoting arbitration fairness. As of this writing, the most recent bills were introduced in 2011. Senator Al Franken (D-MN) has sponsored the Arbitration Fairness Act of 2011,[47] which states that "[n]owithstanding any other provision of this title, no predispute arbitration agreement shall be valid or enforceable if it requires arbitration of an employment dispute, consumer dispute, or civil rights dispute."[48]

---

[43] David Horton, *Arbitration as Delegation*, 86 N.Y.U. L. REV. 437, 447 (2011).

[44] *See* Jean R. Sternlight, *Panacea or Corporate Tool?: Debunking The Supreme Court's Preference for Binding Arbitration*, 74 WASH. U. L.Q. 637, 641 (1996).

[45] *Id.* at 494 (quoting Carnegie v. Household Int'l, Inc., 376 F.3d 656, 661 (7th Cir. 2004); Richard A. Nagareda, *Aggregation and Its Discontents: Class Settlement Pressure, Class-Wide Arbitration, and CAFA*, 106 COLUM. L. REV. 1872, 1904 (2006)).

[46] *Concepcion*, 131 S. Ct. at 1760–61 (Breyer, J., dissenting) ("What rational lawyer would have signed on to represent the Concepcions in litigation for the possibility of fees stemming from a $30.22 claim?").

[47] Arbitration Fairness Act of 2011, S. 987, 112th Cong. (2011).

[48] *Id.* at § 402(a).

That bill has now been referred to the Senate Judiciary Committee. The House of Representatives has introduced a practically identical bill, also known as the Arbitration Fairness Act of 2011.[49] The House bill, sponsored by Representative Hank Johnson (D-GA), uses language identical to the Senate bill to invalidate all arbitration clauses that seek to require arbitration of any consumer, employment, or civil rights disputes, pursuant to an agreement signed before the dispute arose. As of this writing, the bill has been referred to the Courts, Commercial and Administrative Law Subcommittee of the House Judiciary Committee.

Some commentators have warned that the bill would create too draconian an approach to the problem of litigation waivers. Others believe that this legislation would return the FAA to its intended purpose of providing a streamlined mechanism for the resolution of disputes between corporations, but without depriving individuals of their rights to access the courts.[50]

§ 15.04 Indirect purchaser litigation

The question of which parties in the chain of distribution may sue for damages under the federal antitrust laws has been a subject of litigation and debate for decades.[51] In 1968, the Supreme Court took a step toward resolving this issue in *Hanover Shoe, Inc. v. United Shoe Machinery Corp.*[52] In *Hanover Shoe*, the Court held that an antitrust defendant may not assert the defense that the direct purchaser plaintiff passed on that defendant's overcharges to its customers, and therefore, was not harmed by that defendant's antitrust violation.[53]

Then, in the 1977 case *Illinois Brick Co. v. Illinois*, the Supreme Court held that *only* direct purchasers may sue under federal law to recover antitrust overcharges.[54] The Court reasoned that, if defendants could not use the pass-on argument "defensively" against claims by direct purchasers, it would be inconsistent to allow indirect purchasers to use the argument "offensively" to claim that overcharges were, in fact, passed on to them. The Court was also concerned that allowing indirect purchasers to bring antitrust claims "would create a serious risk of multiple liability for defendants."[55]

Justice Brennan, joined by Justices Blackmun and Marshall, issued a strong dissent, stating that the decision "flouts Congress' purpose and severely undermines the effectiveness of the private treble-damages action as an instrument of antitrust enforcement."[56]

---

49 Arbitration Fairness Act of 2011, H.R. 1873, 112th Cong. (2011).

50 Another bill addressing arbitration agreements, the Consumer Mobile Fairness Act of 2011, was introduced in 2011 by Senator Franken and Senator Richard Blumenthal (D-CT). That bill focuses exclusively on arbitration agreements in cellular telephone and mobile data service contracts, stating that "a predispute arbitration agreement between a covered individual and a provider of mobile service shall not be valid or enforceable." S. 1652 112th Cong. § 402(a) (2011). As of this writing, that bill has been referred to the Senate Judiciary Committee.

51 For a full discussion of antitrust standing, see Chapter 3 of this Handbook.

52 392 U.S. 481 (1968).

53 *Id.* at 493–94.

54 431 U.S. 720 (1977).

55 *Id.* at 730.

56 *Id.* at 749 (Brennan, J., dissenting).

The dissenters noted that, in many cases, the harm from antitrust violations is borne almost entirely by the ultimate consumers of a product because overcharges are passed on to them.[57] In those cases, direct purchasers would have little or no incentive to sue the violators. Under the majority's ruling, this circumstance would frustrate congressional intent behind the private enforcement scheme in the antitrust laws, which includes provisions for victim compensation and deterrence of wrongdoers. Justice Blackmun wrote a brief additional dissent, in which he predicted that Congress would enact legislation to overturn *Illinois Brick* to achieve "the obvious congressional aim" of the antitrust laws.[58]

Justice Blackmun was partially correct. Legislation to overturn the decision was introduced and vigorously debated over the course of many Congresses, but it was never enacted. Many states, however, did respond by passing so-called "*Illinois Brick* repealers" that authorized indirect purchasers to recover damages under state antitrust laws. In other cases, state courts issued rulings that allowed indirect purchasers to sue. Currently, over 35 states allow for some type of damage action by indirect purchasers under state antitrust laws.[59]

In 2005, the AMC asked for public comment and proposals for reform regarding indirect purchaser litigation. Many commenters recommended that no changes be made in the law, while others recommended overturning both *Illinois Brick* and *Hanover Shoe*, and still others recommended overturning one but not the other. There were also proposals to allow state indirect purchaser suits to be brought in federal court and consolidated with direct purchaser cases. Many commenters discussed the issue of preempting state indirect purchaser laws because of the danger of duplicative recoveries by direct and indirect purchasers for the same overcharge. No commenters, however, could cite a case in which indirect purchaser litigation had resulted in such duplication, and a recommendation to preempt state laws was not featured in any of the proposed reforms.

The AAI and a number of antitrust practitioners recommended keeping the status quo. These commenters noted that the recently-enacted Class Action Fairness Act (CAFA), which would cause most state law-based class actions to be removed to federal court, would allow indirect purchaser and direct purchaser cases to be consolidated in federal court for pre-trial purposes.[60] They theorized that CAFA would ameliorate the risk that parallel state court and federal court litigation would result in multiple liability for defendants. AAI's submission on this topic stated:

> Congress has just passed major legislation, the Class Action Fairness Act, reforming the handling of class actions. Nearly all antitrust class actions (whether grounded in state or federal law) will be coordinated or consolidated in a single federal court. That should take care of many of the concerns relating to *Illinois Brick*, proliferation of duplicative state and federal suits and inconsistent adjudications. In view of this brand new and revolutionary change, which has not yet been given a chance to work itself out, it would be unwise to recommend additional reformation of the relationship between state and federal law for indirect purchasers at this time.

---

[57] *Id.*

[58] *Id.* at 766 (Blackmun, J., dissenting).

[59] ANTITRUST MODERNIZATION COMMISSION, REPORT AND RECOMMENDATIONS 269 (April 2, 2007).

[60] *See* 28 U.S.C. § 1453. For further discussion of CAFA, see Chapter 4 and Chapter 5 of this Handbook.

Rather, Congress would benefit from a fuller opportunity to witness the actual (as opposed to theoretical) benefits and drawbacks of state indirect purchaser remedies and how in reality they interplay with federal remedies, under the new scheme.[61]

In contrast, the National Association of Attorneys General, representing 50 state attorneys general offices, recommended a full repeal of *Illinois Brick* and a partial repeal of *Hanover Shoe*. Testimony submitted on the association's behalf stated:

The states, in a National Association of Attorneys General resolution, advocate that Congress repeal *Illinois Brick* and provide a federal remedy for downstream purchasers. *Hanover Shoe* should be modified to permit a fair allocation of damages among direct and indirect purchasers when there are multiple levels of claimants. The Attorneys General also oppose preemption of state antitrust laws, including state laws providing downstream purchaser remedies.[62]

The American Bar Association Section of Antitrust Law (ABA) submitted a recommendation intended to balance the competing interests of plaintiffs and defendants in antitrust cases, which consisted of the following five parts:

(1) Repeal *Illinois Brick* to provide indirect purchasers a federal cause of action;
(2) Overrule *Hanover Shoe* to prevent duplicative recoveries;
(3) Relax diversity jurisdiction and allow the cases to be consolidated for pre-trial motions and for trial;
(4) Provide for prejudgment interest on damage awards; and
(5) Do not preempt state laws.[63]

The AMC itself did not issue a unanimous recommendation for reform of indirect purchaser litigation. A majority of the AMC voted for a recommendation very much along the lines of the ABA's proposal. The AMC majority proposed the following:

(1) Overrule *Illinois Brick* and *Hanover Shoe* to the extent necessary to allow both direct and indirect purchasers to sue to recover for actual damages from violations of federal antitrust laws. Damages in such actions could not exceed the overcharges (trebled) incurred by direct purchasers. Damages should be apportioned among all purchaser plaintiffs – both direct and indirect – in full satisfaction of their claims in accordance with the evidence as to the extent of the actual damages they suffered.
(2) Allow removal of indirect purchaser actions brought under state antitrust law to federal court to the full extent permitted under Article III.
(3) Allow consolidation of all direct and indirect purchaser actions in a single federal forum for both pre-trial and trial proceedings.
(4) Allow for certification of classes of direct purchasers, consistent with current practice, without regard to whether the injury alleged was passed on to customers of the direct purchasers.[64]

---

61 Comments of the American Antitrust Institute Working Group on Remedies, 18 (June 17, 2005).

62 *Hearing Concerning Indirect Purchaser Actions Before the Antitrust Modernization Commission*, 109th Cong. 1 (2005) (testimony of Mark J. Bennett and Ellen S. Cooper).

63 *Hearing Concerning Indirect Purchaser Actions Before the Antitrust Modernization Commission*, 109th Cong. 3–4 (2005) (oral testimony of Richard M. Steuer).

64 Antitrust Modernization Commission, *supra* note 56, at 270–71.

As indicated above, however, not every Commissioner of the AMC endorsed each of these proposals. Three Commissioners did not endorse overruling *Illinois Brick* and *Hanover Shoe*. Another Commissioner did not endorse expanding the ability to remove state indirect actions to federal court. Three Commissioners recommended preempting state laws to require that any claim for damages by an indirect purchaser be brought in federal court under federal antitrust law.

There has not been any legislative activity or debate in Congress regarding indirect purchaser litigation since the AMC issued its report.

§ 15.05 Claims reduction and contribution

Under current U.S. law, antitrust defendants are jointly and severally liable for treble damages if they are found to have violated the antitrust laws. In addition, defendants do not have the right to seek contribution from their co-conspirators. When antitrust co-conspirators reach a settlement with the plaintiffs, the liability of the remaining defendants is reduced only by the actual amount of the settlement, after actual damages have been trebled. At times, defendants in antitrust lawsuits have claimed that these rules are unfair and may result in overcompensation to plaintiffs and over-deterrence to legitimate business activity.[65]

During much of the 1980s, Congress considered various bills addressing treble damages, claims reduction, and contribution. The legislative debates were instigated in the aftermath of the Supreme Court's decision in *Texas Industries, Inc. v. Radcliff Materials, Inc.*[66] In that case, Chief Justice Warren Burger delivered a unanimous opinion for the Court, finding that the antitrust laws do not provide for a right of contribution.[67] He went on to state that only Congress, not the courts, has the authority to establish such a right.[68]

Early versions of contribution and claims reduction legislation died because some large firms wanted to apply the new rules retroactively to reduce their liability in pending cases. One academic article stated that over 200 firms were involved in the legislative debate and many of them had a direct stake in the outcome.[69] In most cases, Congress has an aversion to interfering in pending litigation, especially where, as in many antitrust cases, the stakes are high and the issues are complex. Despite hard-fought and well-financed lobbying campaigns, federal legislation regarding claims reduction and contribution never passed the Congress, and proponents of the legislation eventually stopped introducing bills.

In 2005, the AMC revived interest in these issues by requesting testimony on whether the rules should be changed. Predictably, the Commission received a variety of opinions from plaintiff and defense lawyers, a federal judge, the ABA, and the AAI. The comments

---

[65] For further discussion of settlement practice in private antitrust cases, see Chapter 12 of this Handbook.

[66] 451 U.S. 630 (1981).

[67] *Id.* at 639–40.

[68] *Id.* at 646.

[69] Edward D. Cavanagh, *Contribution, Claim Reduction, and Individual Treble Damage Responsibility: Which Path to Reform of Antitrust Remedies?*, 40 VAND. L. REV. 1277, 1281 (1987).

ran the gamut from recommending no changes at all to recommending provisions for contribution and claim reduction among antitrust defendants.

The AAI's Working Group on Remedies, for example, recommended no changes to the current rules. The Working Group reasoned that "[t]he current rules . . . promote the goals of deterrence, victim compensation, settlement, finality and judicial economy" and that "[t]here have been few, if any, reported instances of miscarriages of justice created by these rules."[70]

In contrast, the ABA submitted comments recommending that legislation be enacted to provide for contribution and claim reduction in antitrust cases. The Section cited the following three reasons for its view:

> First, a plaintiff may arbitrarily impose the entire damage award on any one violator, either by suing only it or by enforcing the judgment only against it. Second, as the academic literature has recognized, the combination of the remedial rules discussed above tends to lead to settlements that exceed the risk-adjusted value of cases . . . . Third, the remedial rules tend to create a whipsaw effect that forces defendants to settle even when they are confident that they committed no violation.[71]

The AMC ultimately concluded that the current rules regarding claim reduction and contribution are unfair because they could result in one defendant being responsible for almost all of the damage caused by an antitrust conspiracy. The Commission also found that the rules "create significant pressure on defendants to settle antitrust claims, even those claims of questionable merit, simply to avoid the potential for excessive liability."[72] Therefore, the AMC recommended the following modifications:

> Congress should enact a statute applicable to all antitrust cases involving joint and several liability that would permit non-settling defendants to obtain reduction of the plaintiffs' claims by the amount of the settlement(s) or the allocated share(s) of liability of the settling defendants, whichever is greater. The recommended statute should also allow claims for contribution among non-settling defendants.[73]

In an addendum to its report, the AMC included legislative language that would implement this recommendation. The legislative language was more explicit about how the claim reduction would work. According to the proposed statute, "the court shall reduce the claim of any person releasing any person from liability or potential liability for damages by the greatest of: (1) any amount stipulated for this purpose; (2) the amount of the consideration paid for the release; or (3) treble the actual allocated share of damages of the person released."[74]

In other words, the proposal contemplates that an antitrust plaintiff's claim could be reduced by three times the amount of the allocated share of the settling defendant, calculated on the basis of each defendant's market share, if that amount is greater than the amount of the actual settlement with that defendant.

To date, no legislation has been introduced to implement the AMC's recommendations.

---

[70] Comments of the American Antitrust Institute Working Group on Remedies, at 10.

[71] American Bar Association, Comments of the Section of Antitrust Law, 2 (Dec. 28, 2005).

[72] ANTITRUST MODERNIZATION COMMISSION, *supra* note 56, at 252.

[73] *Id.* (Commissioners Dennis Carlton and Deborah Garza did not join this recommendation with respect to a right of contribution among non-settling defendants).

[74] ANTITRUST MODERNIZATION COMMISSION, *supra* note 56, at 256, Annex A.

§ 15.06 Reverse payments

Reverse payments, which have been used with increasing frequency over the last 10 years to resolve generic drug manufacturers' (generics') challenges to patents held by brand name drug companies, present thorny issues for both judges and litigants.

Challenges to brand name patents arise when generics file Abbreviated New Drug Applications (ANDAs), under procedures established by the Hatch-Waxman Act, to request approval from the Food and Drug Administration (FDA) to manufacture generic versions of a brand name drug.[75] In these ANDAs, many generics assert that their use of the patent held by a brand name drug manufacturer is not infringing because that patent is invalid. Numerous brand name patent holders, concerned by these challenges, offer to settle with generics by paying them in exchange for their relinquishment of their challenges and agreement to stay out of the market for a number of years.

The majority of federal circuit courts examining the propriety of such reverse payments under the antitrust laws have found them to be legal.

However, the first federal court of appeals to opine on this type of agreement, the Sixth Circuit, found reverse payments to be per se illegal under the Sherman Act, holding that such settlements amount to "horizontal agreement[s] to eliminate competition."[76]

Later challenges to such agreements proved less successful. In *Schering-Plough Corp. v. Federal Trade Commission*, the Eleventh Circuit came up with a rule for evaluating reverse payment settlements, holding that in order to determine whether a reverse payment constituted a violation of the antitrust laws, a court must examine "(1) the scope of the exclusionary potential of the patent; (2) the extent to which the agreements exceed that scope; and (3) the resulting anticompetitive effects."[77] Applying this test, the panel stated that the rights granted by the patent included within their scope the right to exclude infringers from the market for the life of the patent and that the settlement did not exceed that scope.[78] The court also held that the restraints resulting from the reverse payment were ancillary and gave rise to procompetitive efficiencies because the resolution of the dispute saved the parties significant costs and permitted further research and development in the field.[79]

The Second Circuit, in an opinion issued one year later, held that a reverse payment settlement was valid as long as there was no fraud, the patent litigation was not objectively baseless, and the settlement did not extend the patent's monopoly beyond its scope.[80] Finding that the Tamoxifen settlement at issue did not meet any of the listed invalidity criteria, the court upheld it.

---

[75] *See generally* Hatch-Waxman Act, 21 U.S.C. § 355 (2008).

[76] *In re* Cardizem CD Antitrust Litig., 332 F.3d 896, 908 (6th Cir. 2003), *cert. denied*, 543 U.S. 939 (2004) (citations omitted).

[77] Schering-Plough Corp. v. Fed. Trade Comm'n, 402 F.3d 1056, 1076 (11th Cir. 2005), *cert. denied*, 548 U.S. 919 (2006).

[78] *Id.* at 1067, 1071.

[79] *Id.* at 1072–75.

[80] *In re* Tamoxifen Citrate Antitrust Litig., 466 F.3d 187, 213 (2d Cir. 2006), *cert. denied*, 551 U.S. 1144 (2007).

Two years later, similarly to the Eleventh Circuit, the Federal Circuit, considering an agreement between Bayer and Barr Labs, held that entering into a reverse payment settlement with Barr Labs was "well within Bayer's rights as the patentee" and that "there is a long-standing policy in the law in favor of settlements."[81]

Both the Department of Justice and the Federal Trade Commission (FTC) have expressed disagreement with the rulings of the Second, Eleventh and Federal Circuits. These agencies have taken the position that reverse settlements constitute illegal agreements under the Sherman Act.[82]

Many others have also attacked the rulings upholding reverse payments, stating that these types of agreements protect invalid patents that would likely have been struck down in litigation. Opponents of these agreements complain that the large dollar amounts of these settlements demonstrate the invalidity of the patents at issue, and raise concerns that most generics presented with the option of taking a large settlement instead of entering the market, will readily agree to the deal. Critics thus argue that this practice violates the legislative intent of the Hatch-Waxman Act, which was enacted to encourage challenges to invalid patents and to increase the presence of generic competitors in the market. The most oft-repeated criticism of these settlements, however, is that they keep the prices of many drugs, including a number of "blockbuster" drugs, unduly high, as they result in the elimination of generic competition. A 2010 FTC report states that "[c]onsumers lose . . . [;] they miss out on generic prices that can be as much as 90 percent less than brand prices. For example, brand-name medication that costs $300 per month might be sold as a generic for as little as $30 per month."[83]

Those who support reverse payment settlements argue that such agreements promote innovation, allowing the patent holder to retain the value of his investment in the development of the patent. Supporters argue further that, if patent holders knew that they would have to face the possibility of losing their patent without the powerful weapon of large money settlements at their disposal, they would lose their incentive to develop new patents. One of the many law review notes commenting on this issue highlights the dilemma as follows:

> Extended market exclusivity is critical because it allows the brand-name to recoup more of its investment. When a brand-name is able to recoup more of its investment, it is able to reinvest more in future development. Without recovering investment, brand-name manufacturers would not be able to produce today's ground-breaking new drugs. It follows that without these brand-name drugs there would be nothing for the generic manufacturers to replicate

---

81 *In re* Ciprofloxacin Hydrochloride Antitrust Litig., 544 F.3d 1323, 1333 (Fed. Cir. 2008), *cert. denied*, 129 S. Ct. 2828 (2009).

82 Brief For the United States, at 21, *In re* Ciprofloxacin Hydrochloride Antitrust Litig., Nos. 05-2852-cv (CON), 05-2863-cv (CON) (2d Cir. July 6, 2009) (stating that reverse payment settlements should be treated as being presumptively unlawful); Brief for the Federal Trade Commission as Amicus at 22, *In re* K-Dur Antitrust Litig., Nos. 10-2077, 10-2078, 10-2079 (3d Cir. May 18, 2011) (stating that exclusionary payments should be treated as presumptively illegal).

83 Federal Trade Commission, Pay for Delay: How Drug Company Pay-Offs Cost Consumers Billions 3 (FTC Staff Report 2010).

> and learn from, but more importantly "there would be little hope of finding new treatments and cures."[84]

Proponents also argue that taking away the tool of reverse payments results in a great disincentive to settle, because staying out of the market is the only value proposition that a generic can offer a brand name manufacturer. Without the possibility of such an offer, the companies would have to litigate – an unfair outcome for the brand name manufacturer because even a victory would require added costs merely to maintain something it already possesses, which is a monopoly over the market granted by the patent.

In light of the controversy over the topic, Senator Herb Kohl (D-WI) has presented a bill that would make it a violation of the laws enforced by the FTC for generics challenging a patent's validity in their FDA approval filings to accept reverse settlements in return for an agreement to stay out of the market.[85] This bill states the following:

> The Federal Trade Commission may initiate a proceeding to enforce the provisions of this section against the parties to any agreement resolving or settling, on a final or interim basis, a patent infringement claim, in connection with the sale of a drug product.
> (2) PRESUMPTION
> (A) IN GENERAL–Subject to subparagraph (B), an agreement shall be presumed to have anticompetitive effects and be unlawful if
> (i) an ANDA filer receives anything of value; and
> (ii) the ANDA filer agrees to limit or forego research, development, manufacturing, marketing, or sales of the ANDA product for any period of time.
> (B) EXCEPTION–The presumption in subparagraph (A) shall not apply if the parties to such agreement demonstrate by clear and convincing evidence that the procompetitive benefits of the agreement outweigh the anticompetitive effects of the agreement.[86]

As of this writing, the bill has passed the Senate Judiciary Committee and has advanced to the full Senate. A similar bill, designating reverse payments as unfair practices, was introduced in 2009, in the House of Representatives by Representative Bobby Rush (D-IL).[87] That bill was referred to the Judiciary Committee and the Energy and Commerce Committee, but it never came up for a vote during the congressional session. It was also incorporated in the House of Representatives' Affordable Healthcare for America Act,[88] which passed the House, but it was not incorporated in the final version of that act. House legislation on reverse payment settlements has not been introduced in the 112th Congress.

§ 15.07 Minimum resale price maintenance

Minimum resale price maintenance refers to agreements between manufacturers and distributors or retailers to establish a minimum retail price for the manufacturers' products.

---

[84] Alex Korona, *Stuck in Neutral: The Future of Reverse Payment Agreements in Hatch-Waxman Litigation*, 7 Seton Hall Cir. Rev. 201, 226 (2010) (internal citation omitted).

[85] Preserve Access to Affordable Generics Act, S. 27, 112th Cong. § 28 (2011).

[86] *Id.*

[87] Protecting Consumer Access to Generic Drugs Act of 2009, H.R. 1706, 111th Cong. (2009).

[88] Affordable Health Care for America Act, H.R. 3962, 111th Cong. § 2573 (2009).

In the 1911 case *Dr. Miles Medical Co. v. John D. Park & Sons*,[89] the Supreme Court ruled that such agreements are per se violations of the Sherman Act. While subsequent Supreme Court decisions found that certain types of restraints on vertical competition did not violate the antitrust laws,[90] the per se rule against minimum resale price maintenance agreements remained the law for almost one hundred years. In 2007, the Court overruled *Dr. Miles* in *Leegin Creative Leather Products, Inc. v. PSKS, Inc.*[91]

In a 5-4 opinion, the *Leegin* Court held that vertical price restraints should be judged by the rule of reason.[92] The Court relied on a prior holding that per se rules should be "confined to restraints . . . 'that would always or almost always tend to restrict competition and decrease output.'"[93] The Court found that a per se rule was inappropriate for resale price maintenance because "[v]ertical retail-price agreements have either procompetitive or anticompetitive effects, depending on the circumstances in which they were formed; and the limited empirical evidence available does not suggest efficient uses of the agreements are infrequent or hypothetical."[94]

Justice Stephen Breyer wrote the dissent, which was largely based on his view that a decision of such long-standing duration should not be overruled absent changed circumstances or other compelling reasons, which he found were not present. He concluded as follows:

> The only safe predictions to make about today's decision are that it will likely raise the price of goods at retail and that it will create considerable legal turbulence as lower courts seek to develop workable principles. I do not believe that the majority has shown new or changed conditions sufficient to warrant overruling a decision of such long standing. All ordinary *stare decisis* considerations indicate the contrary. For these reasons, with respect, I dissent.[95]

Very soon after the *Leegin* decision was issued, Senator Herb Kohl (D-WI), the Chairman of the Subcommittee on Antitrust, Competition Policy and Consumer Rights of the Senate Judiciary Committee, introduced the Discount Pricing Consumer Protection Act to overturn the decision and restore the per se rule.[96] The bill provided that agreements to set a minimum price below which a product or service cannot be sold by a retailer, wholesaler, or distributor would violate the Sherman Act.[97] No action, however, was taken on the bill in the 111th Congress.

The legislation was the subject of hearings in both the House and the Senate, in which various stakeholders testified. The positions that were presented essentially fell into two camps – parties who opposed the *Leegin* decision and supported the legislation, and those who took the opposite view.

---

89 220 U.S. 373 (1911).

90 *See* Continental T.V., Inc. v. GTE Sylvania Inc., 433 U.S. 36 (1977) *and* Monsanto Co. v. Spray-Rite Service Corp., 465 U.S. 752 (1984).

91 551 U.S. 877 (2007).

92 *Id.* at 877.

93 *Id.* at 885 (quoting Business Electronics Corp. v. Sharp Electronics Corp., 485 U.S. 717, 723 (1988)).

94 *Leegin*, 551 U.S. at 891.

95 *Id.* at 900 (Breyer, J., dissenting).

96 Discount Pricing Consumer Protection Act, S. 148, 111th Cong. (2009).

97 *Id.*

Then-FTC Commissioner Pamela Jones Harbour testified on her own behalf in favor of the legislation. She noted that the *Leegin* decision would allow manufacturers to set minimum resale prices for consumer products, and stated the following:

> I believe this outcome is contrary to good economic and legal policy. It gives excessively short shrift to consumer preferences, which are supposed to be the driving force behind healthy, competitive markets. Post-*Leegin*, and absent action by Congress, consumer preferences will be subordinated to the interests of manufacturers and merchants of branded consumer goods.[98]

Richard M. Brunell of the AAI took the same view, stating, "We believe that consumer welfare and economic innovation are best served when retailers are free to engage in discounting, and therefore urge this committee to take action to restore some version of the *per se* rule."[99] The AAI testimony analyzed the cases that had been brought since the *Leegin* decision and concluded "the so-called 'rule of reason' adopted by the Supreme Court for judging RPM agreements amounts to a rule of virtual *per se legality*."[100] AAI commented that lower courts were summarily dismissing resale price maintenance complaints and not allowing plaintiffs the opportunity to even try to prove their cases.

The ABA took the other side. James A. Wilson, then-Chairman of the ABA Section of Antitrust Law testified that the ABA supported the *Leegin* decision and, therefore, was opposed to the pending legislation. In fact, in February 2007, before *Leegin* was decided, the House of Delegates of the ABA adopted the following resolution:

> RESOLVED, That the American Bar Association recommends that the Sherman Act, 15 U.S.C. Section 1, and comparable state and territorial laws should not be interpreted to apply a rule of per se illegality to agreements between a buyer and seller setting the price at which the buyer may resell goods or services purchased from the seller.[101]

In 2011, Senator Kohl re-introduced the "Discount Pricing Consumer Protection Act," but no action has been taken on the measure. House legislation has not been introduced to date.

§ 15.08 The Robinson-Patman Act

The utility and purpose of the Robinson-Patman Act (the Act) have been debated for the majority of its existence. The Act prohibits sellers from engaging in price discrimination

---

98 *Bye Bye Bargain? Retail Price Fixing, the Leegin Decision, and Its Impact on Consumer Prices: Hearing Before the Subcomm. on Courts and Competition Policy, H. Comm. on the Judiciary*, 111th Cong. 9–10 (2009) (statement of Pamela Jones Harbour, Commissioner, Federal Trade Commission).

99 *Bye Bye Bargain? Retail Price Fixing, the Leegin Decision, and Its Impact on Consumer Prices: Hearing Before the Subcomm. on Courts and Competition Policy, H. Comm. on the Judiciary*, 111th Cong. 71 (2009) (testimony of Richard M. Brunell, Director of Legal Advocacy, American Antitrust Institute).

100 *Id.* at 75.

101 *See The Discount Pricing Consumer Protection Act: Do We Need to Restore the Ban on Vertical Price Fixing?: Hearing Before the Subcomm. on Antitrust, Competition Policy and Consumer Rights of the S. Comm. on the Judiciary*, 111th Cong. 1 (2009) (statement of James A. Wilson on Behalf of the American Bar Association).

between competing buyers purchasing "commodities of like grade and quality."[102] Sellers can violate this act by either engaging in predatory pricing, known as "primary line discrimination," or by selling goods to disfavored buyers at higher prices than they charge to favored buyers when the price difference is not justified by actual cost considerations, which is known as "secondary line discrimination."[103] Under the Act, price discrimination can take the form not only of actual price differences, but also of disparate treatment in the extent to which the seller provides or pays for services or facilities associated with the buyer's promotion of the goods being sold.[104] In addition to targeting sellers engaging in discriminatory behavior, the Act is also aimed at favored buyers knowingly inducing discriminatory pricing or knowingly receiving illegally discriminatory prices.[105]

Since the 1950s, the Act has been under attack from a number of groups, including a White House task force and the Department of Justice, who have contended that it was inconsistent with the other antitrust laws in its approach to regulating competition.[106] The Act has also had its supporters, including the AAI and a number of professors, who have contended that it is necessary to protect smaller businesses and control the prices charged to consumers.

In 2005, the AMC took up the issue as part of its investigation into what modifications needed to be made to the antitrust laws, and requested comments from all interested parties.

The AAI responded by pointing out the continued need for the Act's enforcement mechanisms. It argued that a law prohibiting price discrimination was necessary to prevent powerful buyers from exercising their buying power to jettison smaller buyers from the market and raise prices.[107] The AAI also acknowledged that efforts to enforce the Act had had some anticompetitive effects, such as preventing powerful buyers from obtaining discounts that they could then pass on to consumers.[108] To contend with the elements of the Act that made it anticompetitive while preserving its powerful deterrent effects, the AAI recommended the following changes to the price discrimination provisions:

(1) Plaintiffs in secondary line discrimination cases should be required to prove either that the discriminating seller had market power or that the favored buyer had buyer power. This change would not require that plaintiffs show monopoly power or monopsony power.
(2) Defendants should be allowed to establish the cost justification defense if they can prove that the discriminatory price was reasonably related to cost savings realized in dealing with the favored buyer.
(3) Plaintiffs challenging discrimination in promotional allowances or services should be required to show competitive injury.[109]

---

102 The Robinson-Patman Act, 15 U.S.C. § 13(a) (1936).

103 *Id.* at § 13(a).

104 *Id.* at §§ 13(d)–(e).

105 *Id.* at § 13(f).

106 *See* Phil C. Neal et al., Report of the White House Task Force on Antitrust Policy, *reprinted in* 2 Antitrust L. & Econ. Rev. 11, 41 (1968–69); Department of Justice, Department of Justice Report on the Robinson-Patman Act 260 (1977).

107 Comments of the American Antitrust Institute Working Group on the Robinson-Patman Act, 13 (July 1, 2005).

108 *Id.* at 9.

109 *Id.* at 2.

With regard to the Act's predatory pricing provisions, the AAI recommended that Congress remove the criminal penalty accompanying a finding of predation, contained in Section 3 of the Act.[110] It explained that after the Supreme Court's ruling in *Brooke Group Ltd. v. Brown & Williamson Tobacco Corp.*,[111] which created particularly stringent requirements for proving predatory pricing, the Act's predatory pricing provisions were unlikely to be enforced.[112]

The ABA advocated for some of the same modifications in its comments to the AMC. Its first recommendation was that Congress change the standard for demonstrating that a seller has discriminated against a buyer by not providing or not paying for the same services or facilities it offered to another buyer.[113] The ABA suggested that discarding the current per se standard and adopting a standard based on substantial lessening of competition – the standard required for a showing of discrimination based on price – would make those provisions more comprehensible to buyers and more consistent with the rest of the Act.[114]

The ABA also suggested that Section 2(c) of the Act, which makes it illegal to give or receive a commission, except for services rendered, and Section 3, which makes predatory pricing a criminal offense, should be repealed.[115] With regard to Section 2(c) specifically, the ABA stated that "[c]hanges in distribution practices since the section was enacted have rendered it an unneeded anachronism, a potentially anticompetitive deterrent against innovative distribution practices."[116] On the other hand, its argument for the repeal of Section 3 was that "this provision is vague, confusing, and possibly unconstitutional" and, "[m]oreover, as a practical matter, the agency charged with enforcing the statute long ago indicated an unwillingness to do so, resulting in a de facto repeal."[117]

The AMC adopted neither the suggestions of the AAI nor those of the ABA and instead recommended that Congress repeal the Act entirely.[118] The AMC determined that the Act was inconsistent with other antitrust laws and policies, that its use in private damages and public enforcement actions was waning, and that it had negative effects on consumers.[119] Its report stated:

> [T]he Act has had the unintended effect of limiting the extent of discounting generally and therefore has likely caused consumers to pay higher prices than they otherwise would. As one commentator has explained, the Robinson-Patman Act "was designed to protect small businesses from larger, more efficient businesses. A necessary result is higher consumer prices." Moreover,

---

110 *Id.* at 6.

111 509 U.S. 209, 224 (1993).

112 Comments of the American Antitrust Institute Working Group on the Robinson-Patman Act, at 5–6.

113 Comments of the American Bar Association, Antitrust Section, 2 (April 10, 2006).

114 *Id.*

115 *Id.* at 3.

116 *Id.*

117 *Id.*

118 Antitrust Modernization Commission, *supra* note 56, at 312. Once the AMC's report and recommendations came out in 2007, the ABA also suggested that Congress could repeal the Act, as an alternative to modifying it. American Bar Association, Antitrust Section, 2008 Transition Report 60 (Nov. 25, 2008).

119 Antitrust Modernization Commission, *supra* note 56, at 312, 316–17.

> the Act ironically appears increasingly to be ineffective even in protecting small businesses. Over time, many businesses have found ways to comply with the Act by, for example, differentiating products, so they can sell somewhat different products to different purchasers at different prices. Such methods are likely to increase the seller's costs – and thus increase costs to consumers – but do nothing to protect small businesses. The Act generally appears to have failed in achieving its main objective.[120]

Congress, however, never took any action to repeal or modify the Act, and no legislation has been introduced as of this writing.

§ 15.09 The Railroad Antitrust Enforcement Act

In recent years, Congress has considered legislation that would repeal the antitrust exemption for the American freight railroad industry. The railroad antitrust exemption was put in place because the railroads were subject to a comprehensive regulatory scheme, which included prior approval by the Interstate Commerce Commission (ICC), for most of their actions, including setting rates. And although the railroads were largely deregulated in 1980 through the Staggers Rail Act,[121] the antitrust exemptions remained in place. A 2006 report by the Government Accountability Office (GAO) found a lack of competition in the freight rail industry that was resulting in excessive rates for shippers in many geographic areas.[122] Congressional legislation was subsequently introduced to address the problems identified by the GAO.

The Railroad Antitrust Enforcement Act of 2011,[123] introduced by Senator Herb Kohl, passed the Senate Judiciary Committee on March 3, 2011. There is no comparable legislation pending in the House of Representatives at this time.

§ 15.10 The Antitrust Criminal Penalty Enhancement and Reform Act[124]

The only significant legislation affecting private enforcement of the antitrust laws to pass Congress in the last few years was the Antitrust Criminal Penalty Enhancement and Reform Act of 2004 Extension Act,[125] which was enacted on June 9, 2010. Congress passed ACPERA in 2004 to enhance the effectiveness of the Department of Justice's corporate leniency program. Under the leniency program, corporations and individuals who participate in criminal price-fixing schemes can receive amnesty from criminal liability if they are the first to provide information to the Antitrust Division about the illegal activity and if they cooperate fully with the government's investigation and prosecution. ACPERA provided additional incentives for cooperation with the government by limiting damage recoveries in private lawsuits against corporations and executives who receive

---

120 *Id.* at 311 (citations omitted).

121 Pub. L. 96-448, 94 Stat. 1895; 49 U.S.C. § 10101 *et seq.* (1980).

122 U.S. Government Accountability Office, Report to Congressional Requesters, Freight Railroads' Industry Health Has Improved, but Concerns About Competition and Capacity Should Be Addressed 43 (Report No. GAO-07-94, Oct. 2006).

123 S. 49, 112th Cong. (2011).

124 Pub. L. No. 108-237; 15 U.S.C. § 1, note (2004).

125 Pub. L. No. 111-190 (2010).

criminal amnesty. Specifically, ACPERA eliminated treble damages and joint and several liability for corporate amnesty applicants as long as the applicants provided "satisfactory cooperation" to the civil claimants.[126]

When Congress reauthorized ACPERA in 2010, concerns were raised that amnesty applicants were failing to provide full and timely cooperation to private lawsuits brought on behalf of cartel victims. The 2010 amendments clarified that cooperation from amnesty applicants must be made in a timely fashion in order for the applicant to receive the benefit of reduced damages. In addition, the amendments required full and prompt cooperation from applicants after a stay of civil proceedings requested by the Justice Department has been lifted. The amendments reauthorized ACPERA for another 10 years.

§ 15.11 Conclusion

Private antitrust litigation often involves complex legal and economic analysis, fact-intensive investigation and high financial stakes. Important and powerful interests can be found on both sides of the cases. Not surprisingly, the issues involved in private cases often morph into heated and controversial public policy debates that are discussed at the highest levels of government. Multiple Congresses may consider the same issues over and over again. Similarly, blue ribbon commissions have been established time and again to review and analyze the issues in the hopes of finding some kind of consensus for reform. But the consensus is rarely found and proposals for change are rarely enacted. Perhaps this is because, at their core, the antitrust laws provide strong, efficient, and effective tools for private enforcement. At the end of the day, policymakers reject change rather than risk damaging the underlying scheme, which has lasted, after all, for almost 100 years.

---

[126] For further discussion of ACPERA, see Chapter 7 and Chapter 11 of this Handbook.

Index